'91-'92 AUTUMN & WINTER
COLLECTIONS

This special edition is the selection of Six Great Collections (in Madrid, Milan, London, Paris, New York, and Tokyo).

The purpose of this edition is to introduce the great fashion designers and their creativity, and also to record the fashion trends in the world. This volume is compiled as one of reference works for World Fashion, and we promise that we publish this edition continuously as long as Fashion exists.

We hope that it will be qualified to make a contribution to Fashion history and its future.

この特集号は、世界6大コレクション（マドリッド、ミラノ、ロンドン、パリ、ニューヨーク、東京）の代表的デザイナーのそのシーズンの作品を収録。素晴らしいデザイナー達のクリエイティブを掲載すると共に、その時代のモードを紹介することを意図とし、保存版として編集しています。

また、私共はこの特集号を出版しつづけることにより、デザイナーの作品やモードを知る手がかりとなり、ファッションの歴史に貢献する資料となればと考えております。

'91-'92 AUTUMN & WINTER COLLECTIONS
Published by GAP JAPAN Co., Ltd.
Printed in Japan

JUNKO SHIMADA

'91-'92 AUTUMN & WINTER

COLLECTIONS

PARIS/LONDON

HELEN STOREY

CLAUDE MONTANA

'91-'92
AUTUMN & WINTER
PRÊT-Á-PORTER
COLLECTIONS

YVES SAINT LAURENT  | LOLITA LEMPICKA  | BALENCIAGA

CHRISTIAN DIOR  | FREDERIC CASTET  | YUKI TORII

PIERRE BALMAIN  | VIVIENNE WESTWOOD  | DANIEL HECHTER

INDEX

PARIS

JEAN-PAUL GAULTIER ジャン＝ポール・ゴルチエ	13
COMME DES GARÇONS コム・デ・ギャルソン	25
CLAUDE MONTANA クロード・モンタナ	37
THIERRY MUGLER ティエリー・ミュグレー	55
ROMEO GIGLI ロメオ・ジリ	67
CHRISTIAN DIOR クリスチャン・ディオール	79
VIVIENNE WESTWOOD ヴィヴィアン・ウエストウッド	97
KENZO ケンゾー	105
YVES SAINT LAURENT イヴ・サン・ローラン	113
CHANEL シャネル	121
MARTINE SITBON マルティーヌ・シットボン	129
KARL LAGERFELD カール・ラガーフェルド	137
CHRISTIAN LACROIX クリスチャン・ラクロワ	151
ISSEY MIYAKE イッセイ・ミヤケ	159
SONIA RYKIEL ソニア・リキエル	167
MAURIZIO GALANTE マウリツィオ・ガランテ	175
EMANUEL UNGARO エマニュエル・ウンガロ	187
HELMUT LANG ヘルムート・ラング	191
CHANTAL THOMASS シャンタル・トマス	195
YUKI TORII ユキ・トリイ	199
JUNKO SHIMADA ジュンコ・シマダ	203
LOLITA LEMPICKA ロリータ・レンピカ	207
DANIEL HECHTER ダニエル・エシュテル	211
BARBARA BUI バルバラ・ブュイ	215
CHLOÉ クロエ	219
ANGELO TARLAZZI アンジェロ・タルラッツィ	223
DOROTHÉE BIS ドロテ・ビス	227
SYBILLA シビラ	237
MARTIN MARGIELA マルタン・マルジェラ	239
ZUCCA ズッカ	241
JEAN-LOUIS SCHERRER ジャン＝ルイ・シェレル	243
GIVENCHY ジバンシー	245
GUY LAROCHE ギ・ラロッシュ	247
BALENCIAGA バレンシアガ	249
MICHEL KLEIN ミッシェル・クライン	251
MATSUDA マツダ	253
HIROKO KOSHINO ヒロコ・コシノ	255
JIN ABE ジン・アベ	261
PACO RABANNE パコ・ラバンヌ	263
HANAE MORI ハナエ・モリ	265
J. C. DE CASTELBAJAC J. C. ド・カステルバジャック	267
OSCAR DE LA RENTA オスカー・デ・ラ・レンタ	269
GRÉS グレ	271
NINA RICCI ニナ・リッチ	273
BERNARD PERRIS ベルナール・ペリス	275
ENRICO COVERI エンリコ・コーベリ	277
FREDERIC CASTET フレデリック・カステ	279
PIERRE BALMAIN ピエール・バルマン	281
JUNKO KOSHINO ジュンコ・コシノ	283
KANSAI YAMAMOTO カンサイ・ヤマモト	285

LONDON

OZBEK オズベック	293
VAL PIRIOU バル・ピロー	297
TOMASZ STARZEWSKI トーマス・スターゼウスキィ	301
HELEN STOREY ヘレン・ストーリー	305
PAM HOGG パム・ホッグ	309
CAROLINE CHARLES キャロライン・チャールズ	313
ARABELLA POLLEN アラベラ・ポーラン	317
RED OR DEAD レッド・オア・デッド	321
EDINA RONAY エディーナ・ロネイ	325
JACQUELINE HANCHER ジャクリーヌ・ハンチャー	329
PAUL COSTELLOE ポール・コステロ	333
BETTY JACKSON ベティ・ジャクソン	337
JOE CASELY-HAYFORD ジョー・ケイスリー・ヘイフォード	339
ZANDRA RHODES ザンドラ・ローズ	341

SYBILLA

CHANEL

CHRISTIAN DIOR

PARIS

CHANTAL THOMASS

The 1991/'92 Autumn & Winter Paris Collection was held over a 10 day period from the 11th to the 20th March, in the wake of the gulf war. Around 70 maisons held shows.

Paris did not feel the effects of the gulf conflict as severely as collections held in other European countries. This may either be because the Paris Collection was held just after the gulf war, or it may be an indication of the collection's significance. There seemed to be little difference from last year in the numbers of journalists and buyers who were present. An interesting feature of this collection was the participation of a number of new designers, beginning with Vivienne Westwood of London, and including Enrica Massei and two new designers, Sybilla and Maurizio Galante from Milan, as well as Oscar de la Renta of New York. It adds credence to the saying, "Paris is the capital of mode."

Business is not the only reason why world leading names hold their collections in Paris, where buyers and journalists gather from all over the globe. There is another reason: Paris has a reputation of appreciating true originality and creativity. To put it another way, talented designers aim at Paris because they want their creativity recognized in this city. This aim of the designers allowed us to feel the arrival of the "era of creativity and originality" in the 1991/'92 Autumn & Winter Paris Collection.

Gaultier seemed to be the precursor of this era. The collection he displayed this season seemed to contain a treasure chest of ideas. Lap jackets and coats were transformed into long dresses with lengthy trains and jackets shaped at the waist. It really was a lot of fun. Handkerchief skirts were also full of the new mode. Comme des Garçons breathed an entirely new into materials reminiscent of the '60's, such as vinyl and enamel. In their evening dresses, they showed a dress with a full silhouette with a brush stroke print, reminding us of Japanese paintings. Paris gave them thunderous applause, Montana recreated the forms of perfect beauty, which had received overwhelming praise in the previous season's haute-couture. He amazed people with a demonstration of his talent with colors, shown by the radiant shades in the sharp forms of the trapèze and A lines. In Mugler's show only professional photographers were allowed to take photographs. Videos were shown as compensation for buyers and journalists. However, the show was so funky it was a shame that we couldn't see it. Included were a dress with winking eyes — taking its image from Dali's paintings, a pank dress with monkey fur and an enamel dress that looked a second skin. These were all filled with an overwhelming sense of entertainment. In addition, Romeo Gigli, back for the first time in a year, held his show in a vinyl tent in pouring rain. He reminded us of his Milan days, with his unchanged gentle cocoon silhouette, and the further development in his simple and ecological style.

The "Goddess of Revolution", Vivienne Westwood, the leading overseas designer, drew such top designers as Alaia, Gaultier and M. Sitbon to her collection. Although there were no changes in the ideas seen in the corsets and bustiers, her power was second to none. Galante, a new designer from Milan, caused a modest sensation in Paris with his exquisite and innocent style. Meanwhile, Sybilla held a show at a crowded party, thrown to make the opening of her Paris shop. She is popular as a promising designer.

The debut in Paris by overseas designers adds excitement, and at the same time, shows that Paris is truly the capital of mode.

The significance and the creativity of the Paris Collection. as seen in the succession of designer debuts.

パリ・デビューを飾るデザイナーたちの続出にみる、パリ・コレクションの重要性とクリエイティビティ

'91-'92年秋冬パリ・コレクションは、湾岸戦争終結直後の3月11日より20日の10日間にわたり、約70メゾンがショーを開催した。

戦争直後とあってか、ファッション界のパリ・コレクションの重要度のためか、他国のヨーロッパ・コレクションのように多大な戦争の影響は見受けられない。ジャーナリストやバイヤーの足並みも、ほぼ前シーズン並に出揃った感がある。そして興味深いことに、ロンドンのヴィヴィアン・ウエストウッドを筆頭に、ミラノからはシビラ、マウリツィオ・ガランテの新鋭たちとエンリカ・マッセイが、ニューヨークからはオスカー・デ・ラ・レンタが参加。"モードの都・パリ"の印象を深くした。

このように世界のビッグネームたちがパリでコレクションを開催する由縁は、パリに世界のバイヤーとジャーナリストが集まるというビジネス的な一面に加え、パリが真のクリエイティブとオリジナリティを評価するという伝統的な気質を備えているからであろうか。逆説的に言えば優秀な才能たちがパリを目指すのは、自らのクリエイティブをパリで認知されたいということであろう。こうしたデザイナー個人の願望の中にも、"クリエイティブとオリジナリティの時代"の到来を予感することが出来る、'91-'92秋冬パリ・コレクションである。

その時代を予言するかのように、今シーズンのゴルチエはアイディアの宝庫とも言えるようなコレクションを展開。ラップ・ジャケットやコートは長くトレーンを引くロング・ドレスに変身したり、ウエストで結んだジャケットに変身したりと楽しさ満載。ハンカチーフ・スカートもニューモードの香りいっぱい。コム・デ・ギャルソンは、'60年代を彷彿させる素材、ビニールやエナメルに全く新しい時代の息吹を吹き込んだ。イヴニングには日本画を連想させるブラッシュ・ストローク・プリントを施したフルシルエットのドレスを展開、パリに拍手の渦を巻き起こした。モンタナは前シーズンのオートクチュールで絶大な評価を得た、完璧な造形美の世界を再現。トラペーズやAラインのシャープなフォルムを輝くようなカラーで見せ、色の才能にも驚嘆を招いた。ミュグレーは、カメラマン撮影のみ許可するショーを開催。バイヤーやジャーナリストにもビデオで対応を図った。が、ショーを見られないのが残念なくらいのファンキーさ。ダリをイメージしたというウインクする眼のついたドレスやモンキー・ファーのパンク・ドレス、セカンド・スキンのエナメル・ドレスと過激なエンターテイメント性に満ちている。そして、ロメオ・ジリも一年振りに強雨のふり注ぐビニール・テントでショーを開催。コクーン・シルエットの優しさはそのまま、ずっとシンプルでエコロジカル性を増し、ミラノ時代のロメオ・ジリを彷彿させた。

また他国からのデザイナーの筆頭、"革新の女神"ヴィヴィアン・ウエストウッドのコレクションにはアライアやゴルチエ、M.シットボンなど錚々たるデザイナーの顔が見かけられた。コルセットやビュスティエ等、アイディアは先シーズンと変化はないが、モード・パワーはピカ一的存在。ミラノの新鋭ガランテは、その繊細でナイーブなスタイルでパリに静かな感動を呼び起こした。一方シビラは、パリ・ショップ・オープンのパーティの人波の中でコレクションを開催。期待されるデザイナーとしての人気を見せた。

こうした他国のデザイナーのパリ・デビューは刺激であると同時に、"モードのパリ"を確固として位置づけるものであろう。

ENRICO COVERI

JUNKO SHIMADA

VALENTINO

KANSAI YAMAMOTO

BARBARA BUI

'91-'92 AUTUMN & WINTER COLLECTIONS

PARIS

JUNKO SHIMADA

CHANEL

YVES SAINT LAURENT

PARIS-1

JEAN-PAUL GAULTIER

ジャン＝ポール・ゴルチエ

ラップ・ジャケットやラップ・コートが長くトレーンを引くドレスやウエストで縛ったジャケットに変身。マジックのような斬新で楽しいクリエイティブに脱帽。

Transforming lap jackets and to dresses with long trains and jackets with a shaped waist,
his creativity could only be termed magnificent.

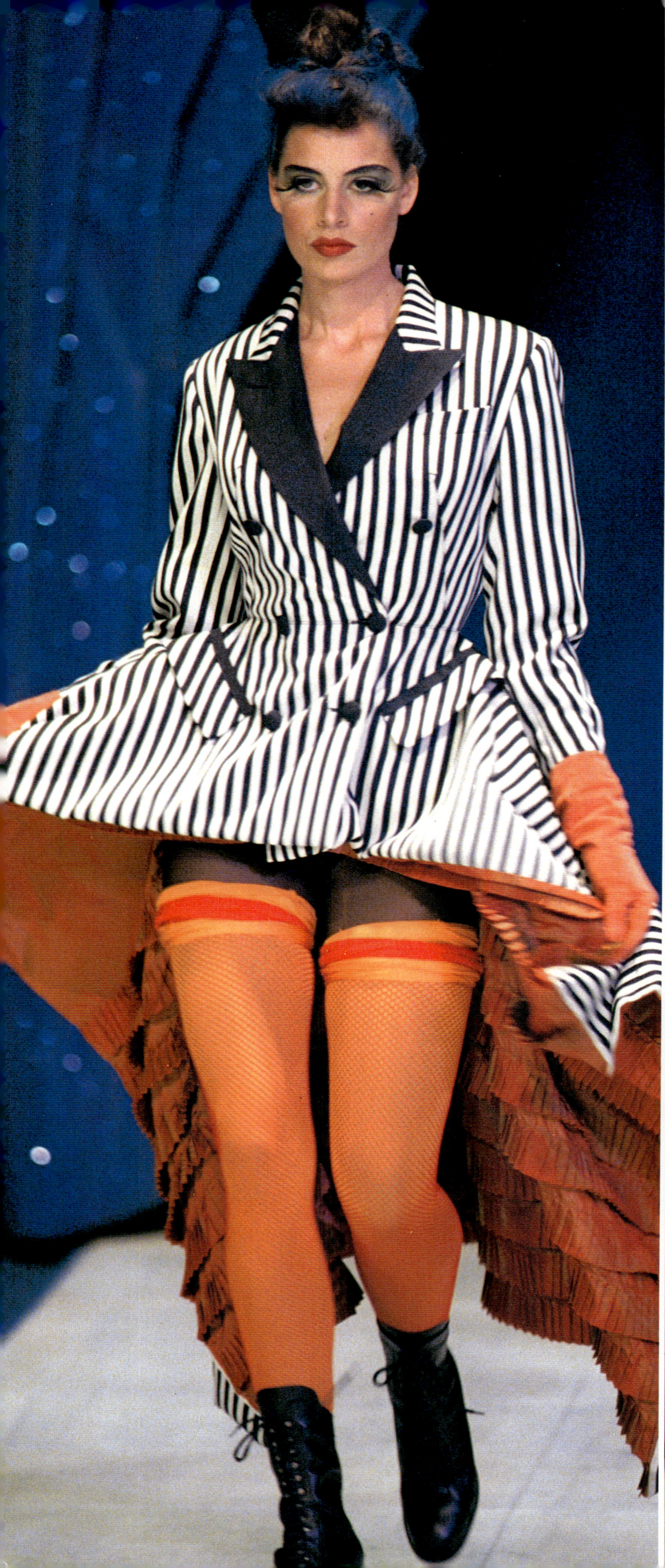
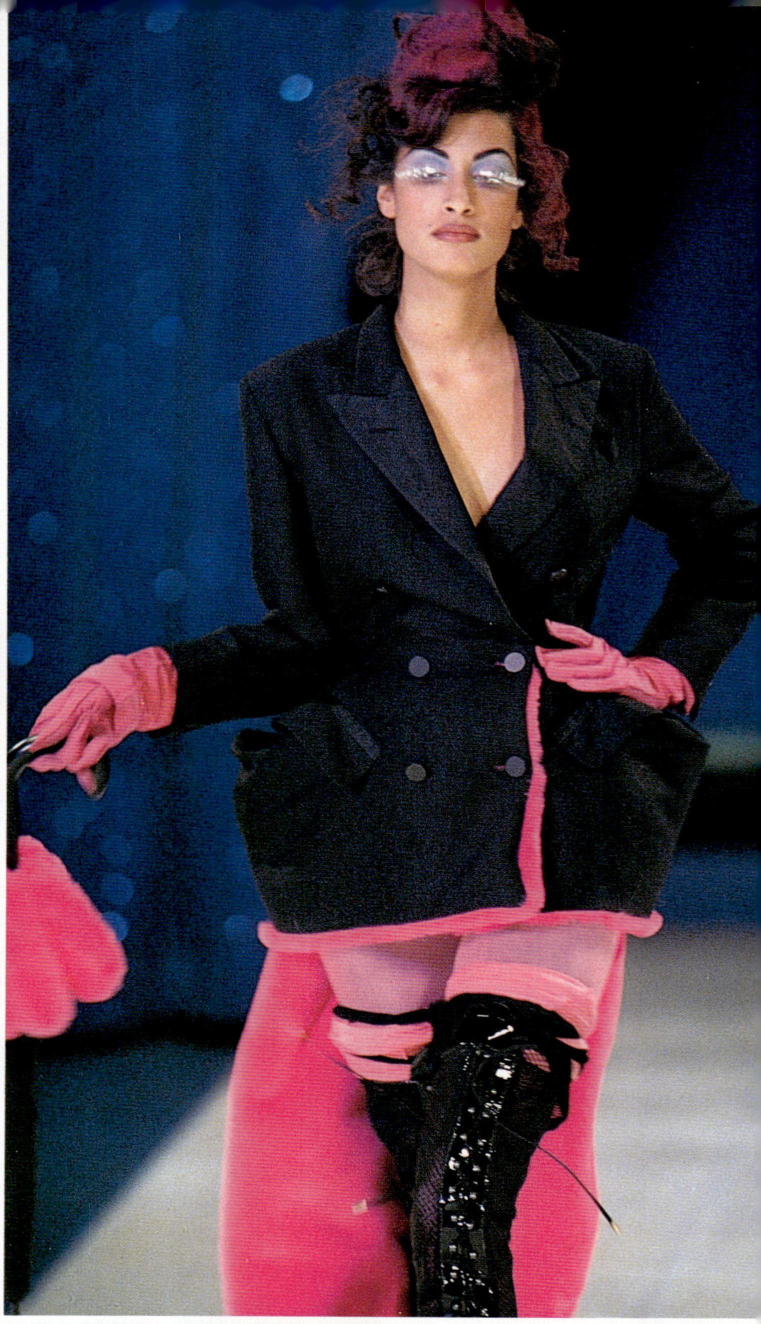
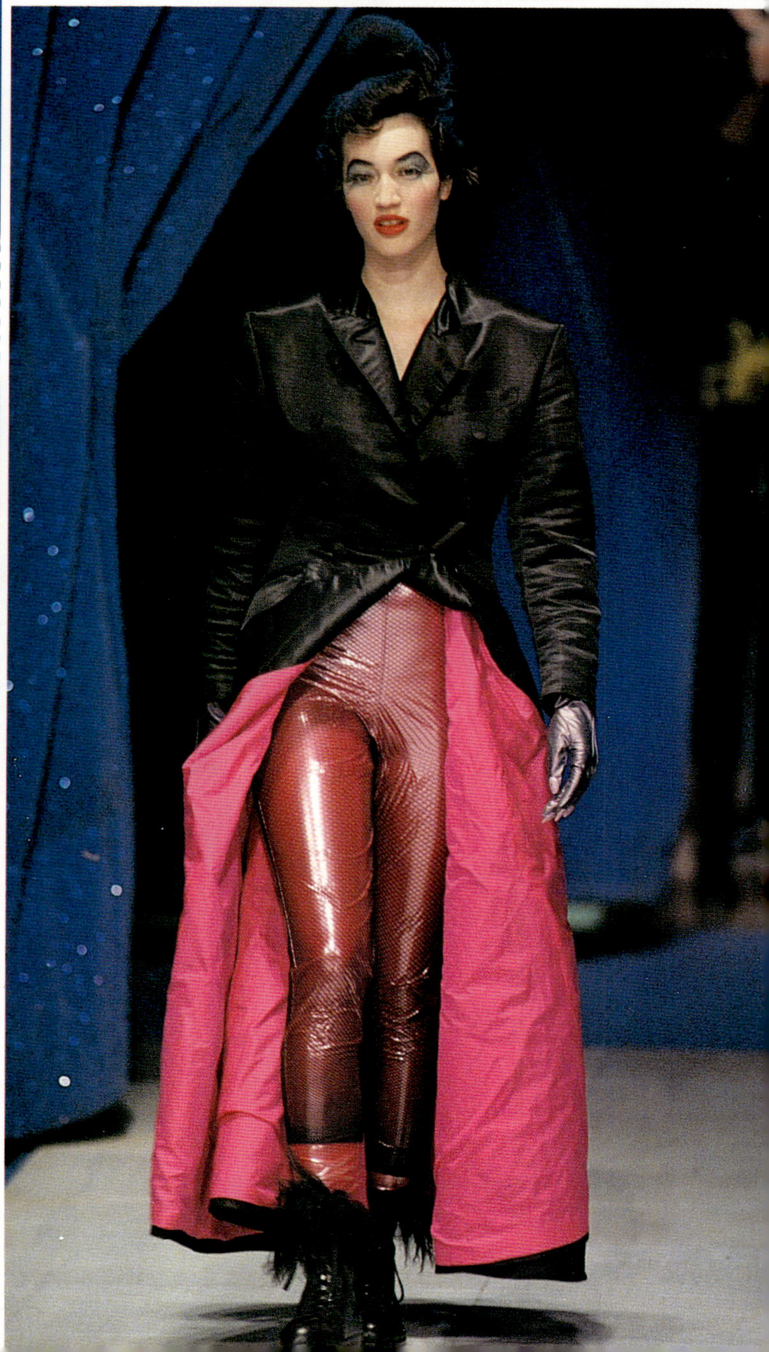

JEAN-PAUL GAULTIER

15

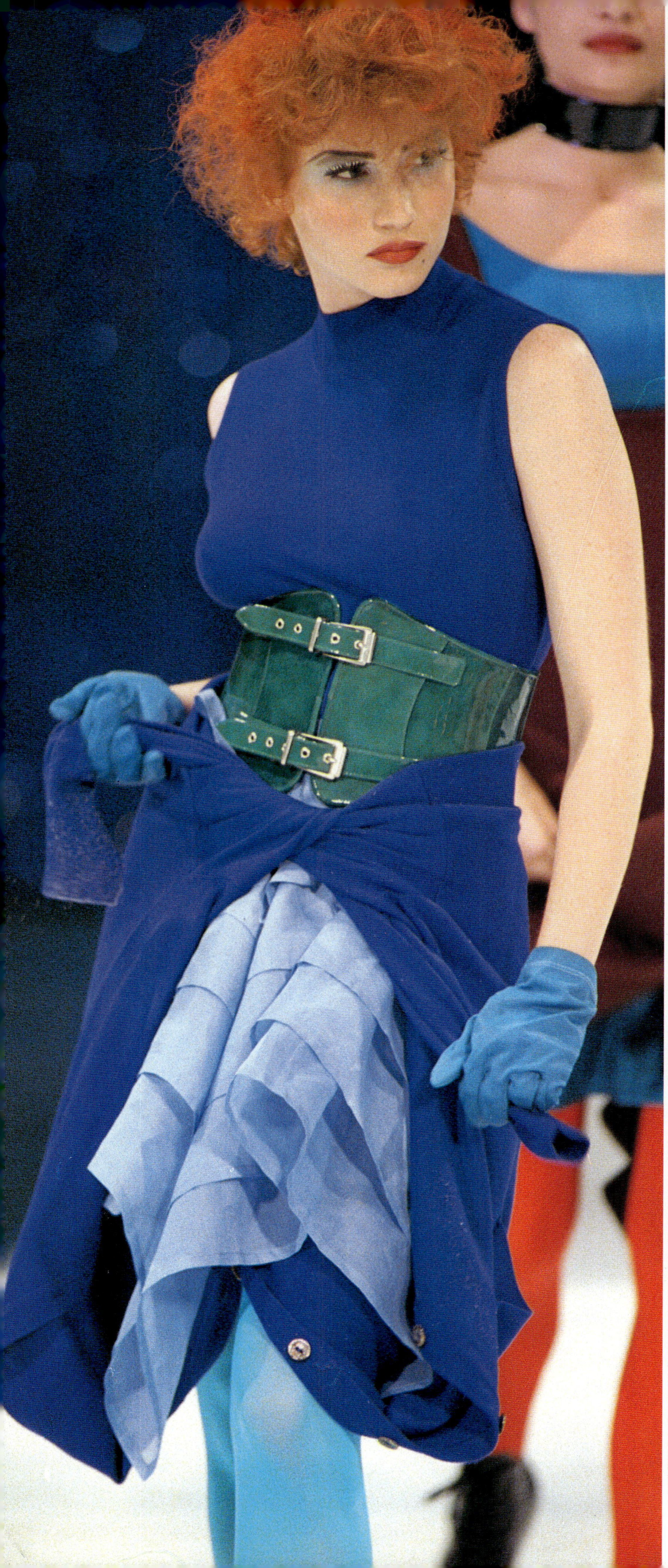
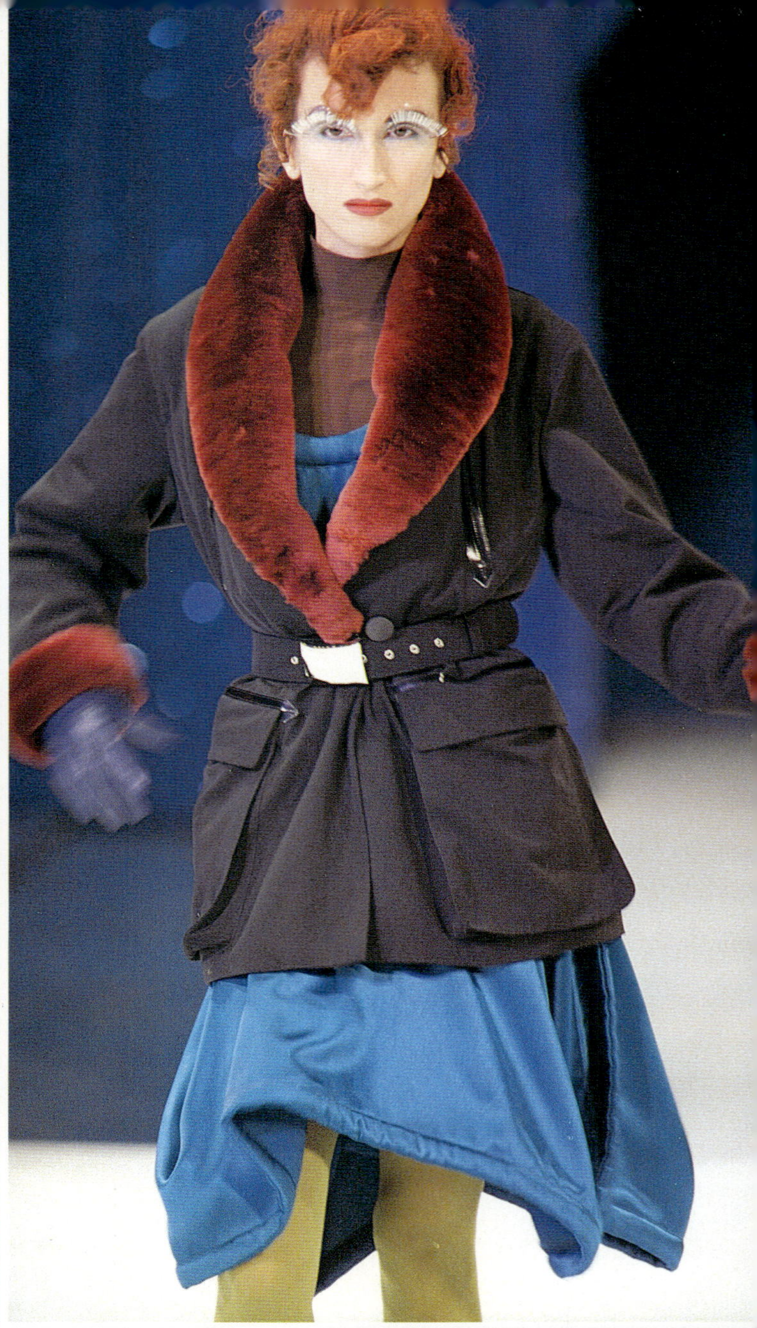
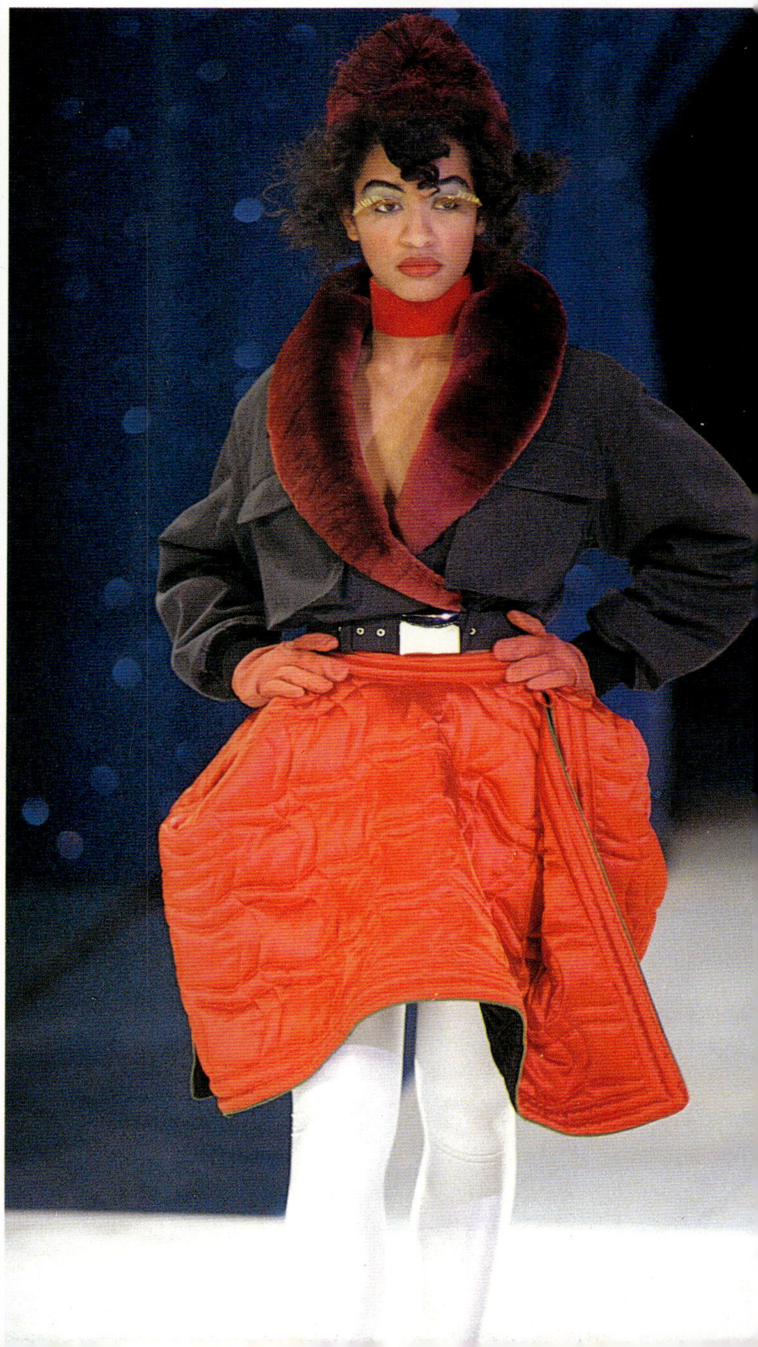

JEAN-PAUL GAULTIER

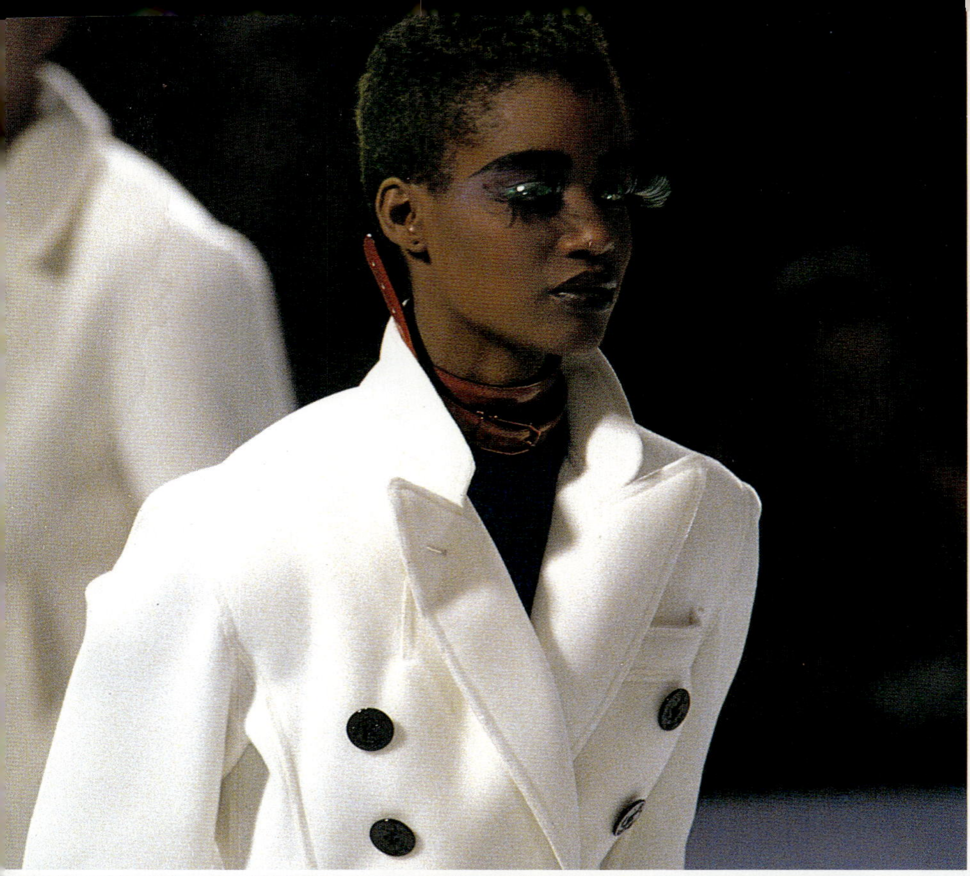
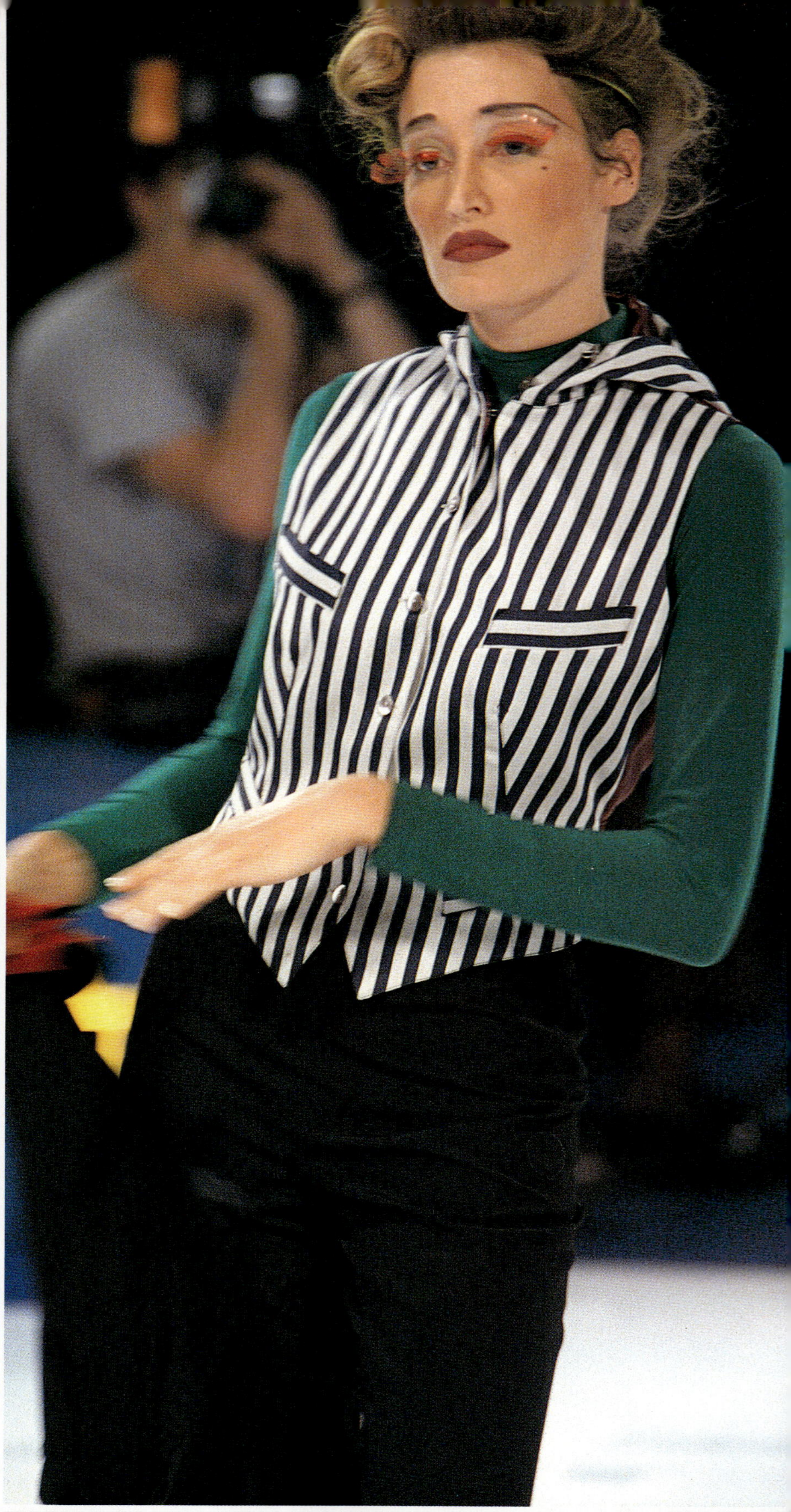
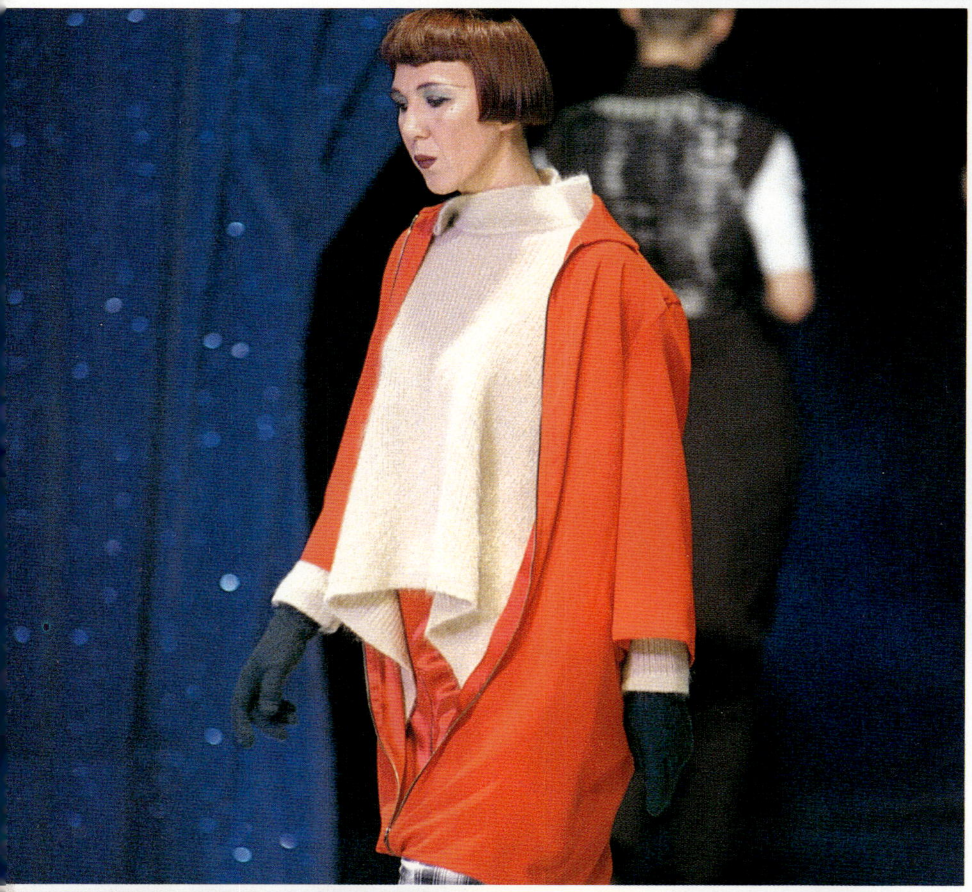
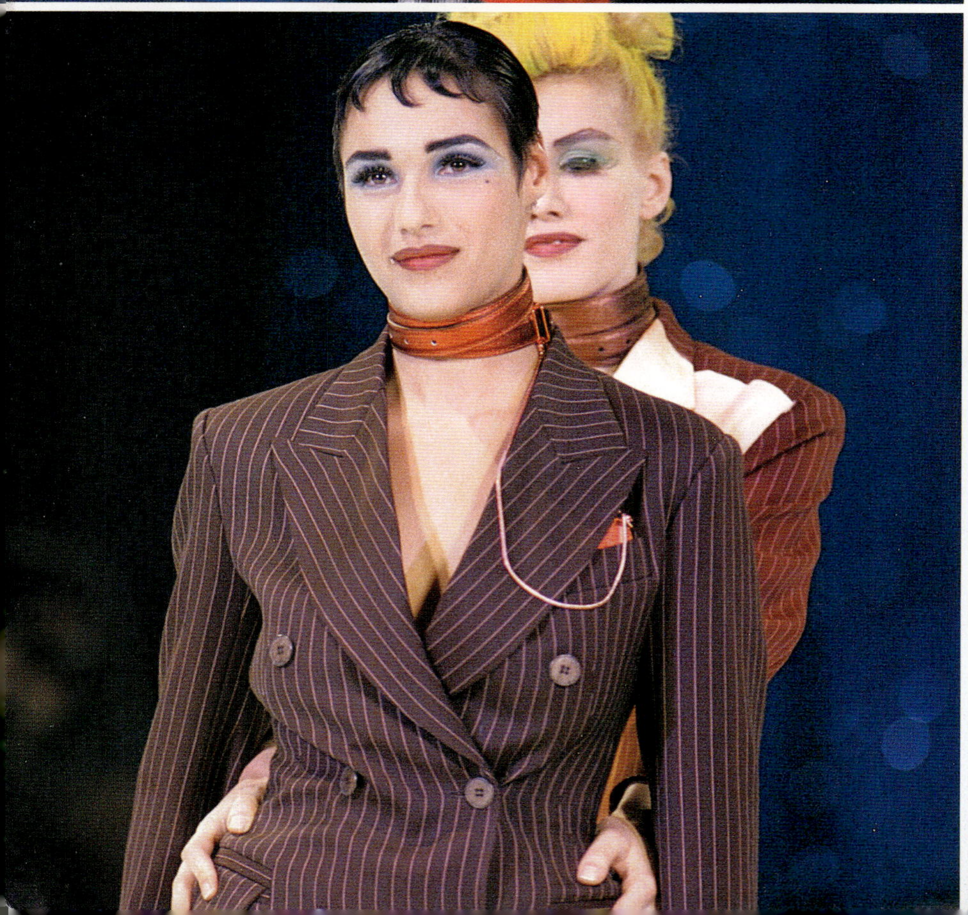
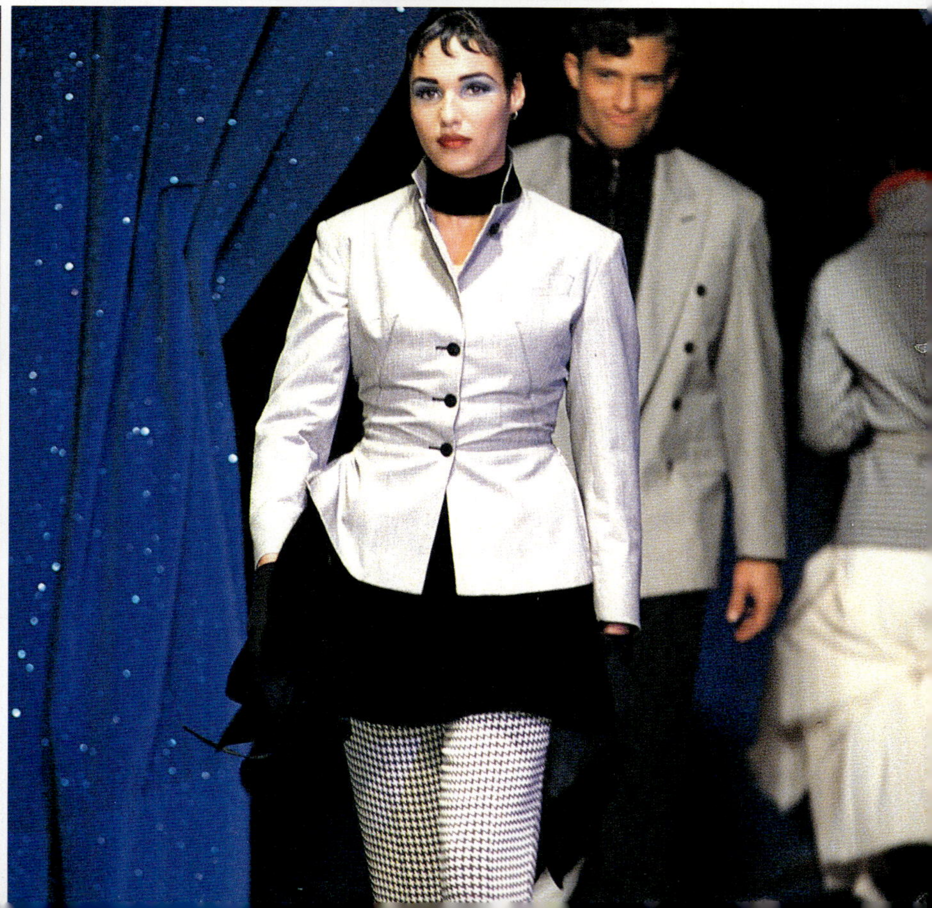

JEAN-PAUL GAULTIER

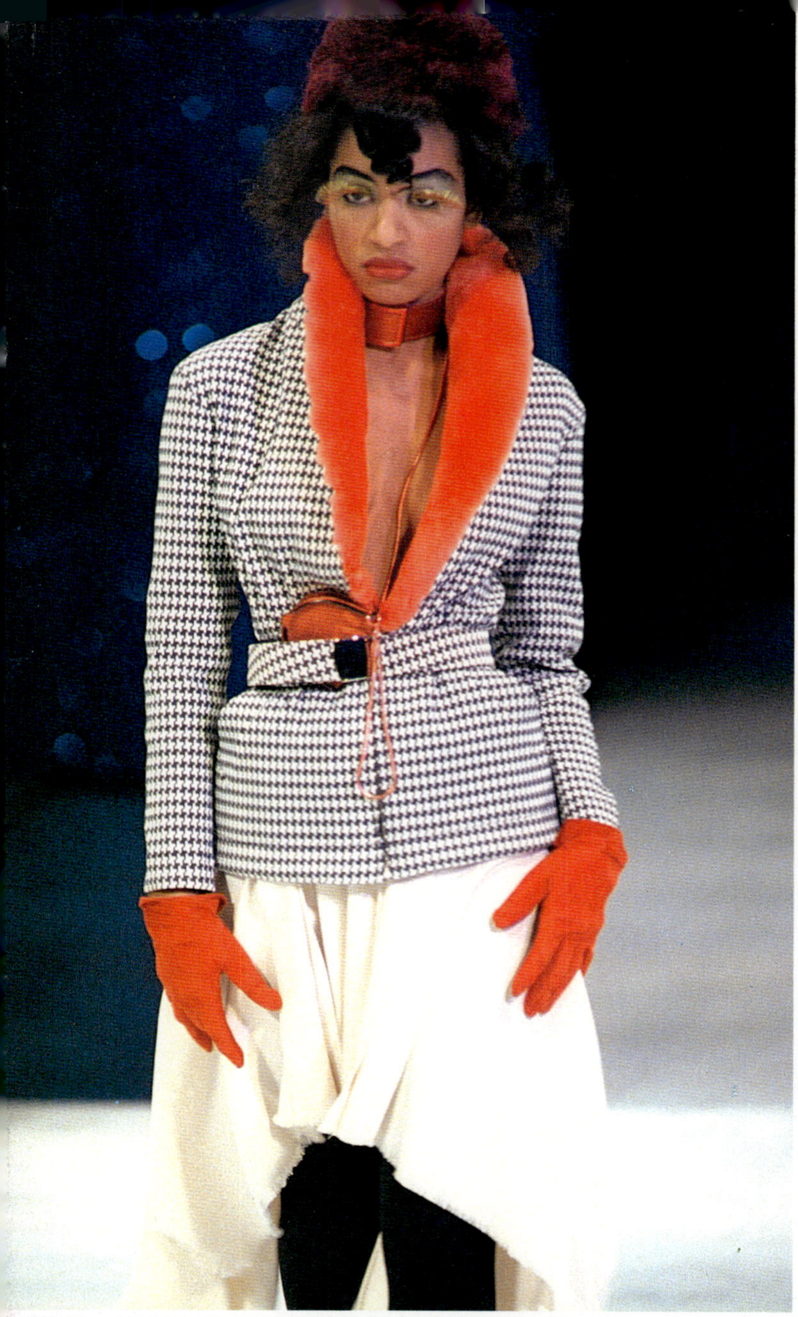
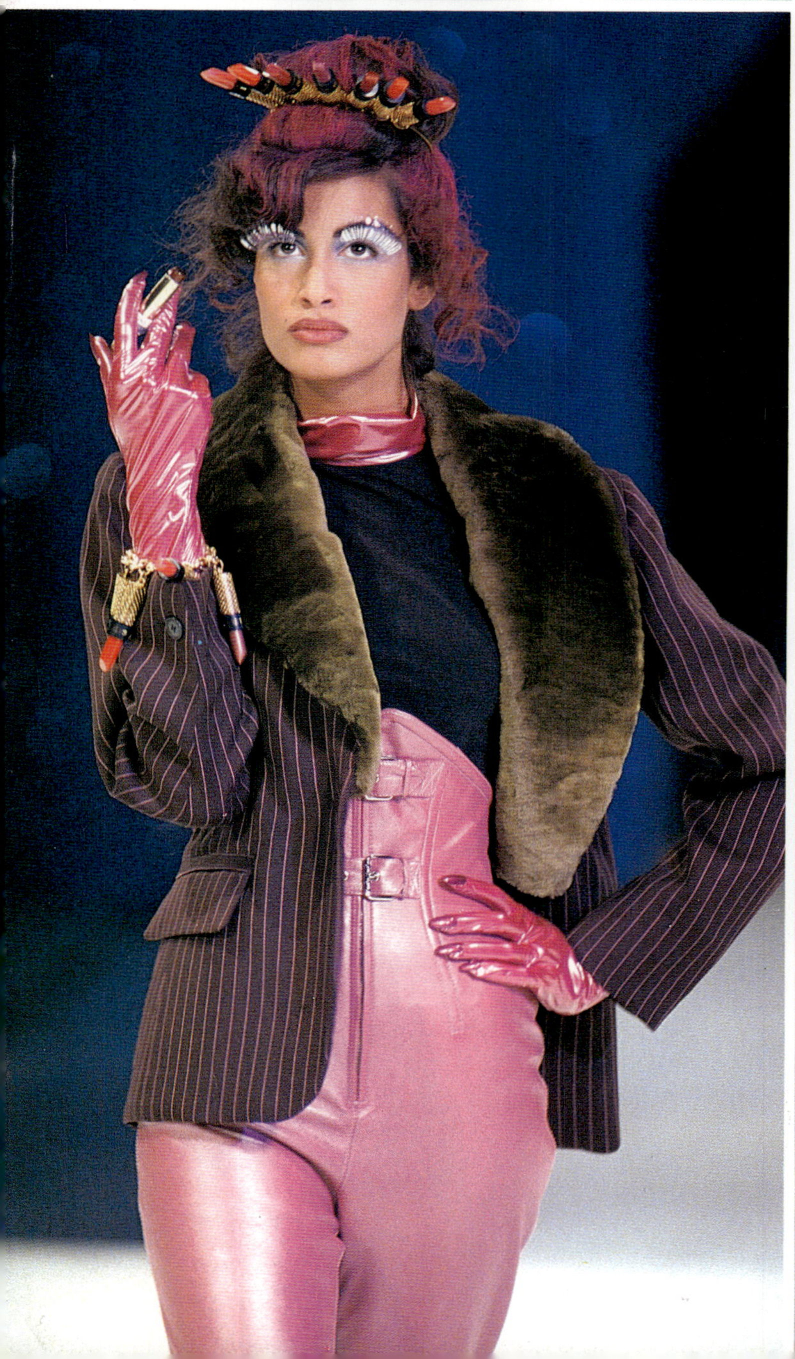
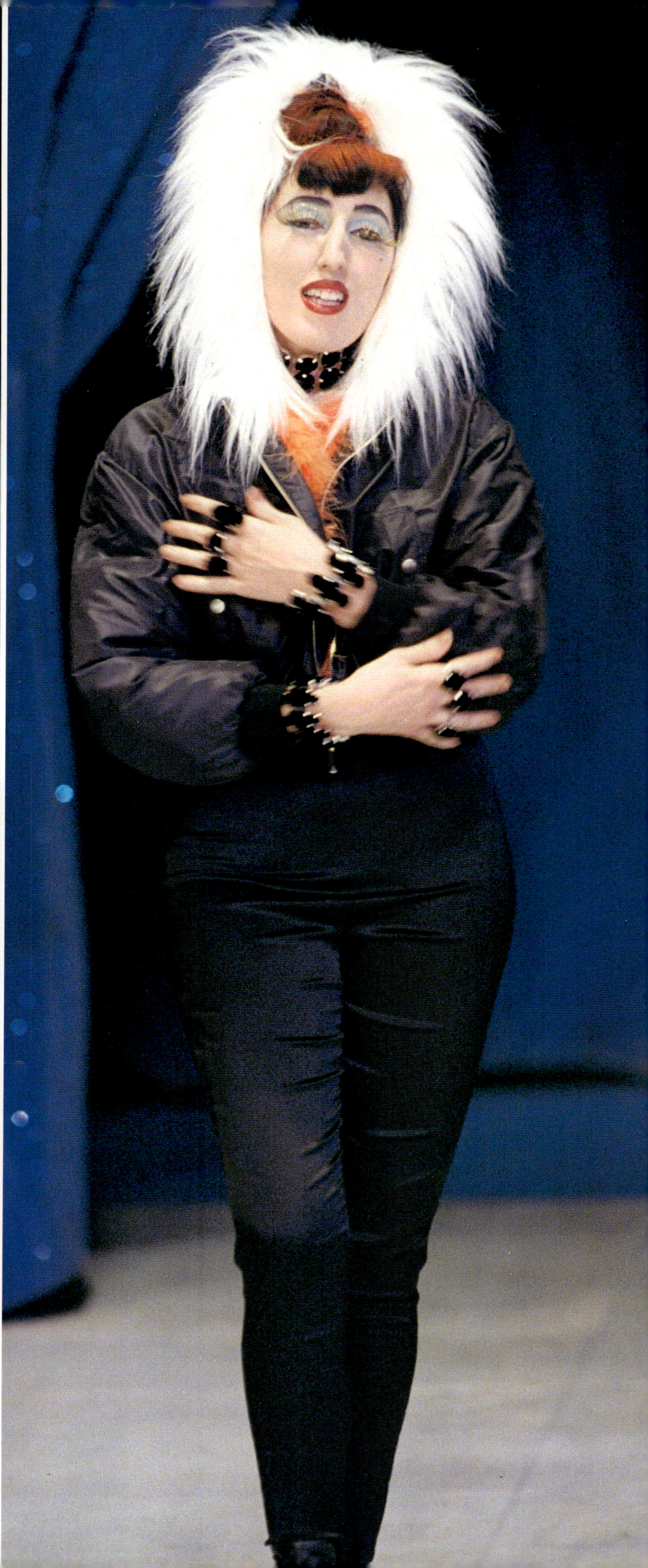

JEAN-PAUL GAULTIER

21

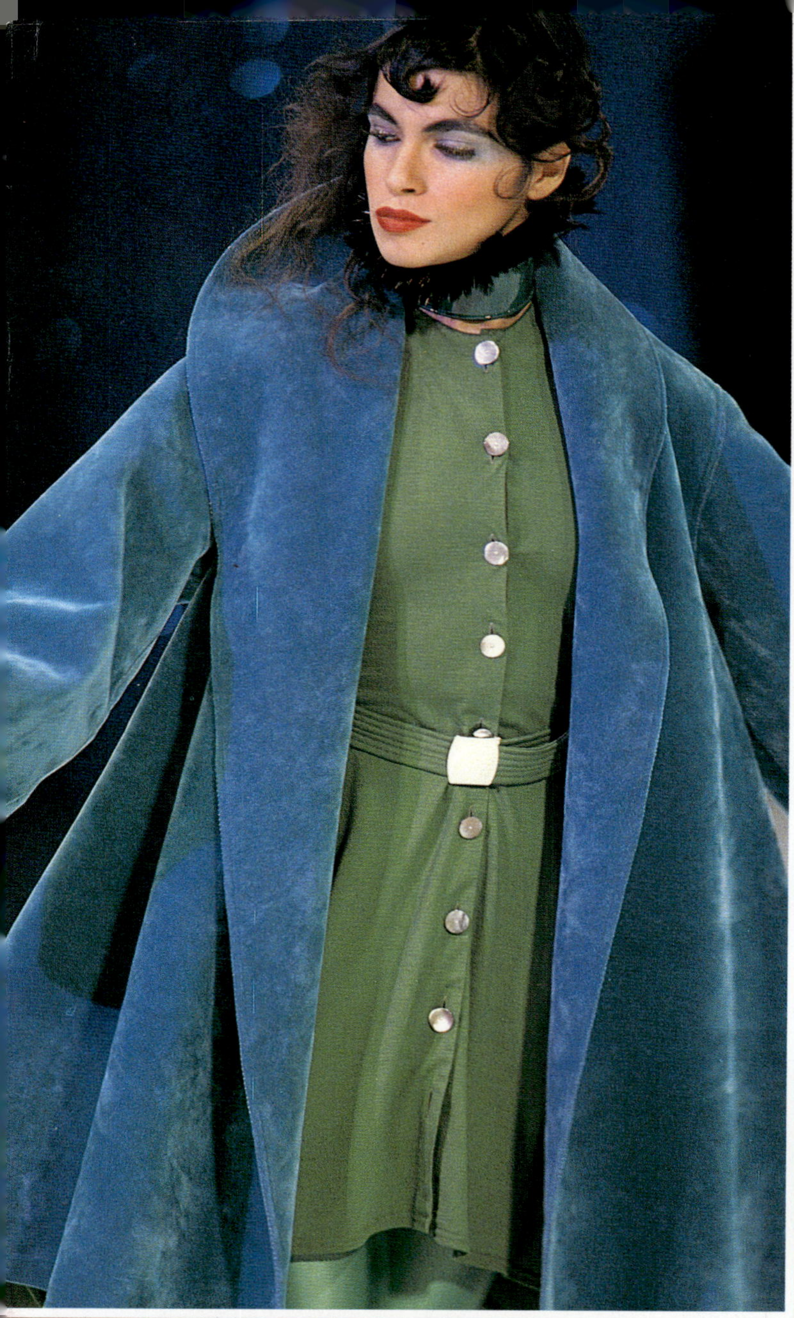
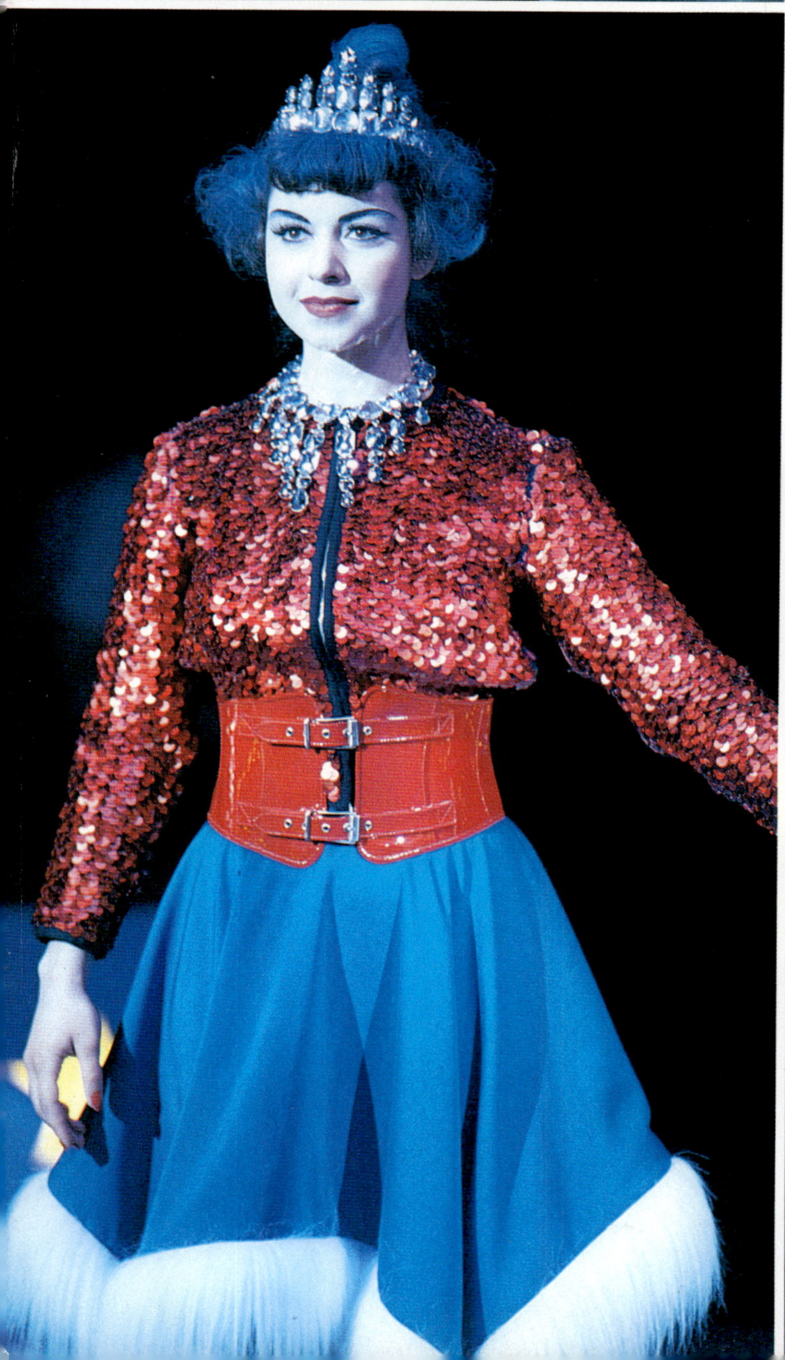
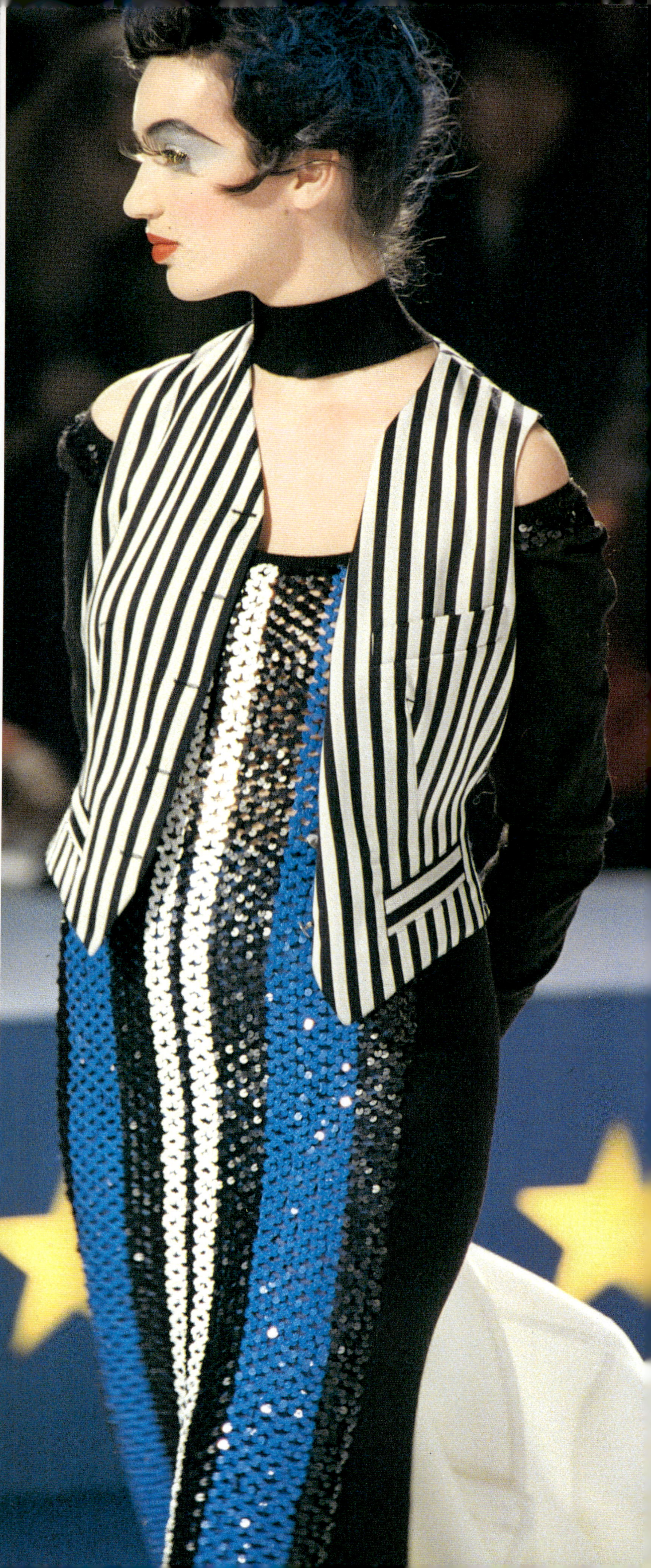

JEAN-PAUL GAULTIER

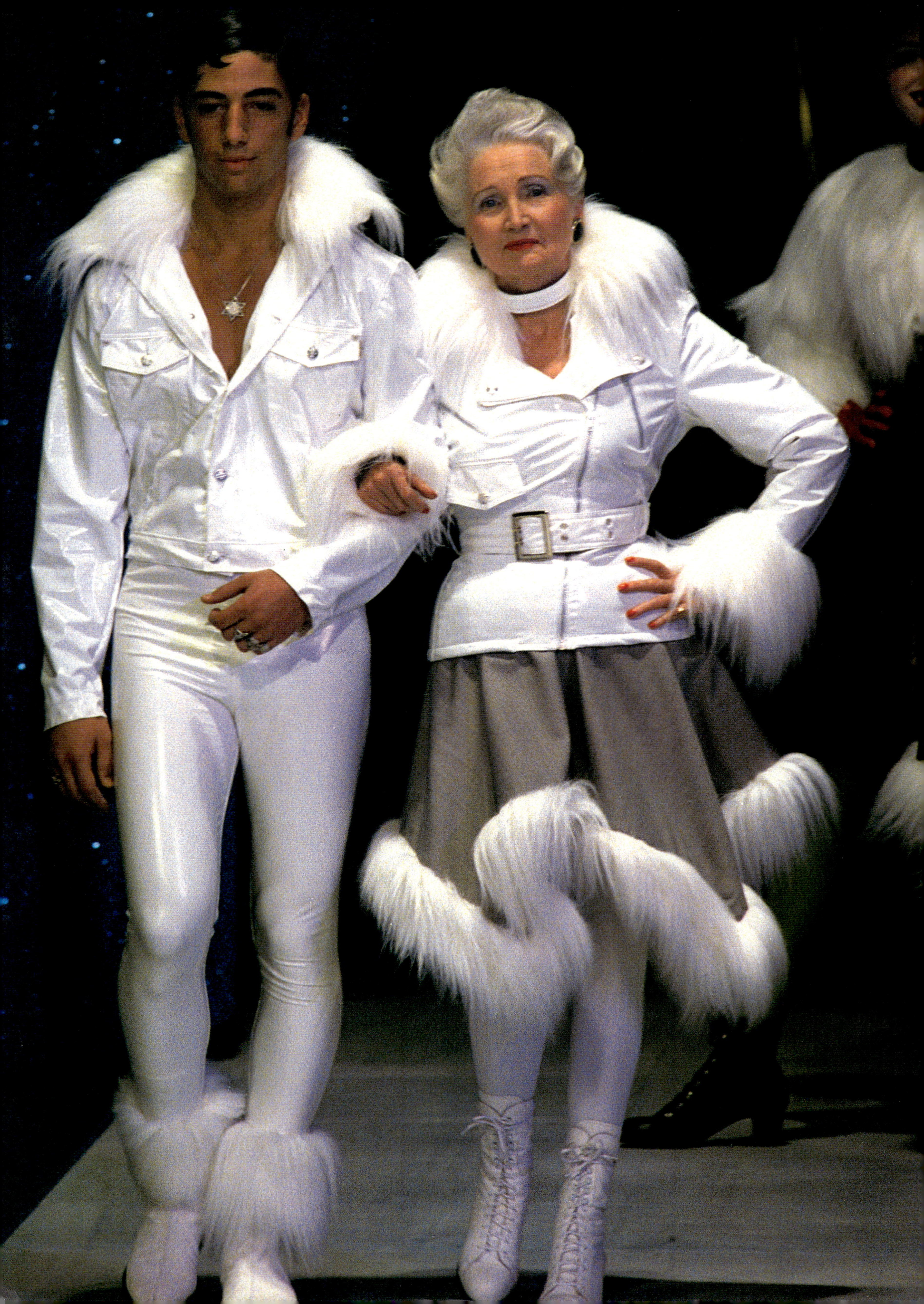

PARIS-2

COMME DES GARÇONS

コム・デ・ギャルソン

ビニール素材のディテール使いや異素材コンビネーションにクリエイティブ力が漲る秀逸なコレクション。日本画を想起させるフル・ドレスのプリントは絶賛の的。
An excellent collection, demonstrating superb creativty in its use of vinyl materials in the details, and its combination of different materials. The full dress prints, reminiscent of Japanese paintings, drew great applause.

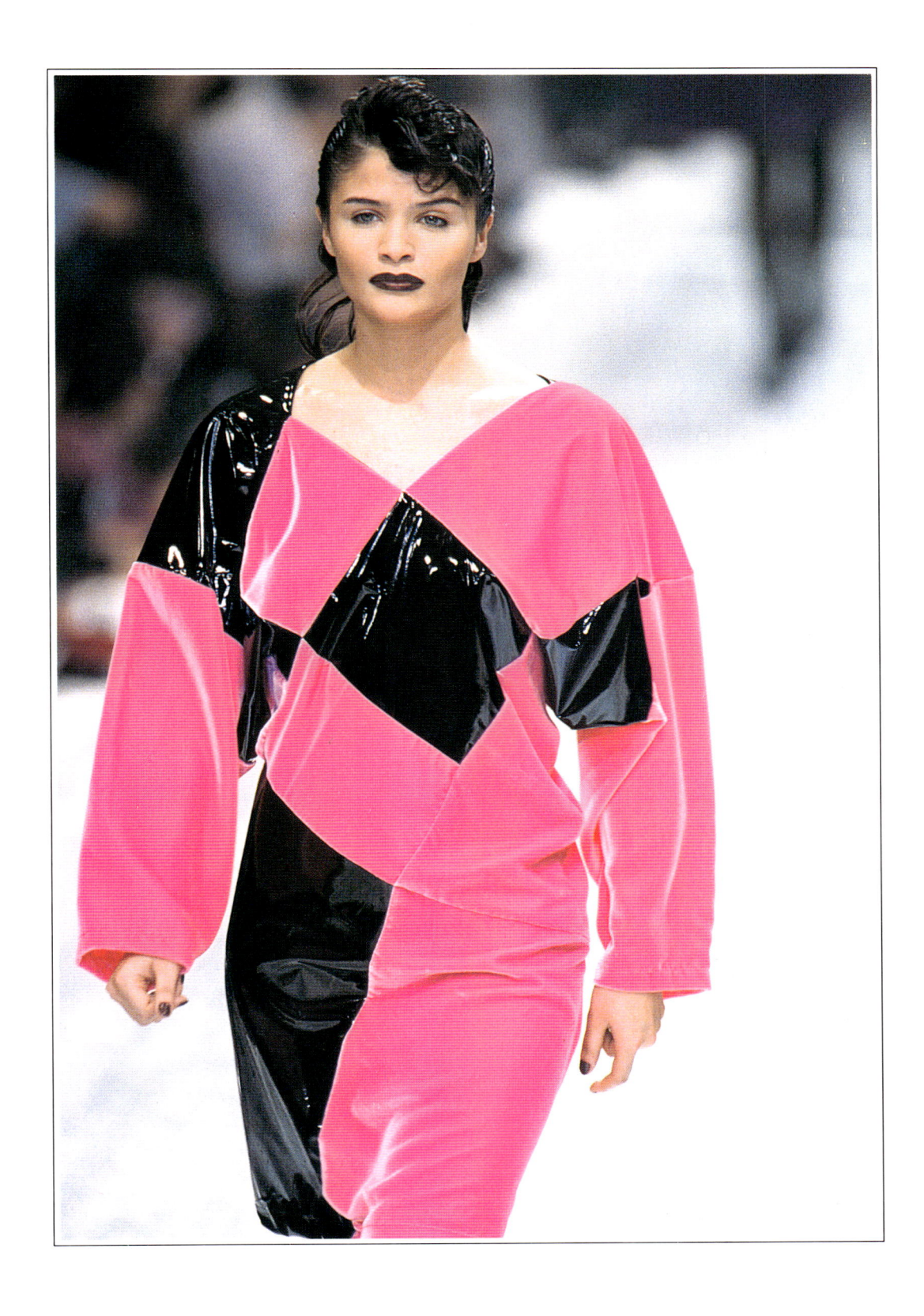

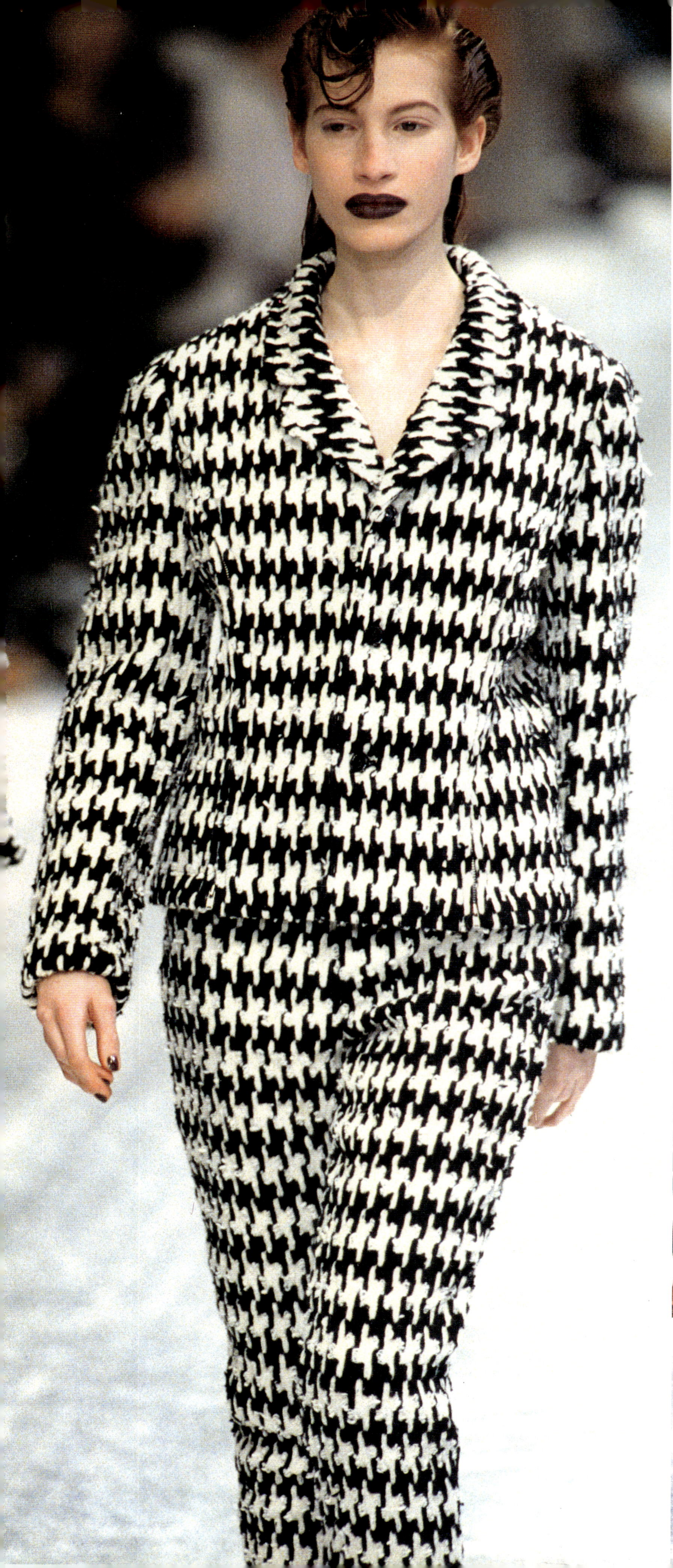
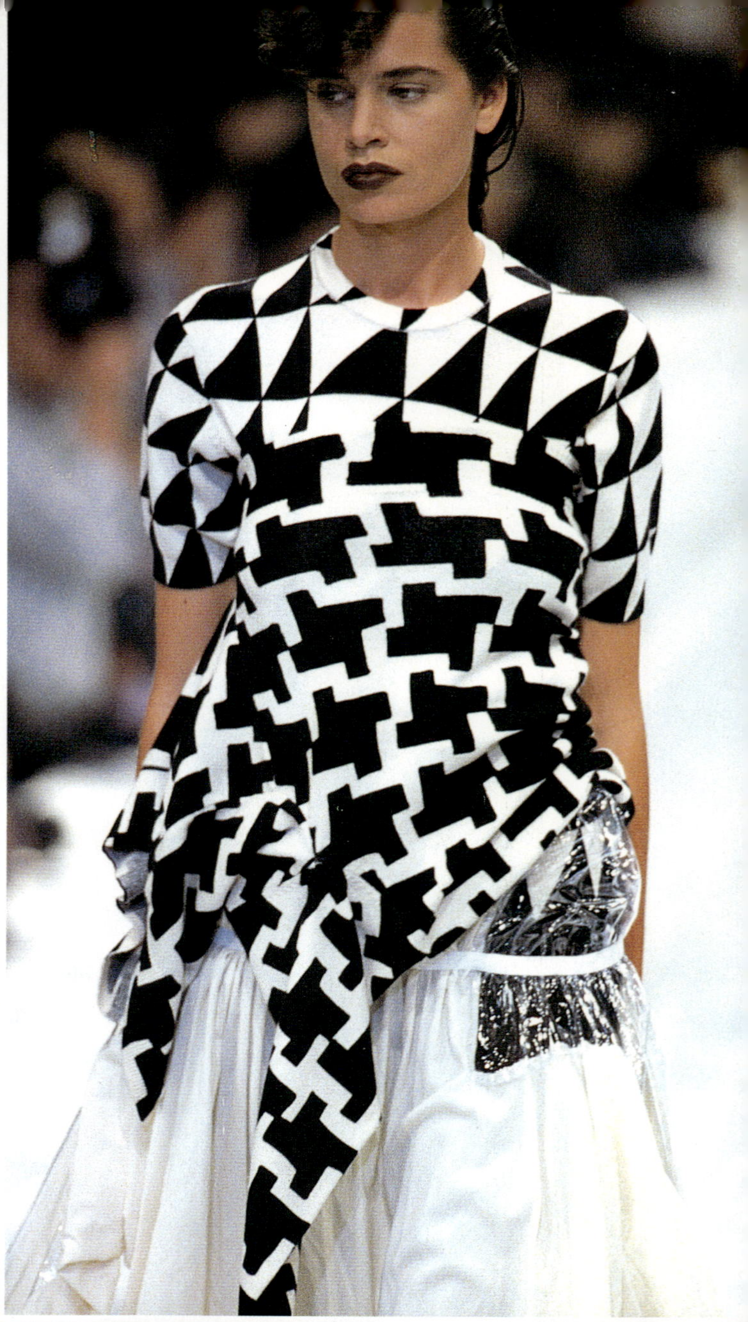
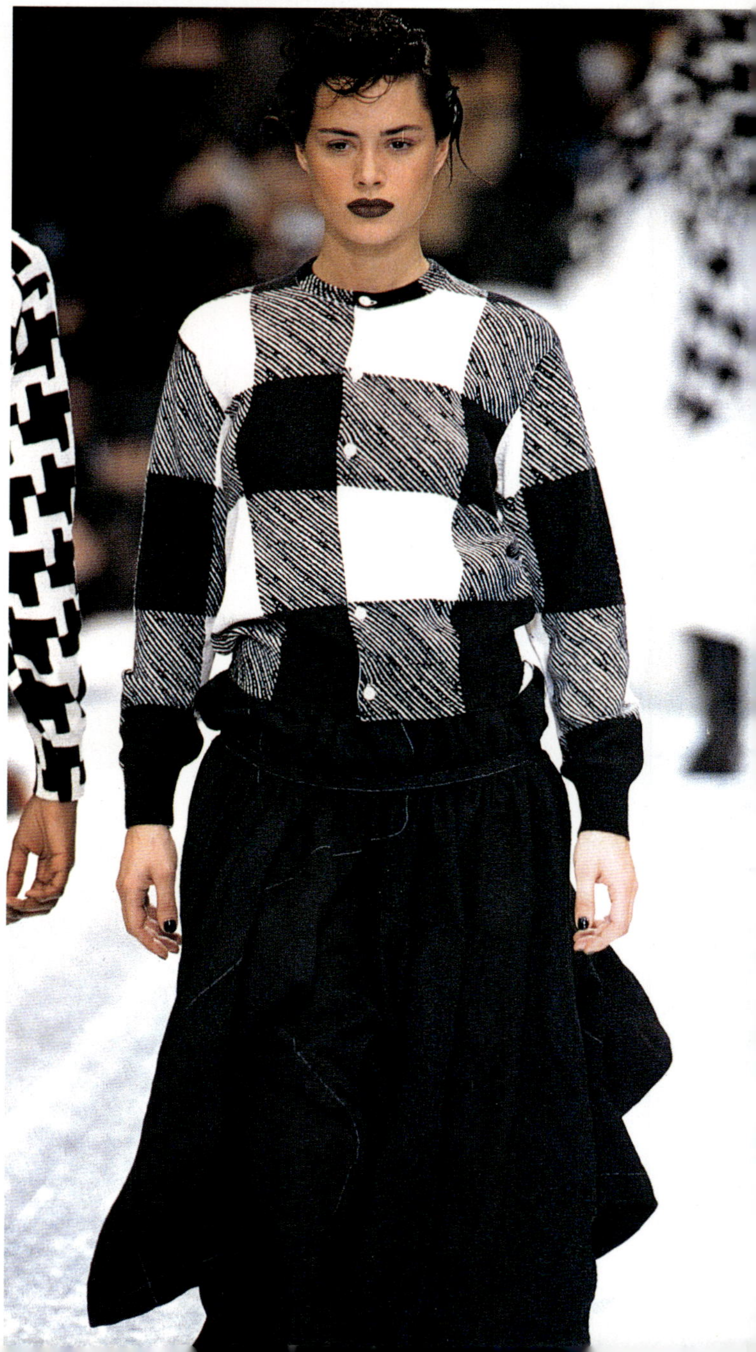

COMME DES GARÇONS

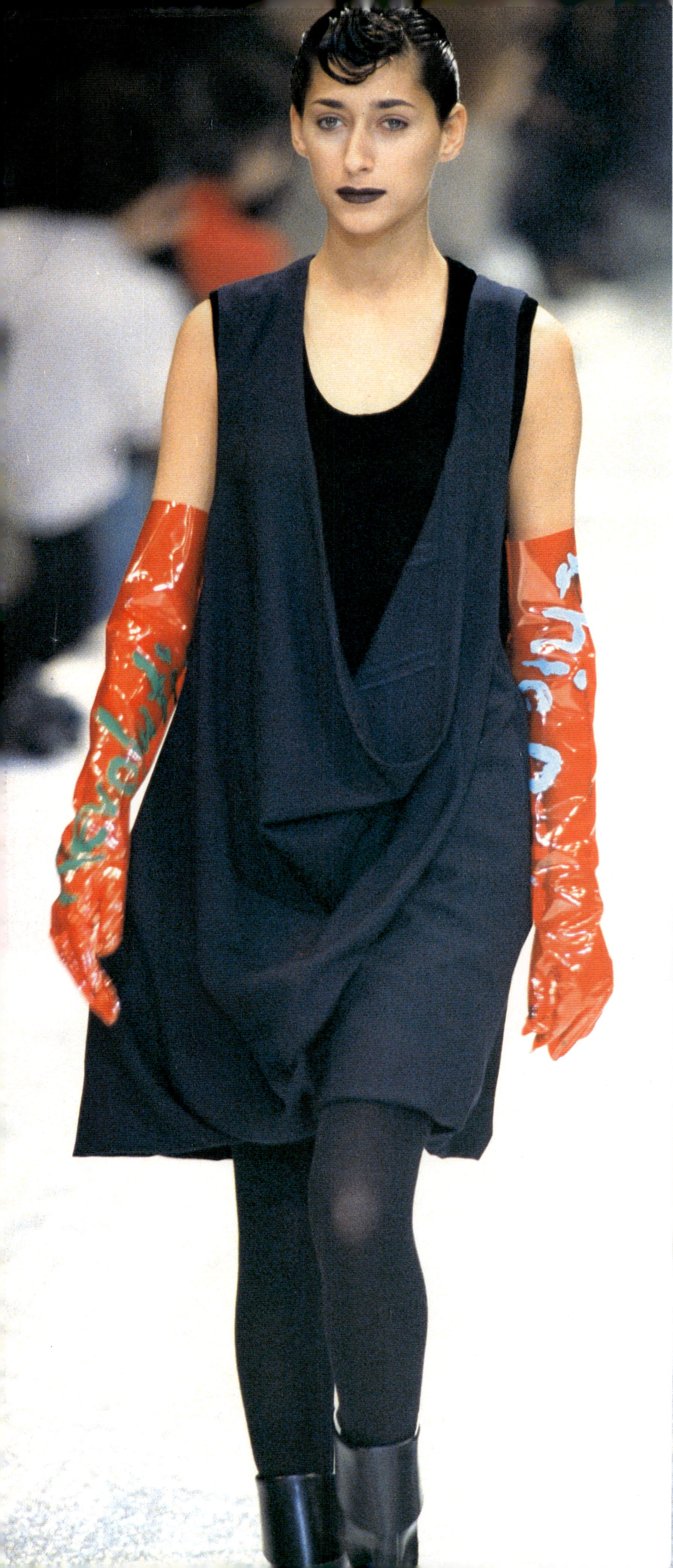

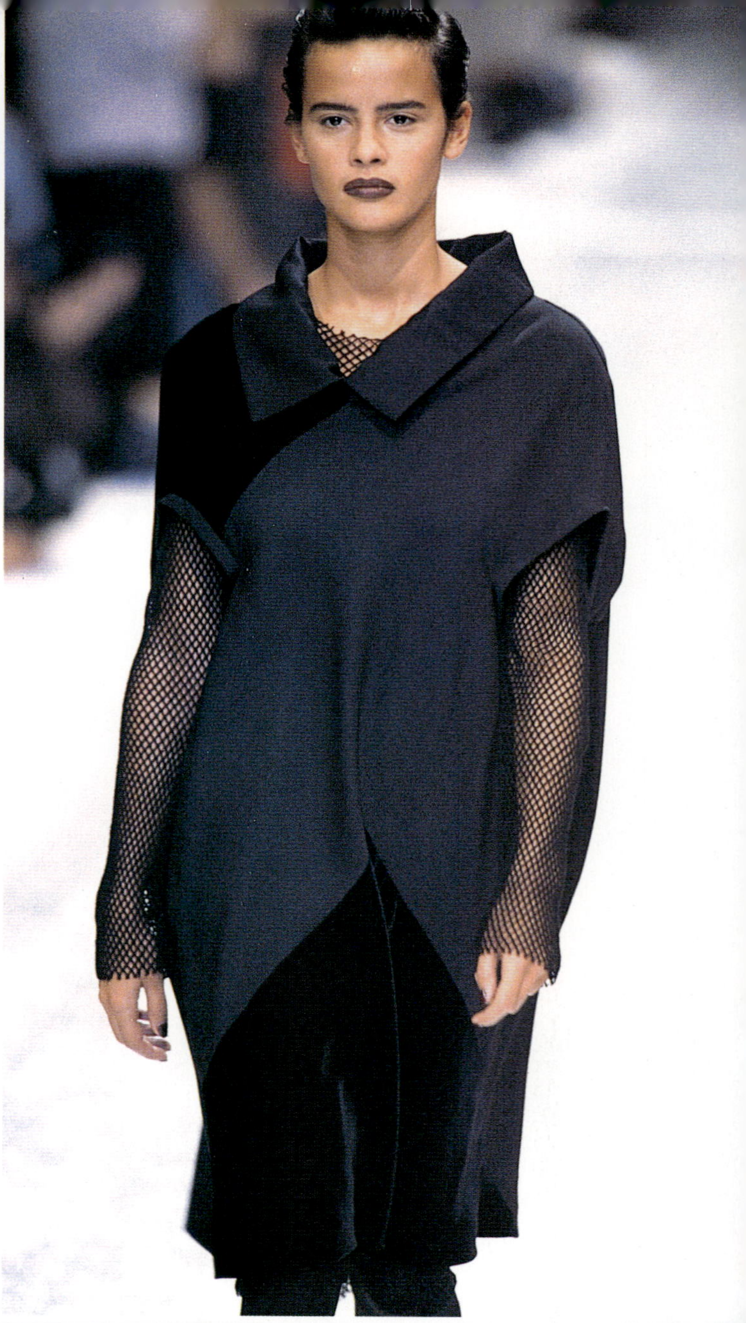

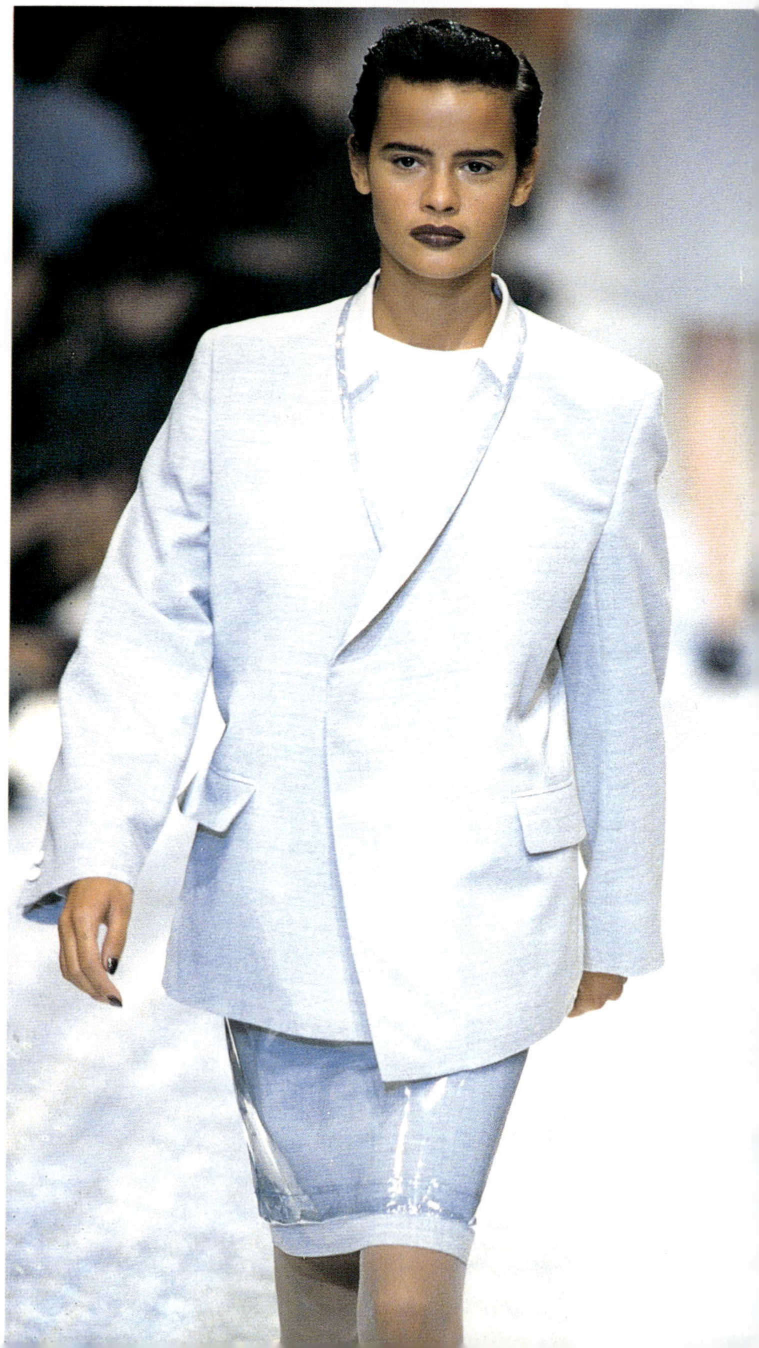

COMME DES GARCONS

29

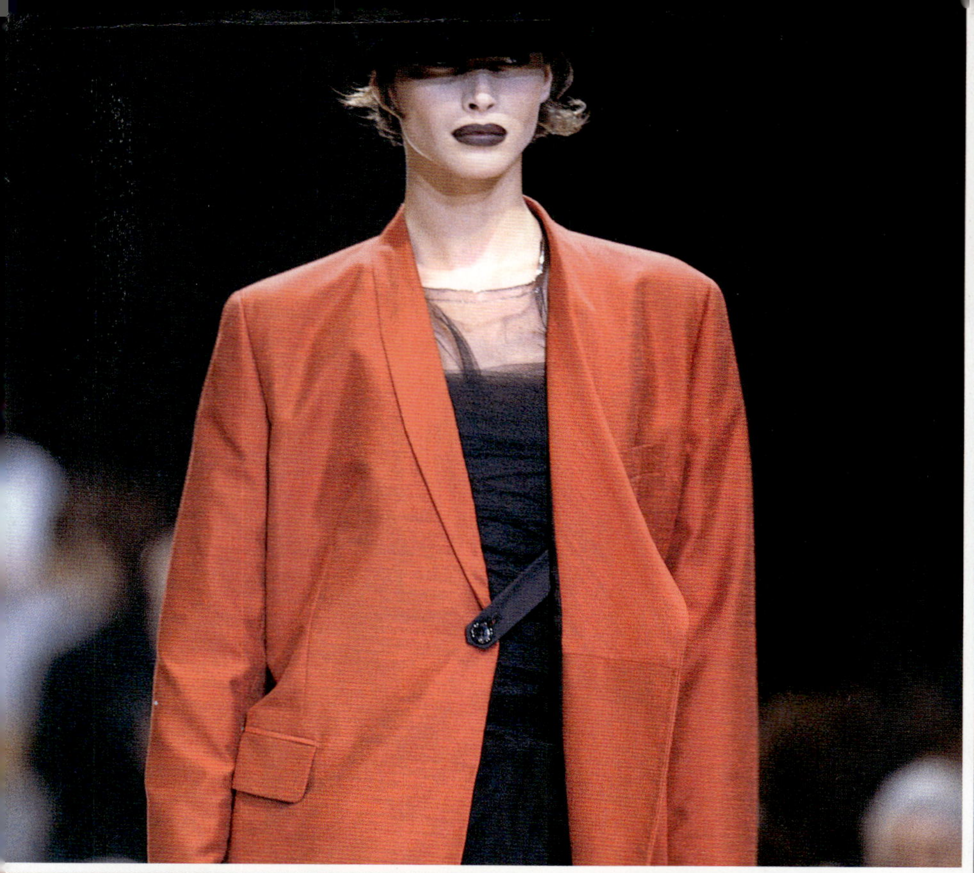
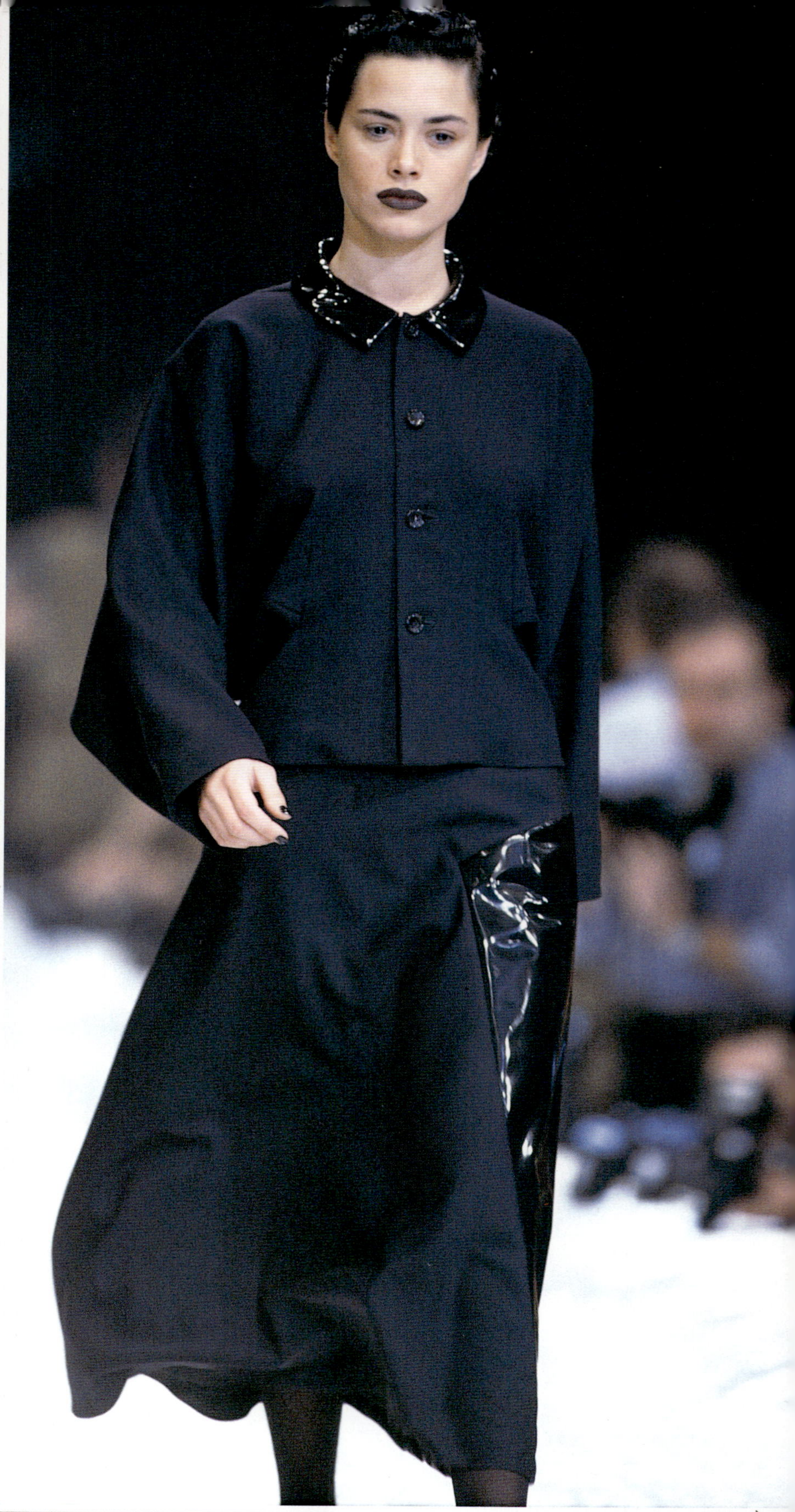
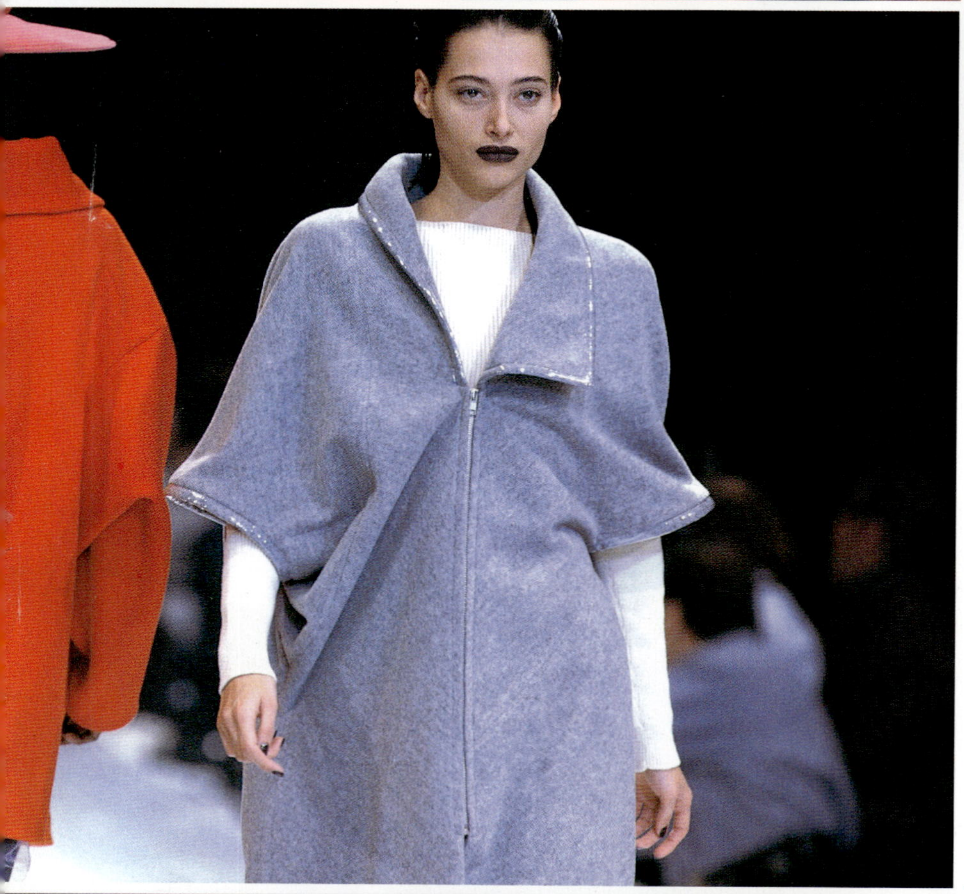
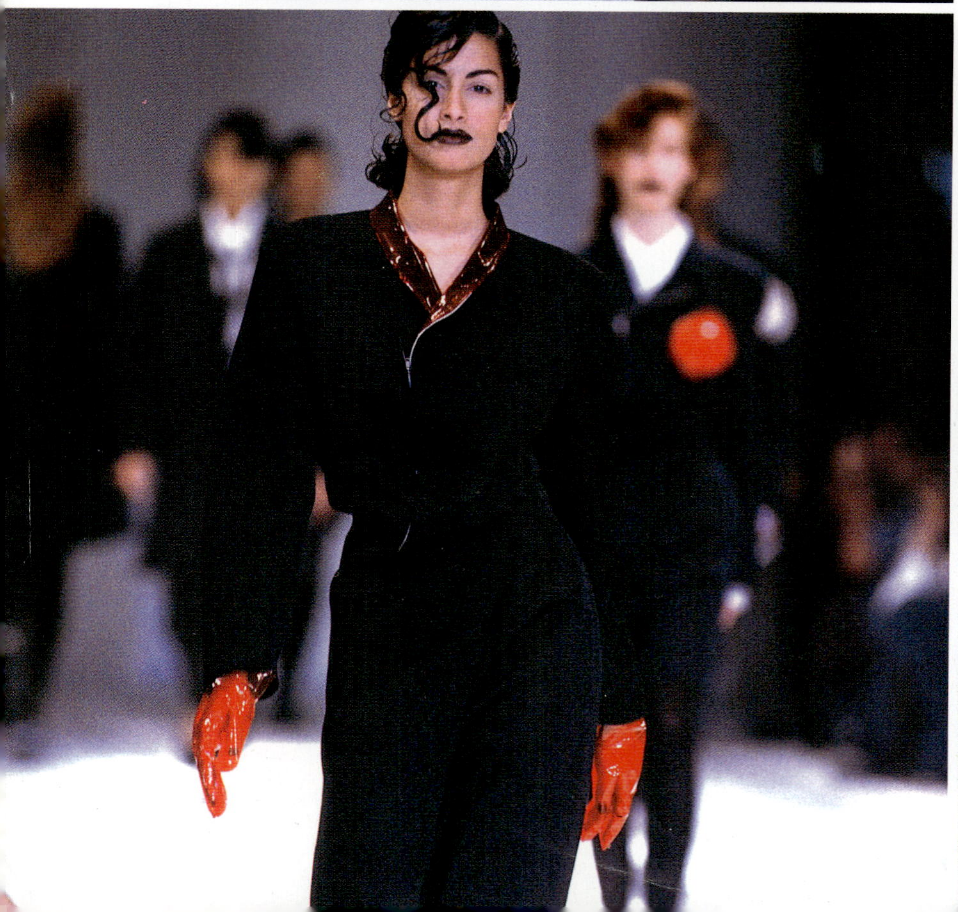
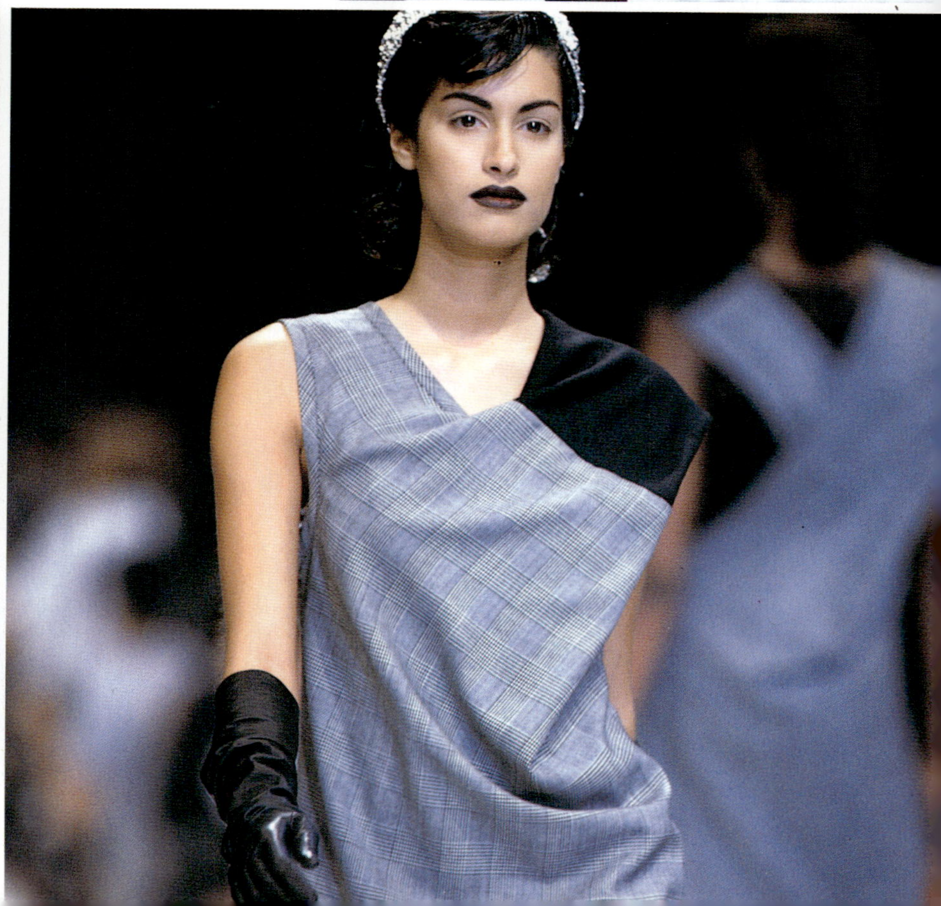

COMME DES GARÇONS

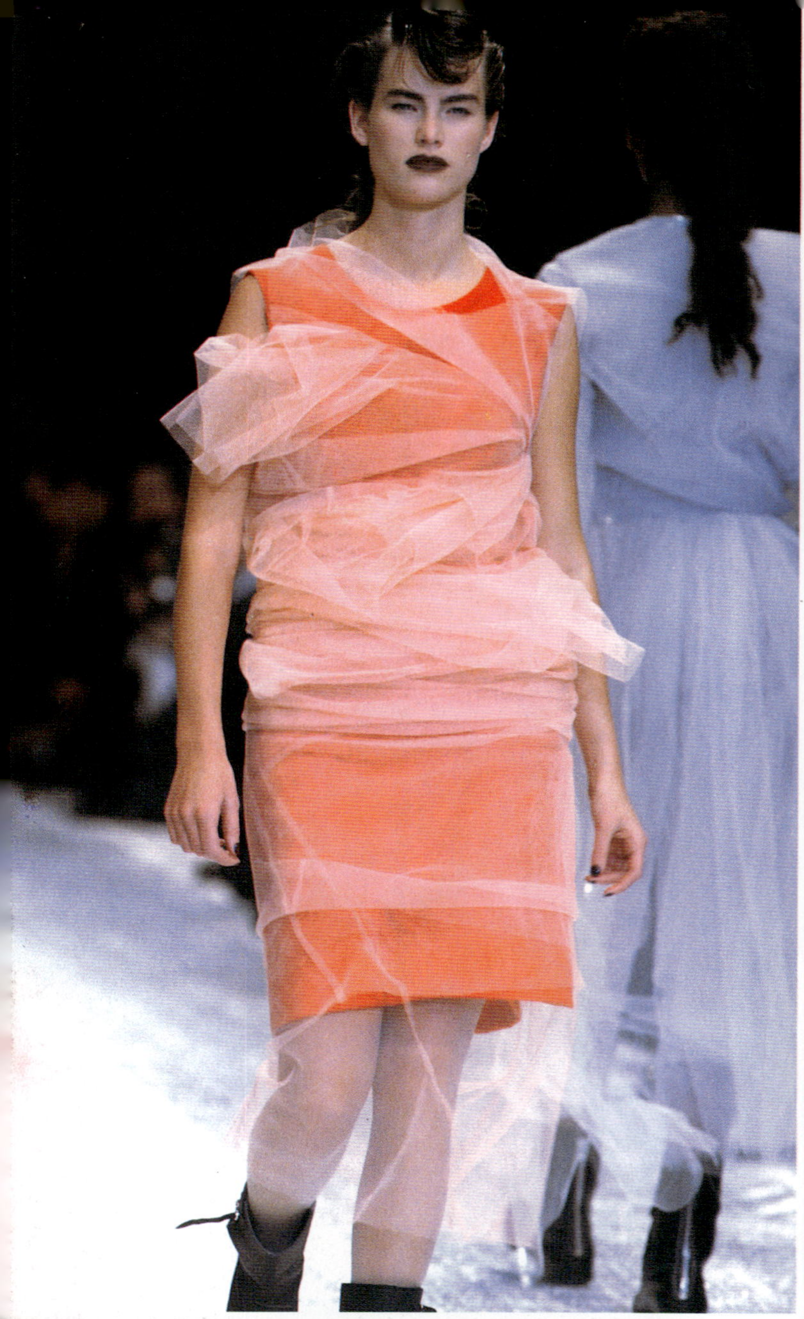
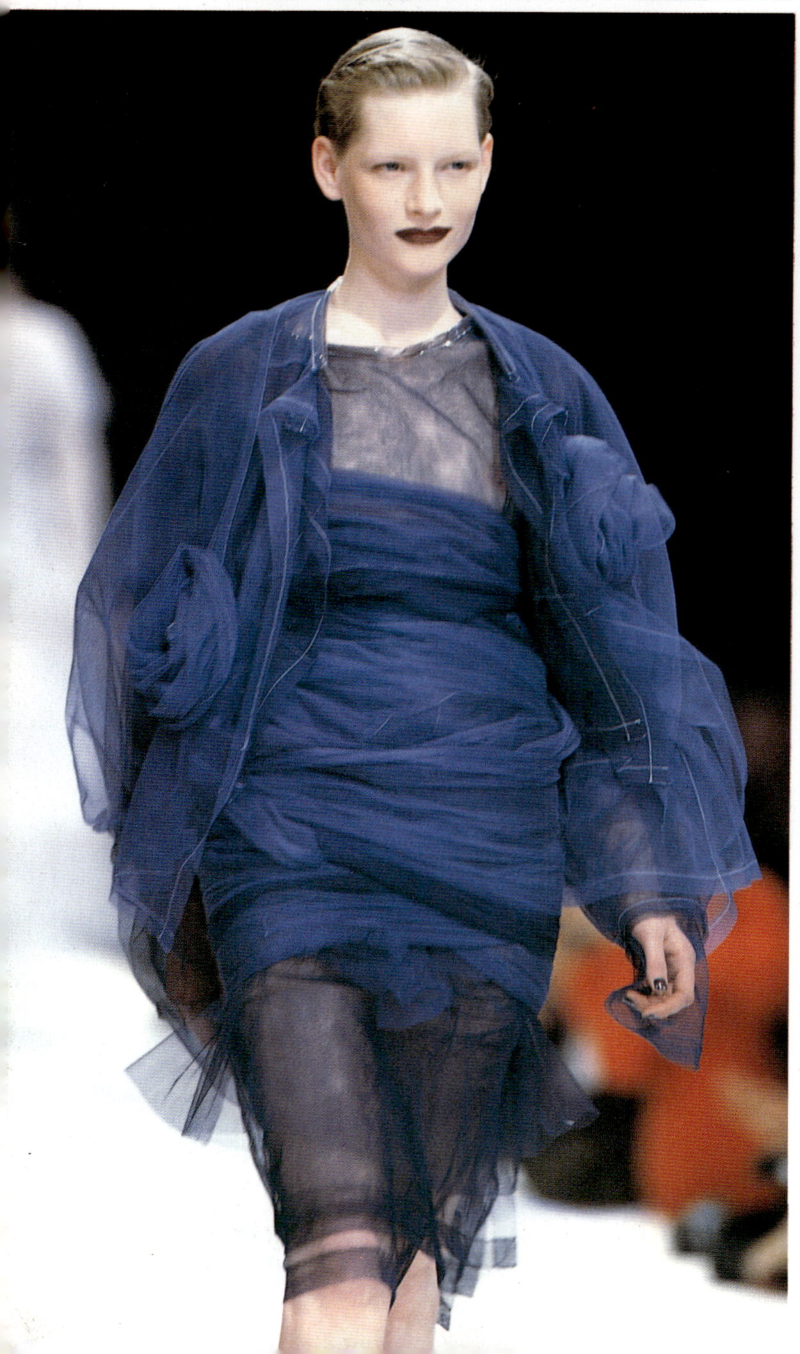
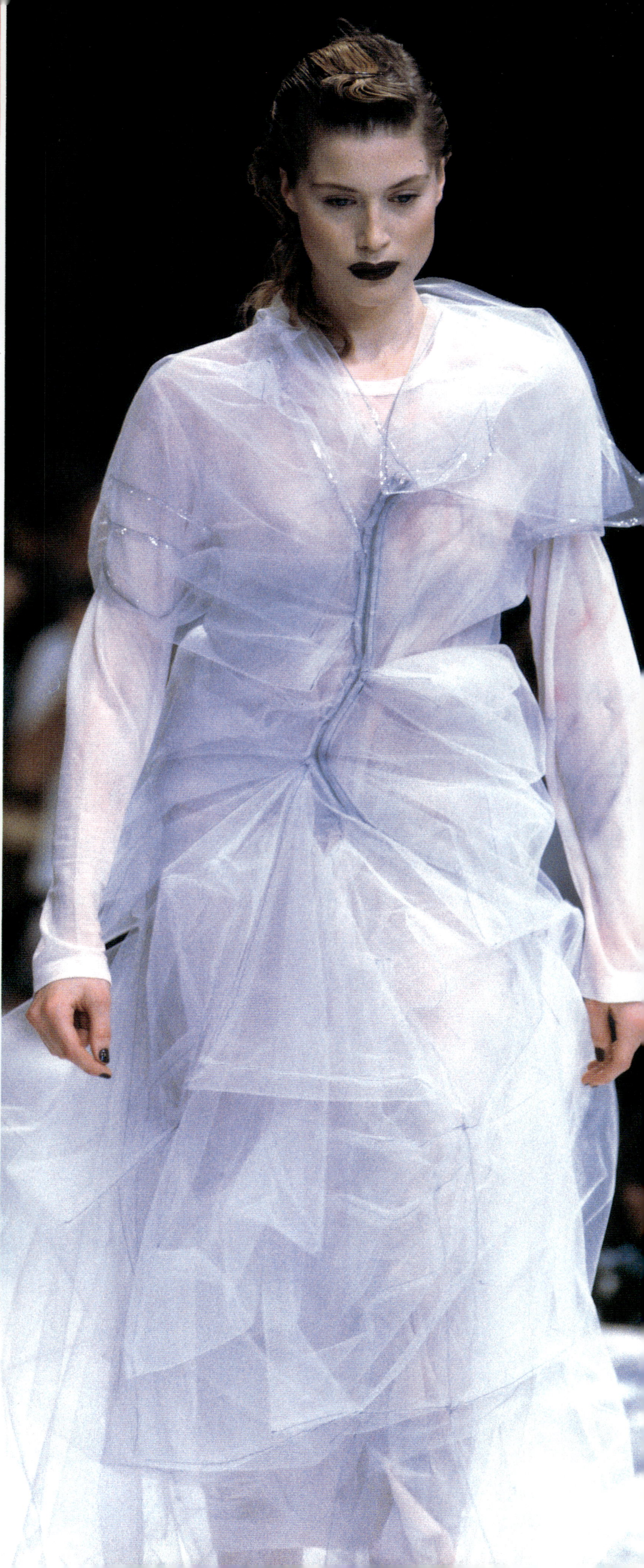

COMME DES GARÇONS

33

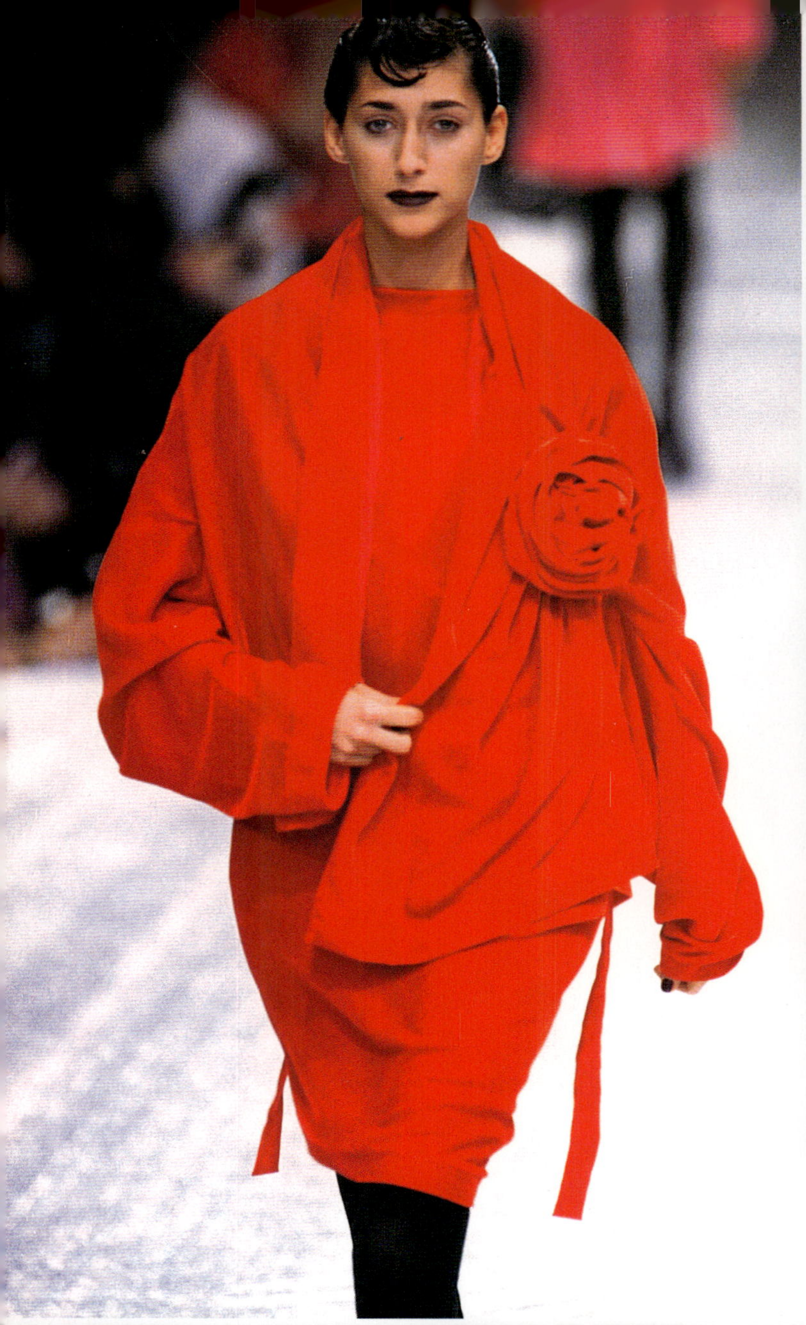
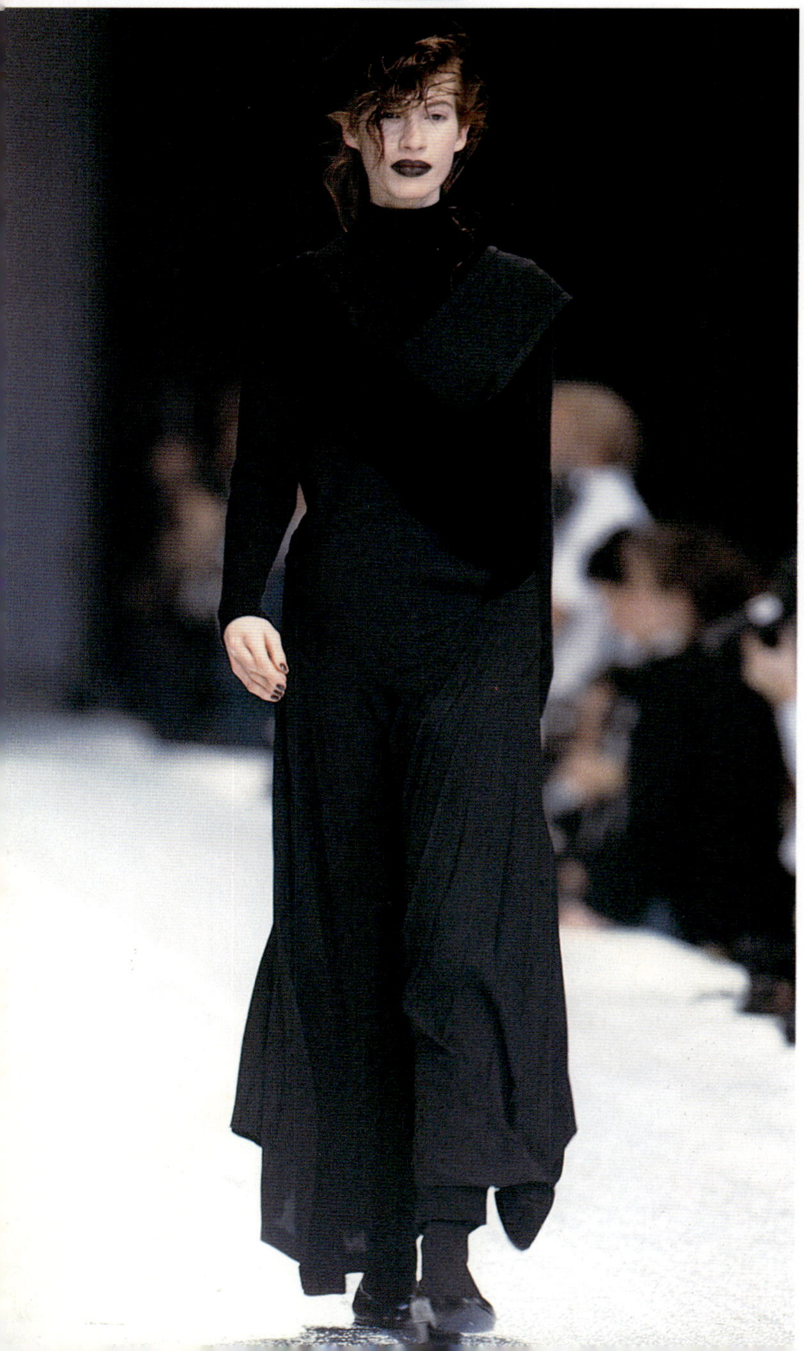
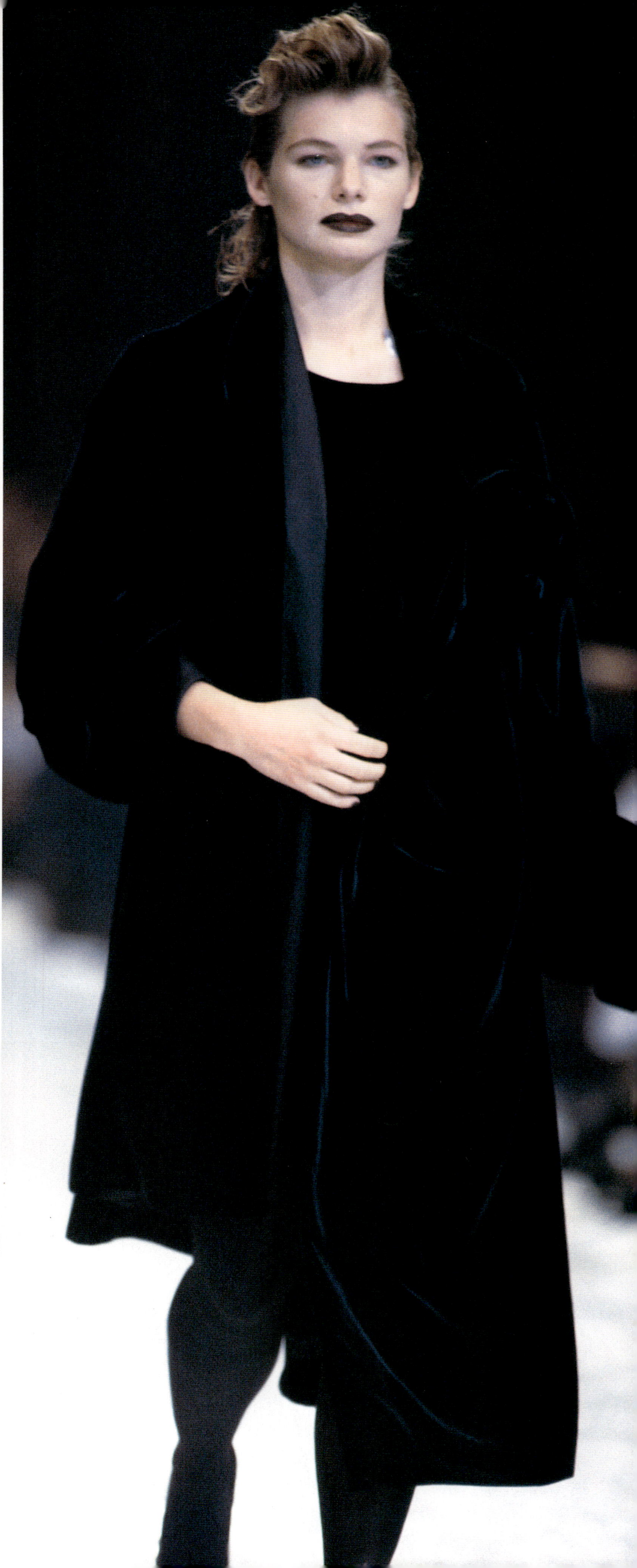

COMME DES GARÇONS

35

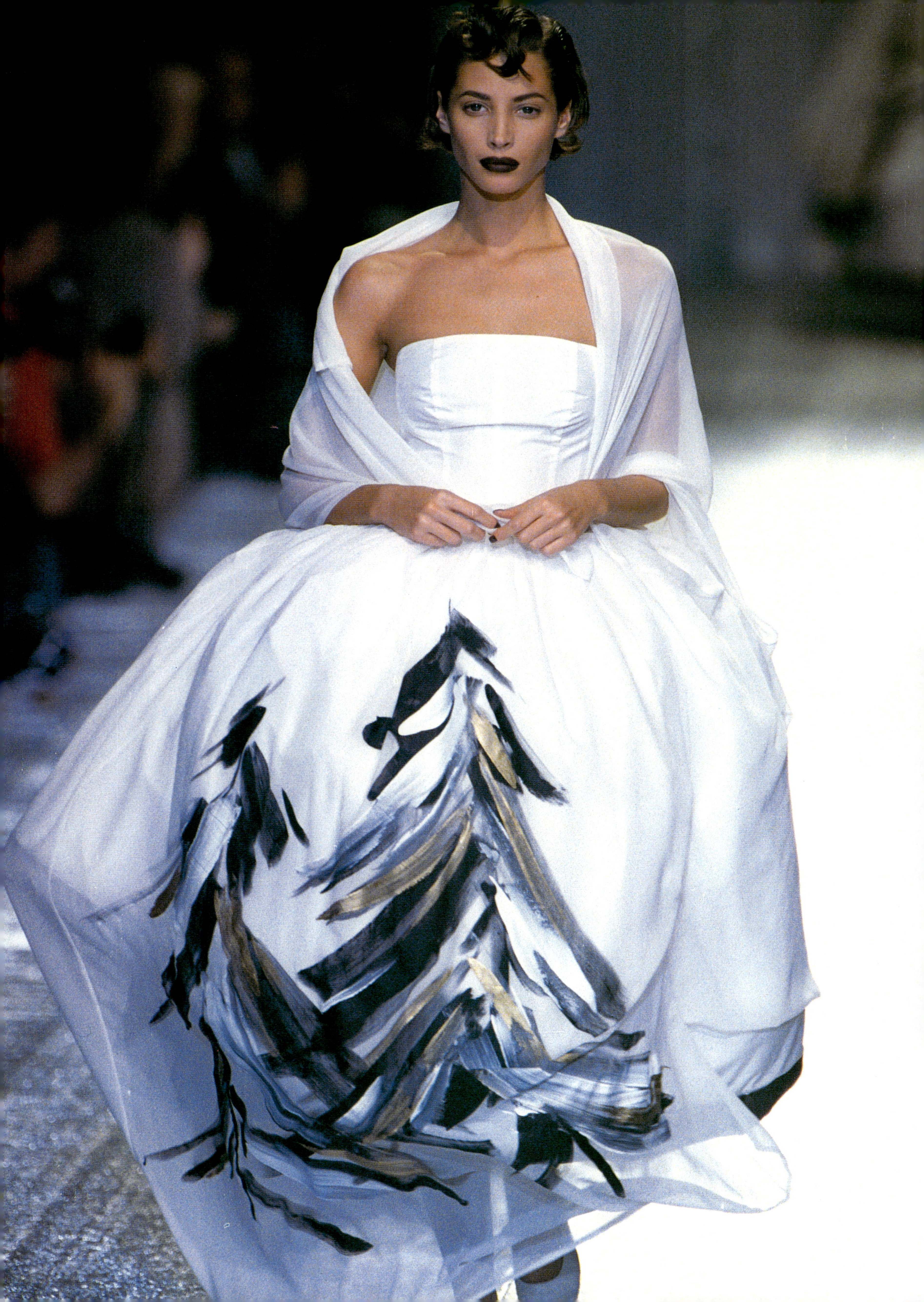

CLAUDE MONTANA

クロード・モンタナ

色彩と造形美の天才、クロード・モンタナの今シーズンは、シャープなシルエットとブライト・カラーの見事な調和。スラッシュを入れた大胆なヘムが新しい。
A genius in the creation of beauty in colors and shapes, this season Claude Montana demonstrated excellent harmony with sharp silhouettes and bright colors. Also a new addition, a hem with a bold slash.

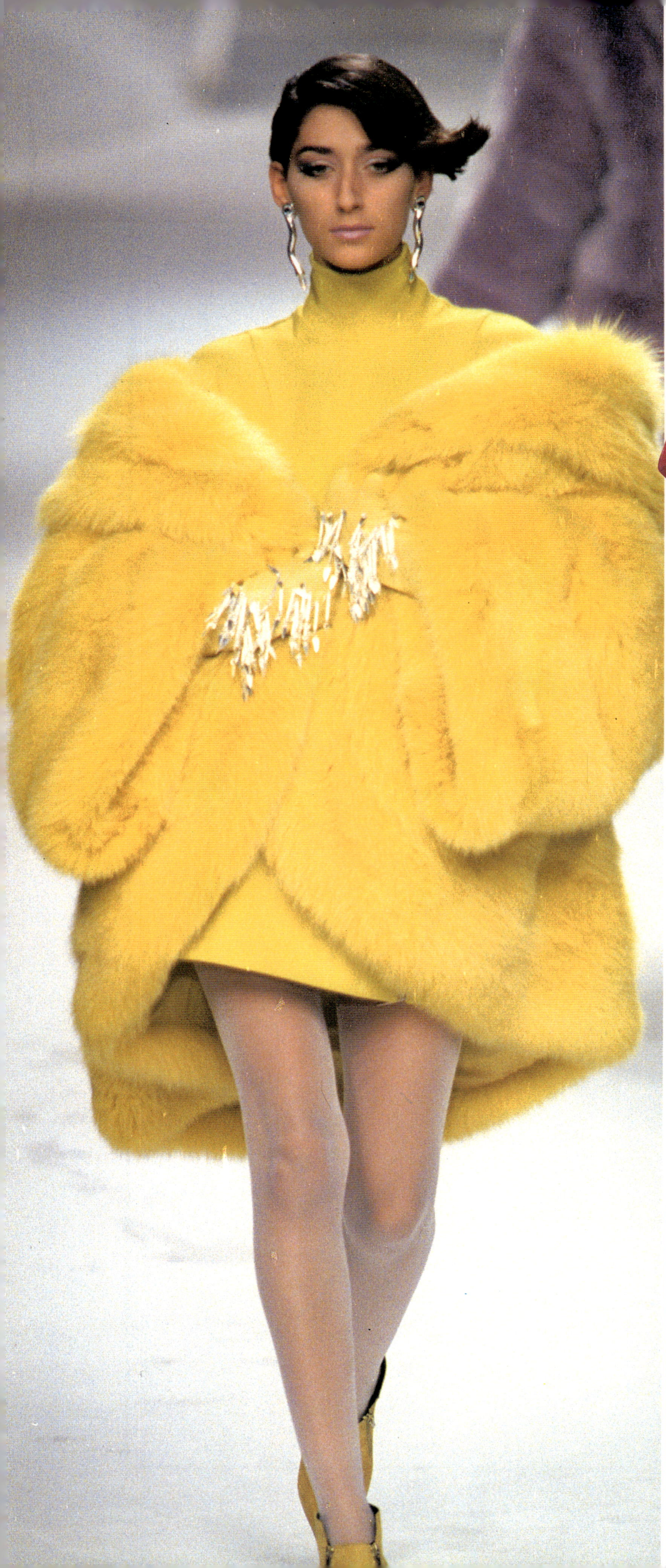
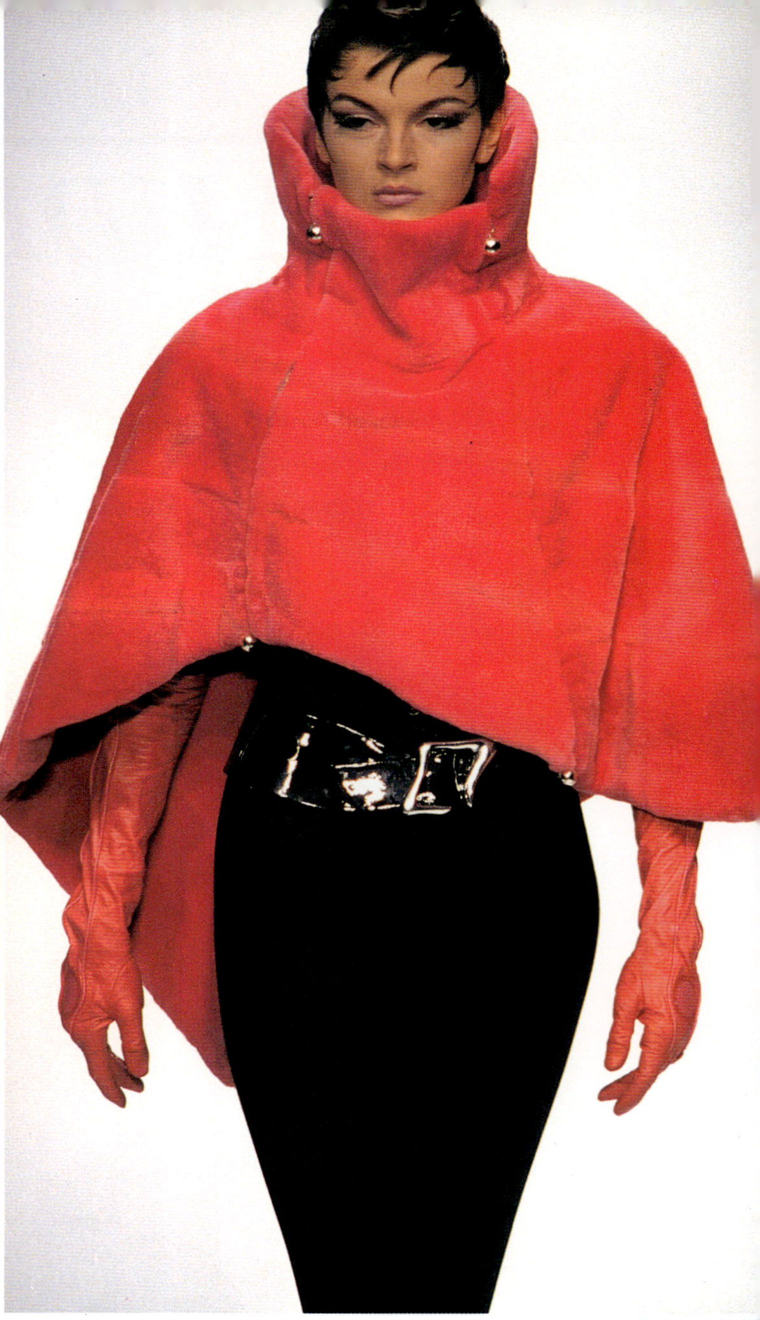
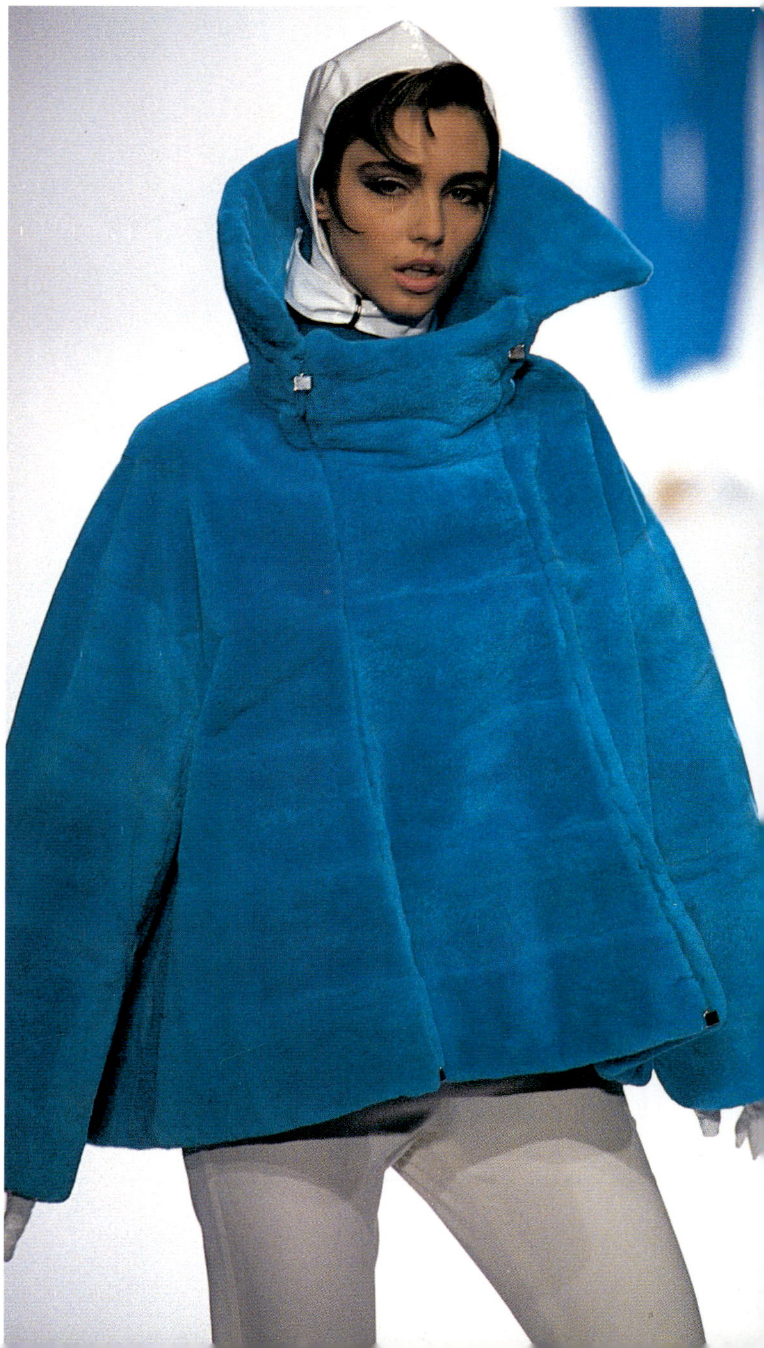

CLAUDE MONTANA

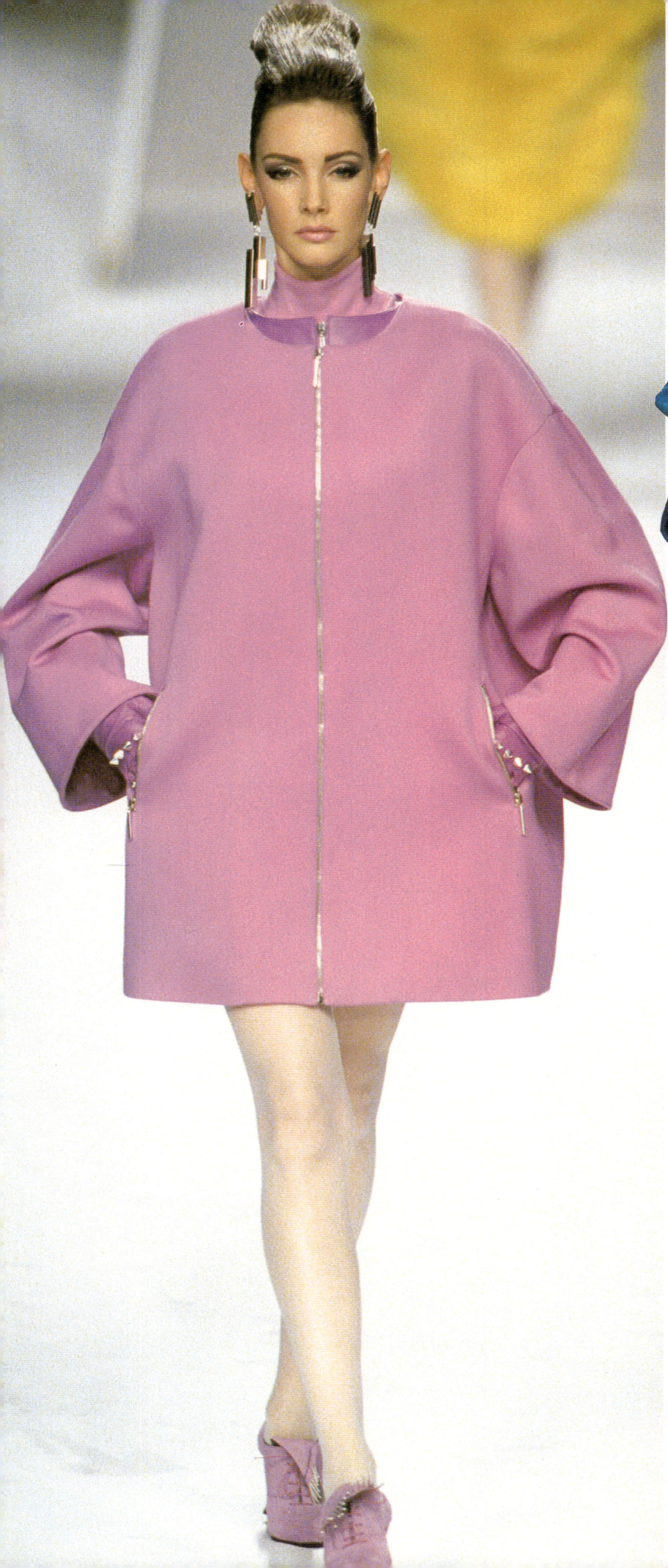
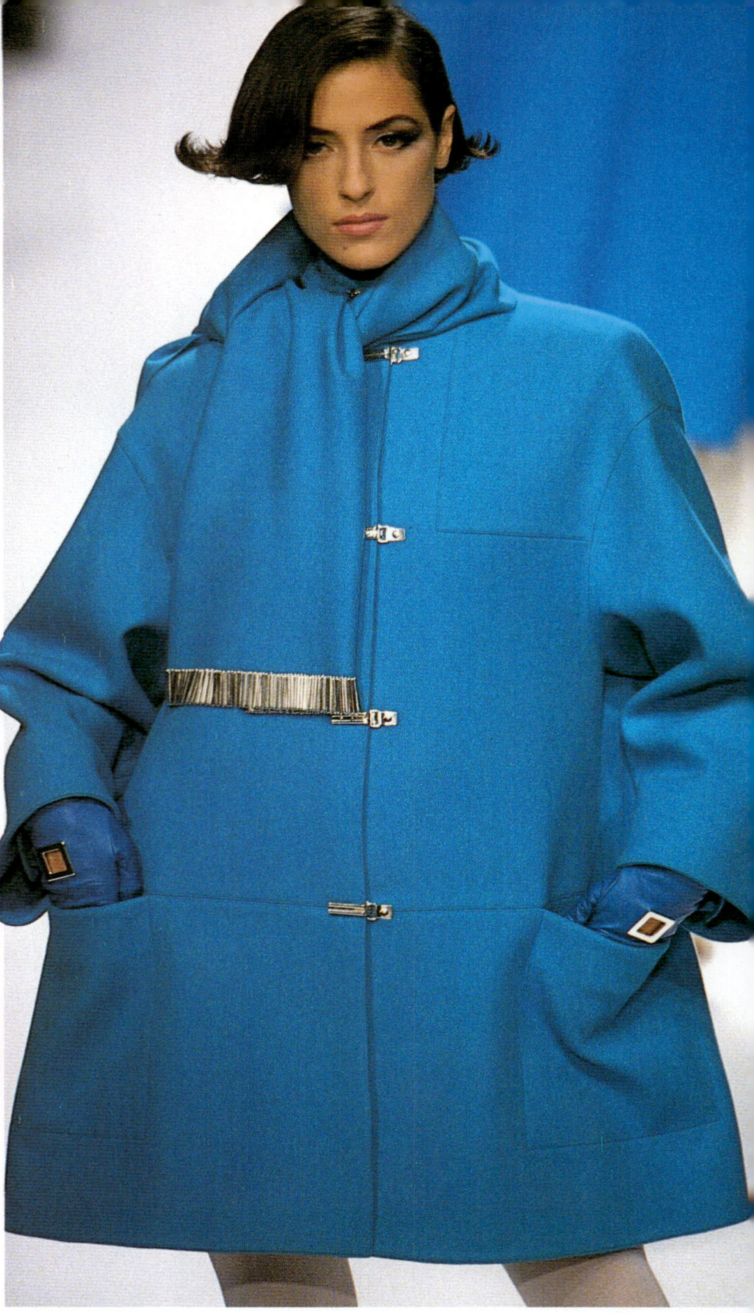
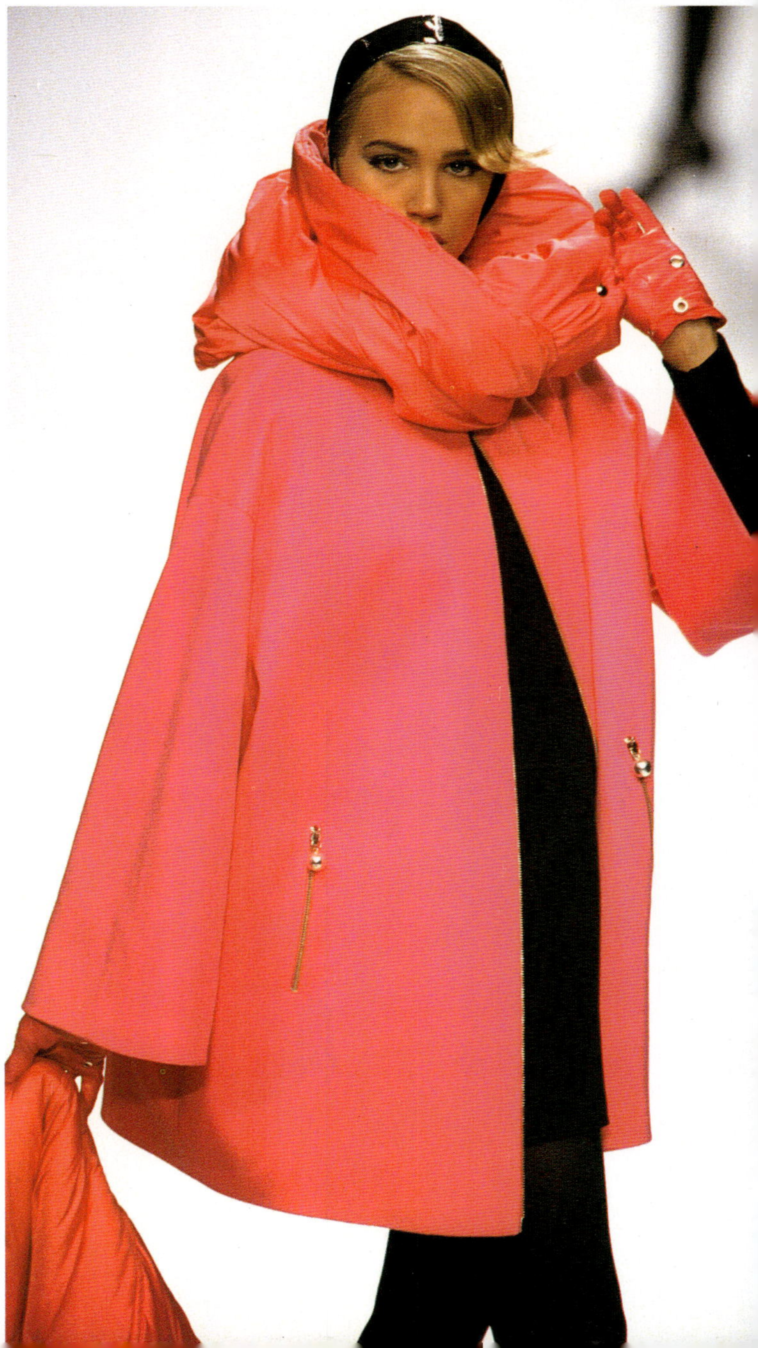

CLAUDE MONTANA

41

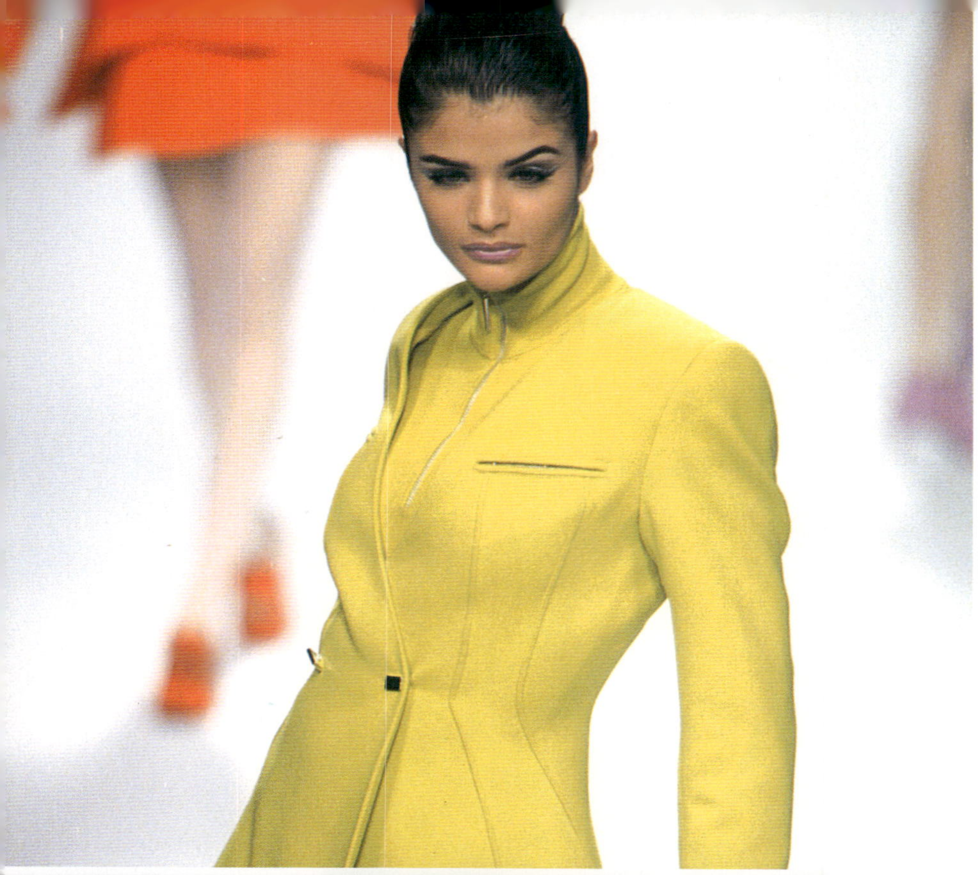
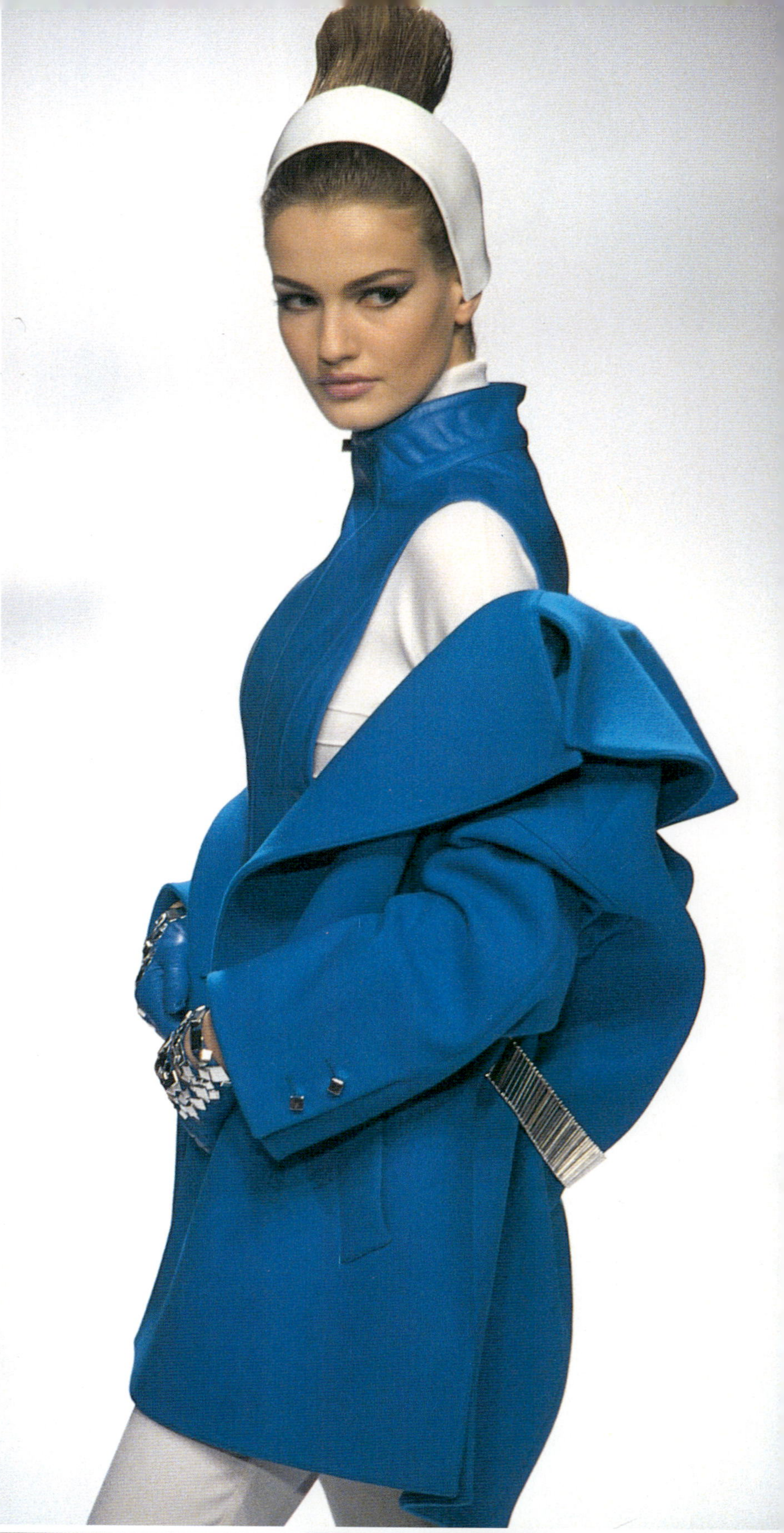
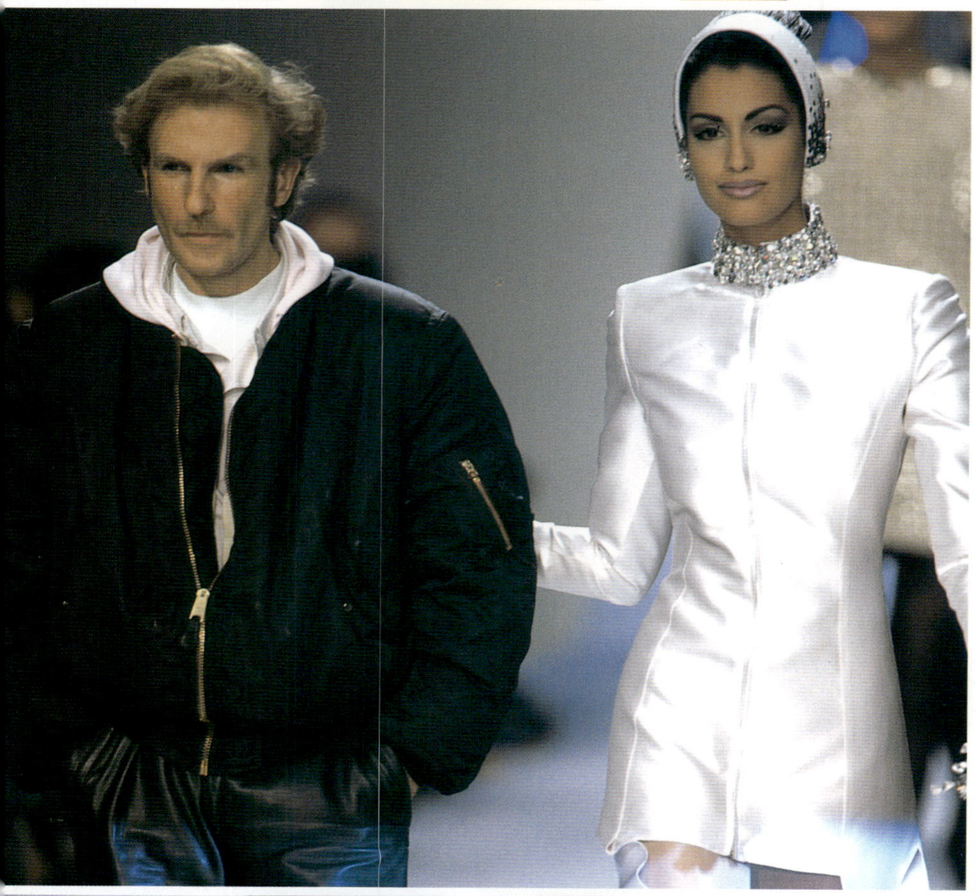
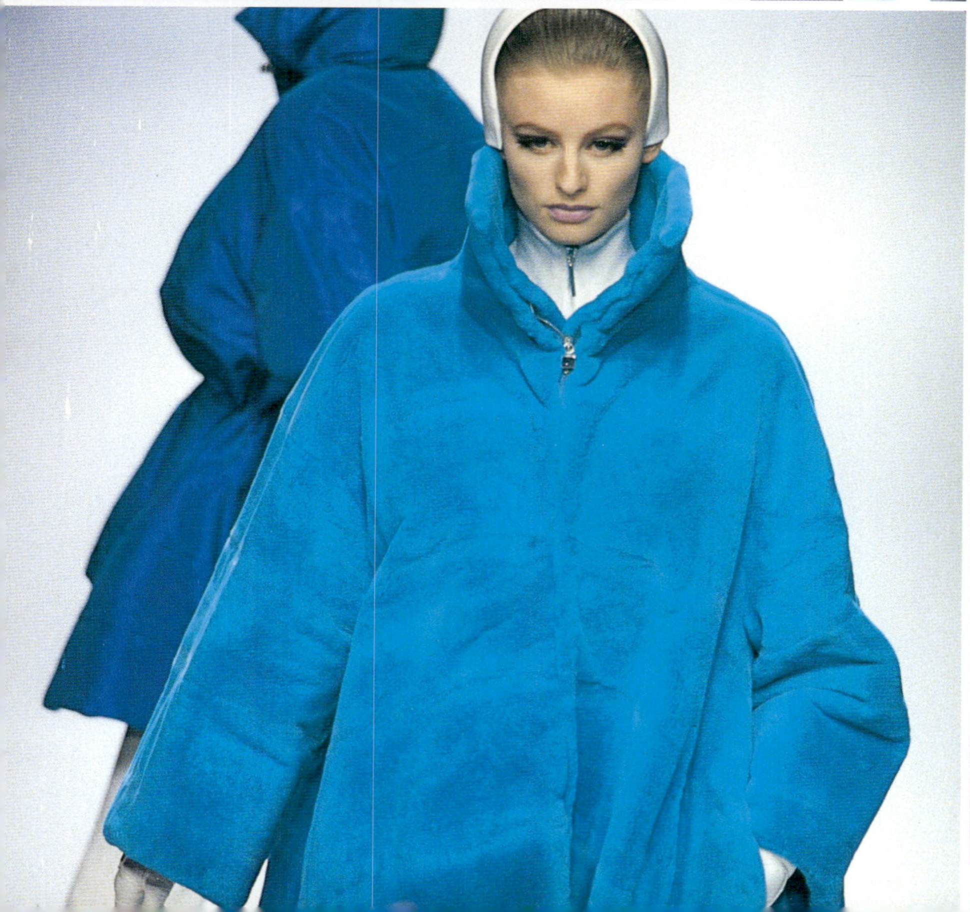
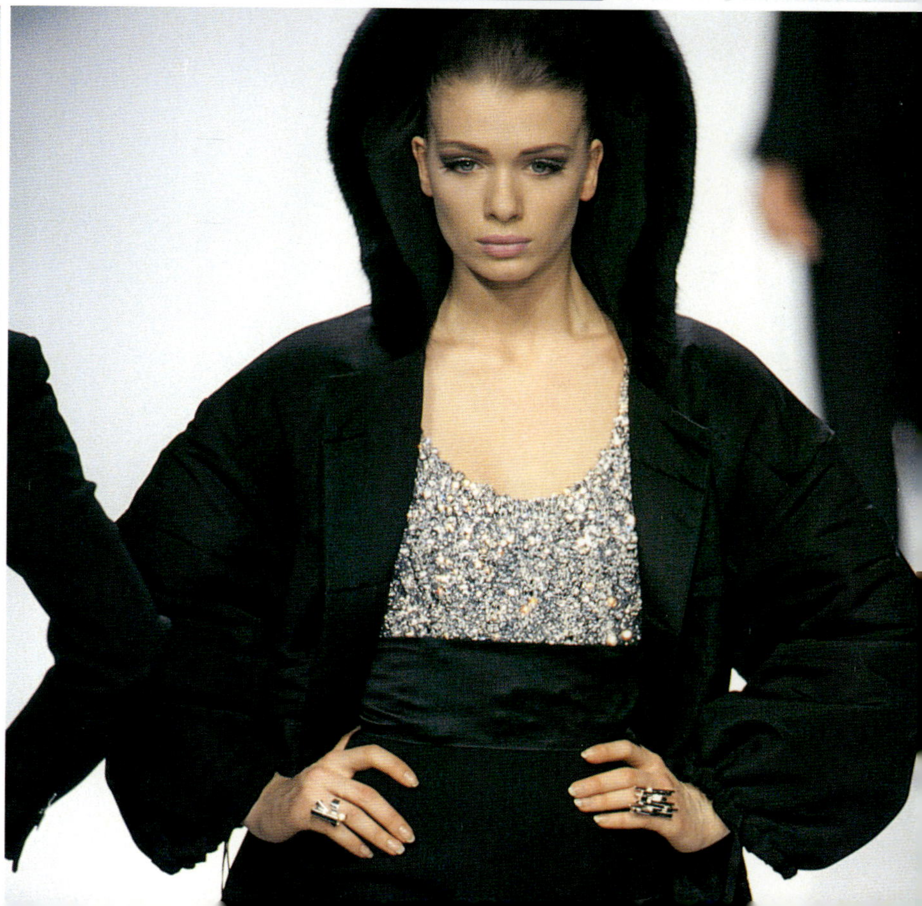

CLAUDE MONTANA

43

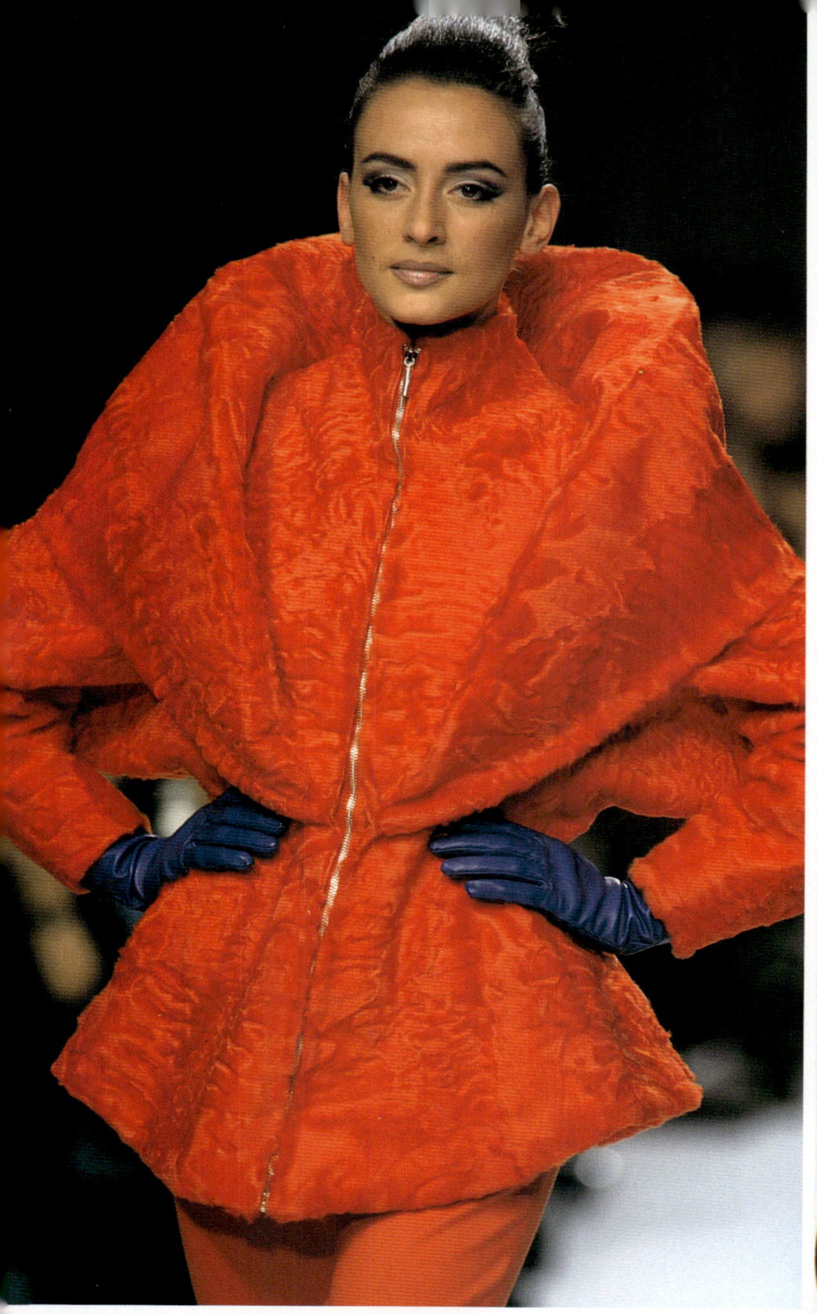

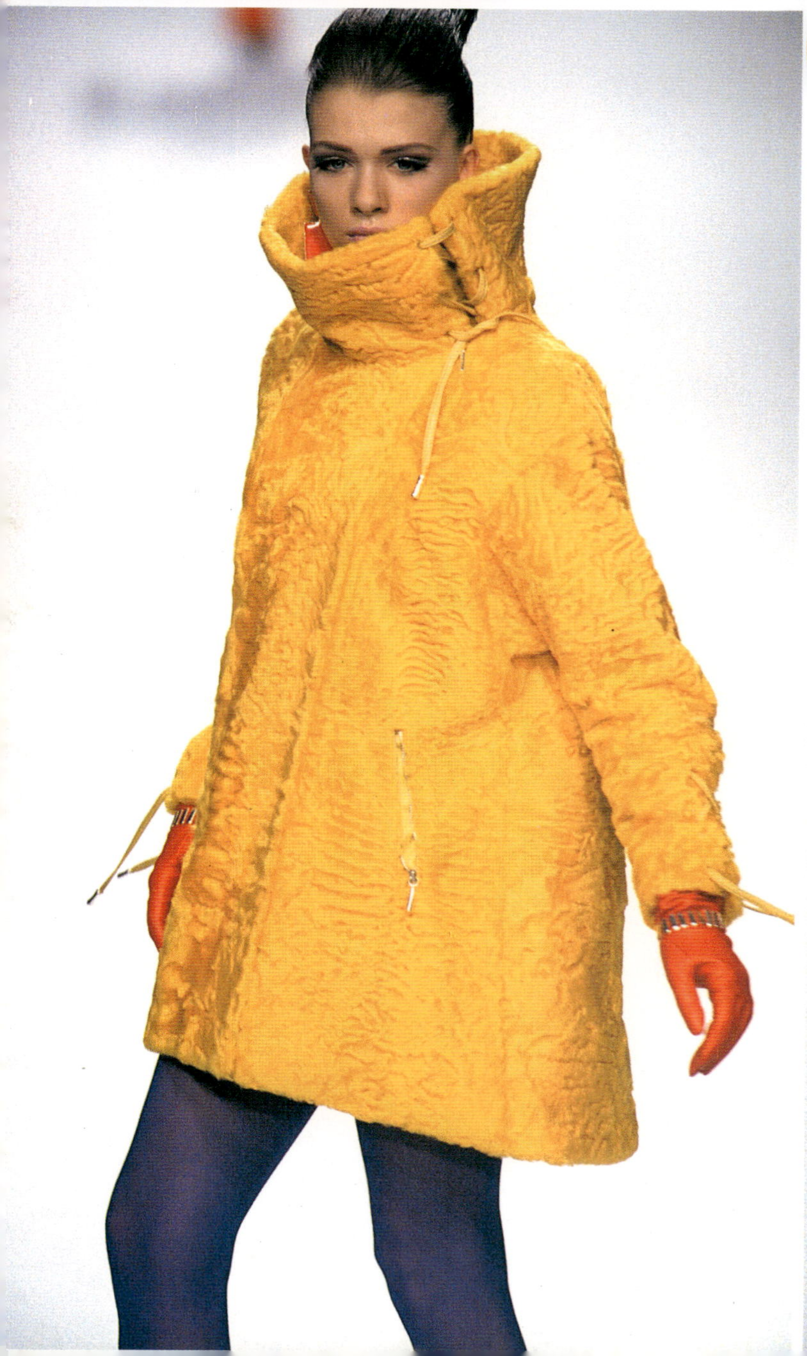

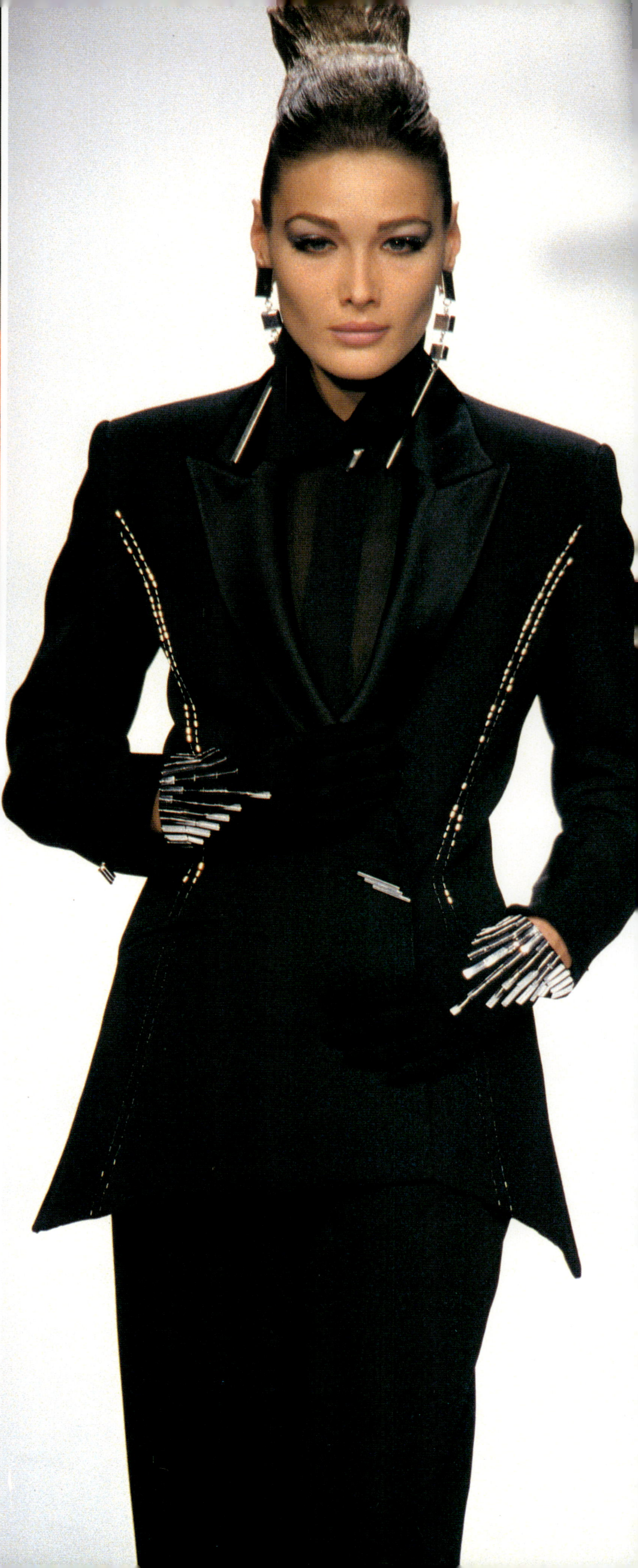

CLAUDE MONTANA

45

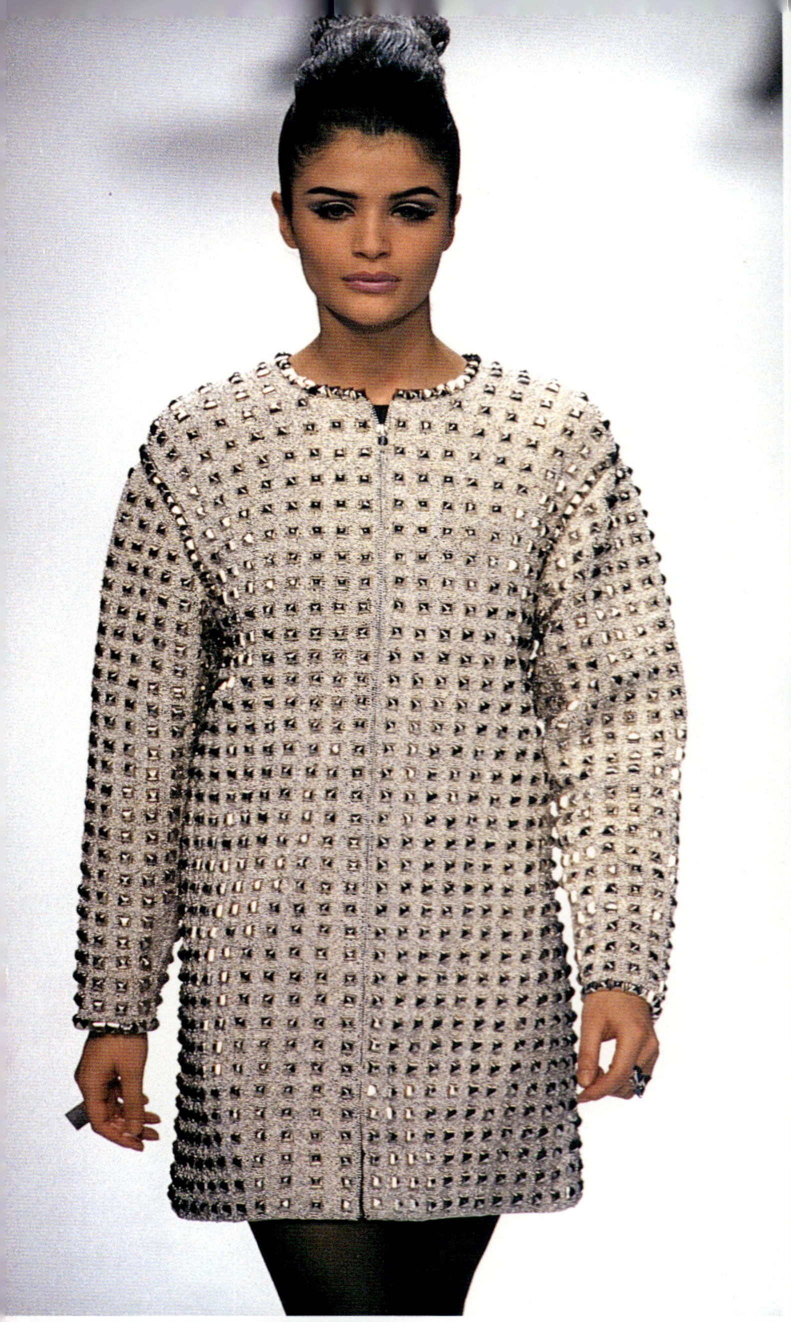

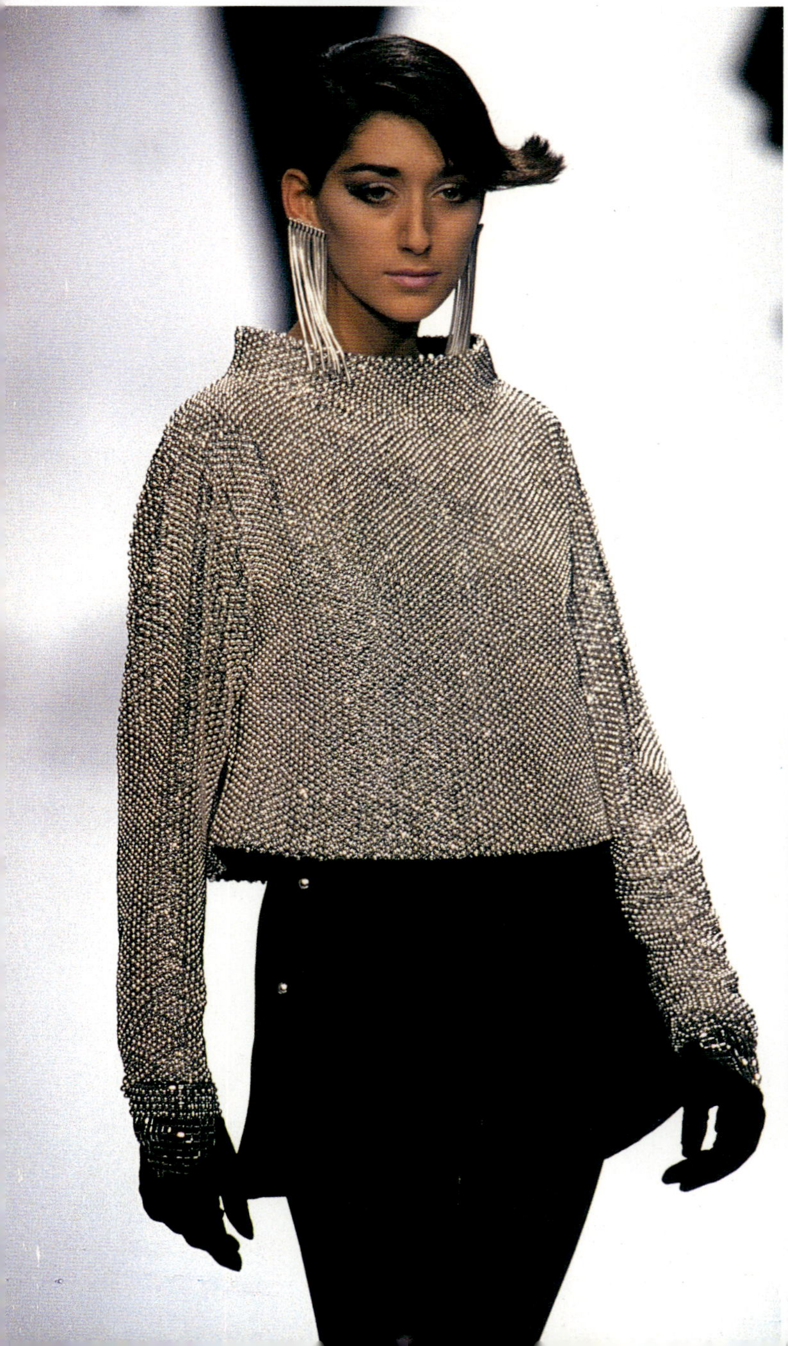

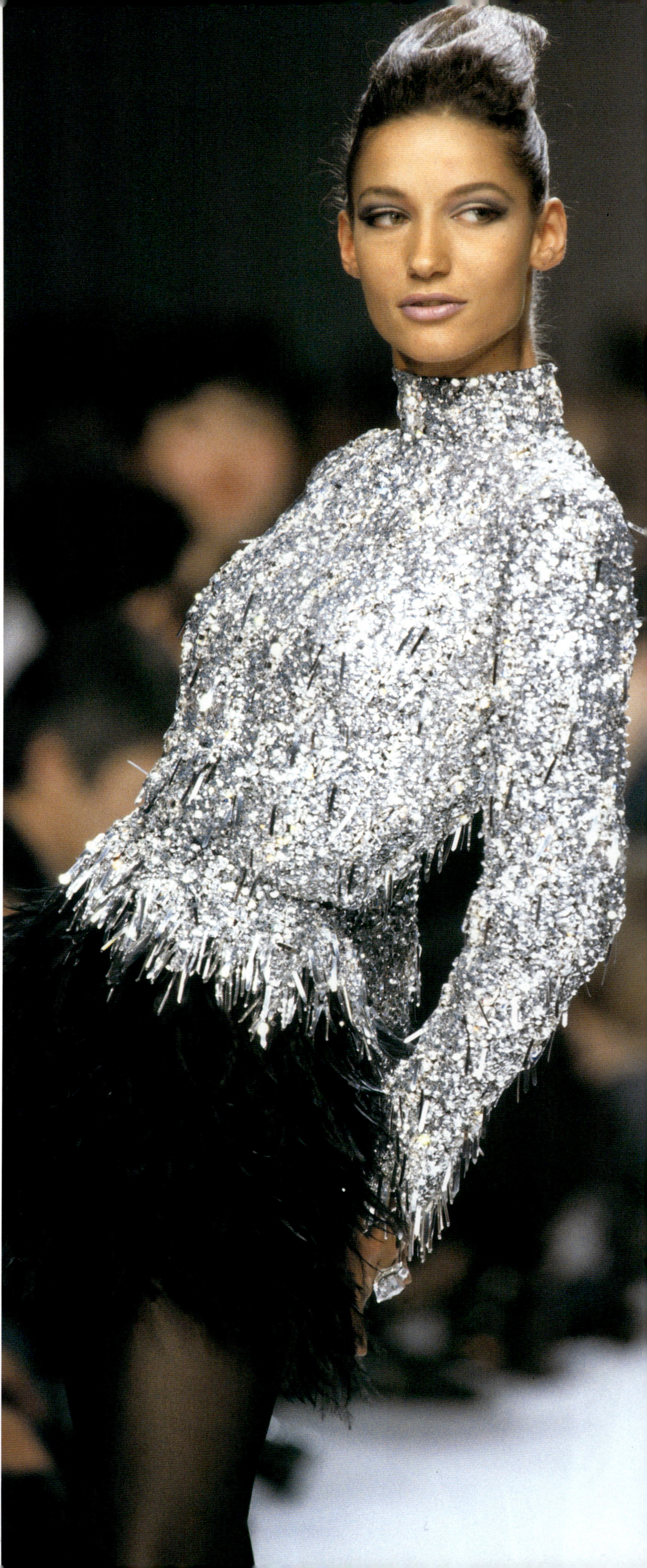

CLAUDE MONTANA

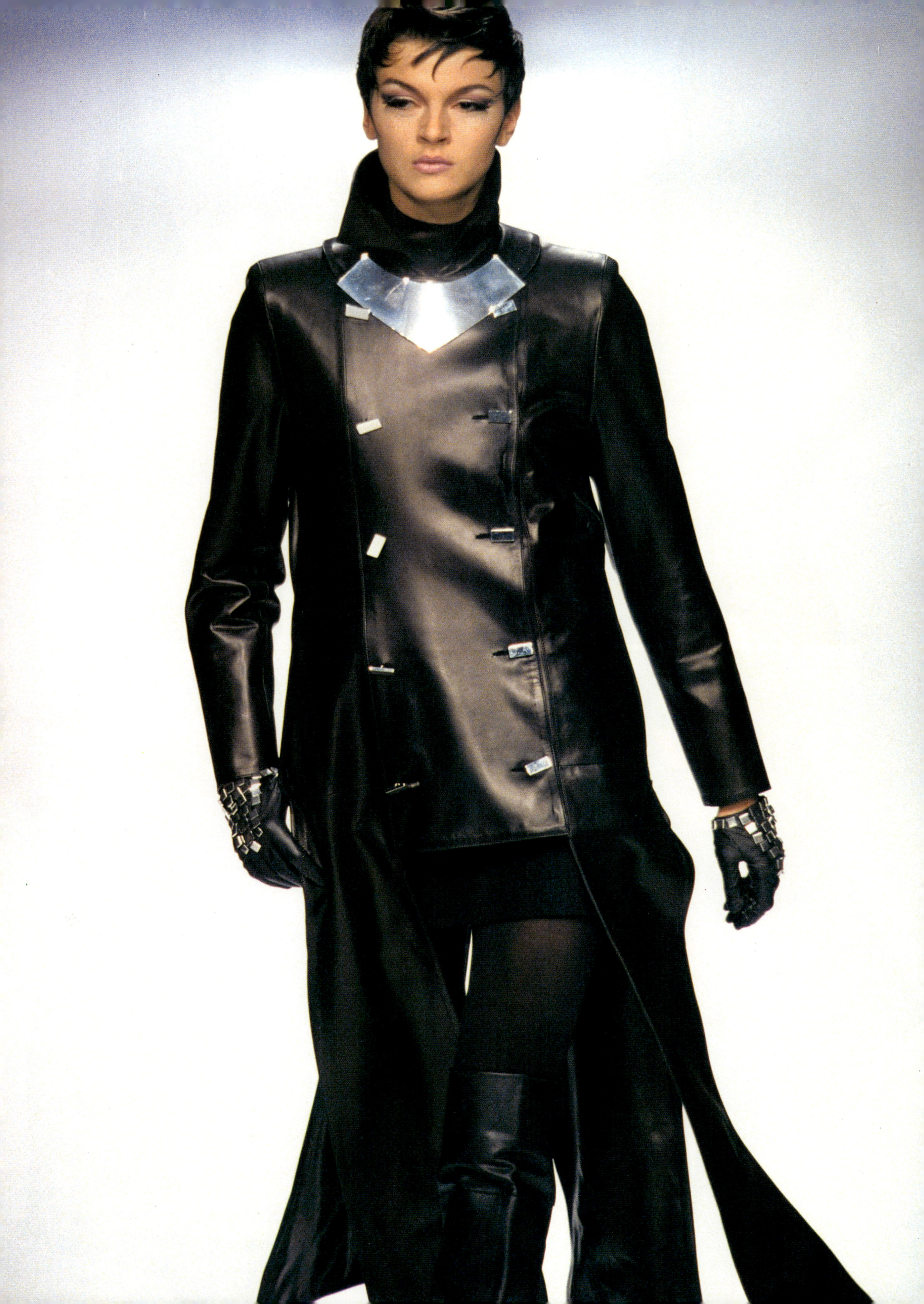

CHANTAL THOMASS

GIVENCHY

'91-'92 AUTUMN & WINTER

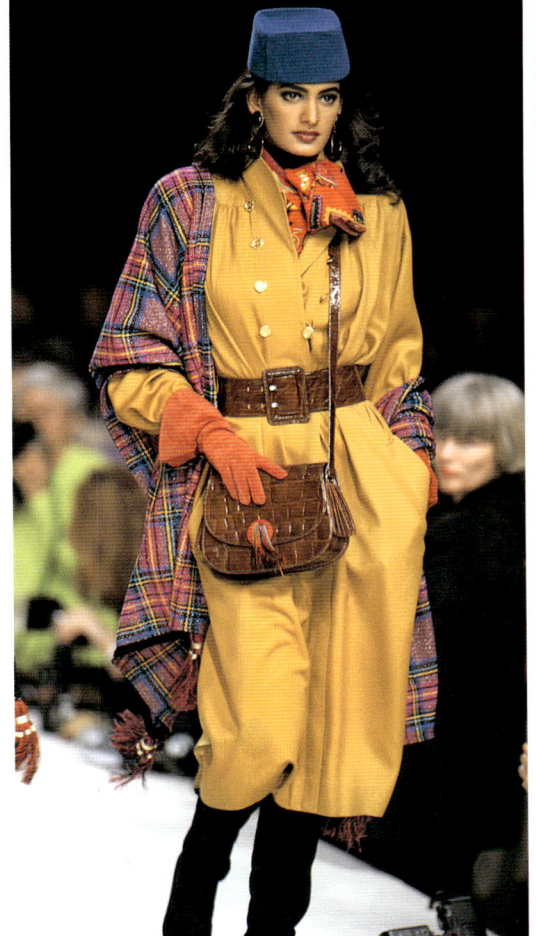

PREÊ-Á-PORTER COLLECTIONS

JUNKO SHIMADA

EMANUEL UNGARO

ANGELO TARLAZZI

CHANTAL THOMASS

EMANUEL UNGARO

'91-'92 AUTUMN & WINTER PRÊT-Á-PORTER COLLECTIONS

JUNKO SHIMADA

VALENTINO

'91-'92
AUTUMN & WINTER
PRÊT-Á-PORTER
COLLECTIONS

NINA RICCI

CHANTAL THOMASS	CHANEL	 NINA RICCI
 J. C. DE CASTELBAJAC	 KENZO	 EMANUEL UNGARO
 JIN ABE	 PIERRE BALMAIN	 NINA RICCI

THIERRY MUGLER

THIERRY MUGLER

THIERRY MUGLER

ティエリー・ミュグレー

ミュグレーの過激でアバンギャルドなセクシー・スタイルは、ユーモアいっぱい。バストにつけられた眼がウインクするドレスやモンキー・ファーのアクセントが楽しい。

Mugler's heavy accent on a sexy avant-garde stye is full of humour.
For example, a dress with winking eyes attached to the bust, and an monkey fur accent.

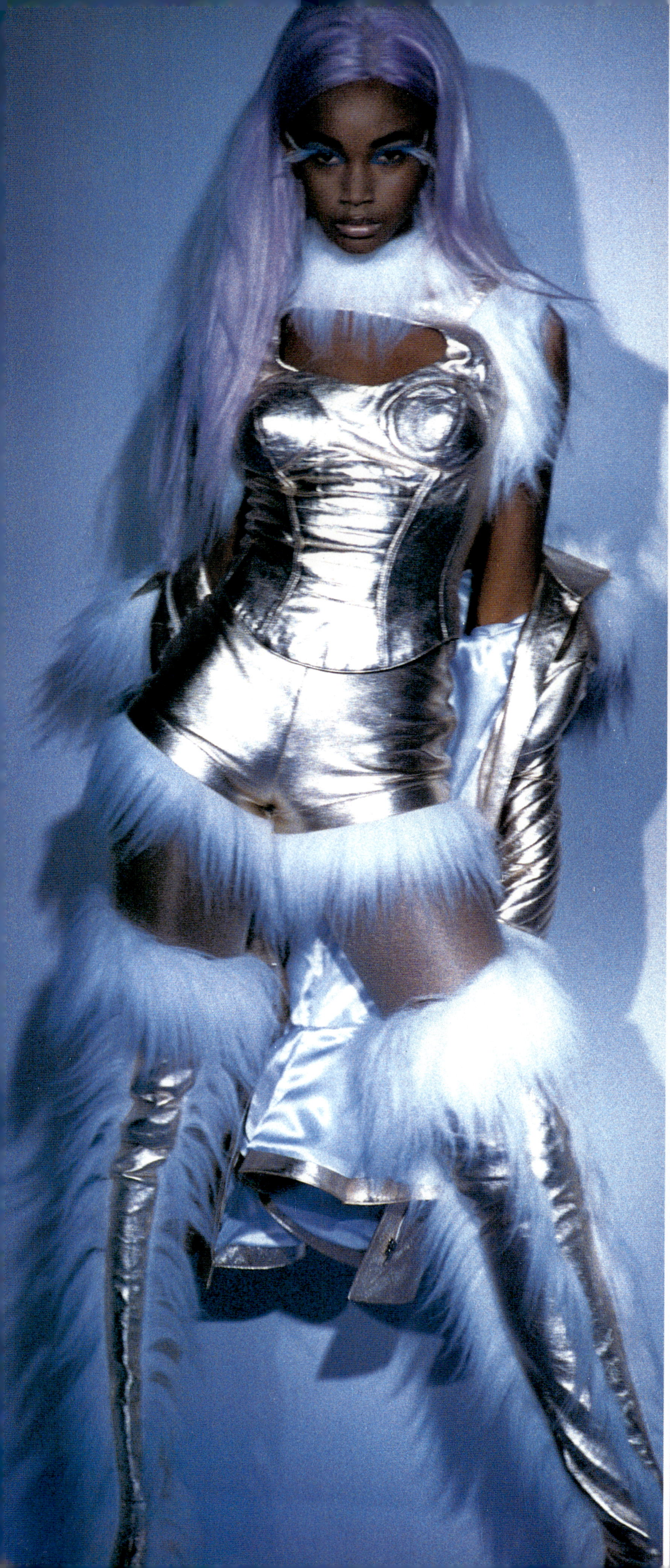
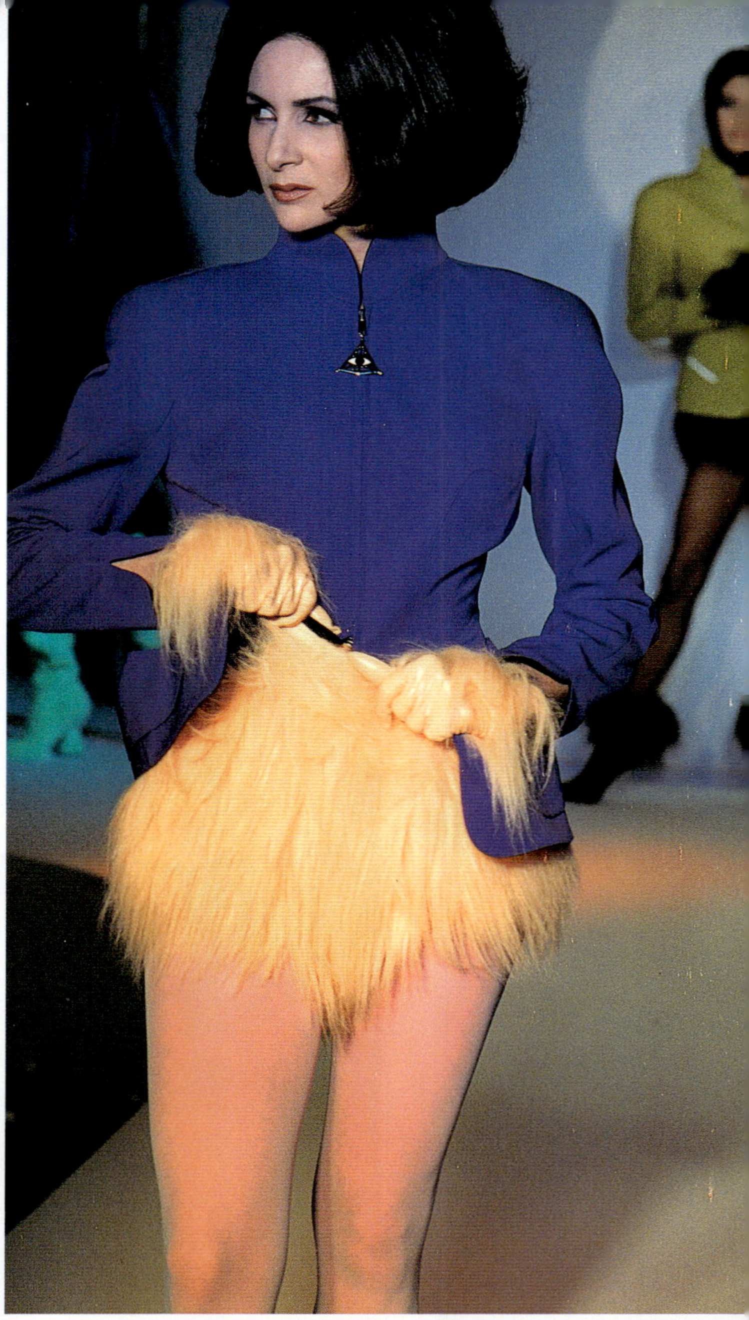
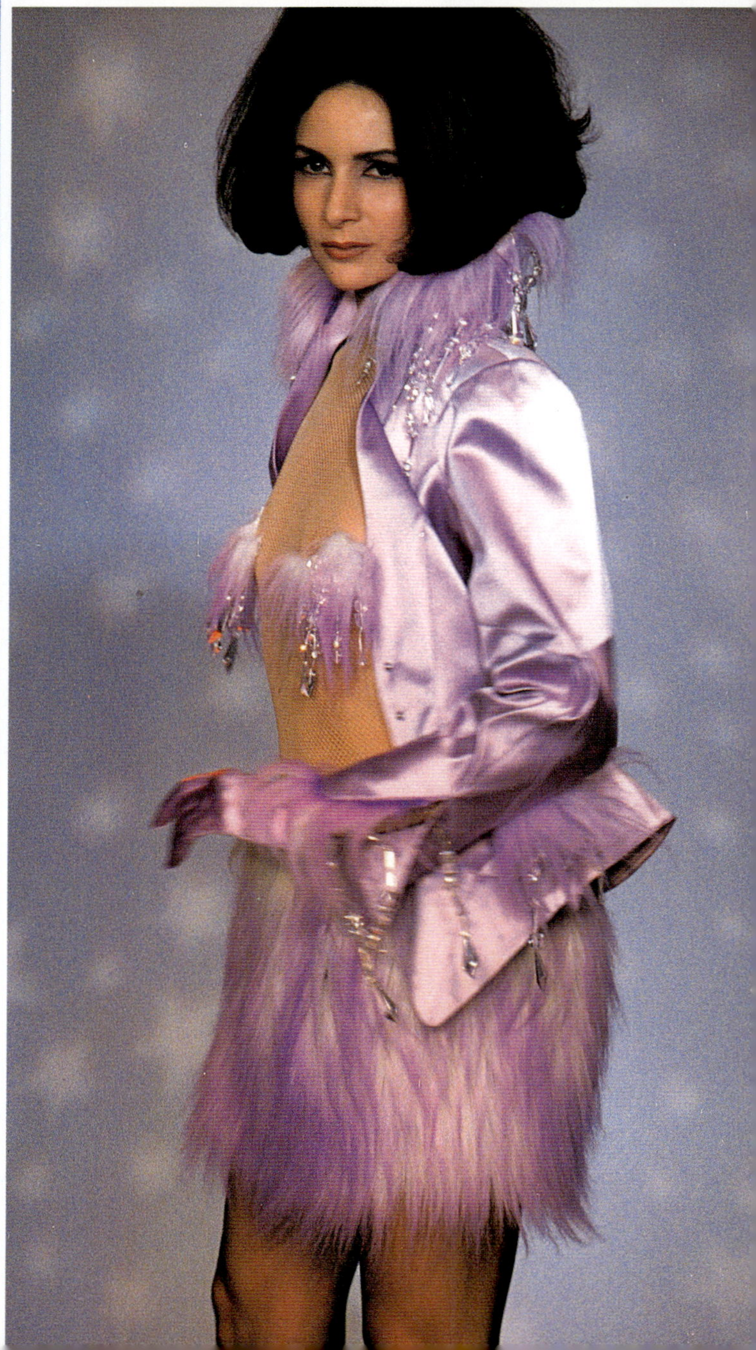

THIERRY MUGLER

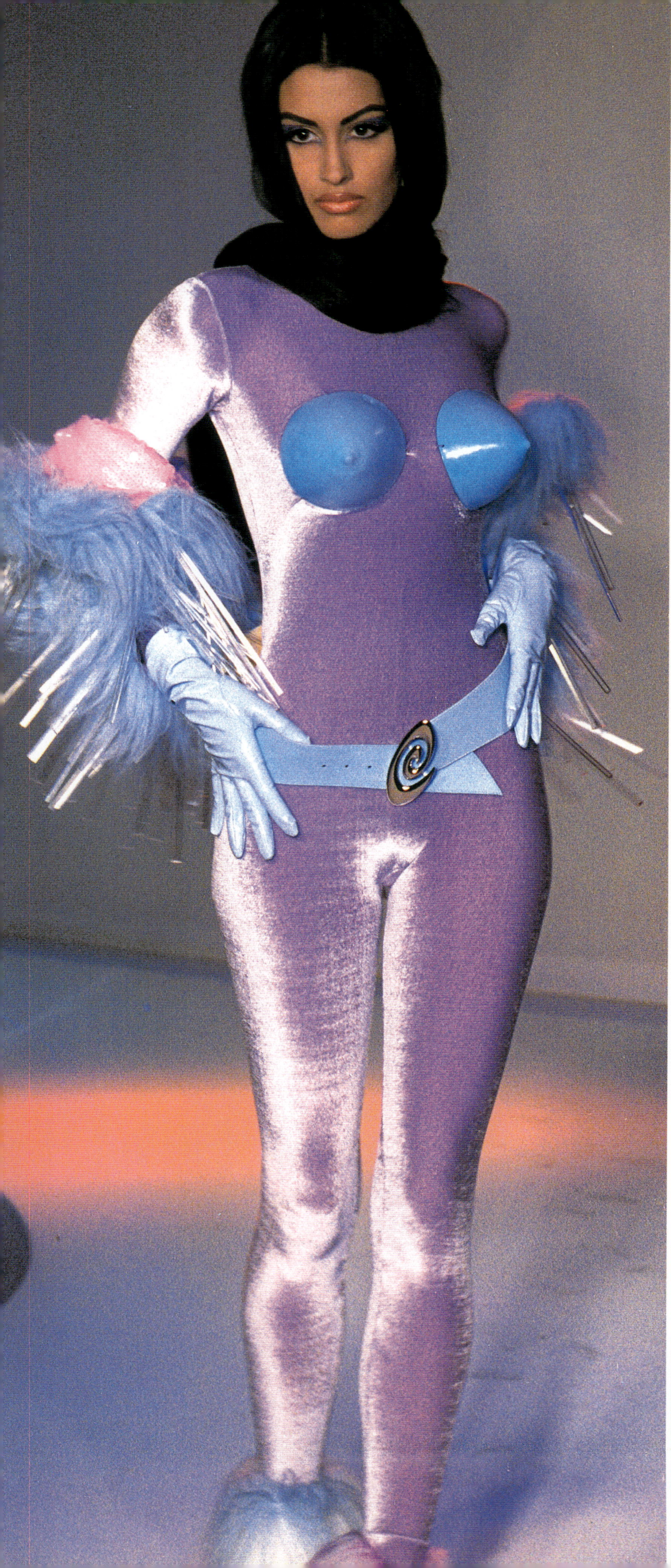
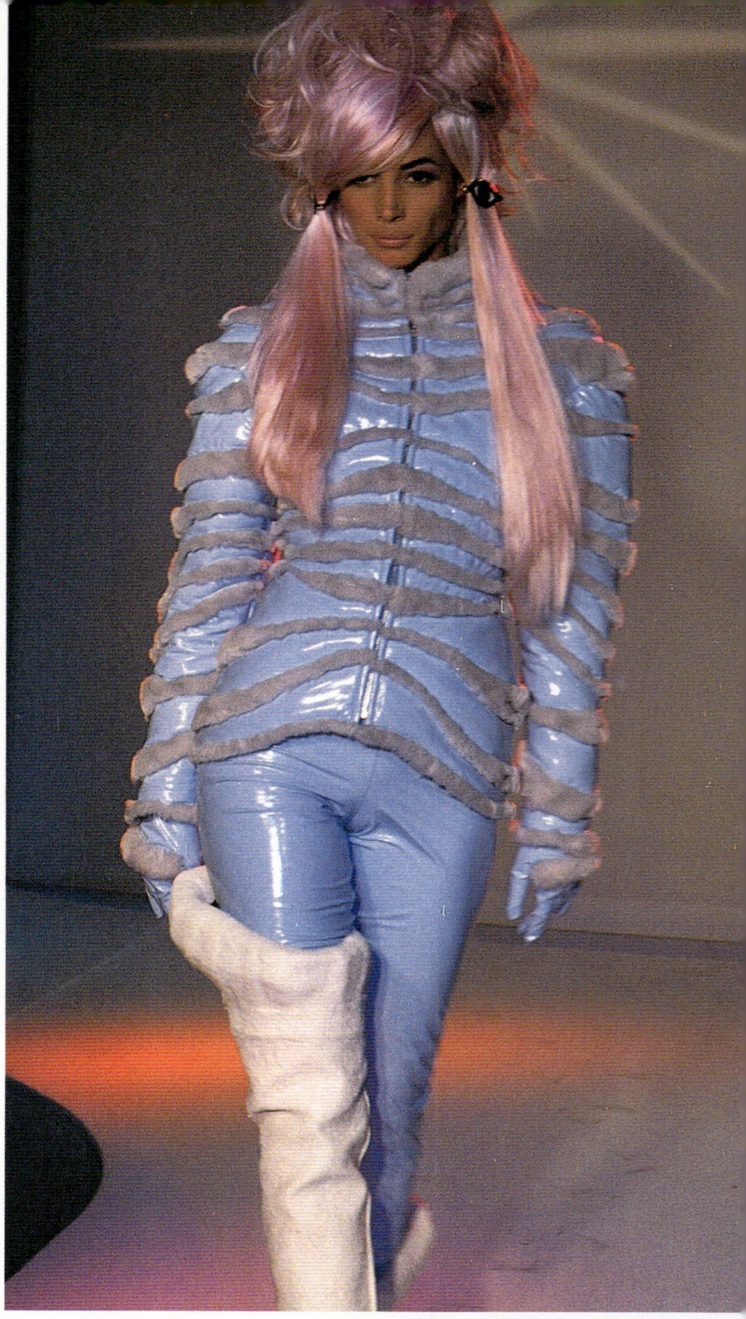
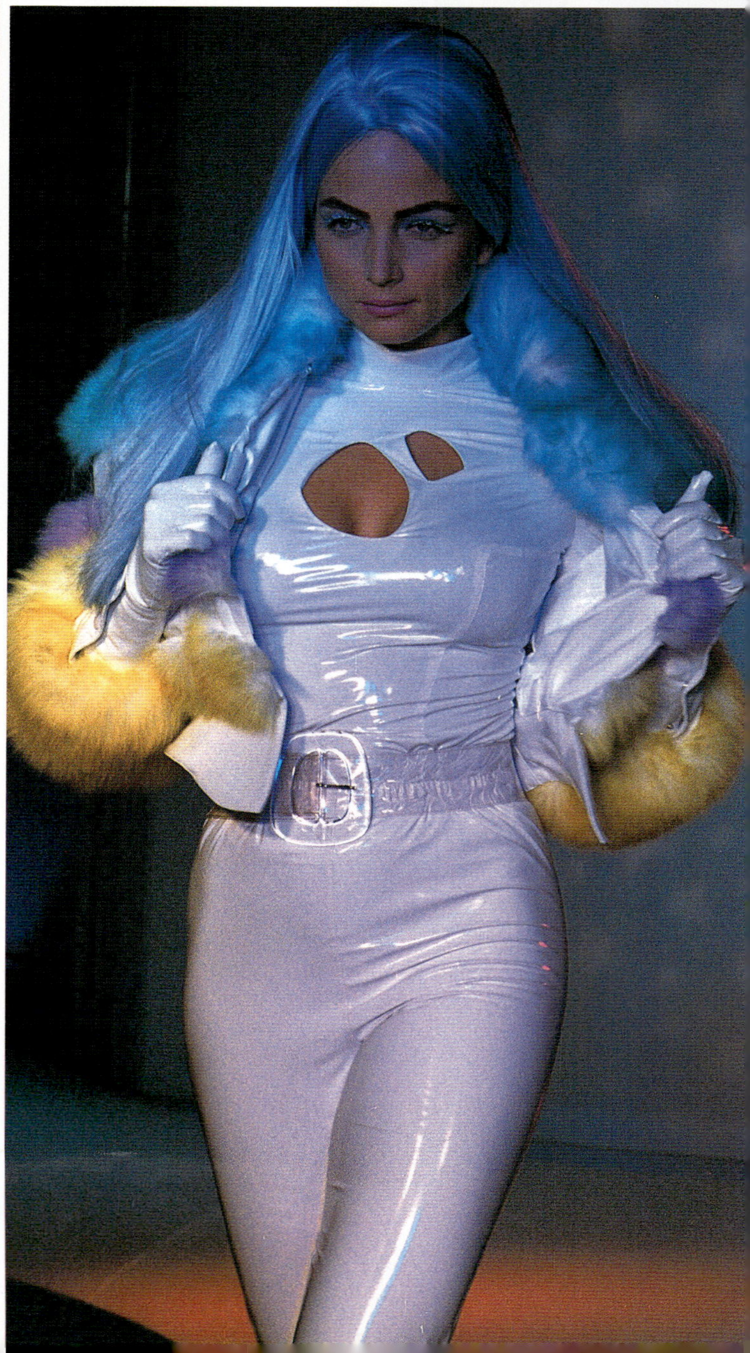

THIERRY MUGLER

59

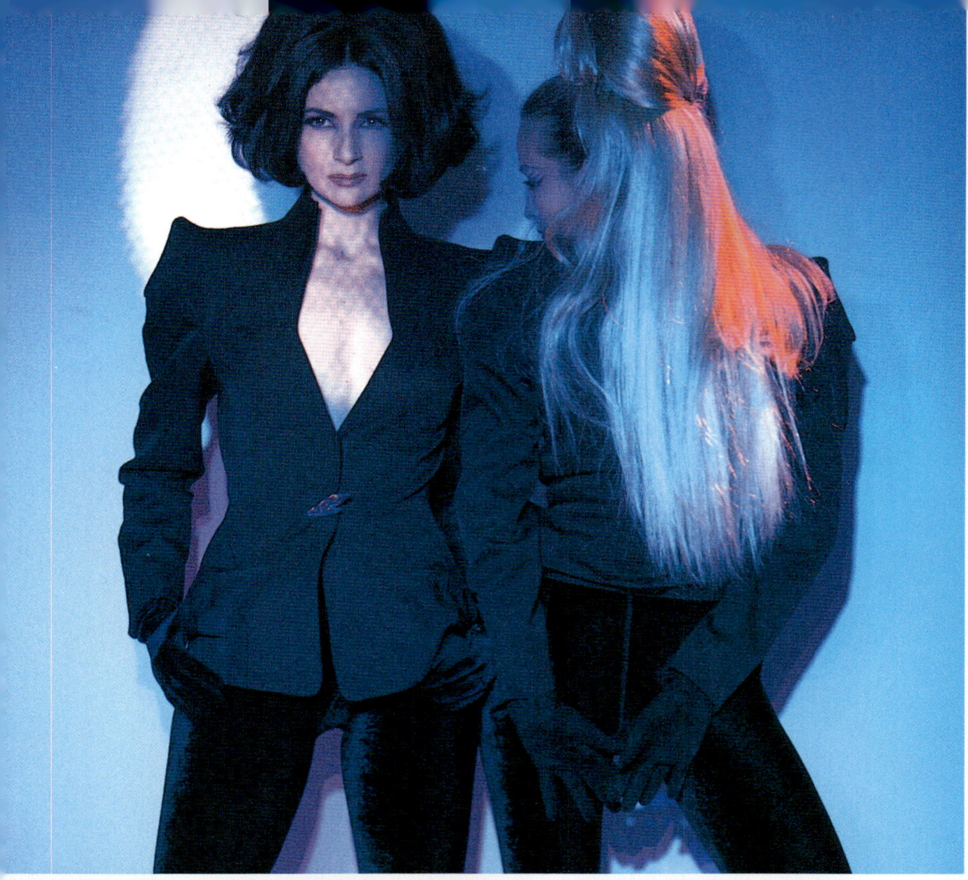

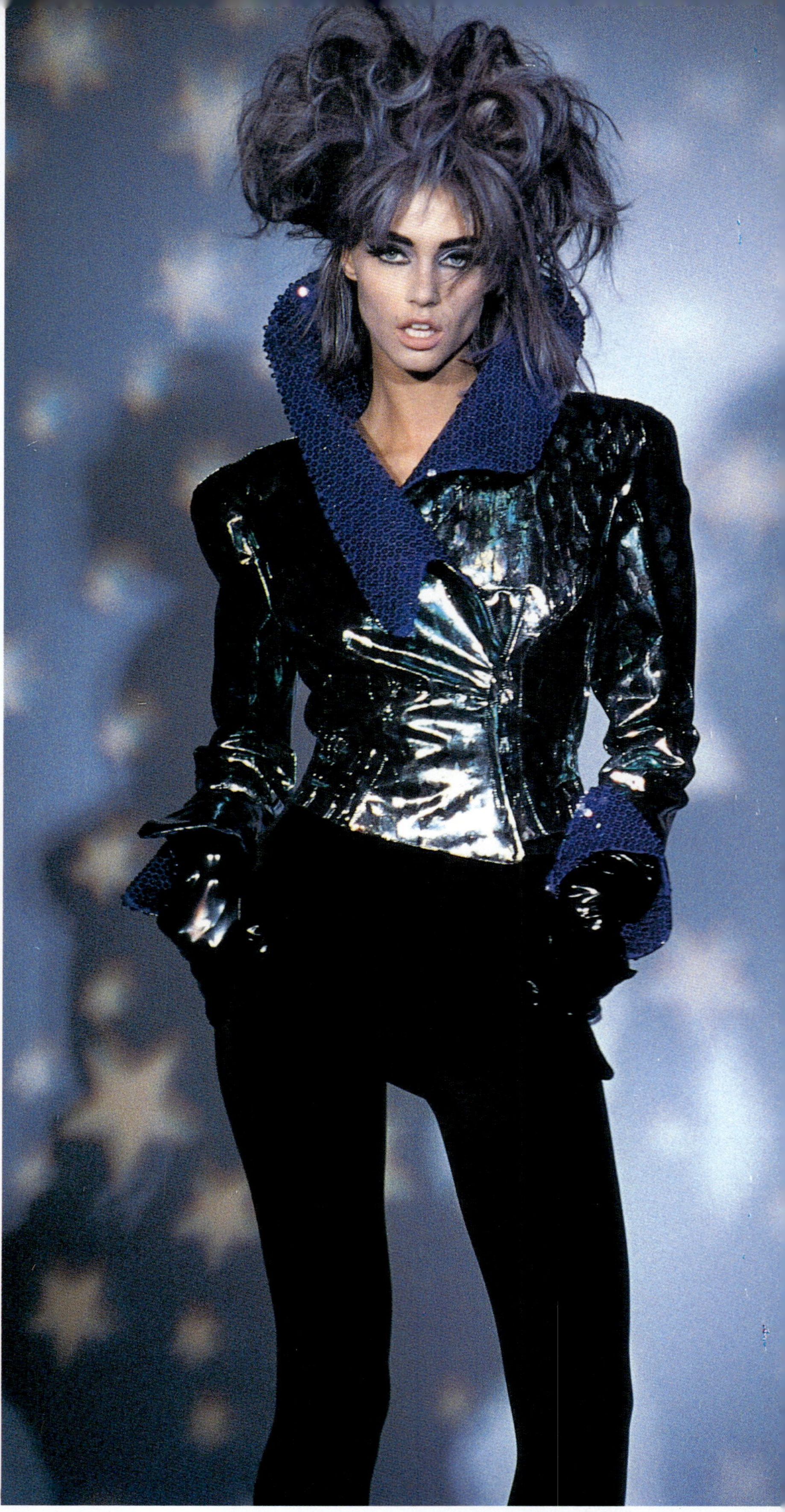

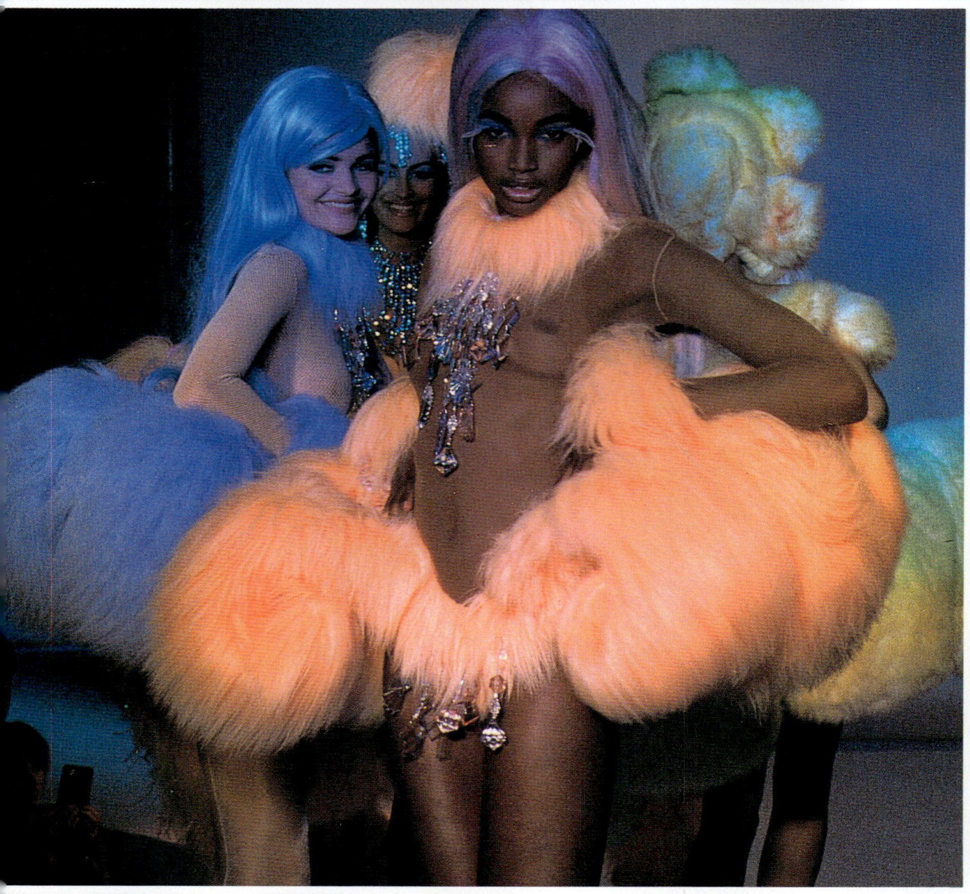

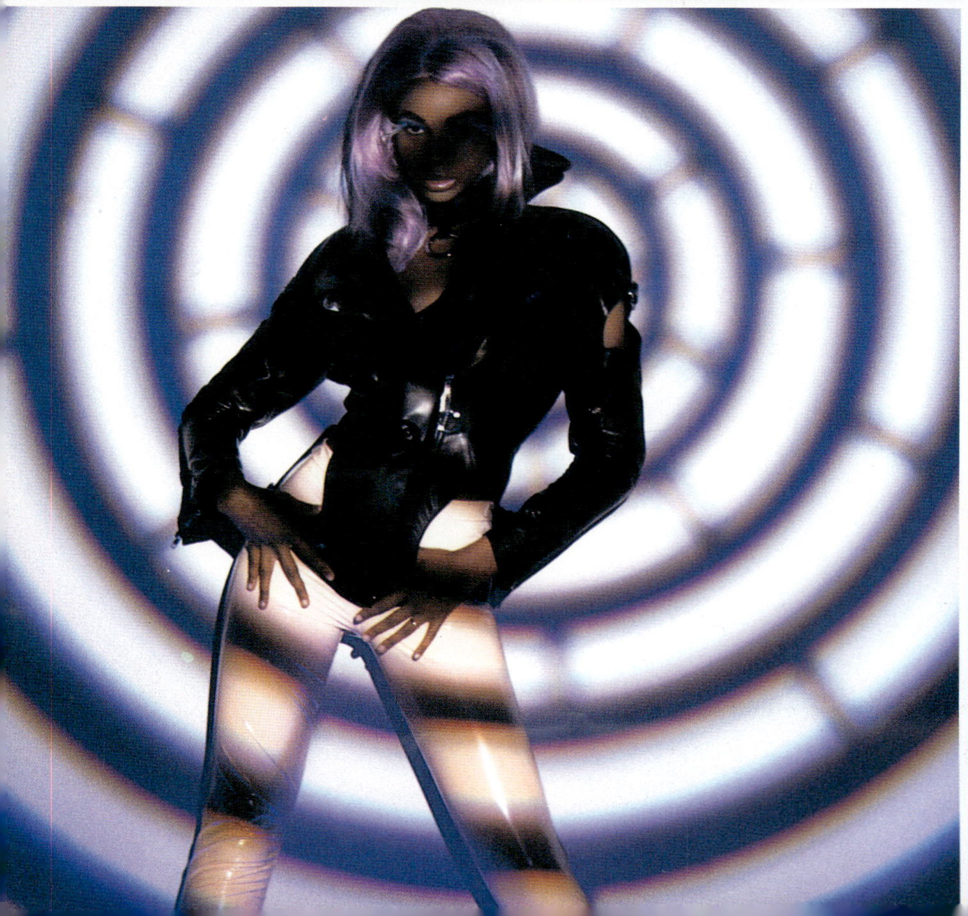

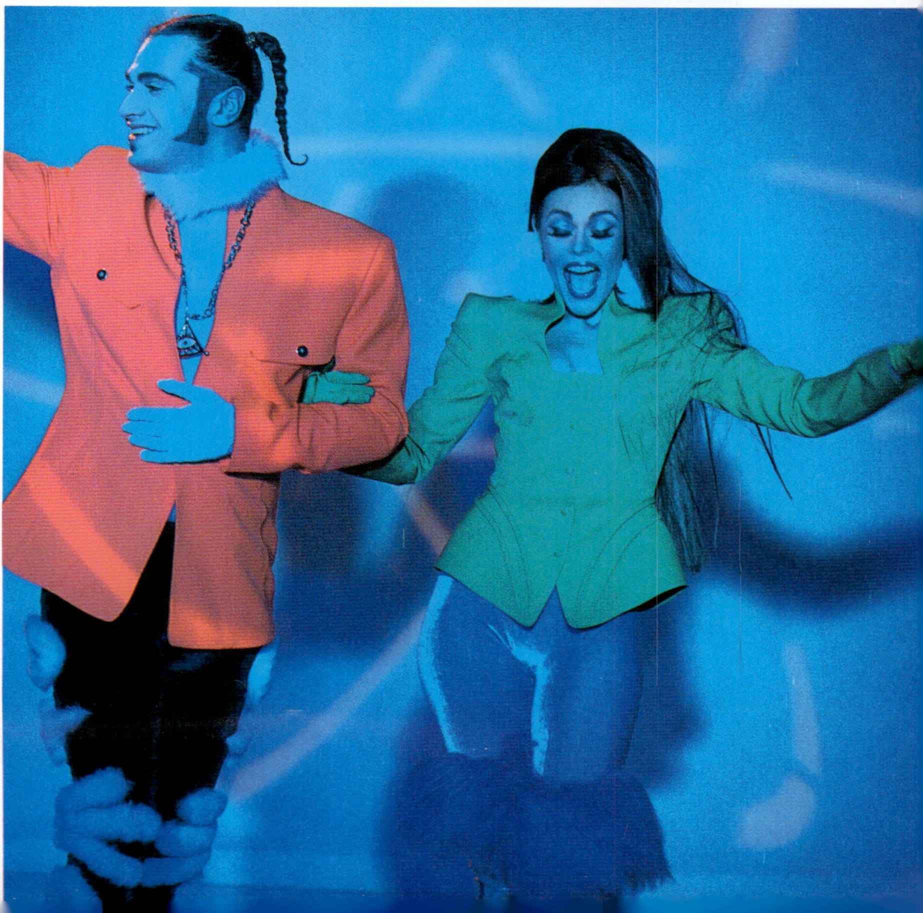

THIERRY MUGLER

61

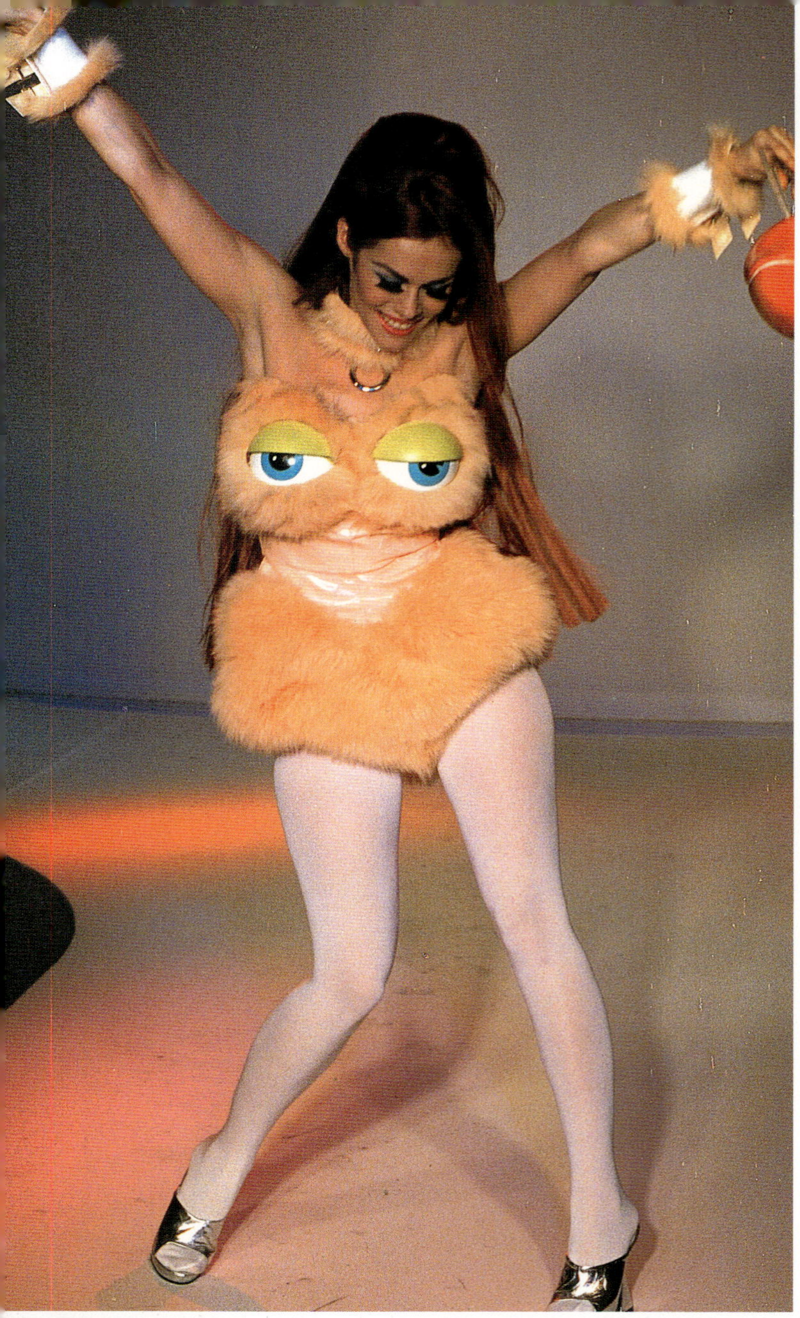

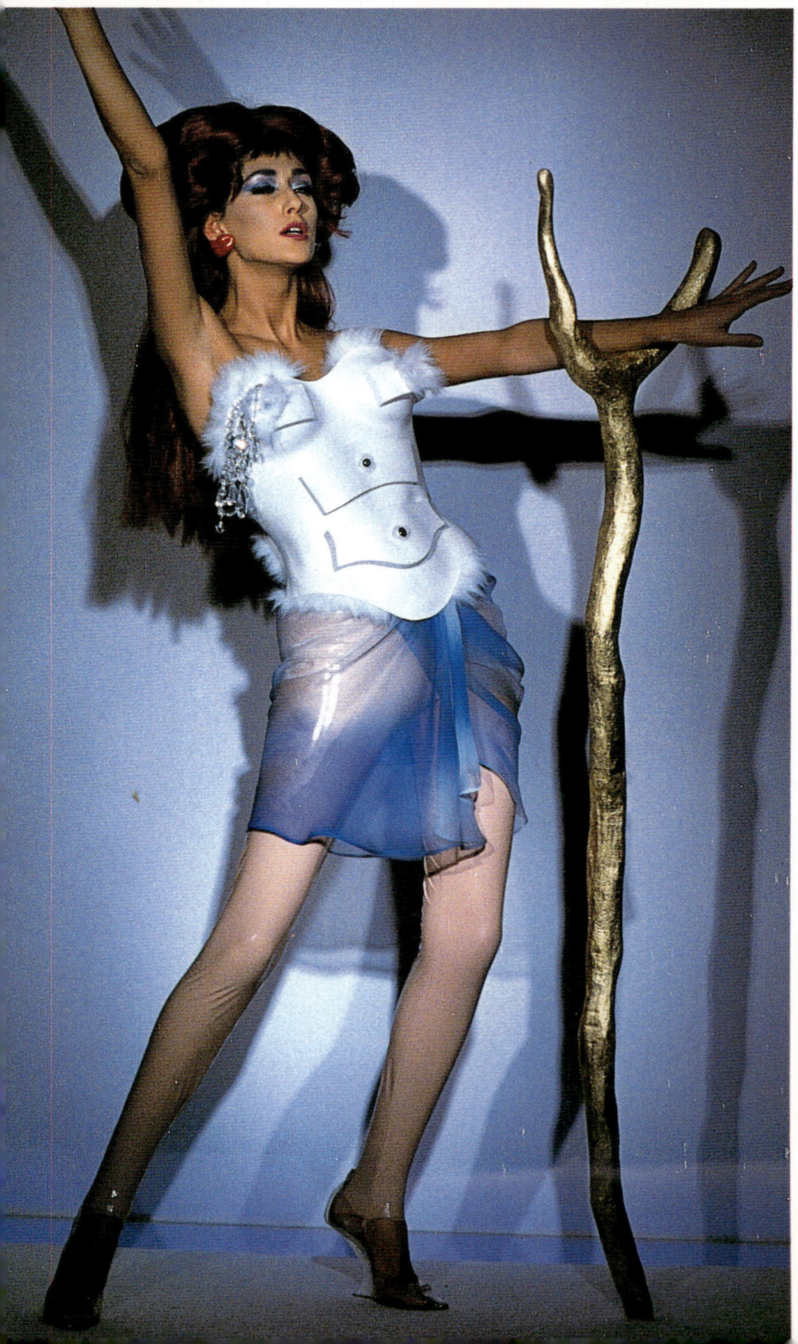

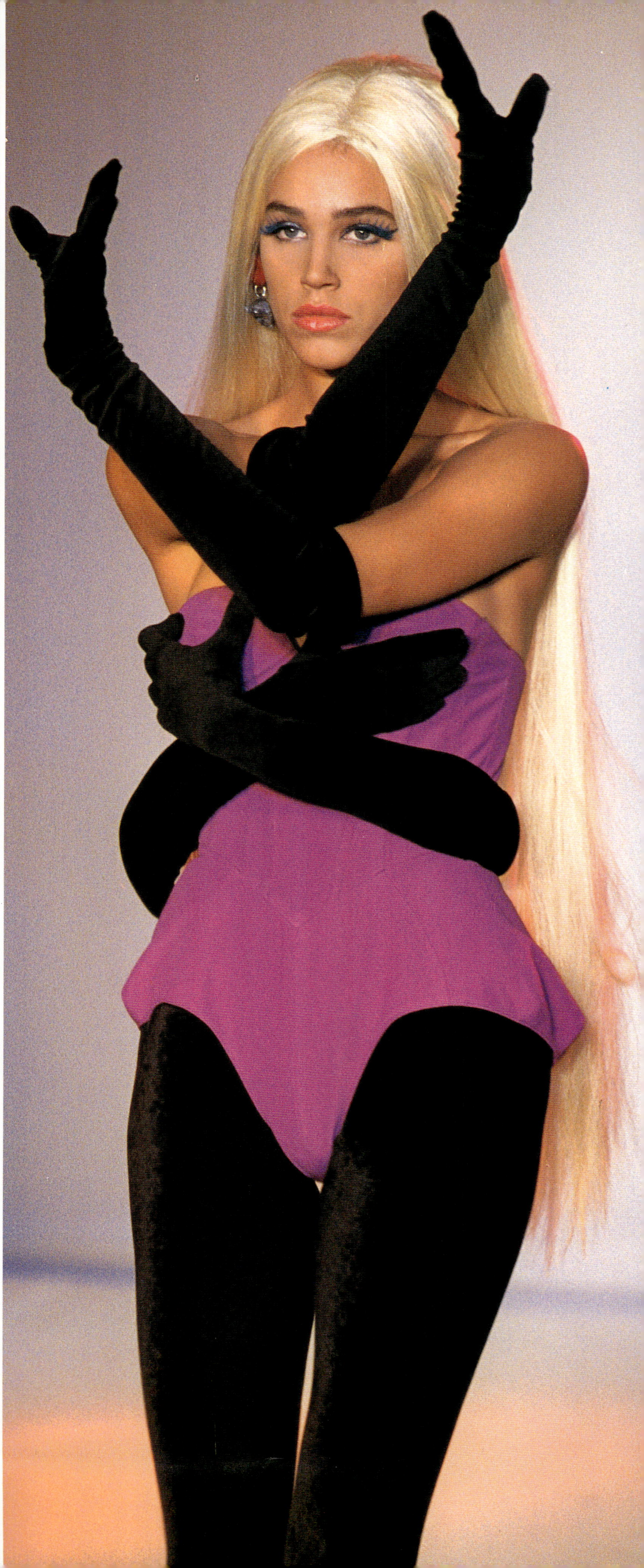

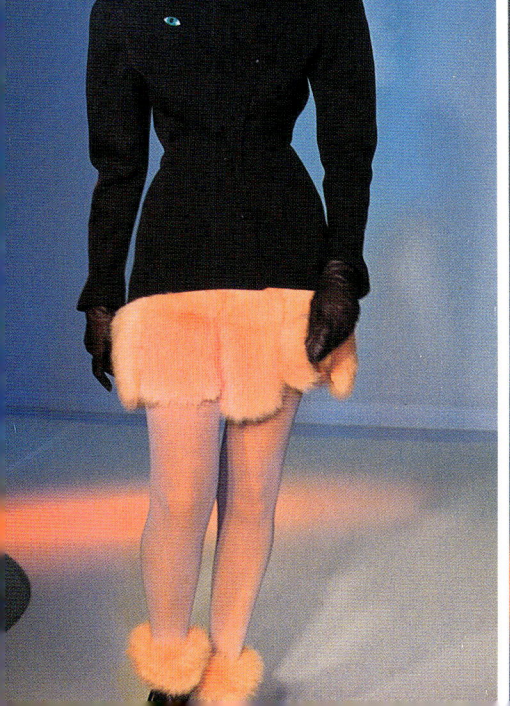

THIERRY MUGLER

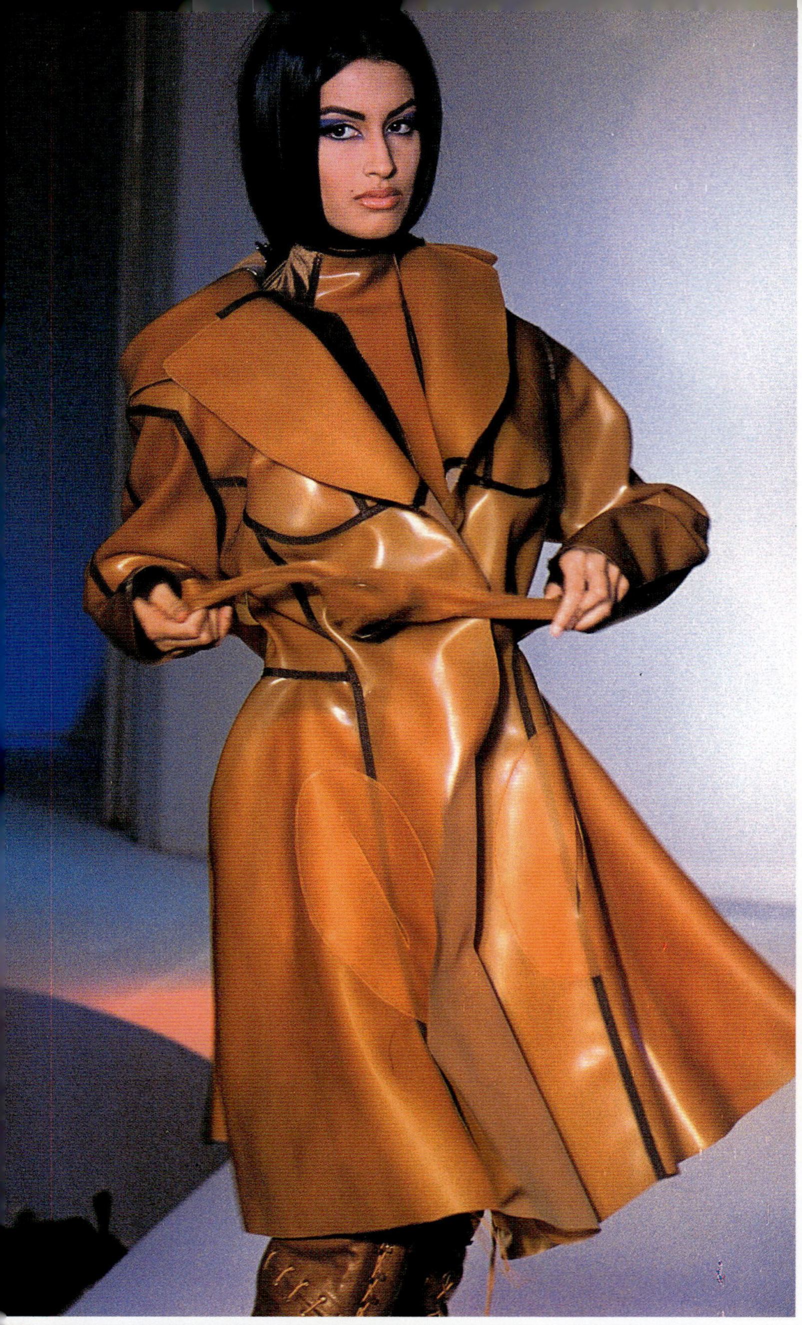

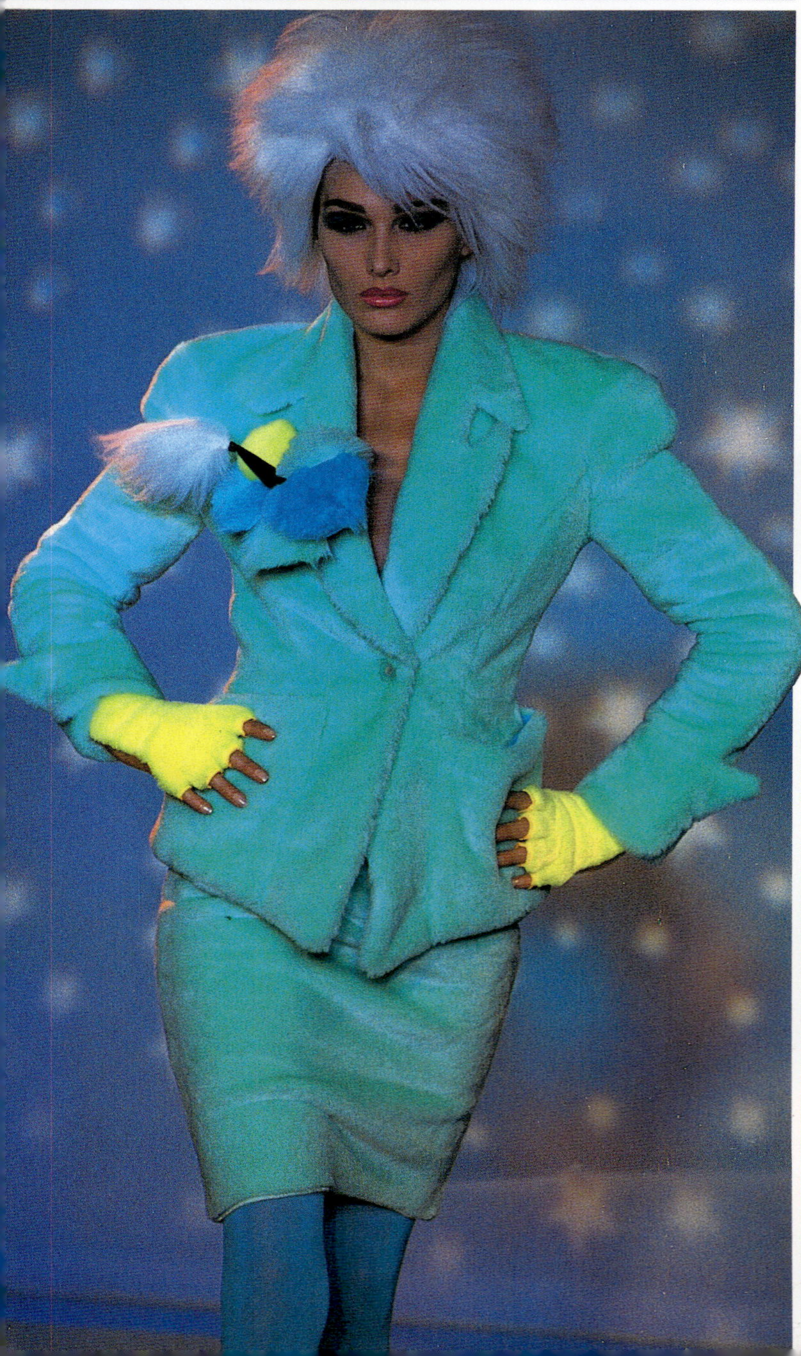

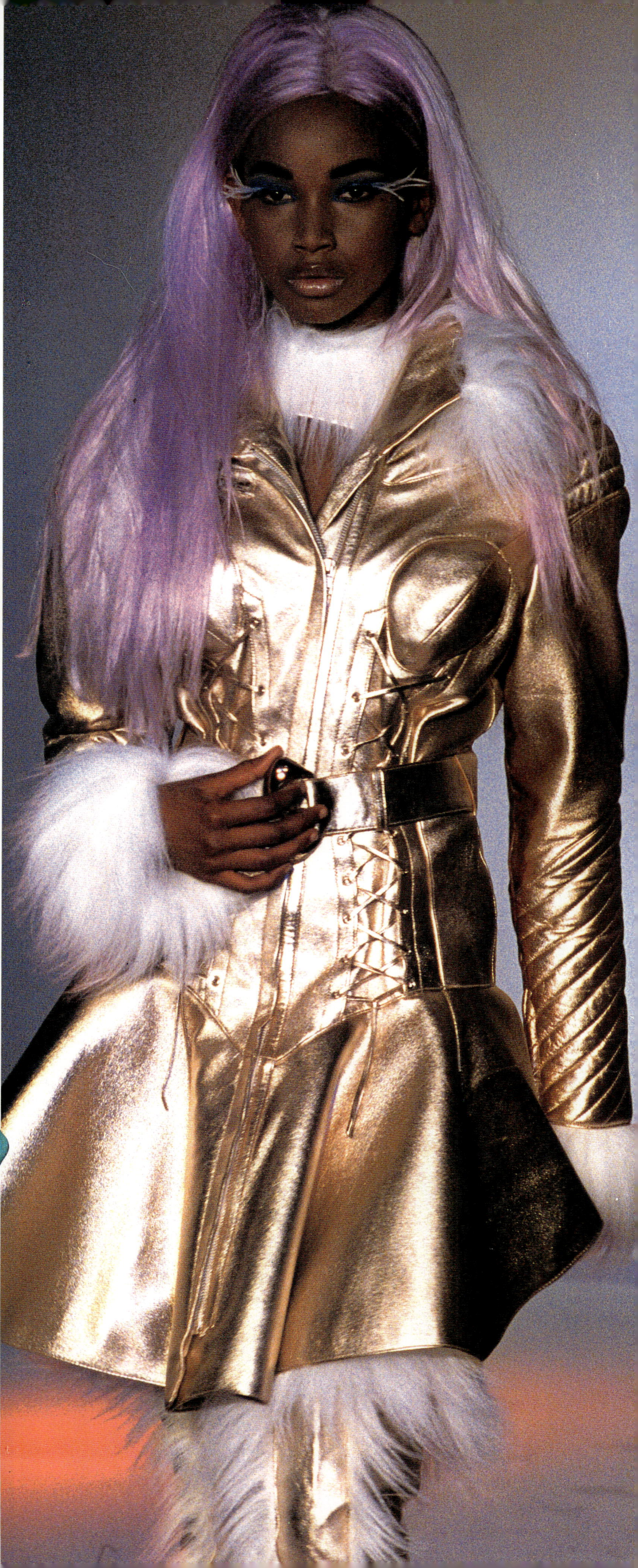

THIERRY MUGLER

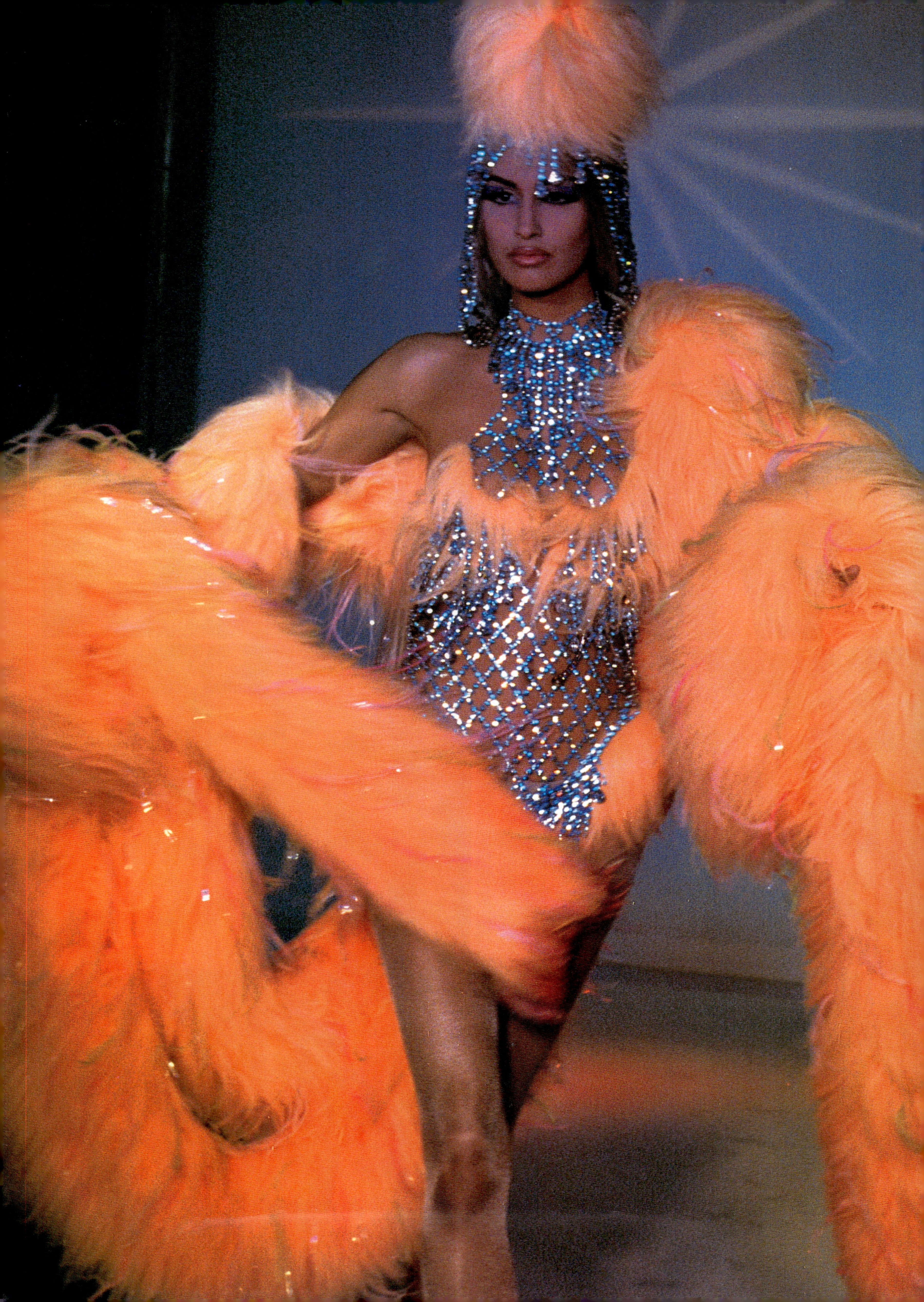

ROMEO GIGLI

ロメオ・ジリ

一年ぶりのコレクション。コクーン・ラインの優しさや素材の素晴らしさはそのままに、シンプルにナイーブに、そして美しく、ミラノ時代のロメオ・ジリを彷彿させる。

His first collection in a year. The gentle, cocoon lines and the excellent quality of the materials haven't changed. The simple, innocent and beautiful style remind us of Romeo Gigli in his Milan day.

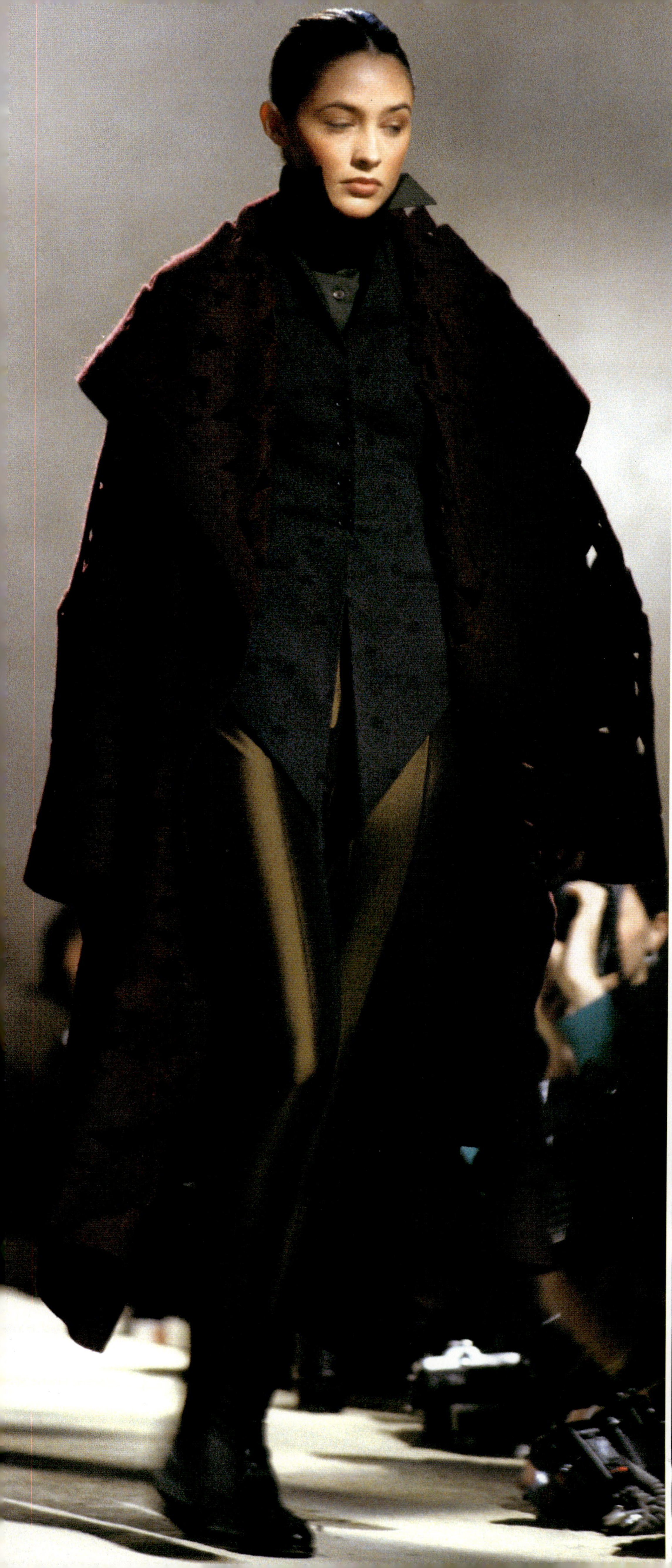
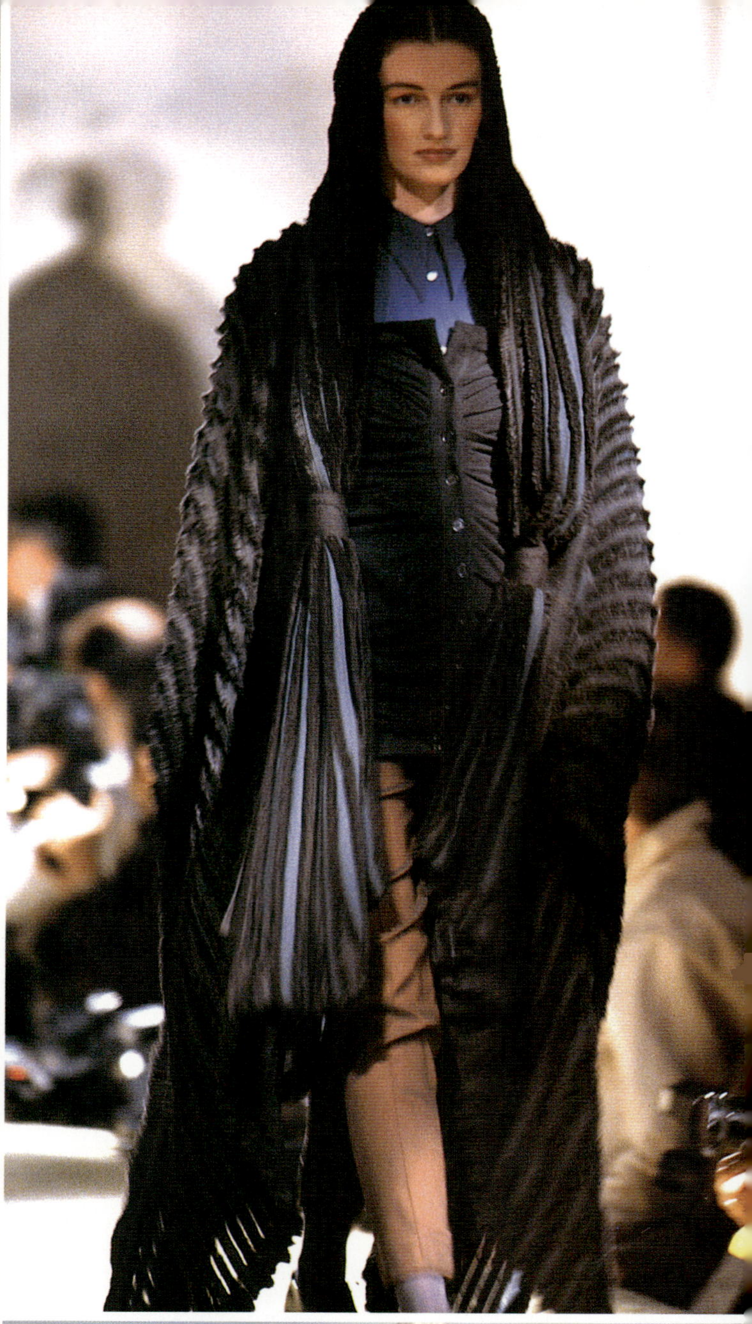
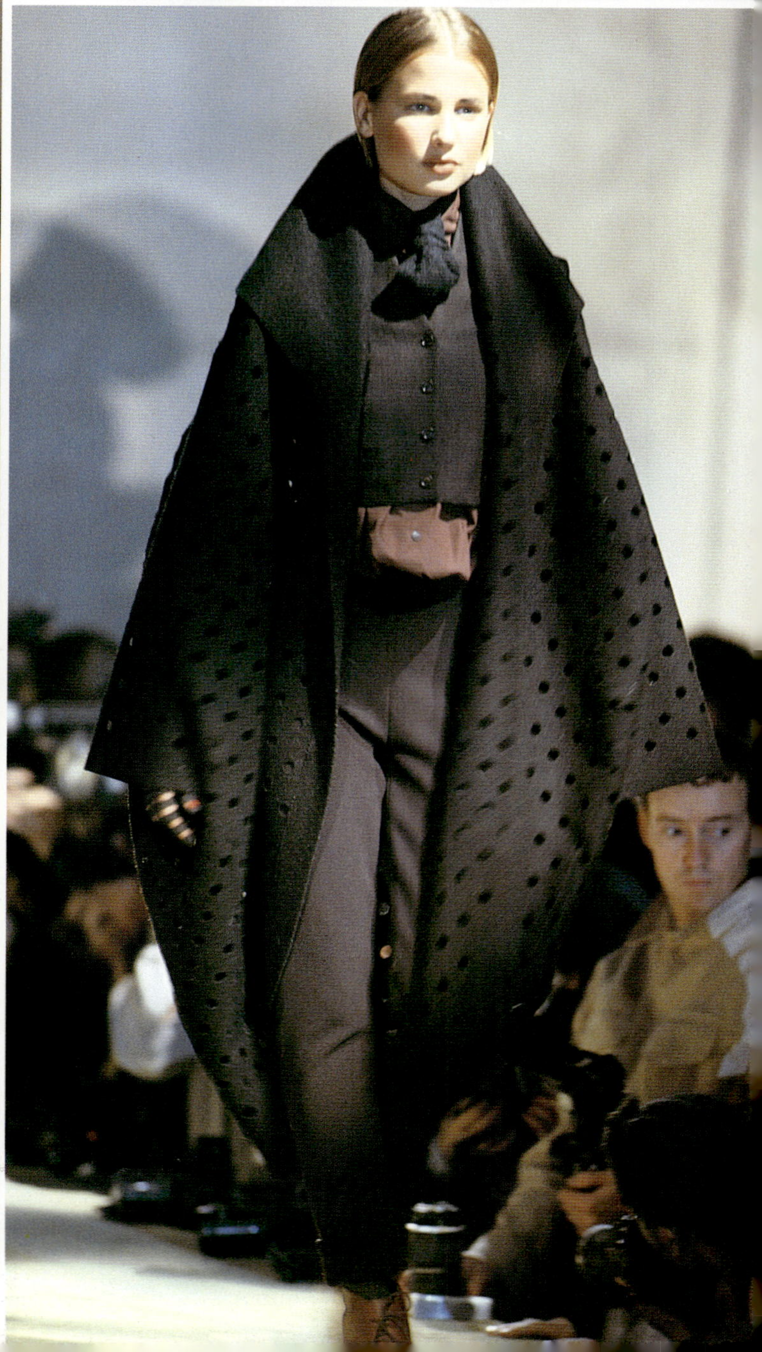

ROMEO GIGLI

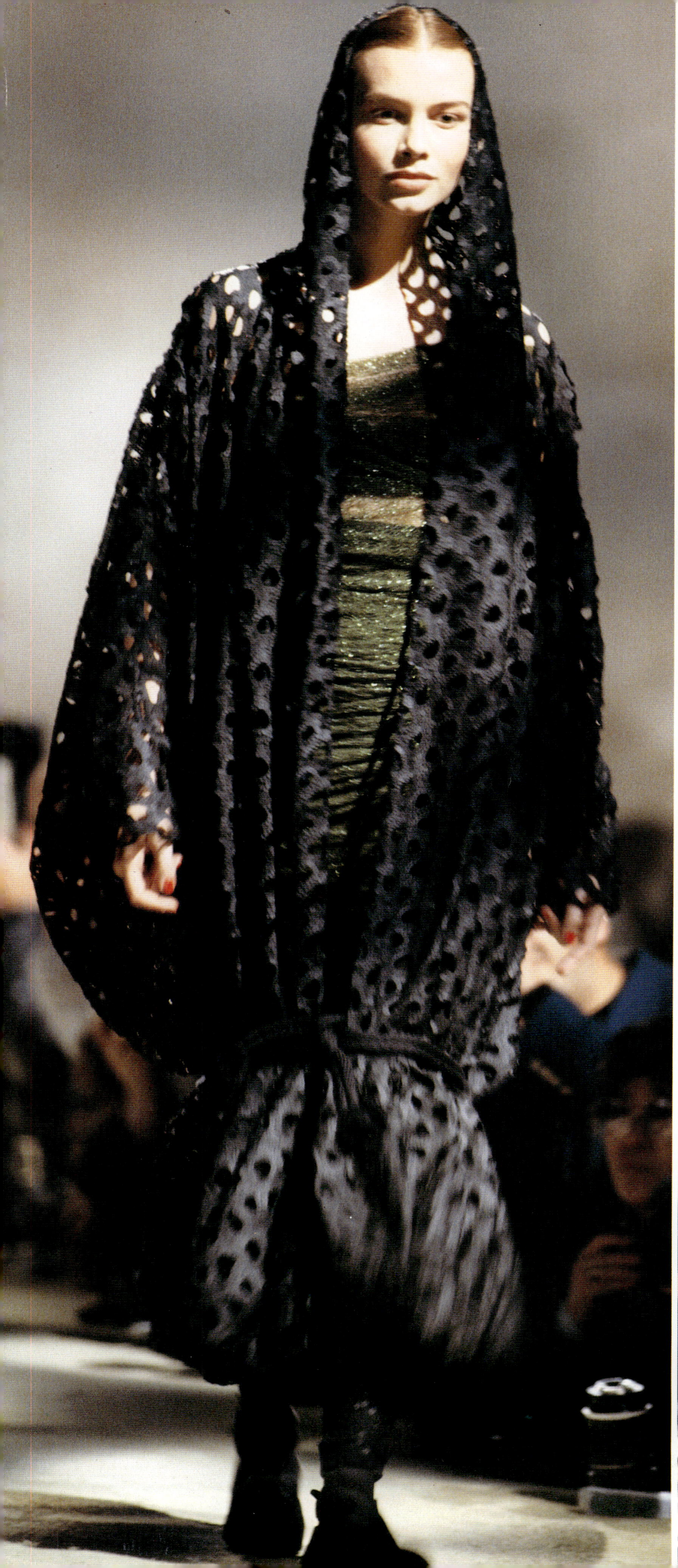

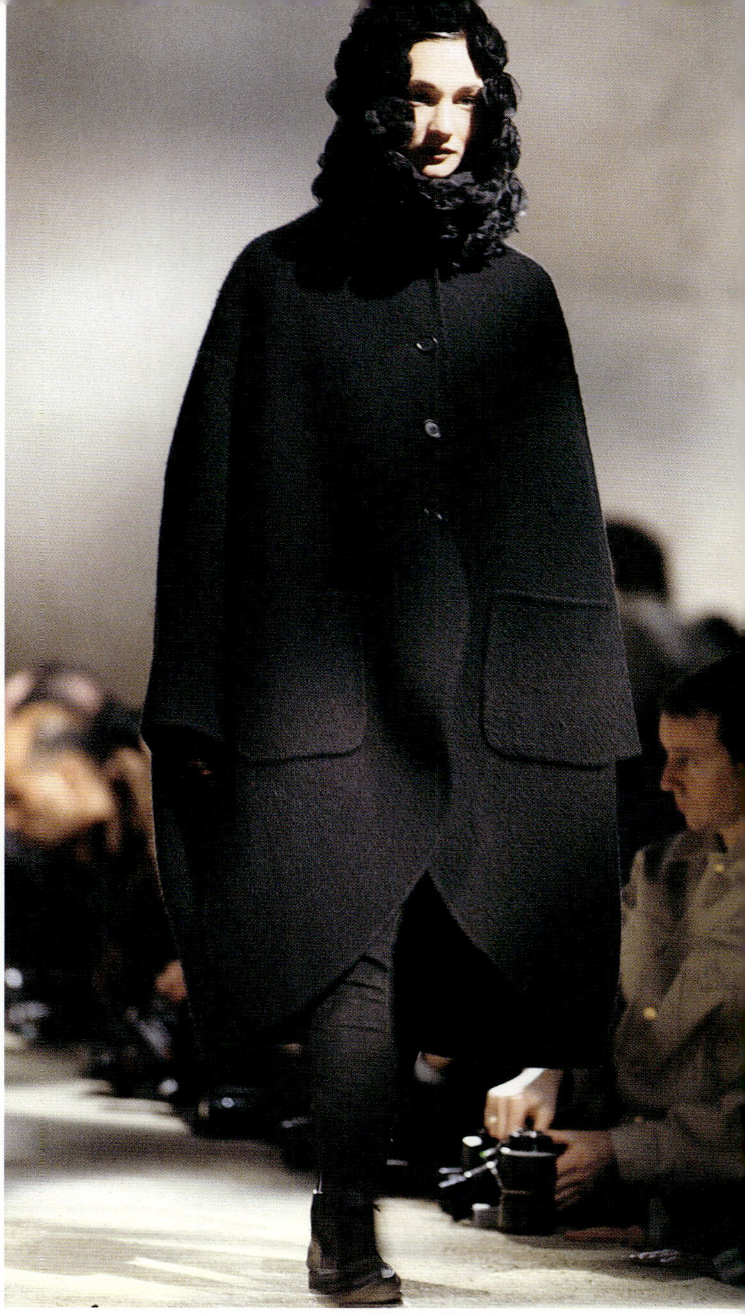

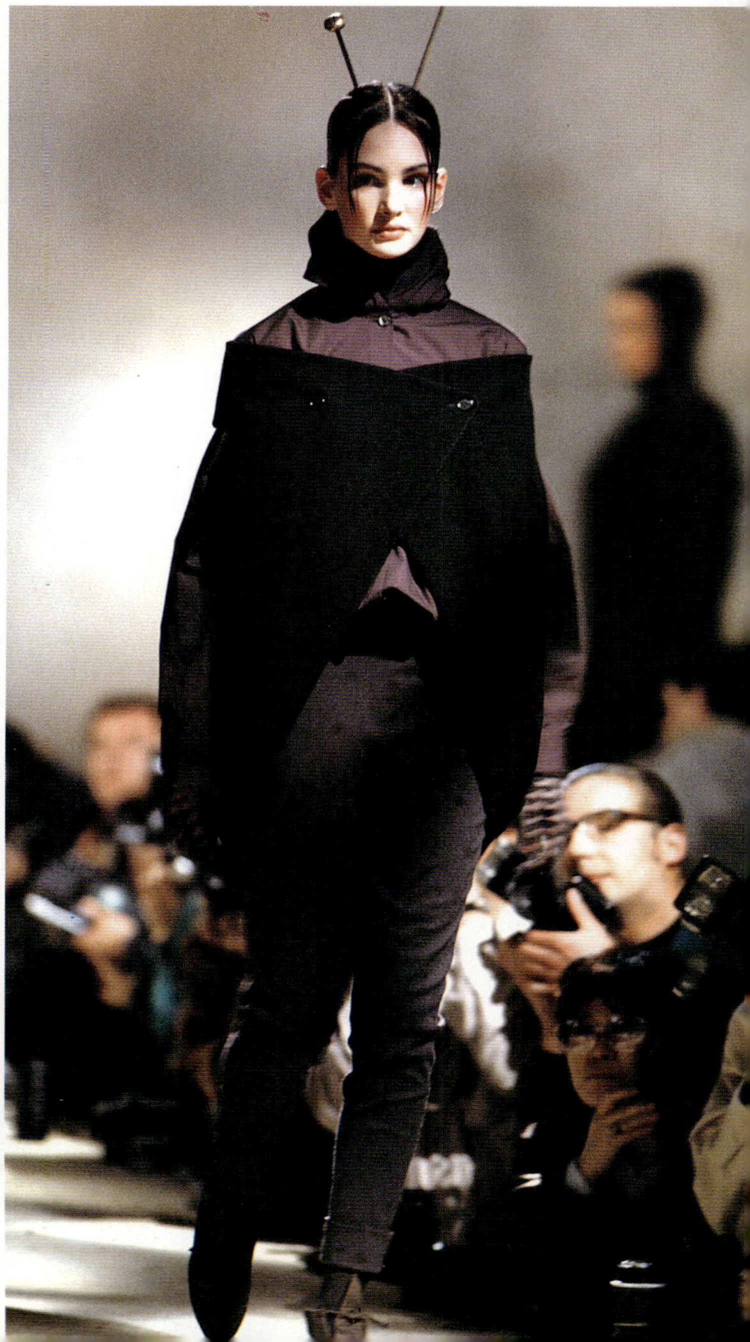

ROMEO GIGLI

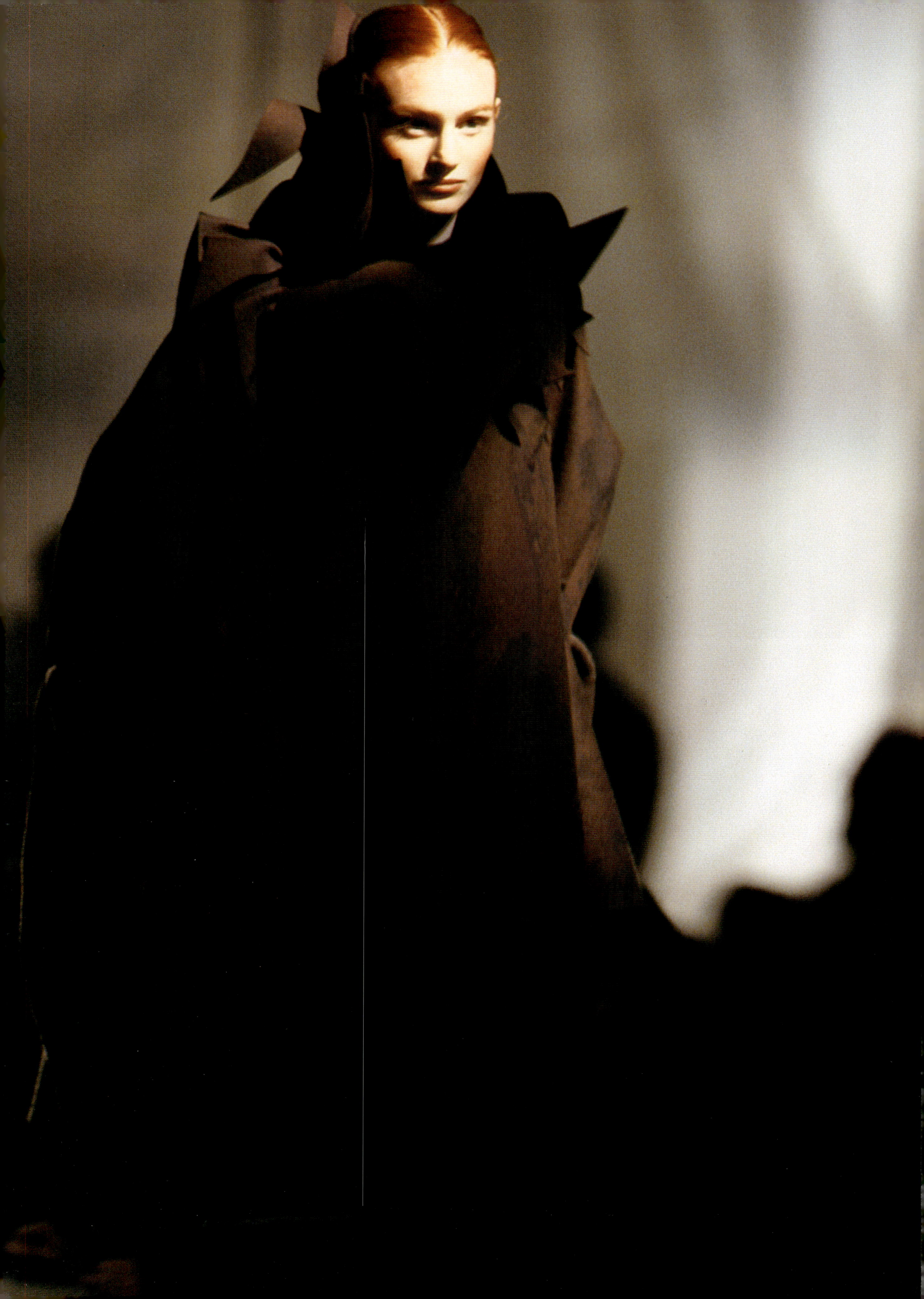

ROMEO GIGLI

73

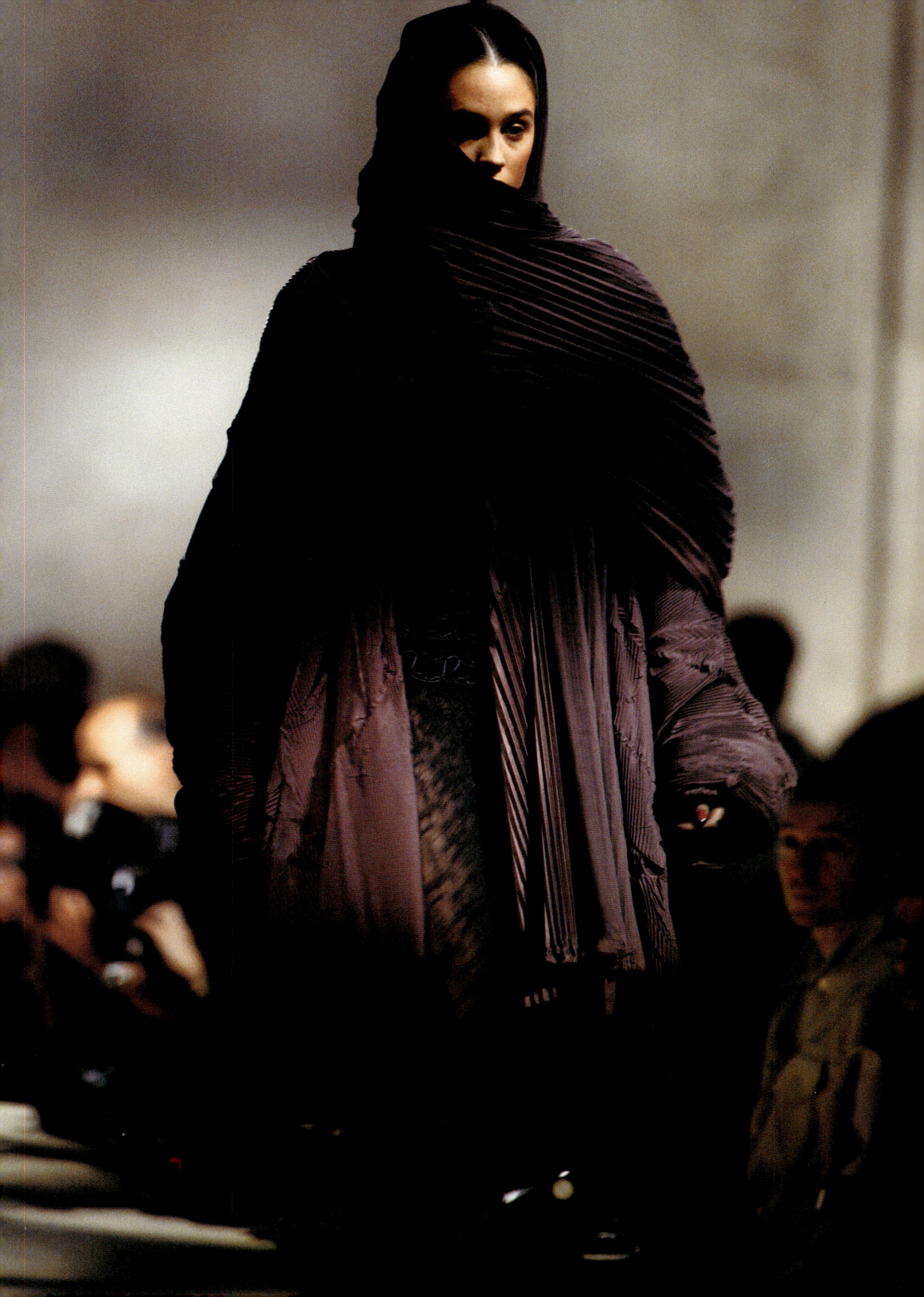

ROMEO GIGLI

75

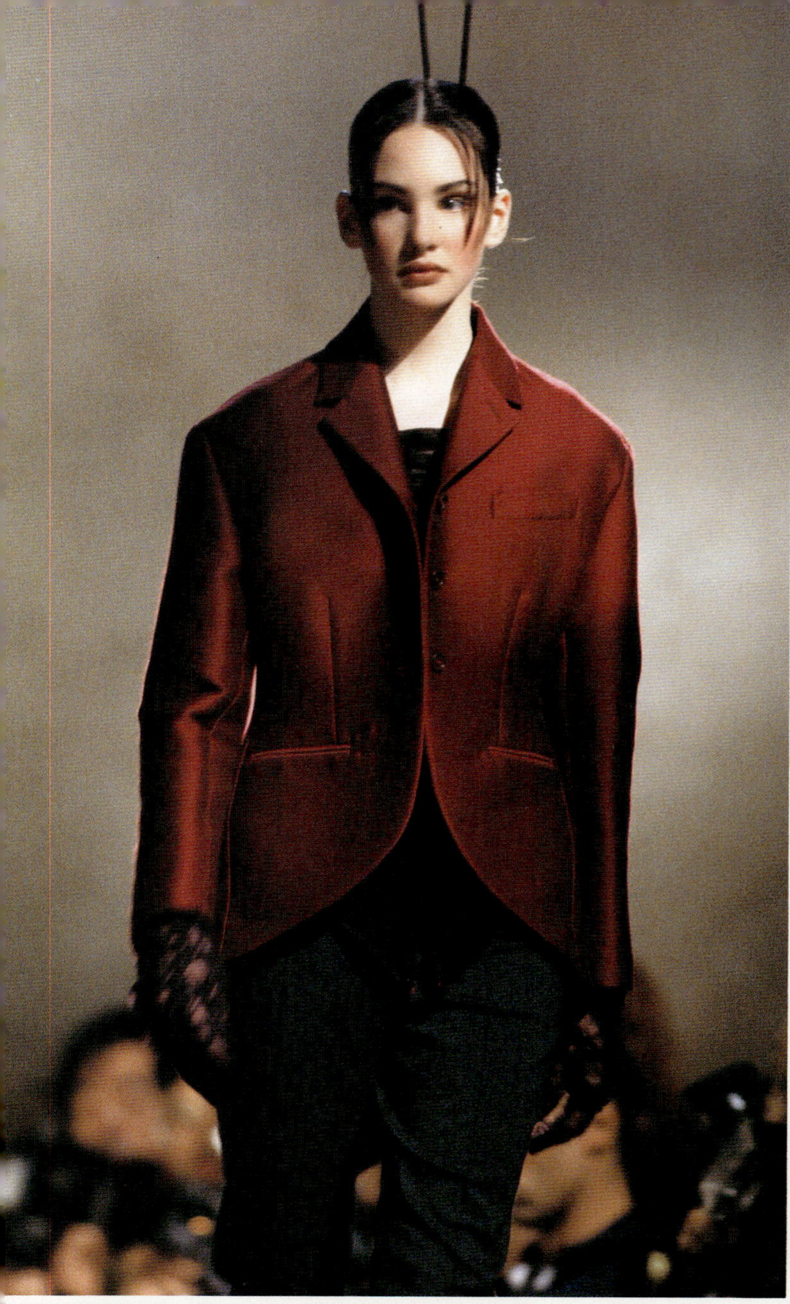
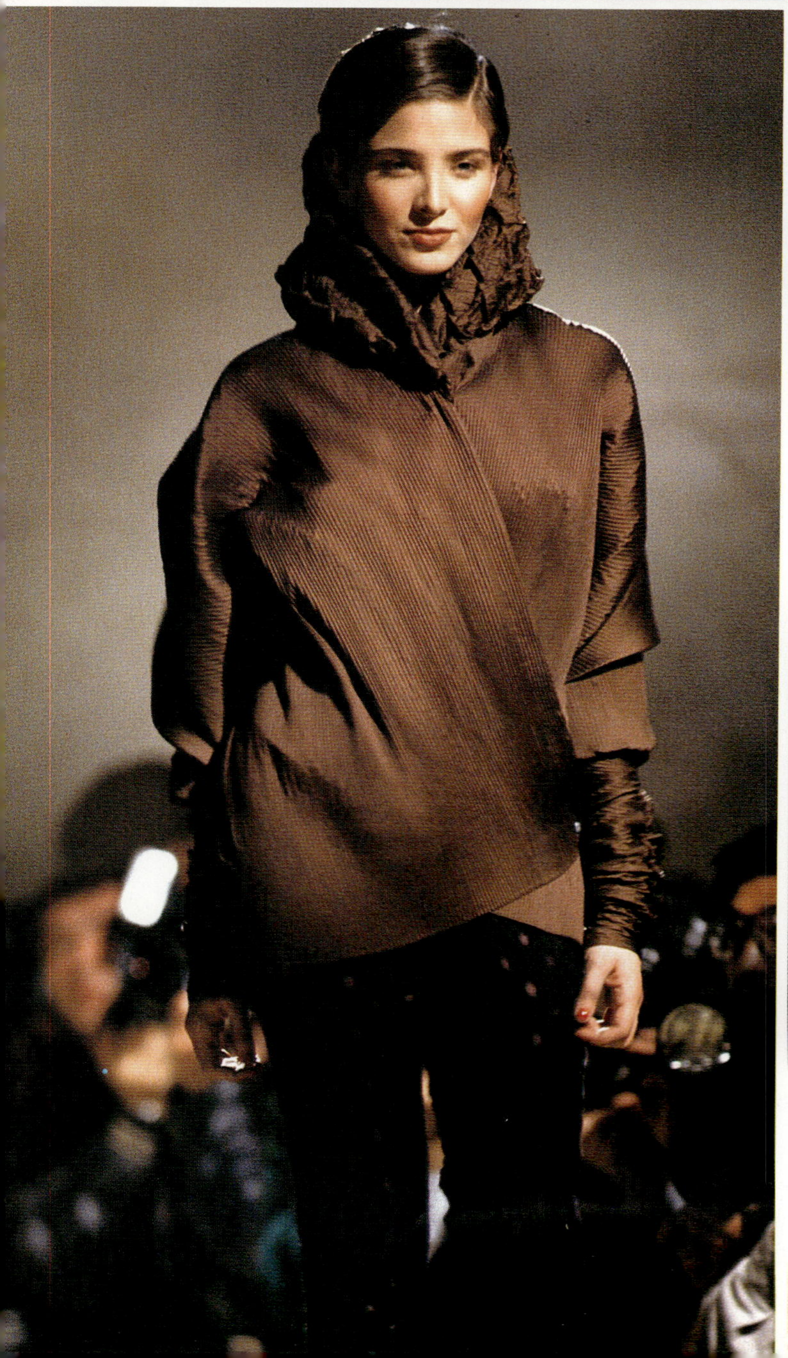
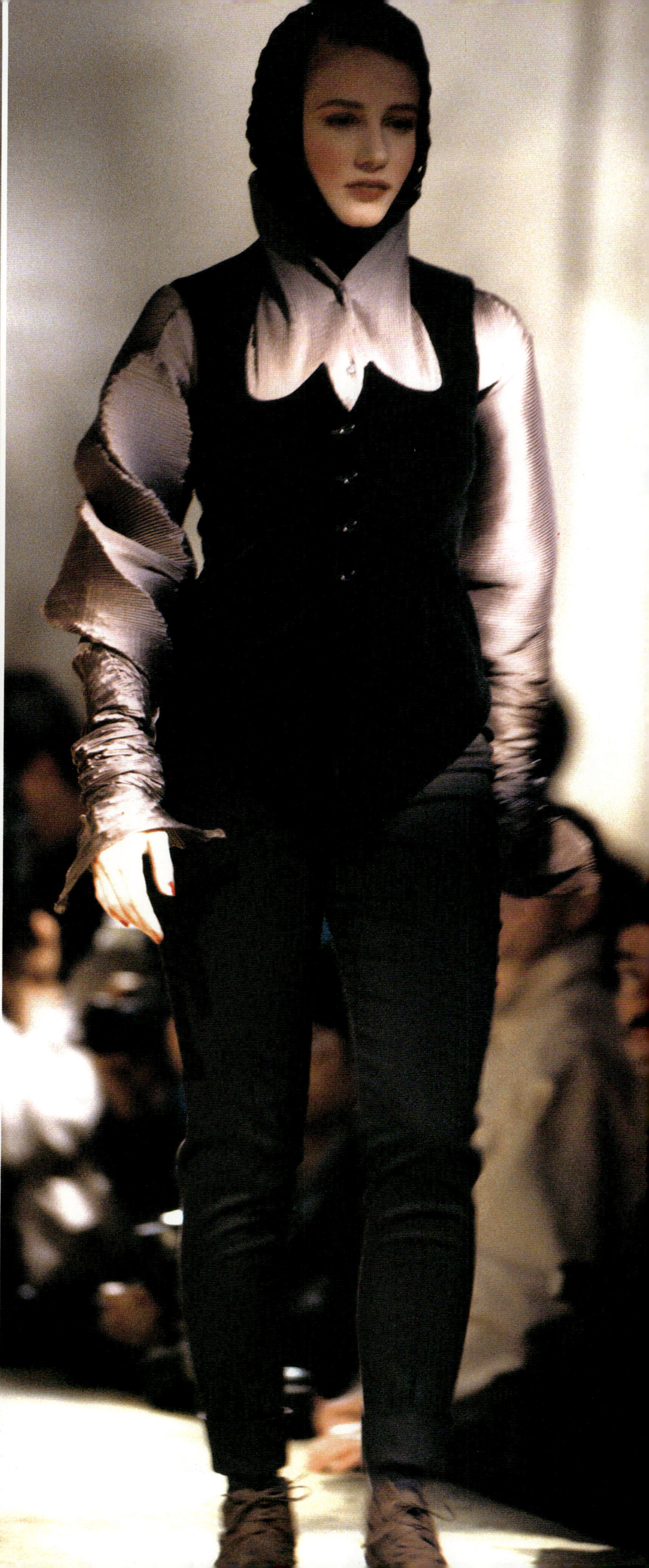

ROMEO GIGLI

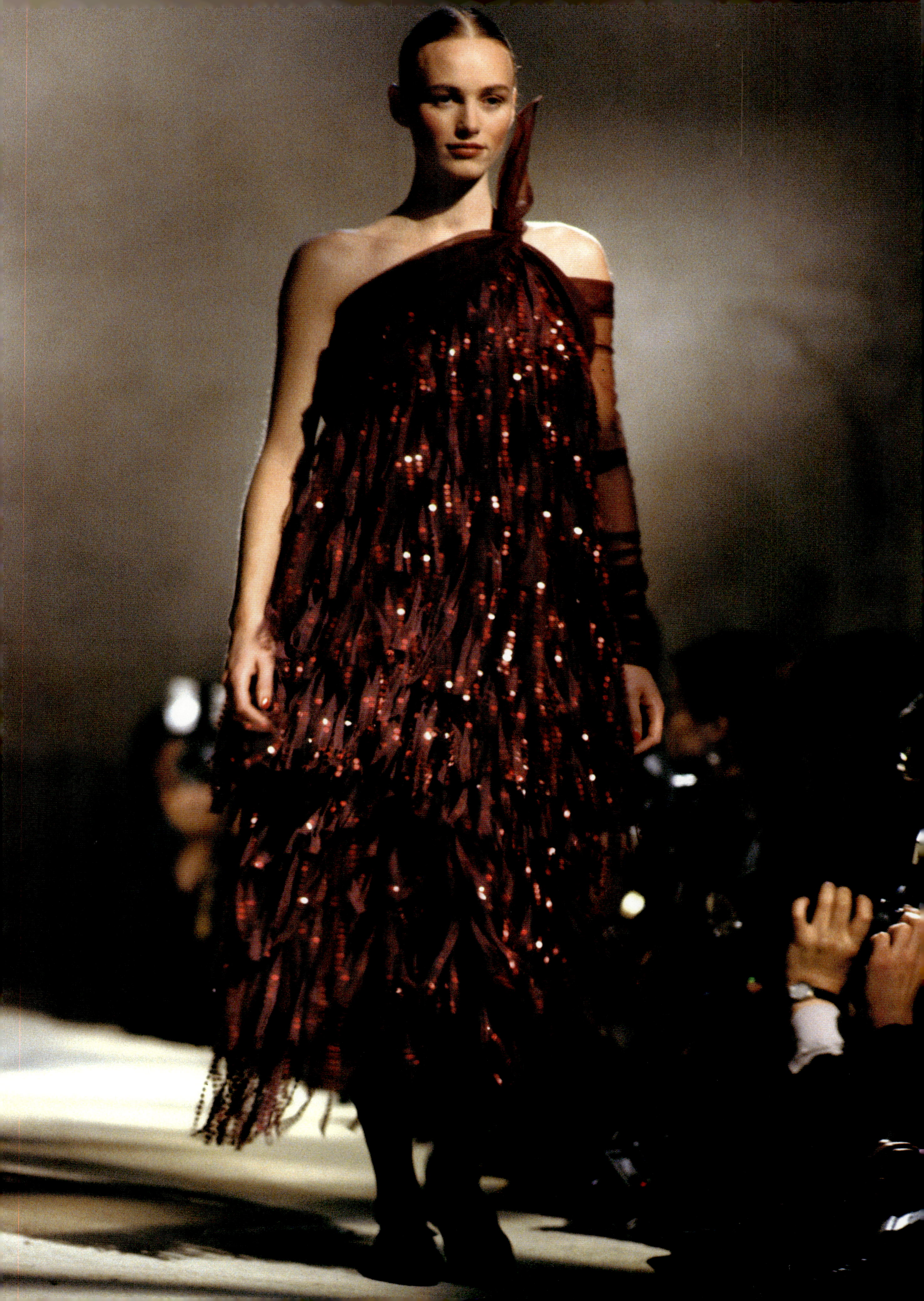

CHRISTIAN DIOR

クリスチャン・ディオール

オリエンタル的なパターンやダイヤゴナル、ベルベットなどを駆使し、華麗なダイナミズムを表現。エンディングはピンク系の色彩のエレガントなドレスのパレードで。

With Oriental patterns, diagonals and velvet, he demonstrated an elegant dynamism.
The conclusion saw a parade of elegant dresses in various shades of pink.

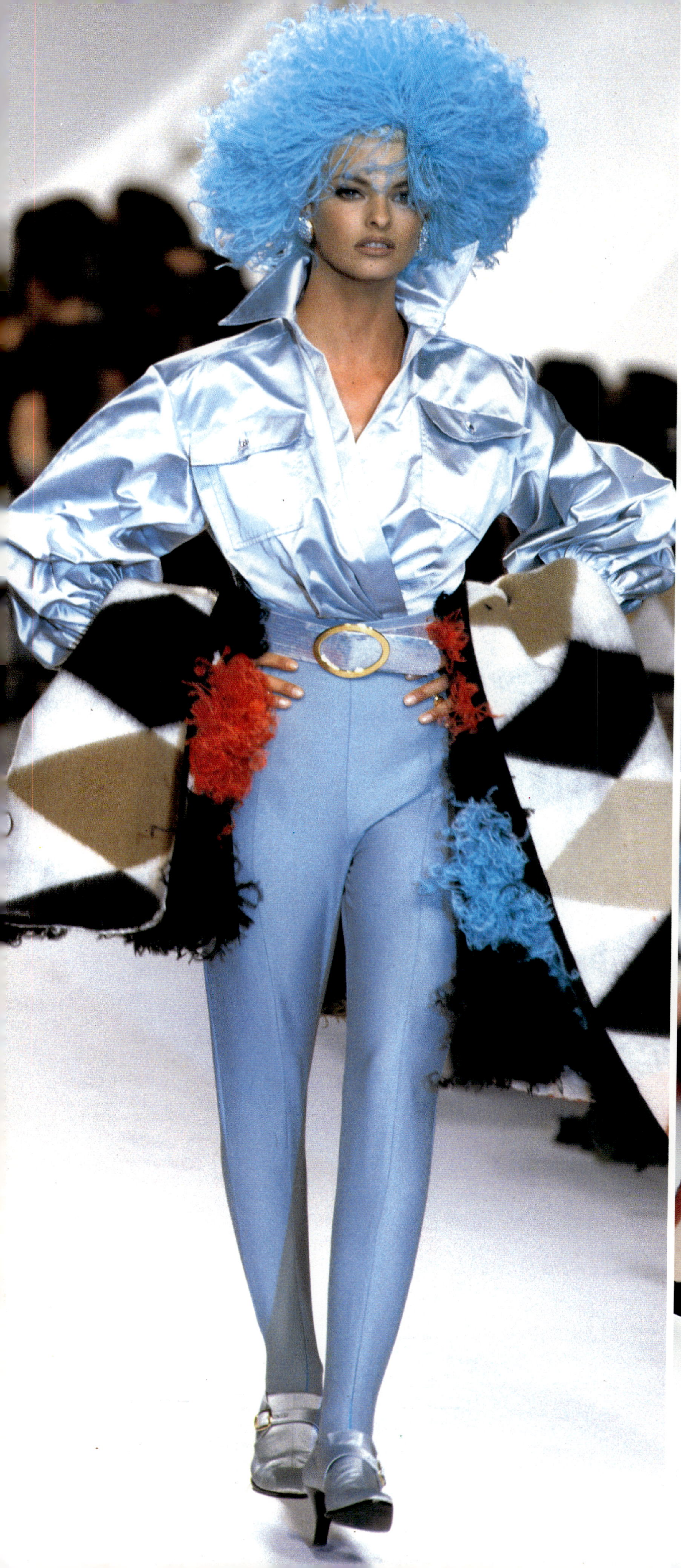
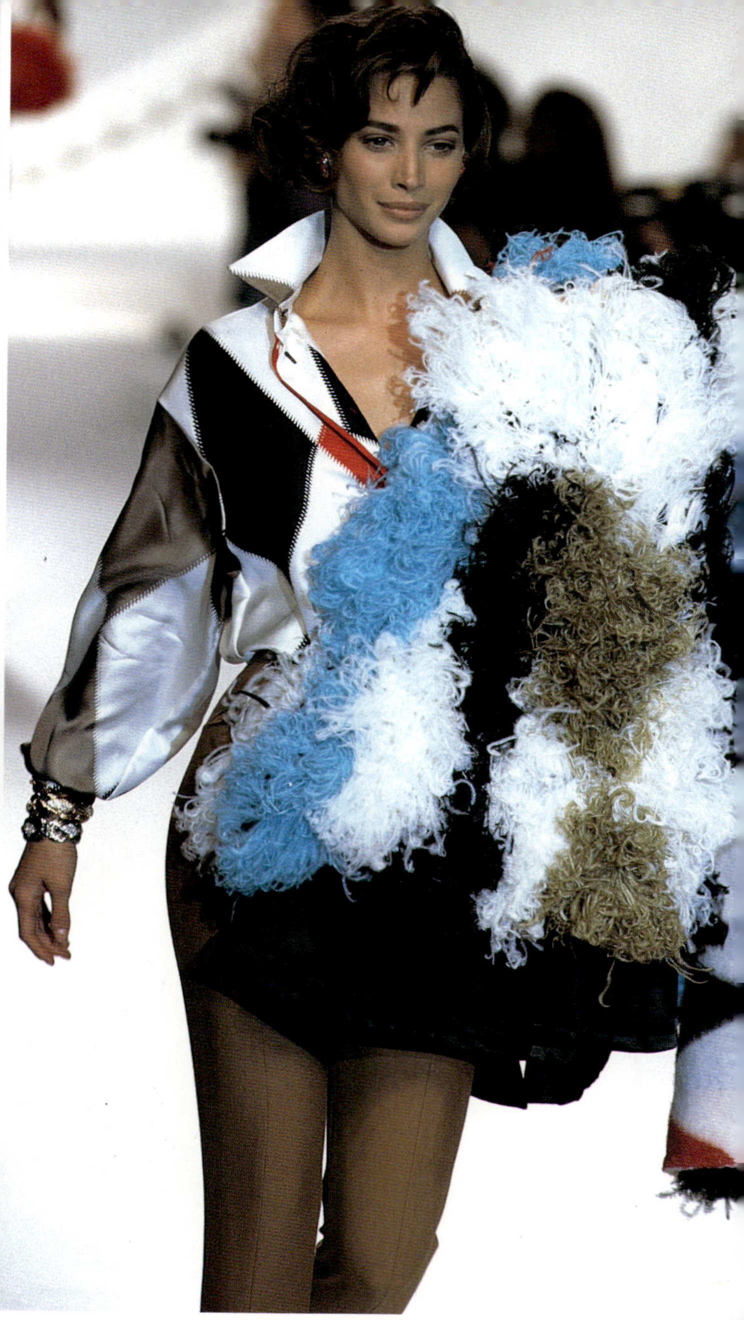
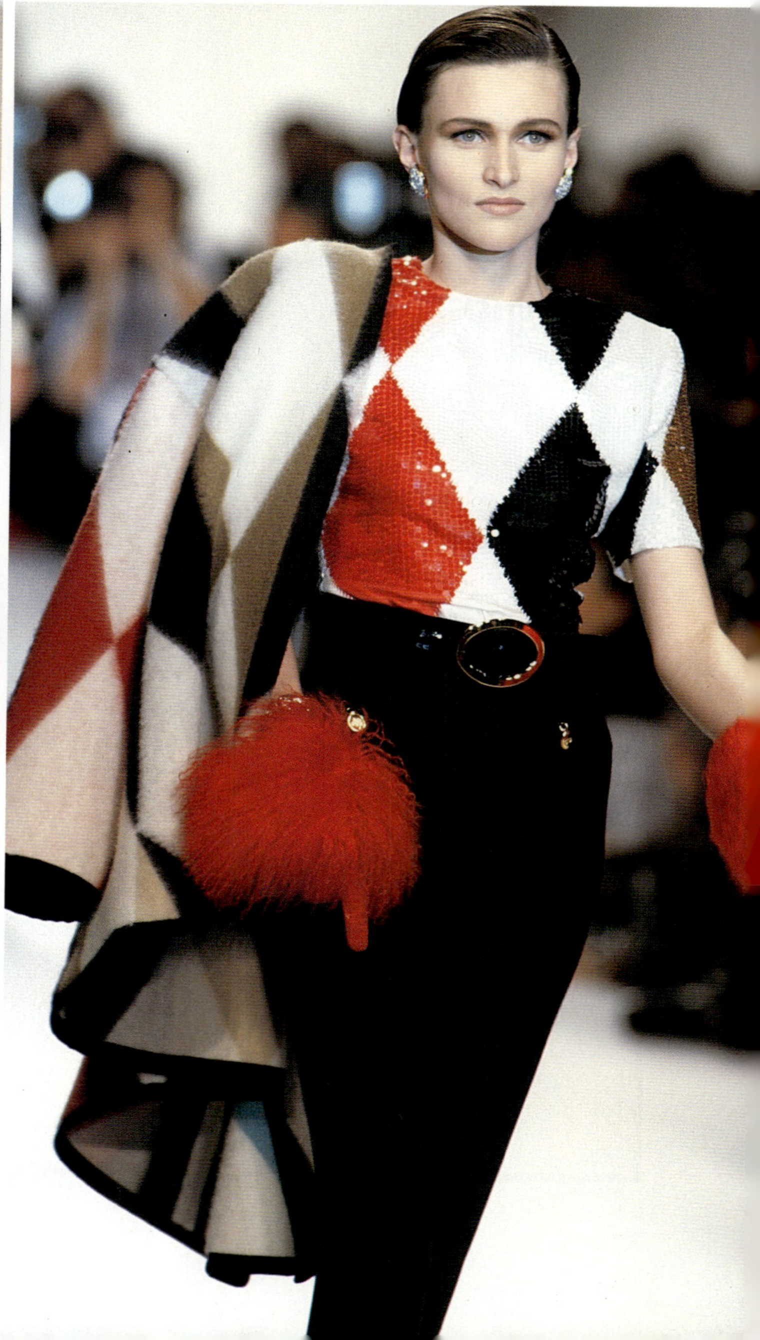

CHRISTIAN DIOR

81

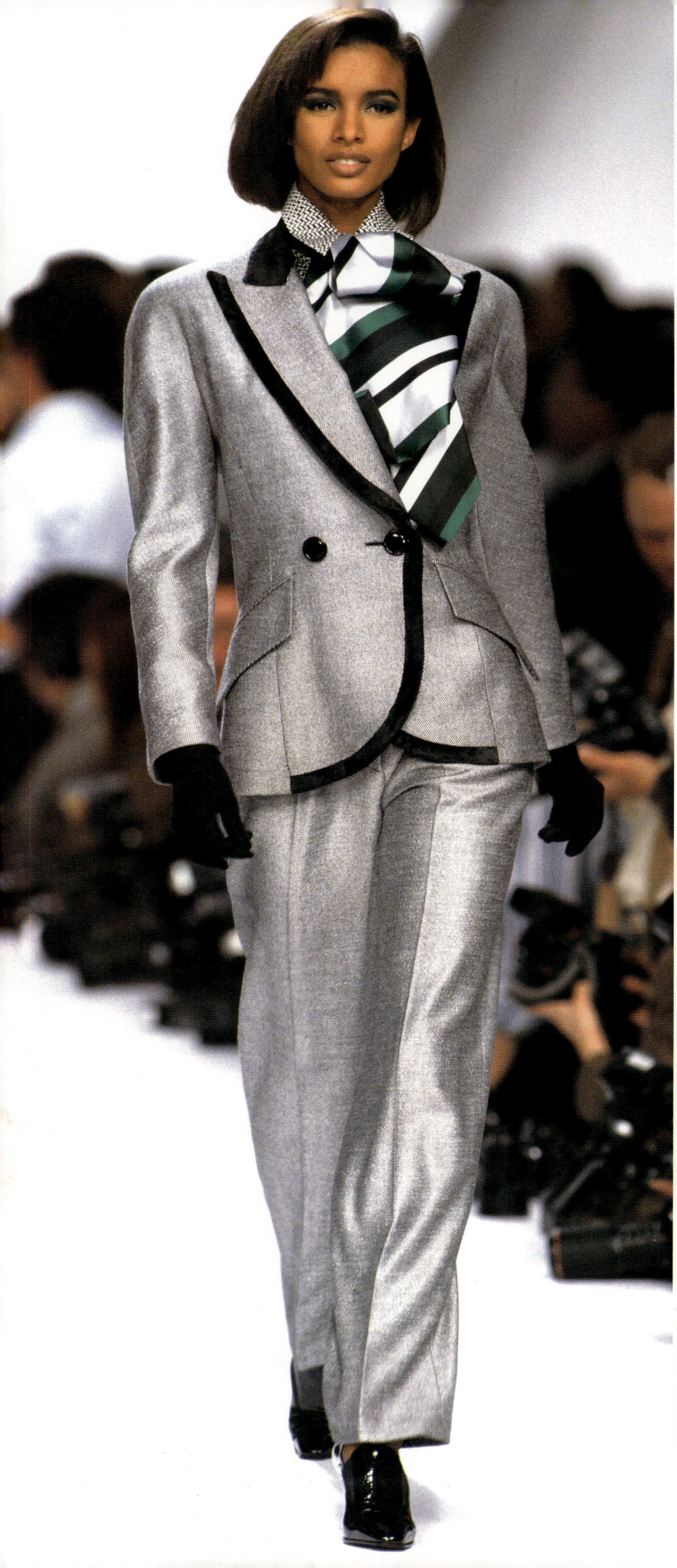
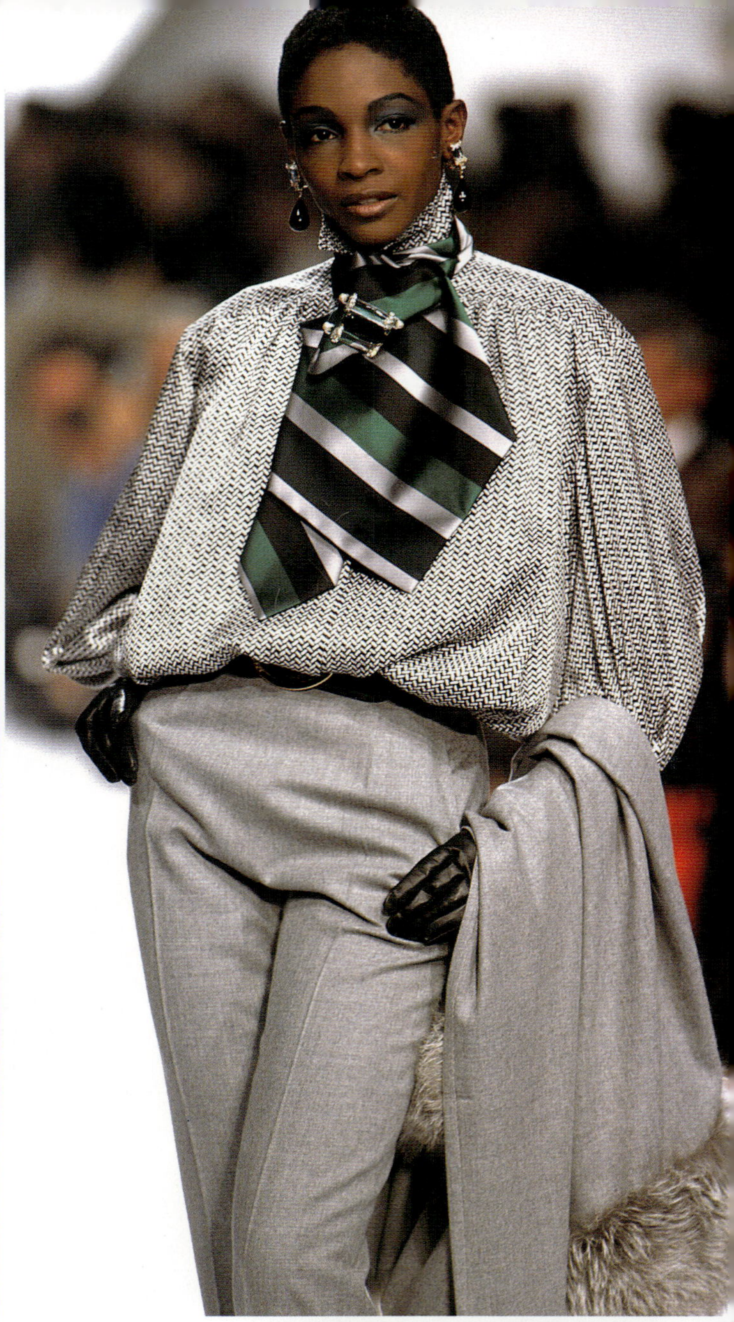
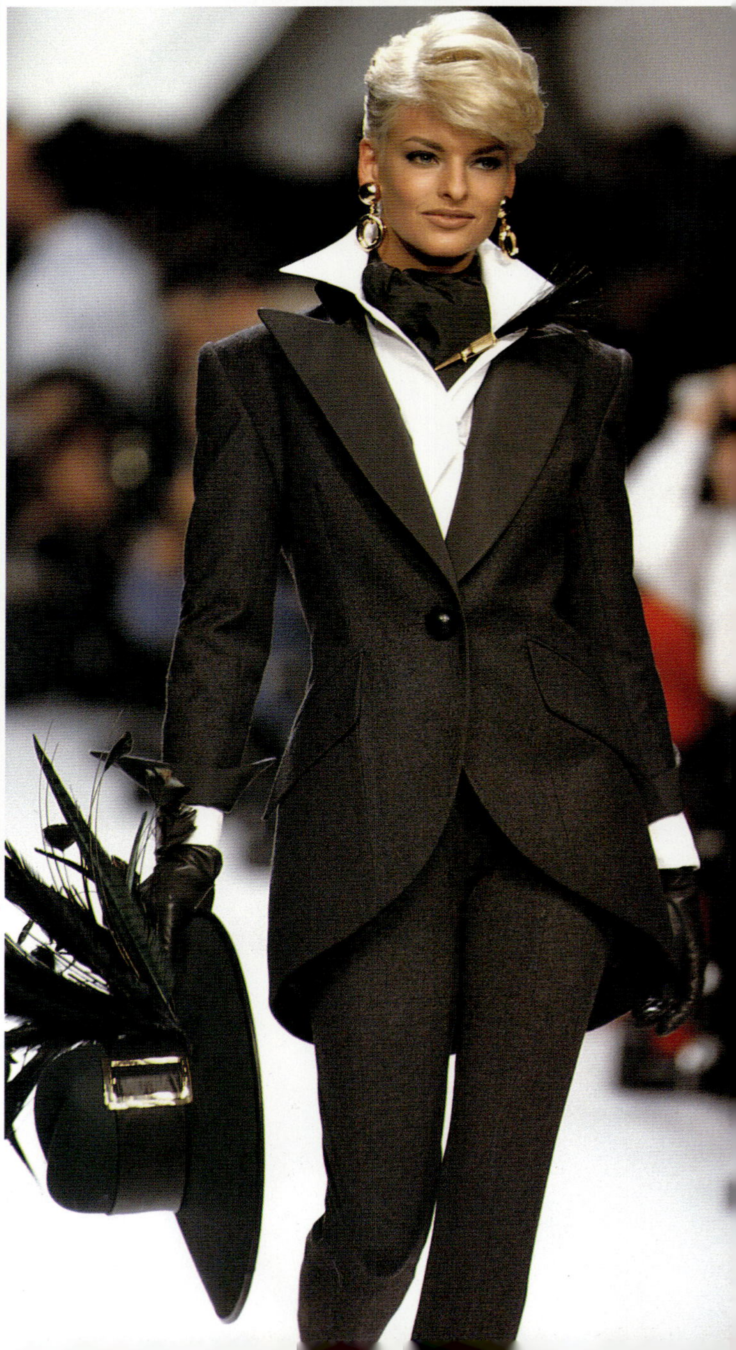

CHRISTIAN DIOR

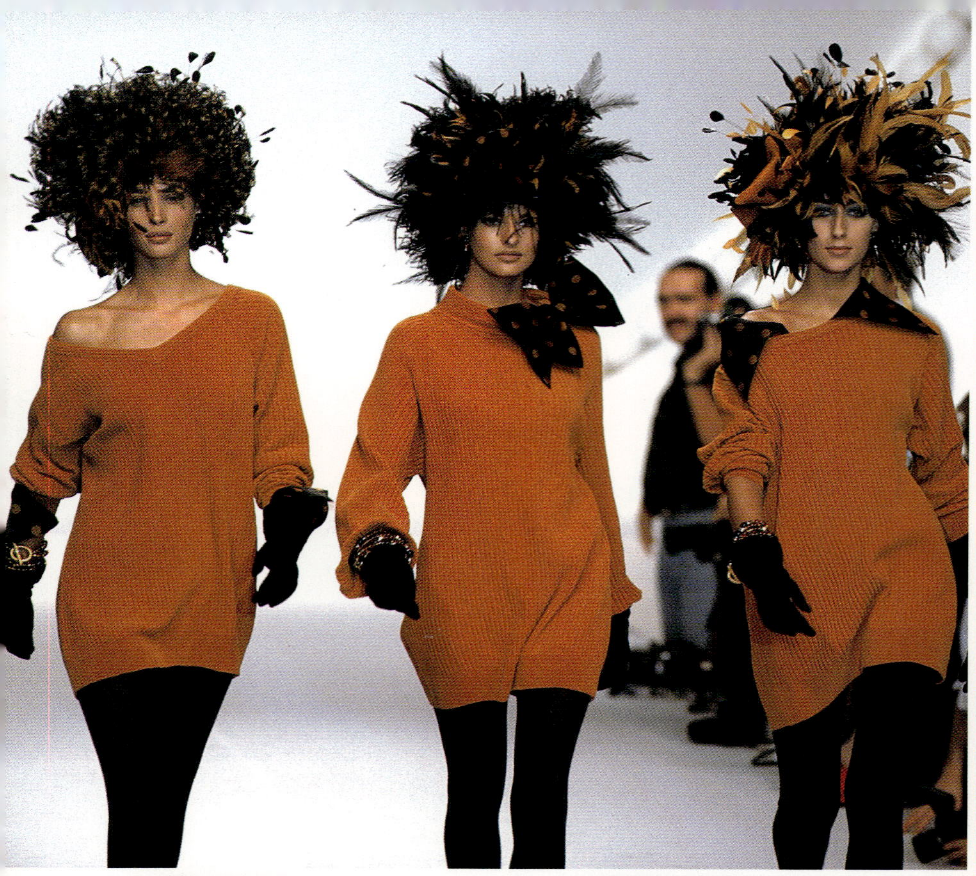

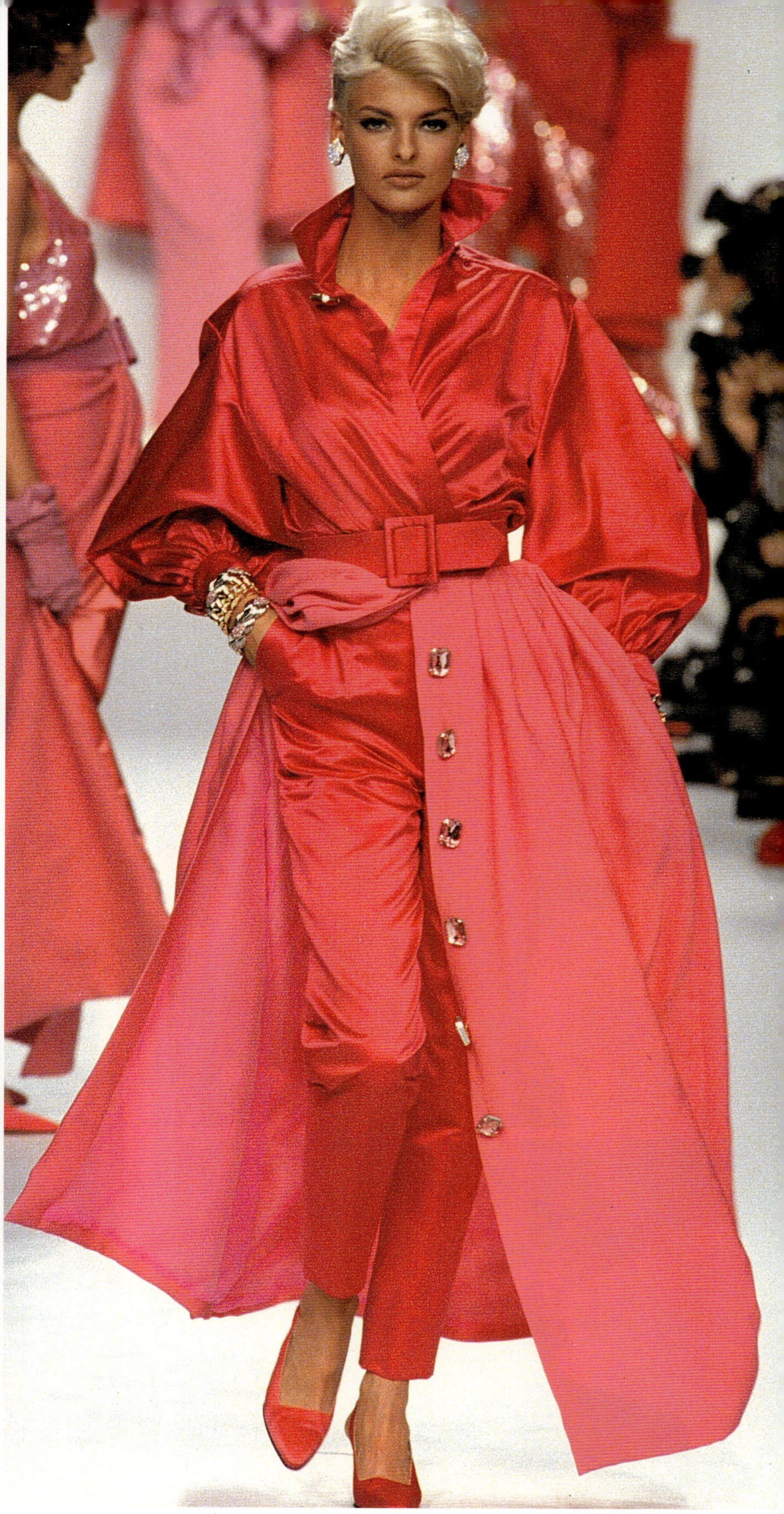

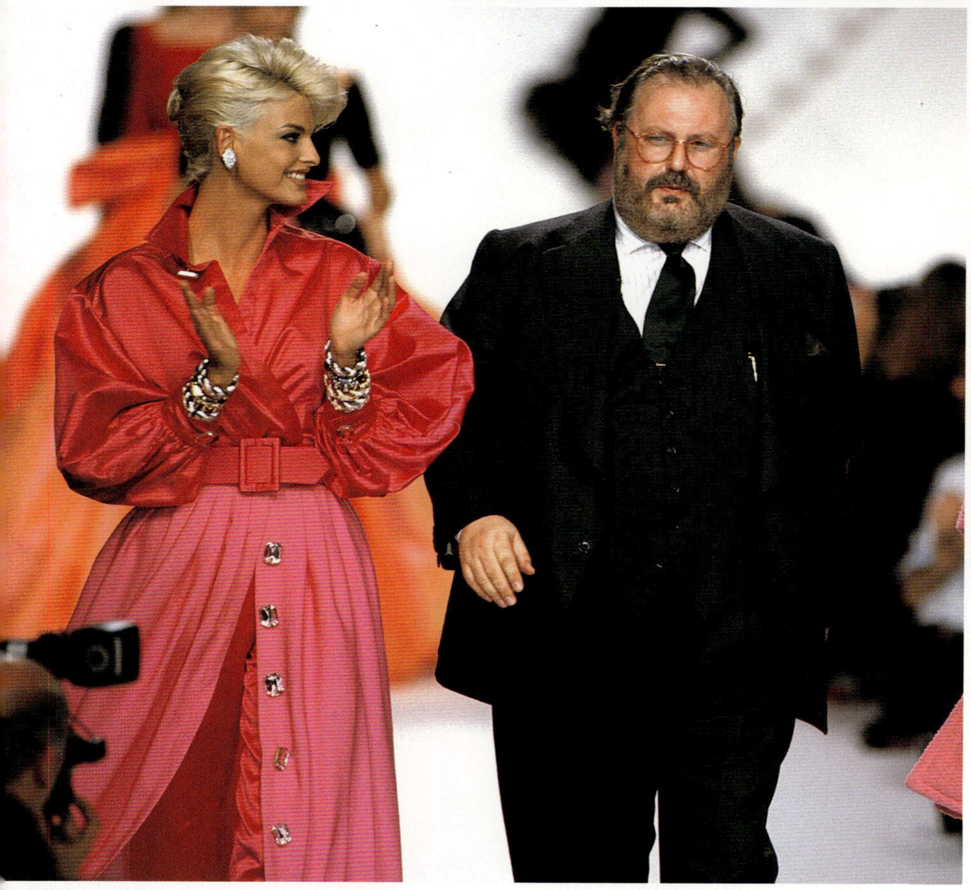

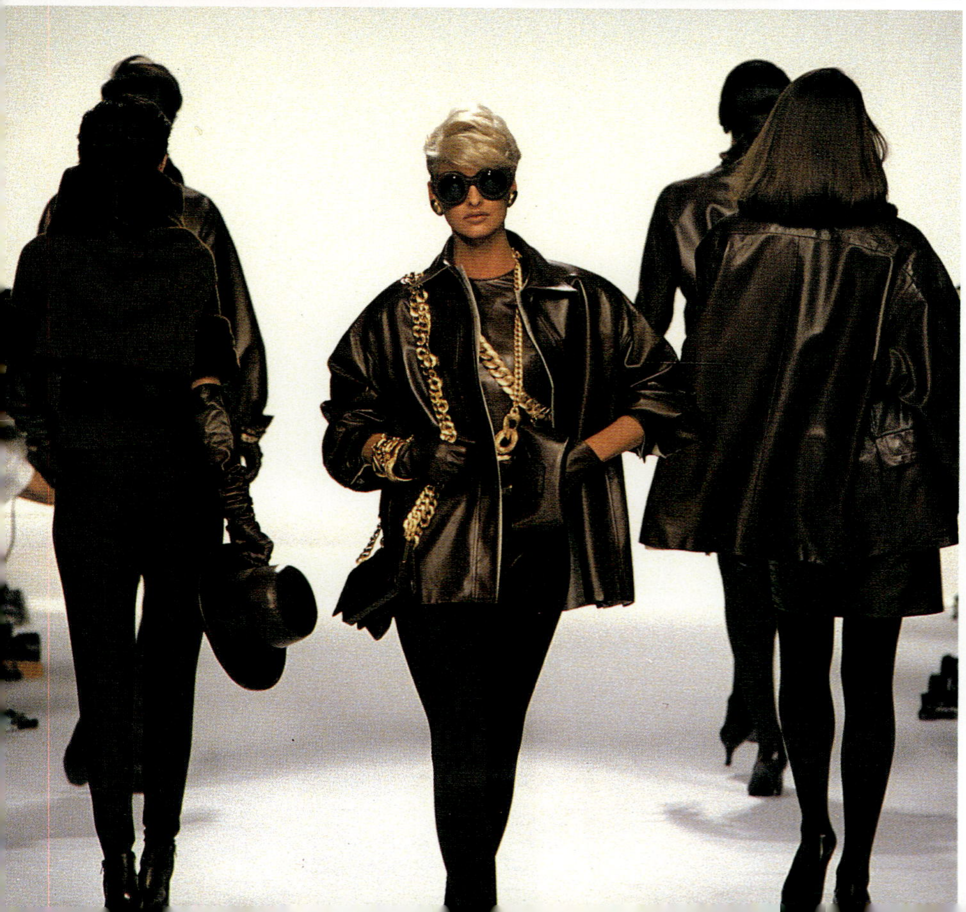

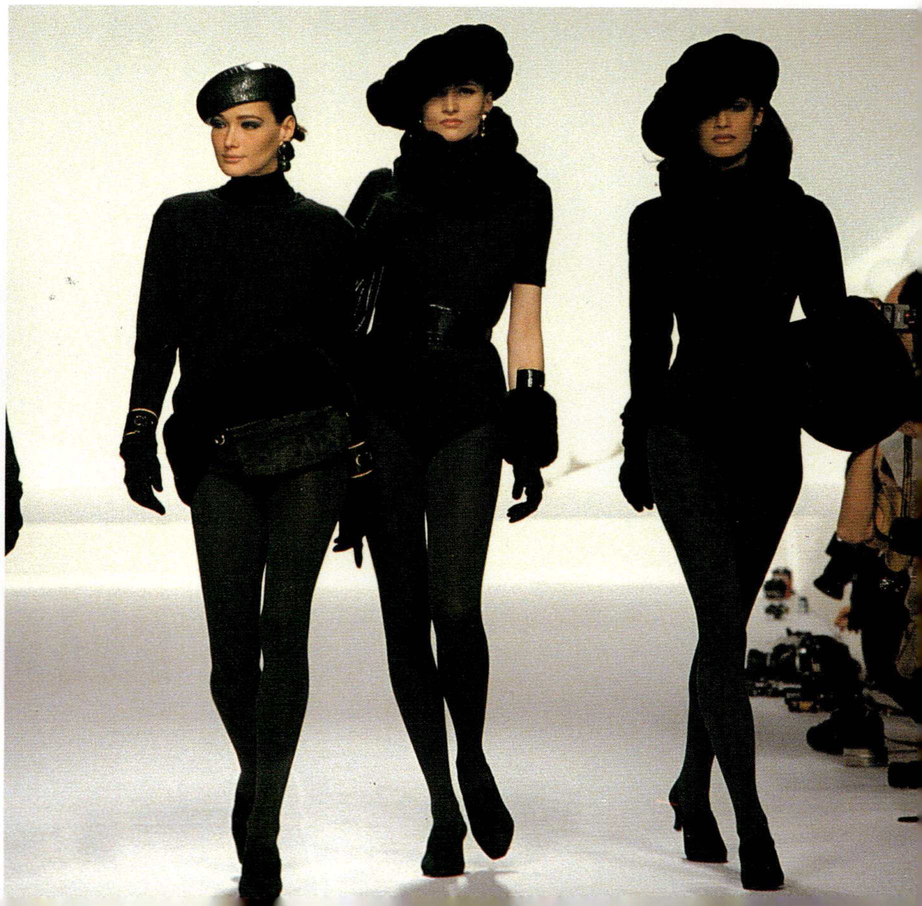

CHRISTIAN DIOR

85

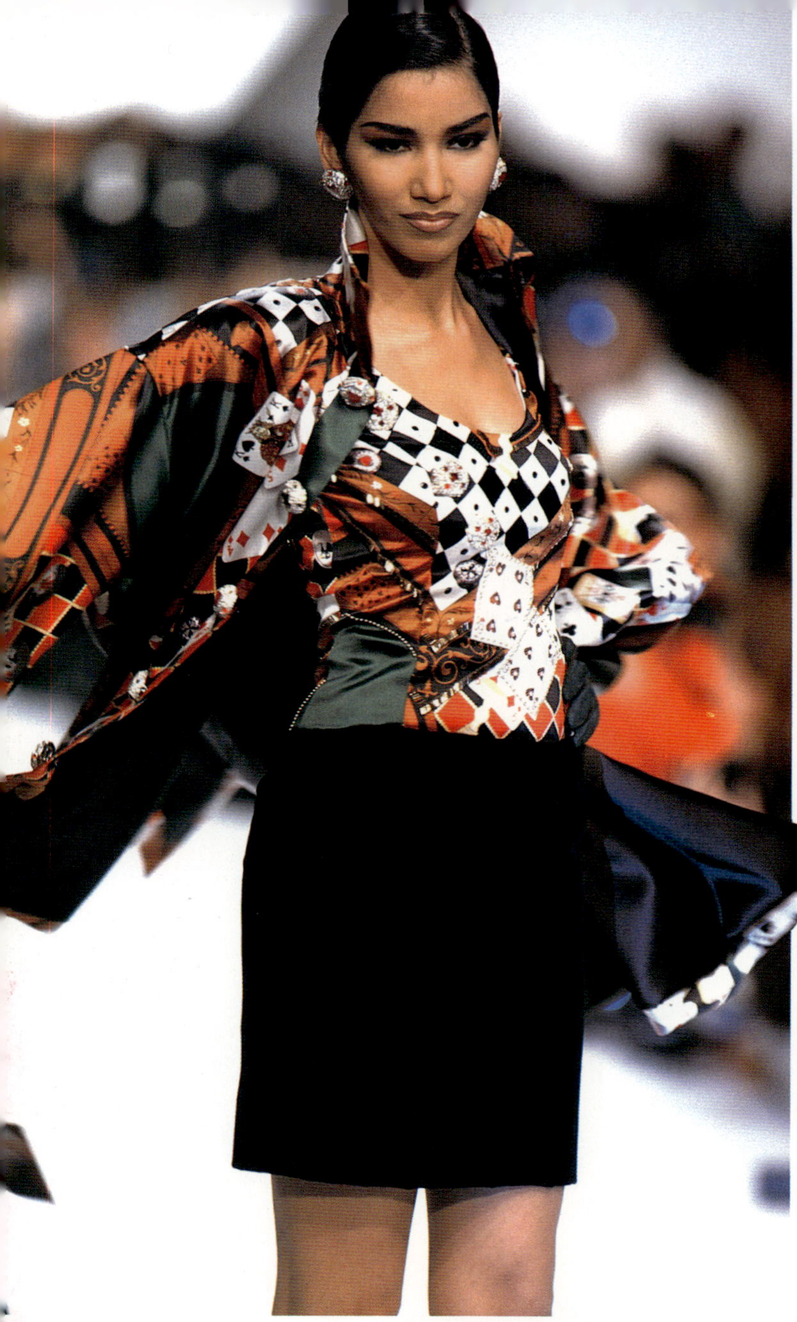

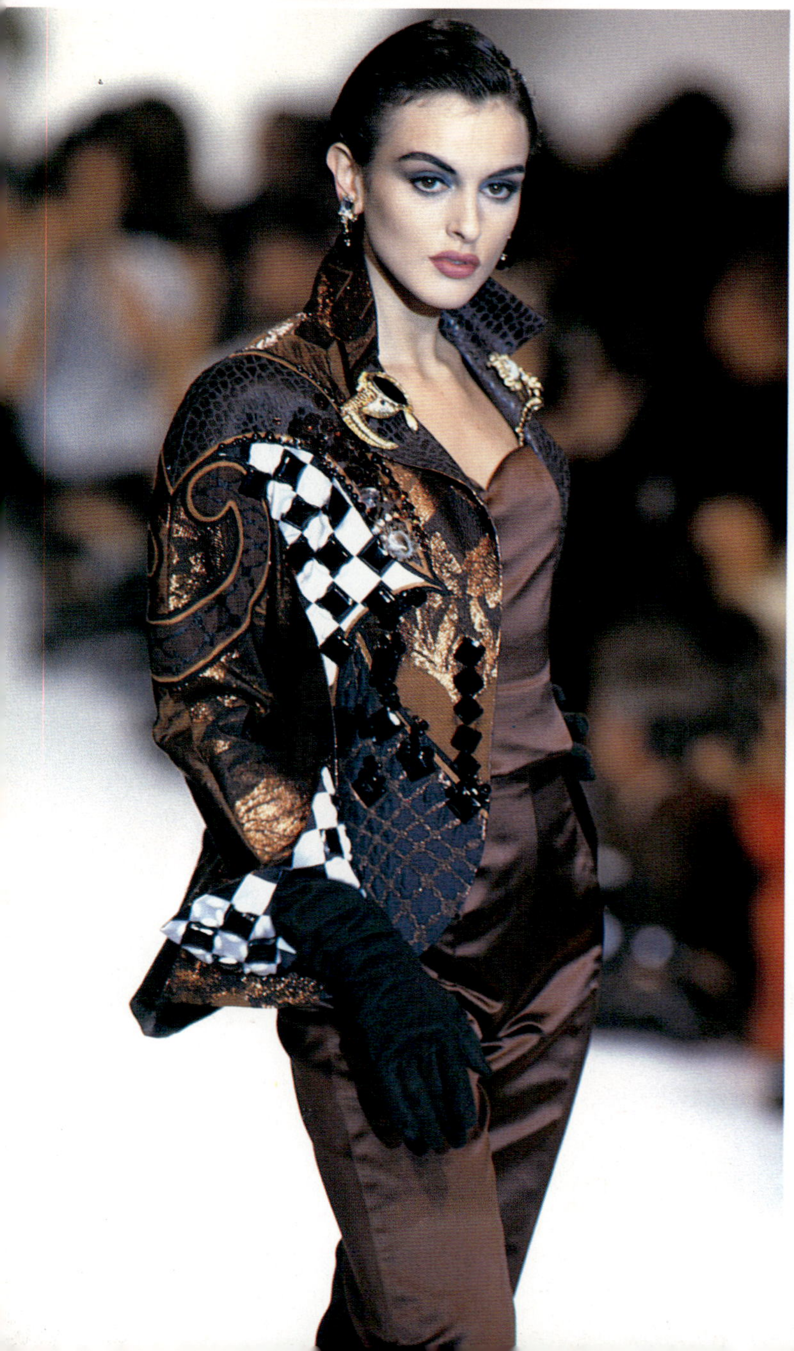

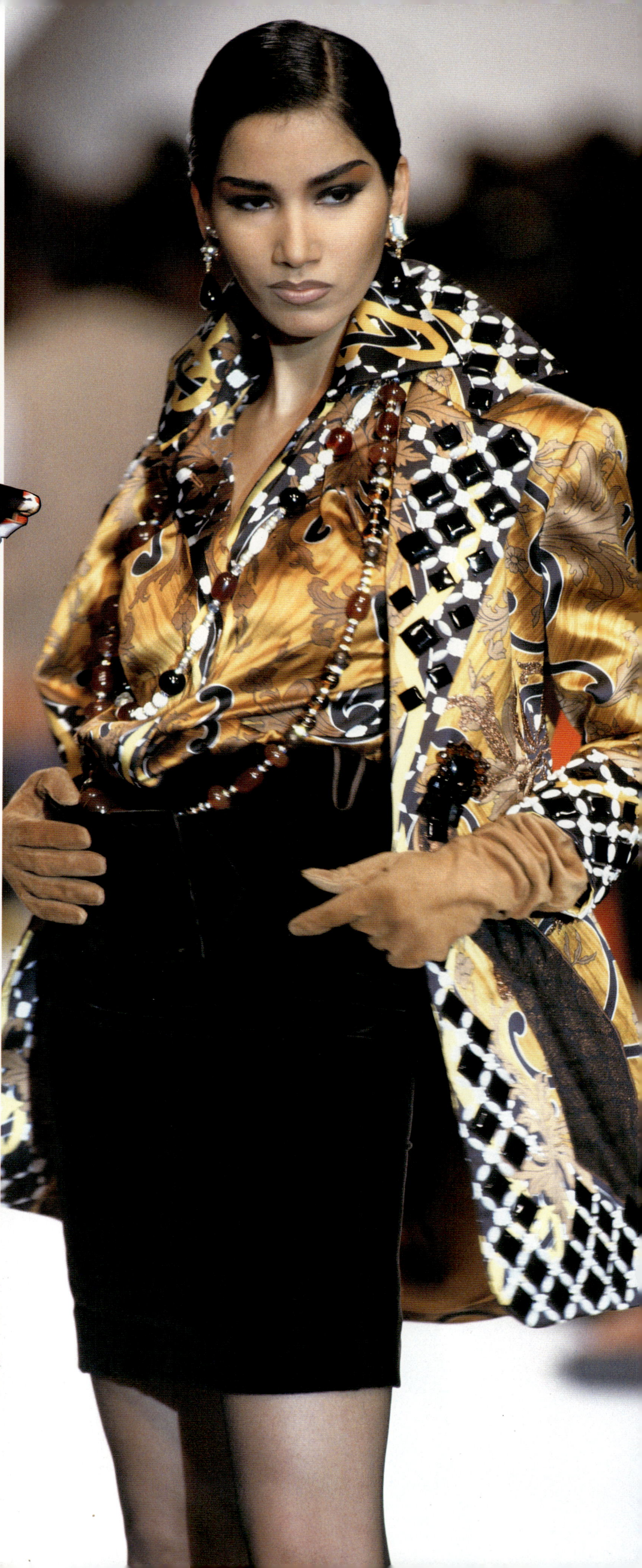

CHRISTIAN DIOR

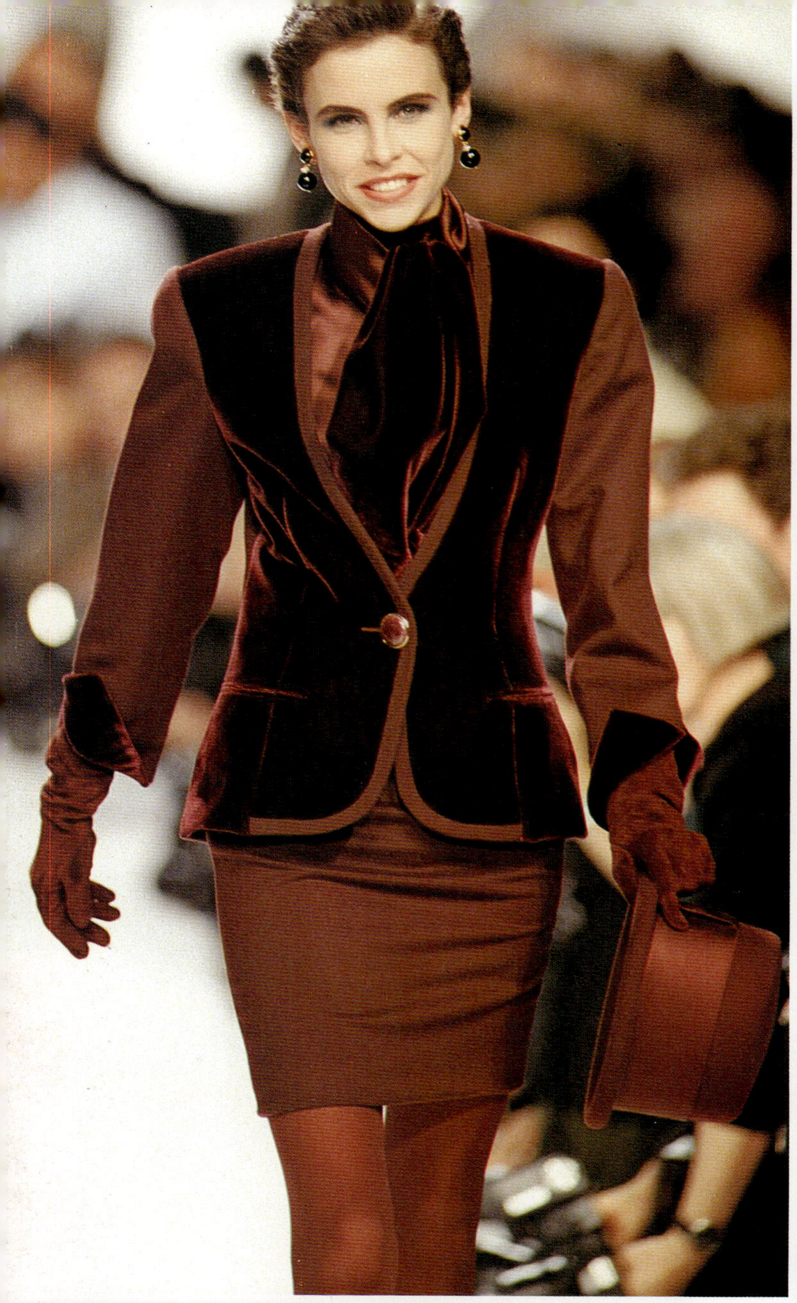
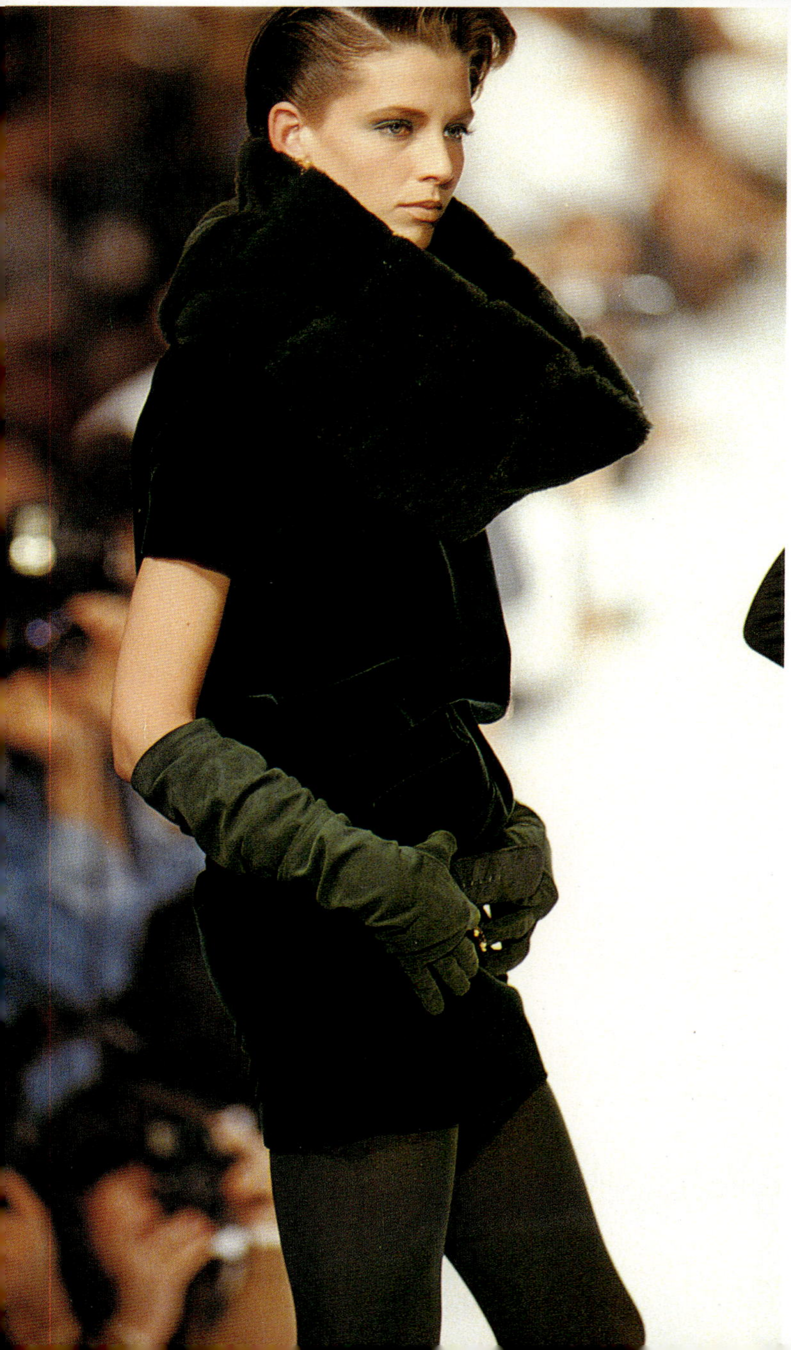
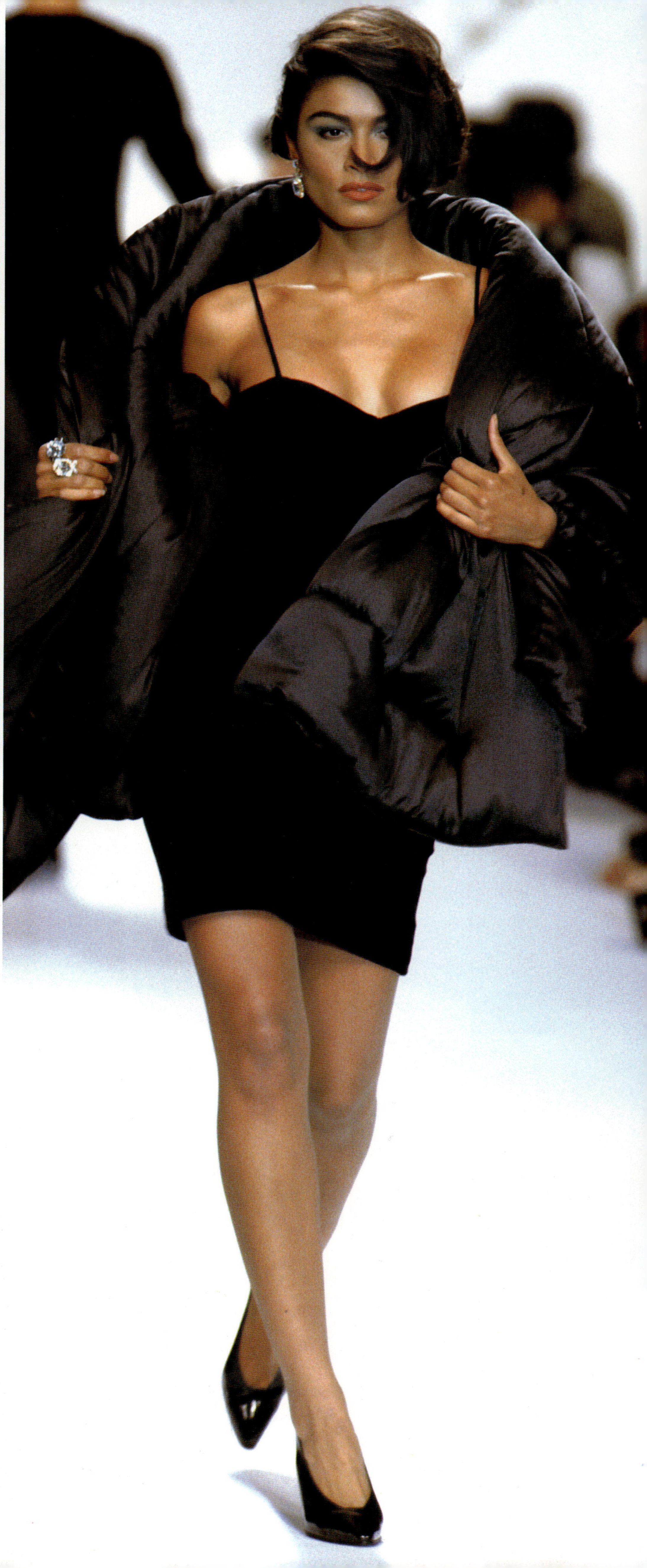

CHRISTIAN DIOR

89

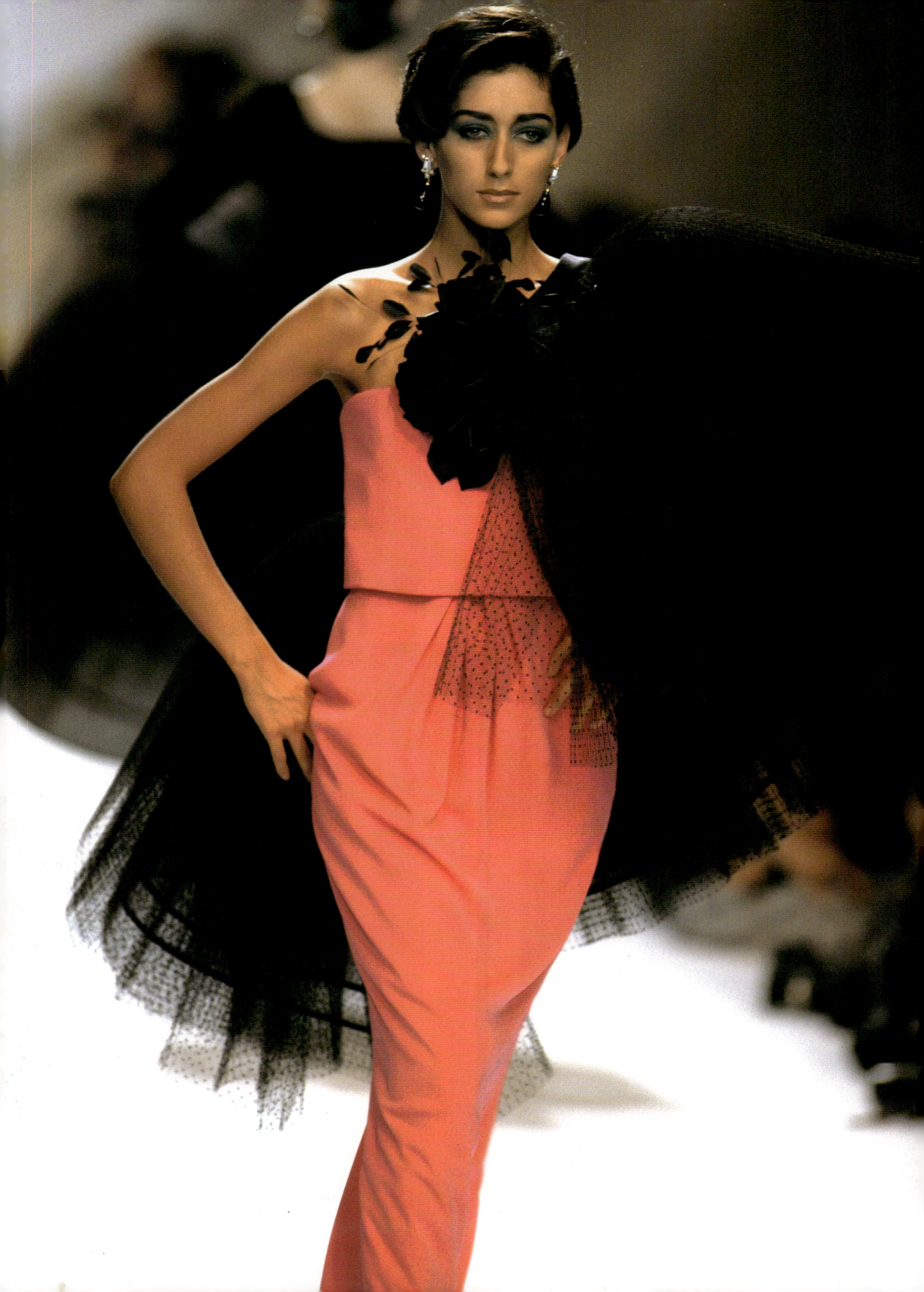

ANGELO TARLAZZI

GIVENCHY

'91-'92 AUTUMN & WINTER

PRÊT-Á-PORTER COLLECTIONS

JUNKO SHIMADA

PIERRE BALMAIN

J. C. DE CASTELBAJAC

'91-'92
AUTUMN & WINTER
PRÊT-À-PORTER
COLLECTIONS

JUNKO SHIMADA

GIVENCHY	JUNKO SHIMADA	GIVENCHY
EMANUEL UNGARO	YUKI TORII	HELMUT LANG
GIVENCHY	ENRICO COVERI	DANIEL HECHTER

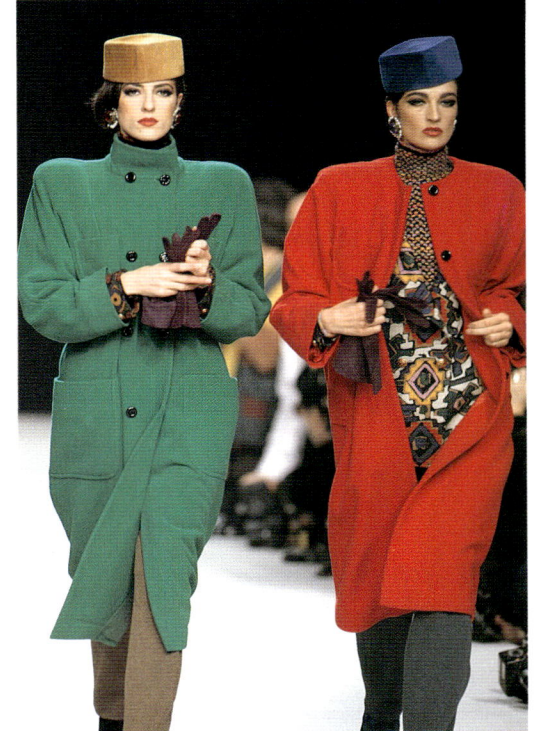

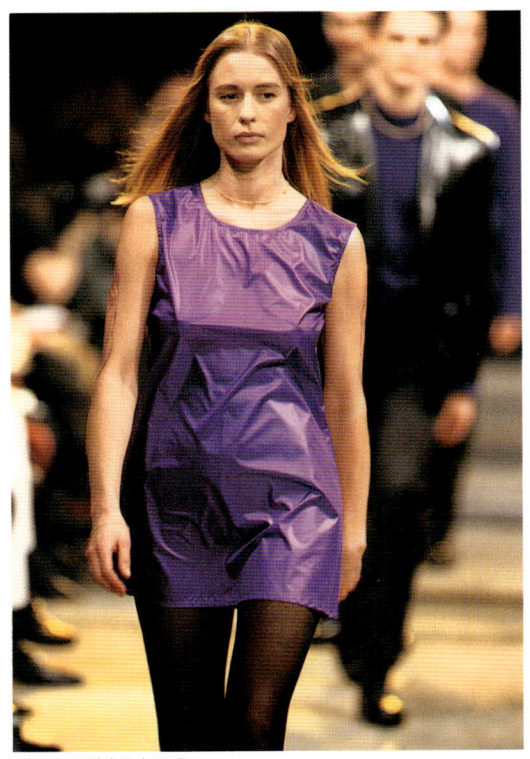

SONIA RYKIEL

EMANUEL UNGARO

'91-'92 AUTUMN & WINTER PREÊT-Á-PORTER COLLECTIONS

GIVENCHY

NINA RICCI

BARBARA BUI

BARBARA BUI

VIVIENNE WESTWOOD

ヴィヴィアン・ウエストウッド

ヴィヴィアンの革新的でクリエイティブなパワーが漲った注目のコレクション。下着ルックはより過激でそしてユーモラスに、クラシックはより新鮮な魅力で映る。

An attention-getting collection filled with Vivienne's revolutionary and creative power.
A style with the appearance of undergarments was shown with even more expression and humour. Also refreshing was her classic style.

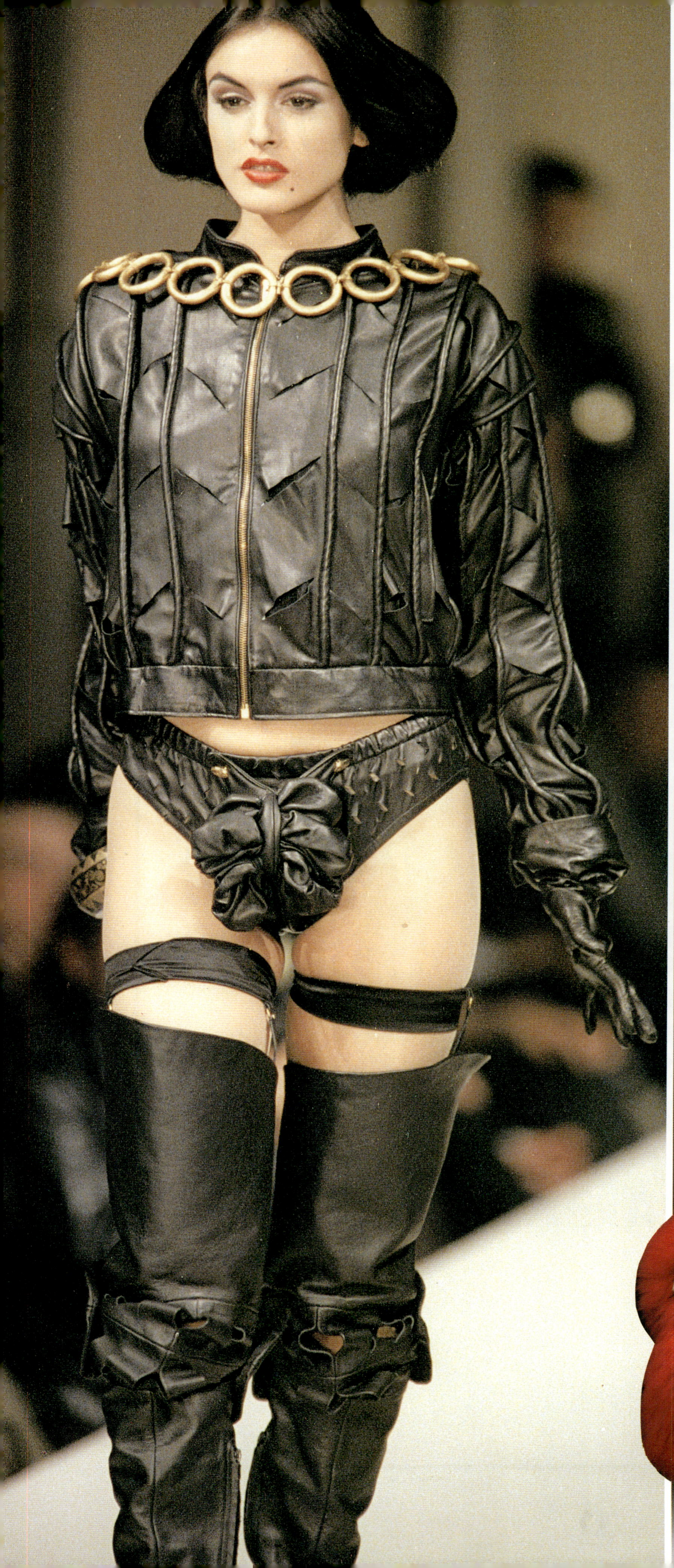
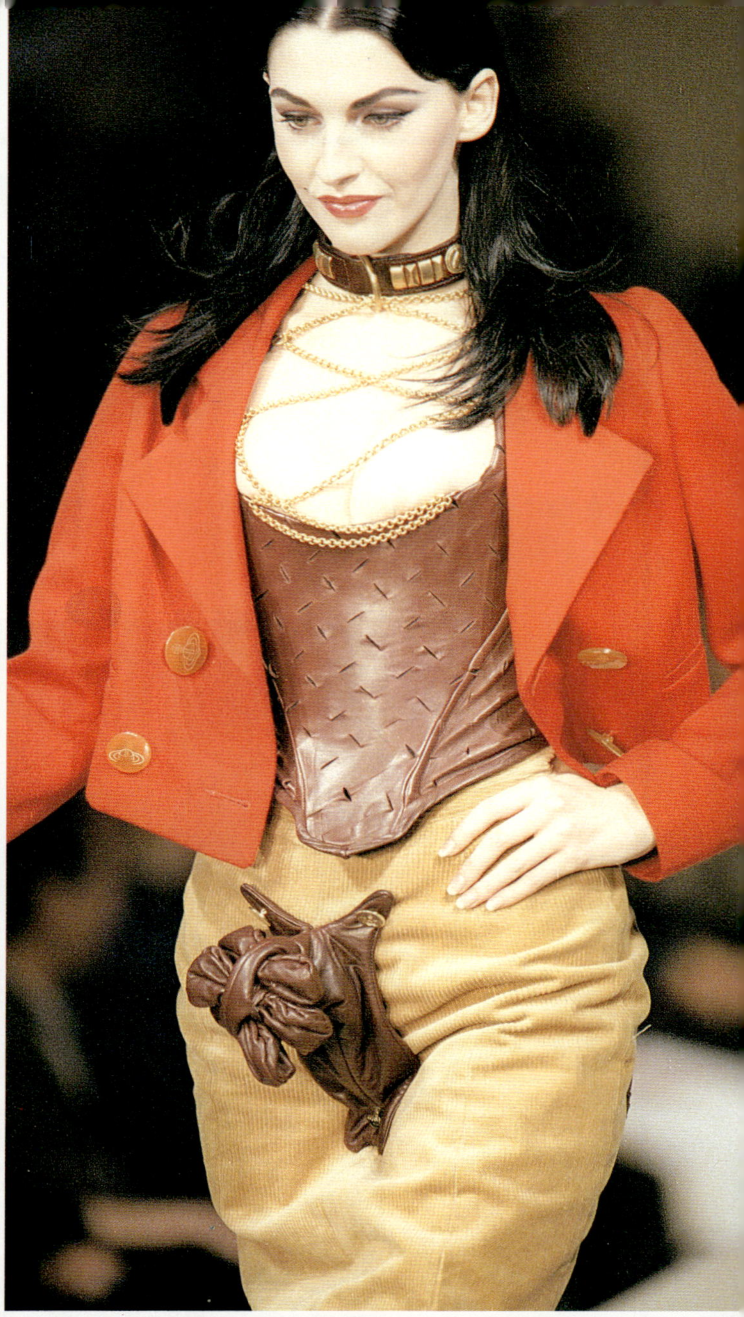
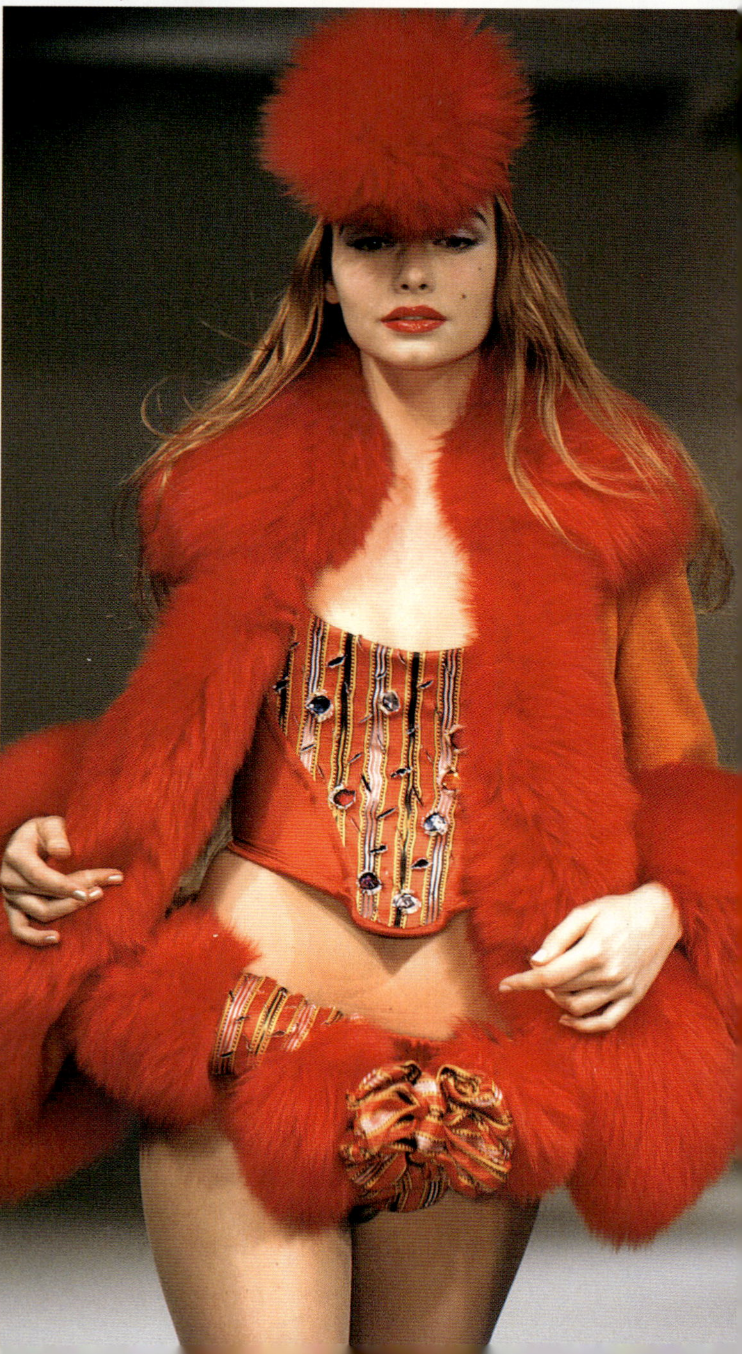

VIVIENNE WESTWOOD

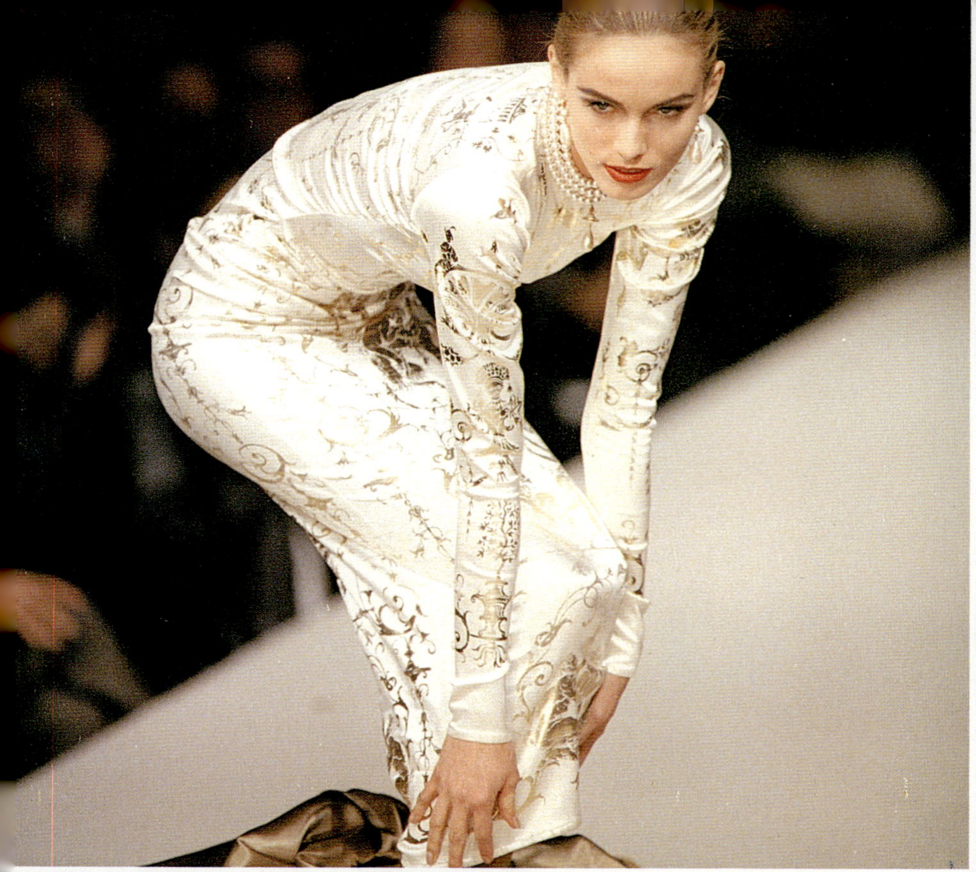
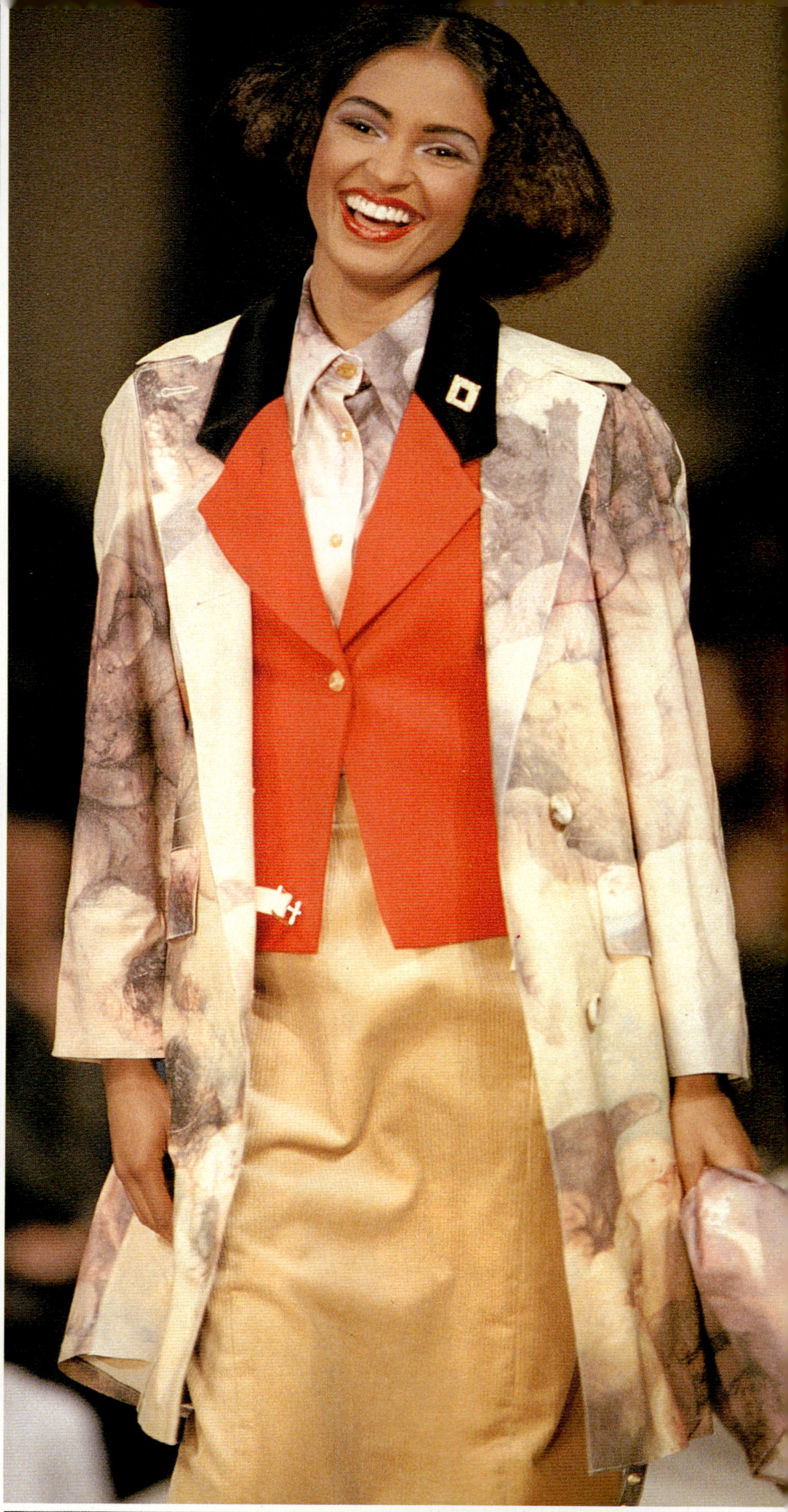
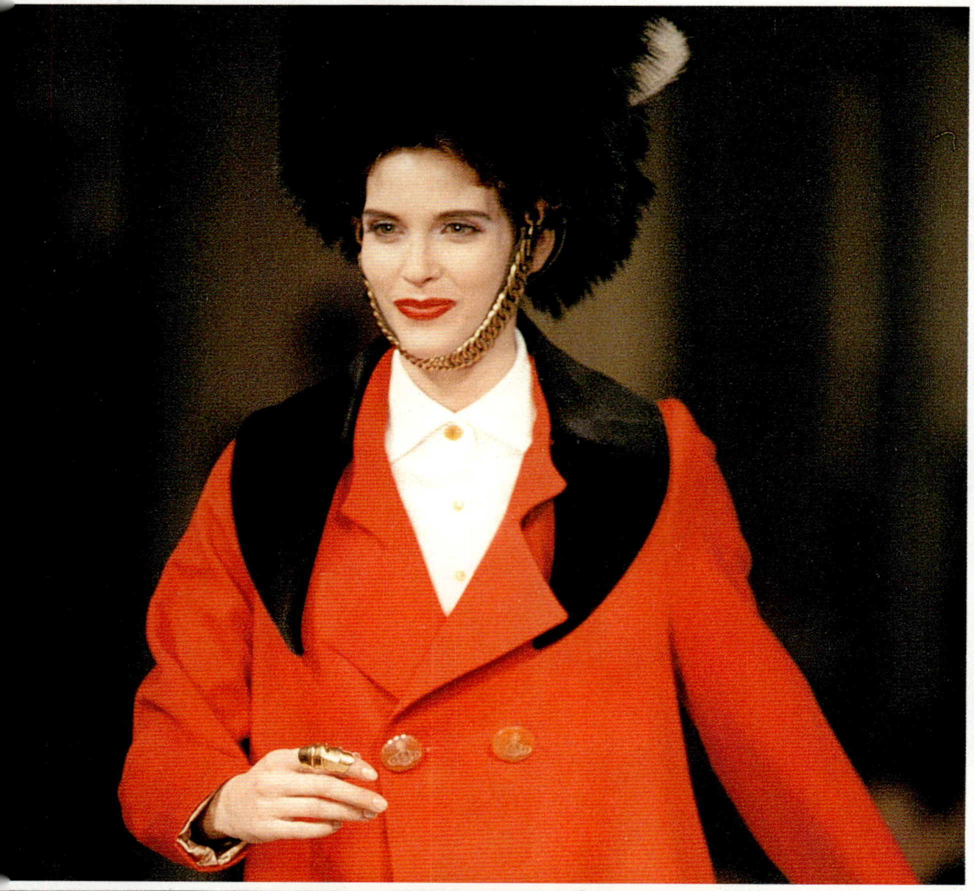
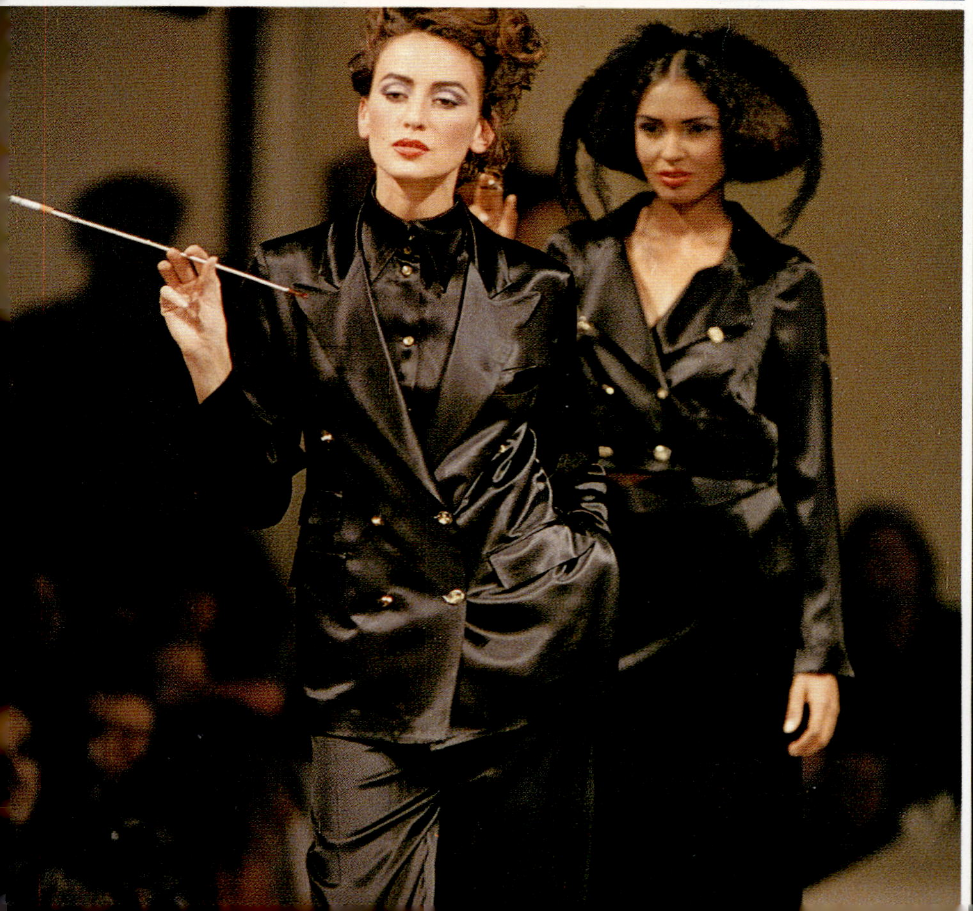
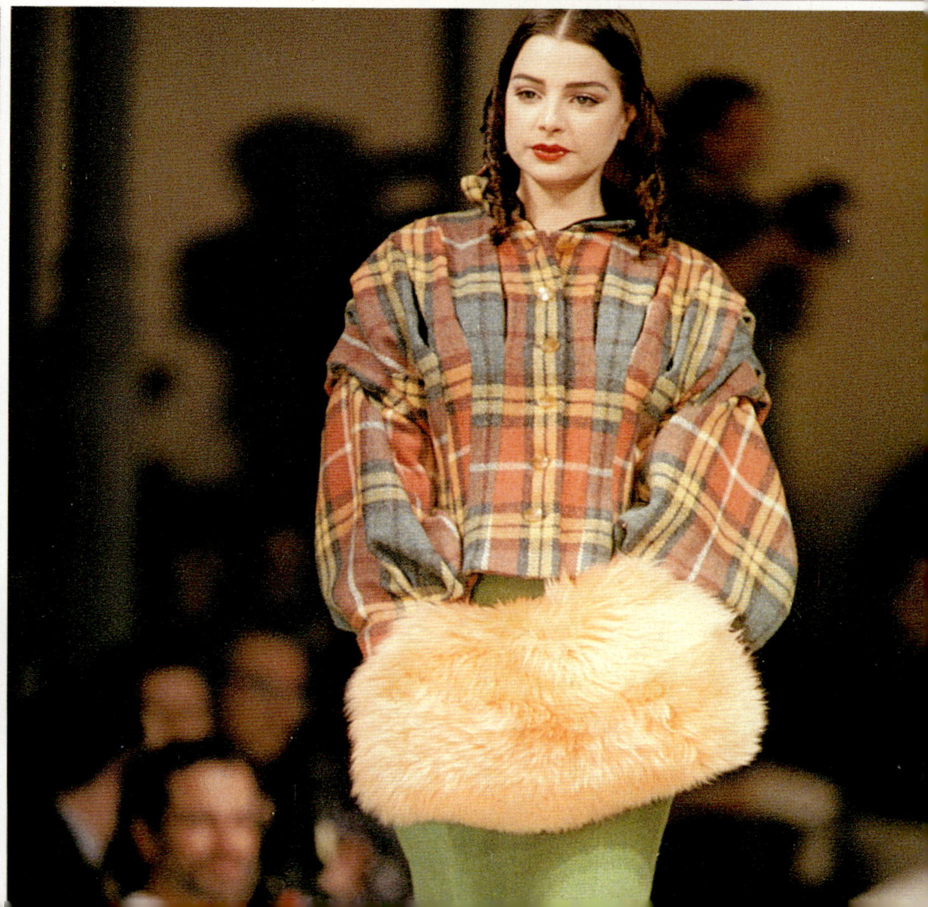

VIVIENNE WESTWOOD

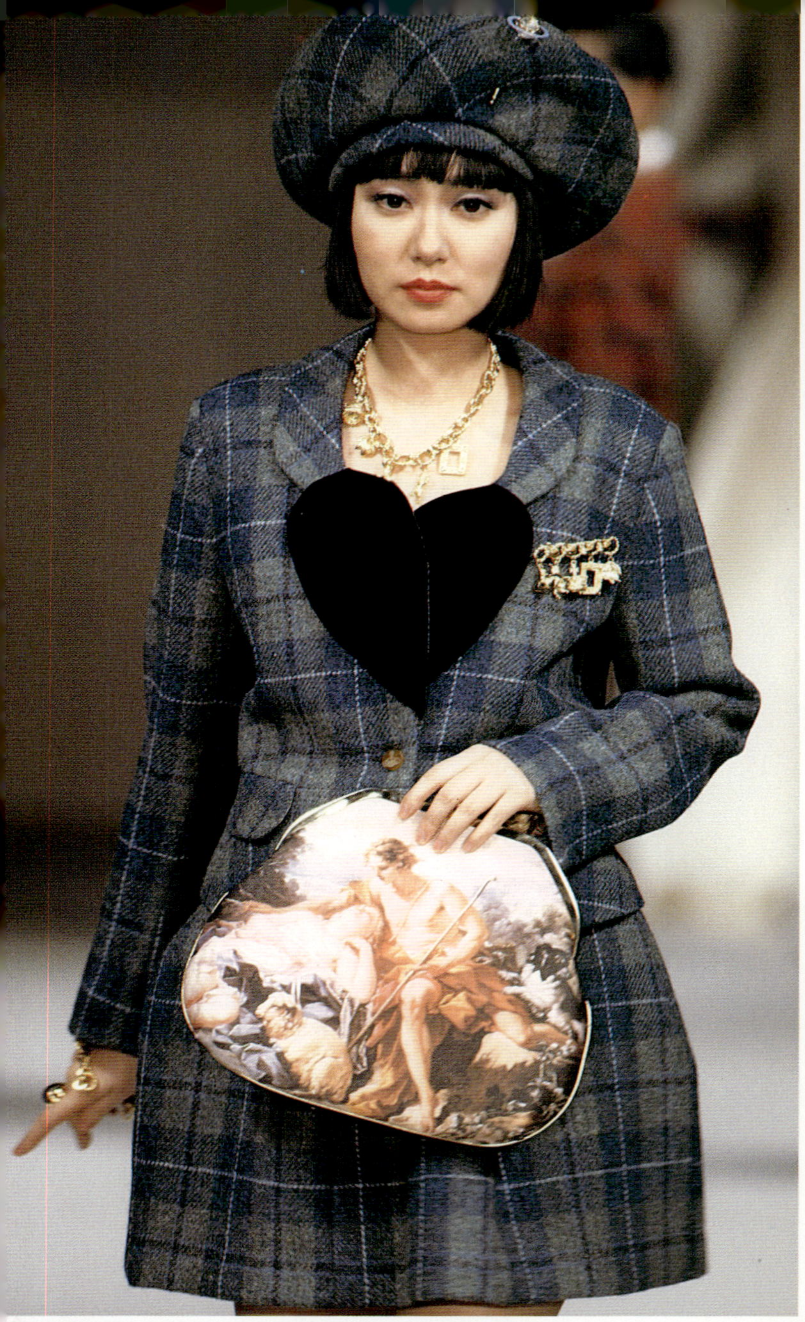
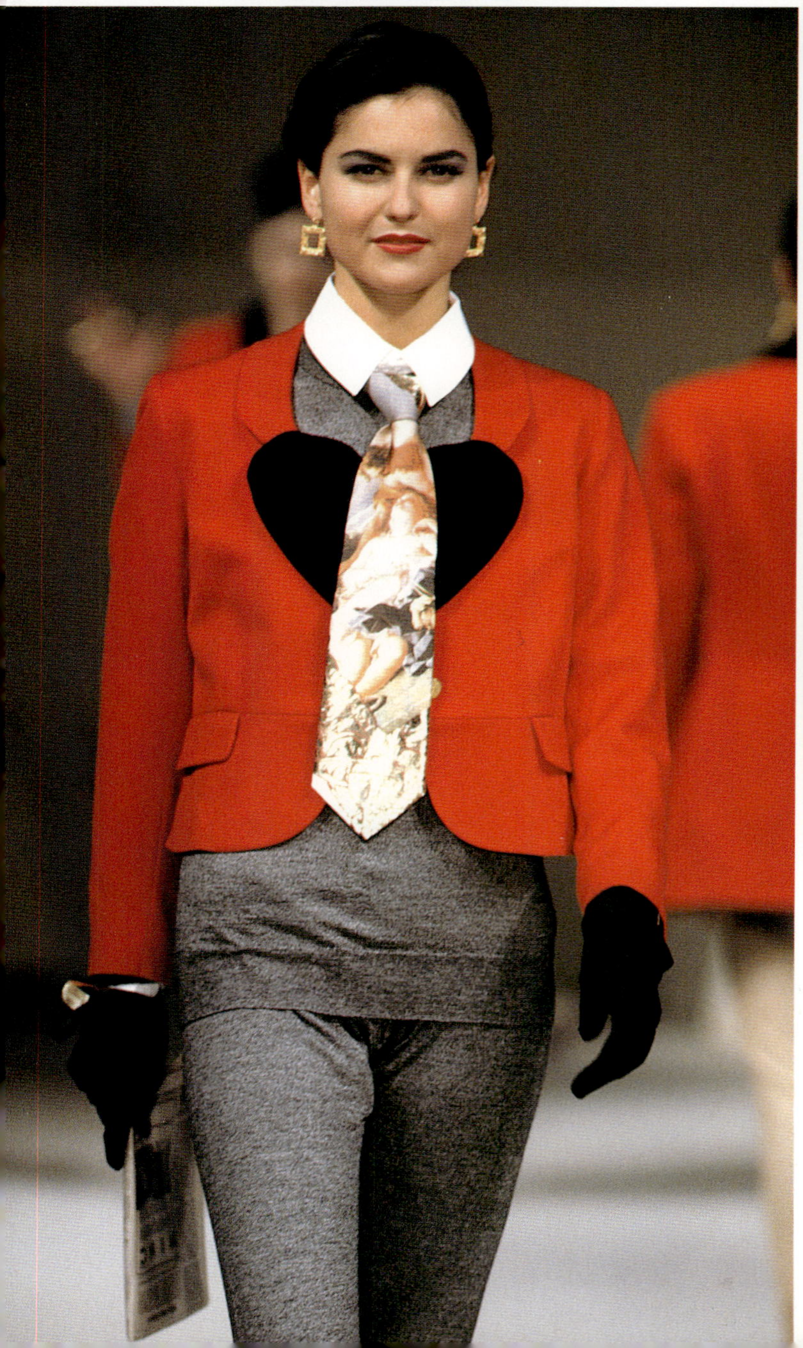
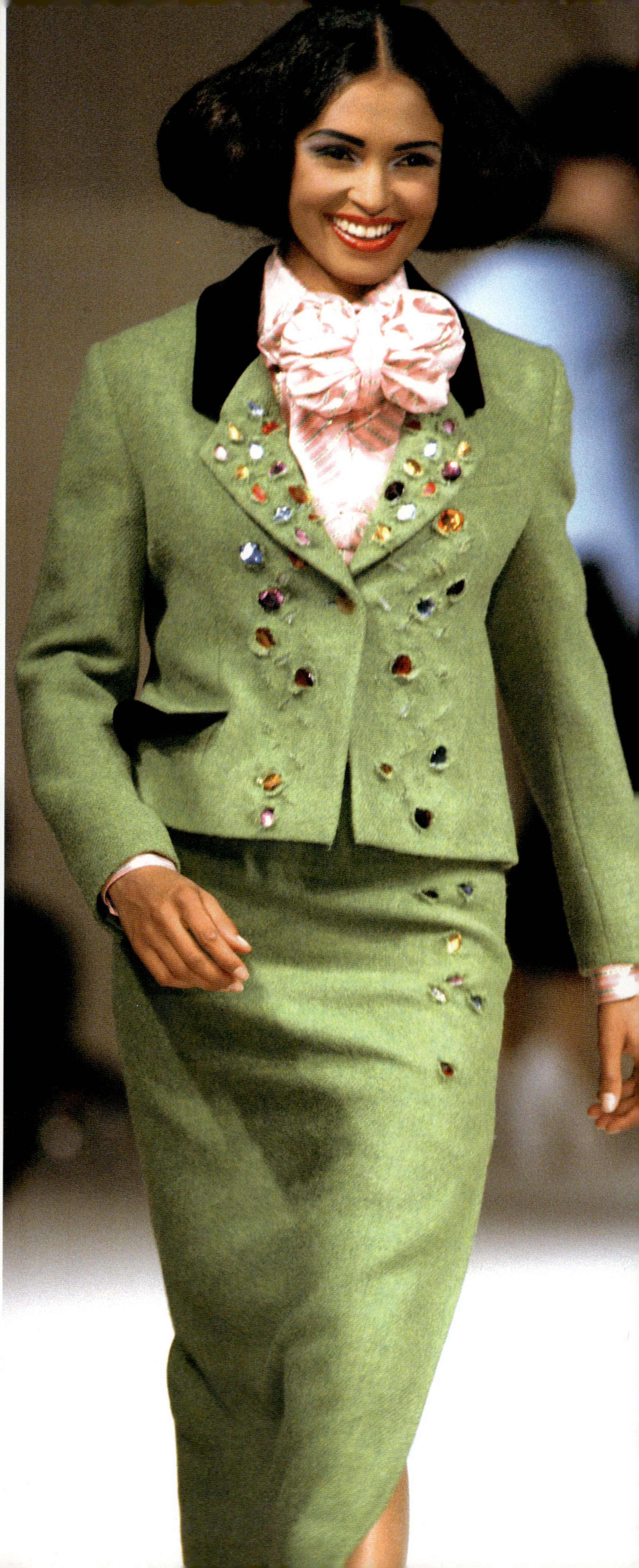

VIVIENNE WESTWOOD

103

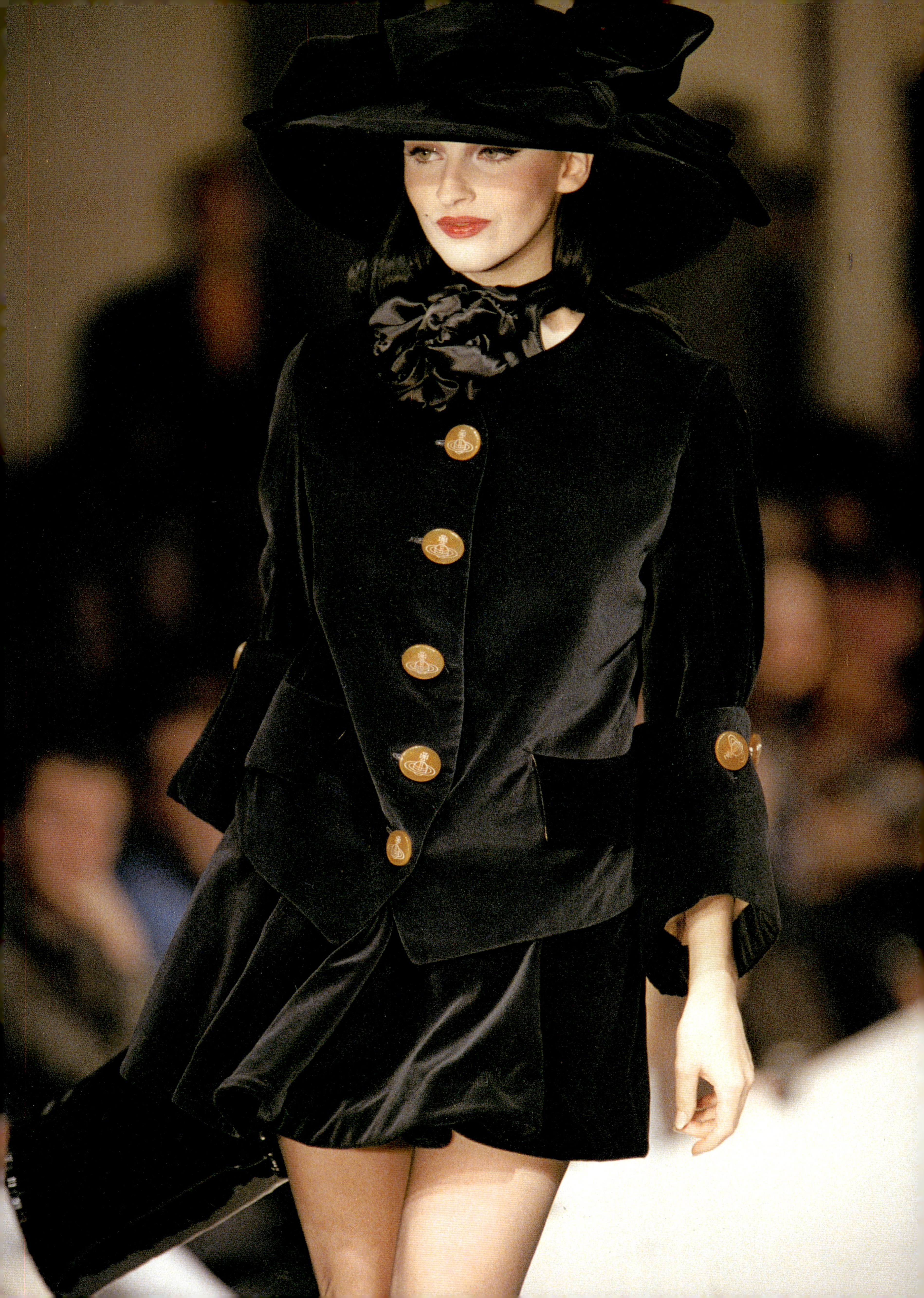

KENZO

ケンゾー

久しぶりにルーブルに戻ってきたケンゾー。色とパターンの楽しさで見せるケンゾーのコレクションは、いつもながら心わくわく。拍手の嵐で迎えられた。
Back in Louvre after a period of abscence. His collection is always exciting, with excellent colors and patterns. He welcomed by a storm of applause.

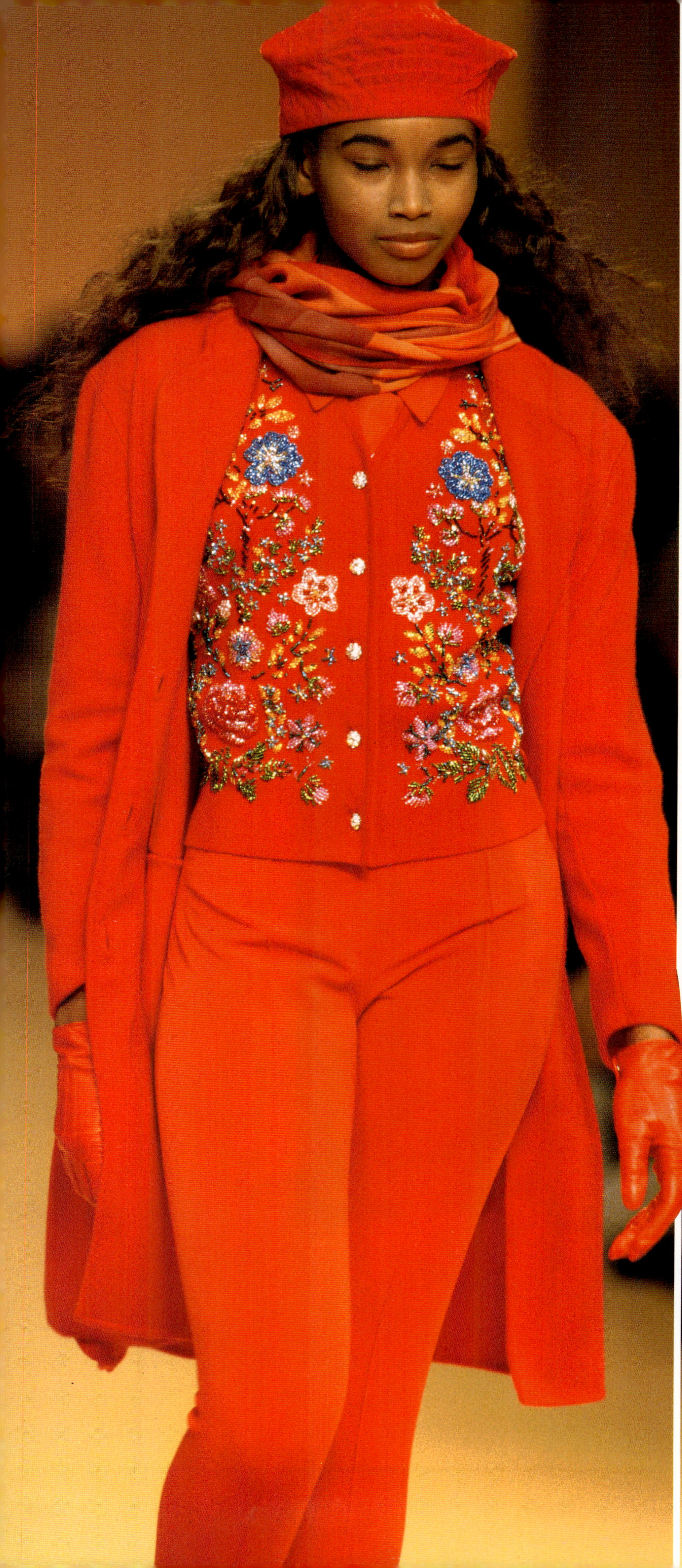
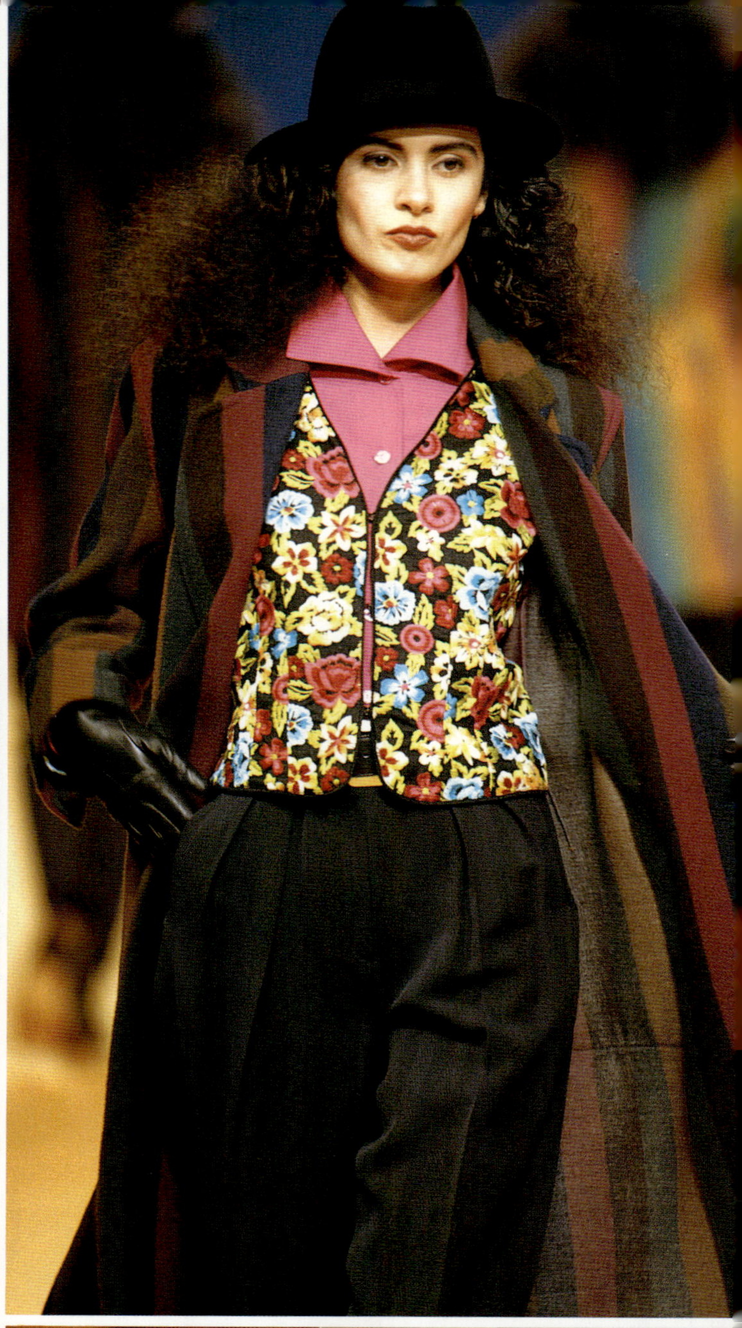
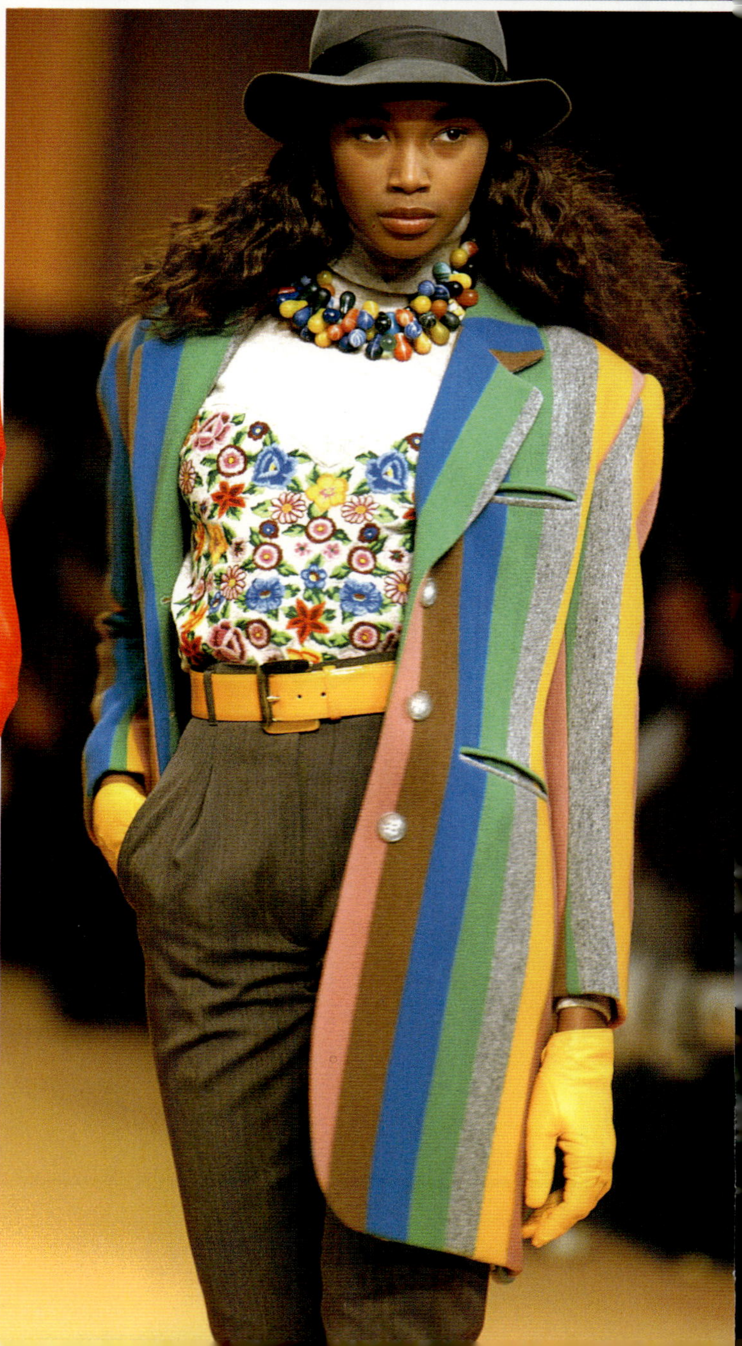

KENZO

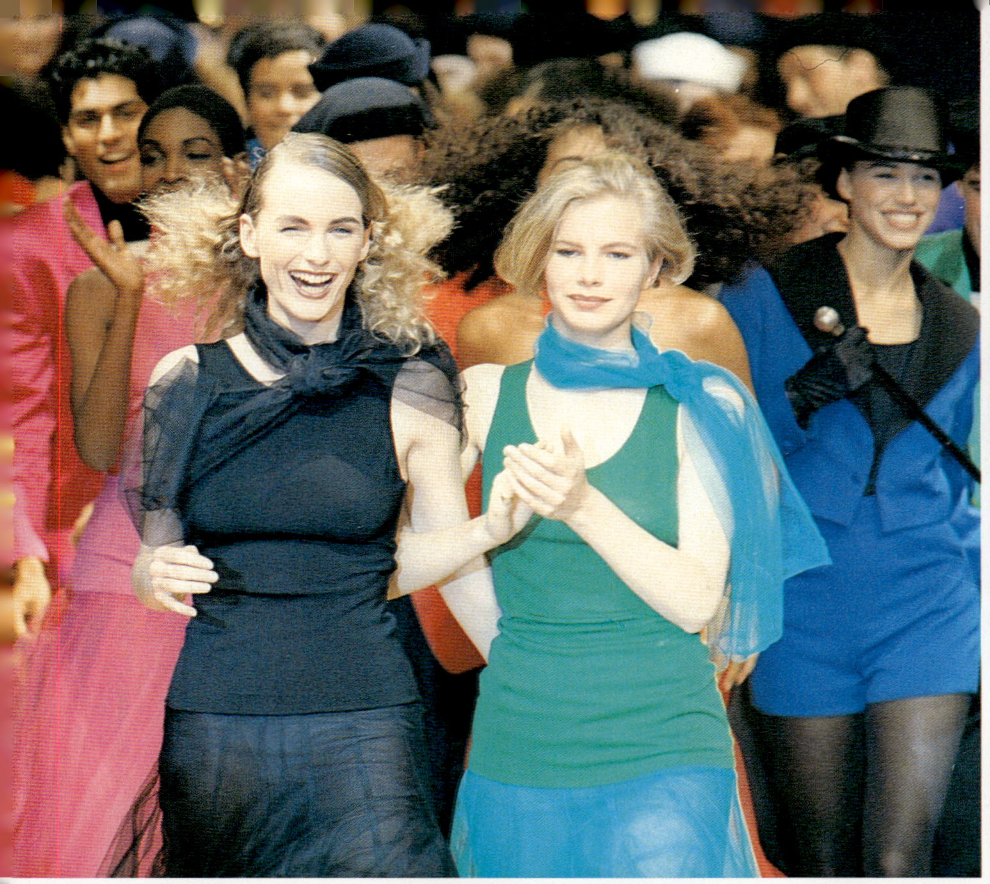
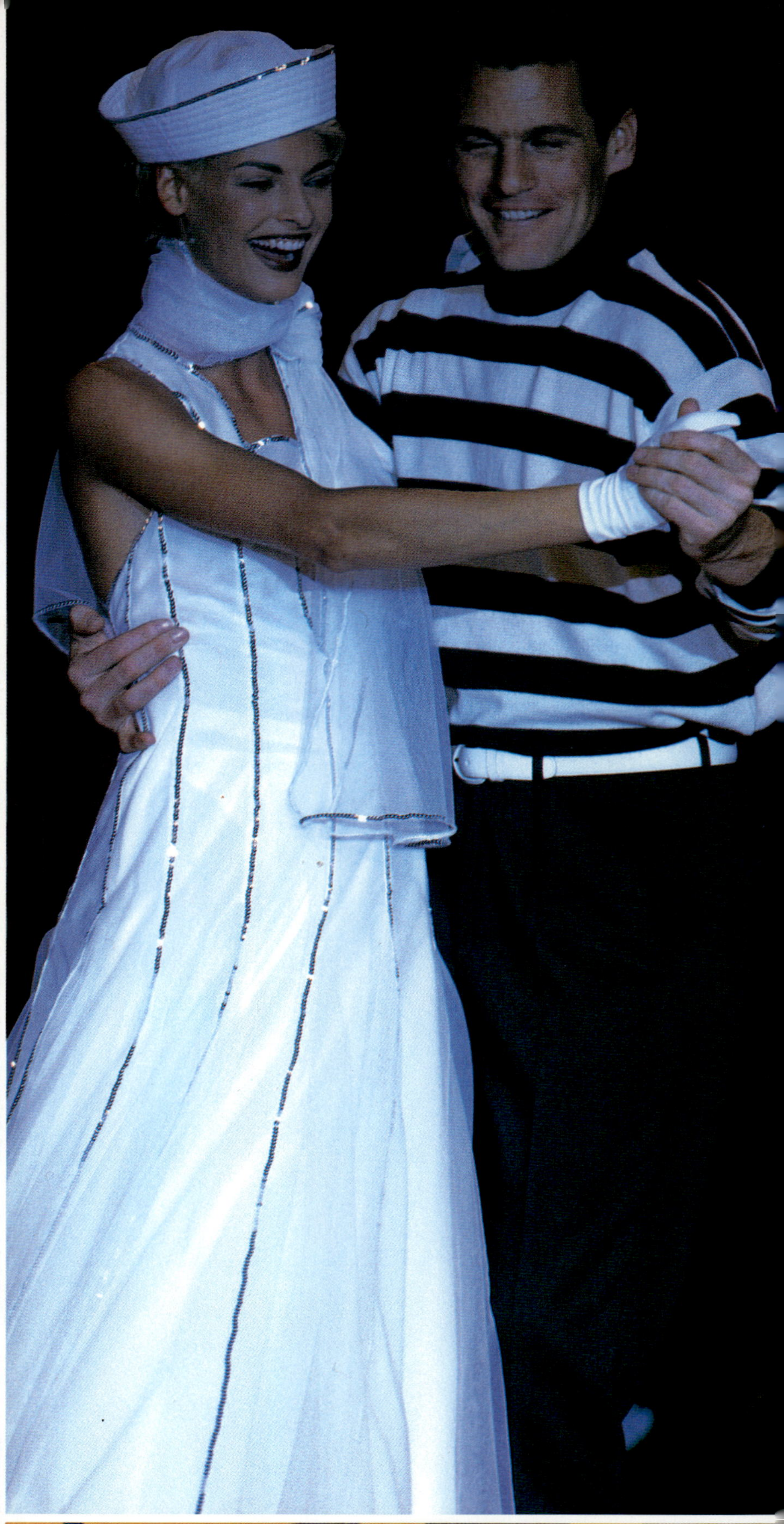
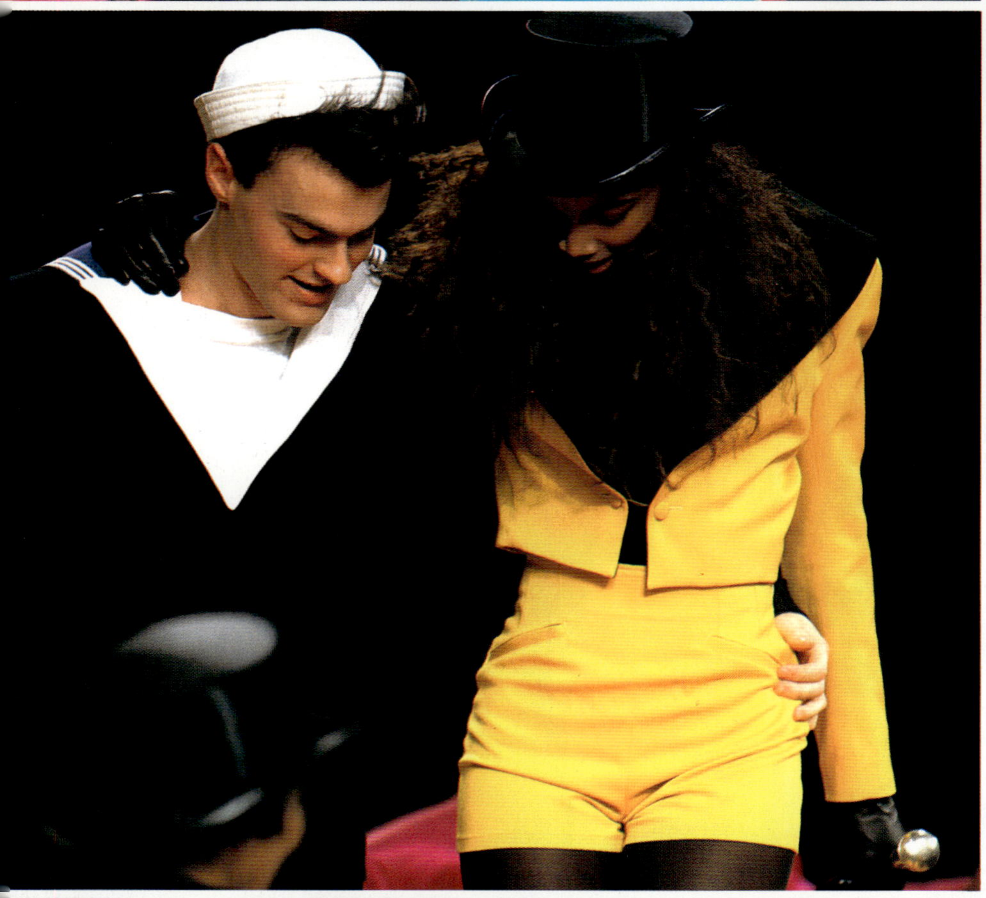
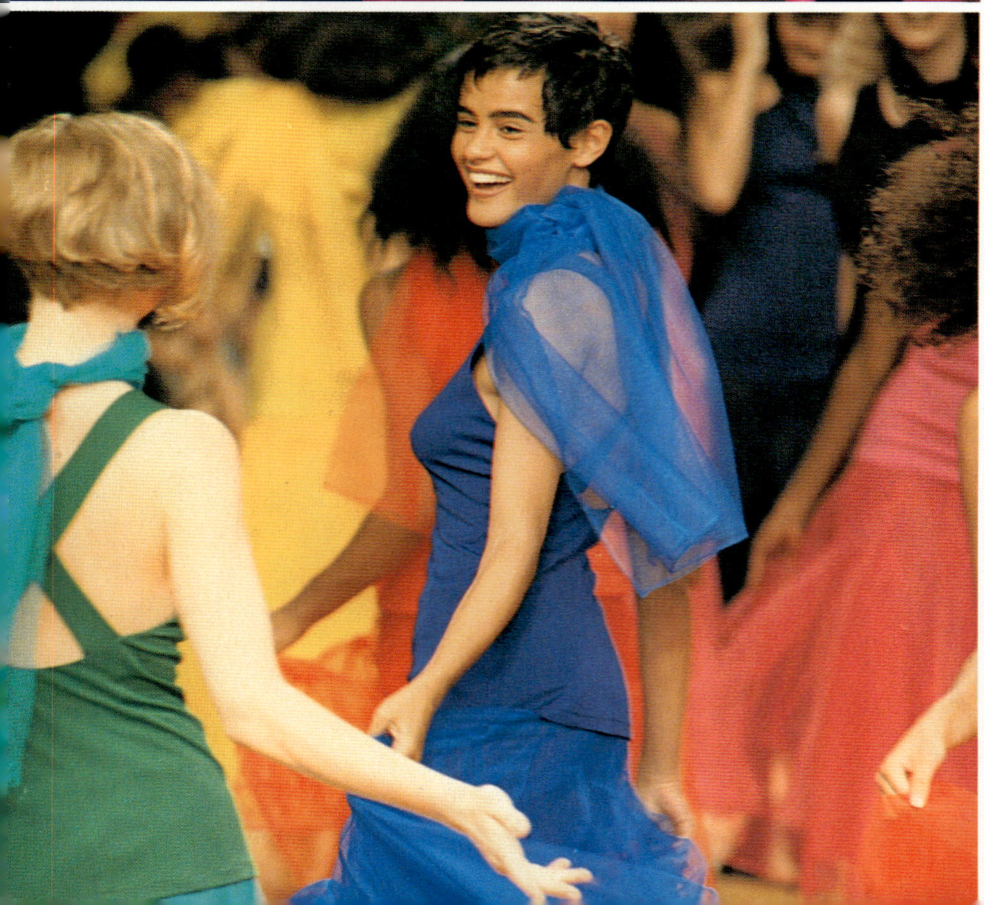
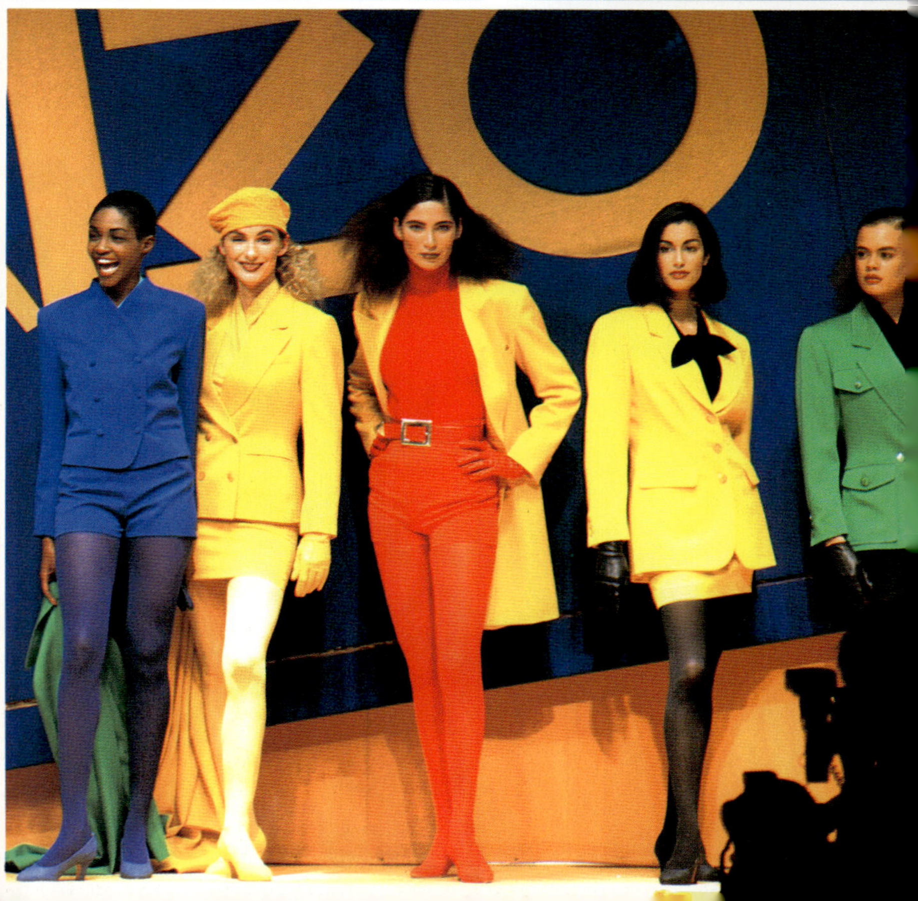

KENZO

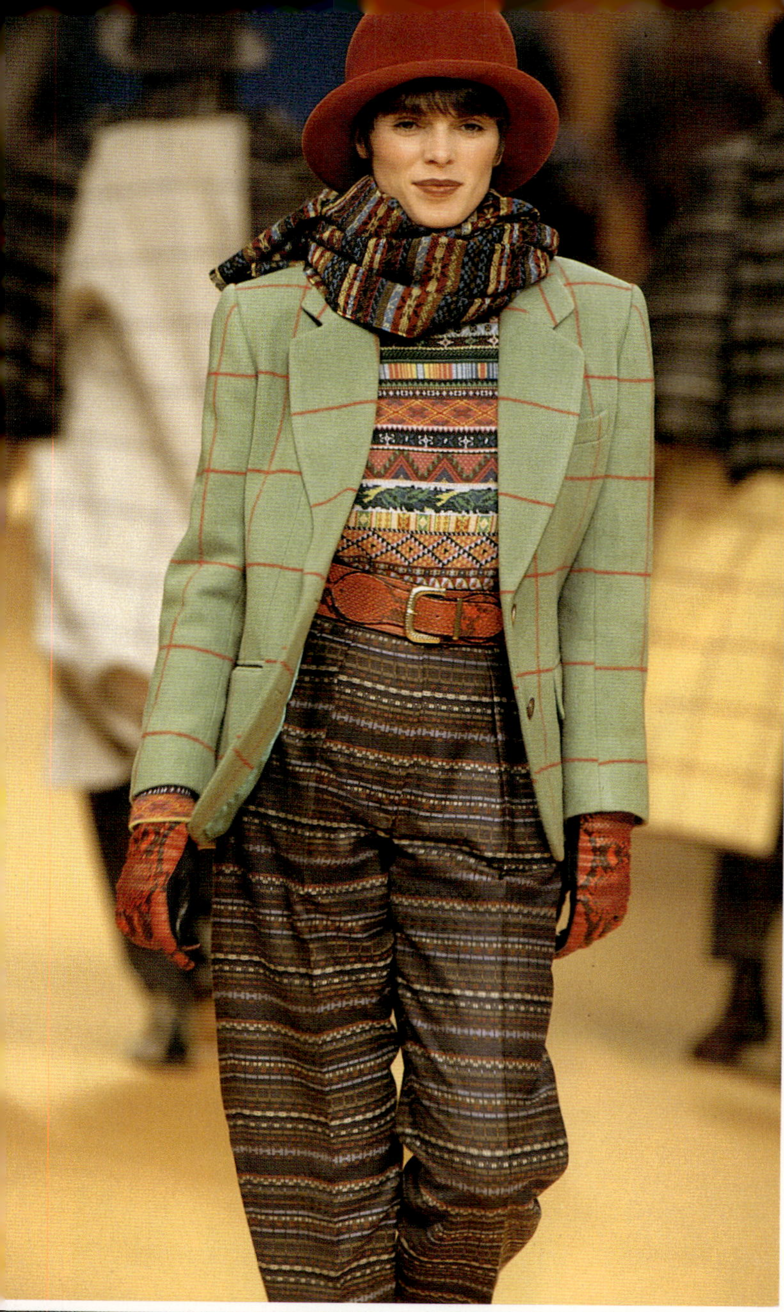
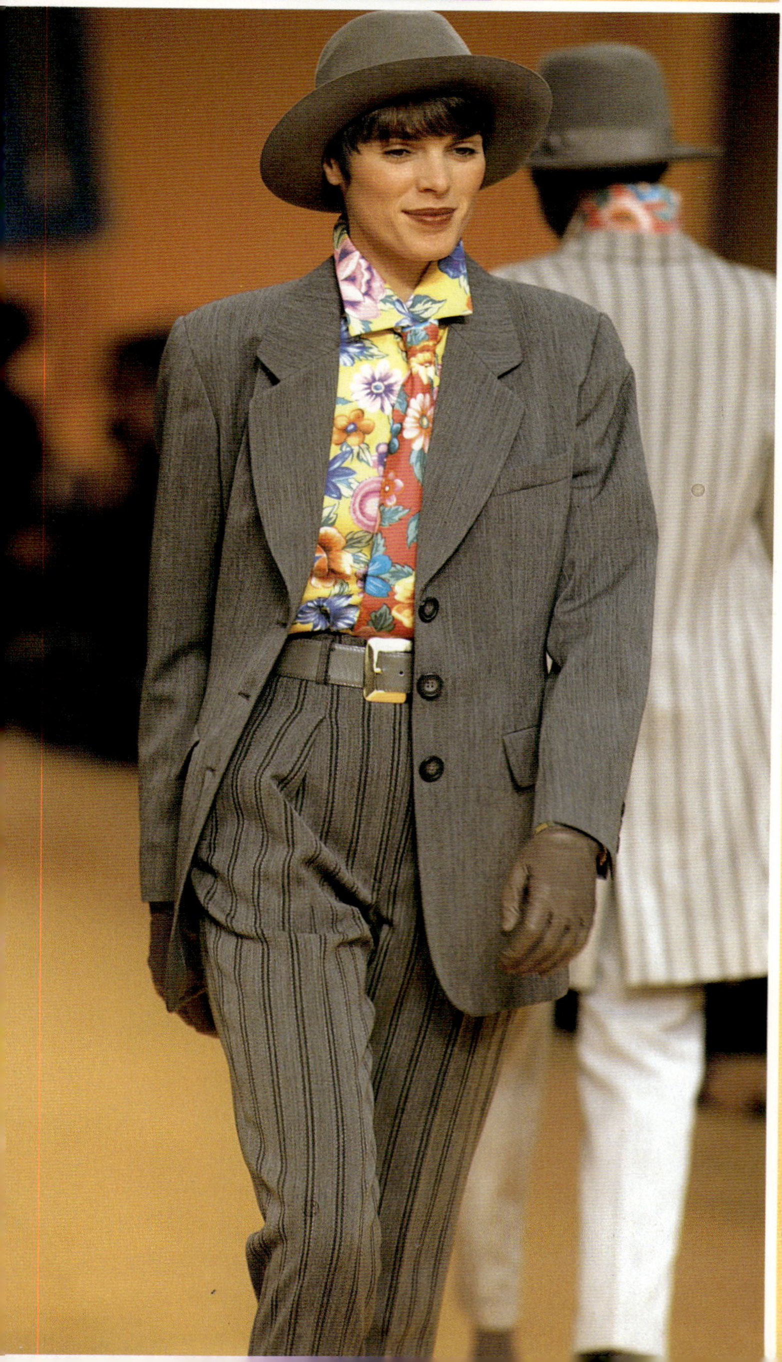
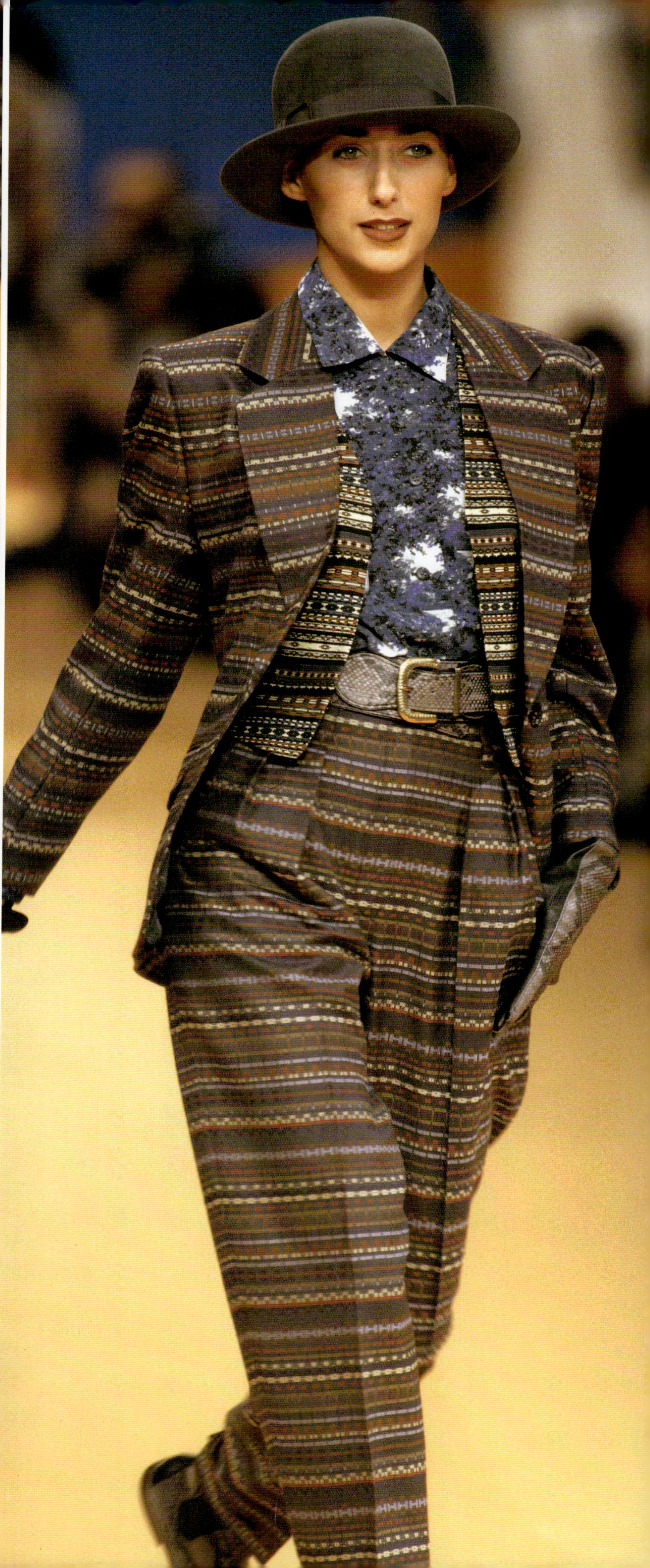

KENZO

111

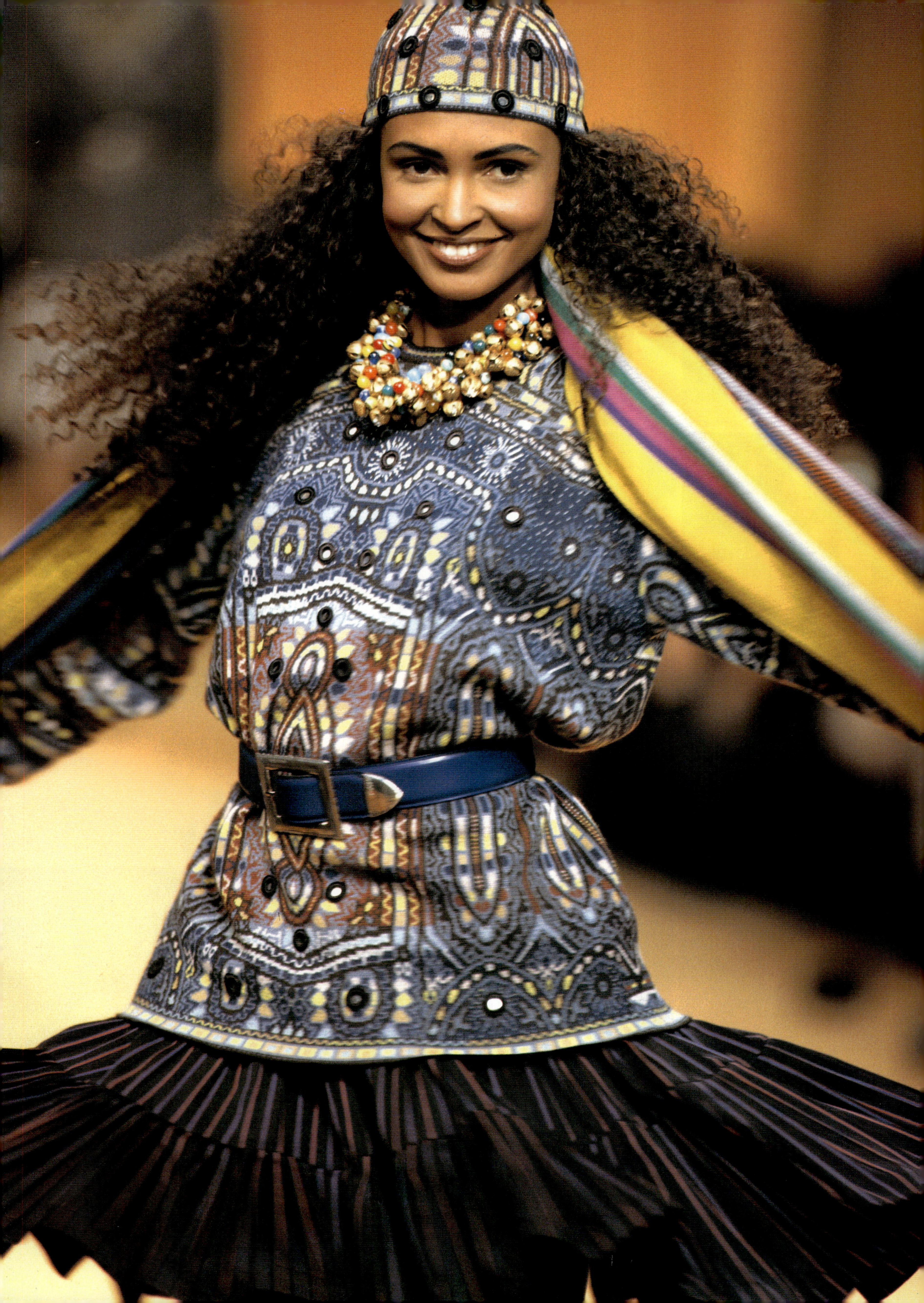

… PARIS-9

YVES SAINT LAURENT

イヴ・サン・ローラン

伝統のタータンを品良く、現代にアレンジしたスタイルが映える、今シーズン。イヴニングにはゴールドの輝きのドレープ・ドレスを。

He presented modern and chic style using tartan-check this season.
Dresses using drape technique are made with gold metalic materials for the evening.

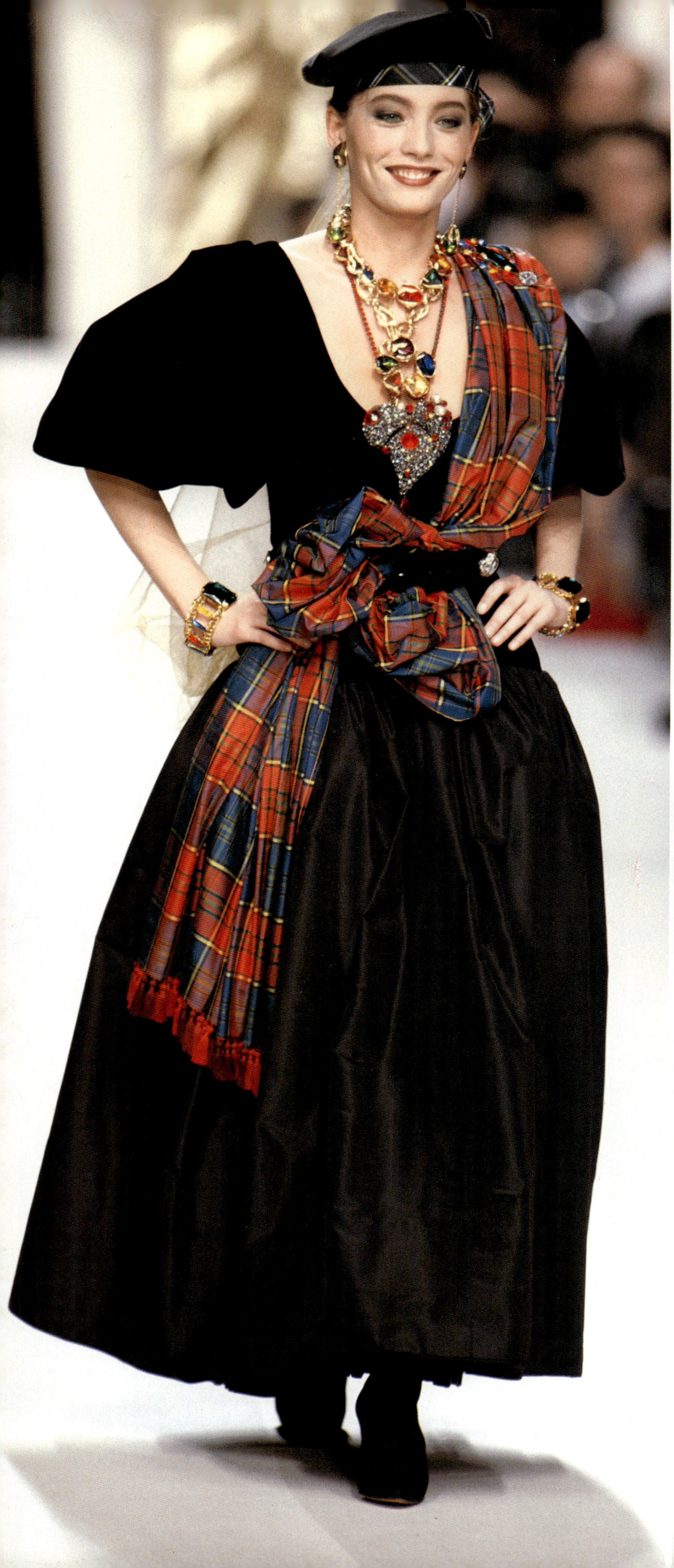

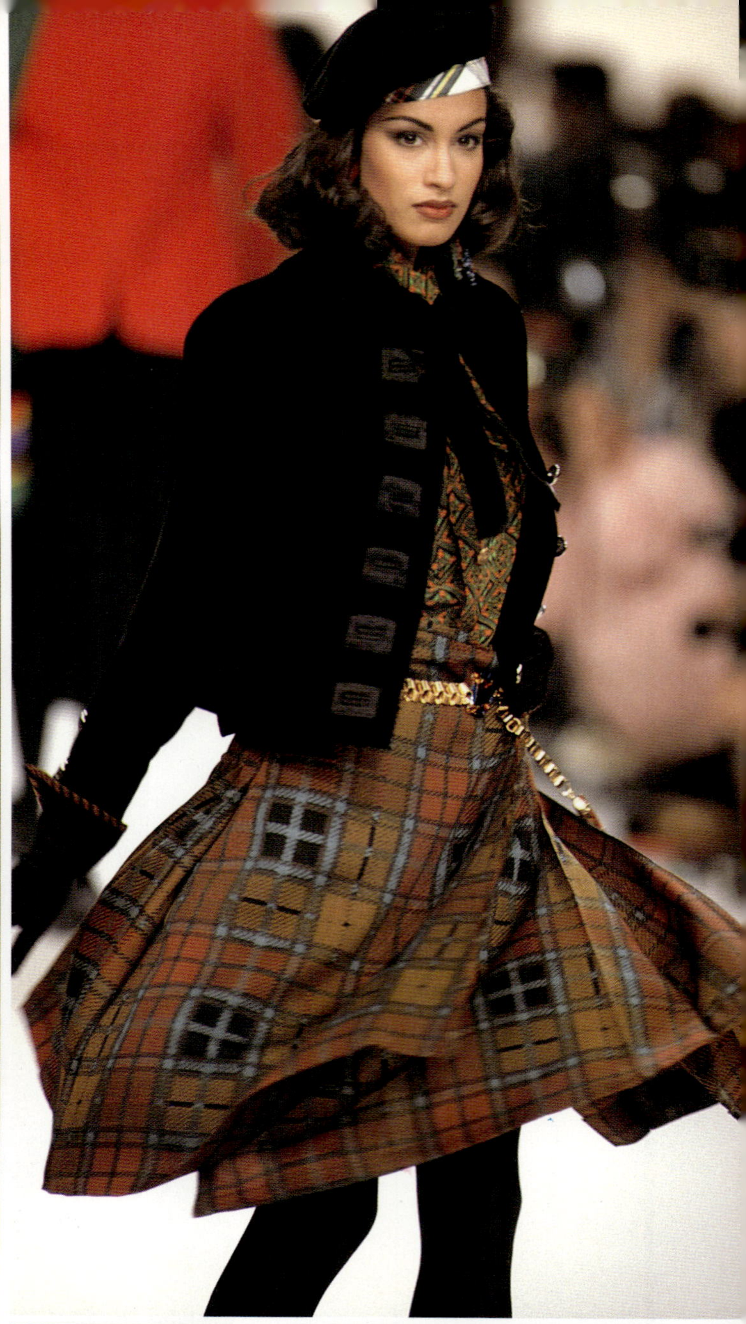

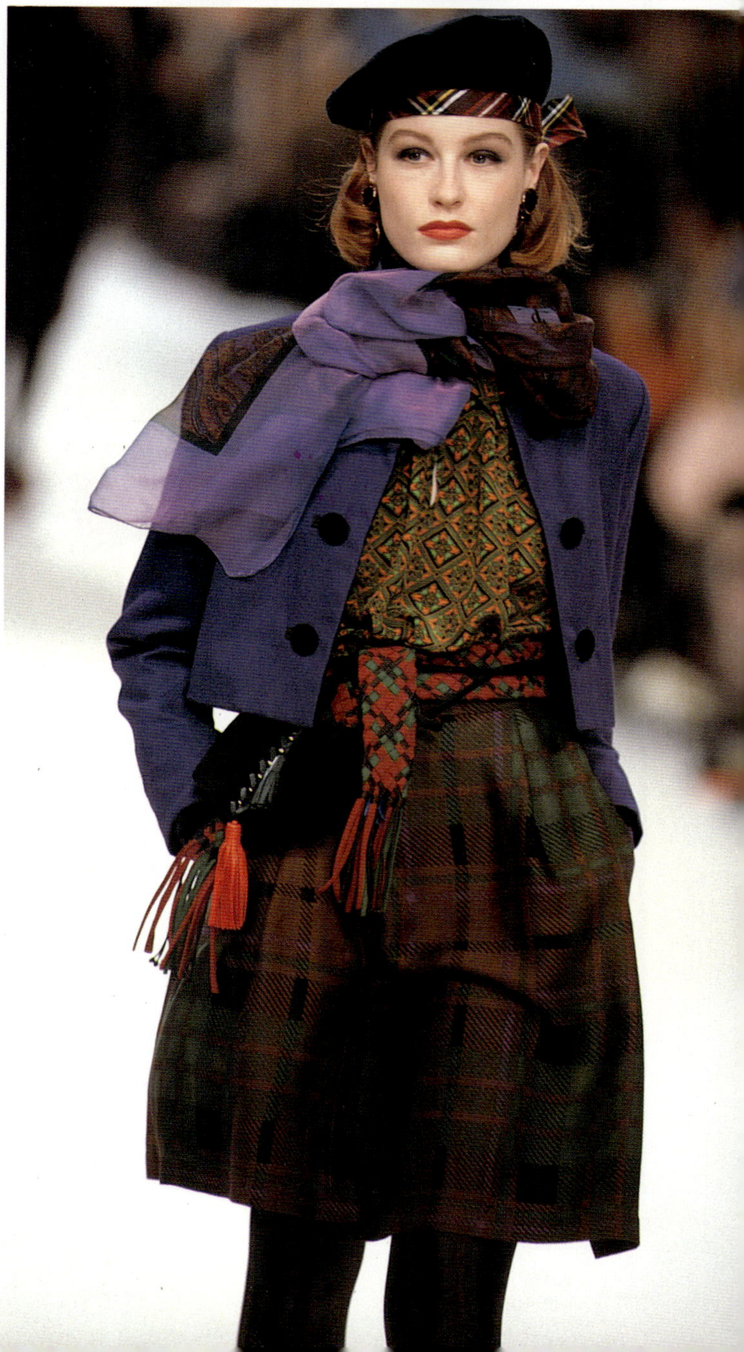

YVES SAINT LAURENT

115

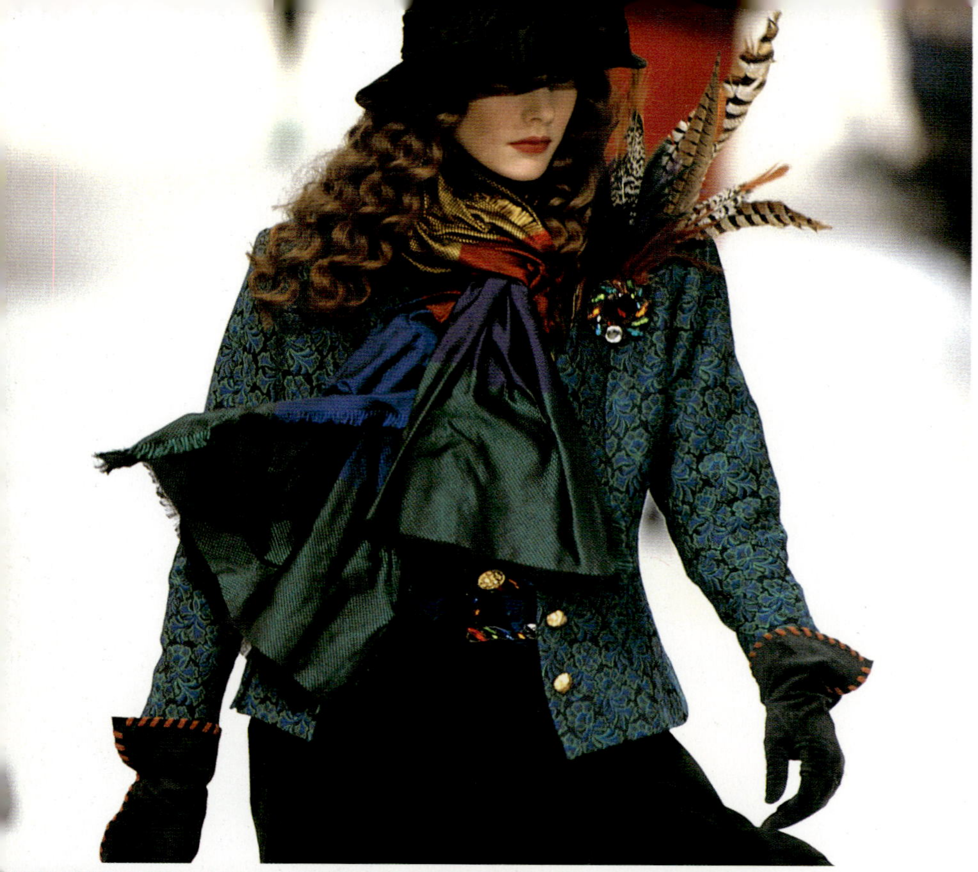
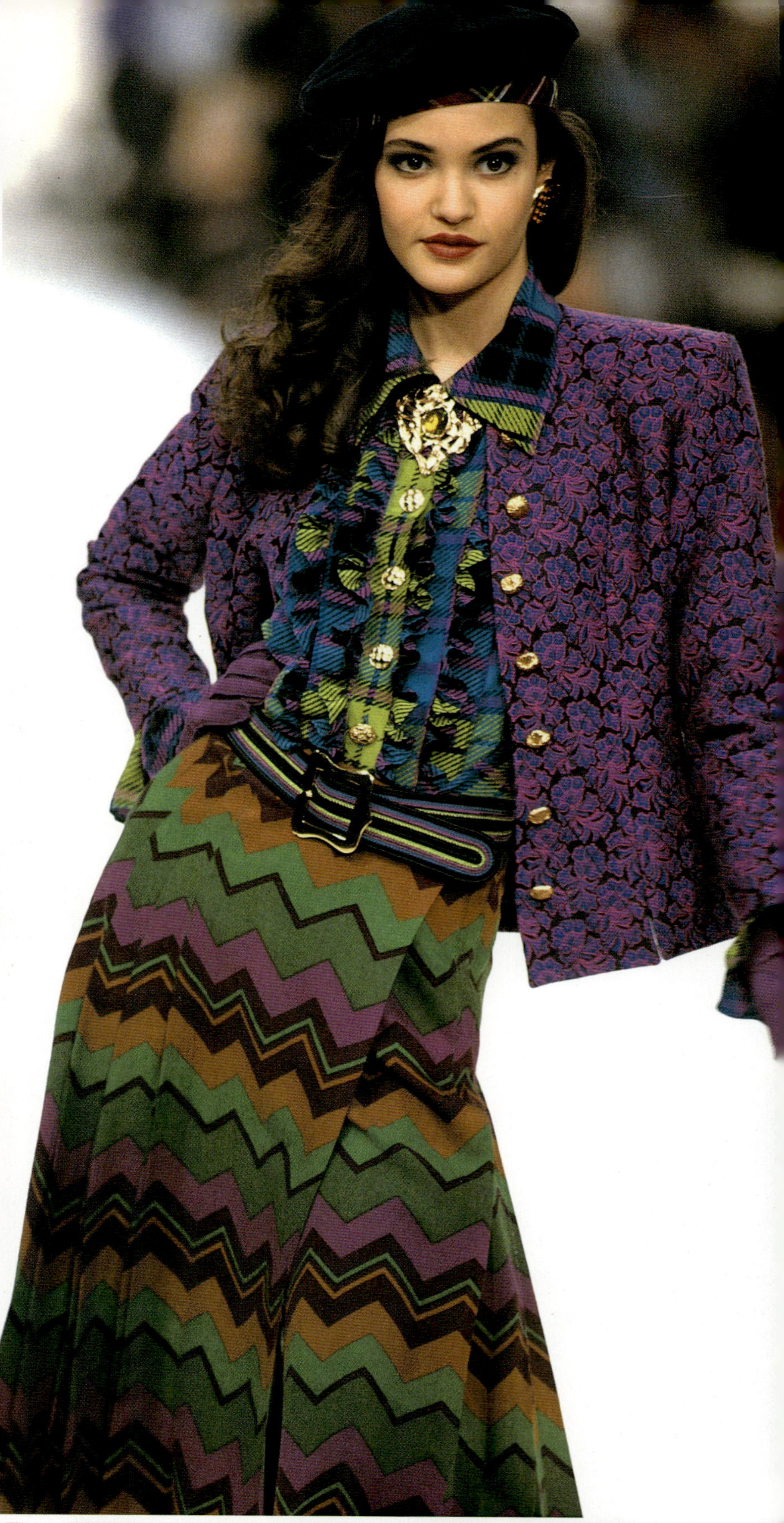
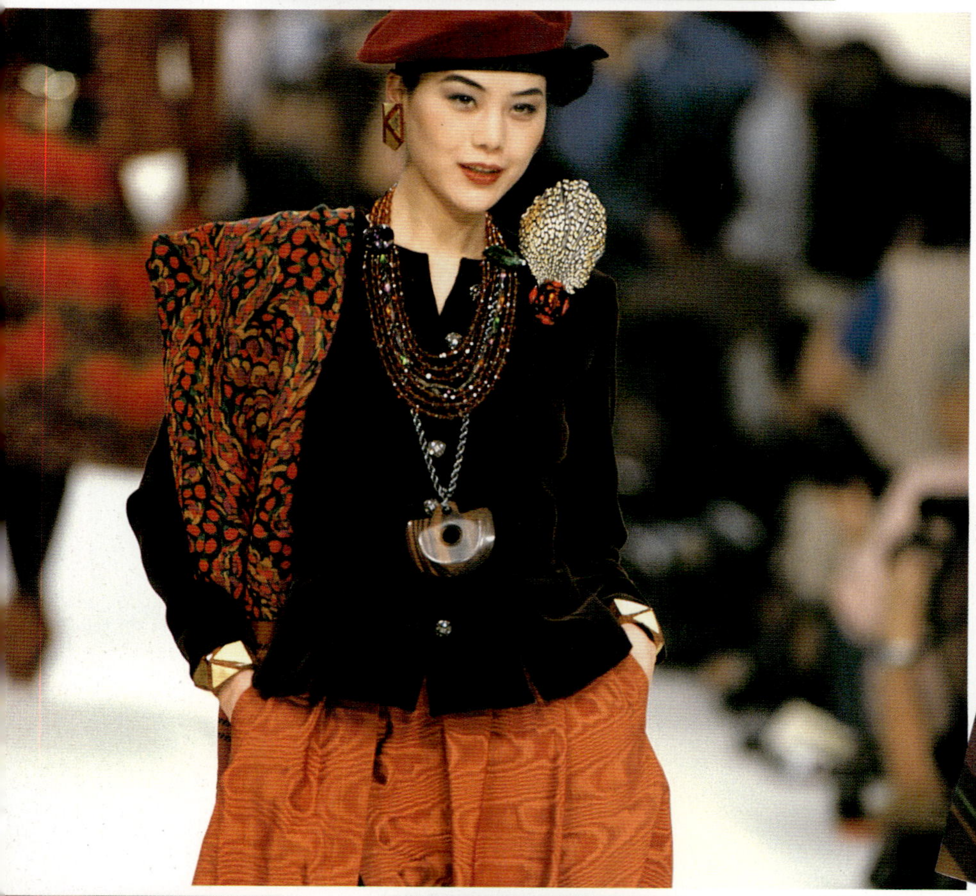
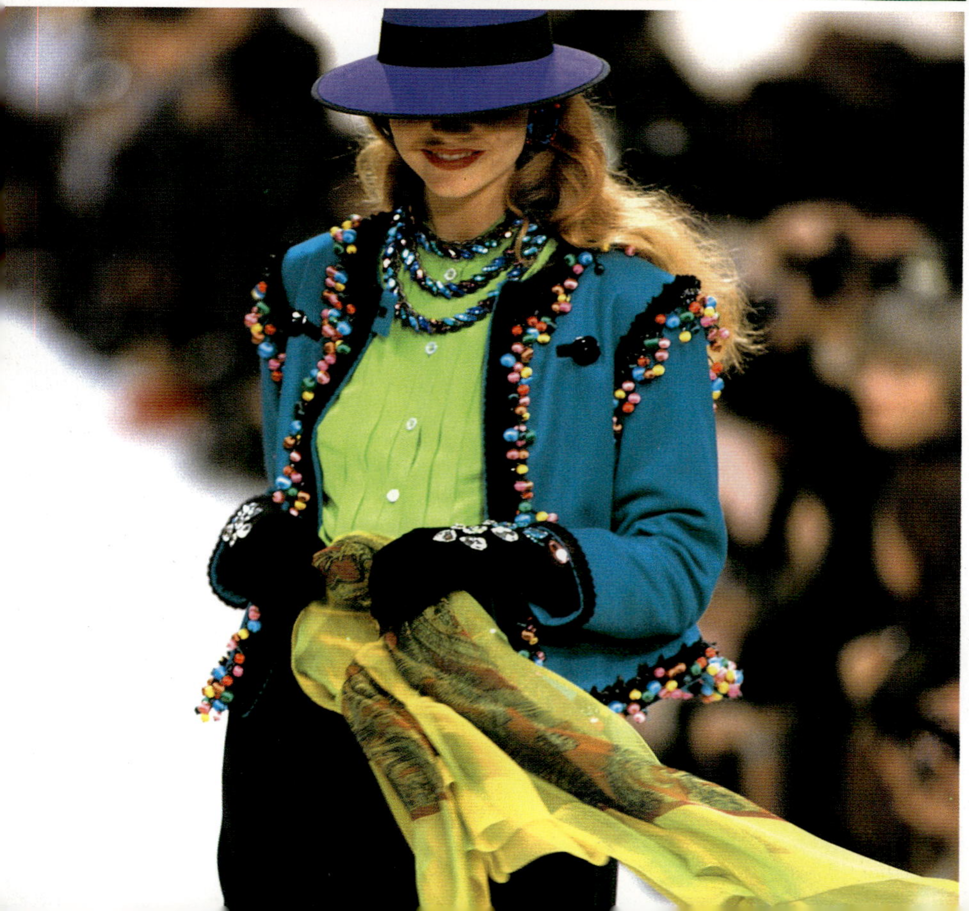
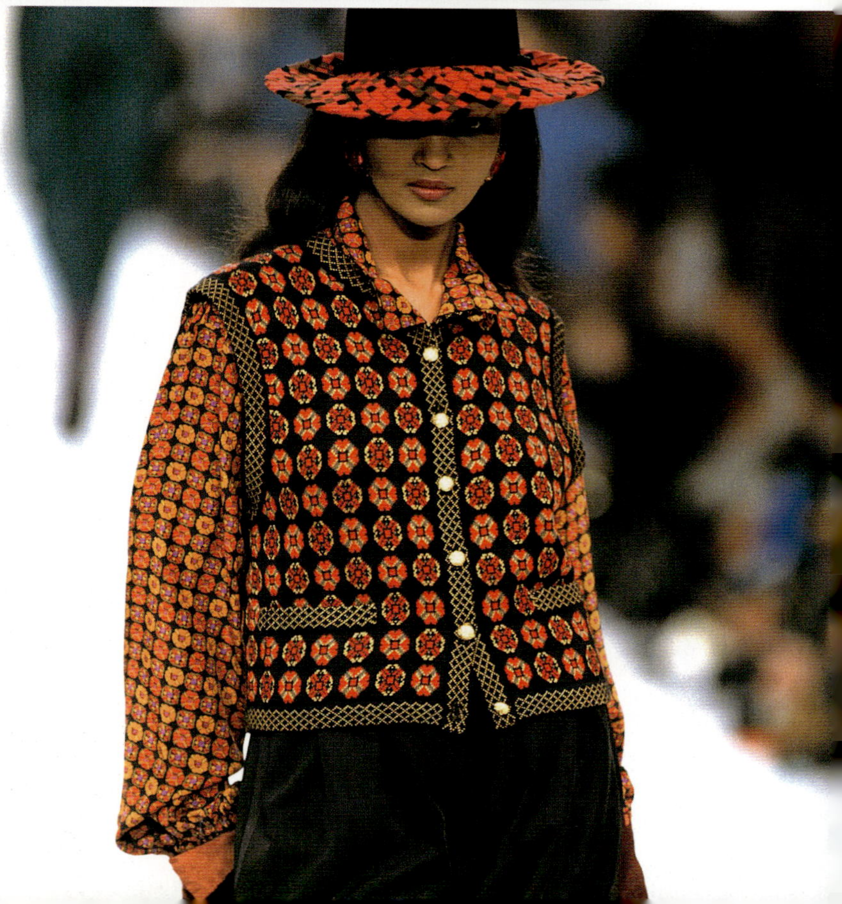

YVES SAINT LAURENT

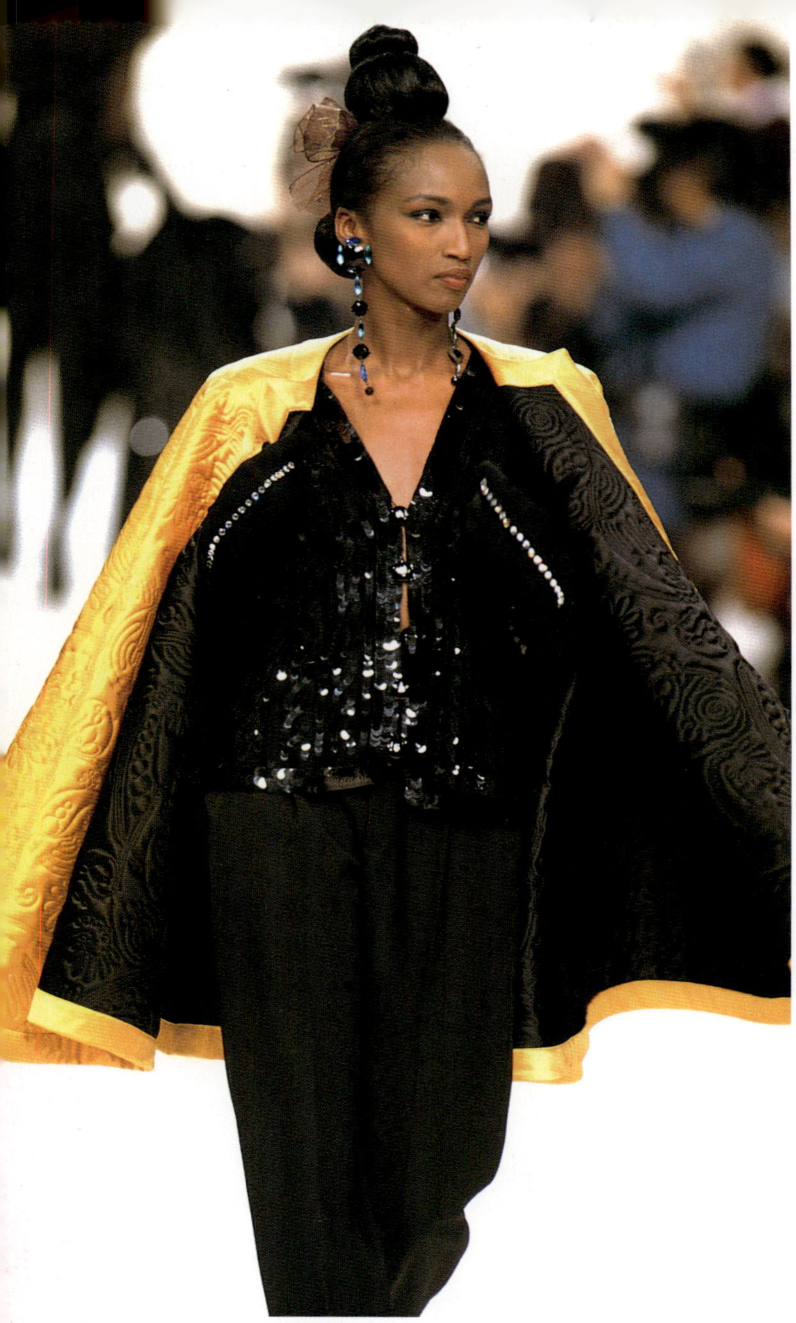

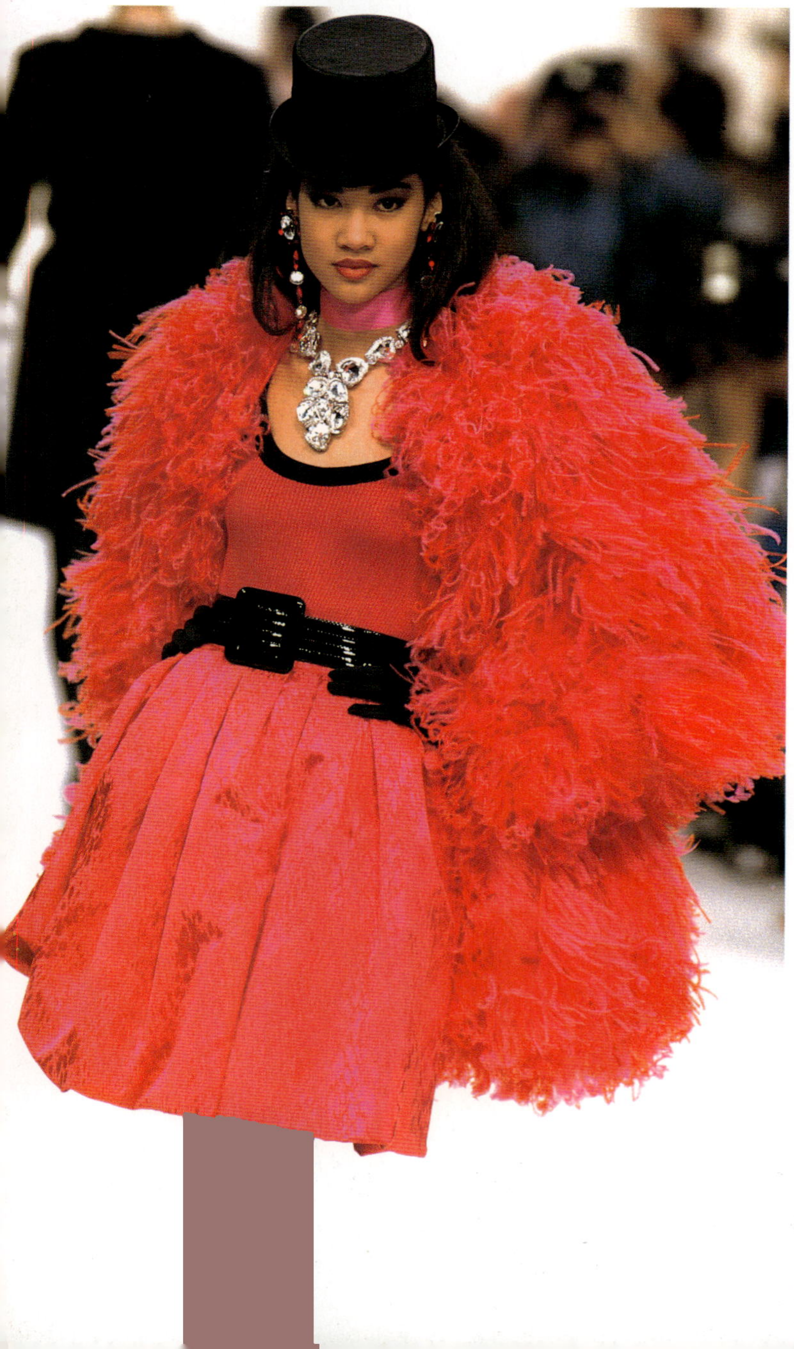

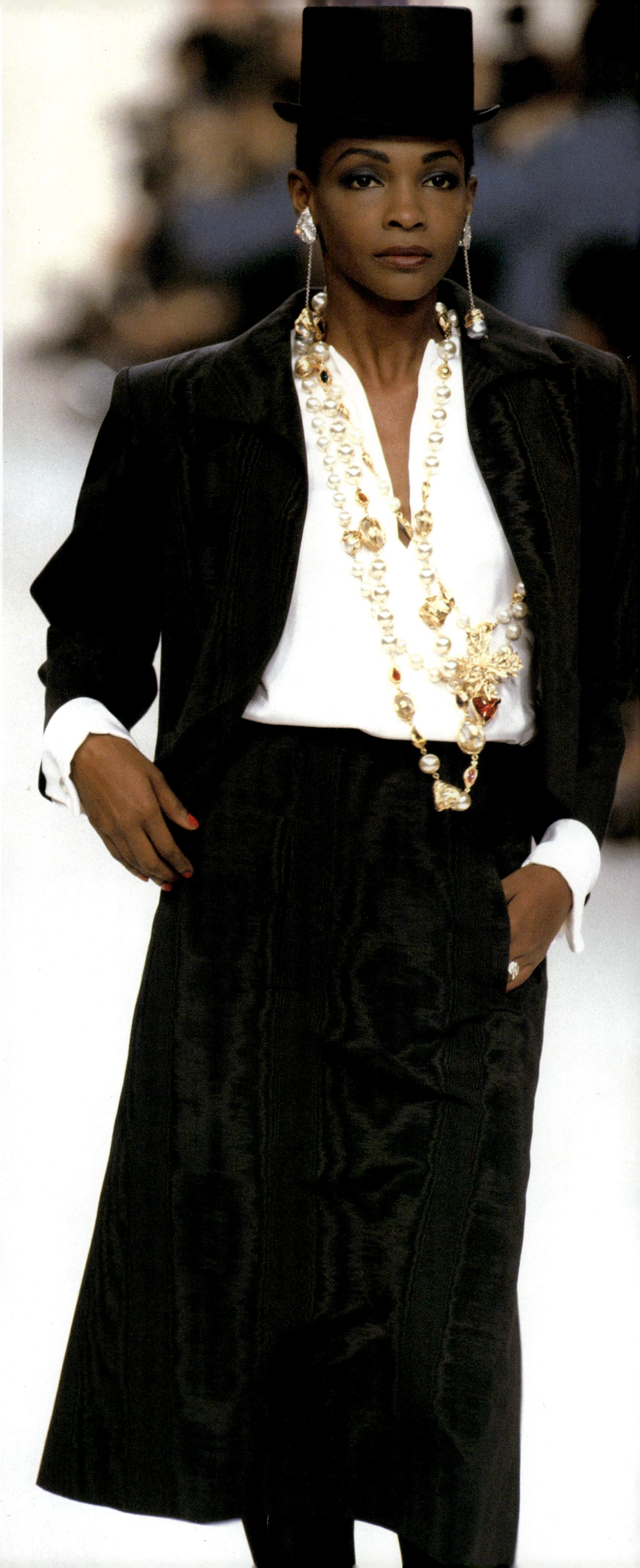

YVES SAINT LAURENT

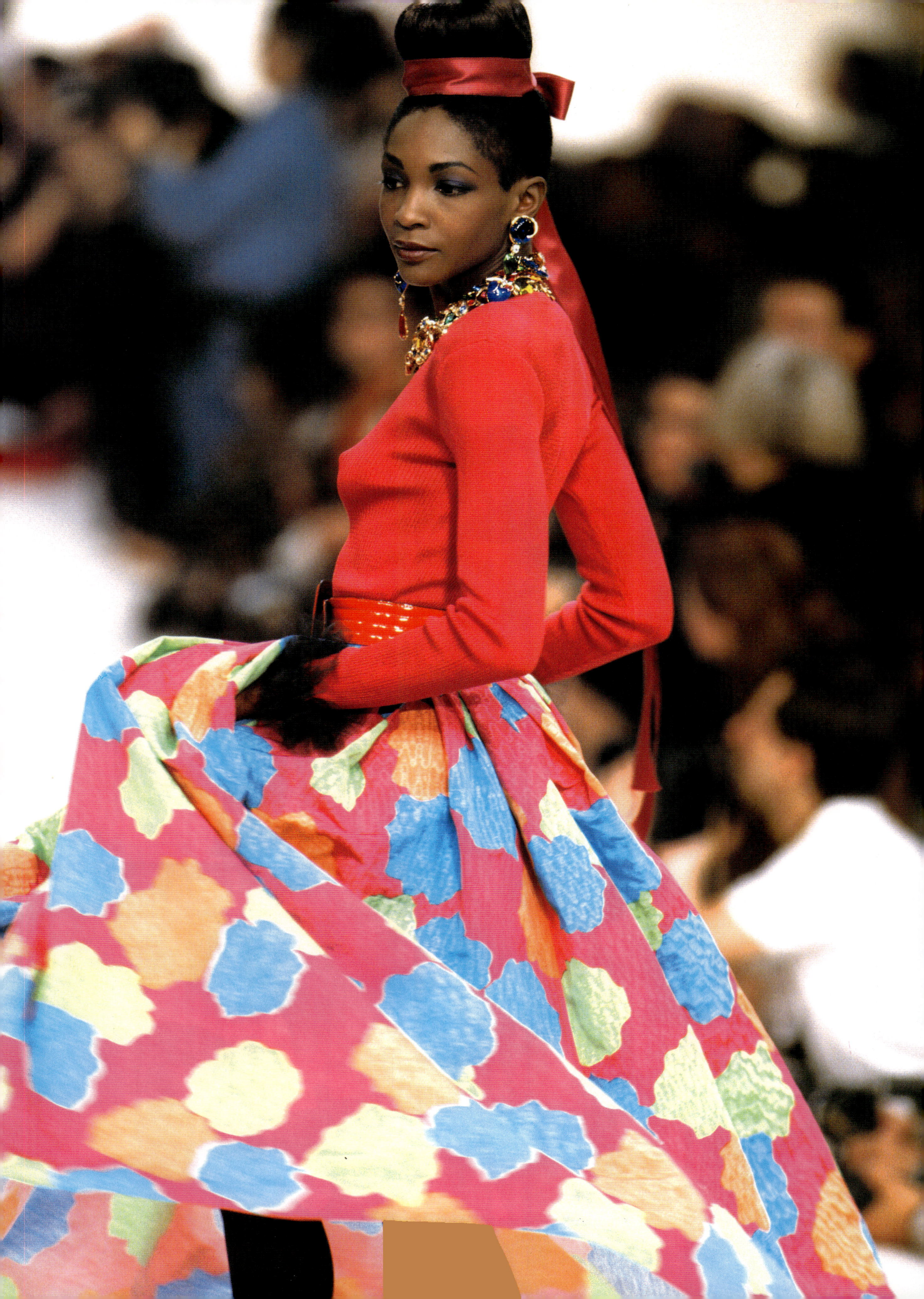

CHANEL

シャネル

若々しいエレガントさで人気を誇るシャネル。今シーズンはウォッシュ・アウトされたデニムが大活躍。異素材コンビネーションやスラッシュ・スカートも新鮮。
Chanel's popularity derives from its youthful elegance. Playing a major role this season were washed out jeans.
The combination of different materials and slash skirts looked refreshing.

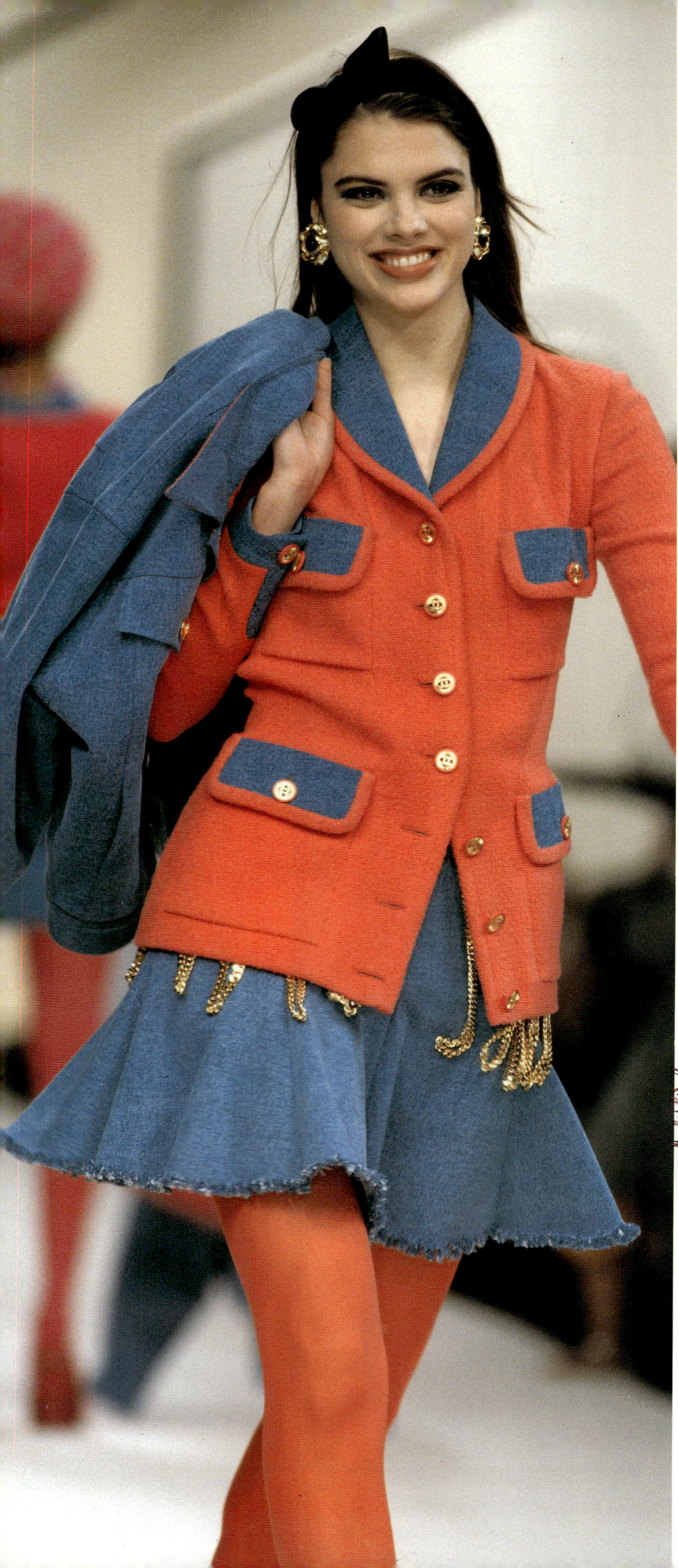
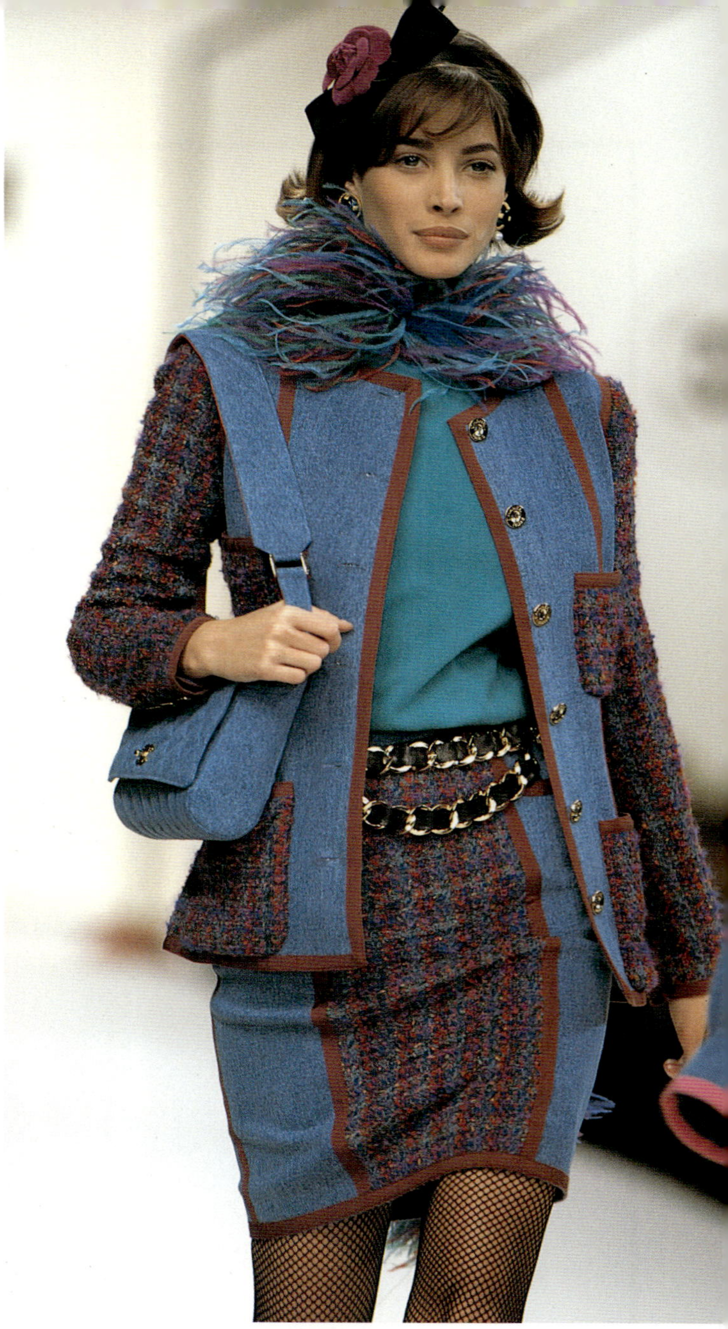
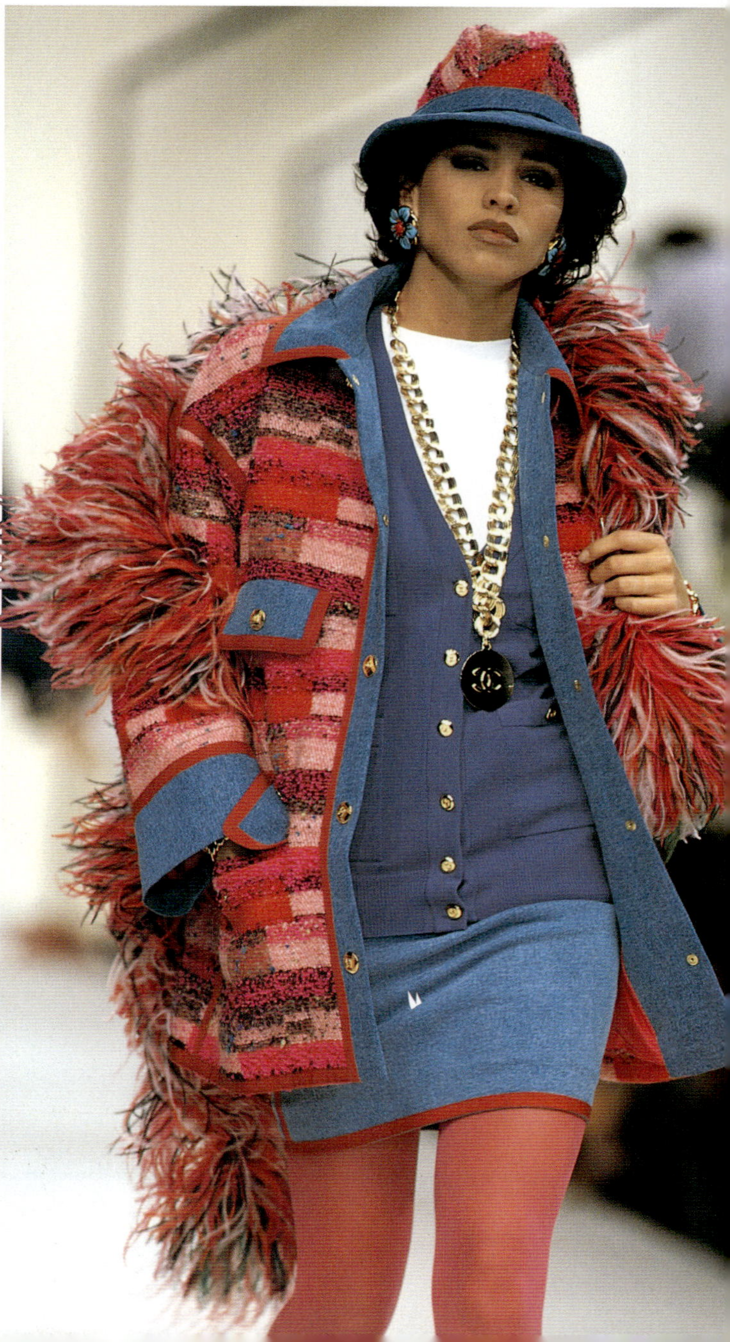

CHANEL

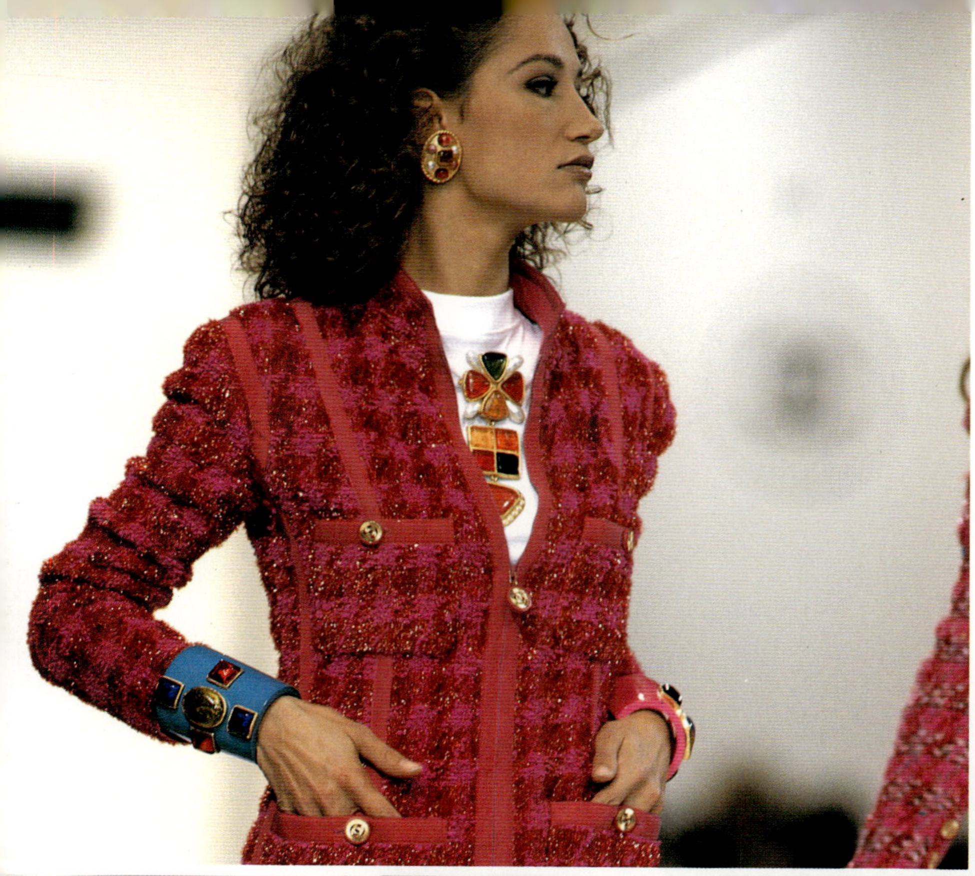

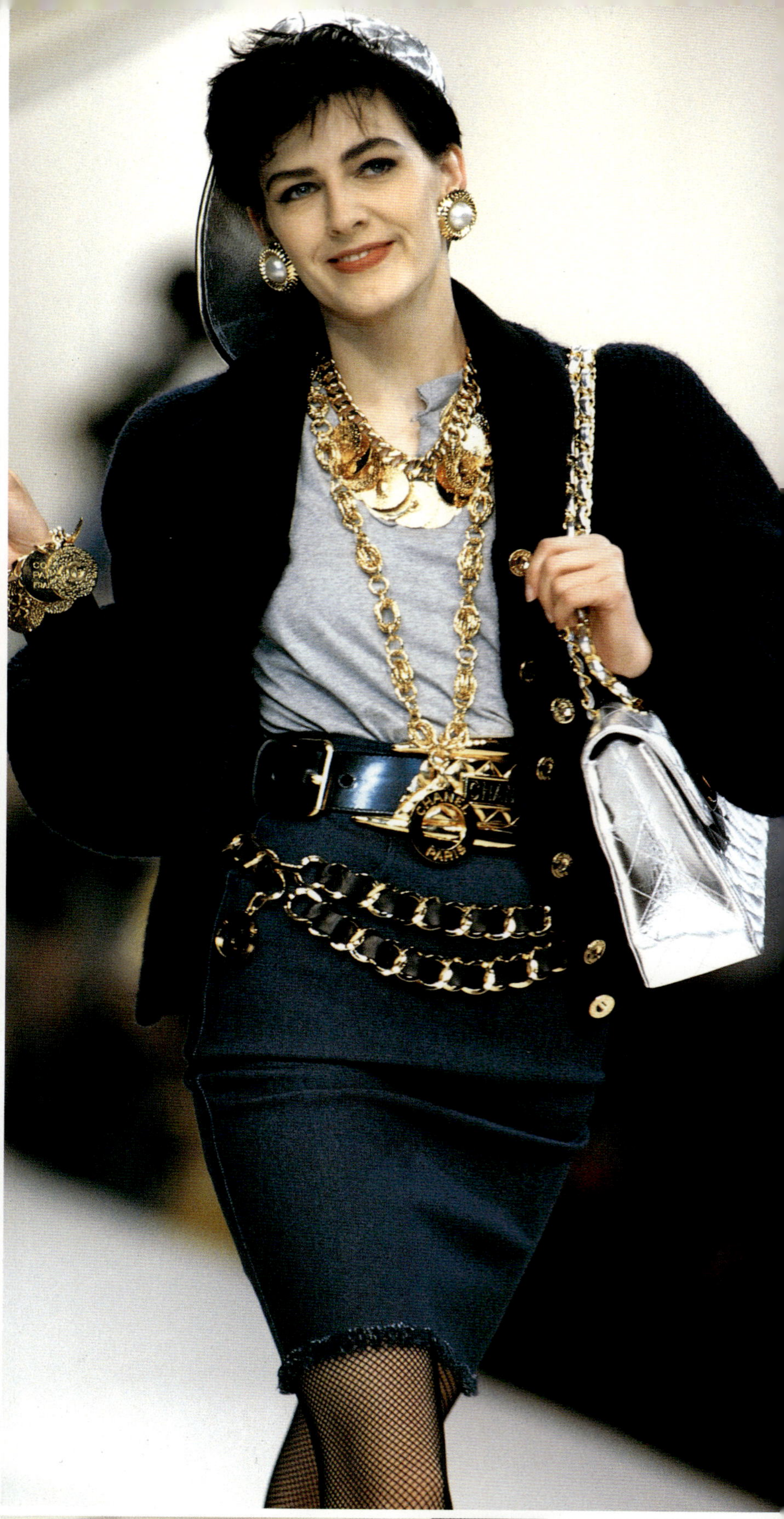

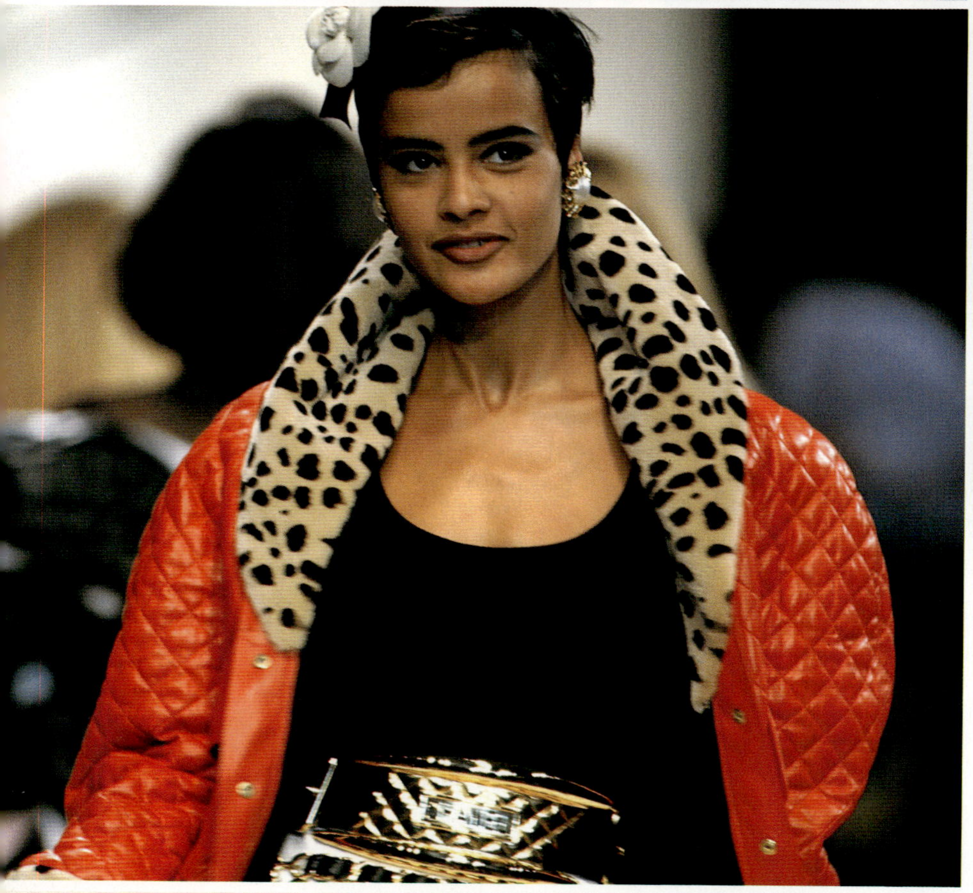

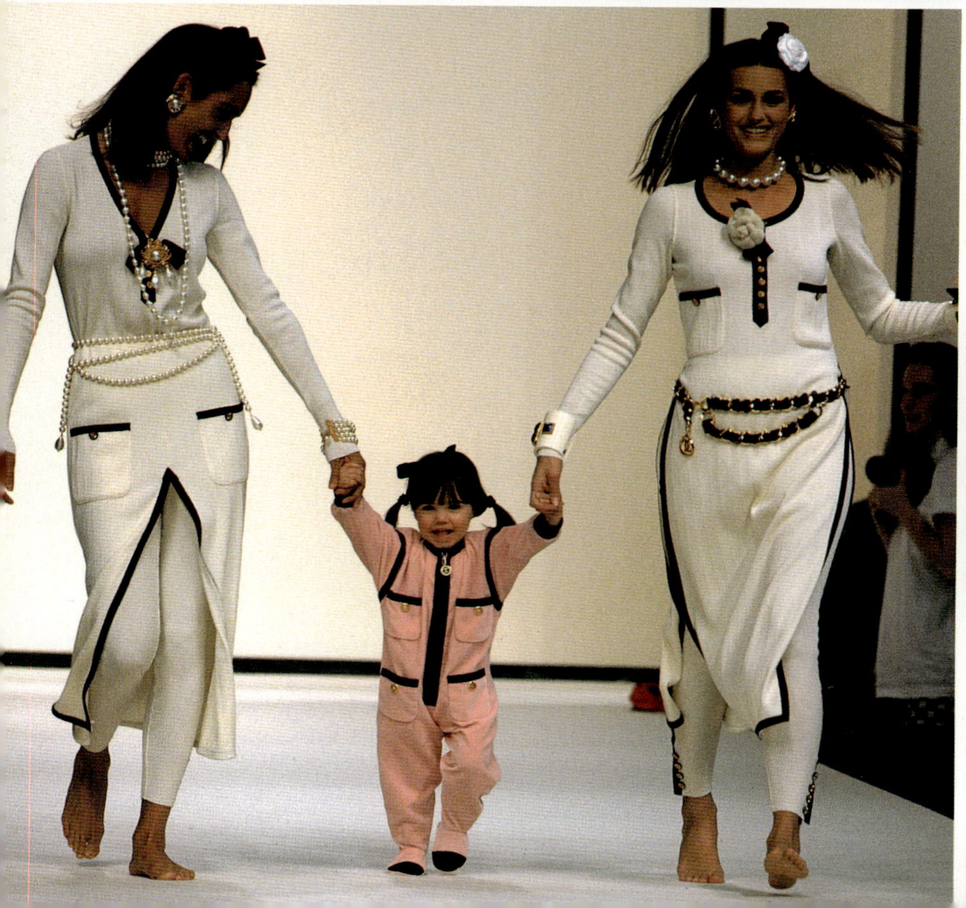

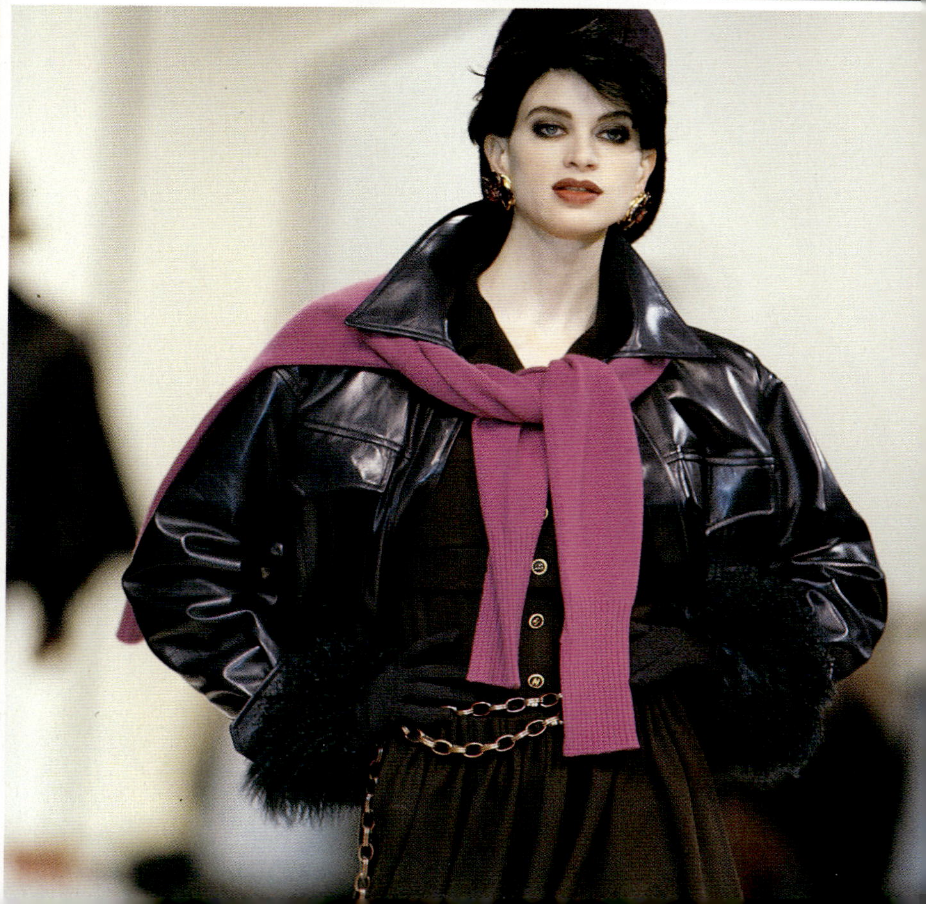

CHANEL

125

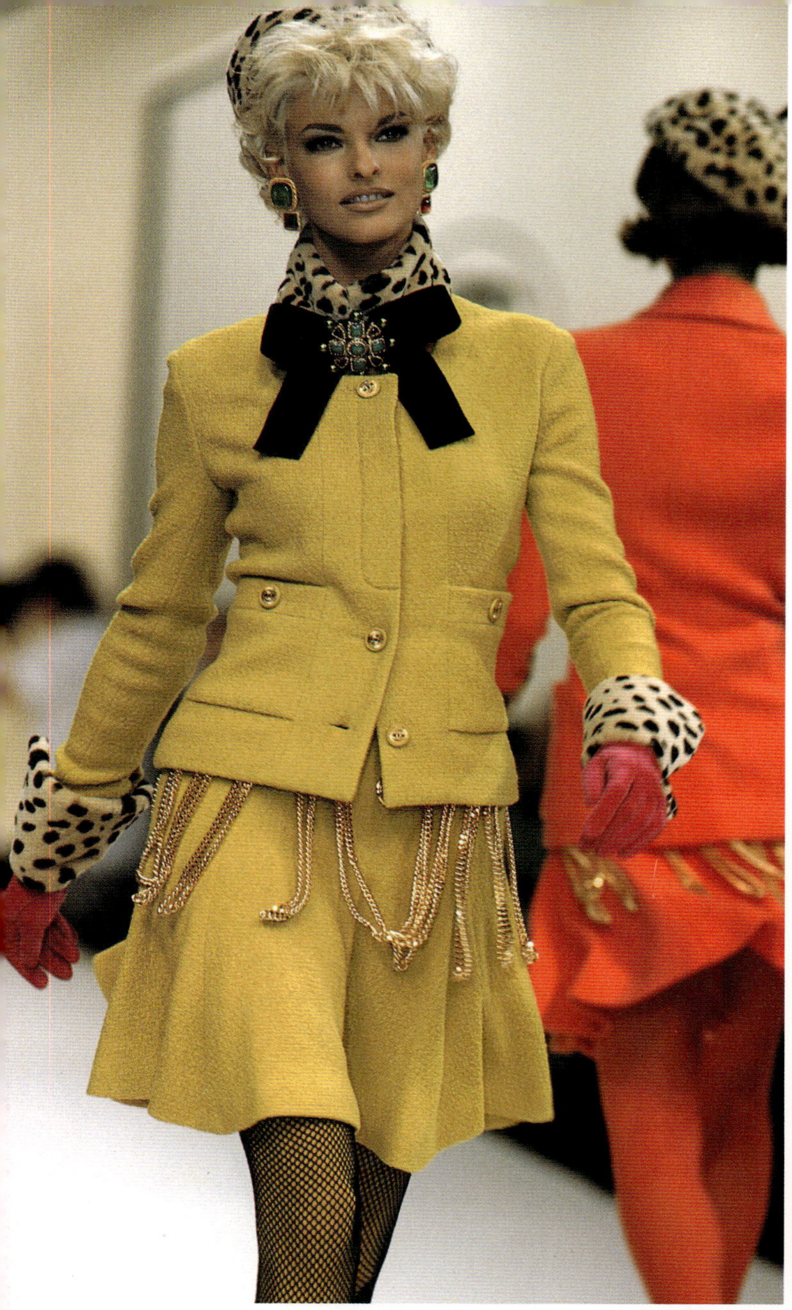

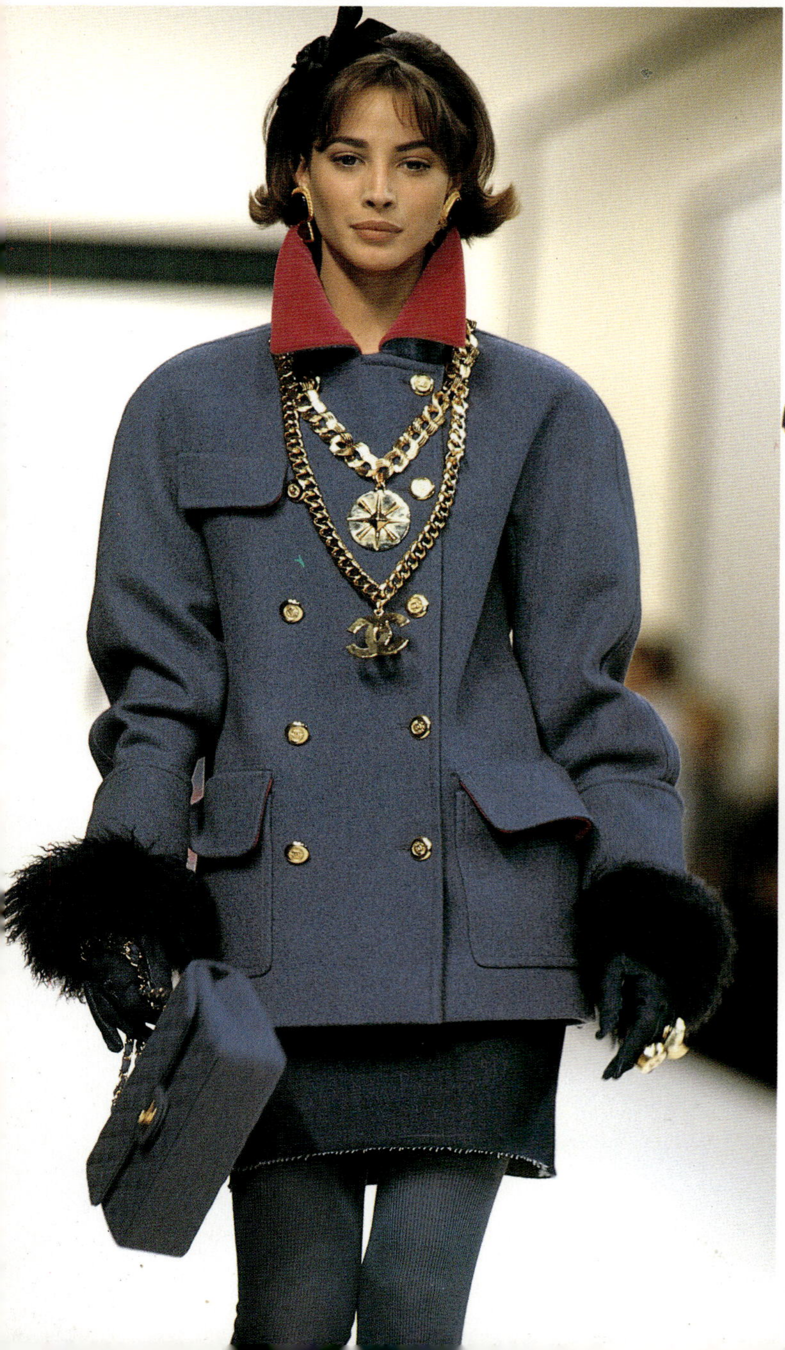

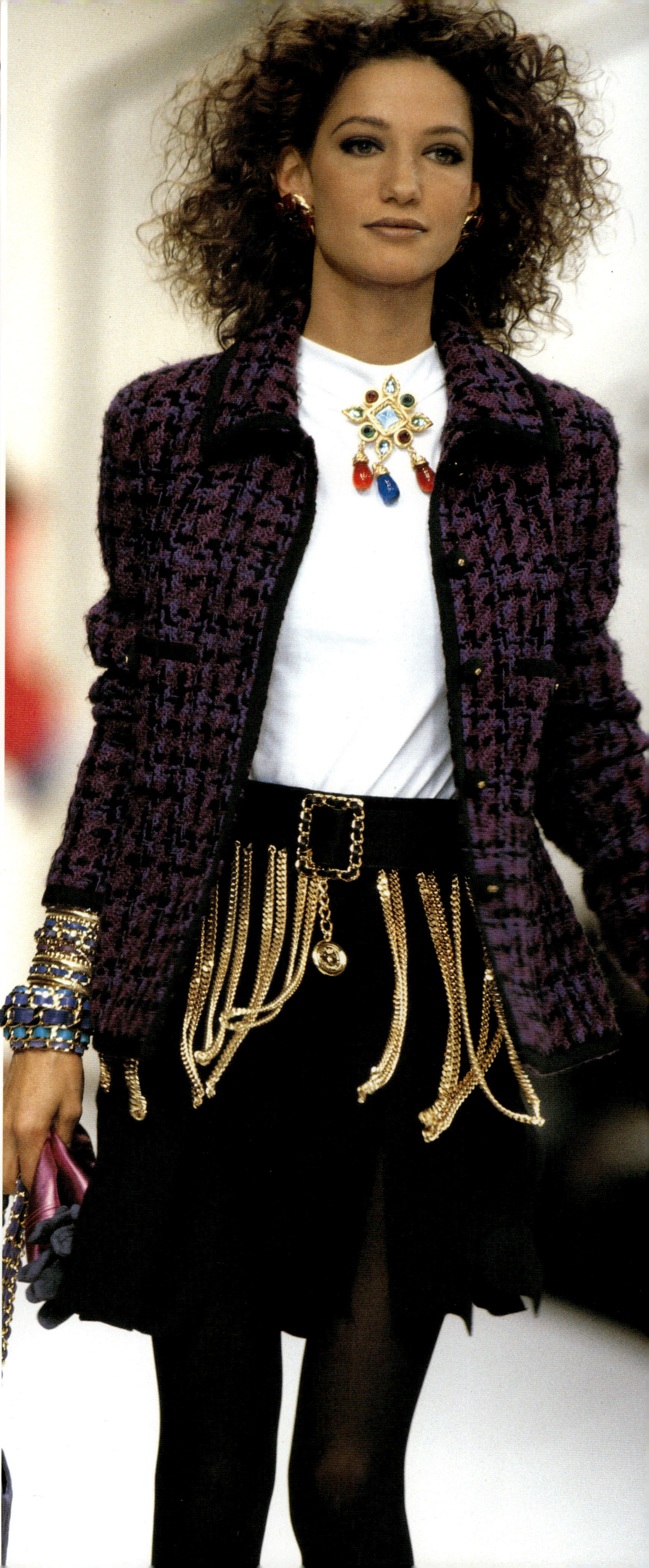

CHANEL

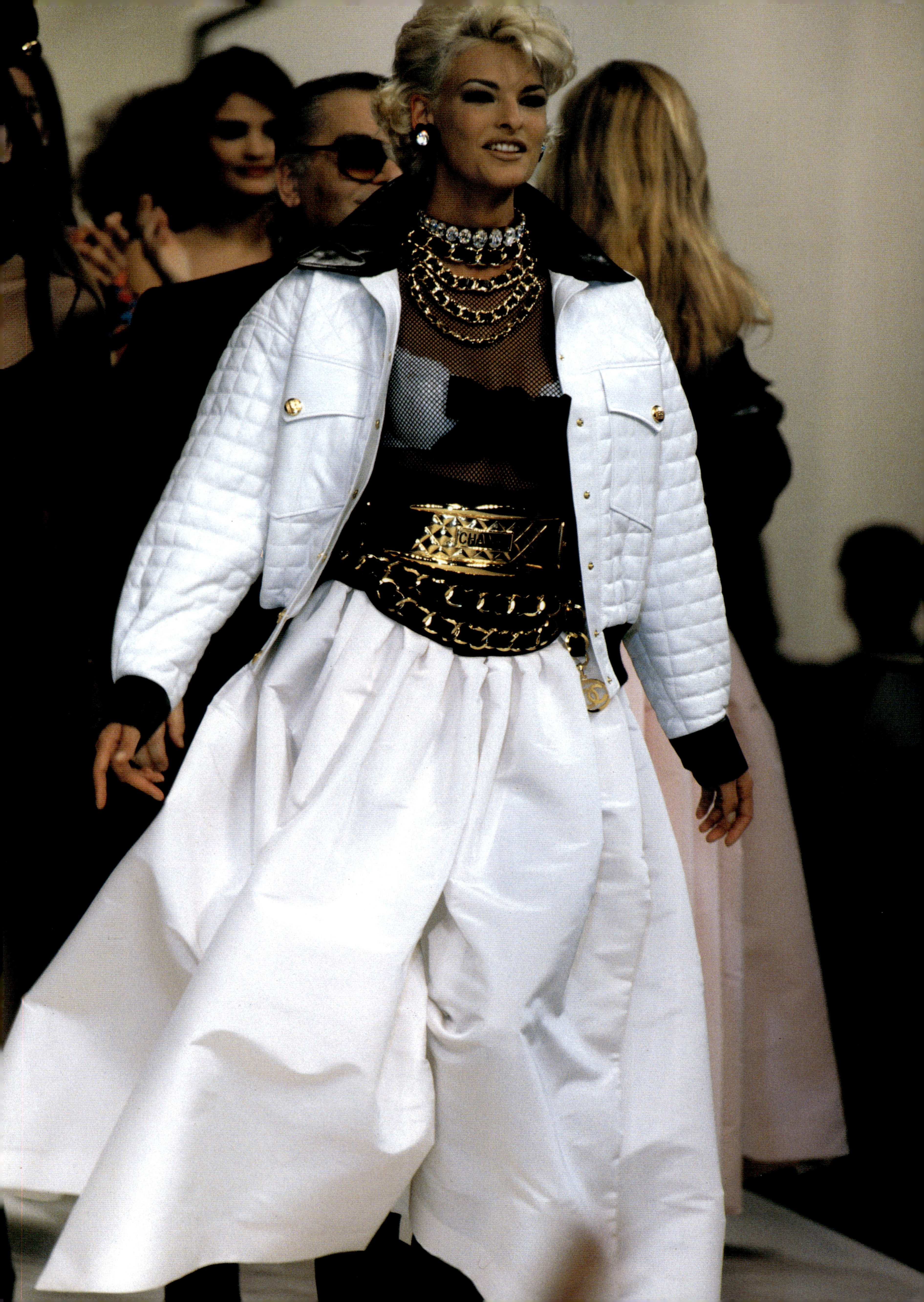

MARTINE SITBON

マルティーヌ・シットボン

トランスペアレント効果や下着のインスピレーションのセクシーさを残したまま、ティアードやラッフル、プリーツなどの袖の効果で美しさを増している。

The underwear-inspired transparent effect and sexiness has been kept,
and the beauty has been enhanced sleeves with the effect of tiered, ruffles, pleats.

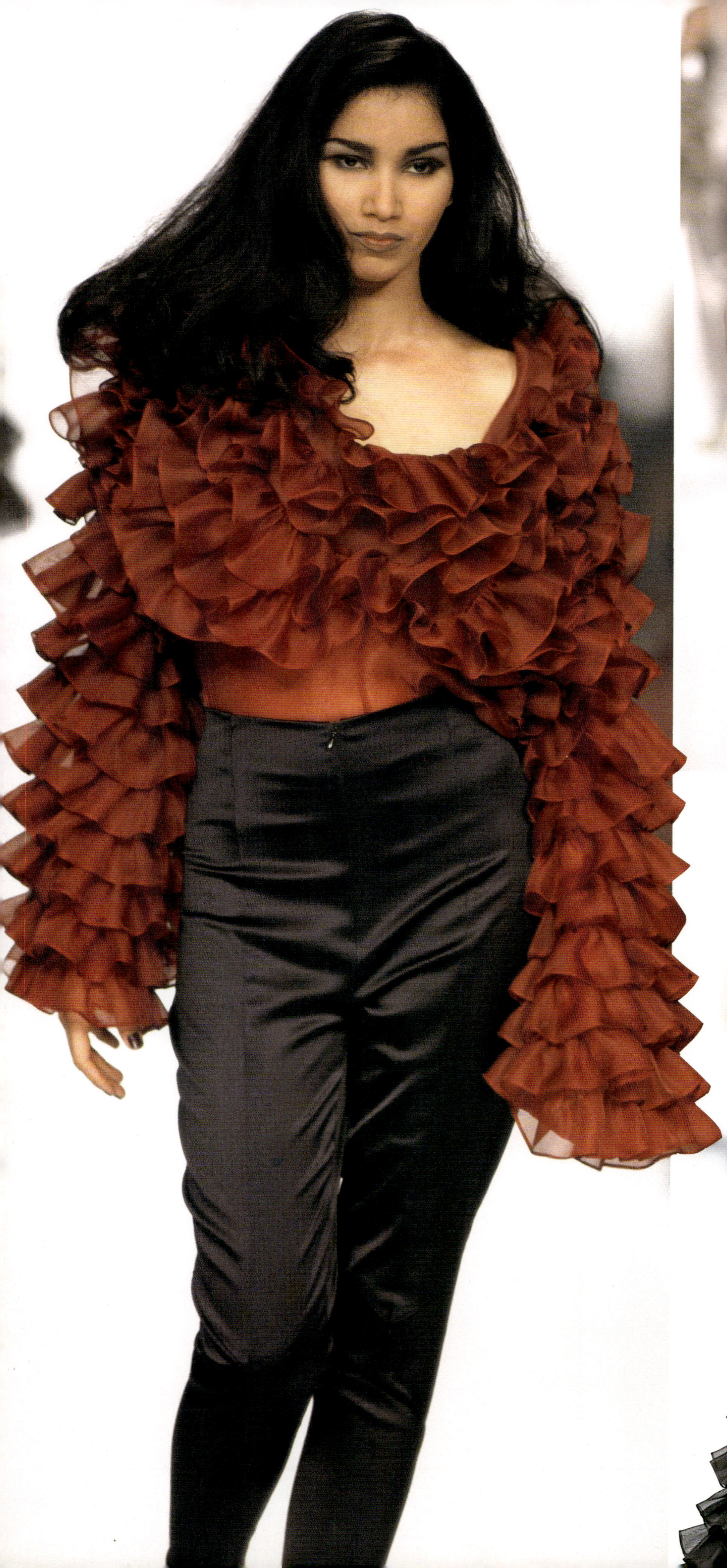
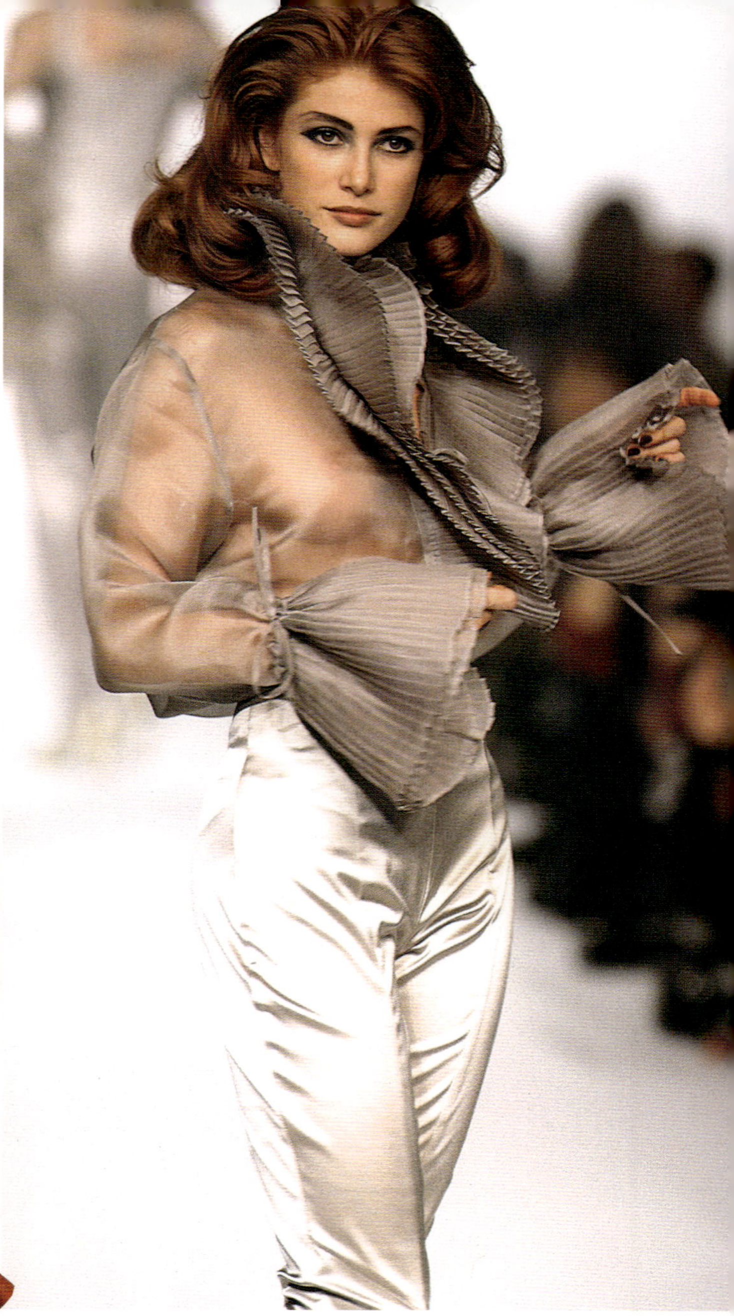
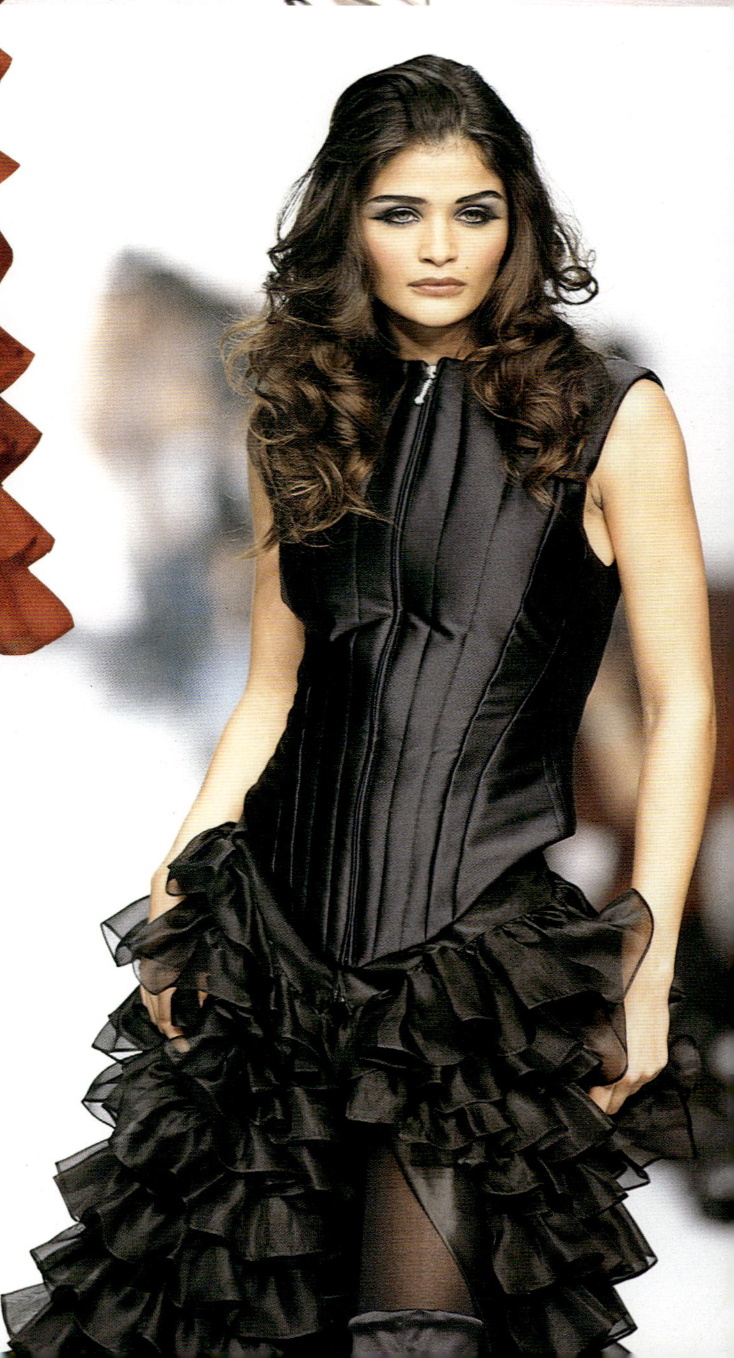

MARTINE SITBON

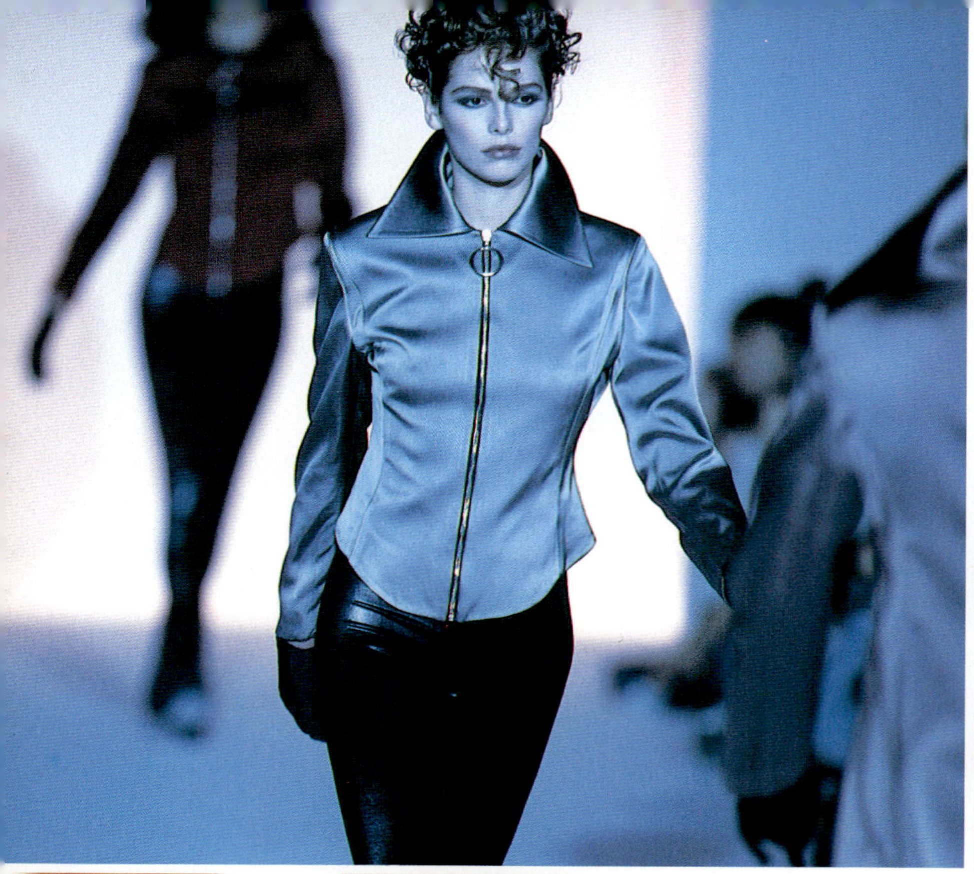
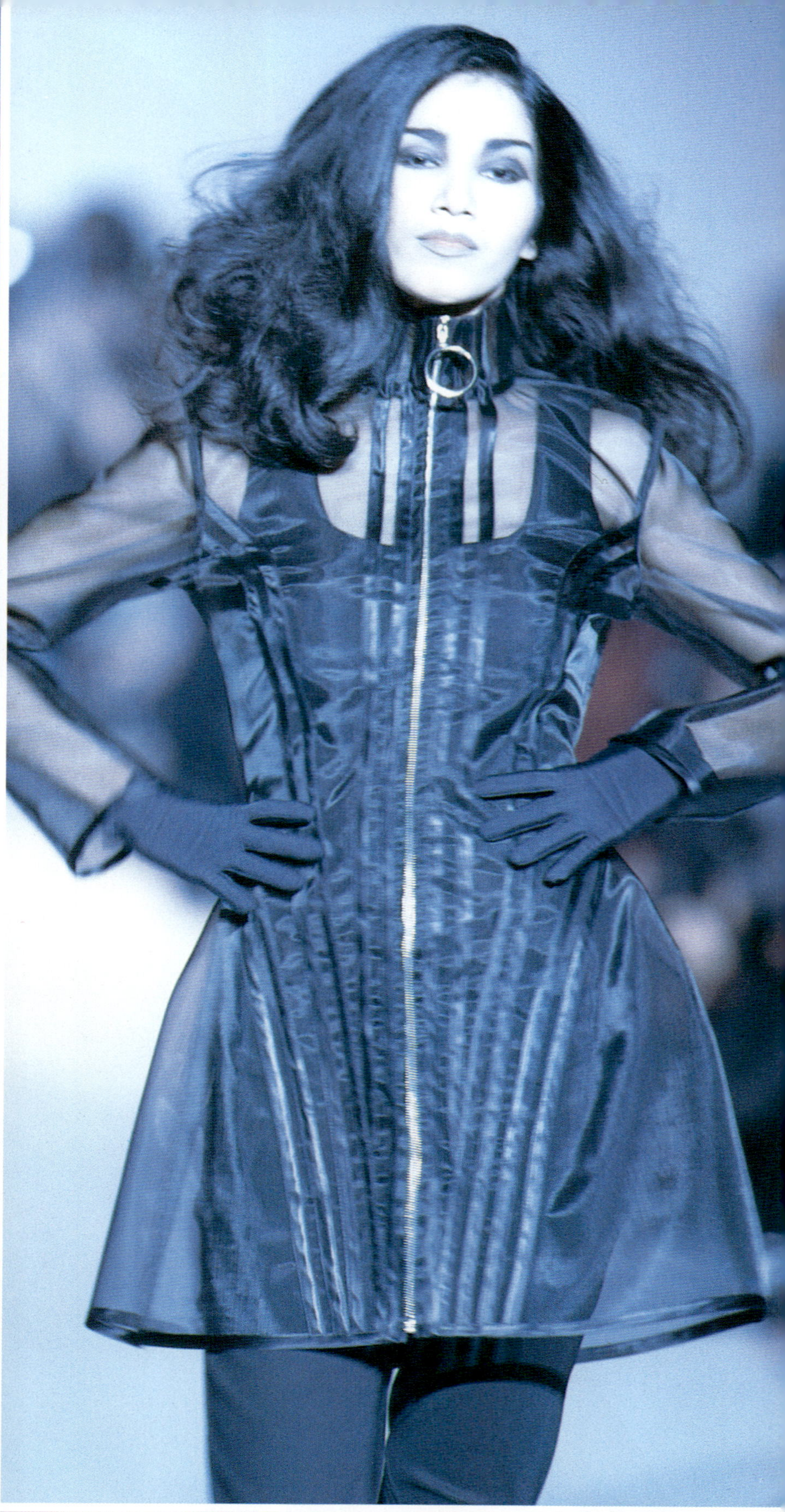
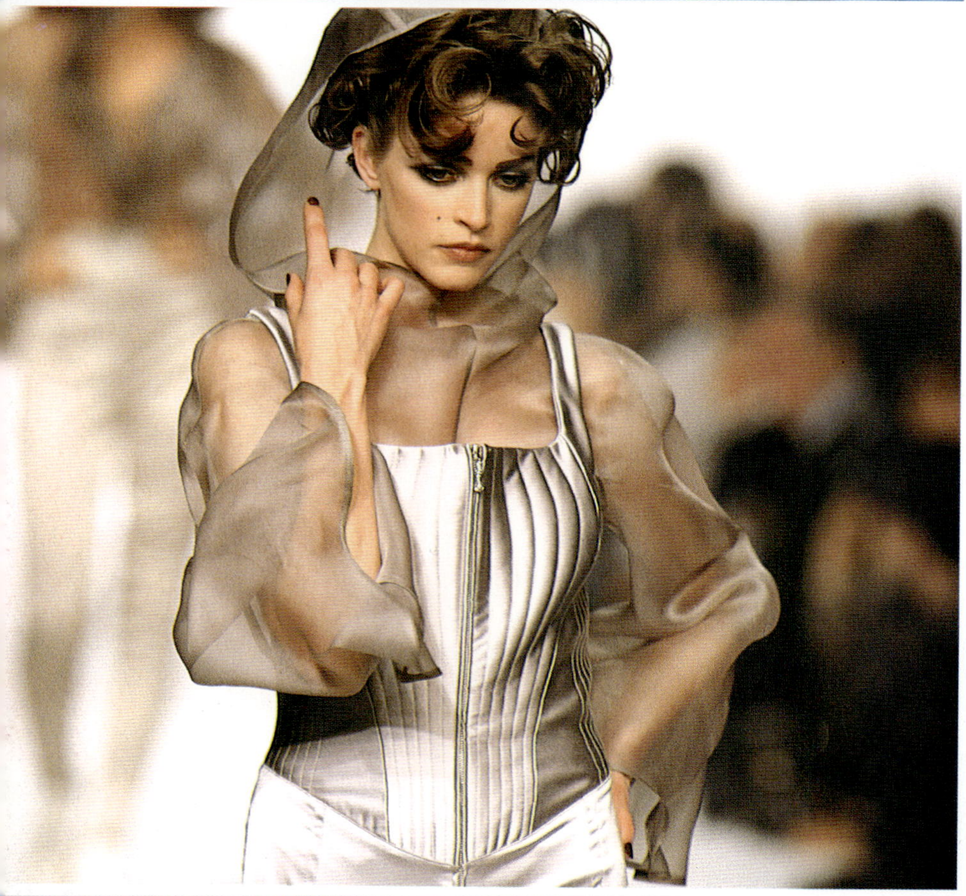
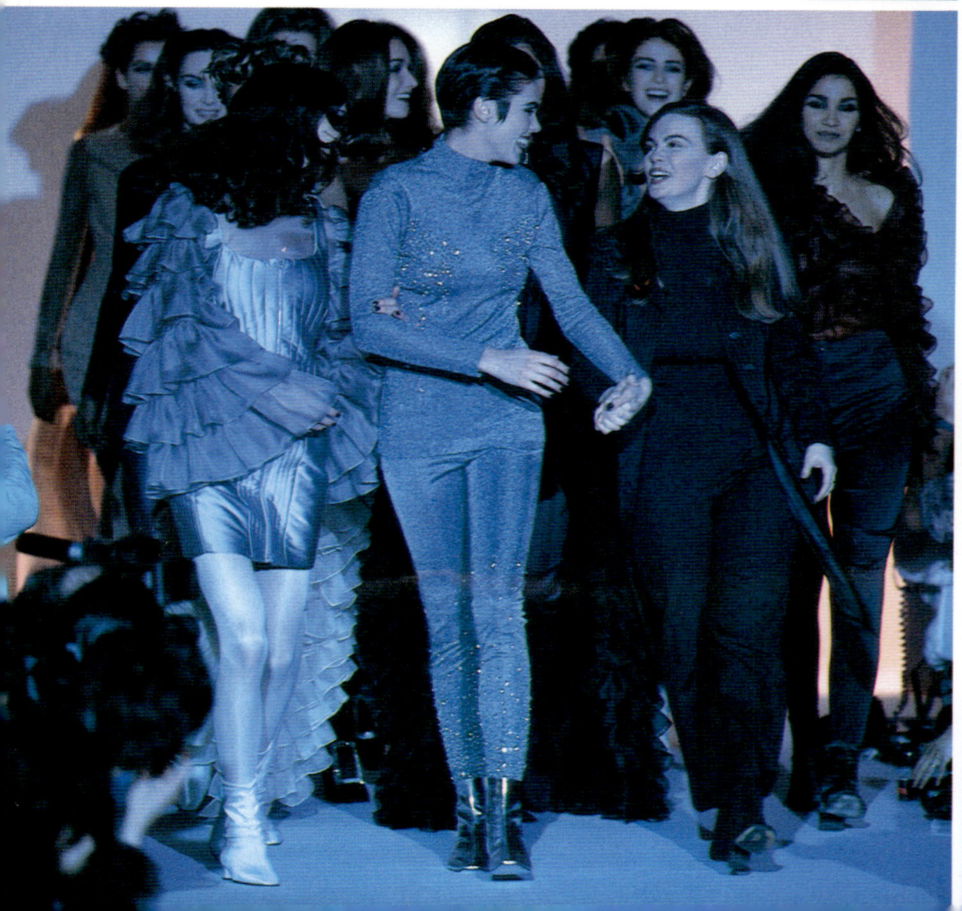
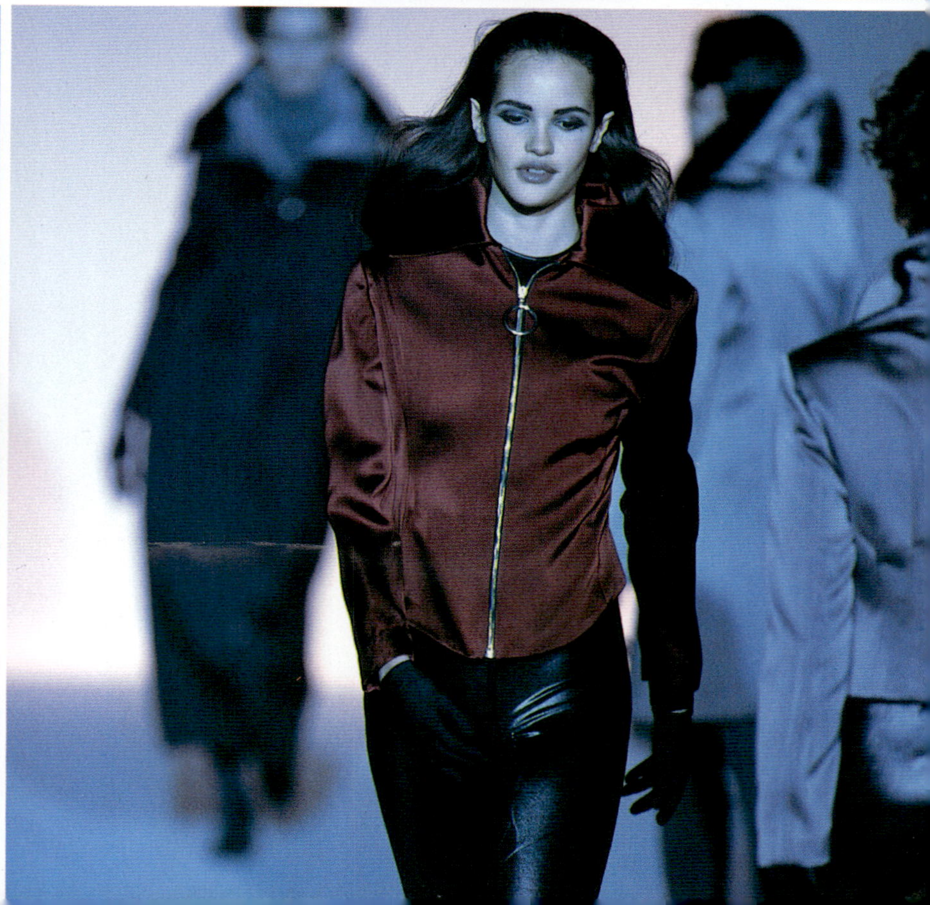

MARTINE SITBON

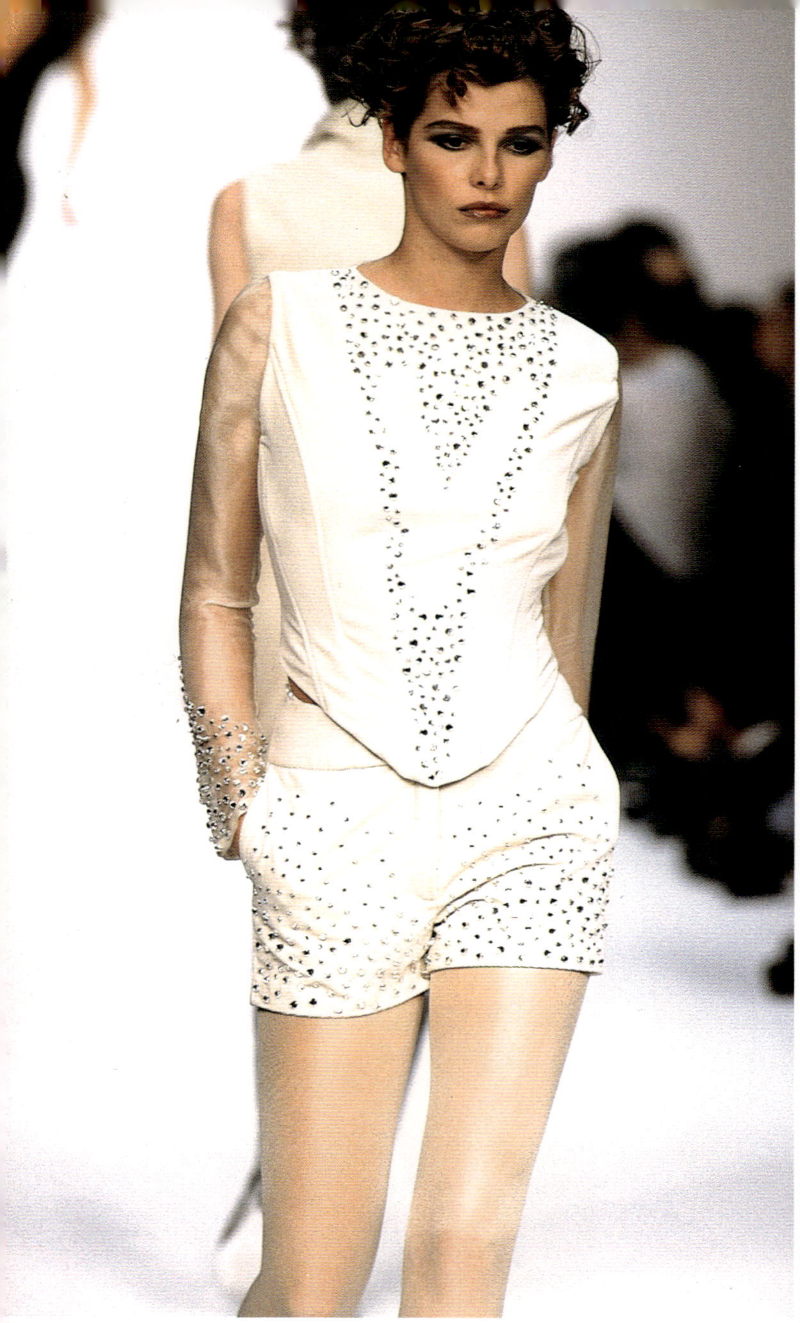
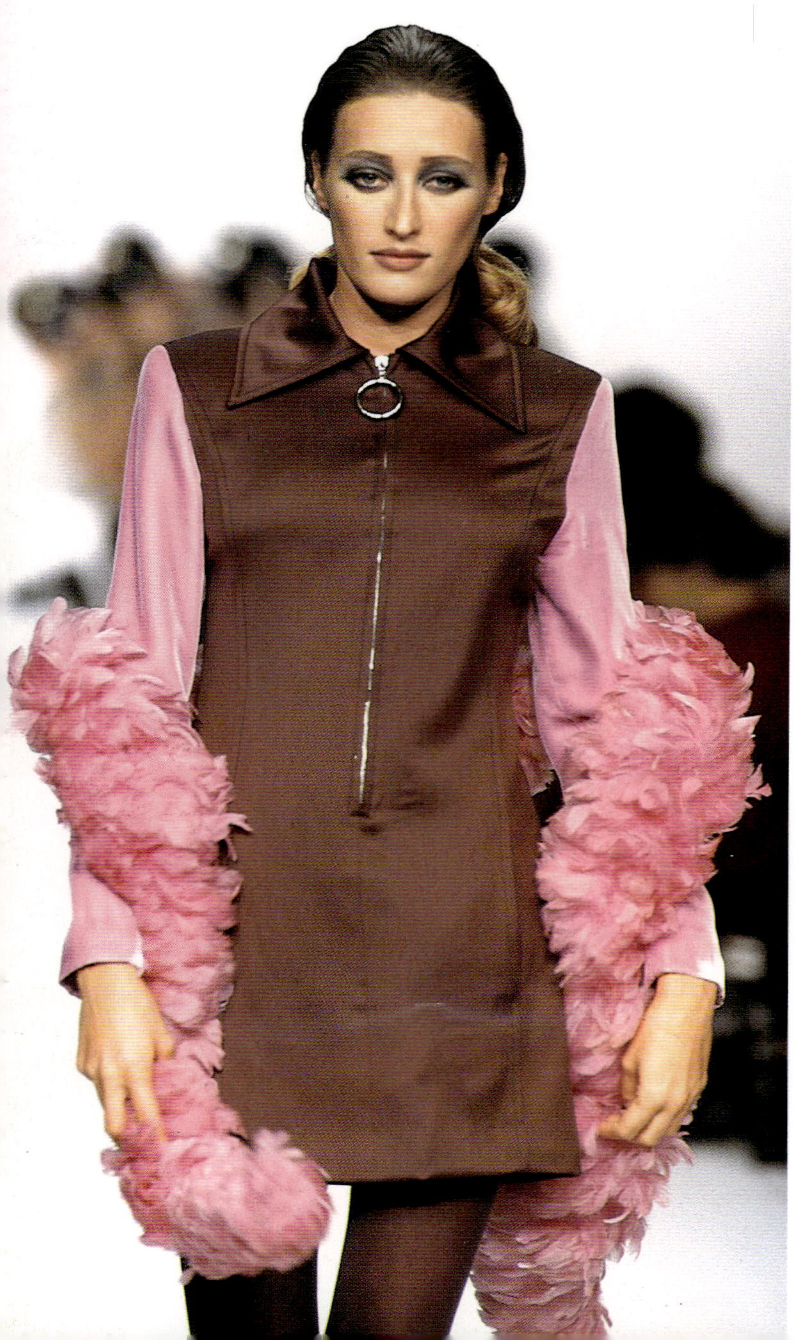
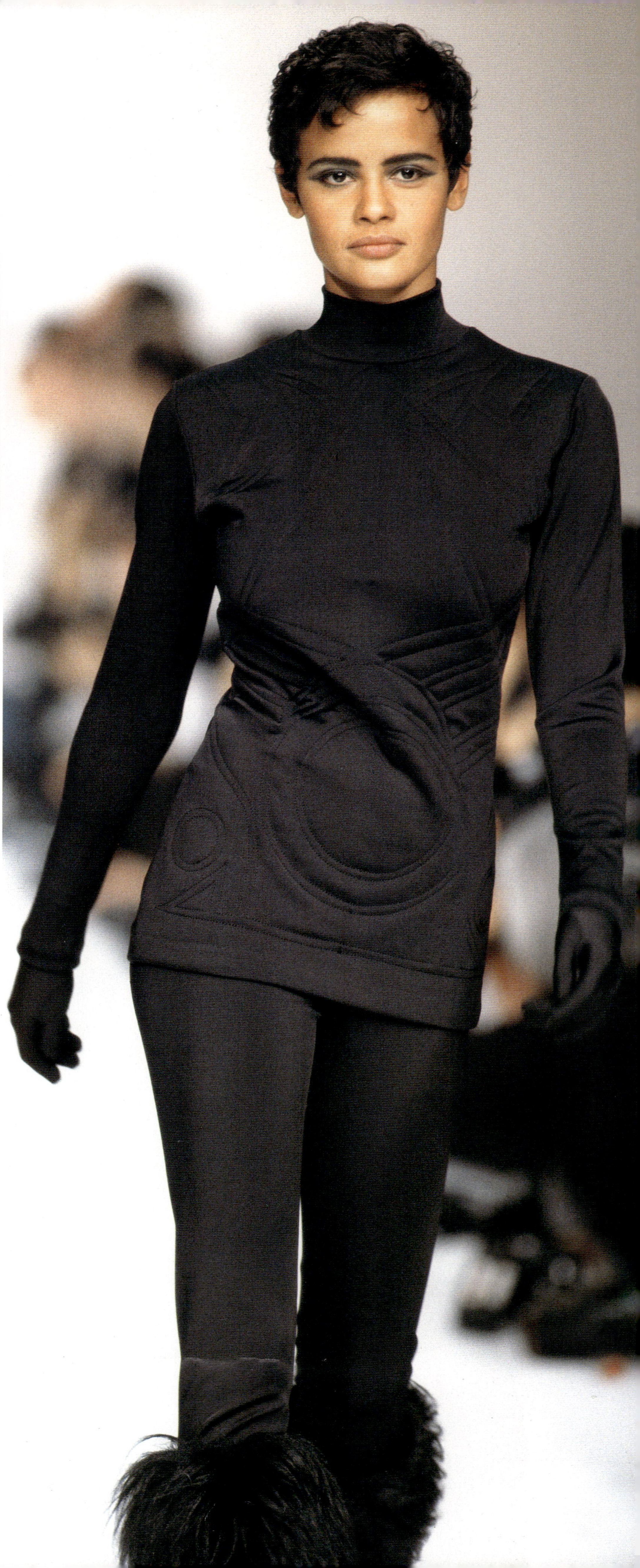

MARTINE SITBON

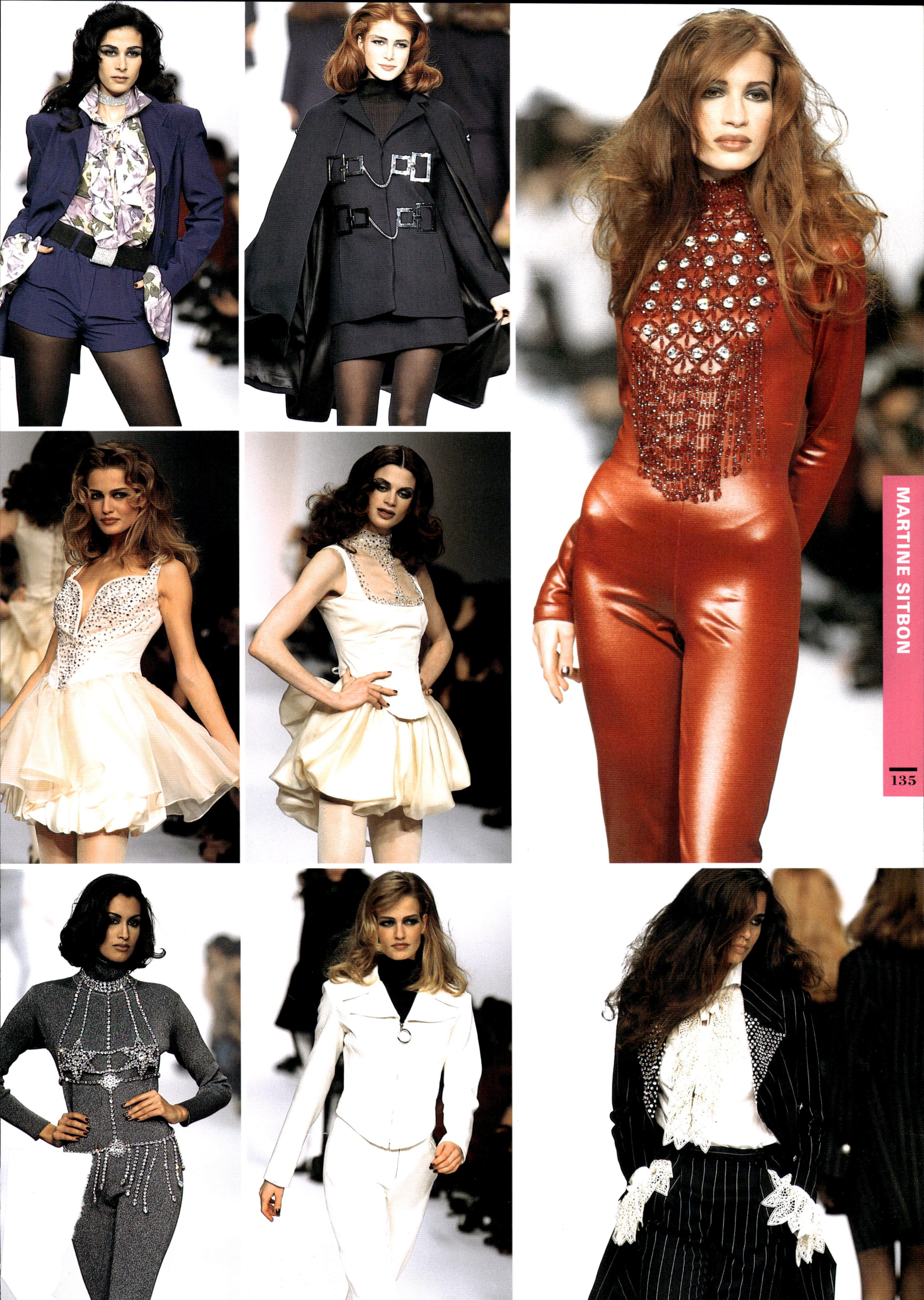

135

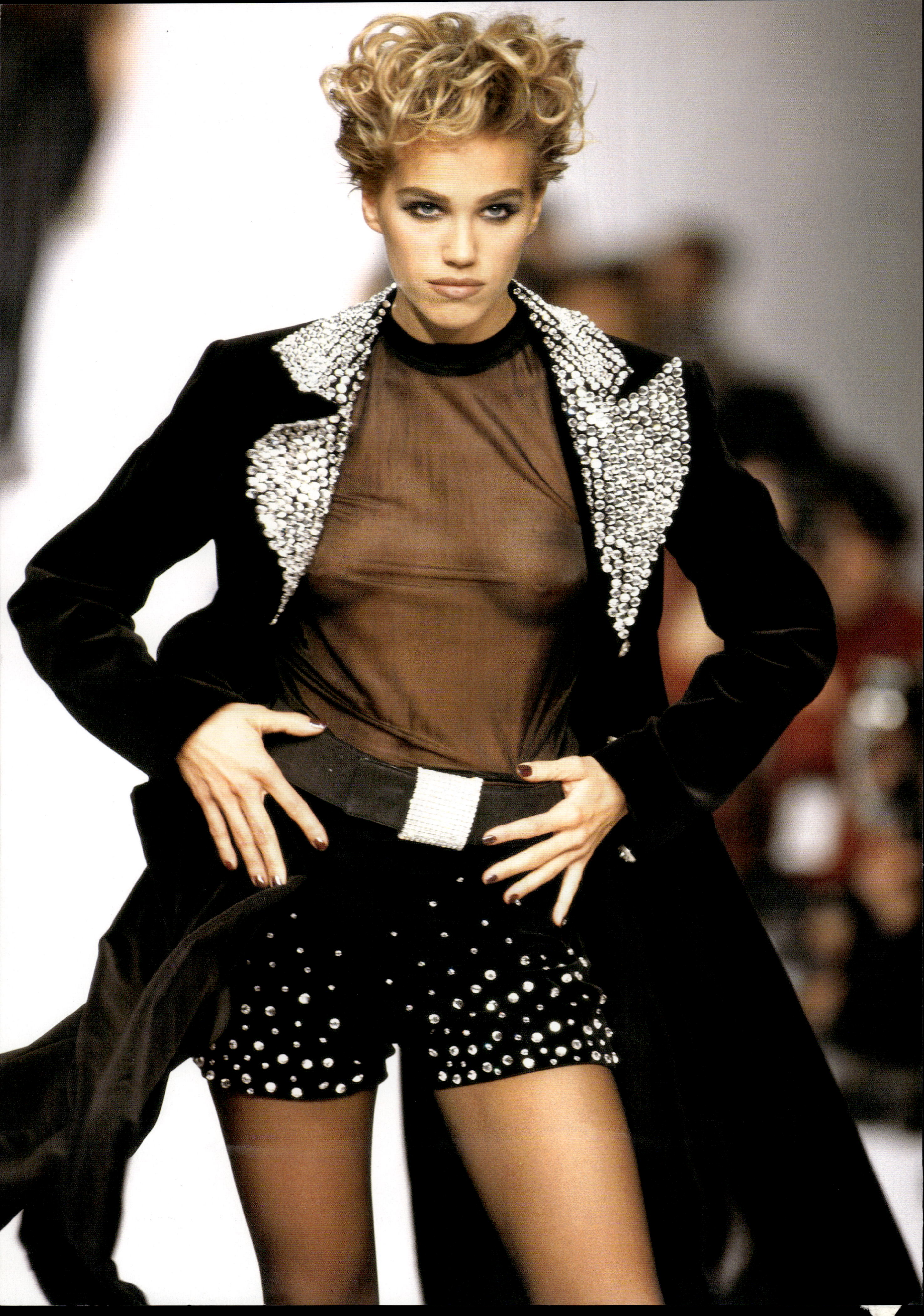

KARL LAGERFELD

カール・ラガーフェルド

全てのスカートの下に、ボディにぴったりしたストレッチのエナメル・パンツをコーディネイト。デニム素材も加わり、セクシーな若々しさを増した。

Coordinated underneath all the skirts, stretch enamel pants, conforming to the body.
The sexy youthfulness was enhanced with an addition of denim material.

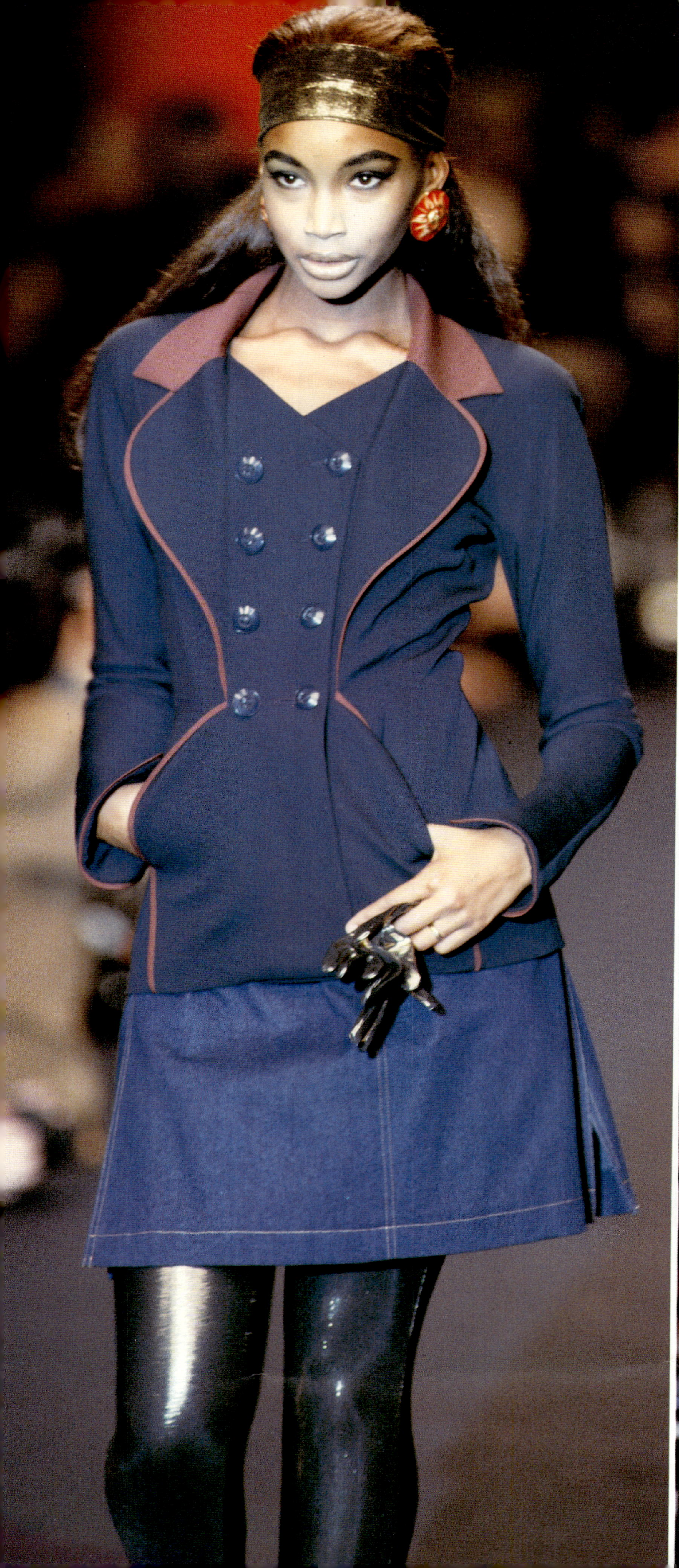
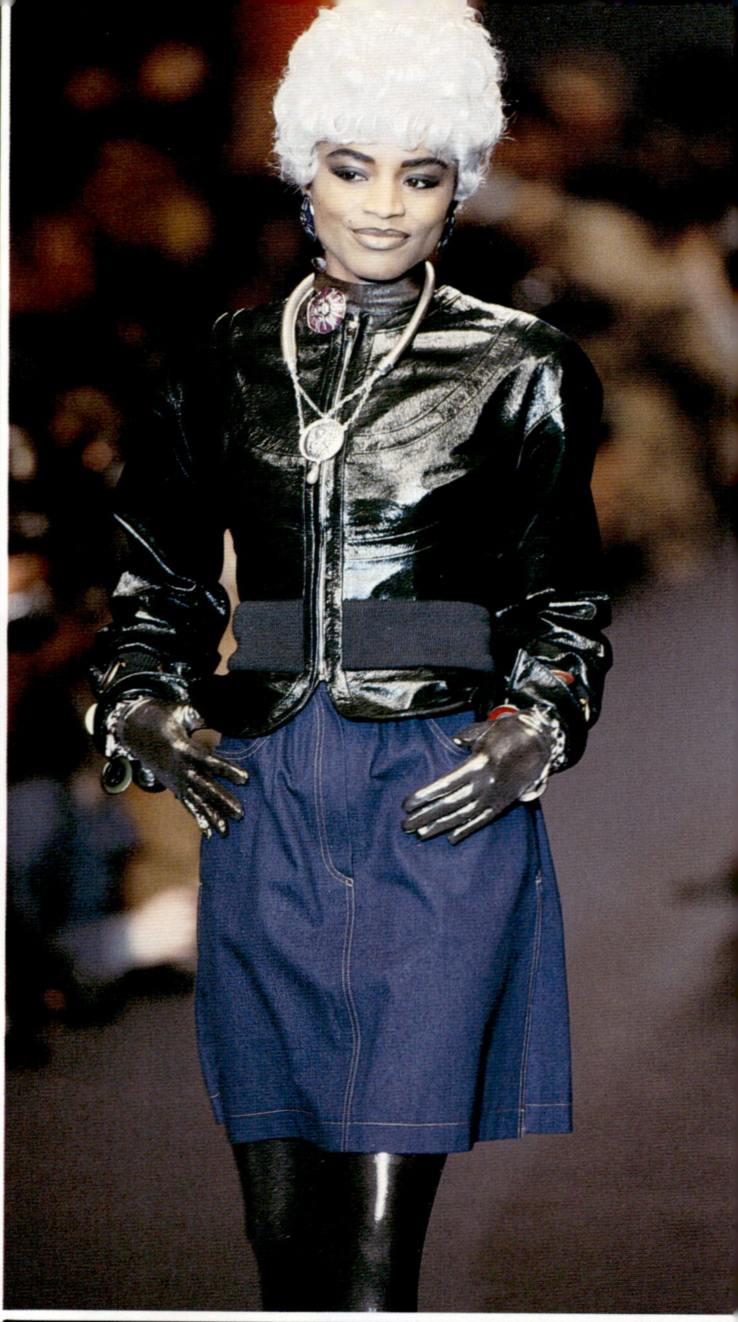
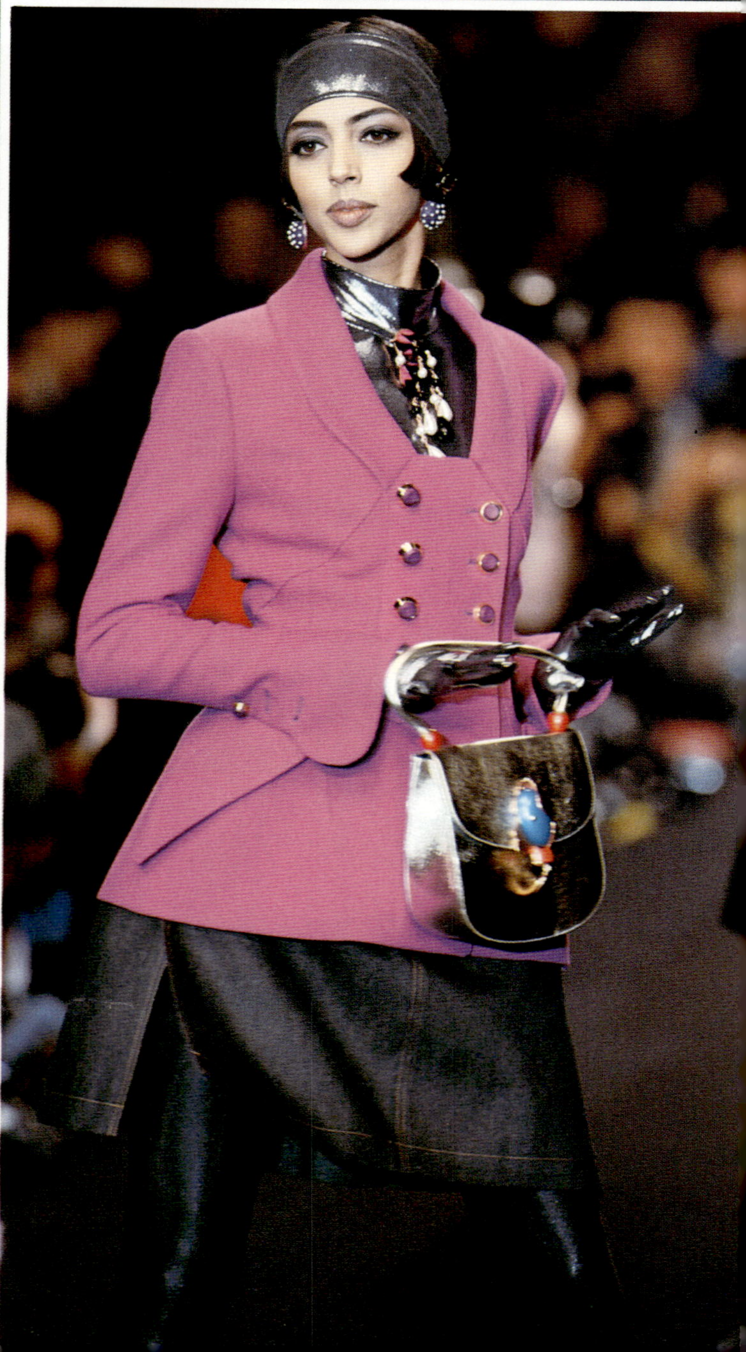

KARL LAGERFELD

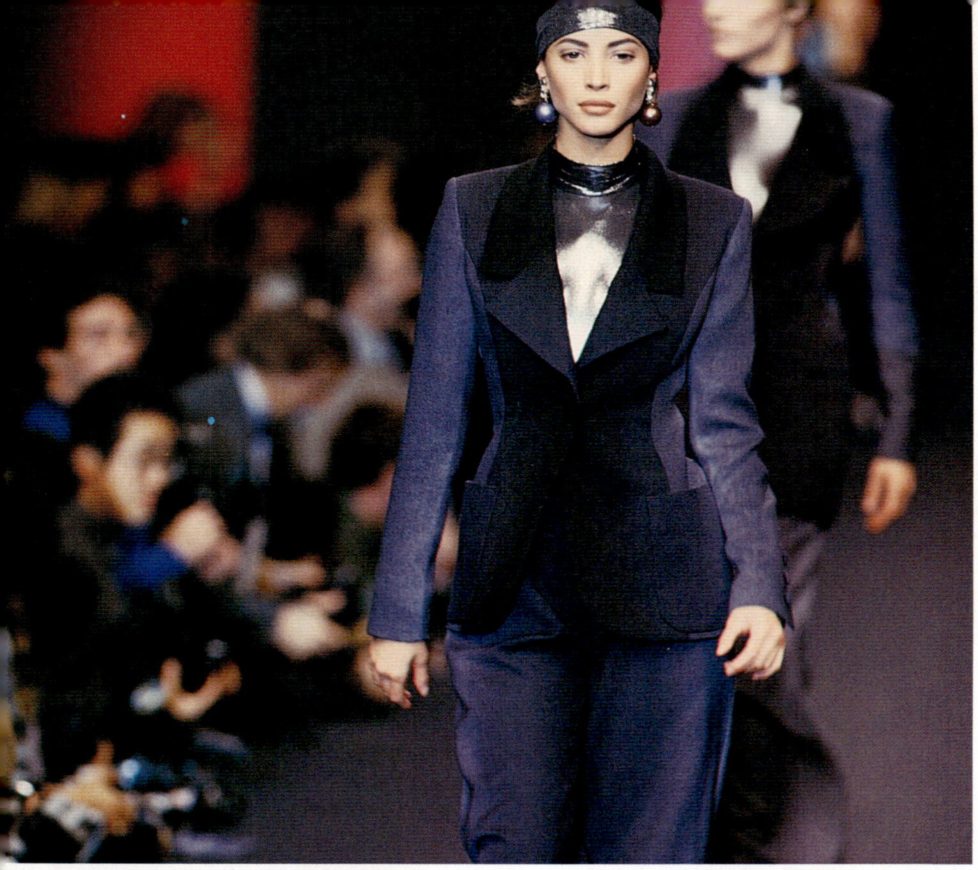
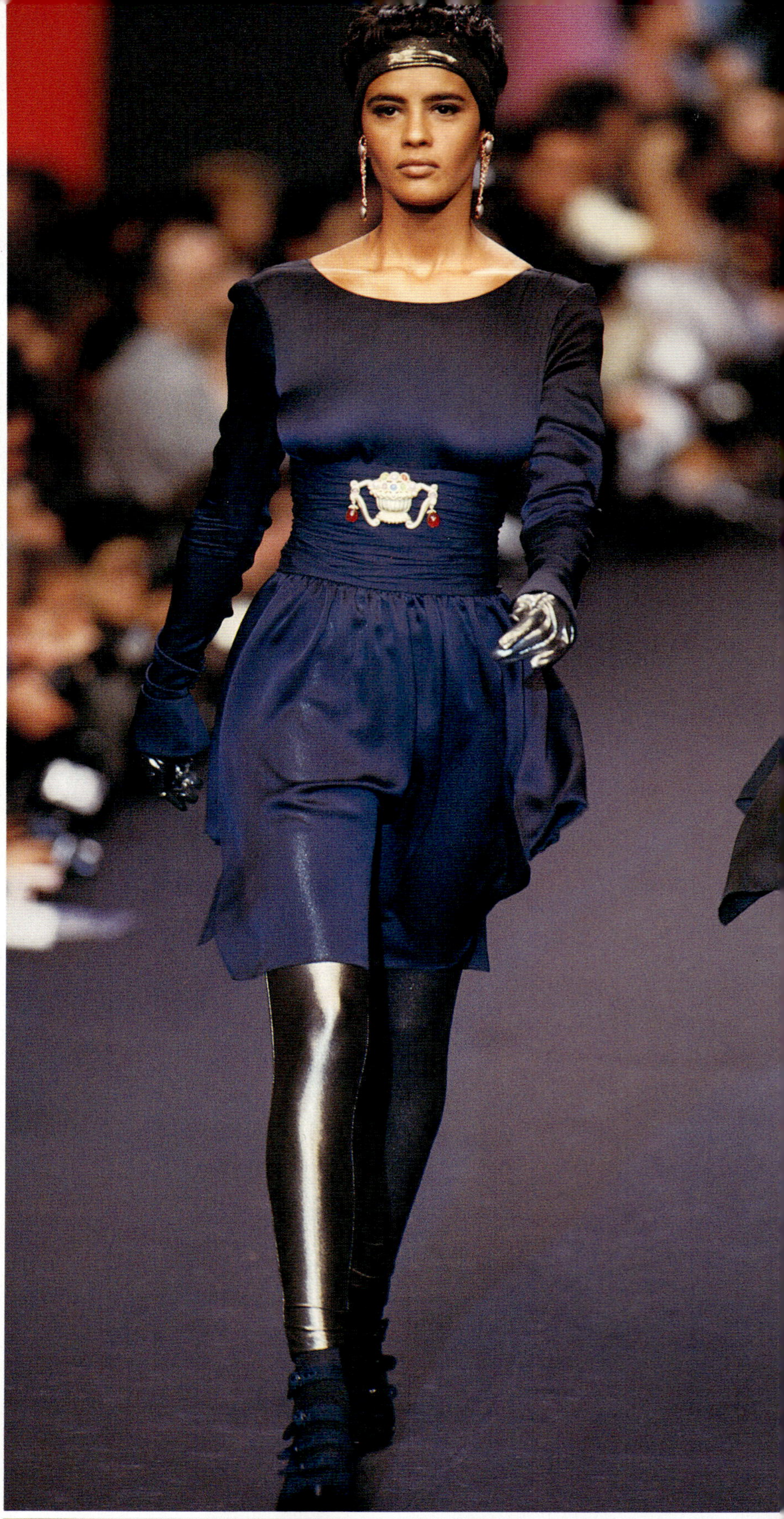
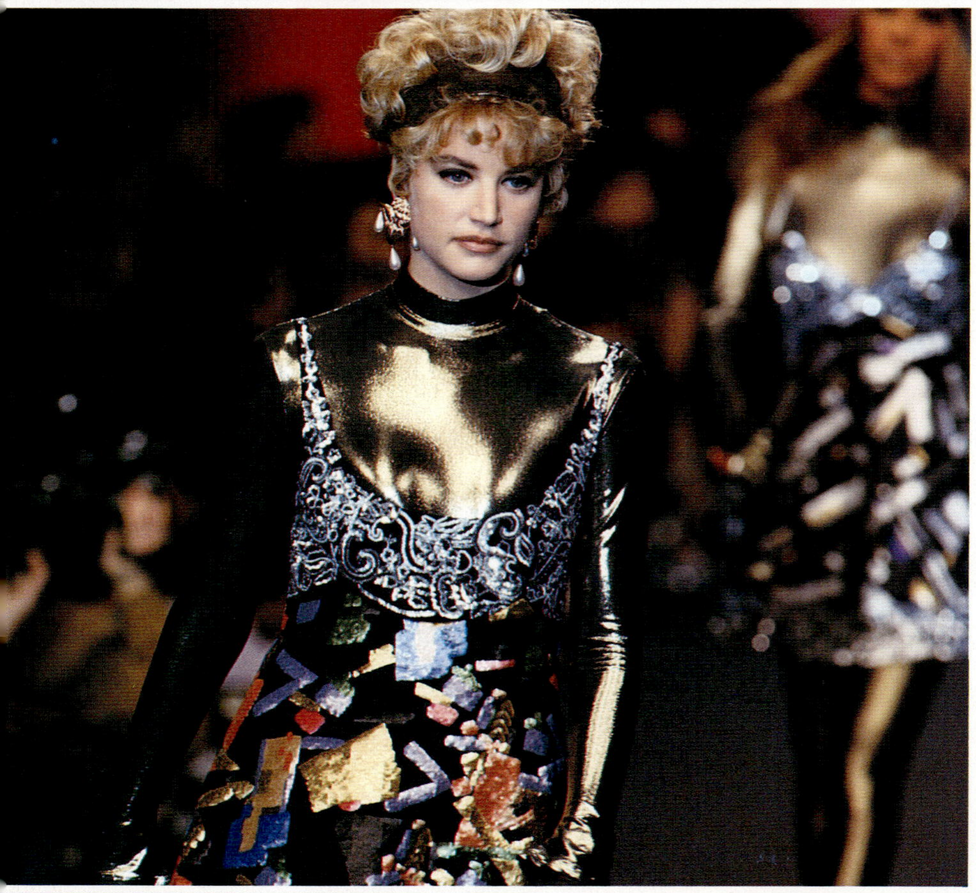
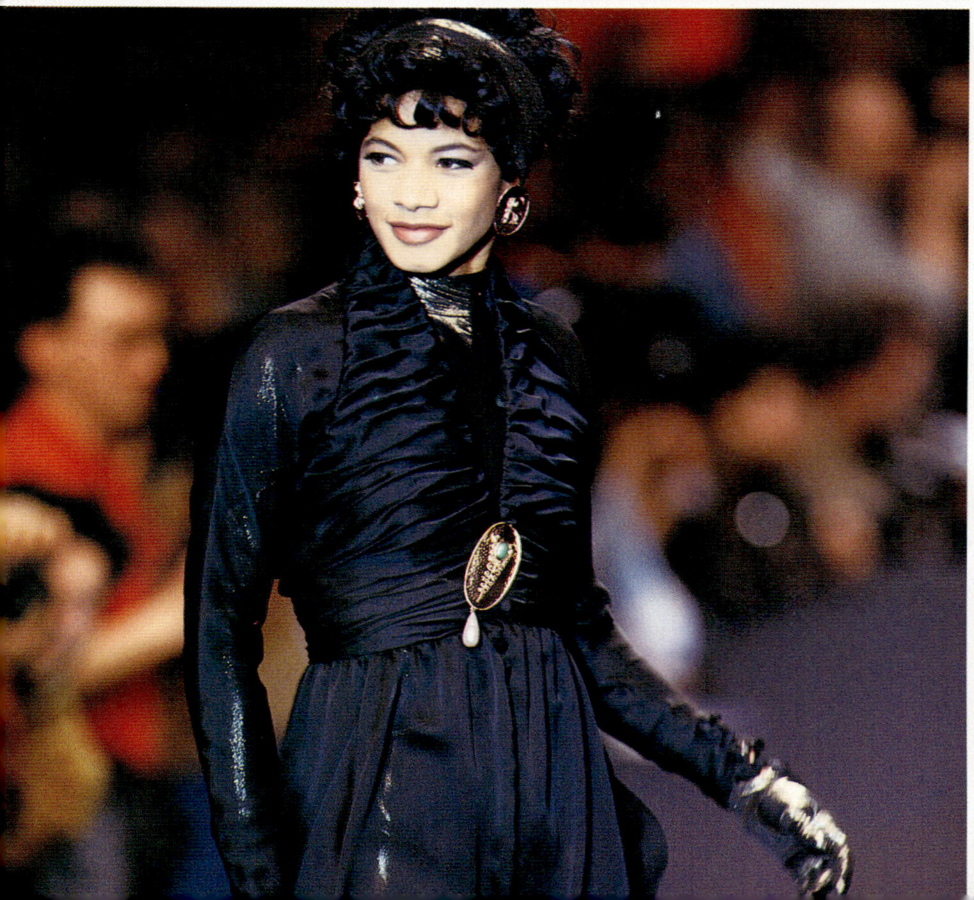
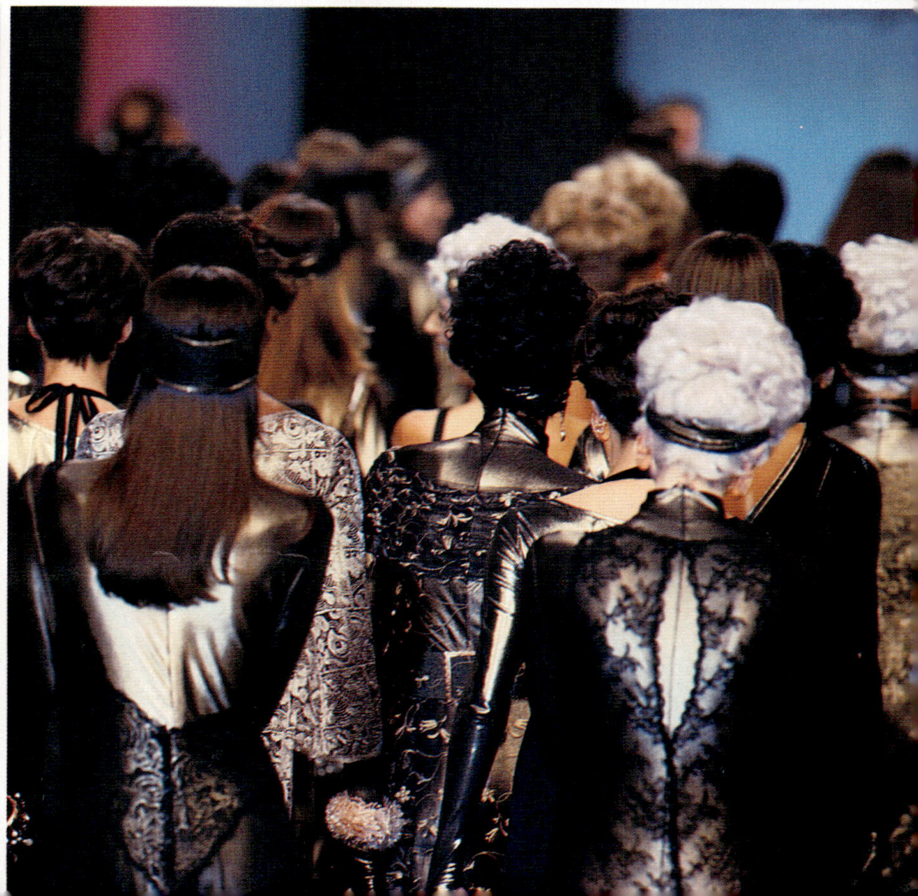

KARL LAGERFELD

141

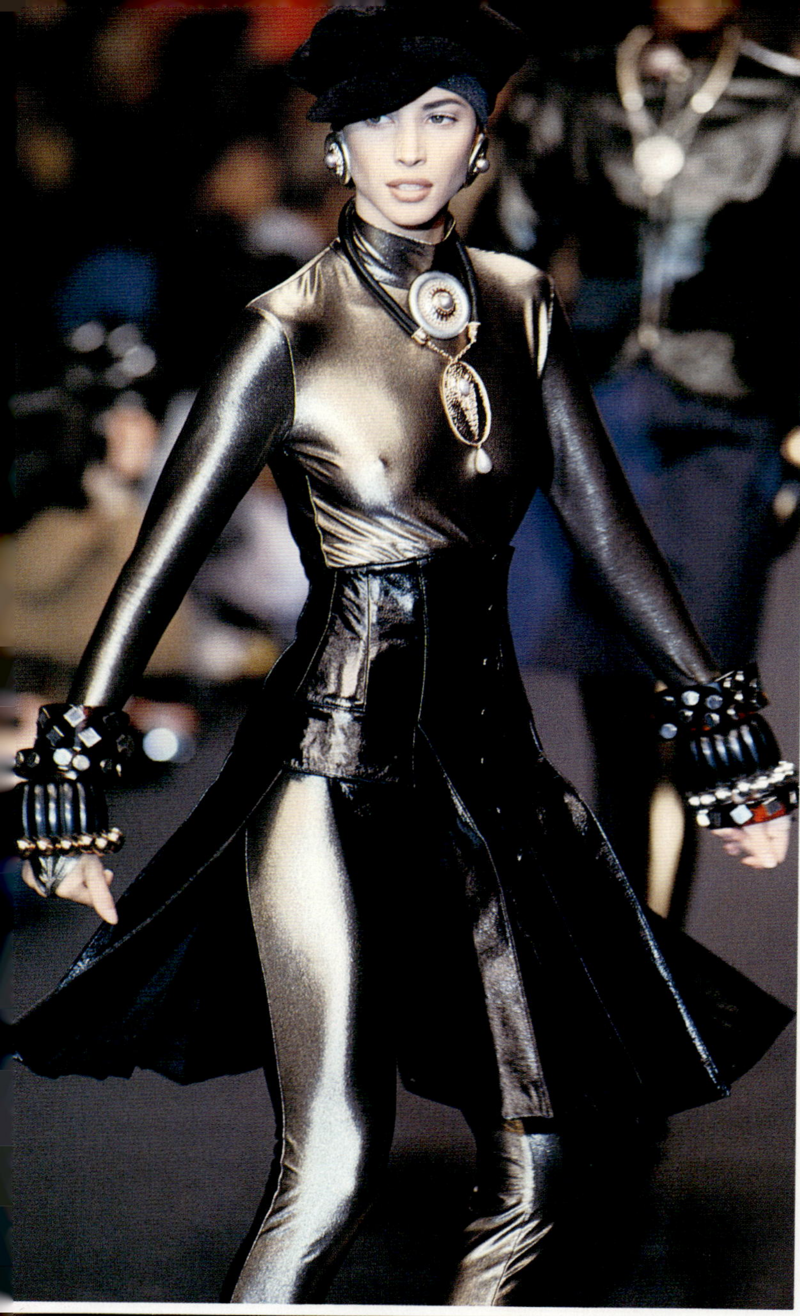
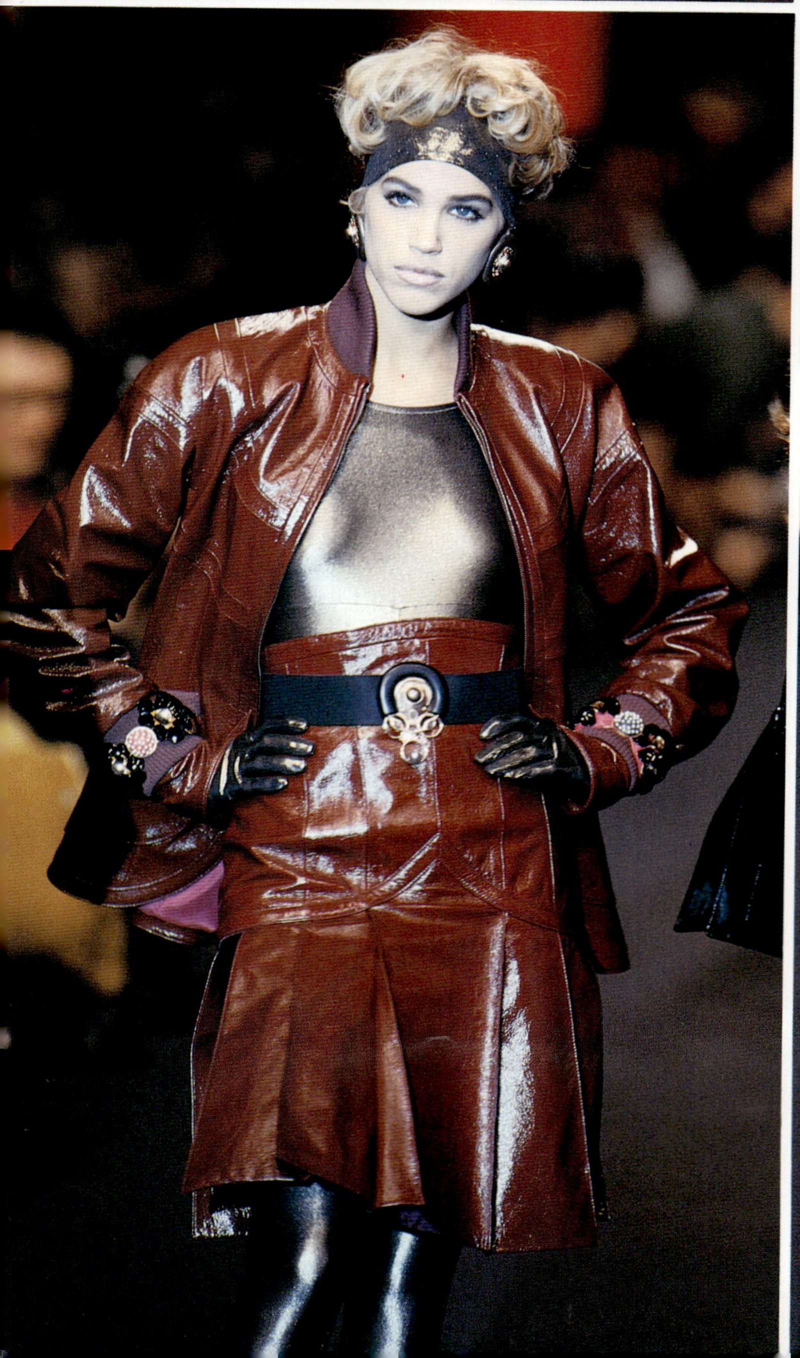
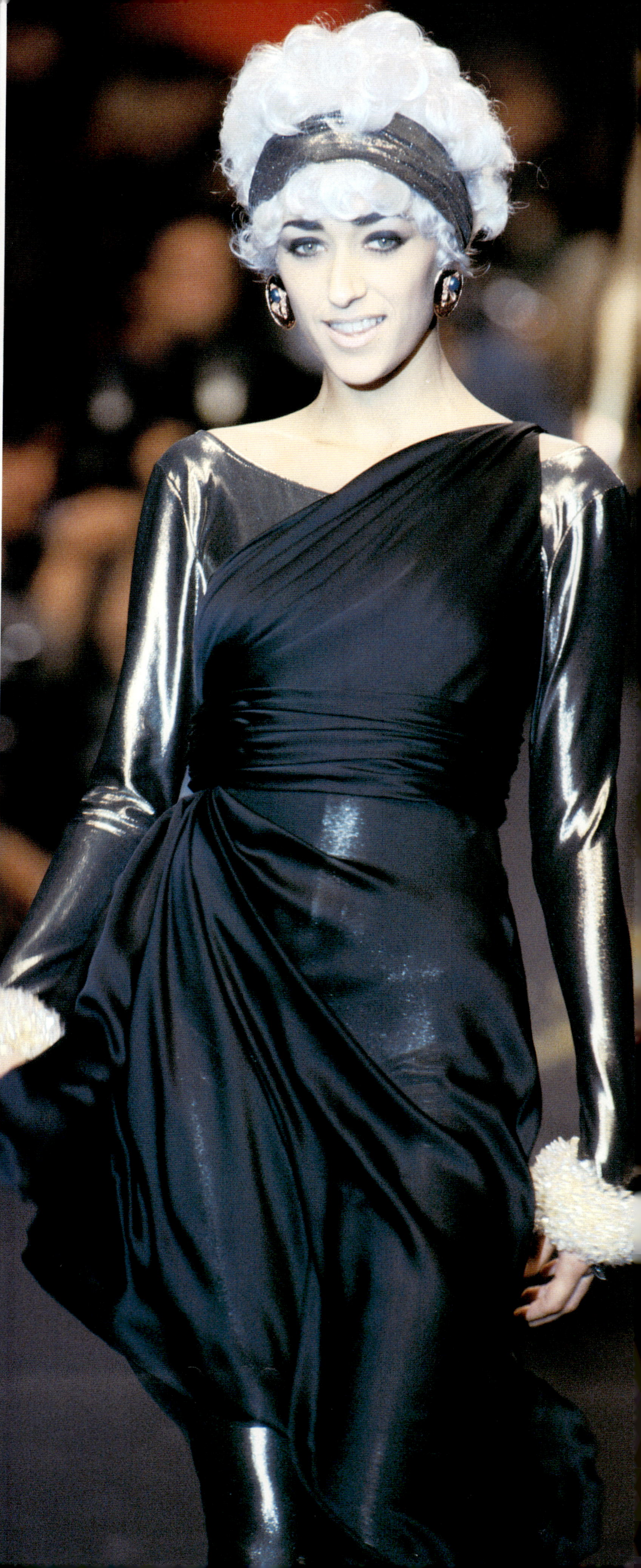

KARL LAGERFELD

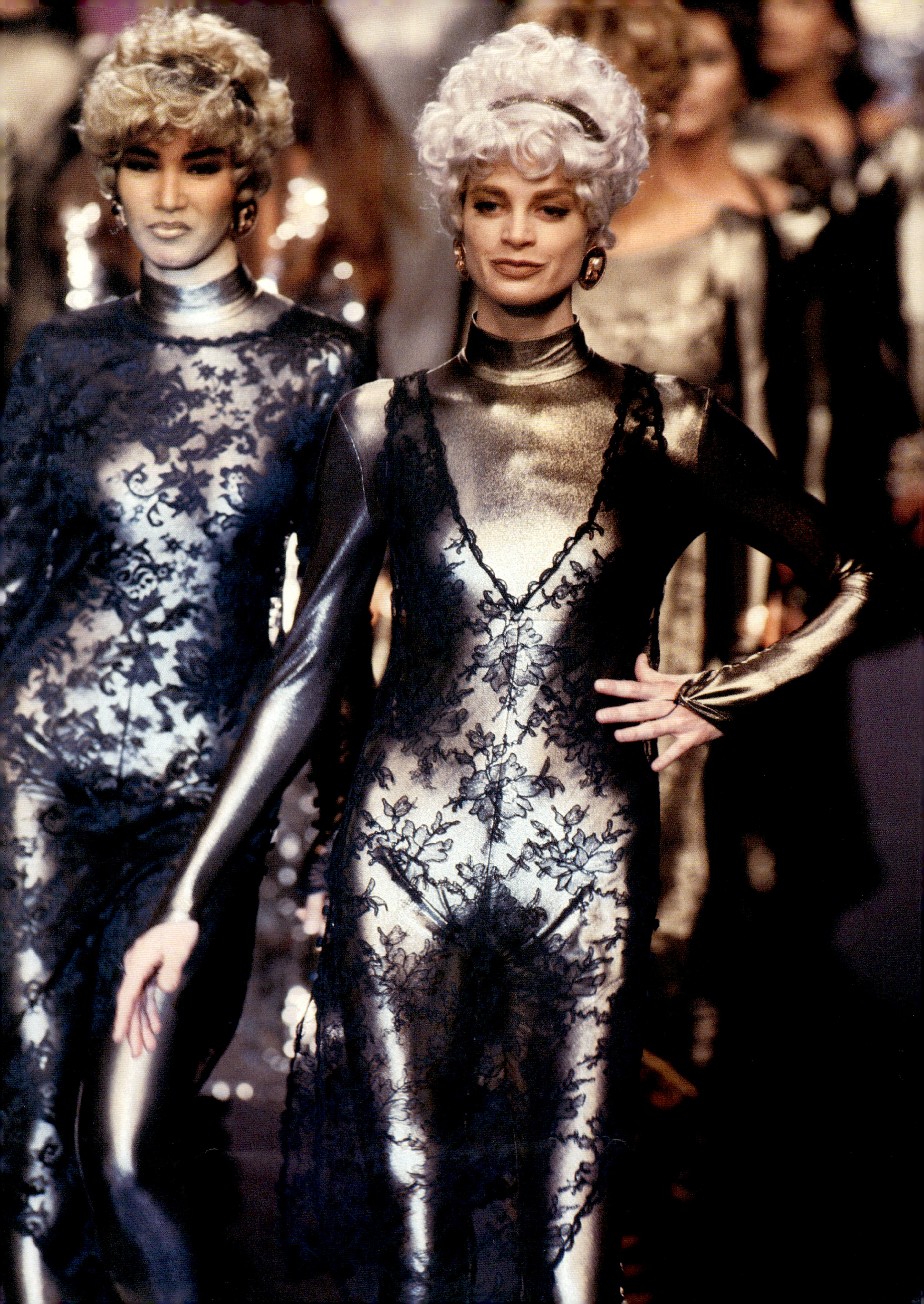

HANAE MORI

PIERRE BALMAIN

'91-'92 AUTUMN & WINTER

PREÎ-Á-PORTER COLLECTIONS

GIVENCHY

EMANUEL UNGARO

CHANEL

'91-'92
AUTUMN & WINTER
PRÊT-Á-PORTER
COLLECTIONS

GIVENCHY

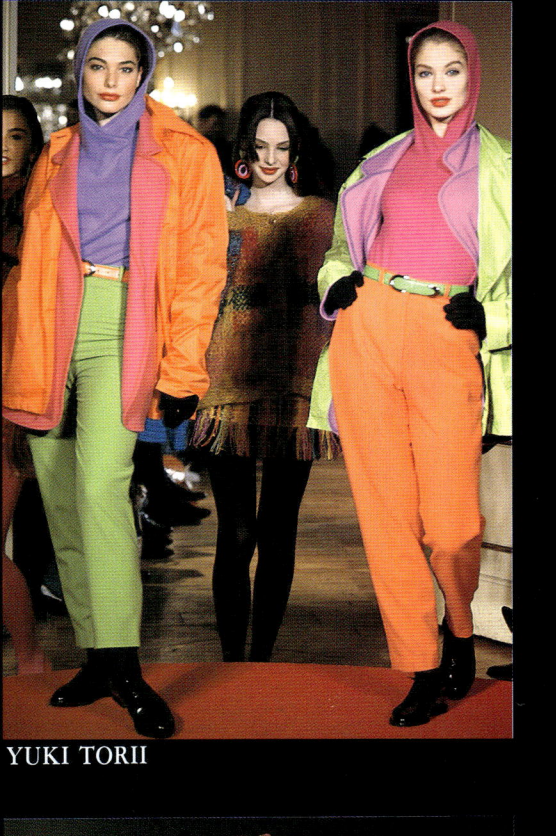

YUKI TORII

GIVENCHY

JUNKO SHIMADA

GIVENCHY

JUNKO SHIMADA

SYBILLA

YUKI TORII

SONIA RYKIEL

GIVENCHY

ENRICO COVERI

DANIEL HECHTER

'91-'92 AUTUMN & WINTER PRET-Á-PORTER COLLECTIONS

ANGELO TARLAZZI

SONIA RYKIEL

JUNKO KOSHINO

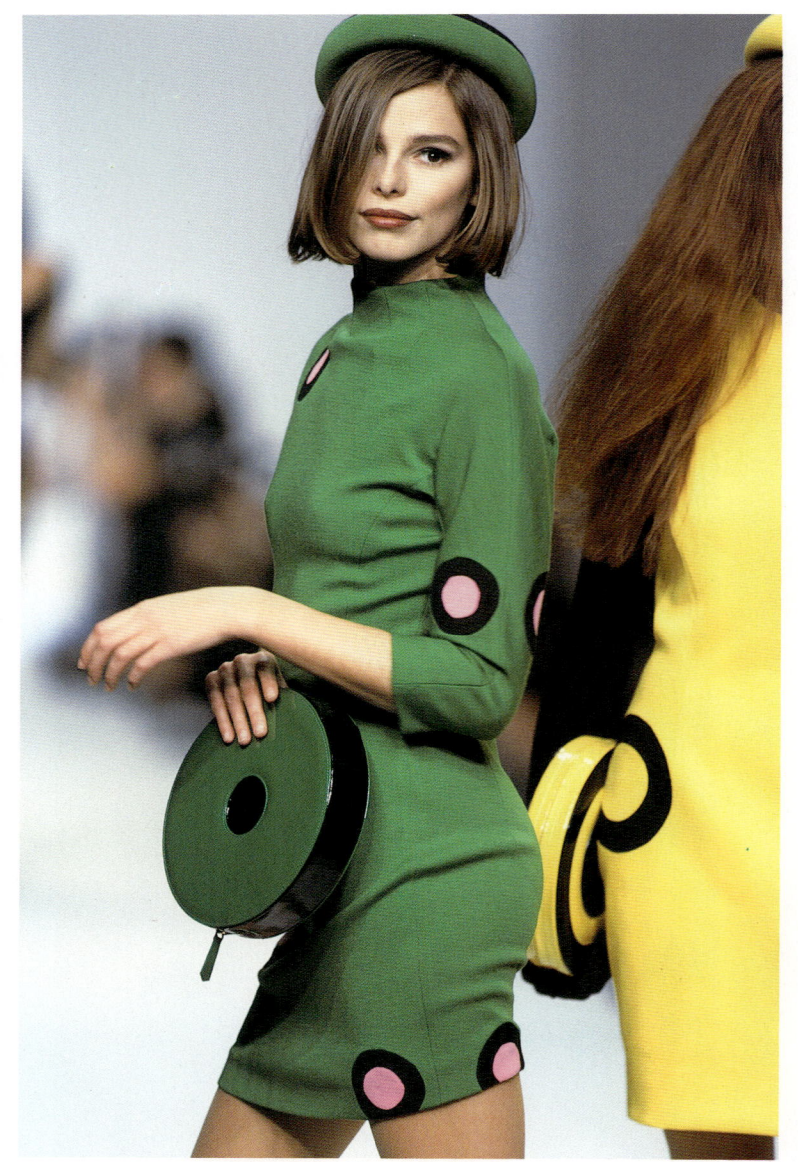

JUNKO KOSHINO

CHRISTIAN LACROIX

クリスチャン・ラクロワ

花やジオメトリックのパターン・ミックスで、革新的なエレガンスを表現するラクロワ。モザイク風やアブストラクトなモチーフが新鮮。
Mixing flower and geometric patterns, Lacroix displayed a revolutionary elegance.
Abstract and mosaic-looking motifs were refreshing.

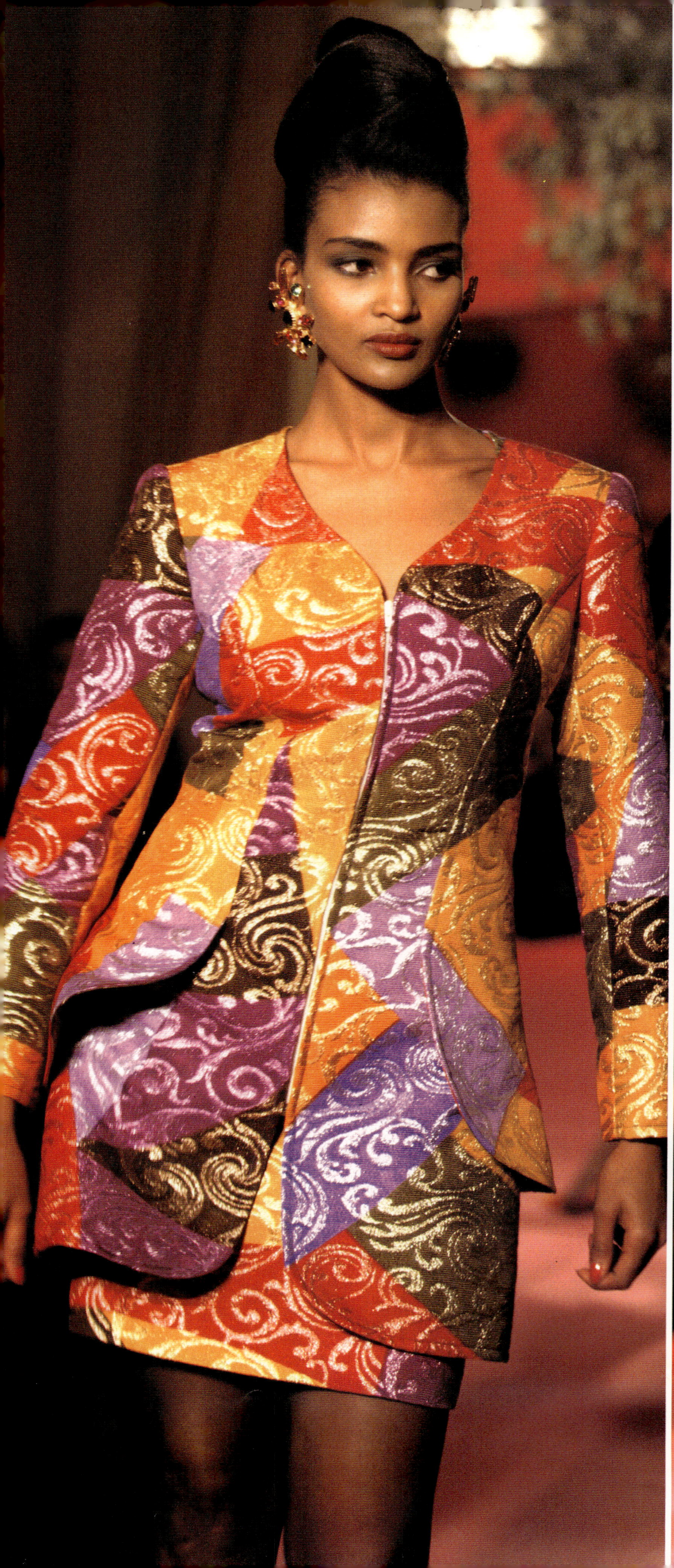
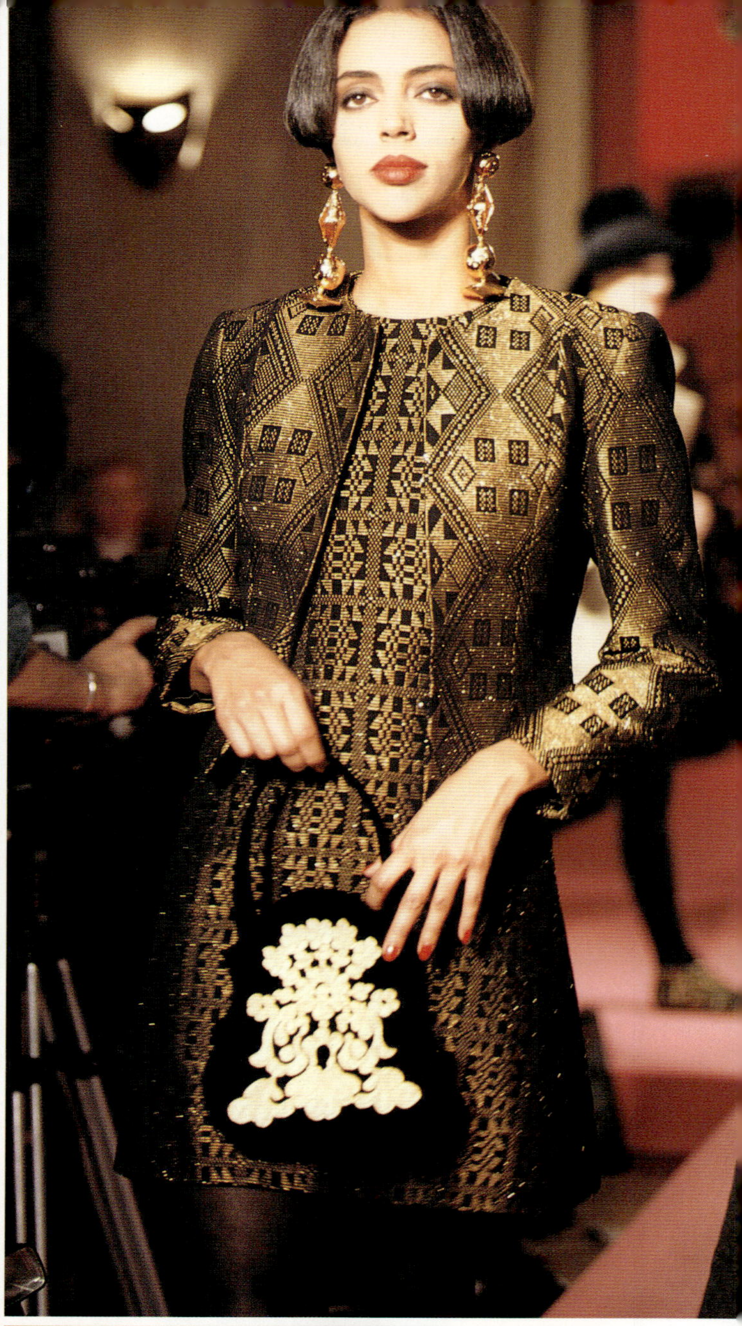
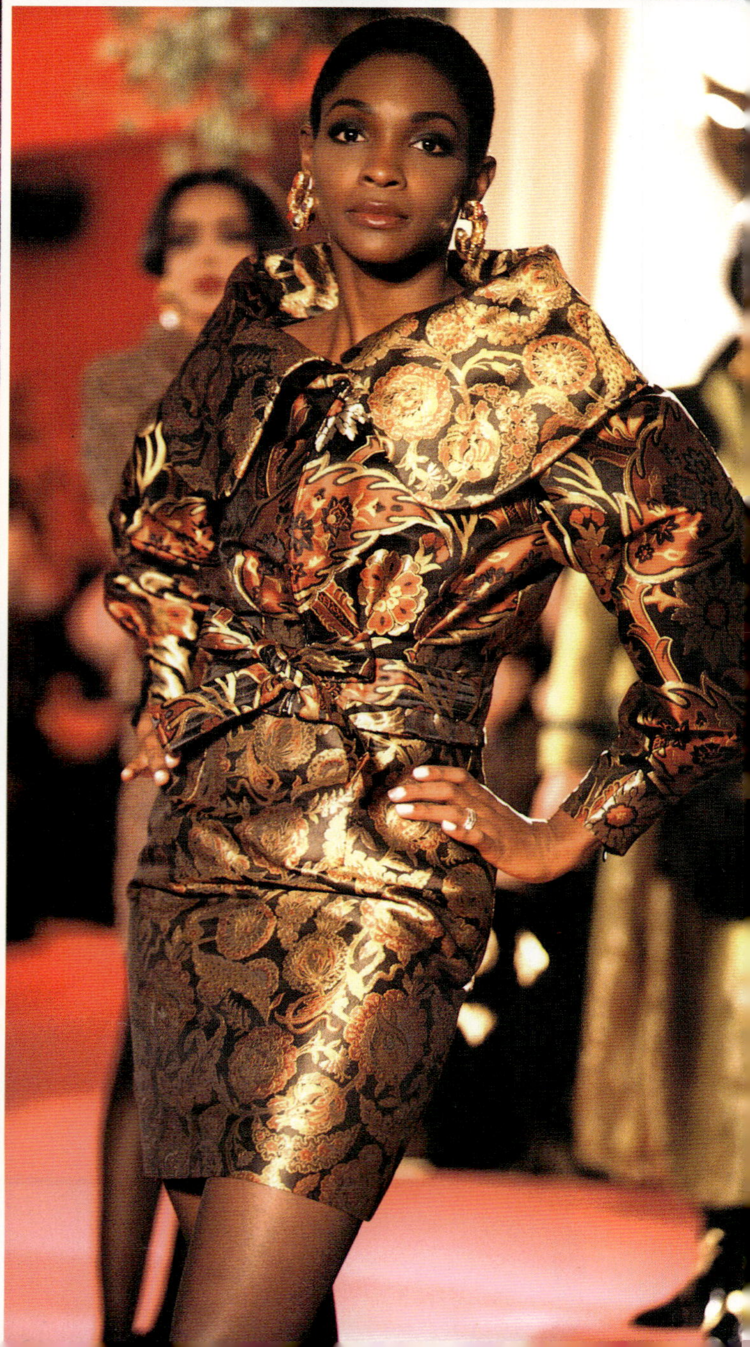

CHRISTIAN LACROIX

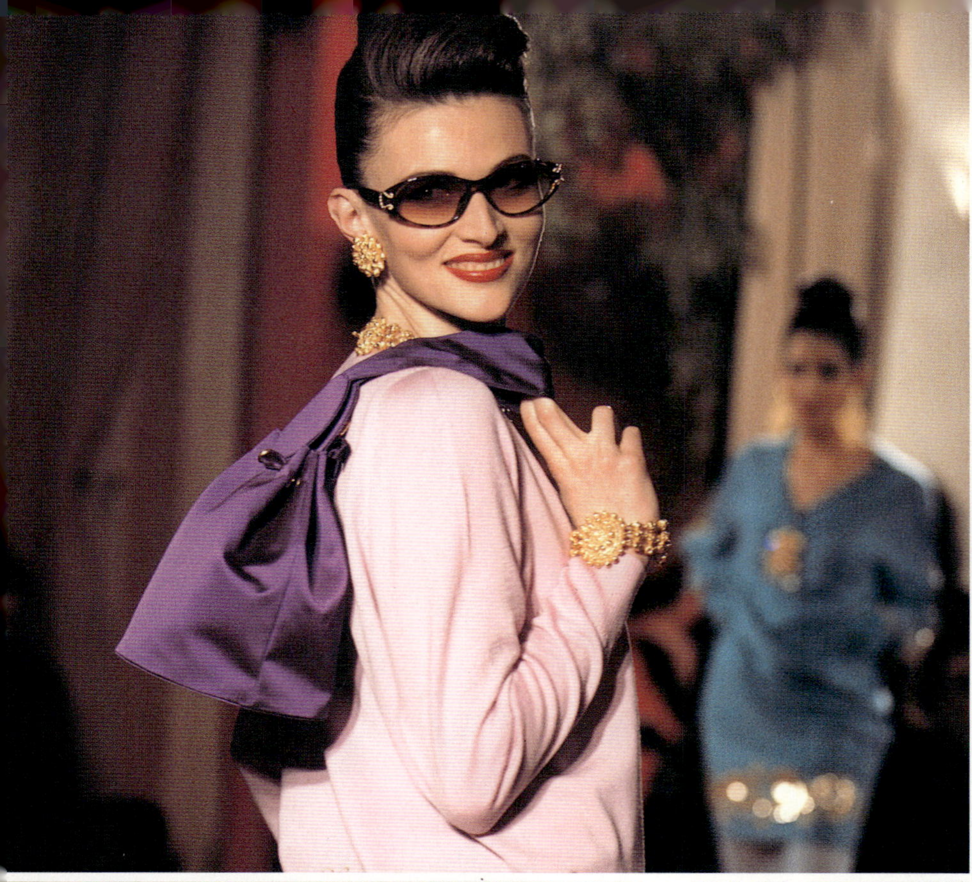
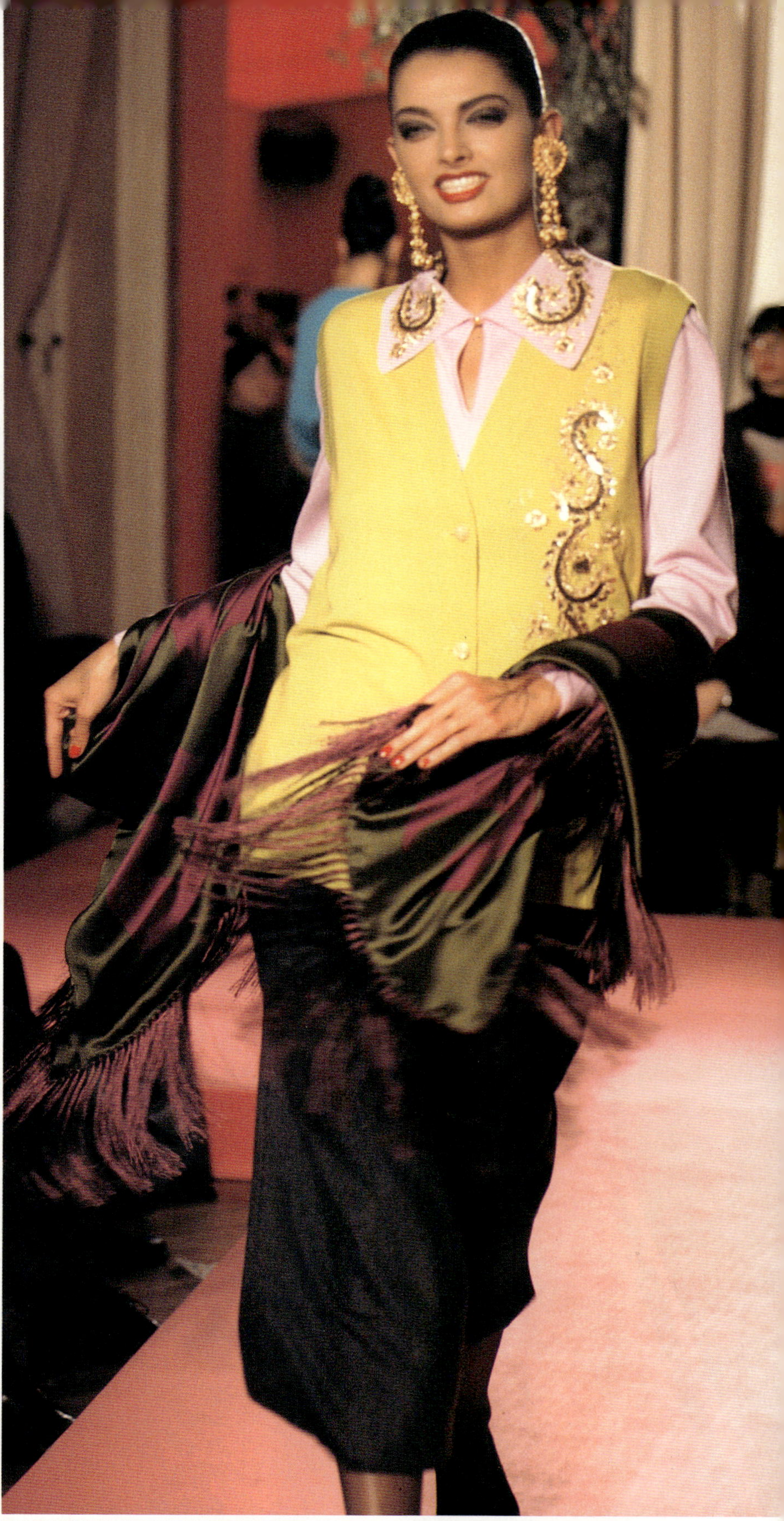
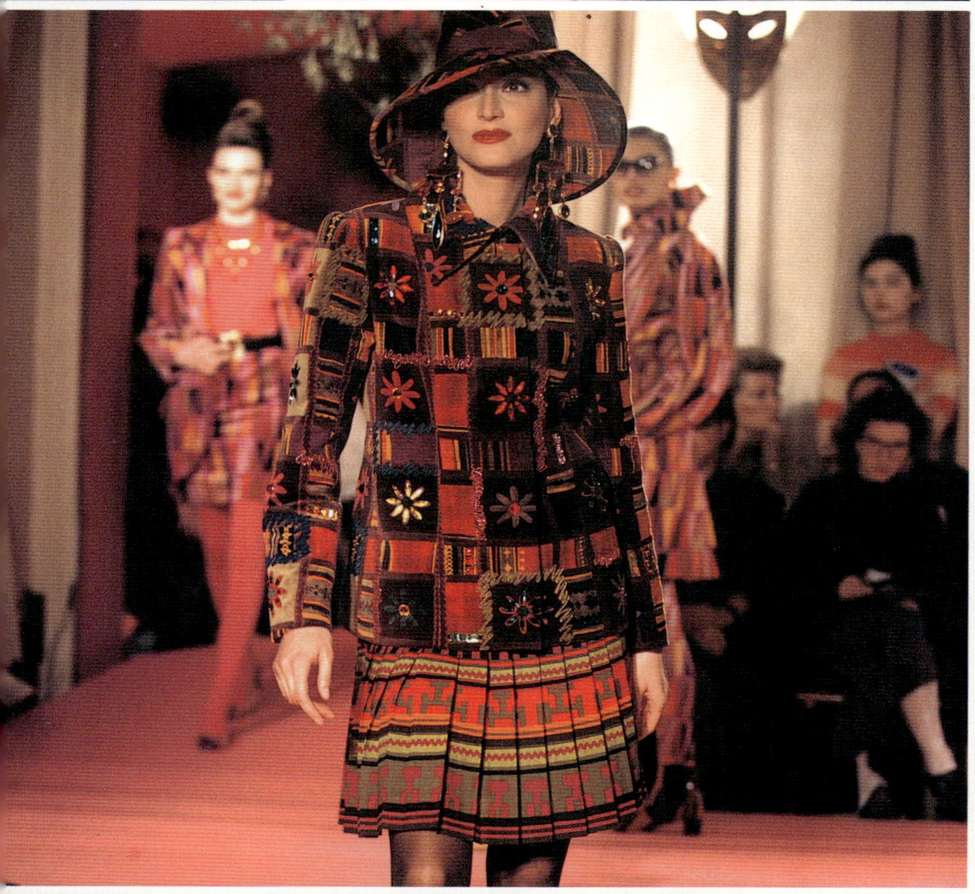
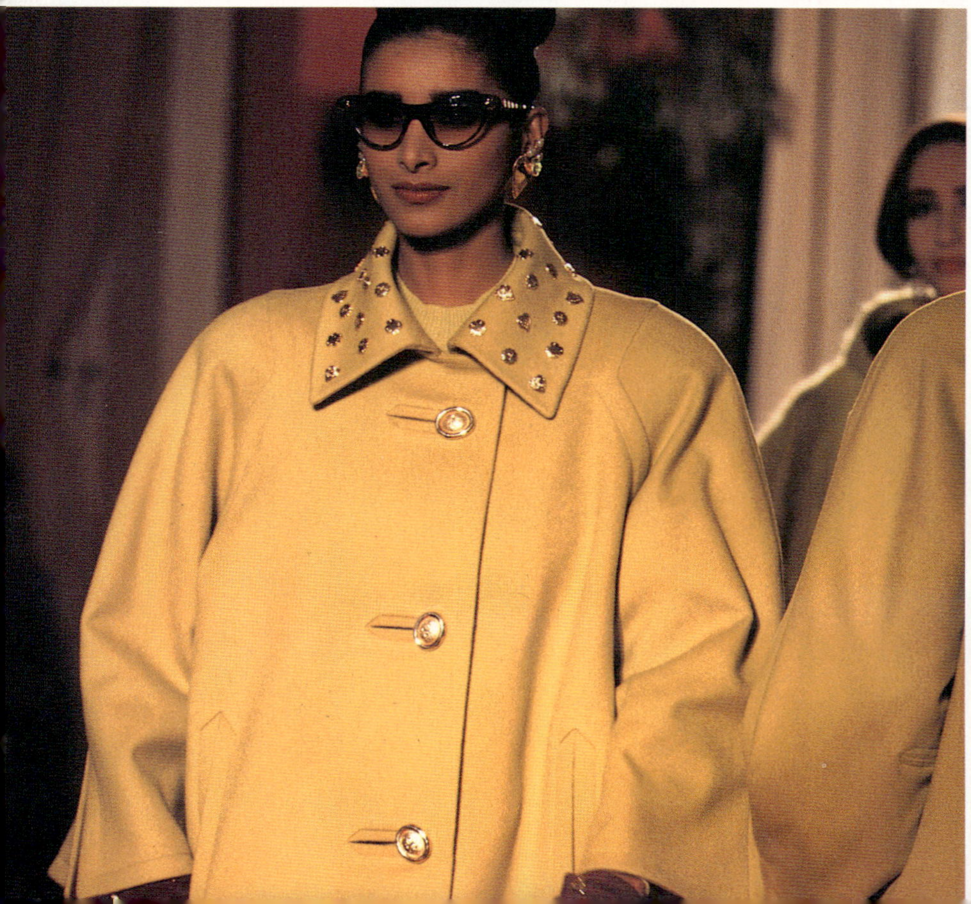
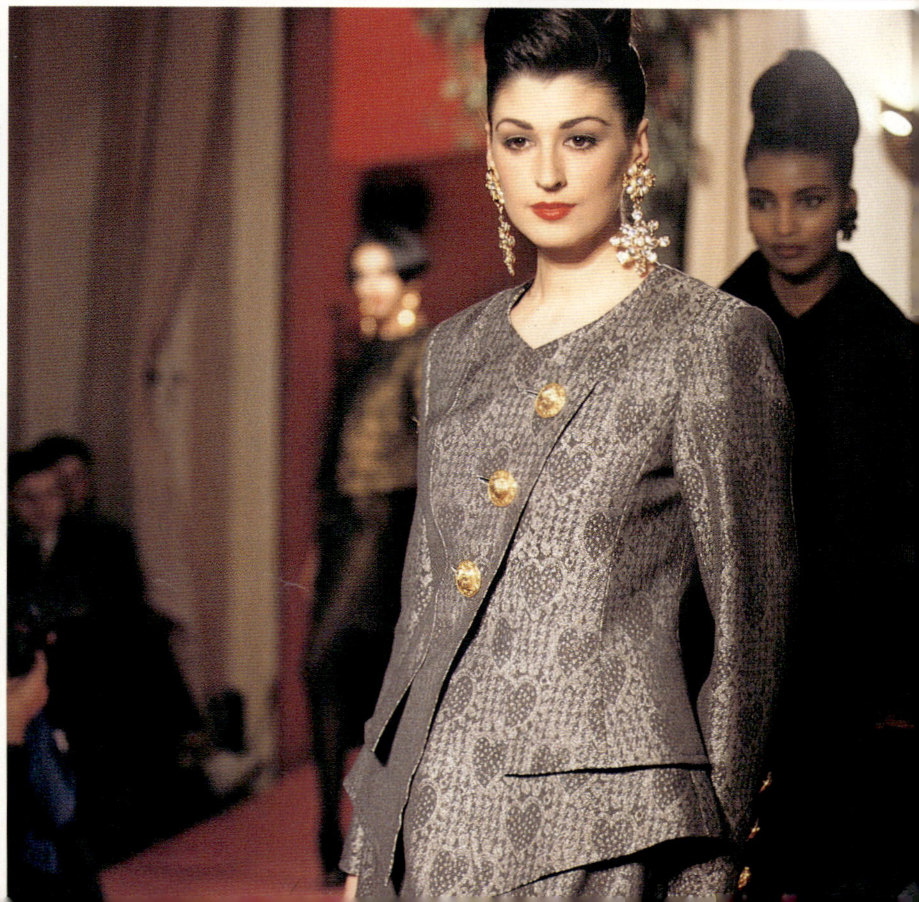

CHRISTIAN LACROIX

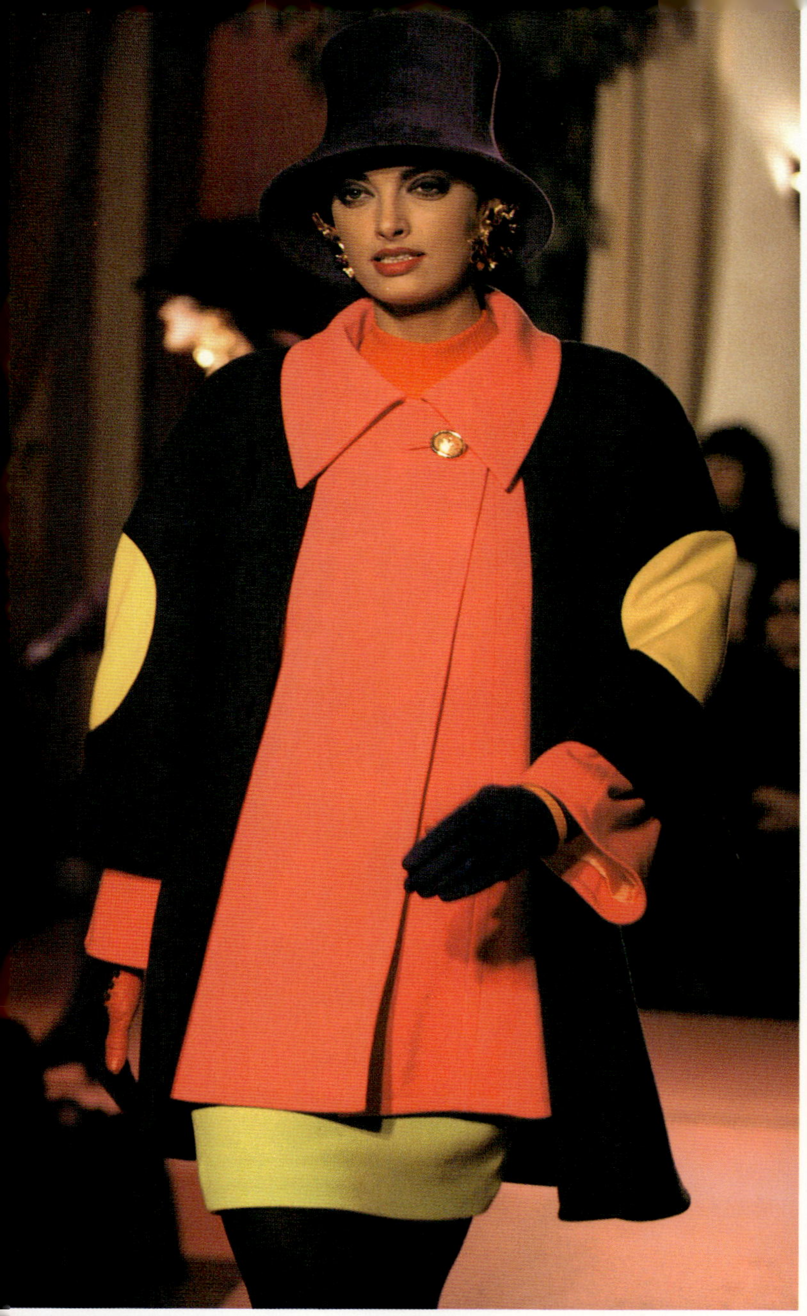
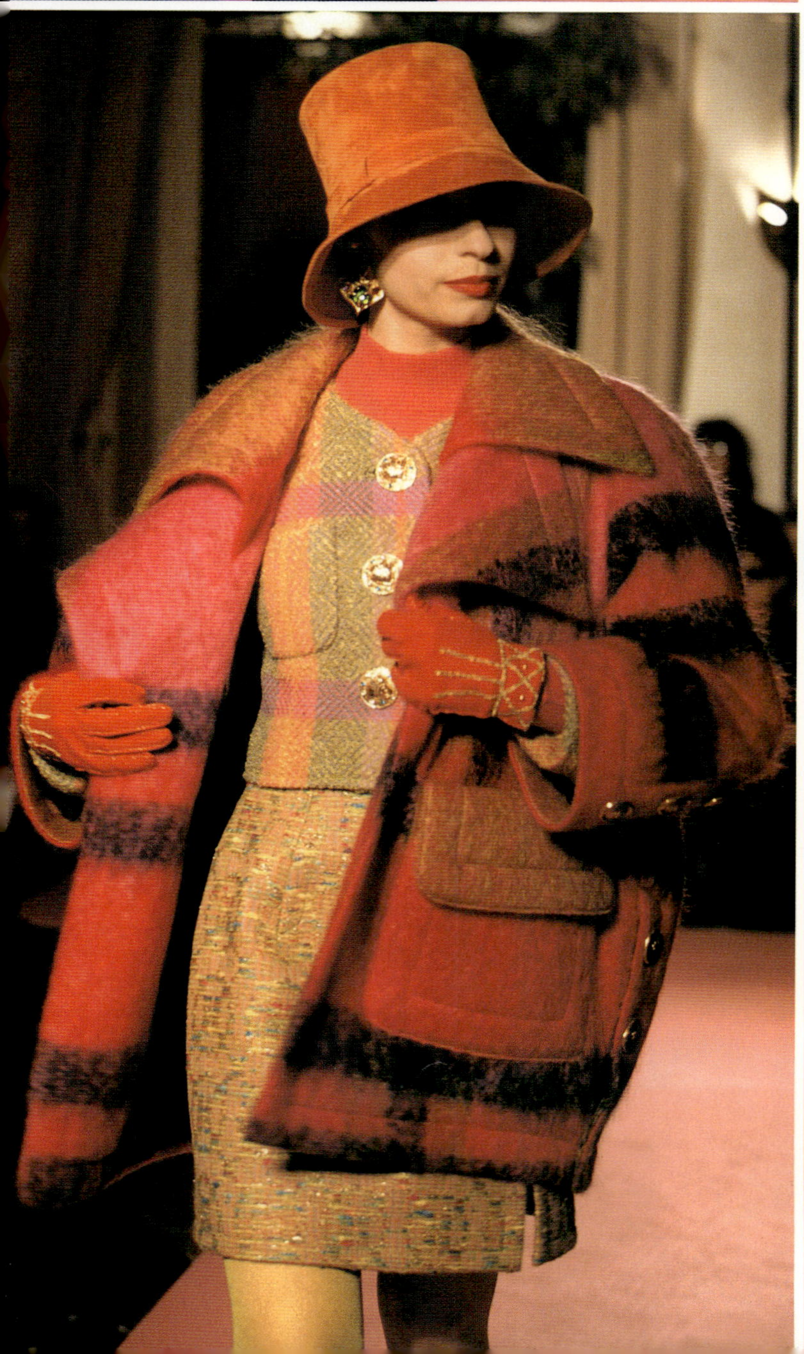
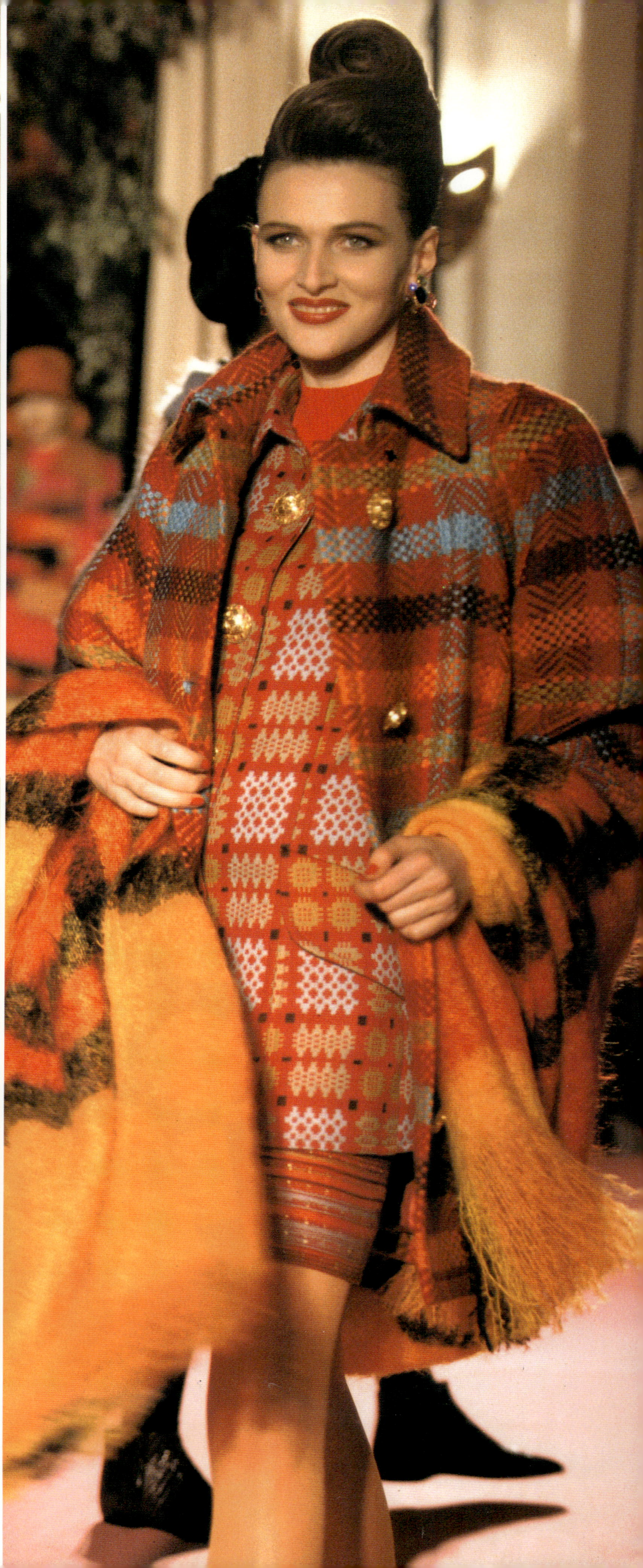

CHRISTIAN LACROIX

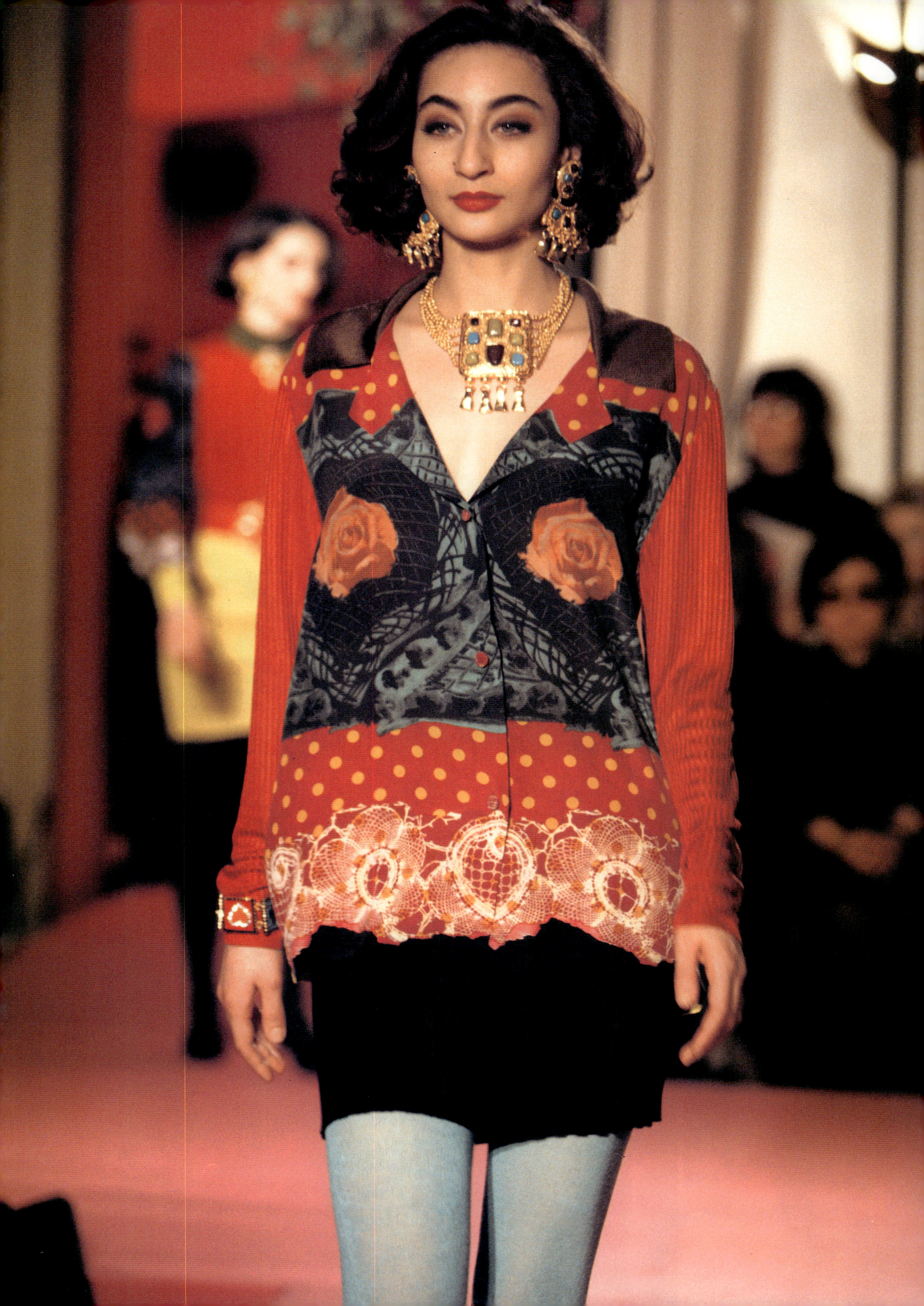

PARIS-14

ISSEY MIYAKE

イッセイ・ミヤケ

見事なプリーツやジップ・アクセントを駆使した、スポーティ感覚溢れる一生ならではのコレクション。四角の布を重ねたカバー・ジャケットのアイディアに拍手の渦。
A collection that could only be created by Issey, full with a sporty feel, employing an excellent accent on pleats and zips.
The idea of cover jackets with layers of square cloth met with thunderous applause.

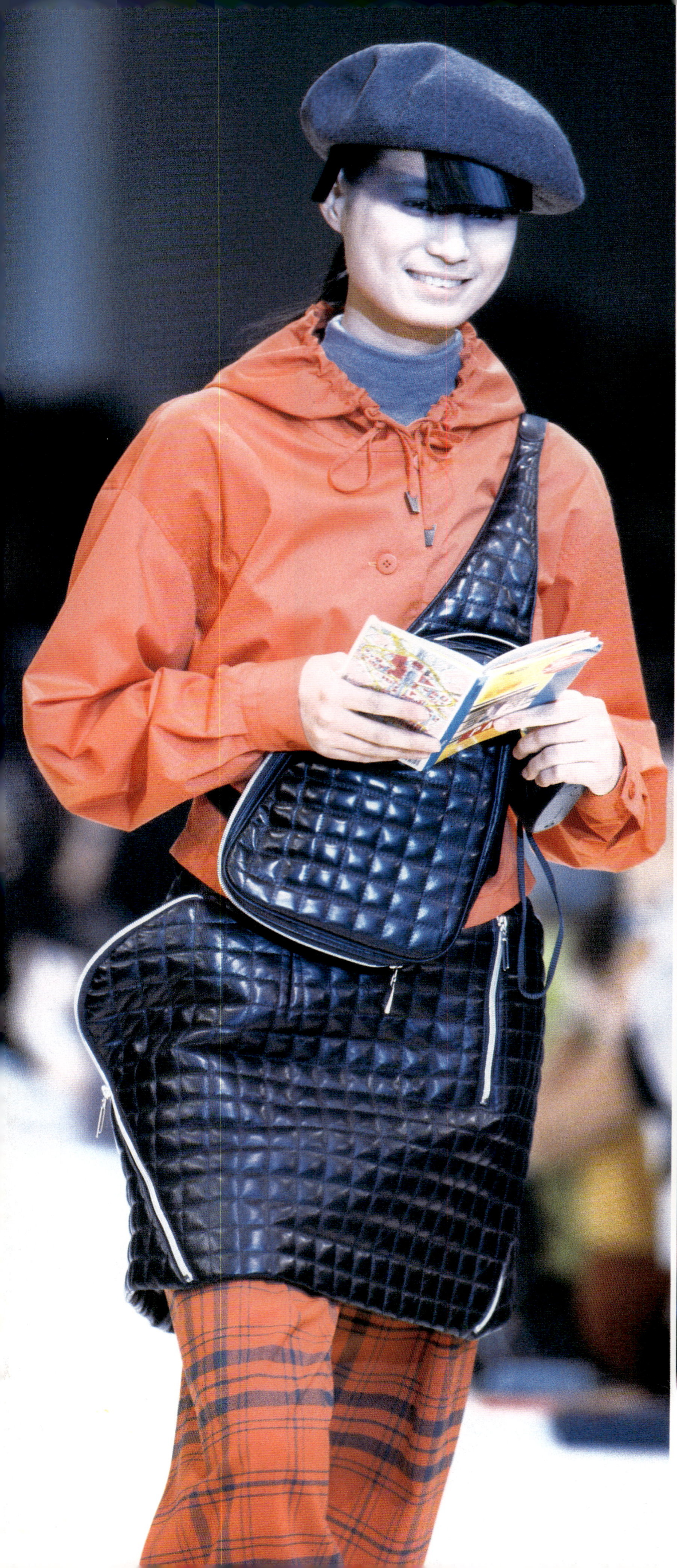
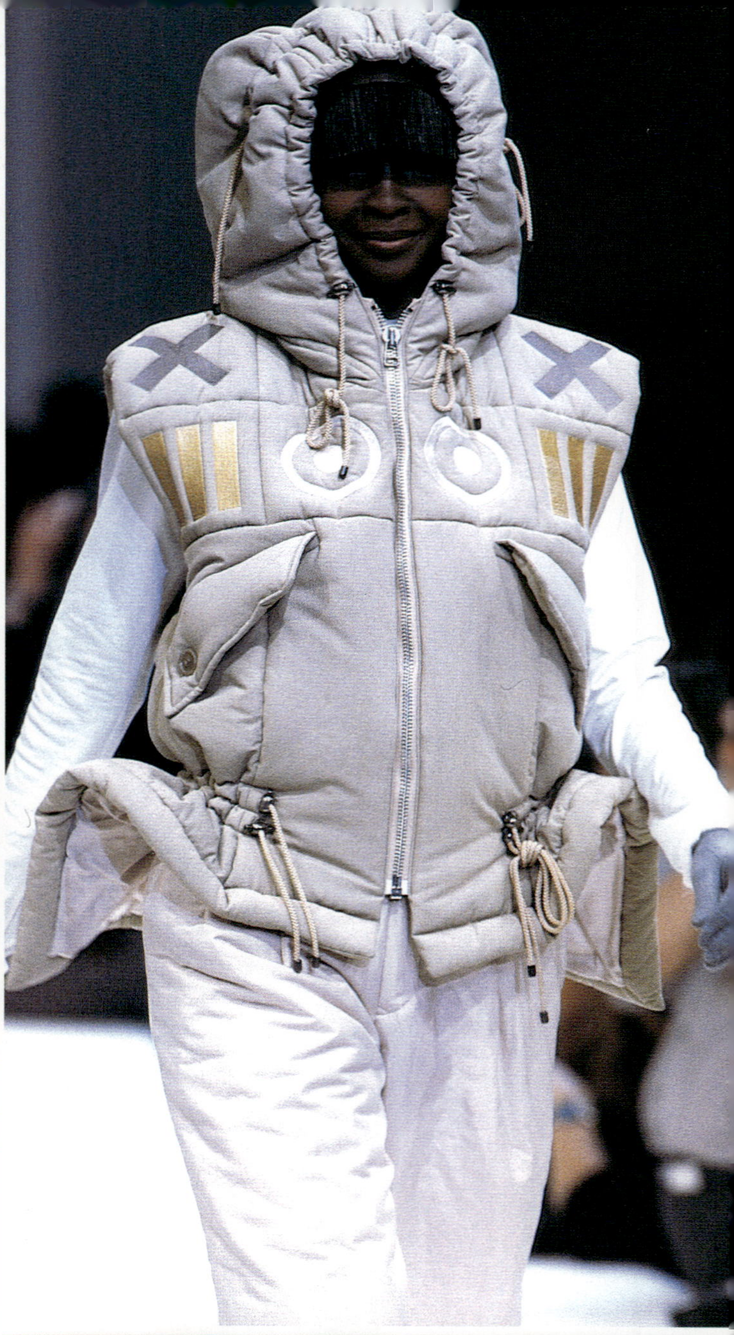
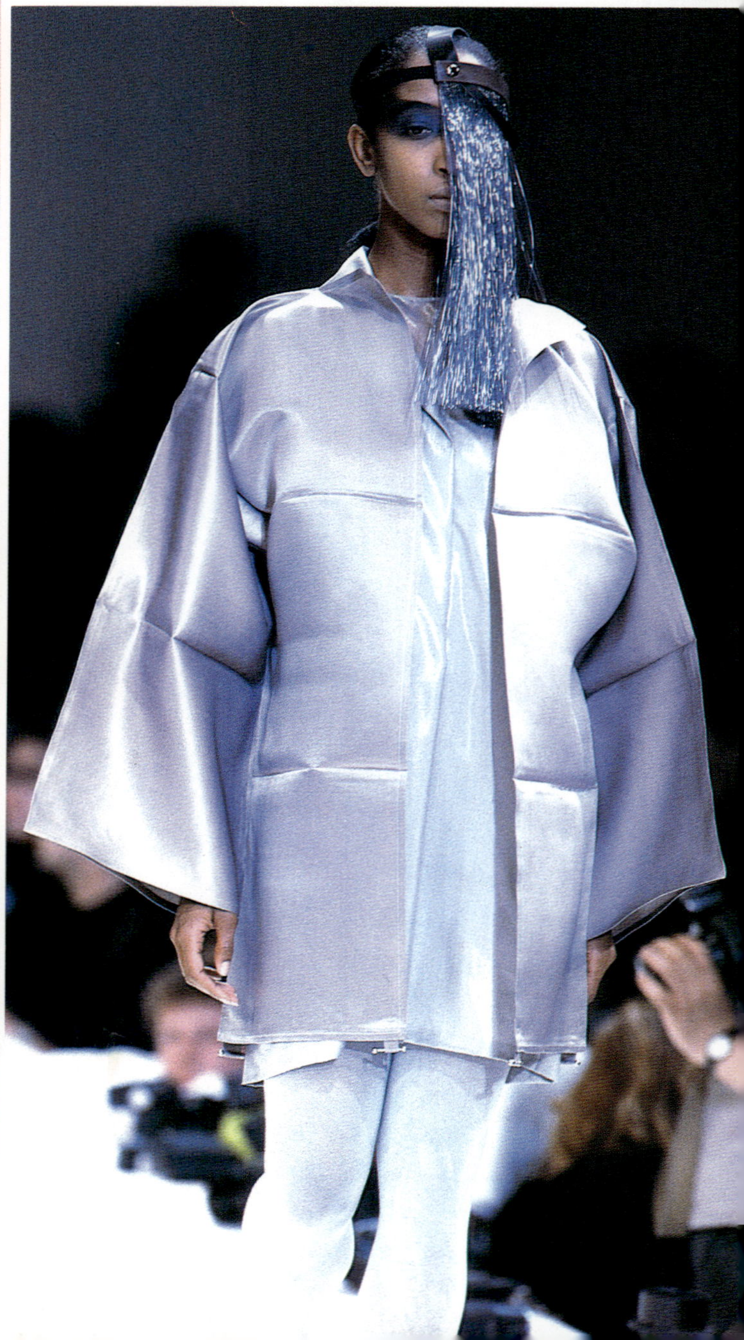

ISSEY MIYAKE

161

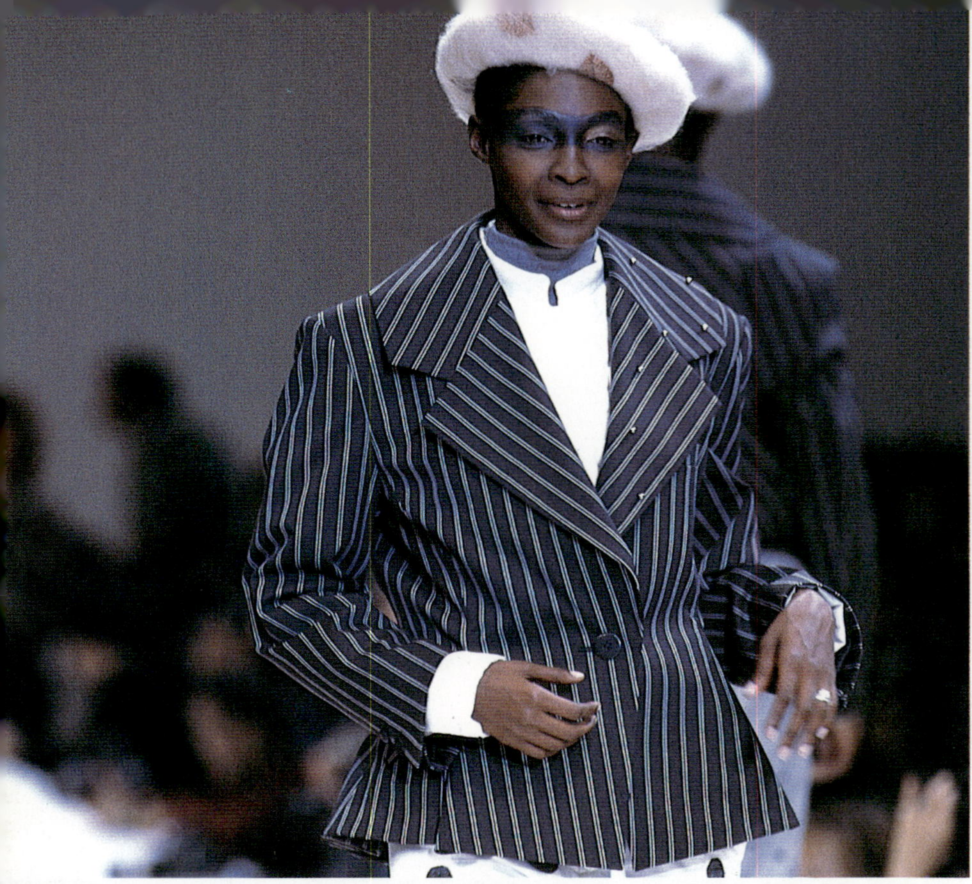
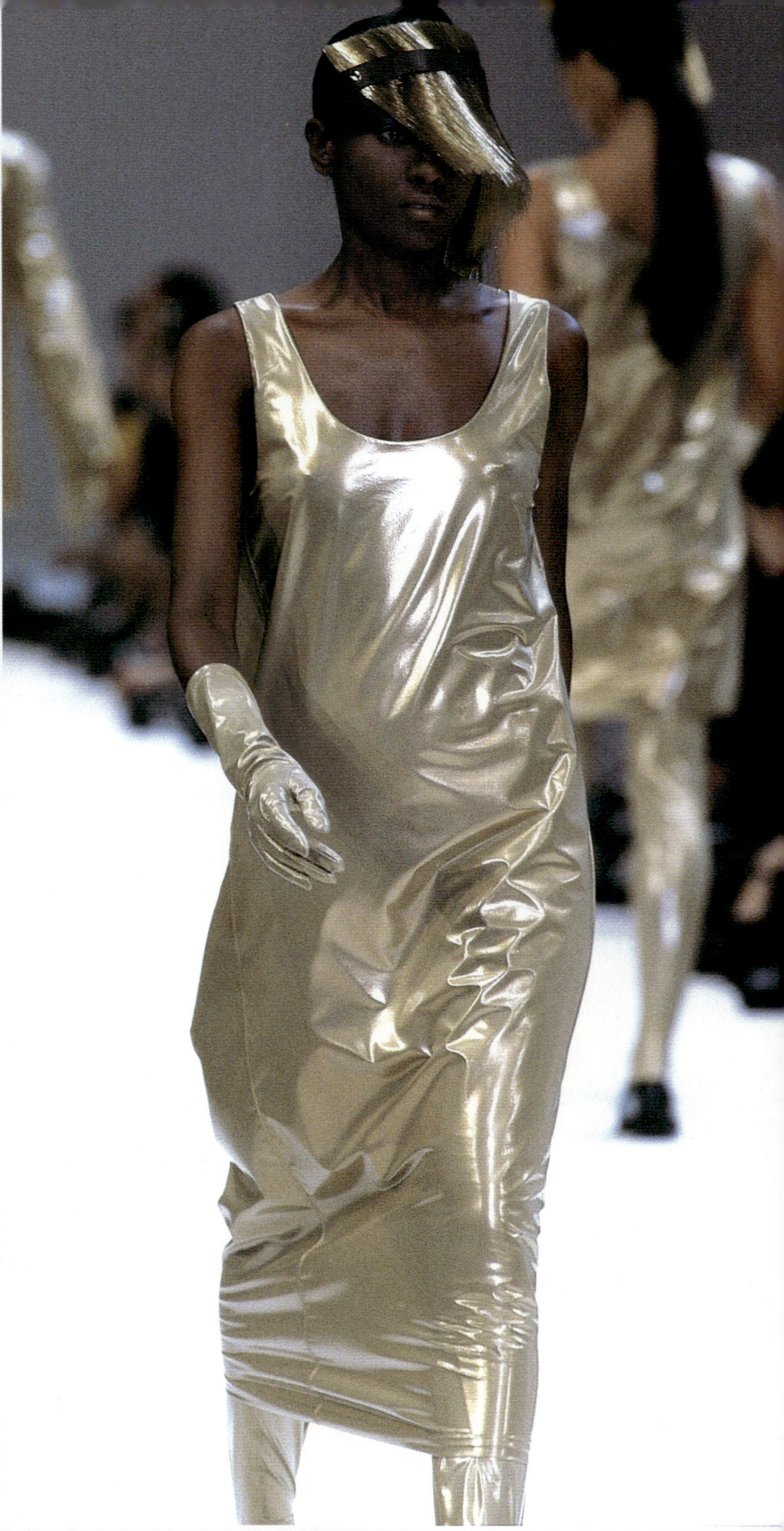
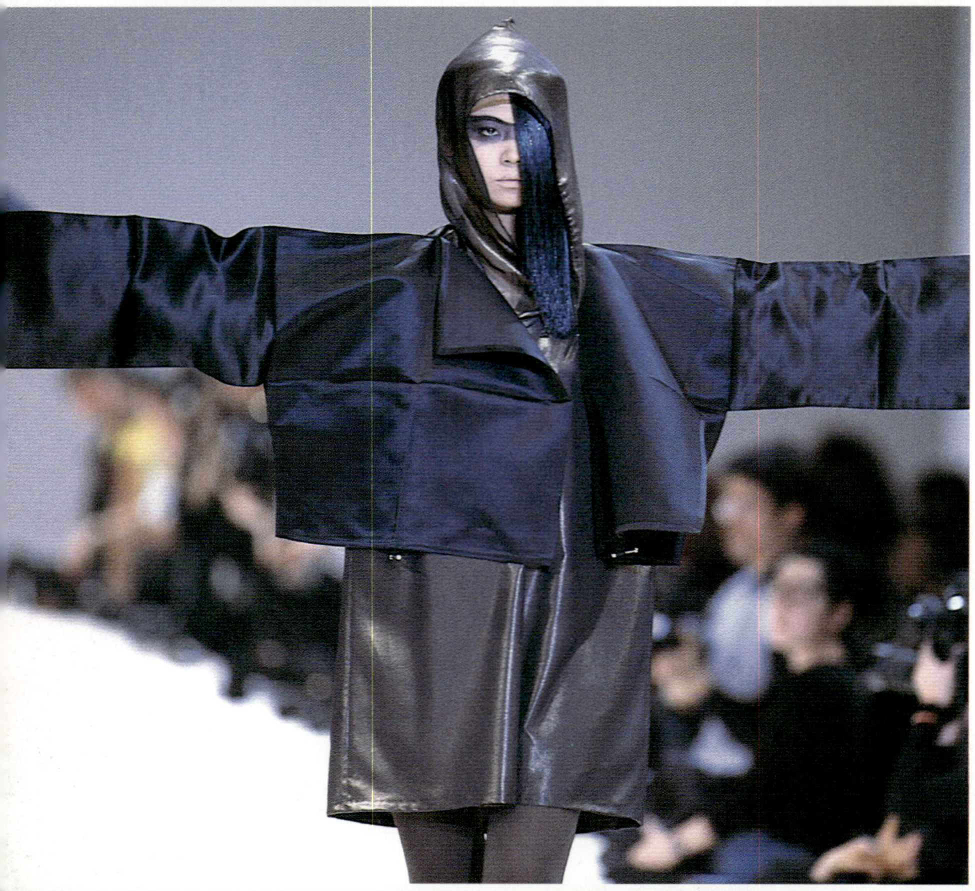
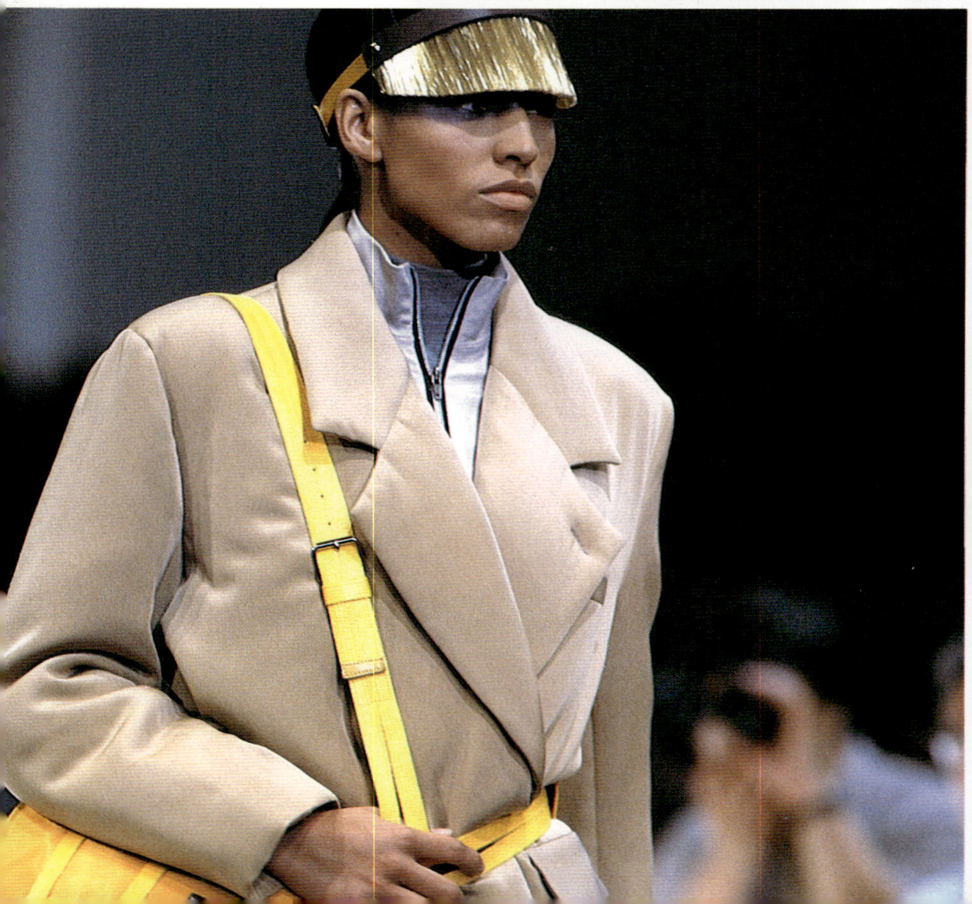
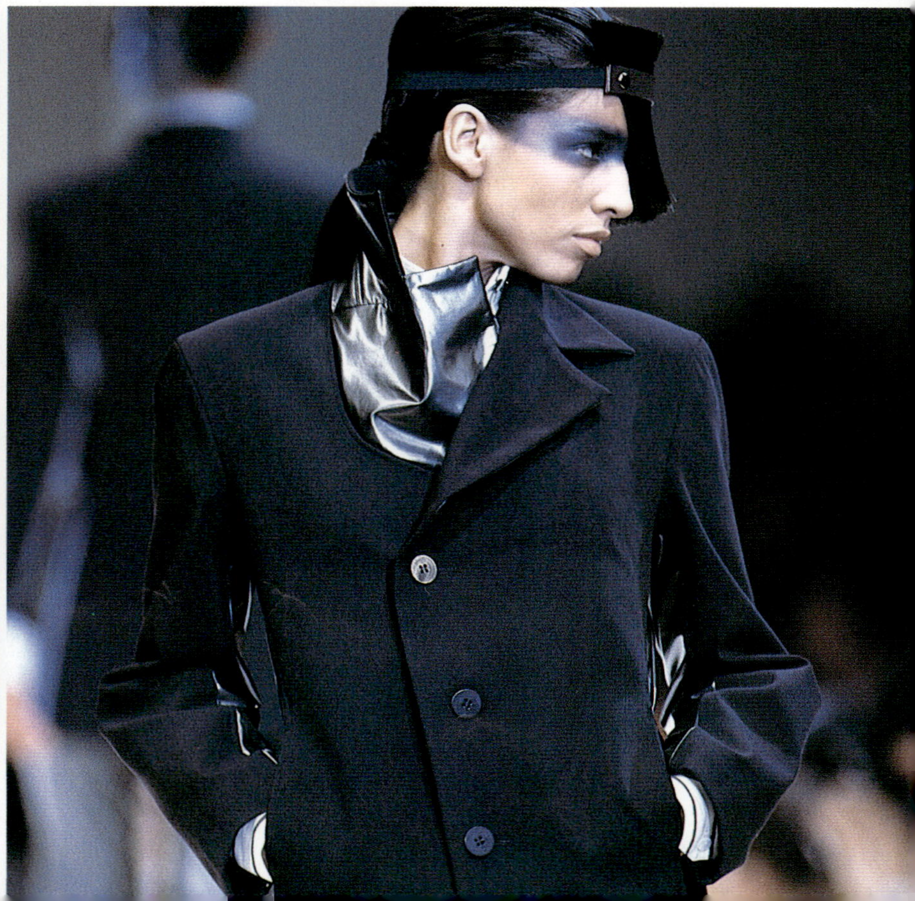

ISSEY MIYAKE

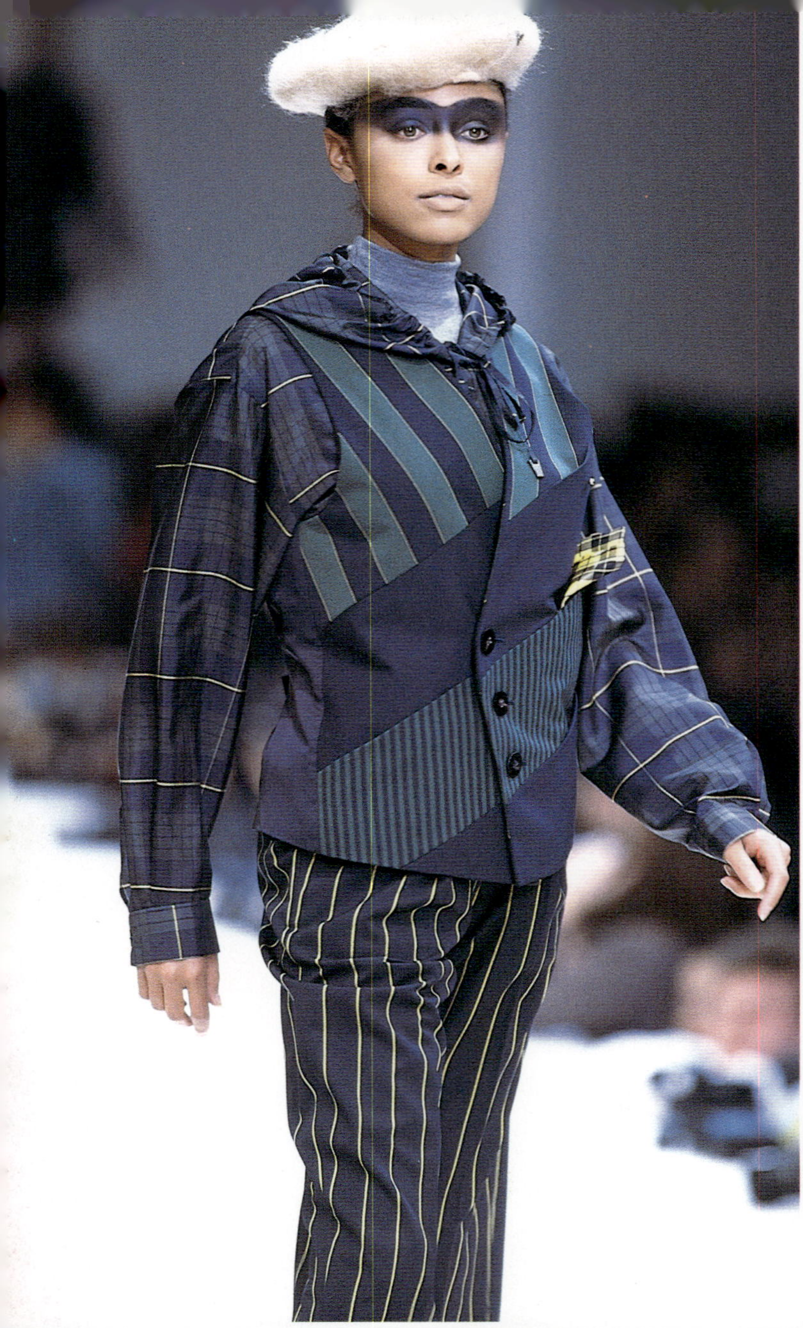
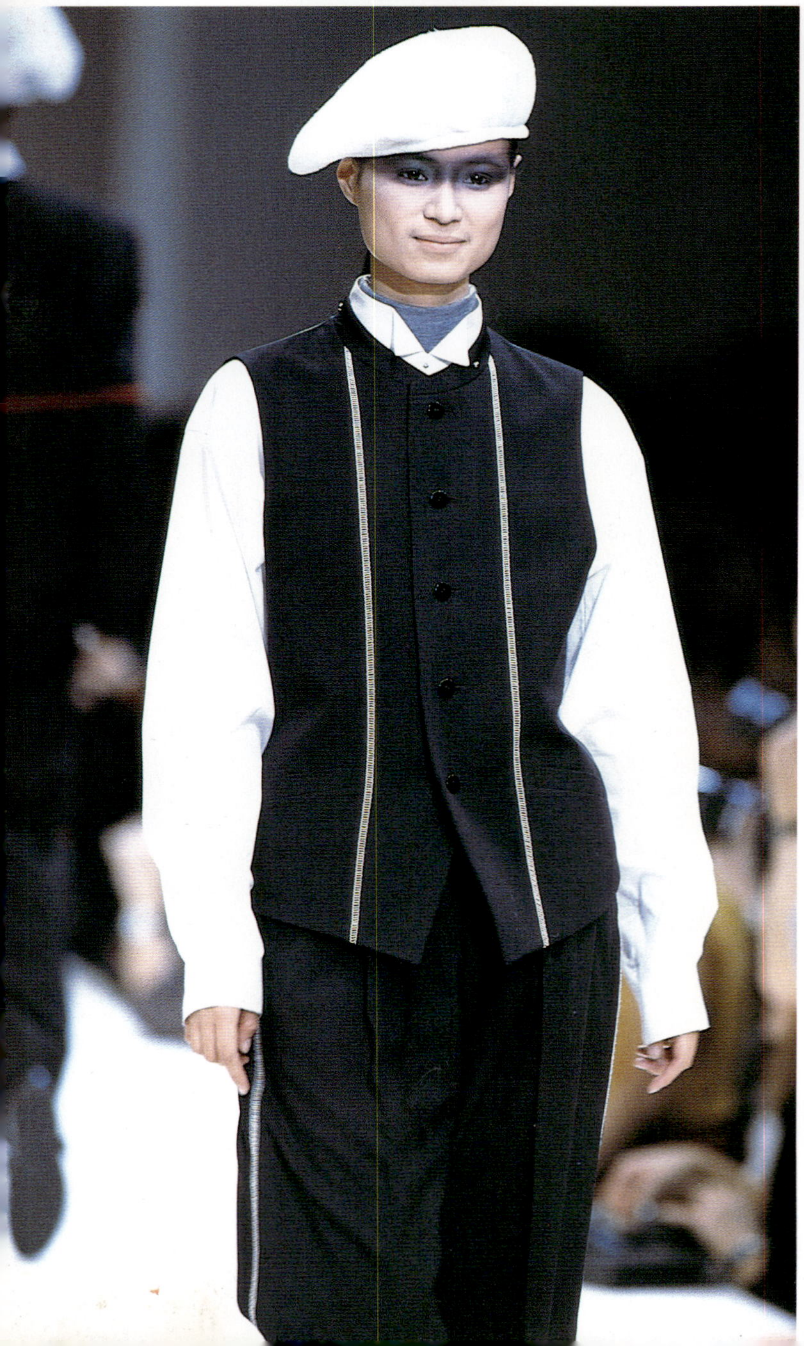
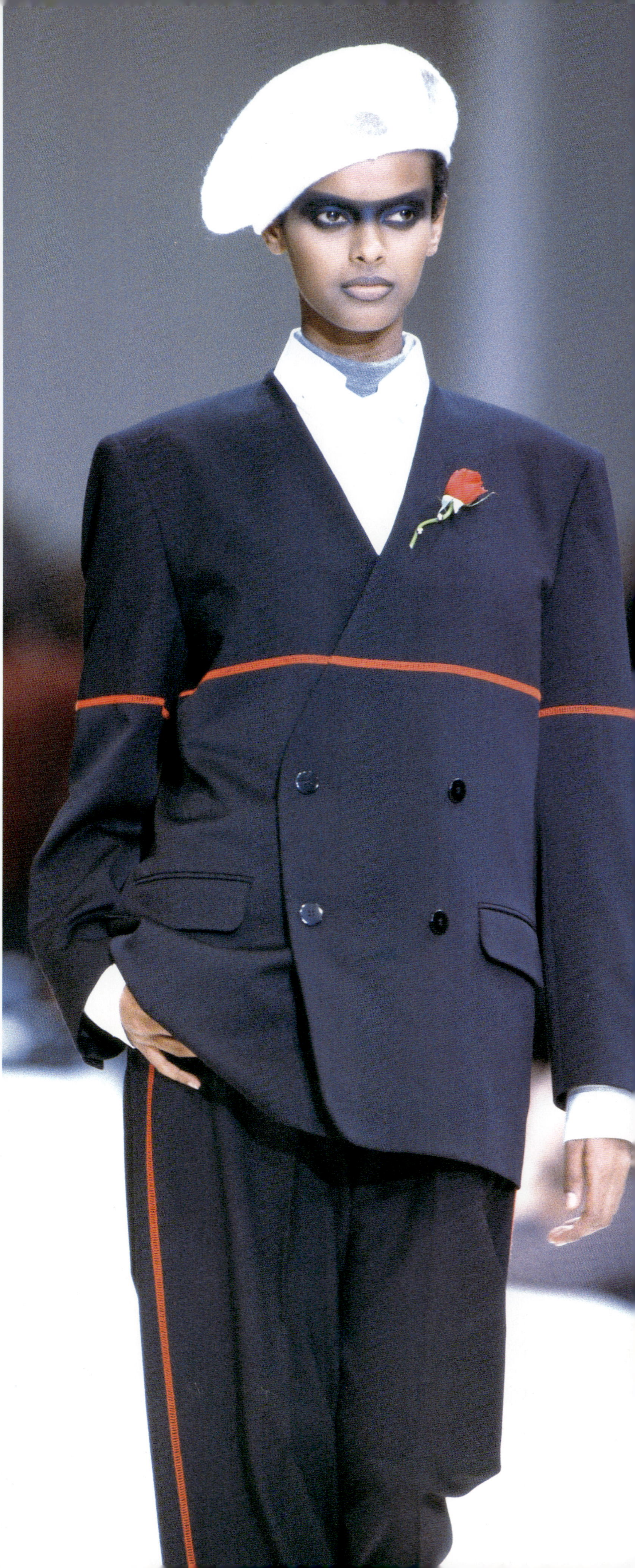

ISSEY MIYAKE

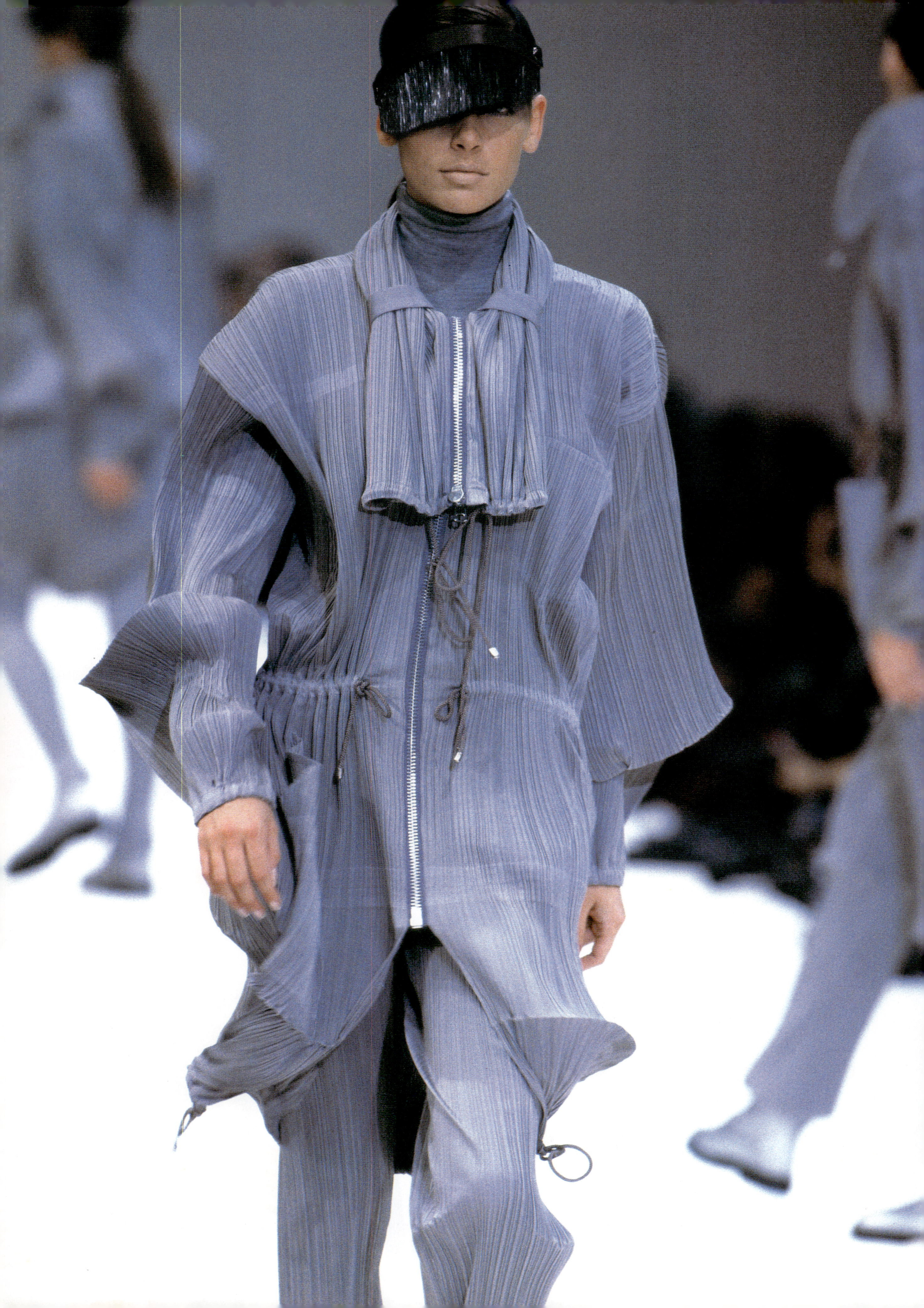

SONIA RYKIEL

ソニア・リキエル

ケープ・コートやマント・コートのスイングする美しさ、ニット・アイテムの粋さはソニアならでは。フェイク・ファーやキルティング・コートのライニングに注目。

Only Sonia creates beautiful swinging cape and mantle coats along with the chic knit items.
Also worthy of note, the fake fur lining and the kilting coats.

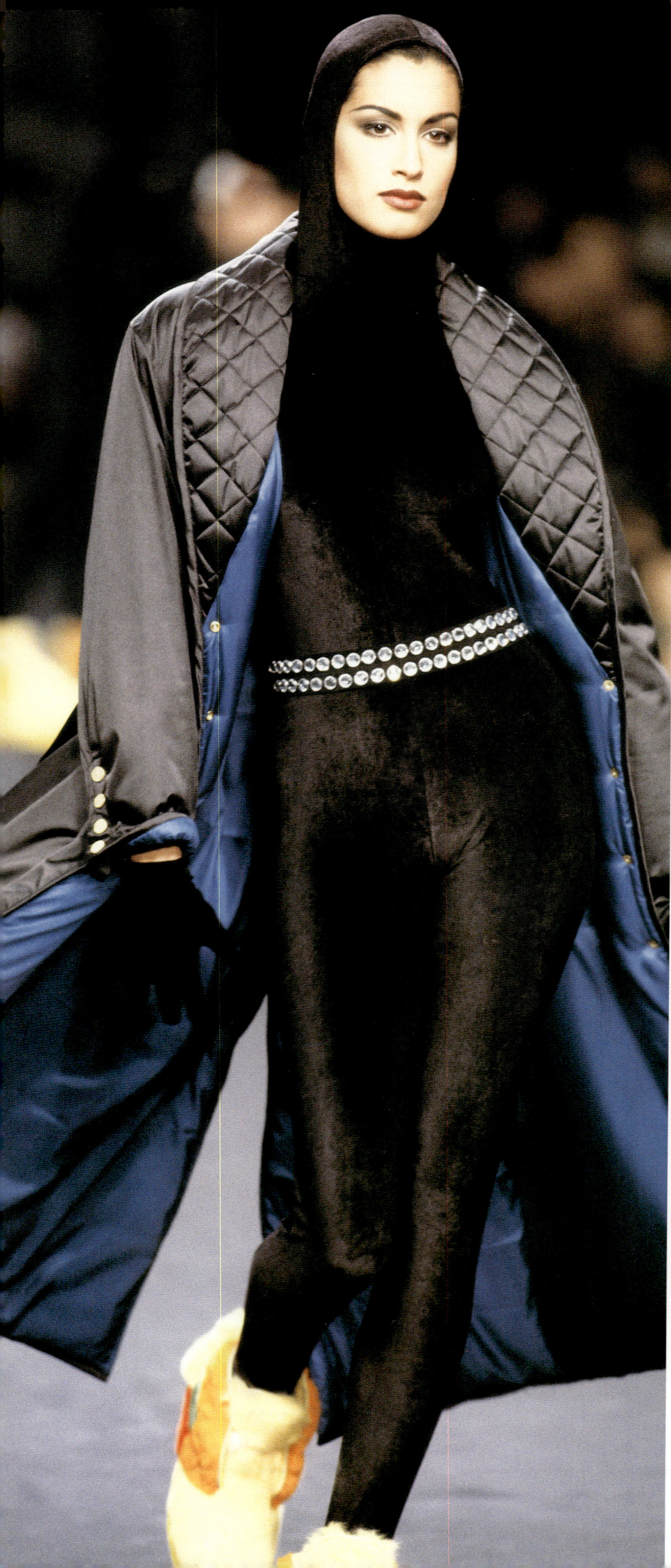
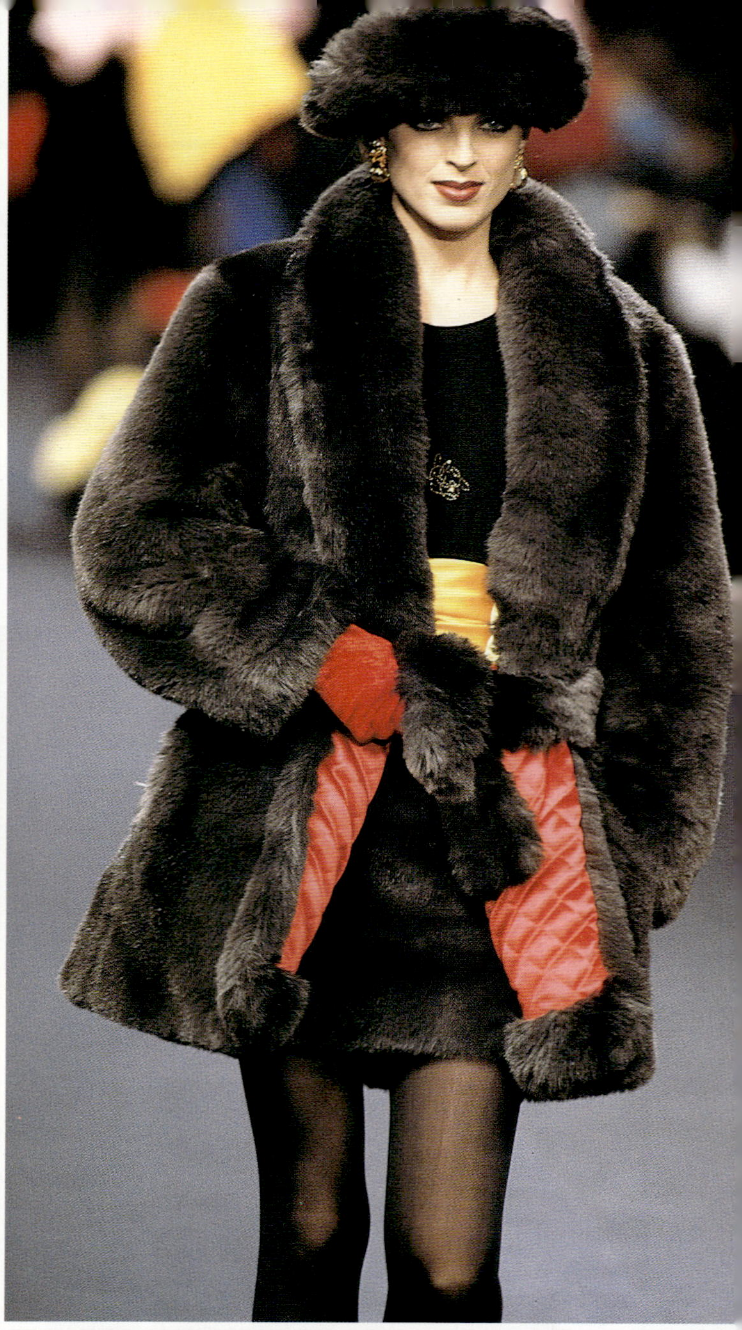
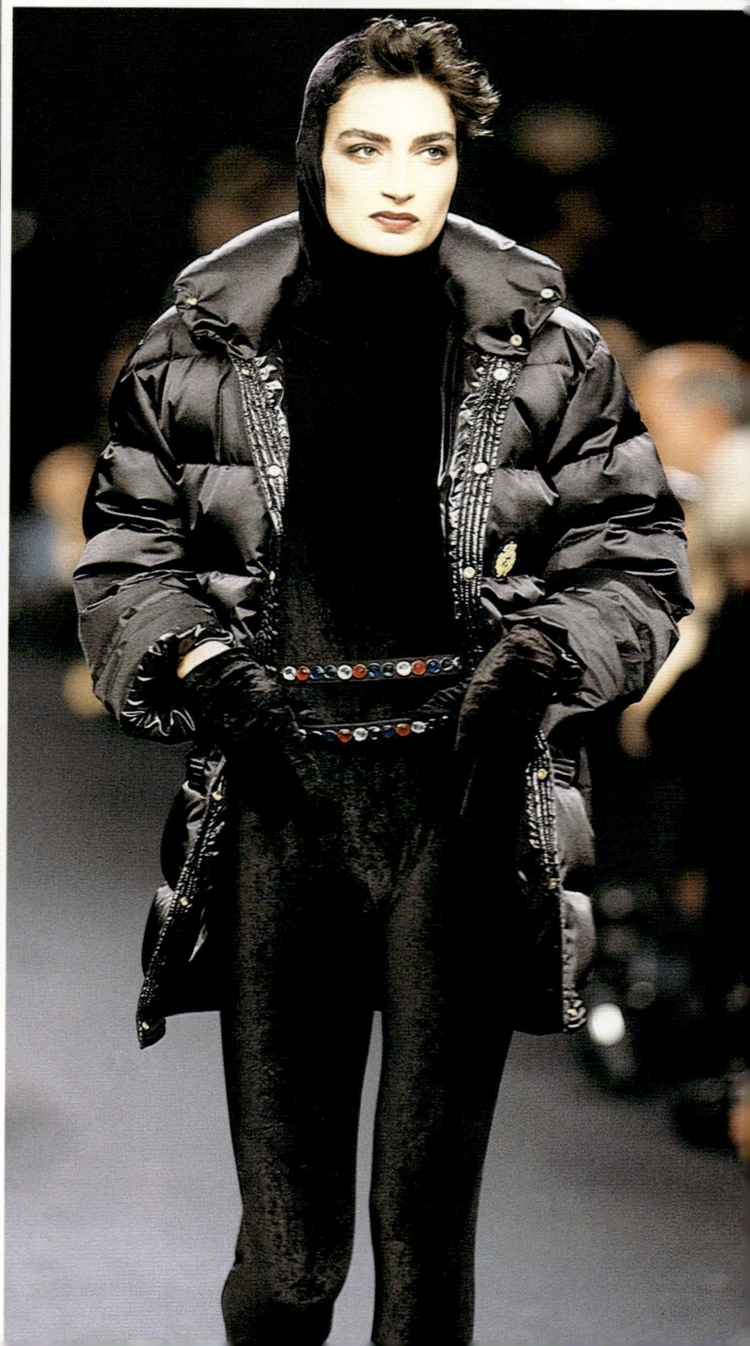

SONIA RYKIEL

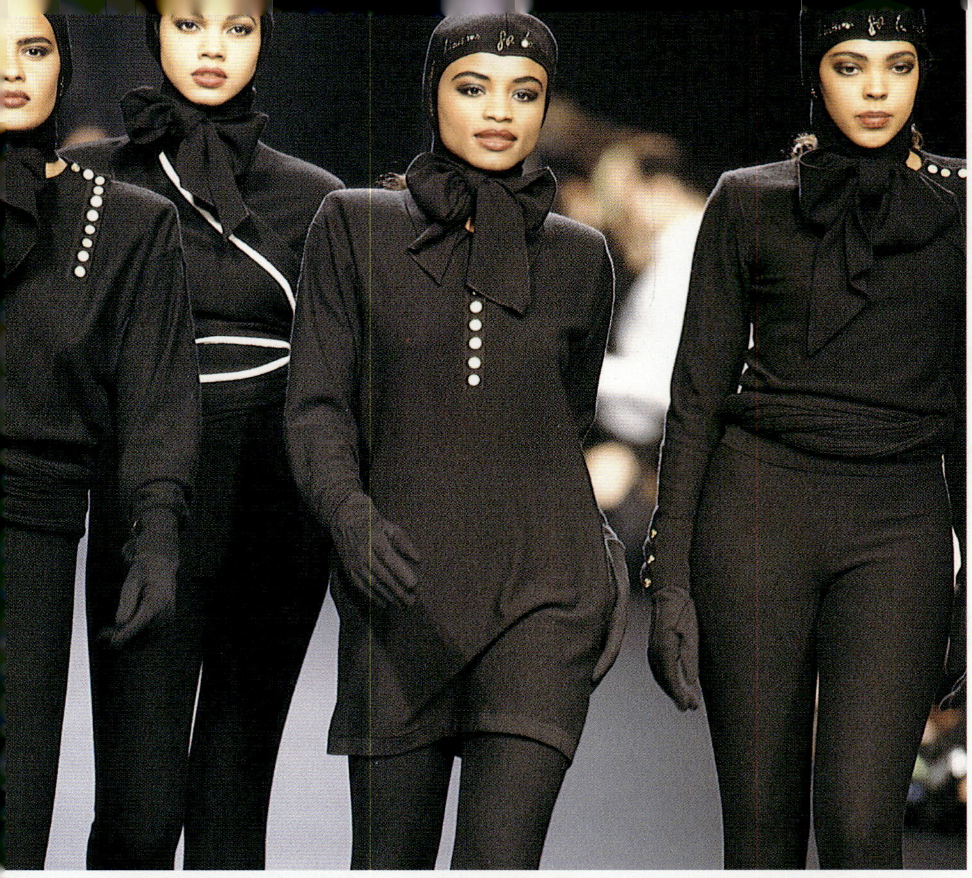

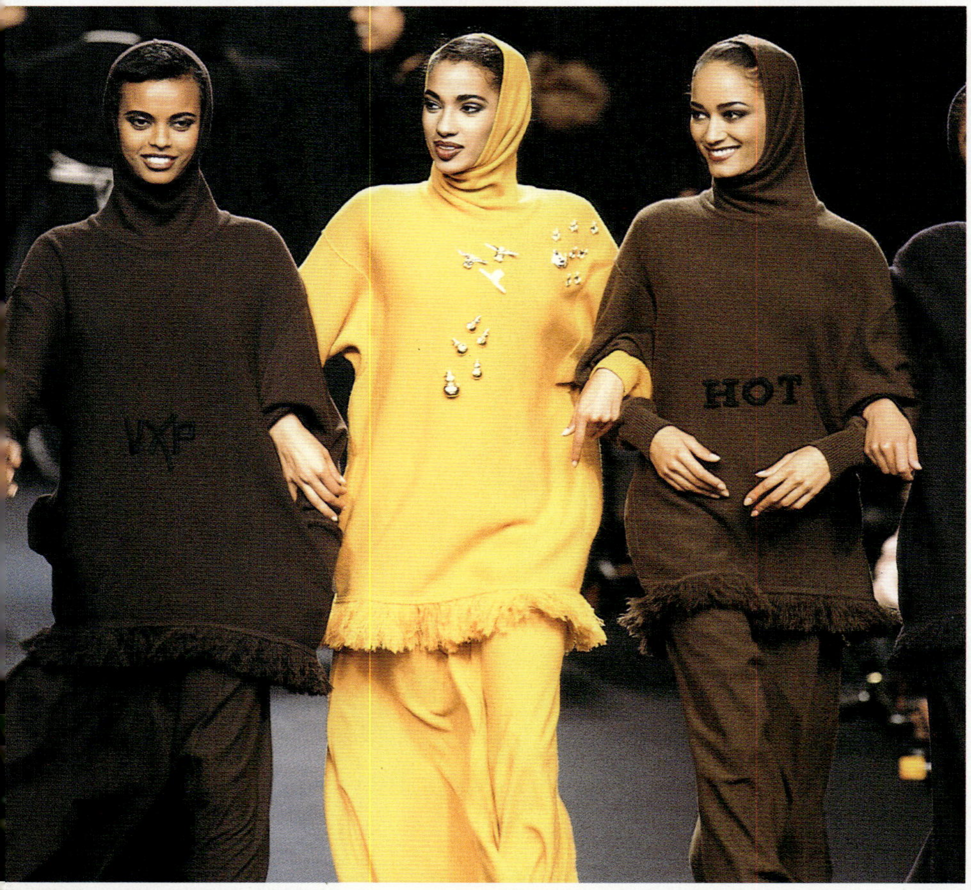
HOT

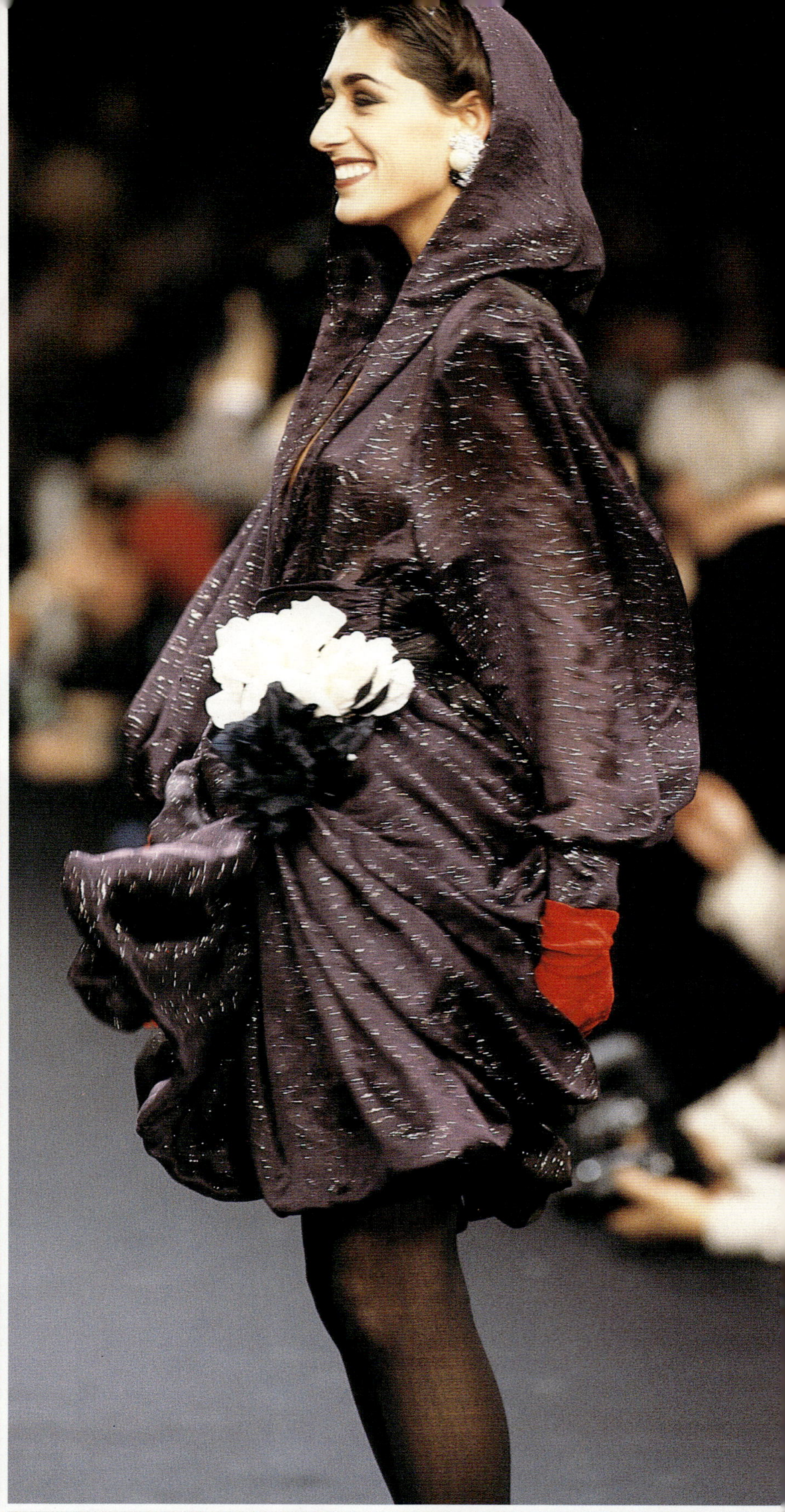

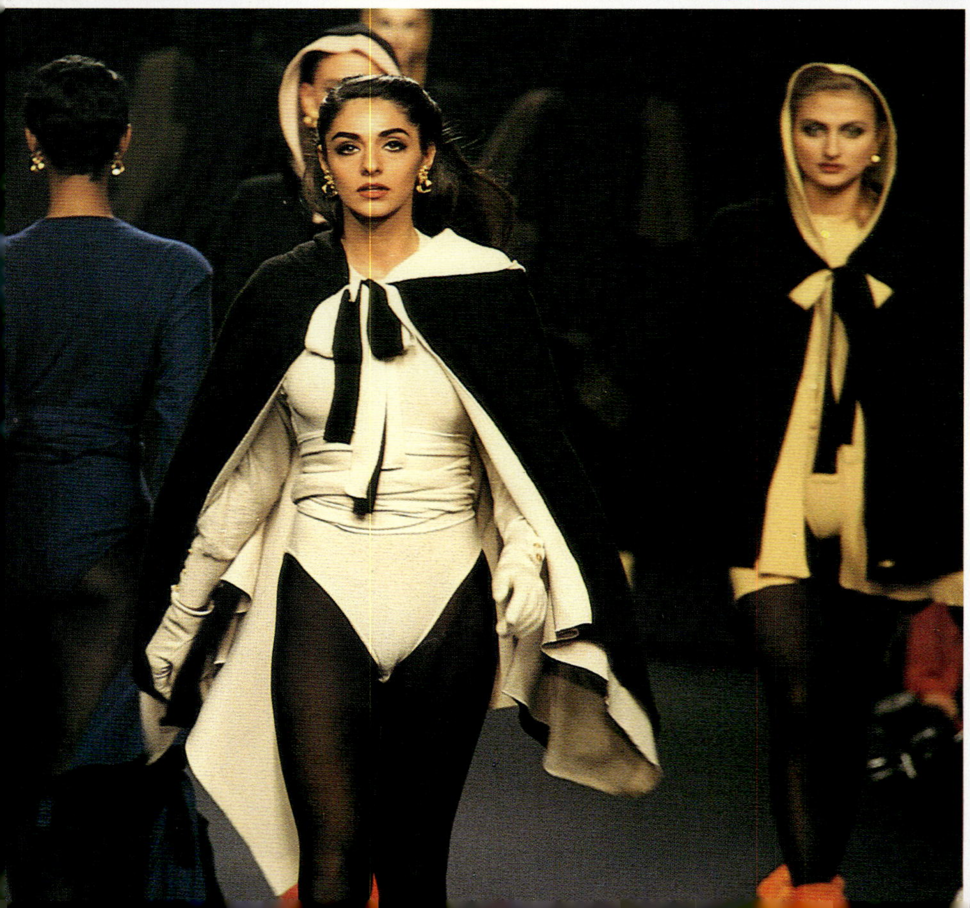

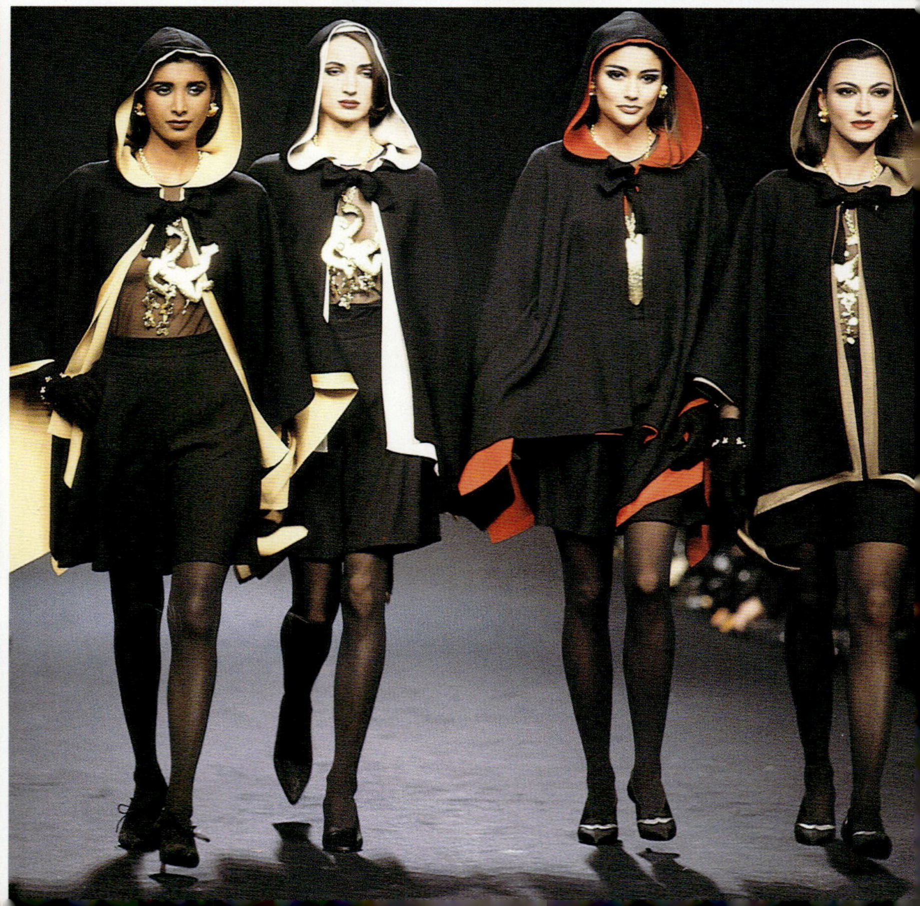

SONIA RYKIEL

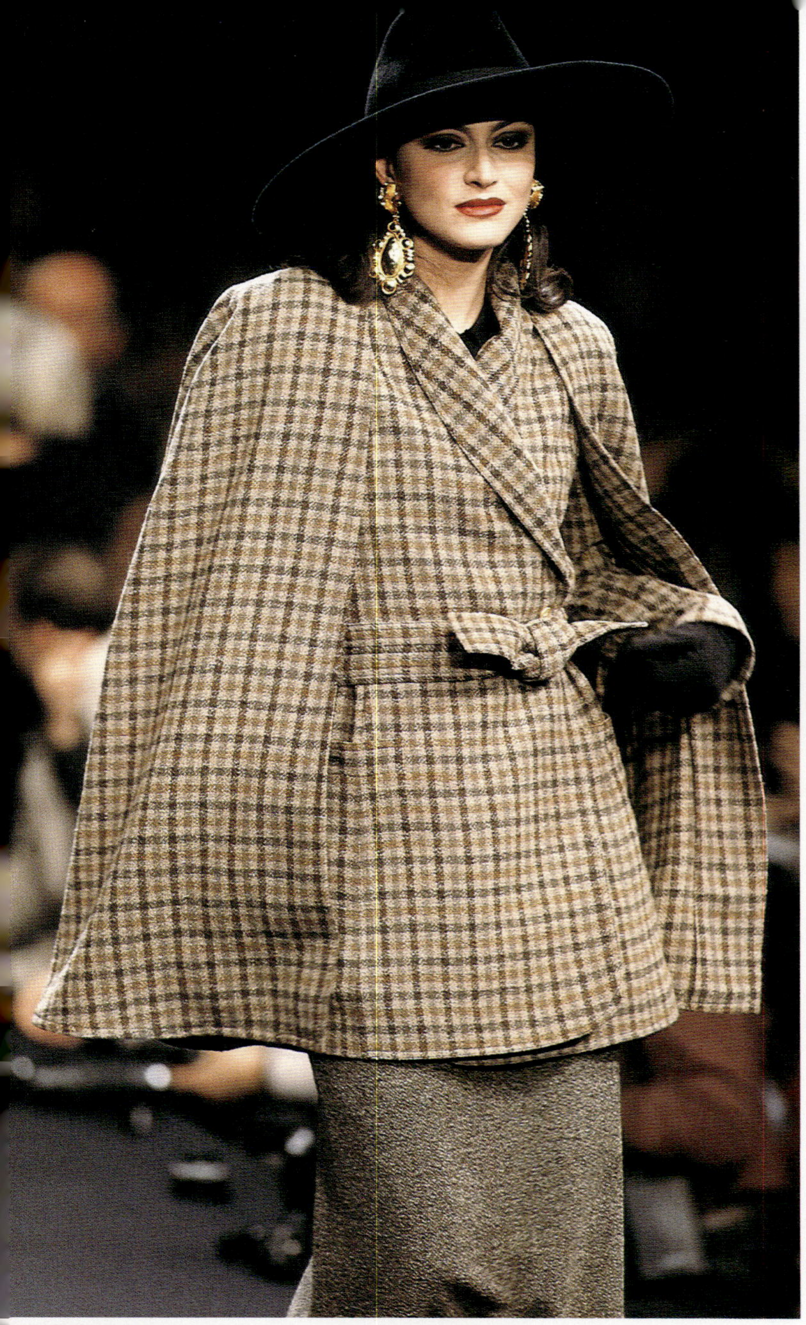

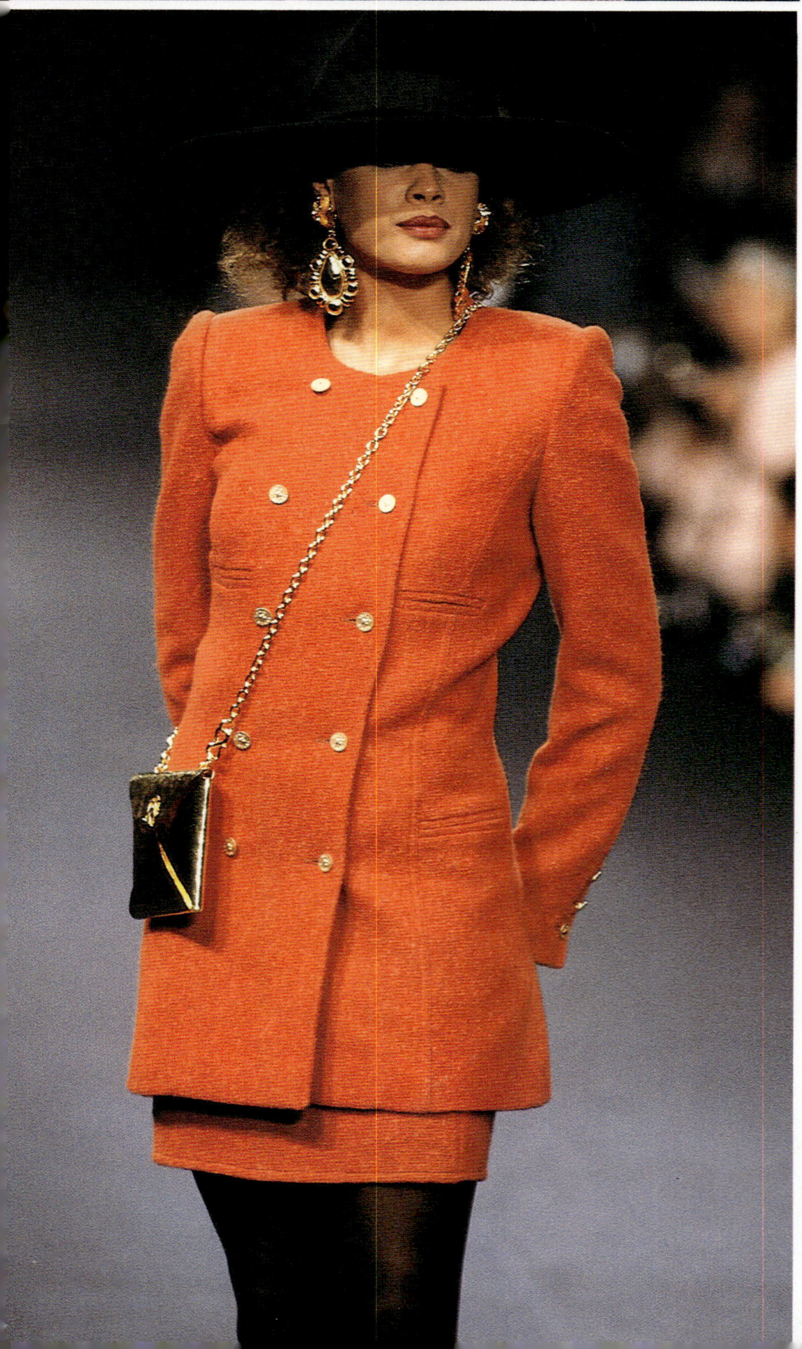

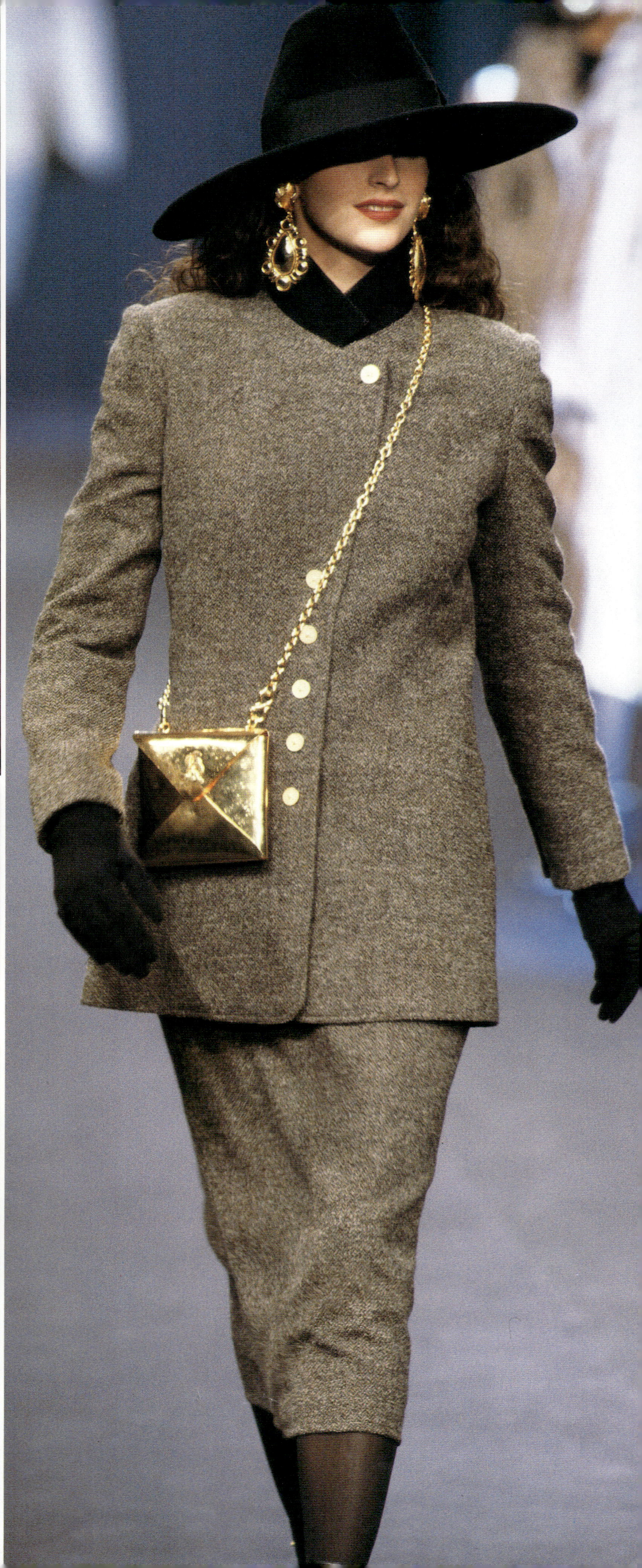

SONIA RYKIEL

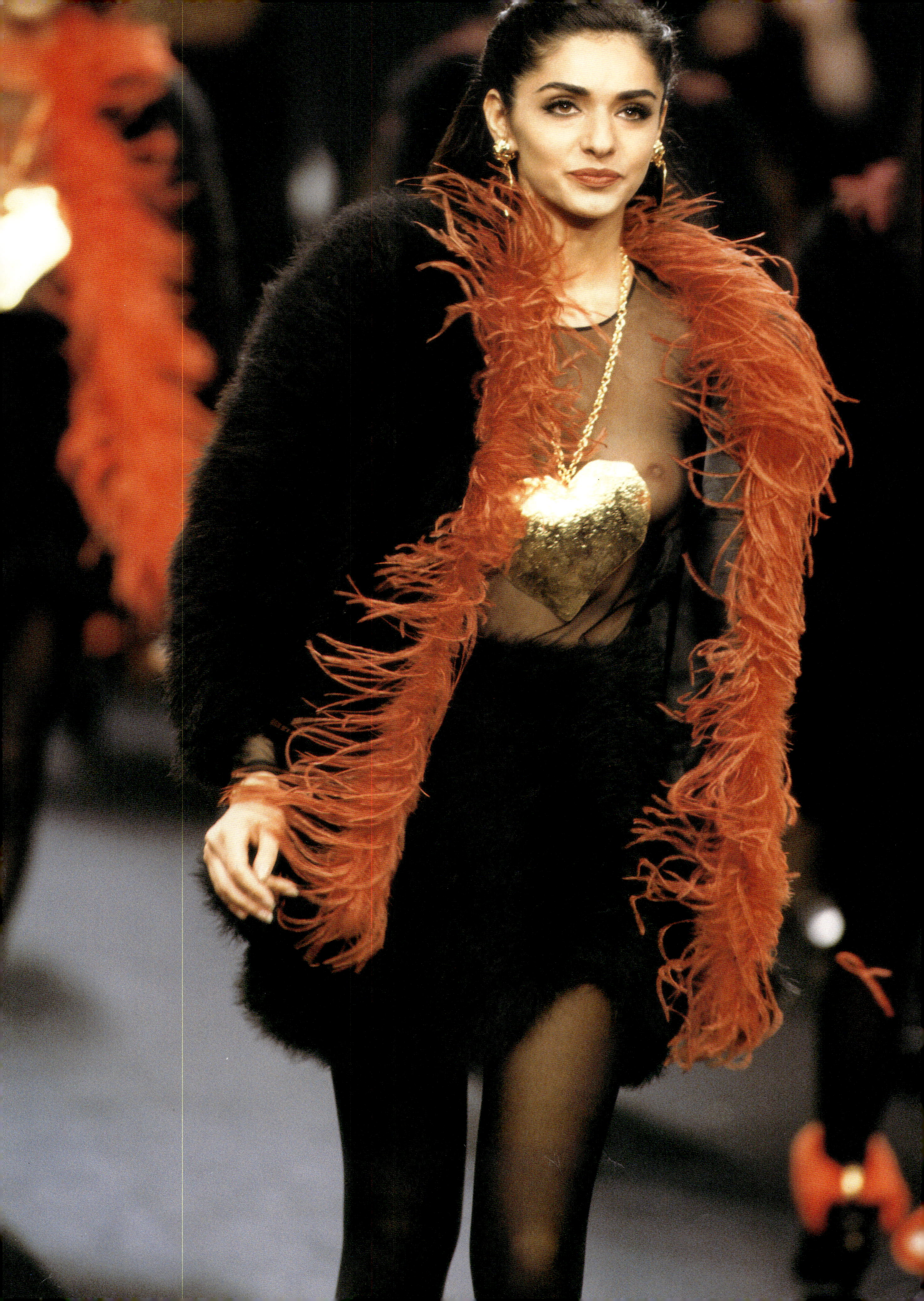

MAURIZIO GALANTE

マウリツィオ・ガランテ

パリコレ・デビューを果したミラノの新鋭デザイナー、マウリツィオ・ガランテ。彼独特のオリジナルで繊細なフォルムの美しさは、パリを感動させた。

Making his debut in the Paris collection, Maurizio Galante is a new designer from Milan.
Paris was moved by his unique and exquisite beauty.

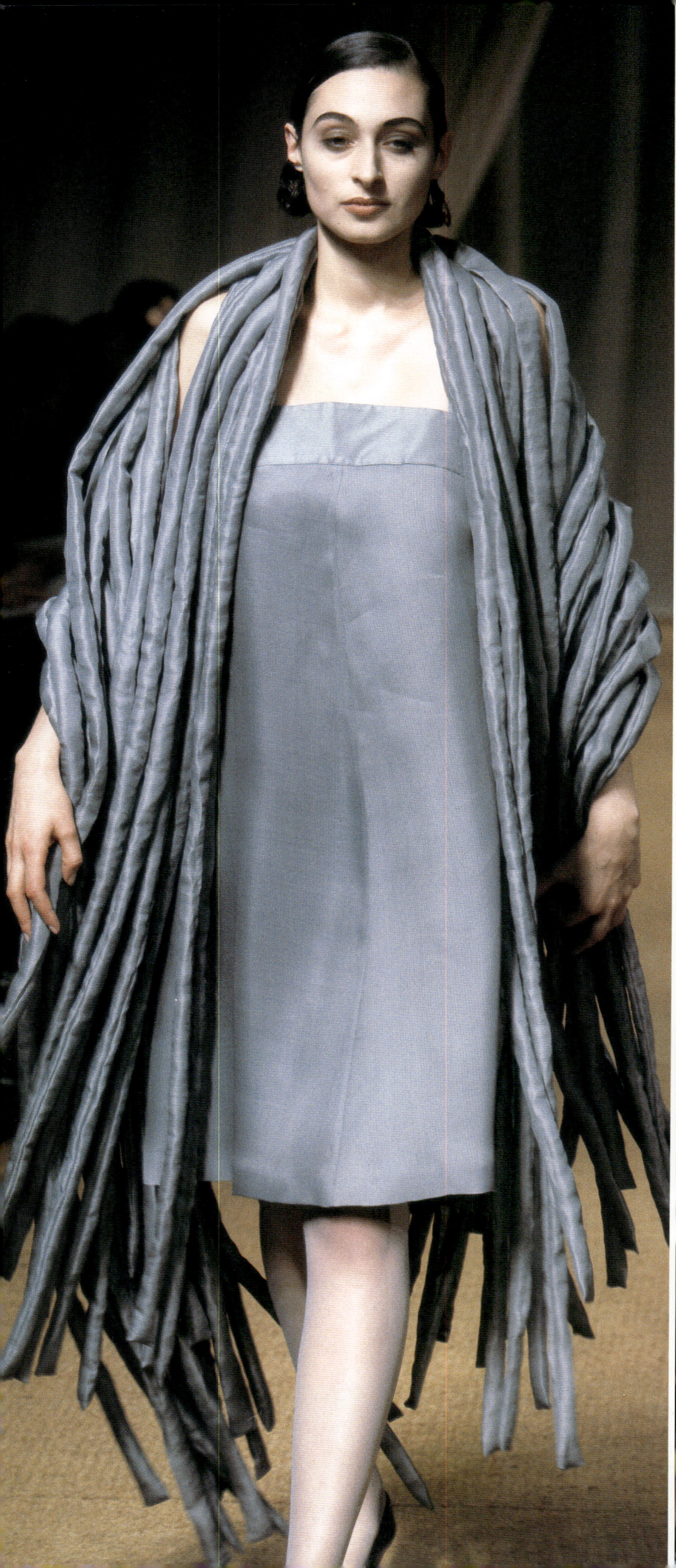
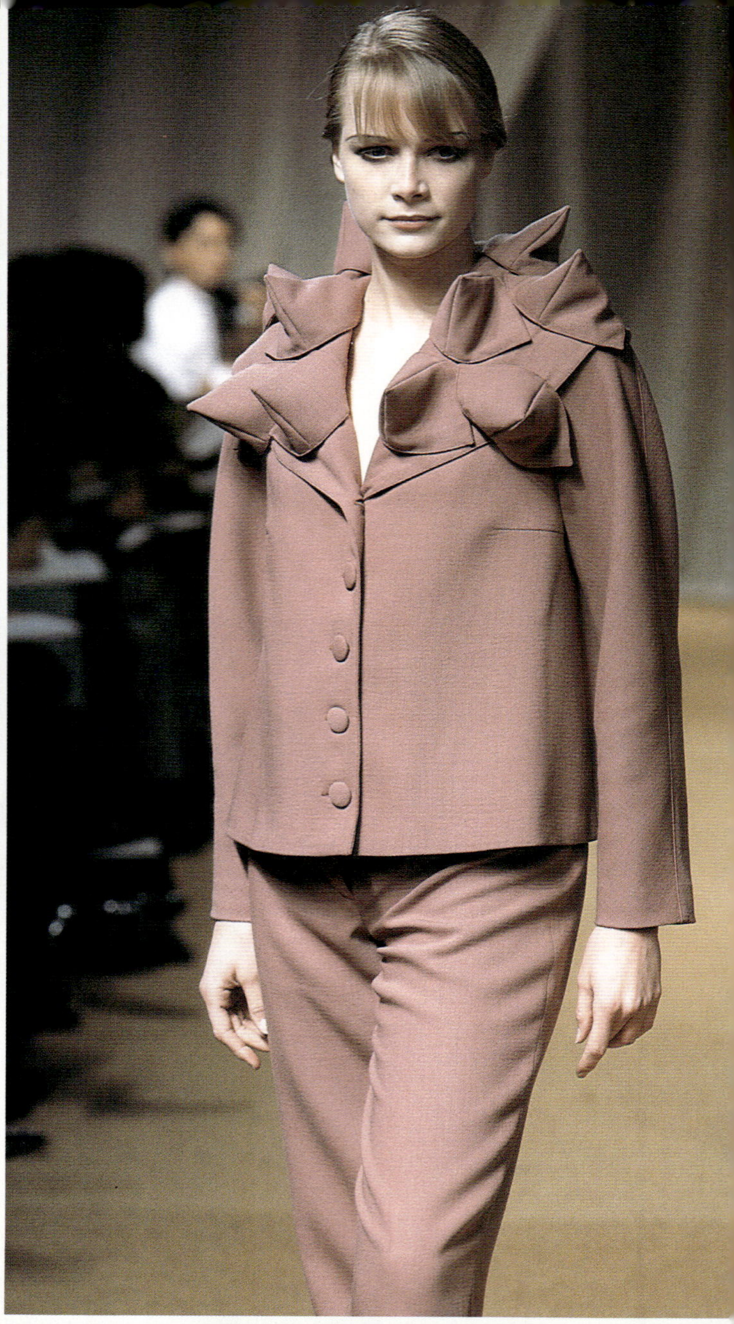
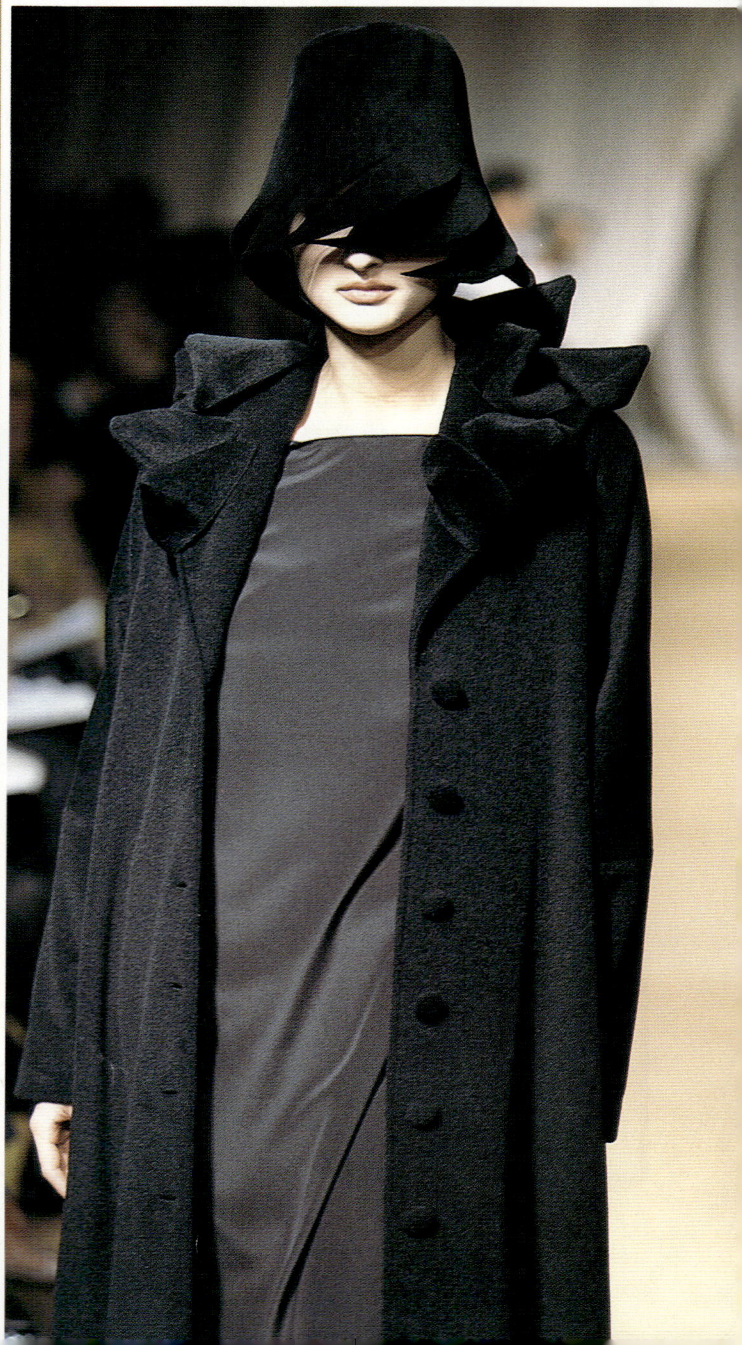

MAURIZIO GALANTE

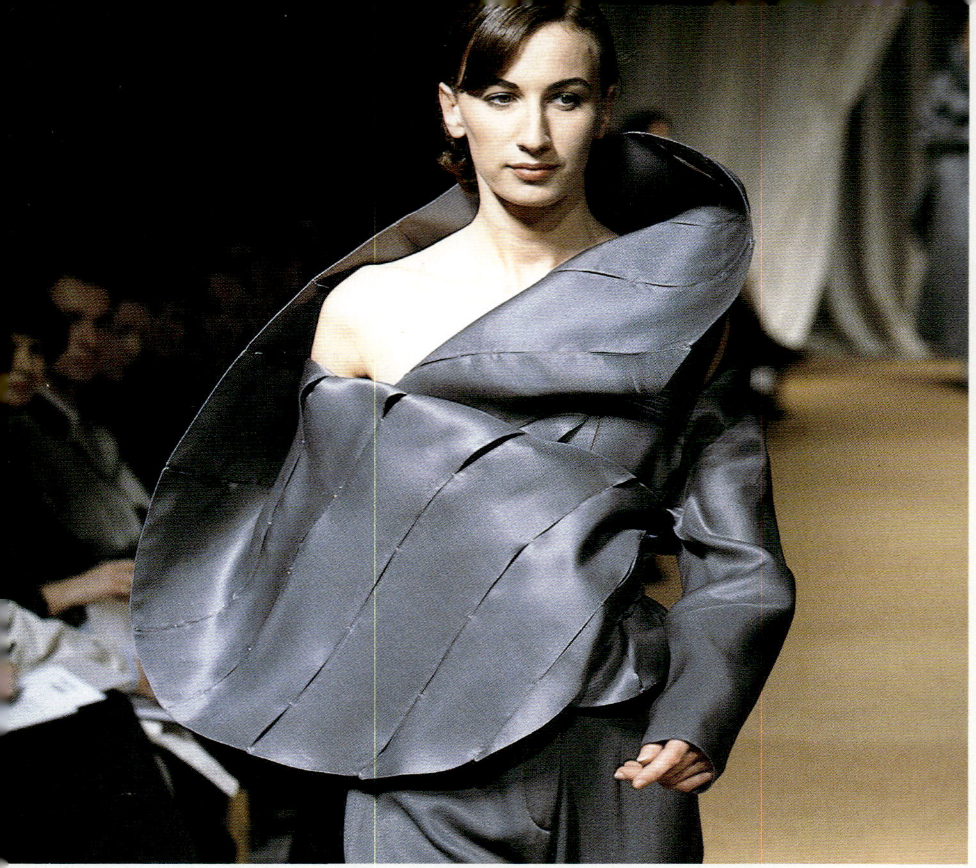
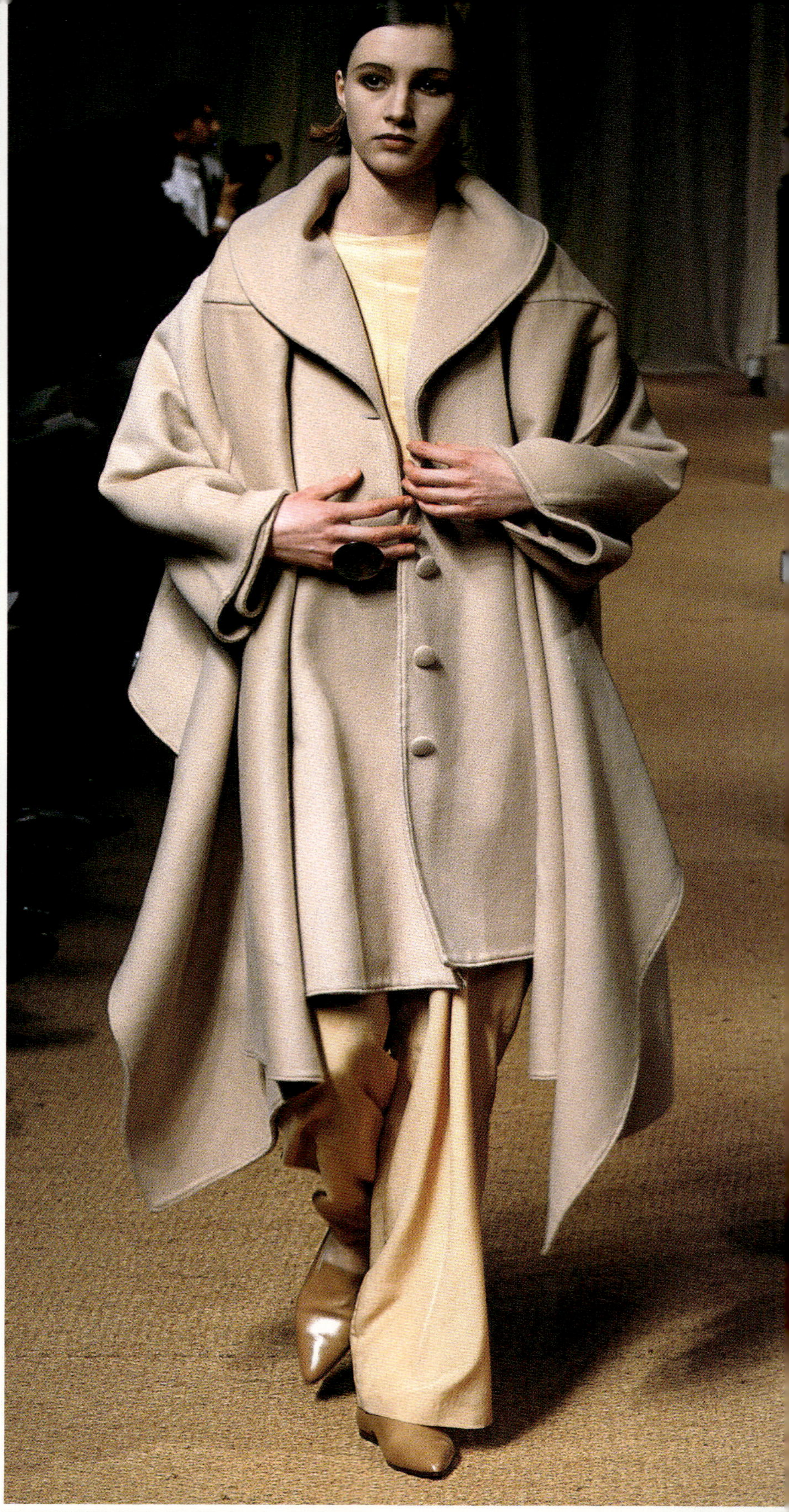
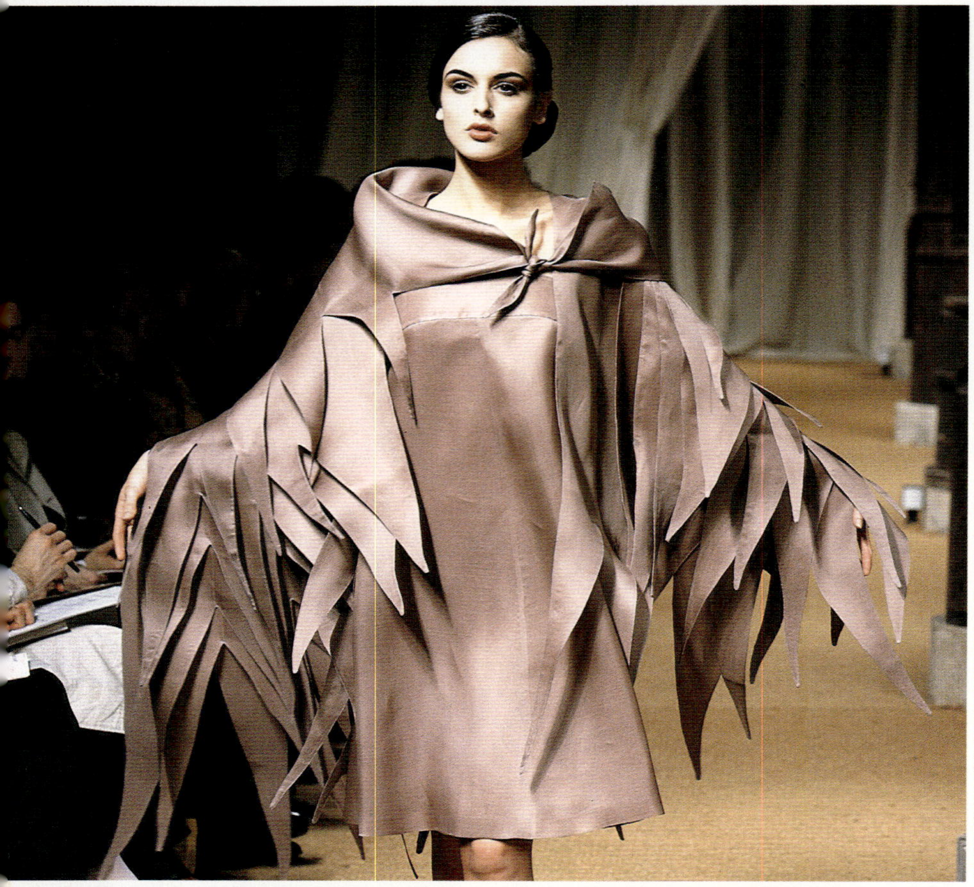
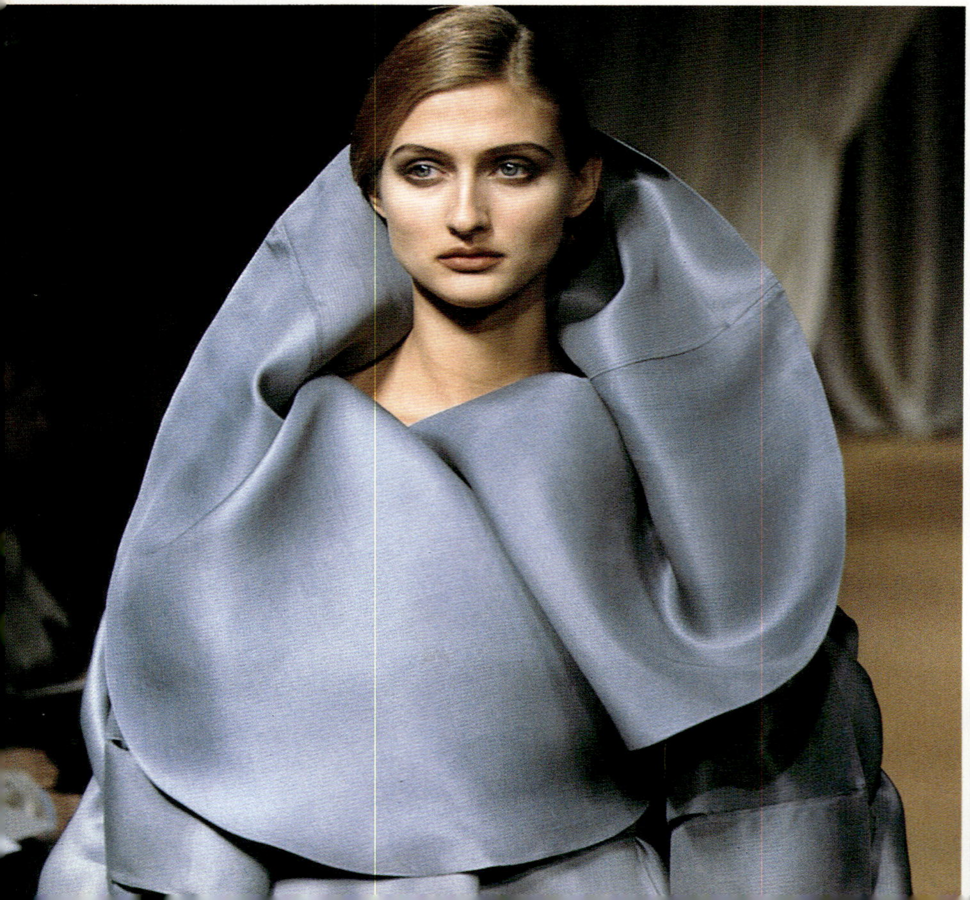
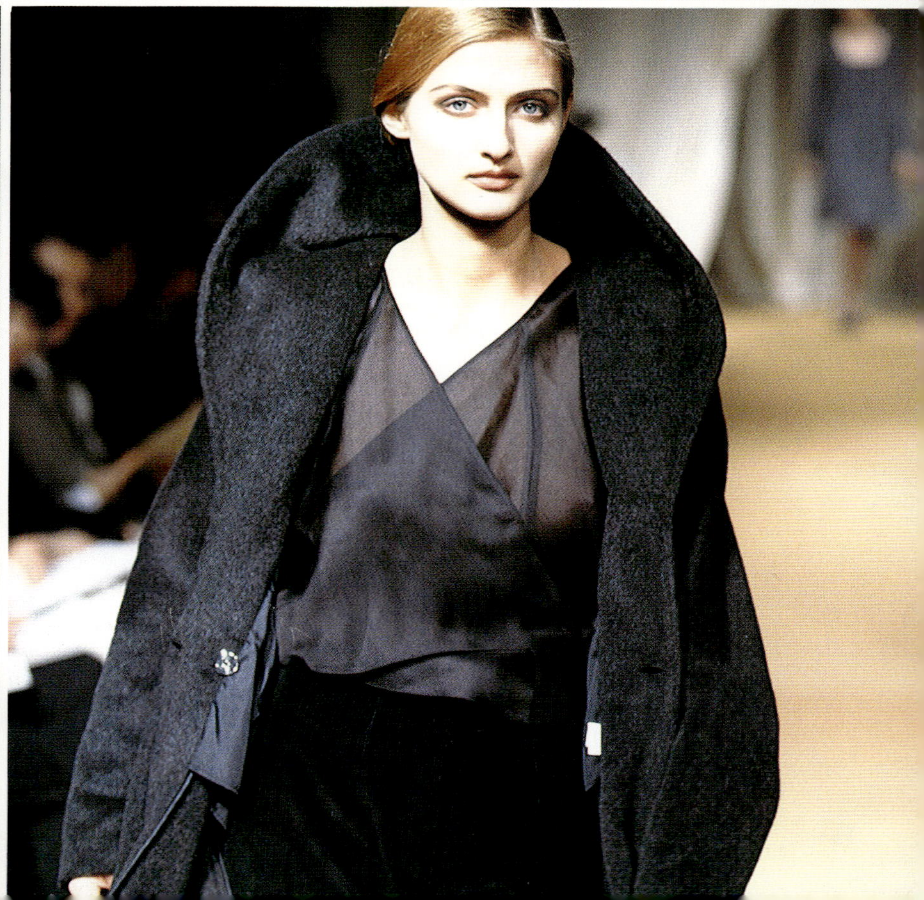

MAURIZIO GALANTE

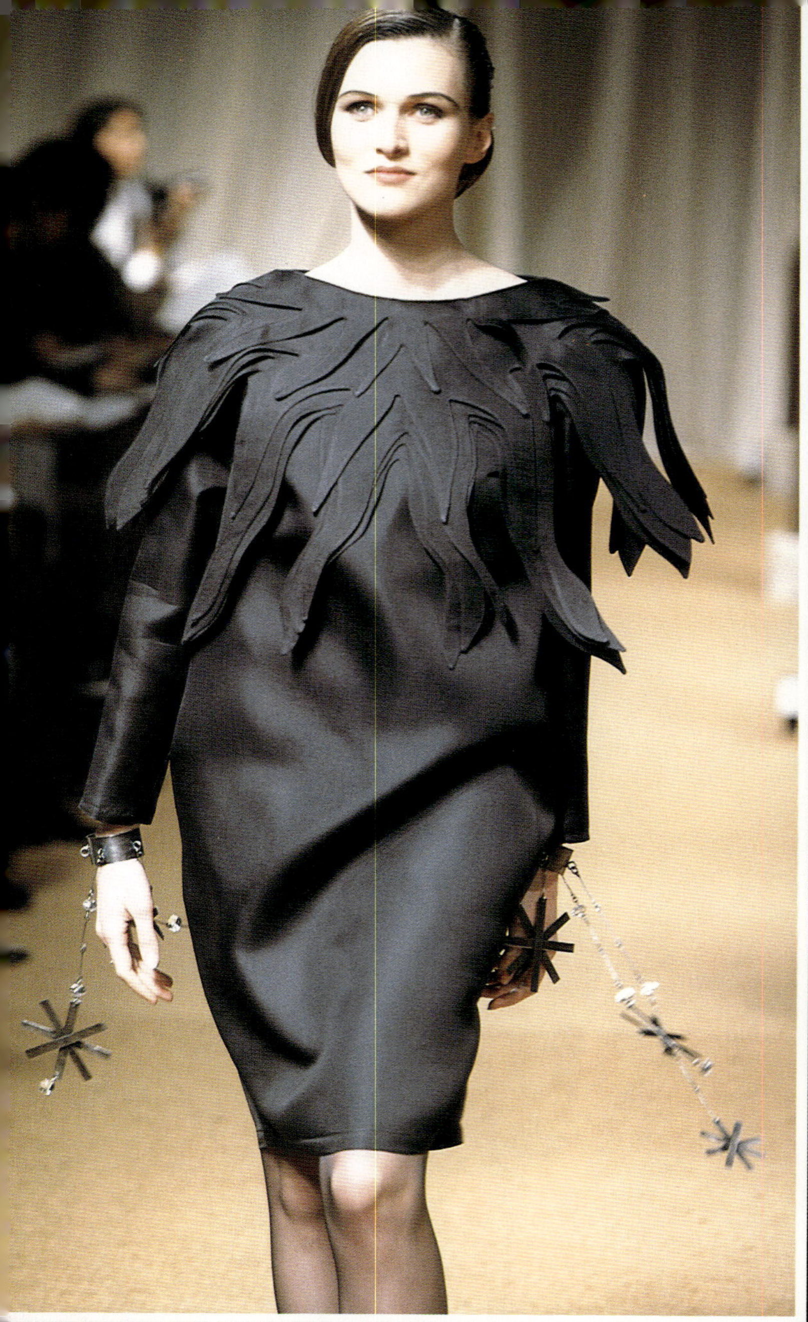
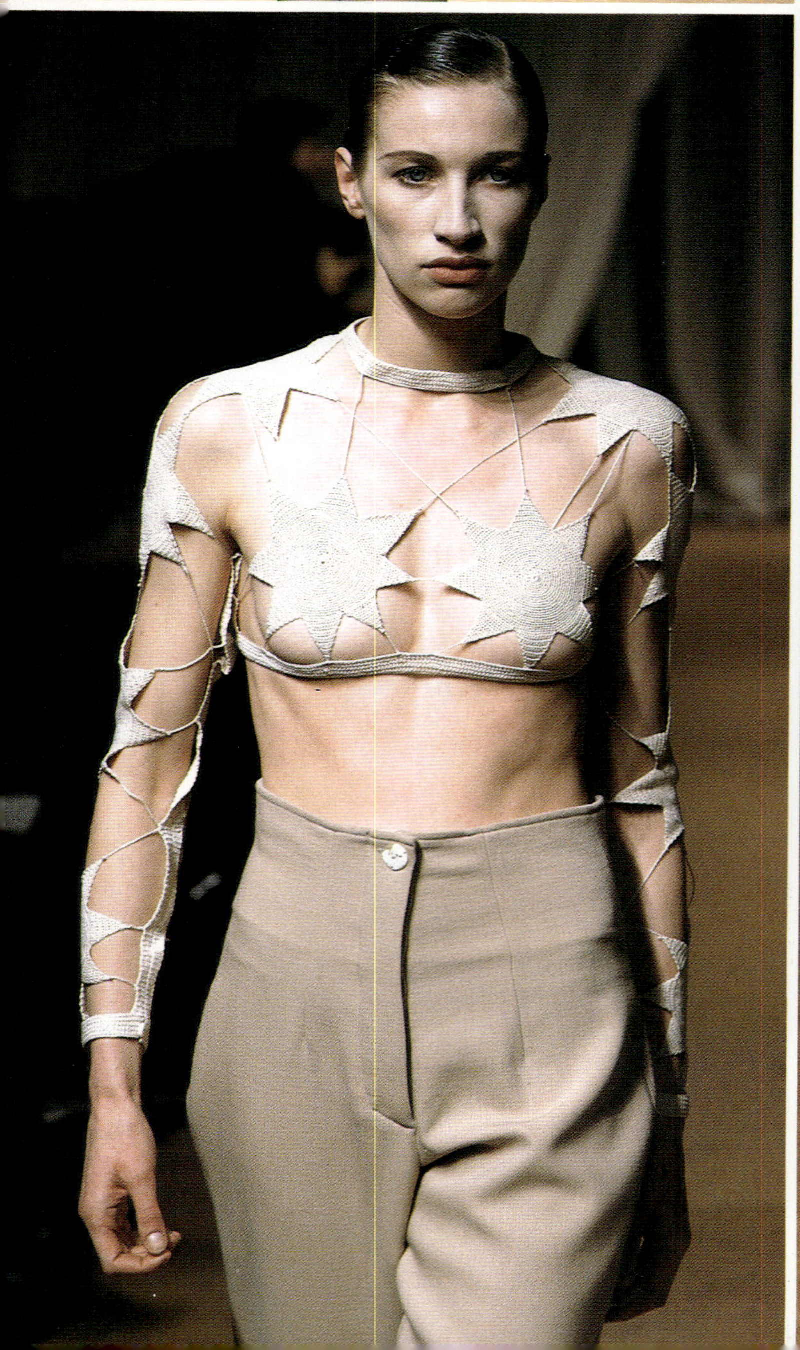
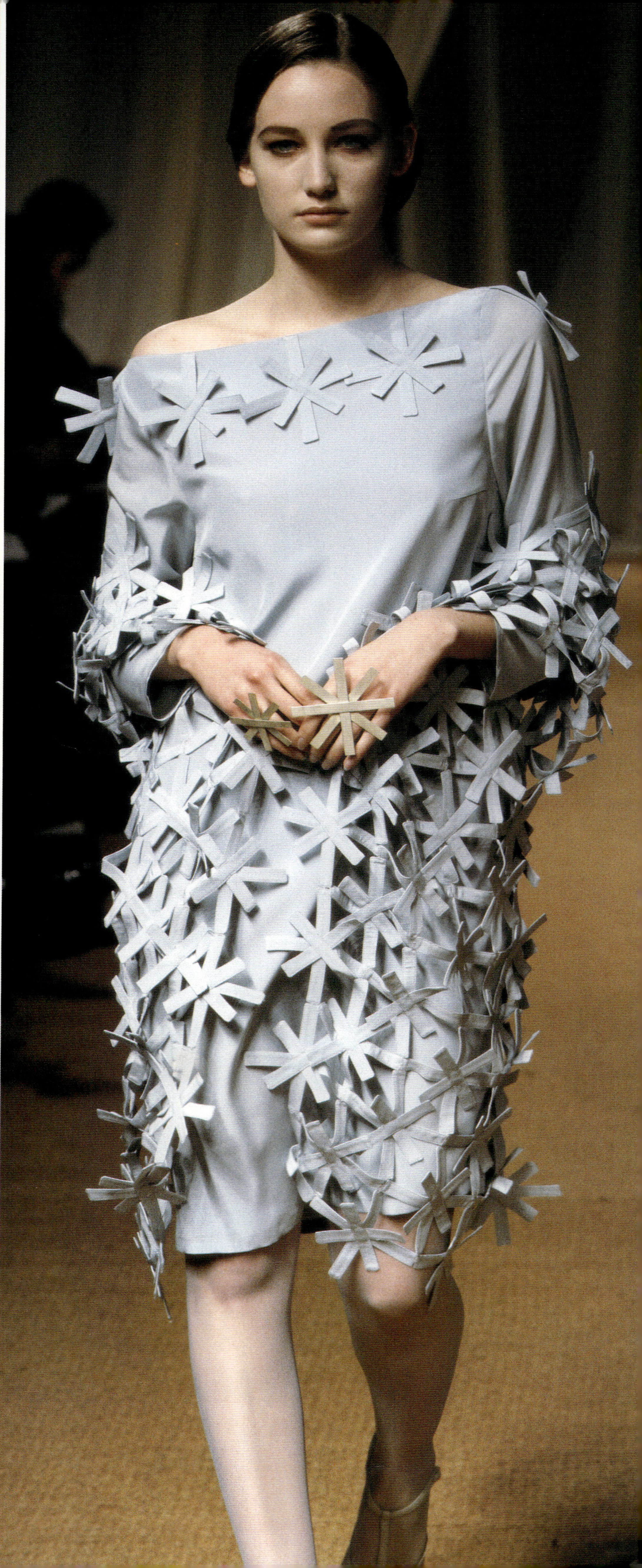

MAURIZIO GALANTE

181

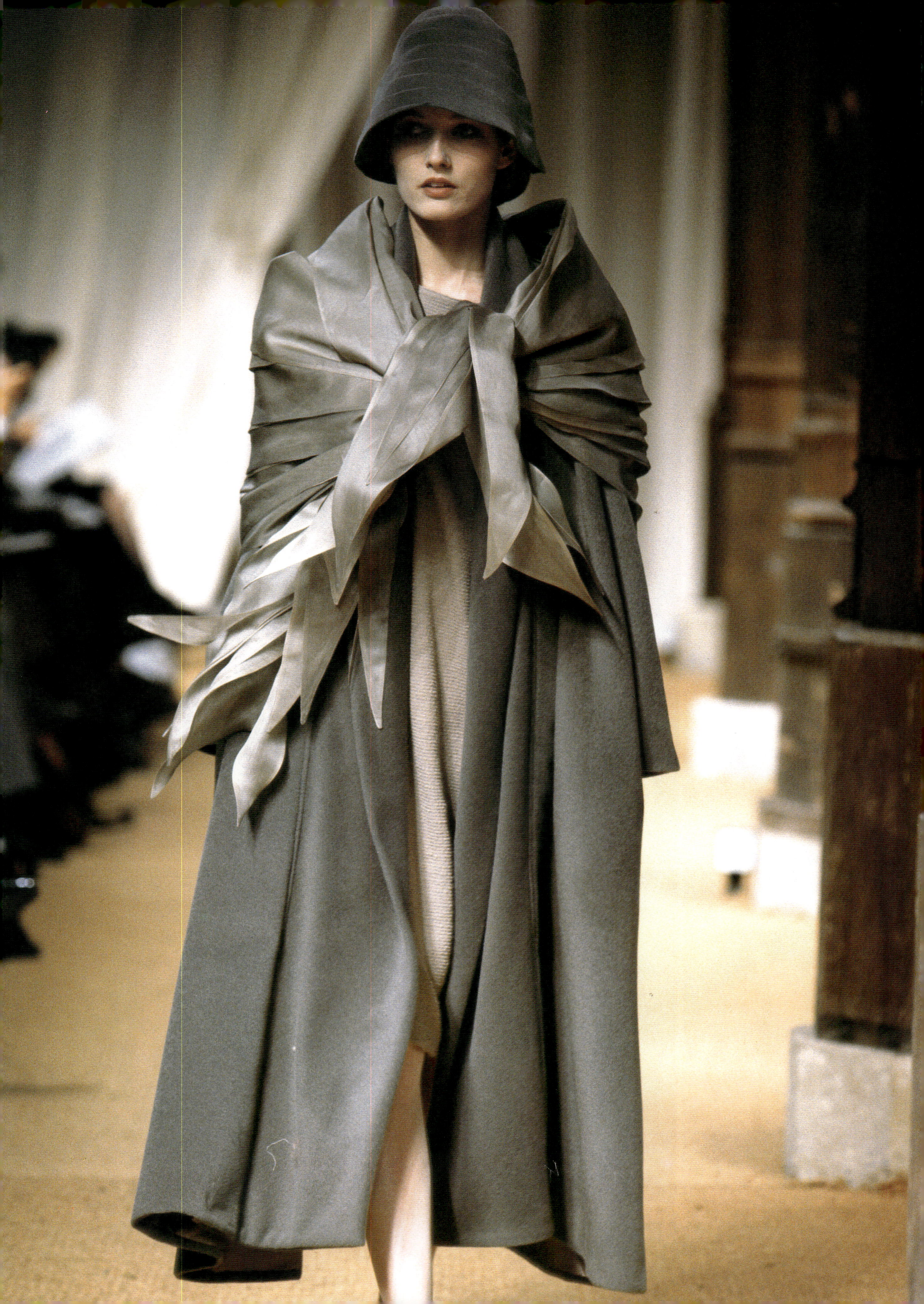

PIERRE BALMAIN

EMANUEL UNGARO

'91-'92 AUTUMN & WINTER

PRÊT-Á-PORTER COLLECTIONS

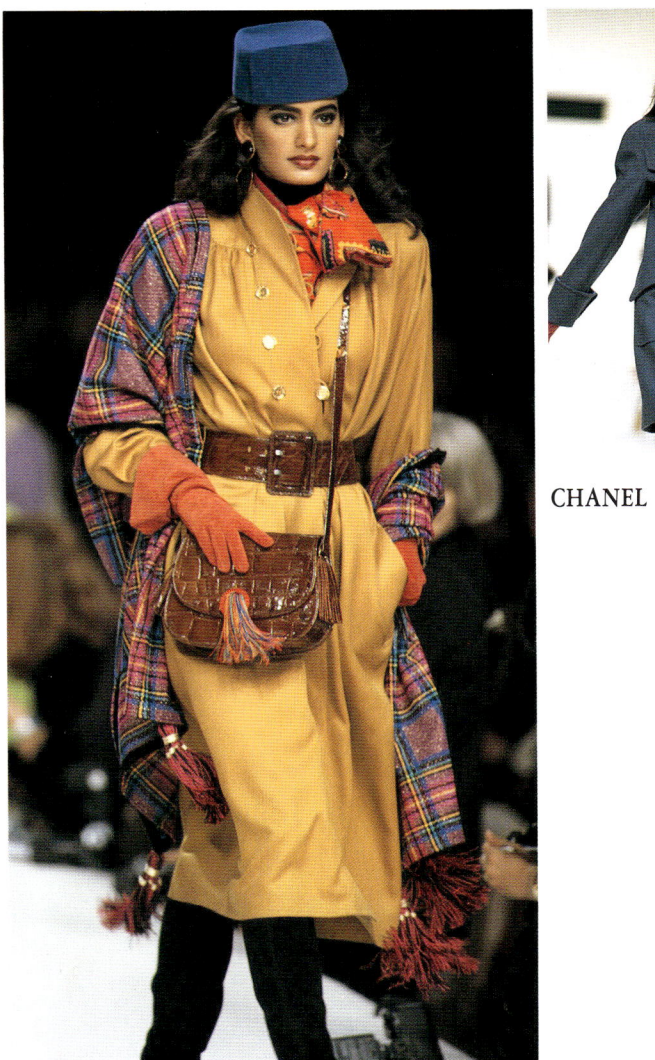

CHANEL

KENZO

EMANUEL UNGARO

GIVENCHY

GIVENCHY

CHANEL

EMANUEL UNGARO

'91-'92 AUTUMN & WINTER

PRÊT-Á-PORTER COLLECTIONS

CHANTAL THOMASS

YVES SAINT LAURENT

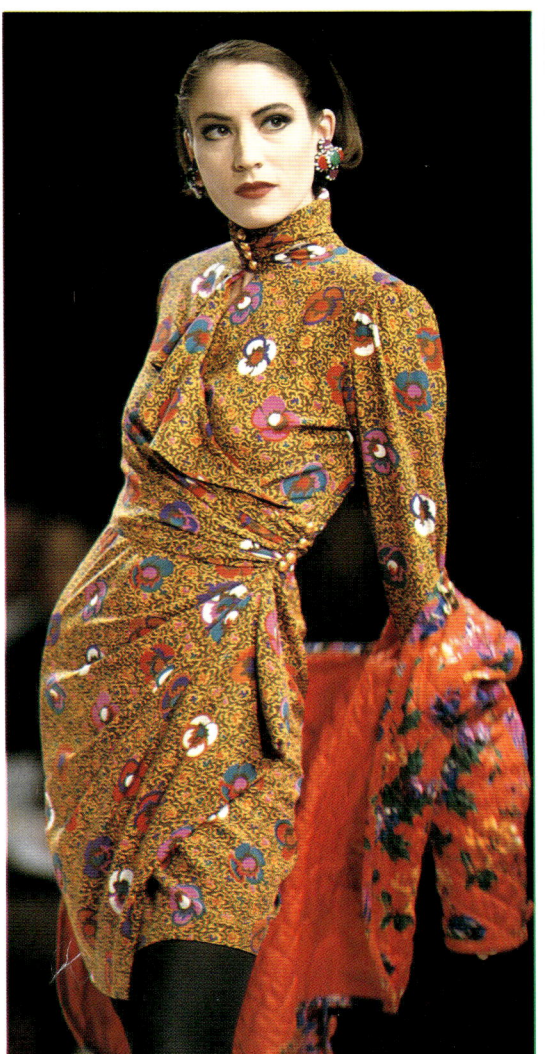

EMANUEL UNGARO

JUNKO SHIMADA

YUKI TORII

EMANUEL UNGARO

エマニュエル・ウンガロ

タータン・チェックとフラワー・プリントやアブストラクト・プリントのパターン・ミックスで、華麗でエレガントなウンガロの世界を披露。ロング・スカートも登場。
Ungaro demonstrated a world of elegance, using tartan checks and mixing abstract and flower print patterns.
Also displayed were long skirts.

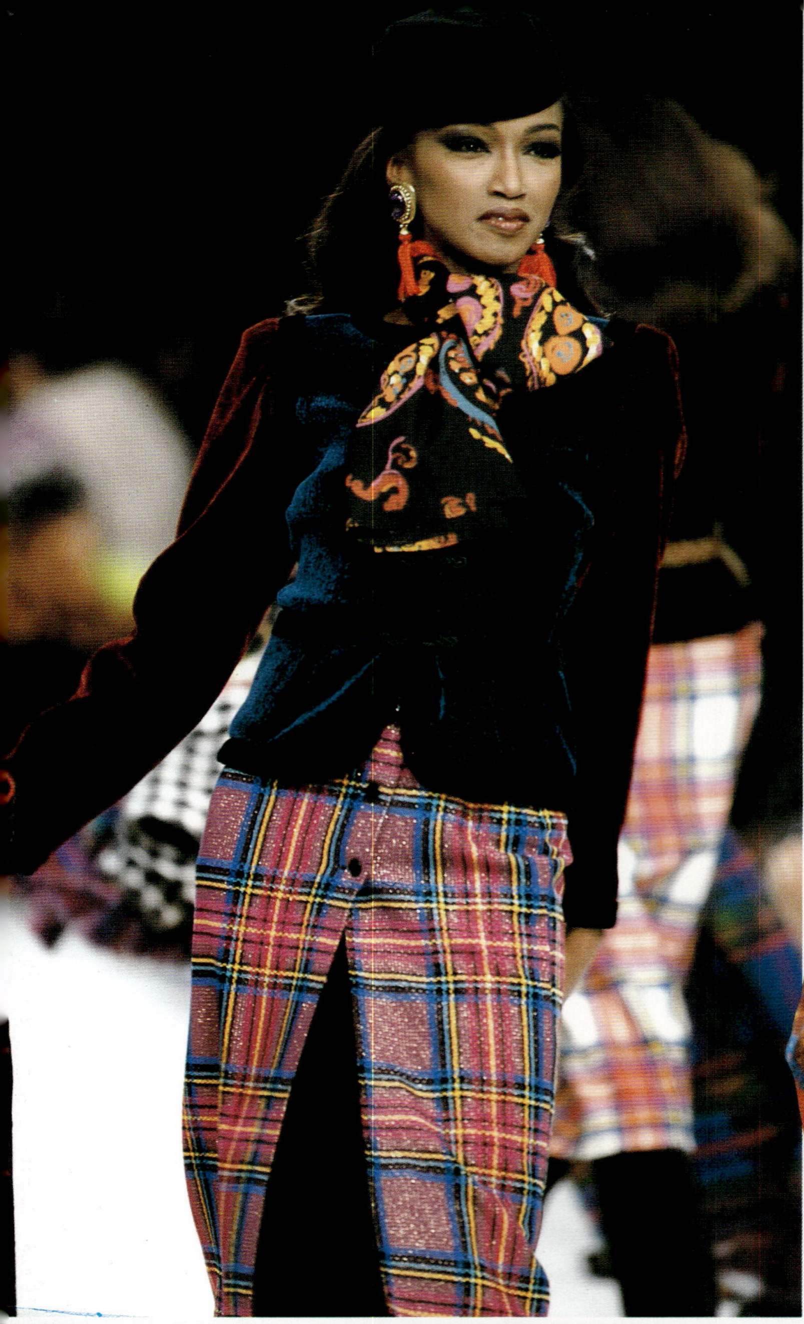

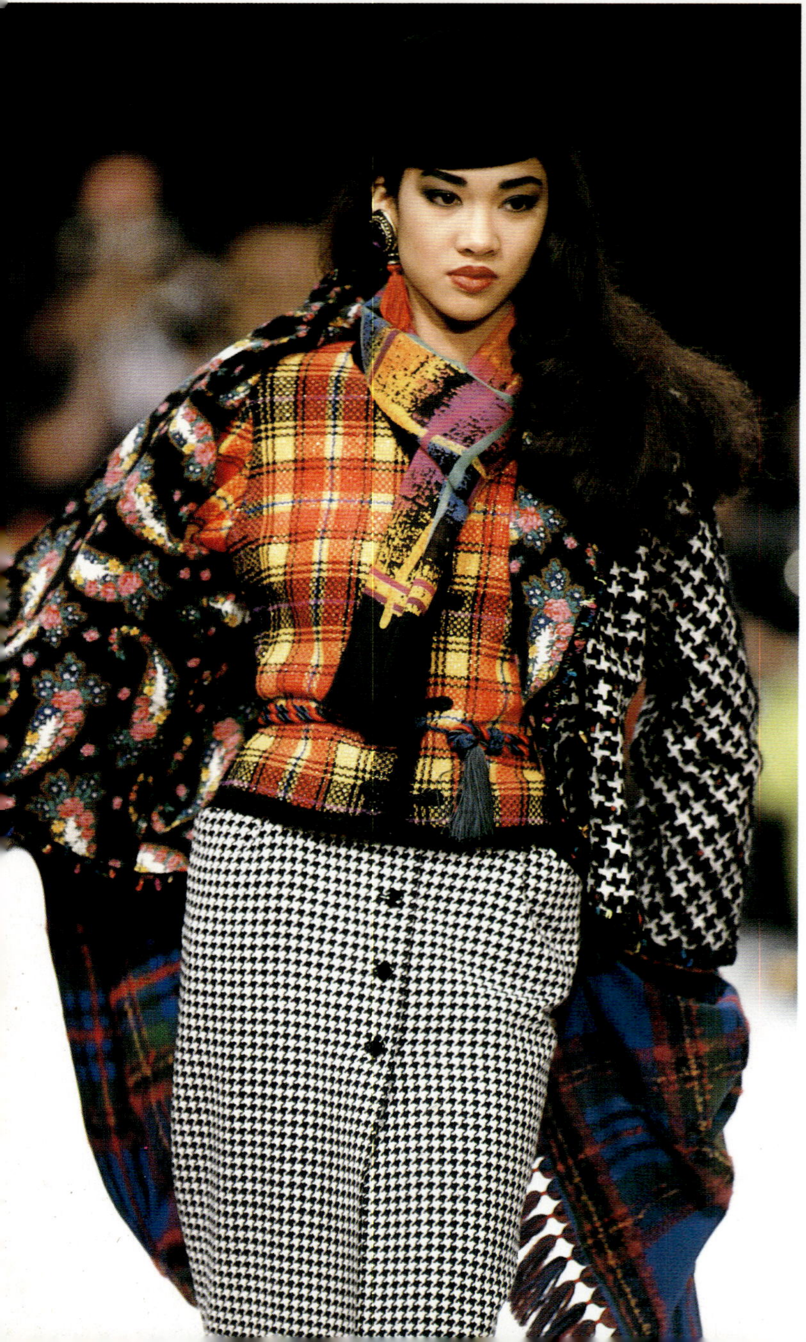

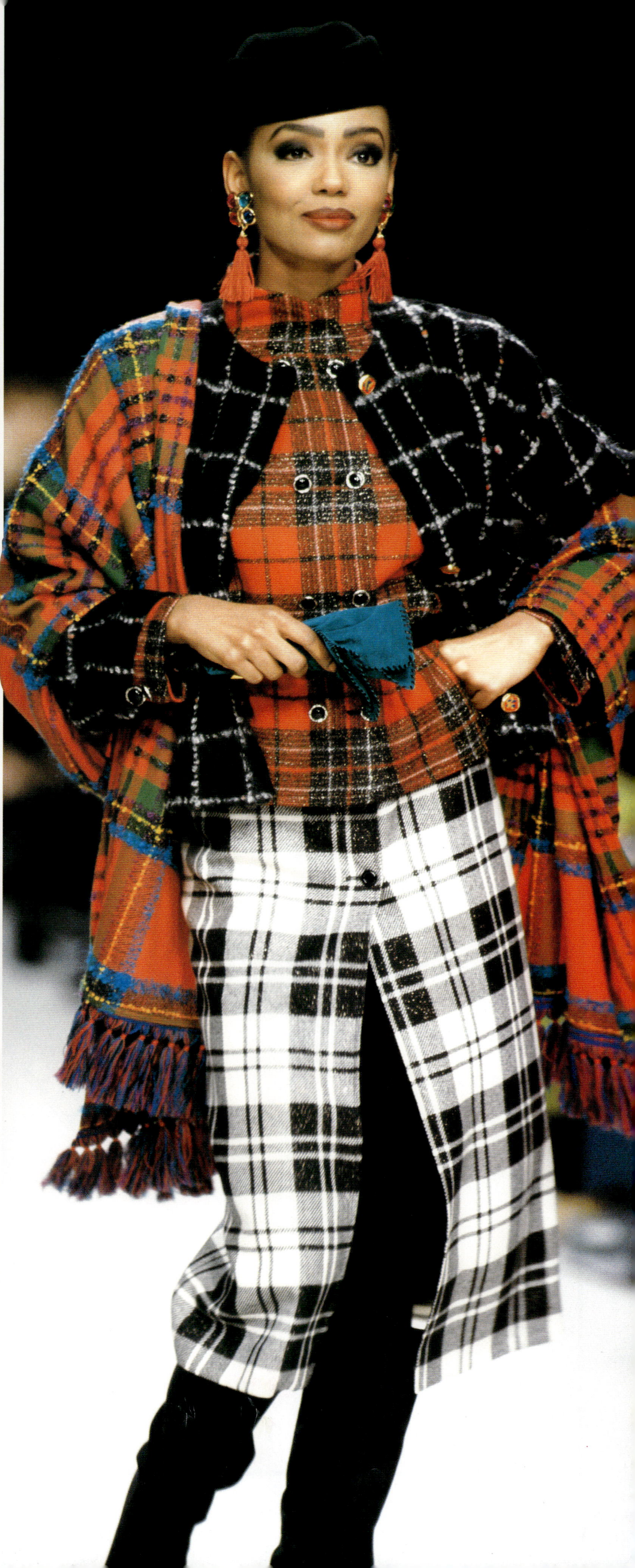

EMANUEL UNGARO

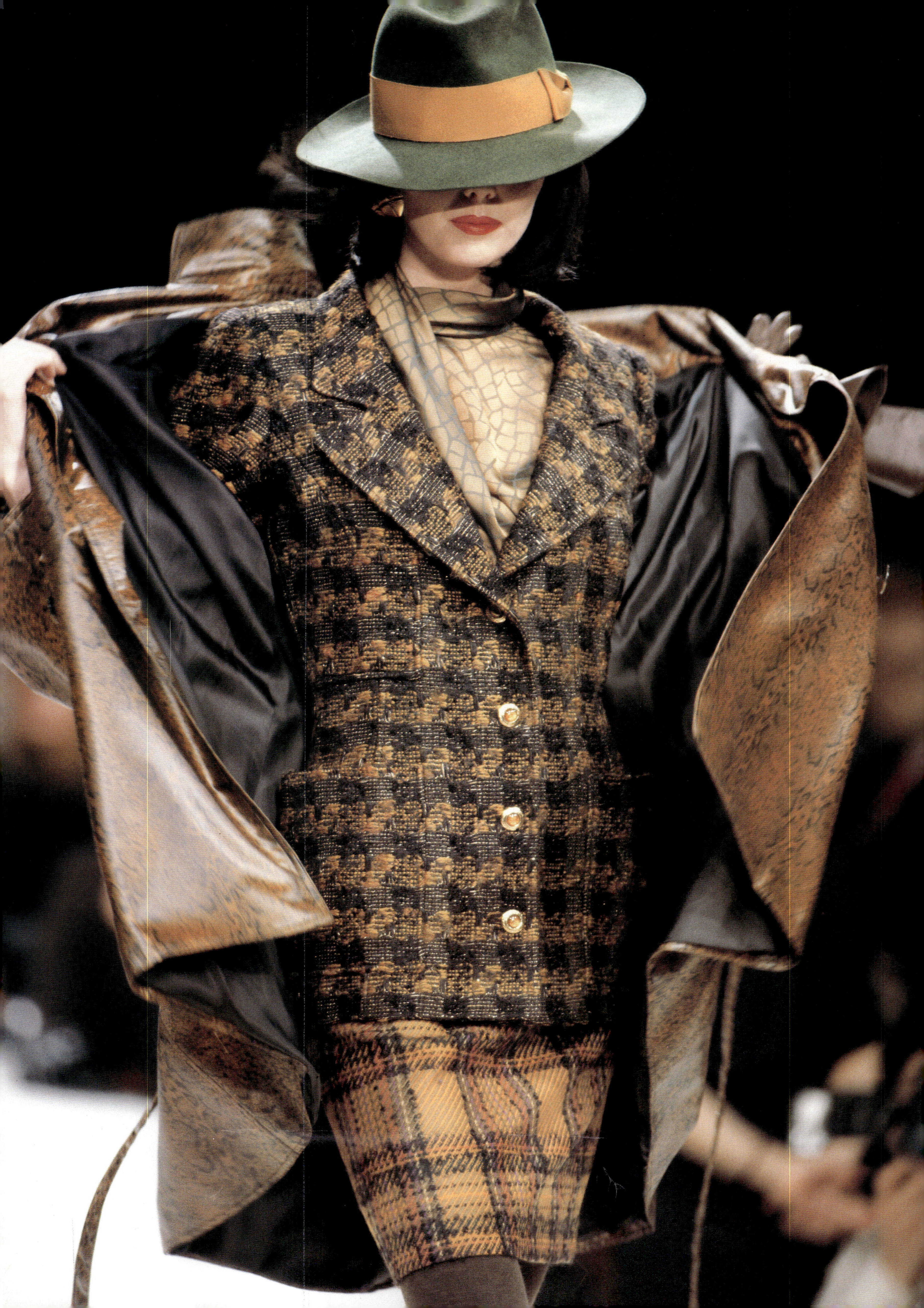

PARIS-18

HELMUT LANG

ヘルムト・ラング

透ける素材とトラペーズ・シルエットのナイーブな効果が魅力。今シーズンはメッシュが透ける素材に加わっている。

Transparent and innocent-looking trapèze silhouettes and charming.
This season, mesh was added to the range of transparent materials.

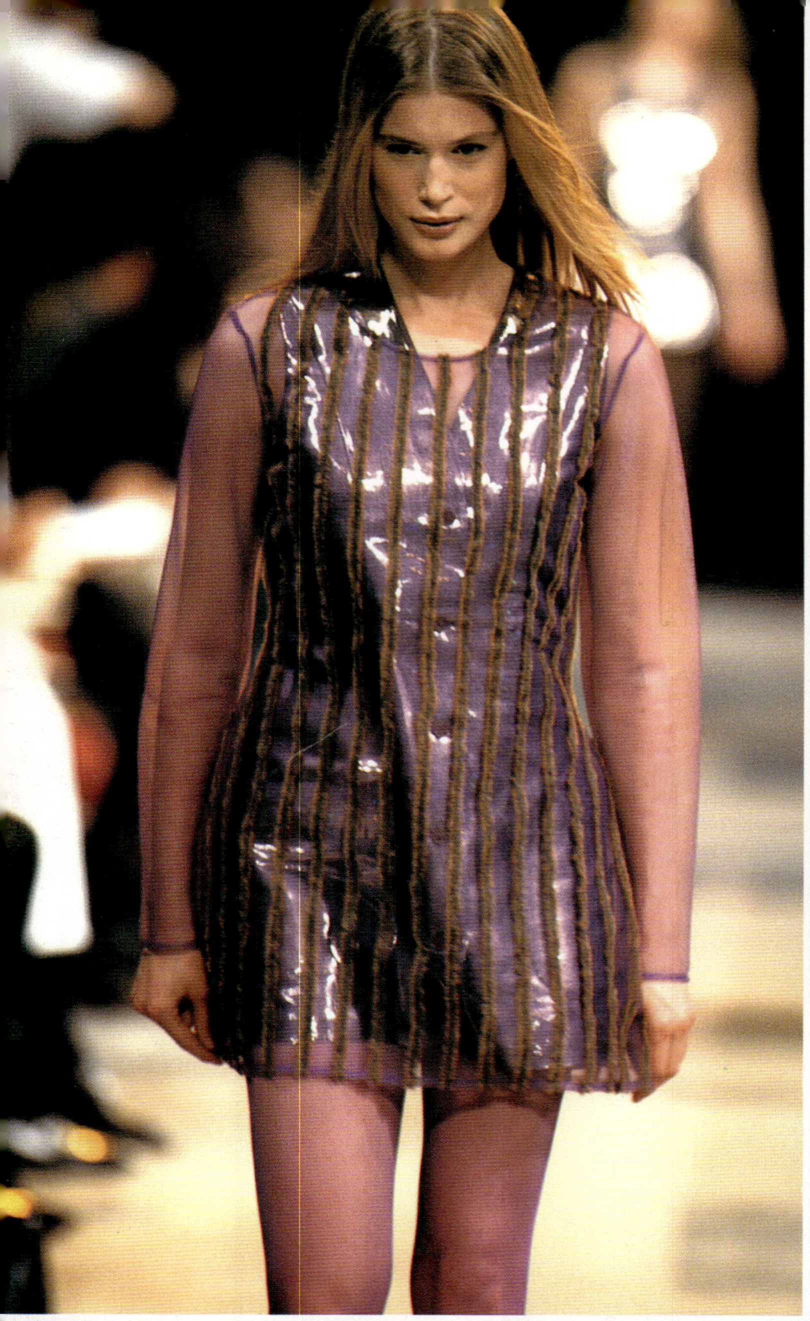
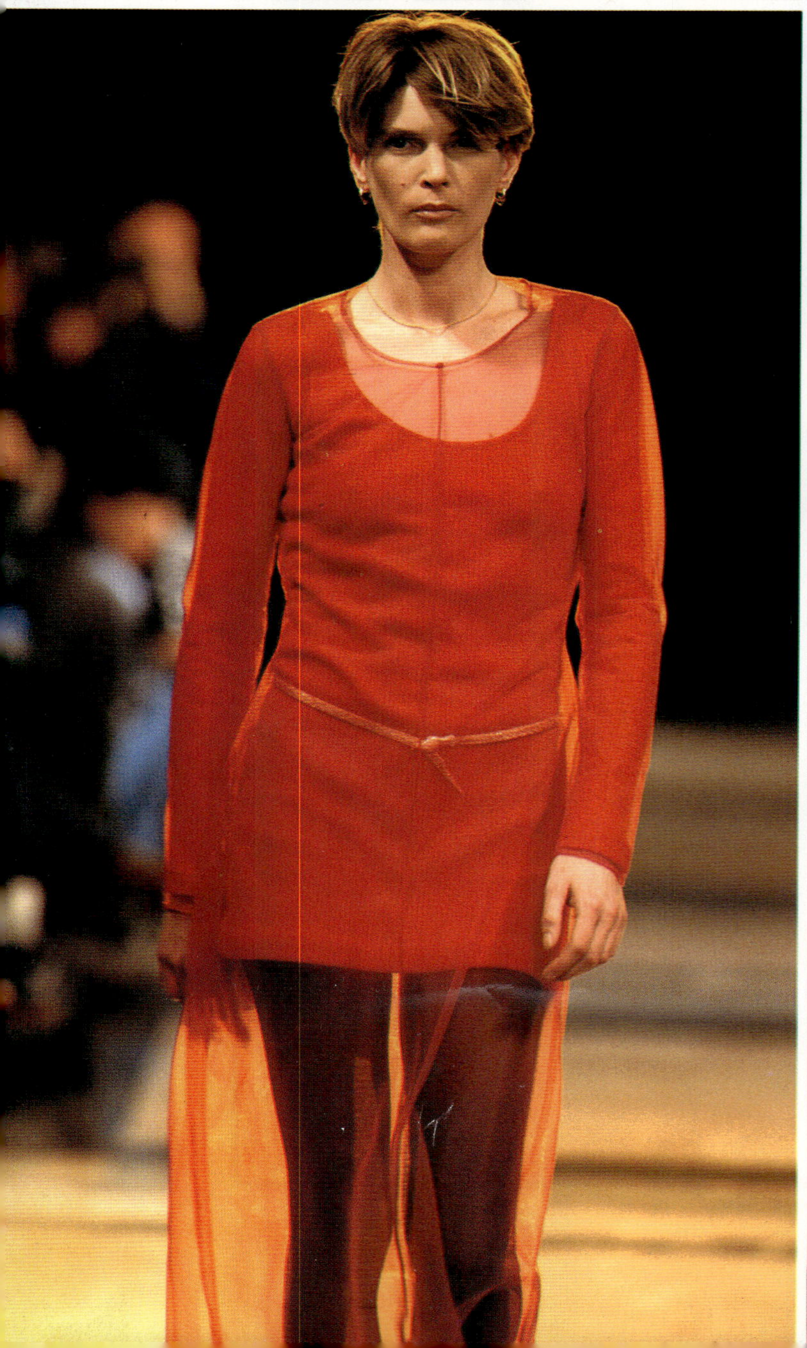
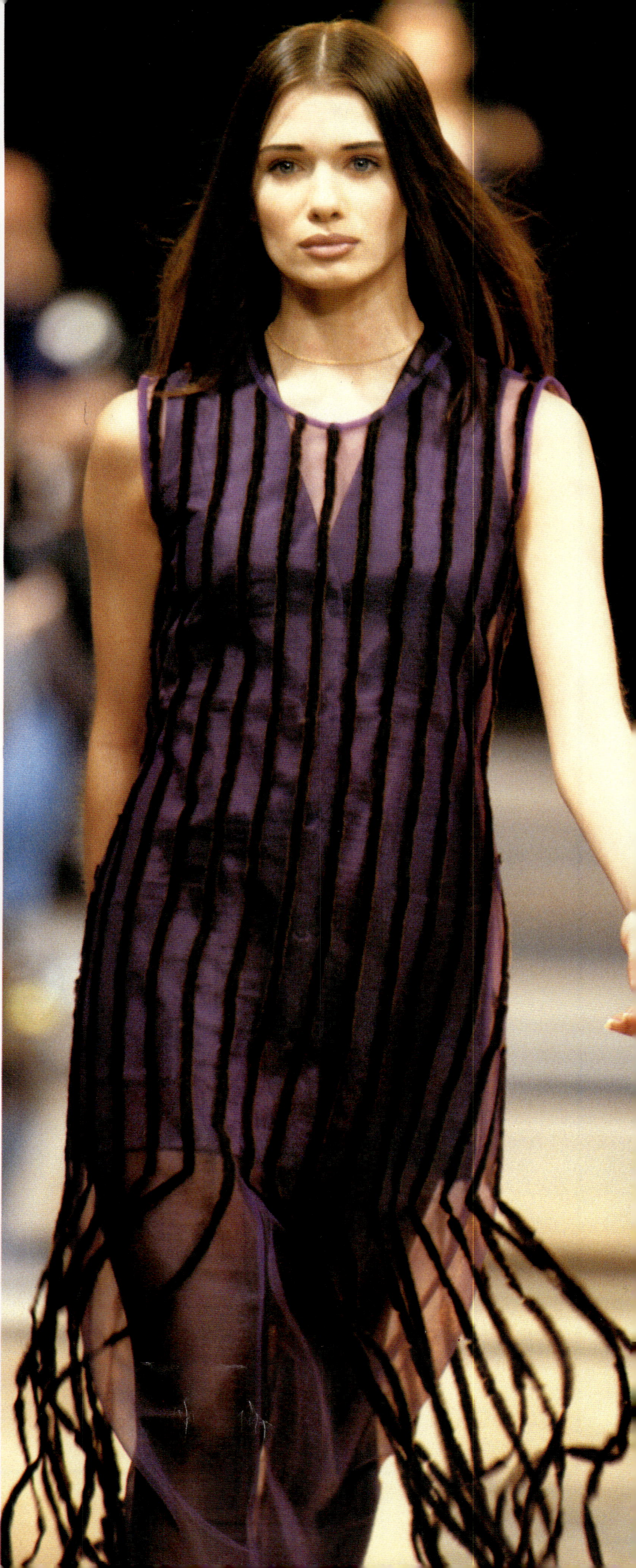

HELMUT LANG

193

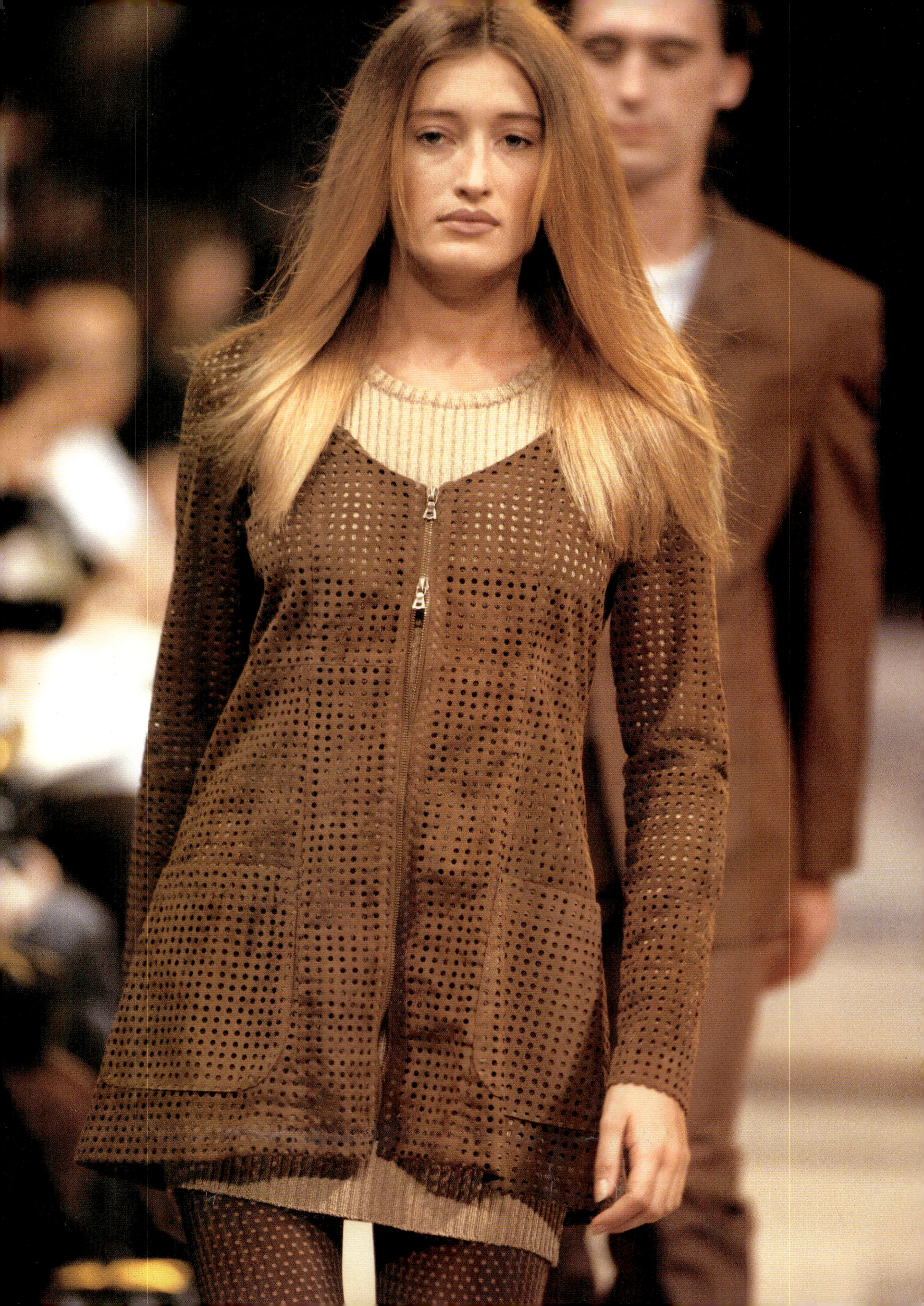

CHANTAL THOMASS

シャンタル・トマス

下着ルックはシャンタル・トマス得意の世界。今シーズンもセクシーな下着をインスピレーションにしたスタイルや乗馬ルックを提案。

Chantal Thomass is an expert at creating a world of undergarment-looking fashion.
Again this season, the styles she brought out were inspired by sexy underwear and horse riding fashion.

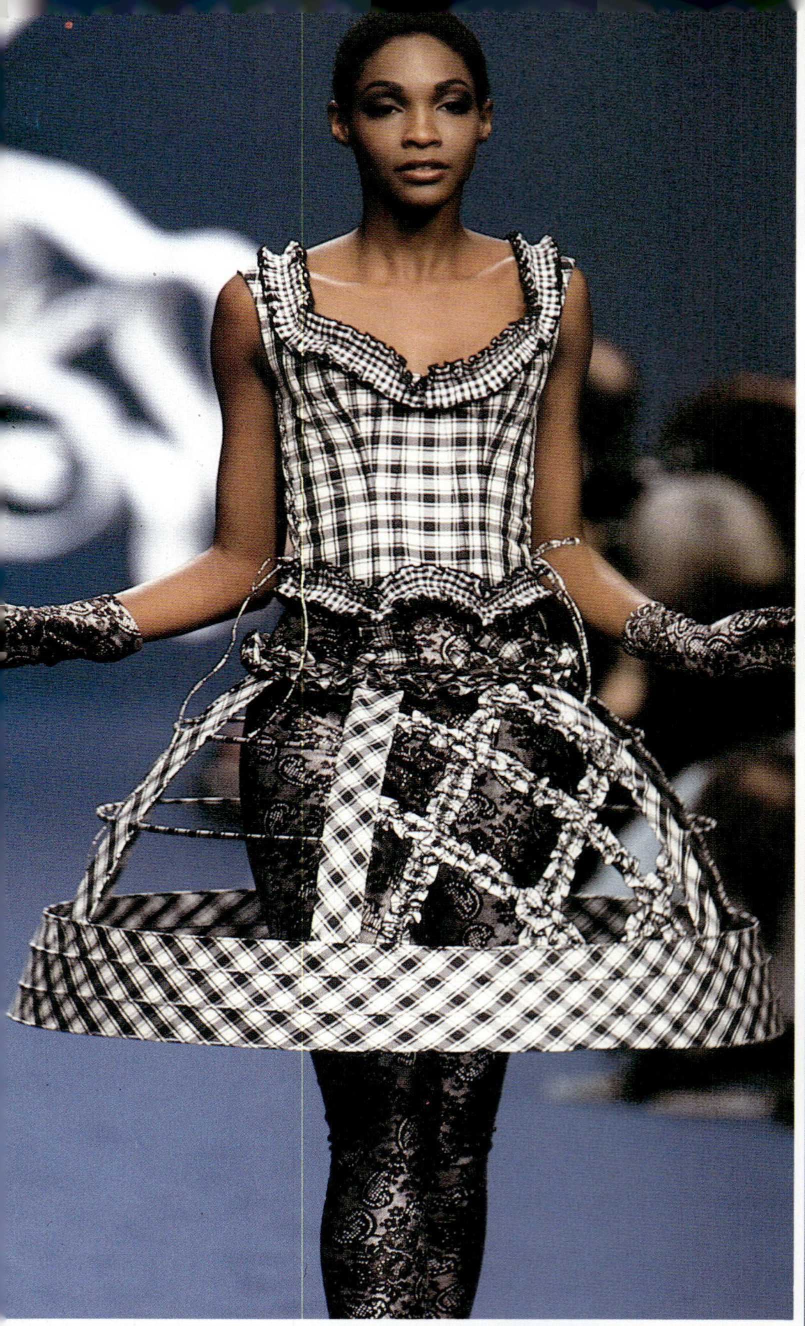
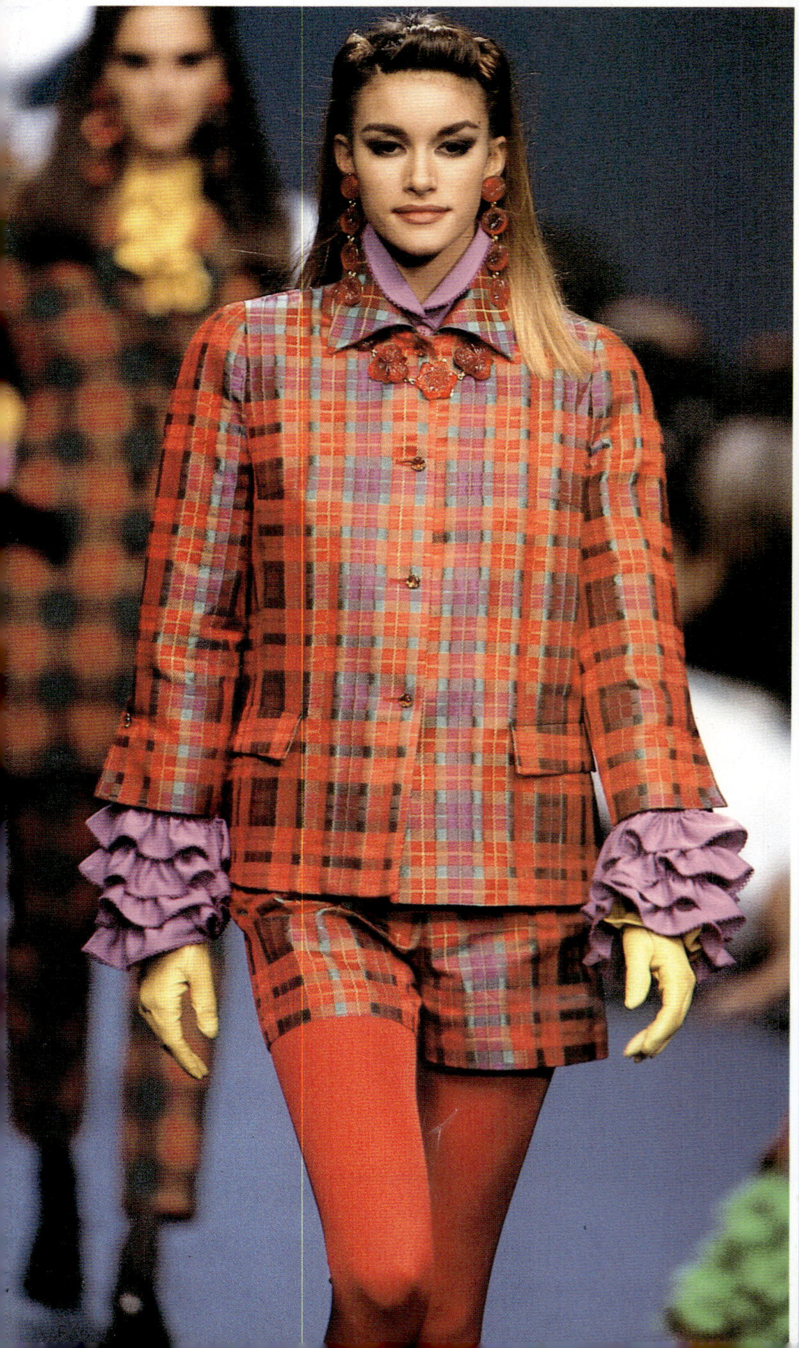
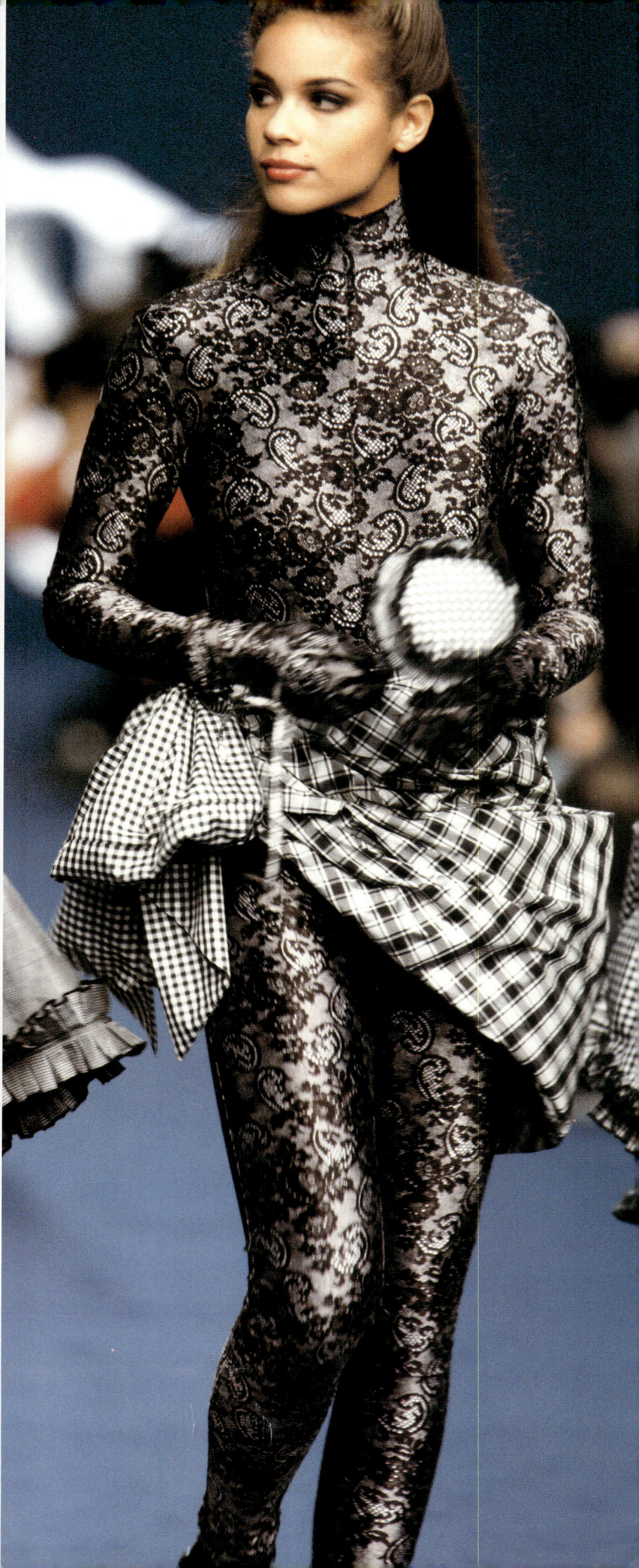

CHANTAL THOMASS

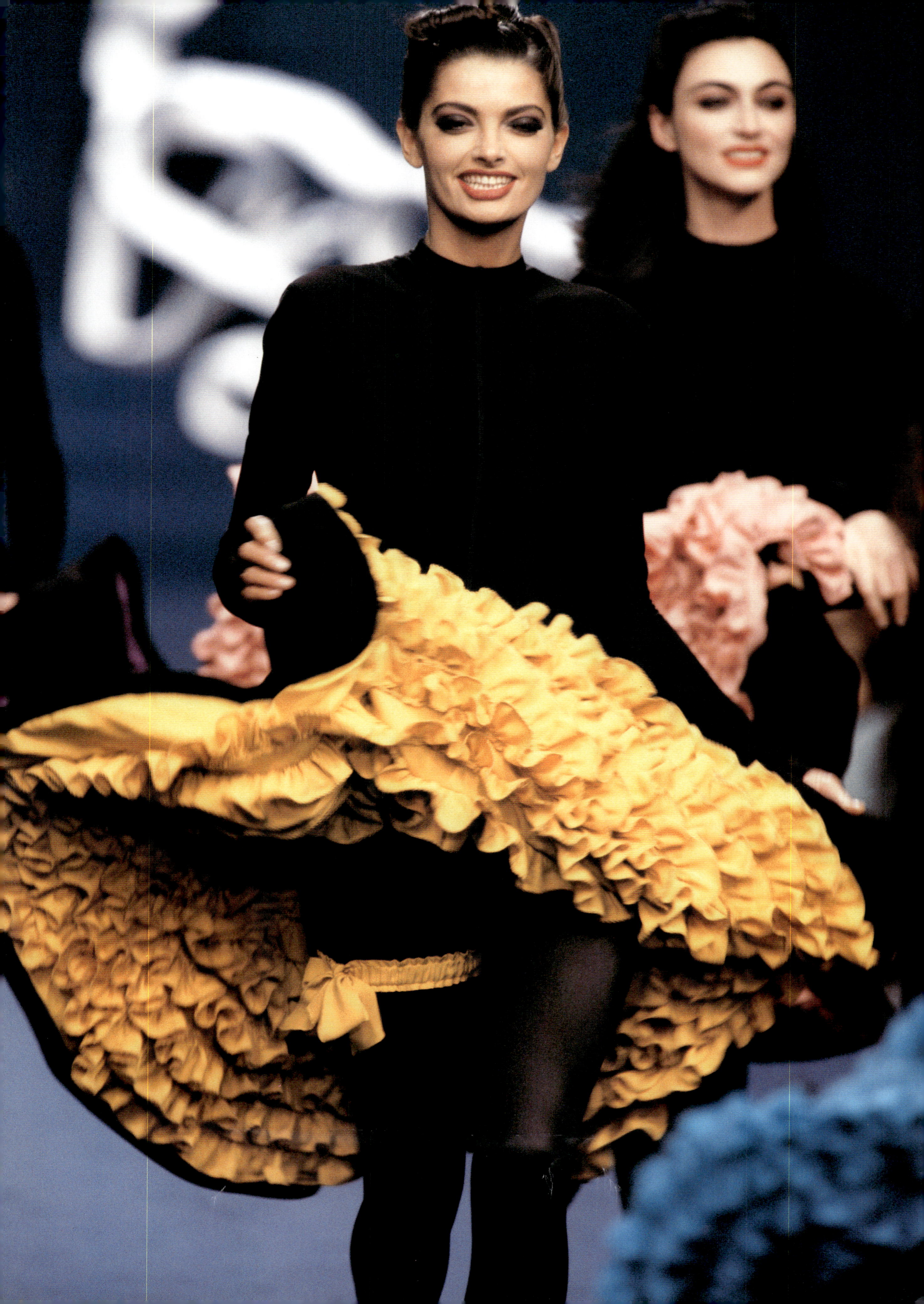

YUKI TORII

ユキ・トリヰ

リ・カラーされた新鮮なチェック・パターンやフリンジが若々しさを表現。ジッパーやステッチ、トリミングのディテールを駆使して、彩りをそえている。

Refreshing re-colored check patterns and fringes applied in a display of youthfulness.
Adding color, details such as zips, stitches and trimmings.

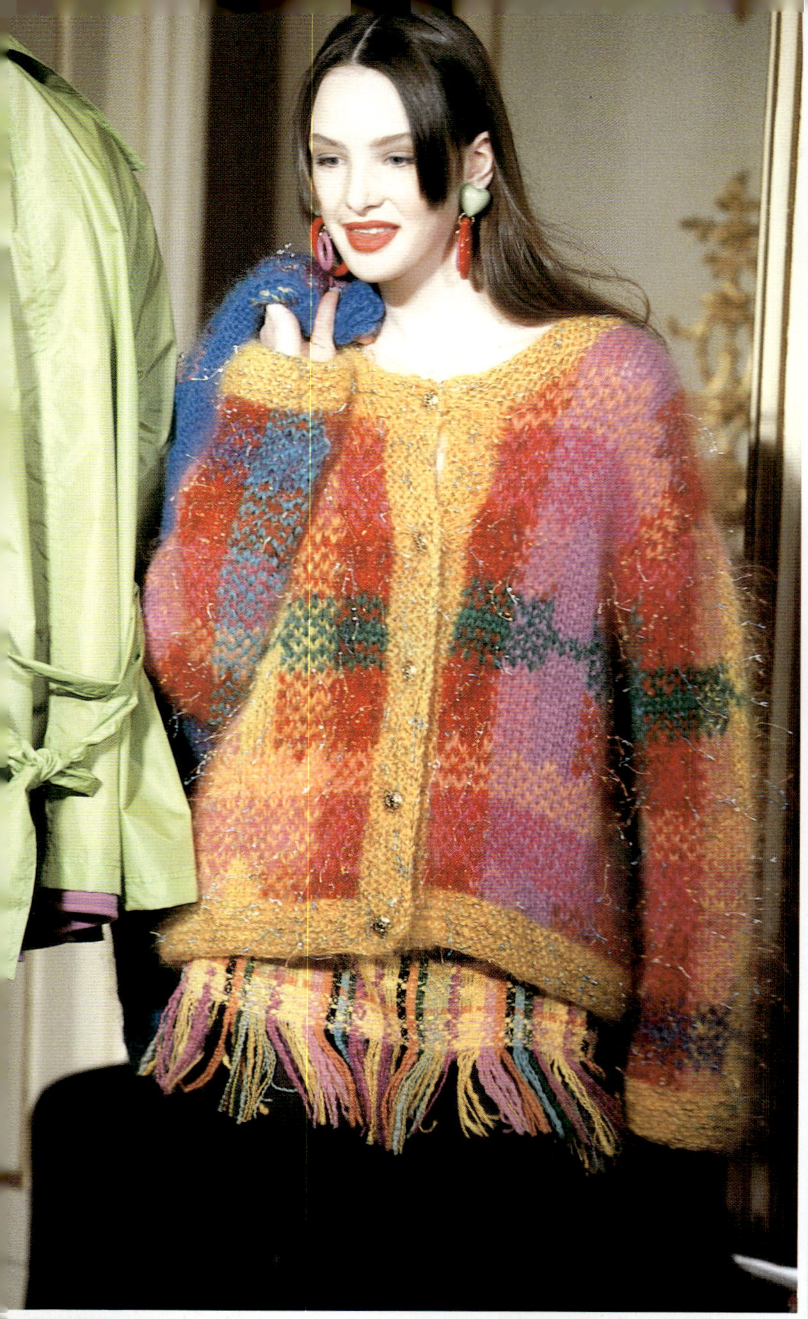
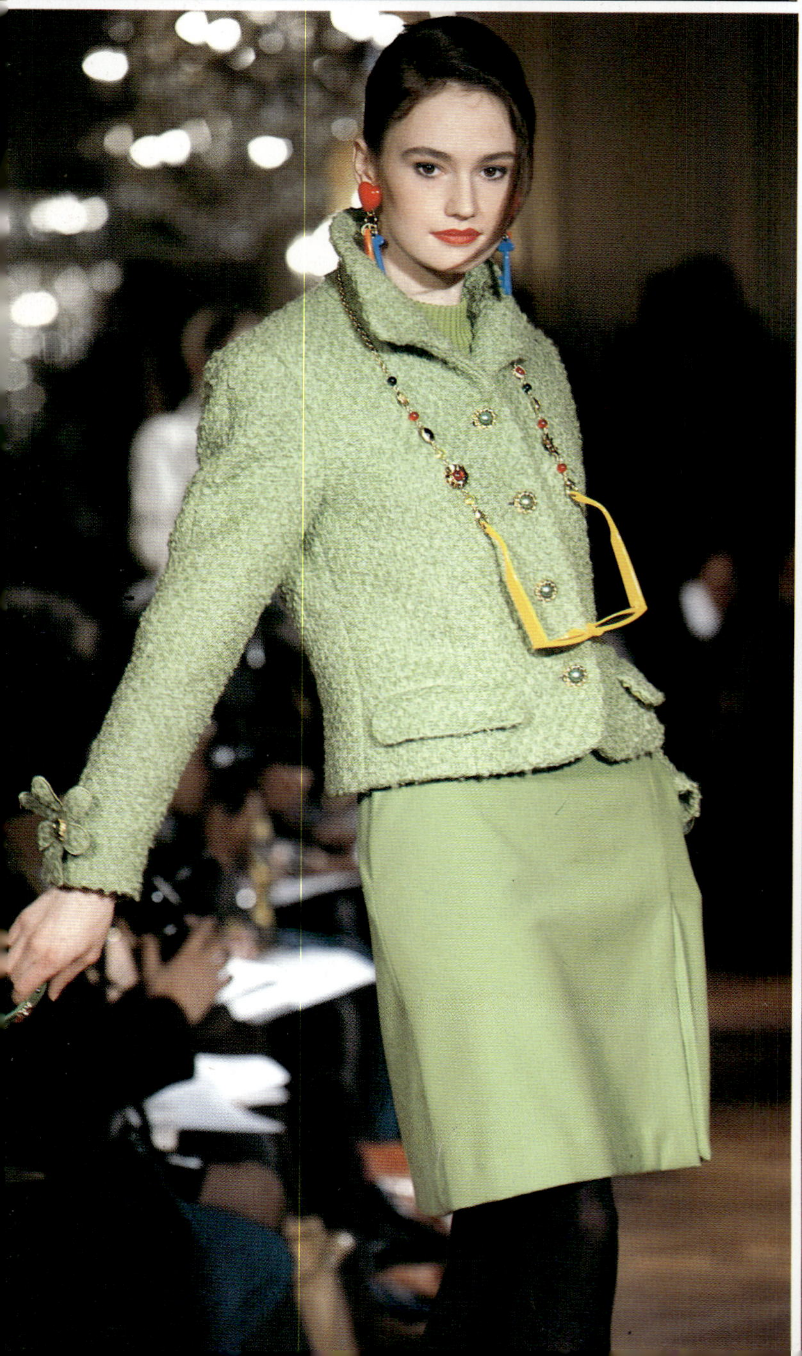
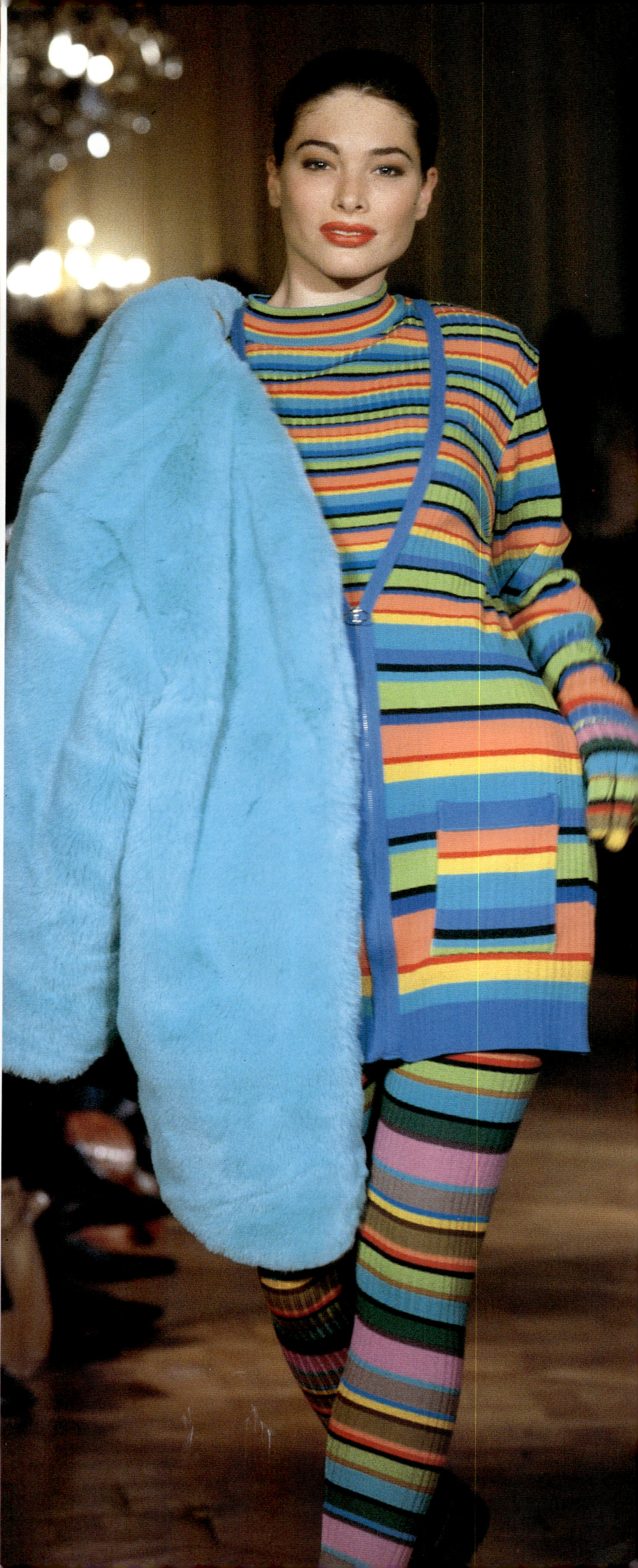

YUKI TORII

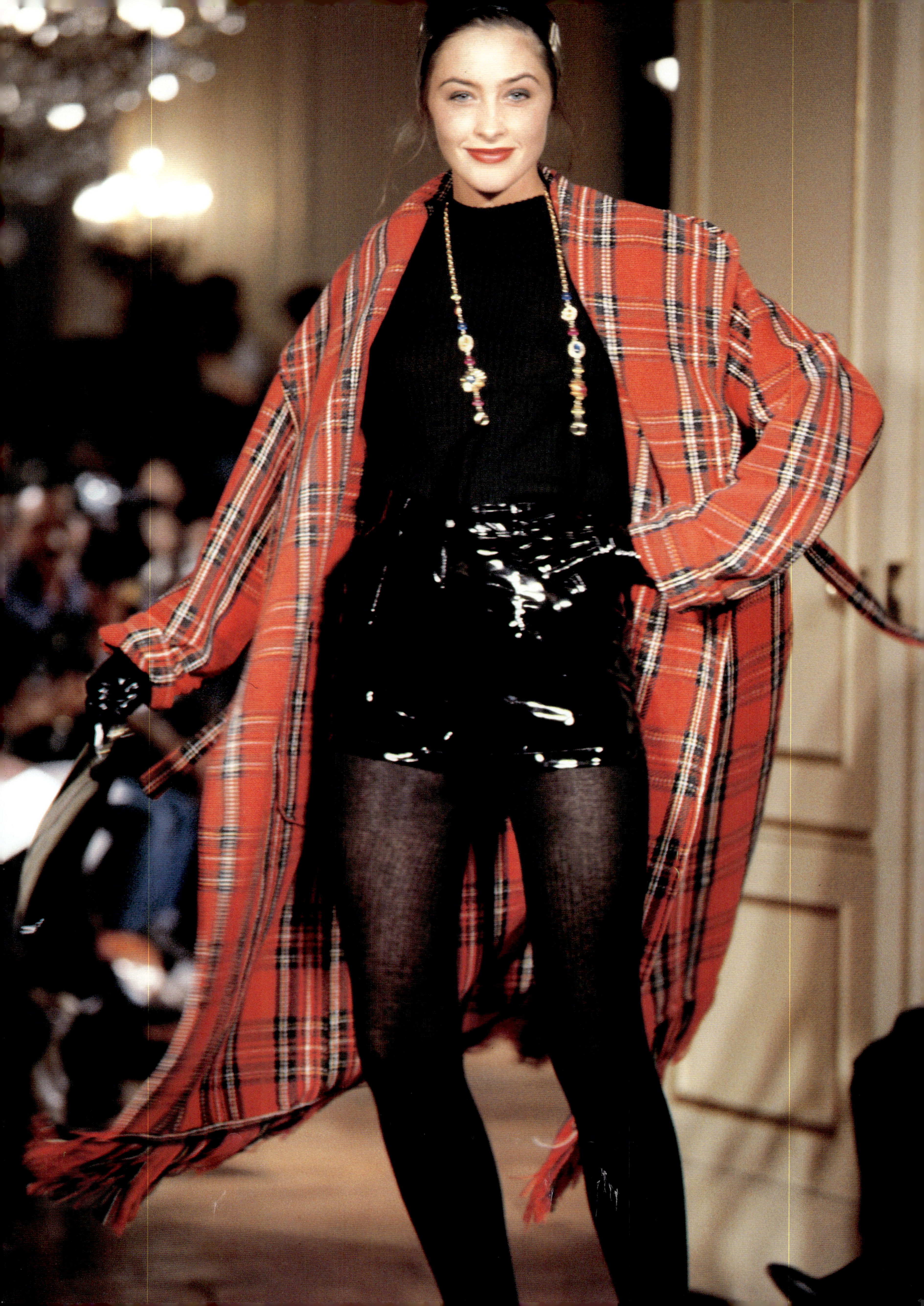

JUNKO SHIMADA

ジュンコ・シマダ

カウガールやカウボーイ、アリゾナなどをテーマに、島田順子らしいセクシーで粋な昇華。レース・アップ・ディテールをふんだんに使ったチューブラー・シルエットも魅力。
With great success, Junko Shimada has created a sexy and chic fashion, based on the Arizona cowboy/cowgirl theme.
Also charming, the tubular silhouette with generous lace-up detail applied.

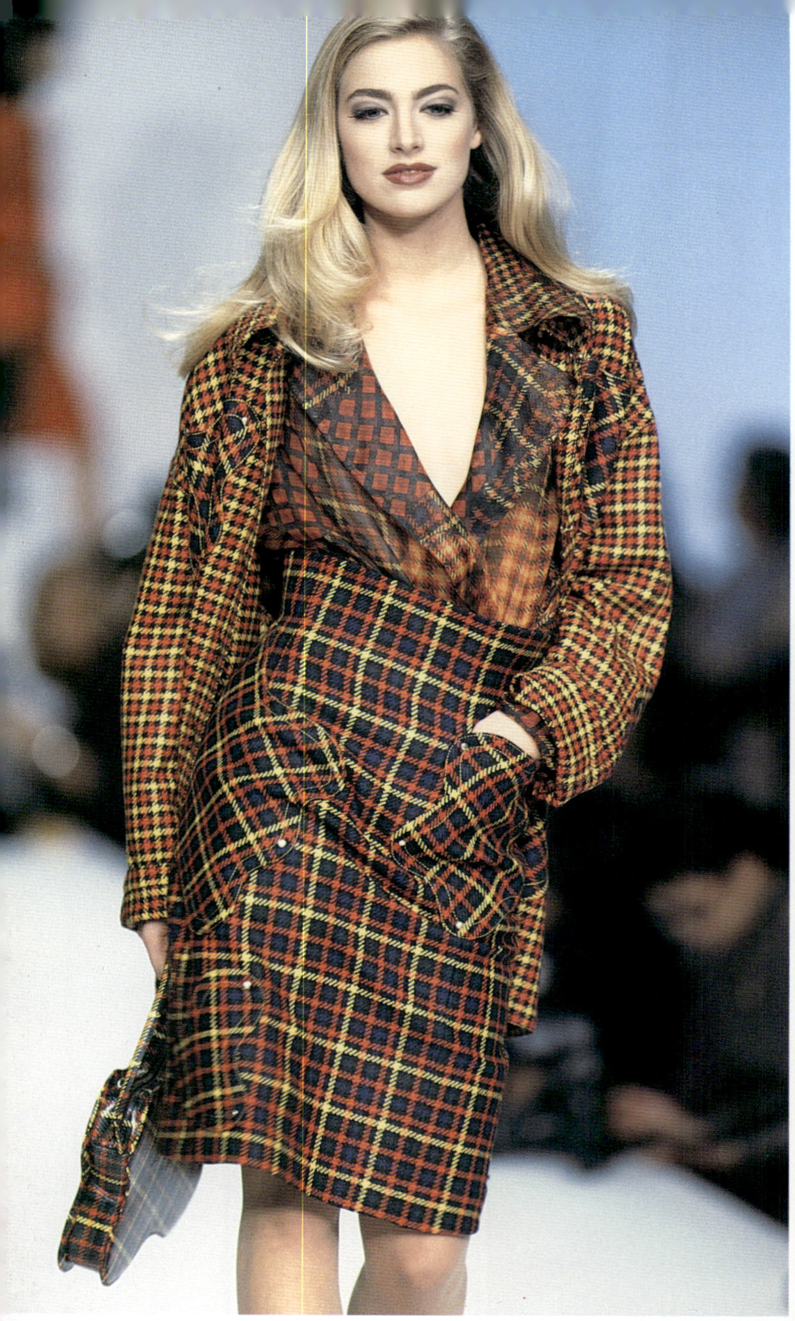

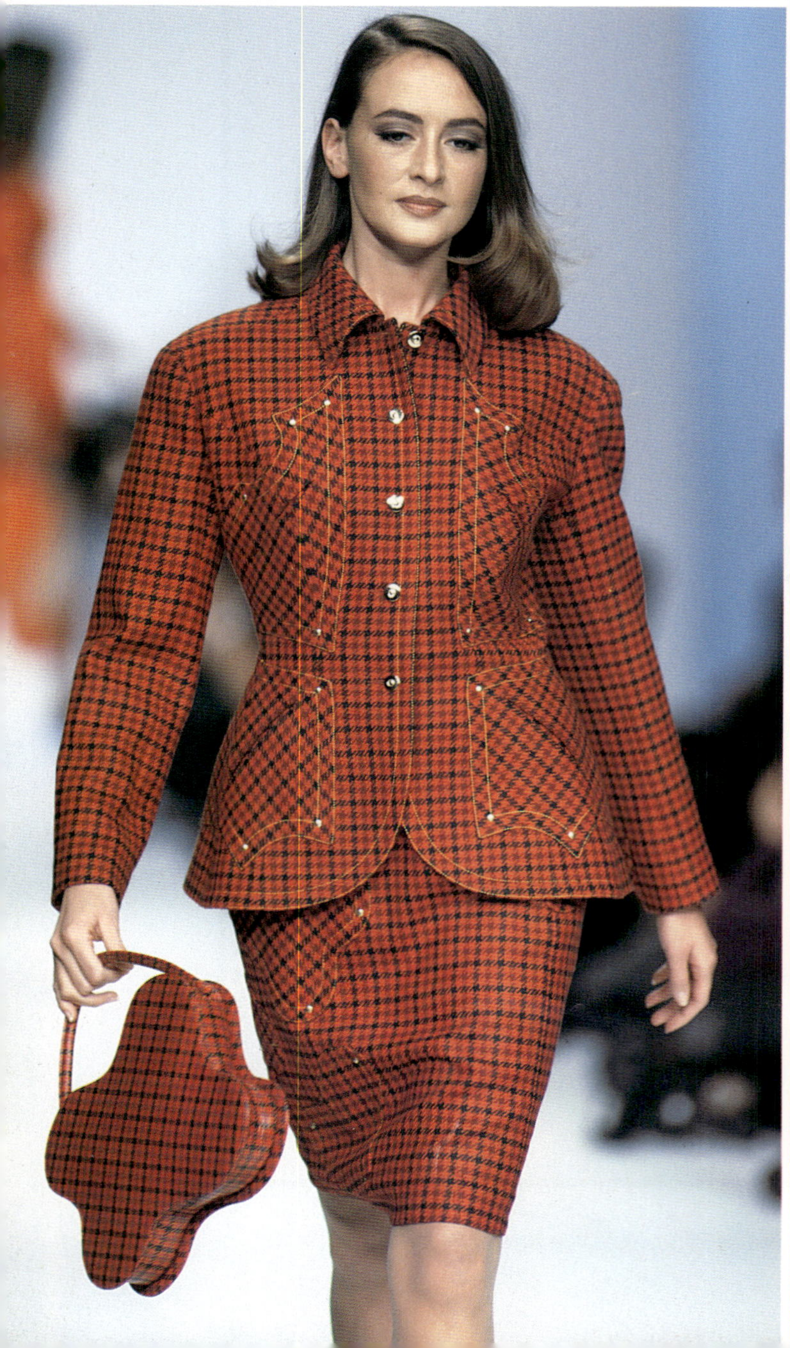

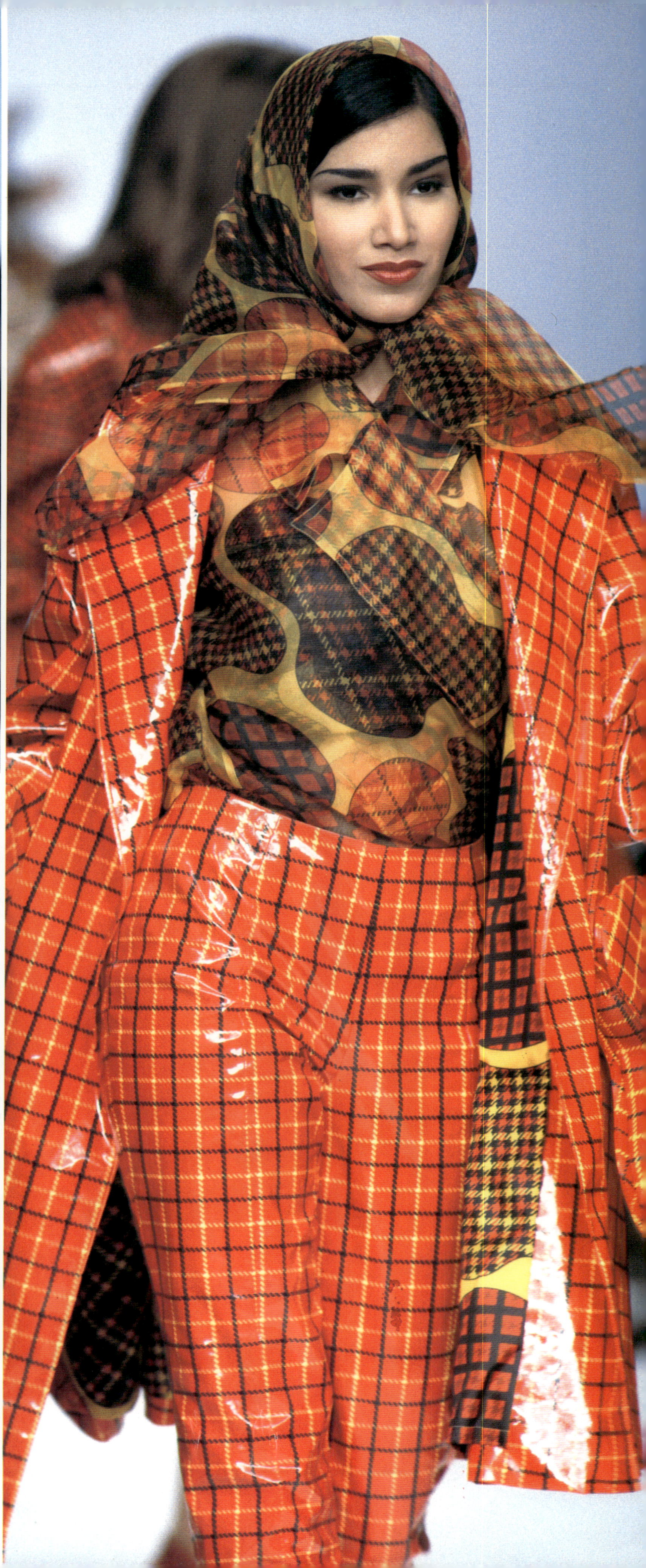

JUNKO SHIMADA

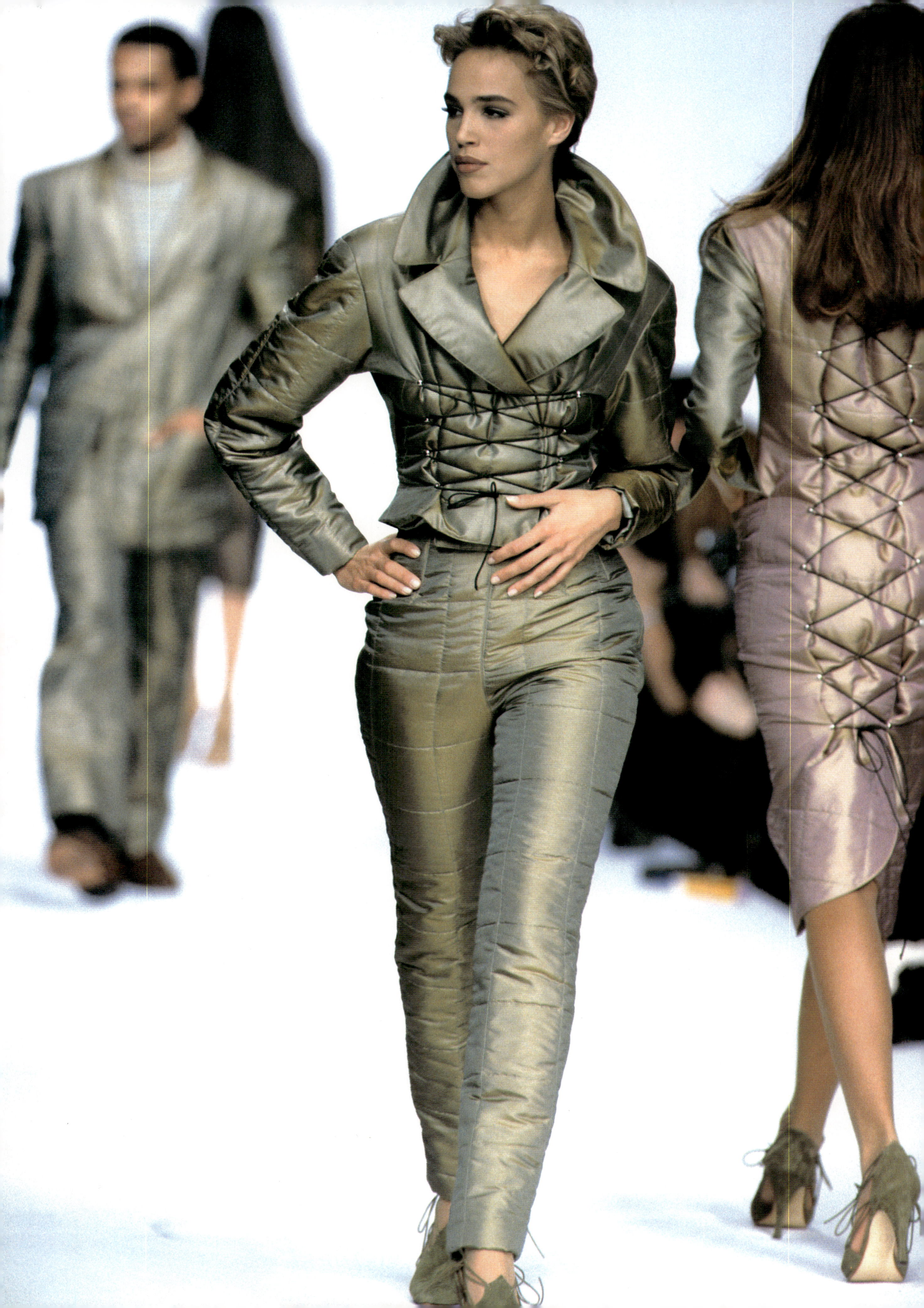

LOLITA LEMPICKA

ロリータ・レンピカ

ボディコンシャス・シルエットが基本のライン。ジャケットもよりボディにクローズ。インパクトあるブライト・カラーとトリミングがシルエットに表情を与えている。

Line jackets, based on a body conscious silhouette, were brought even closer to the body.
Adding expression to the silhouette, bright colors with impact and trimmings,

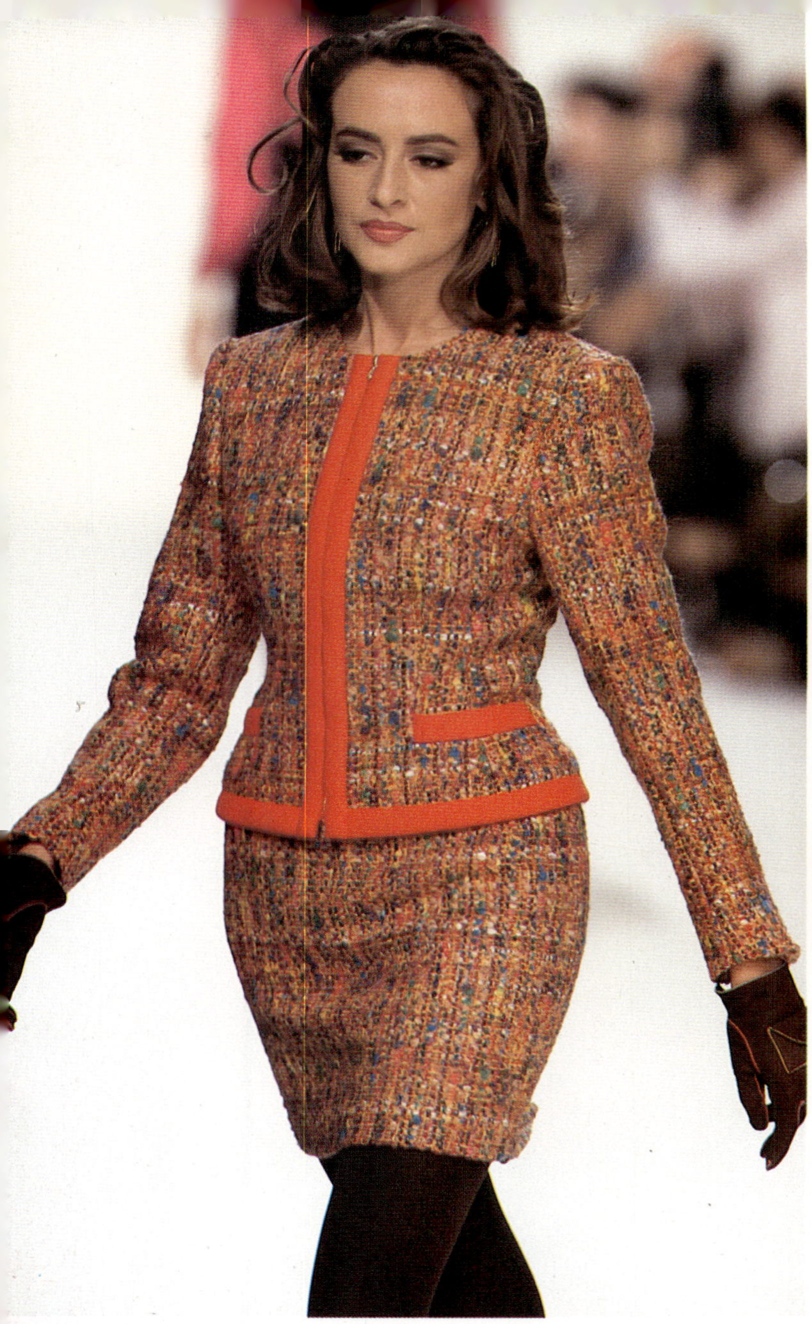
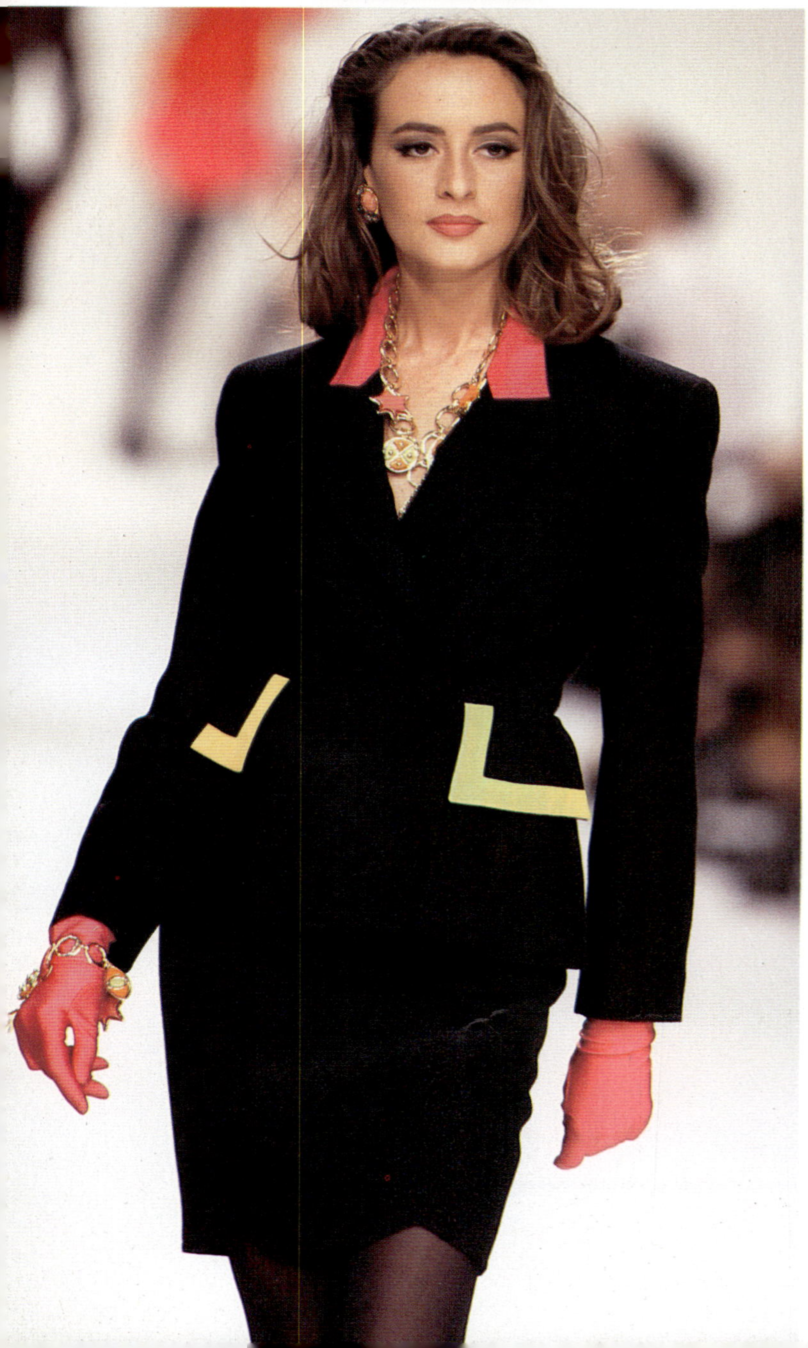
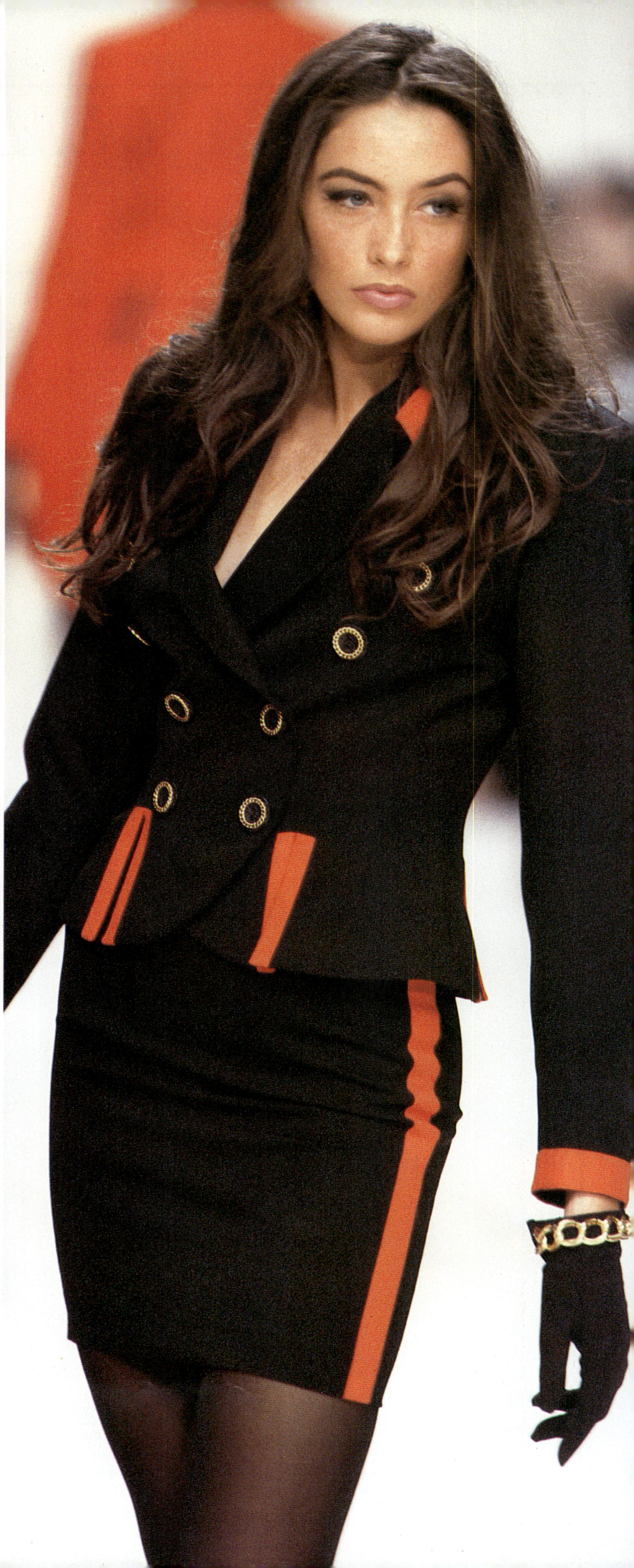

LOLITA LEMPICKA

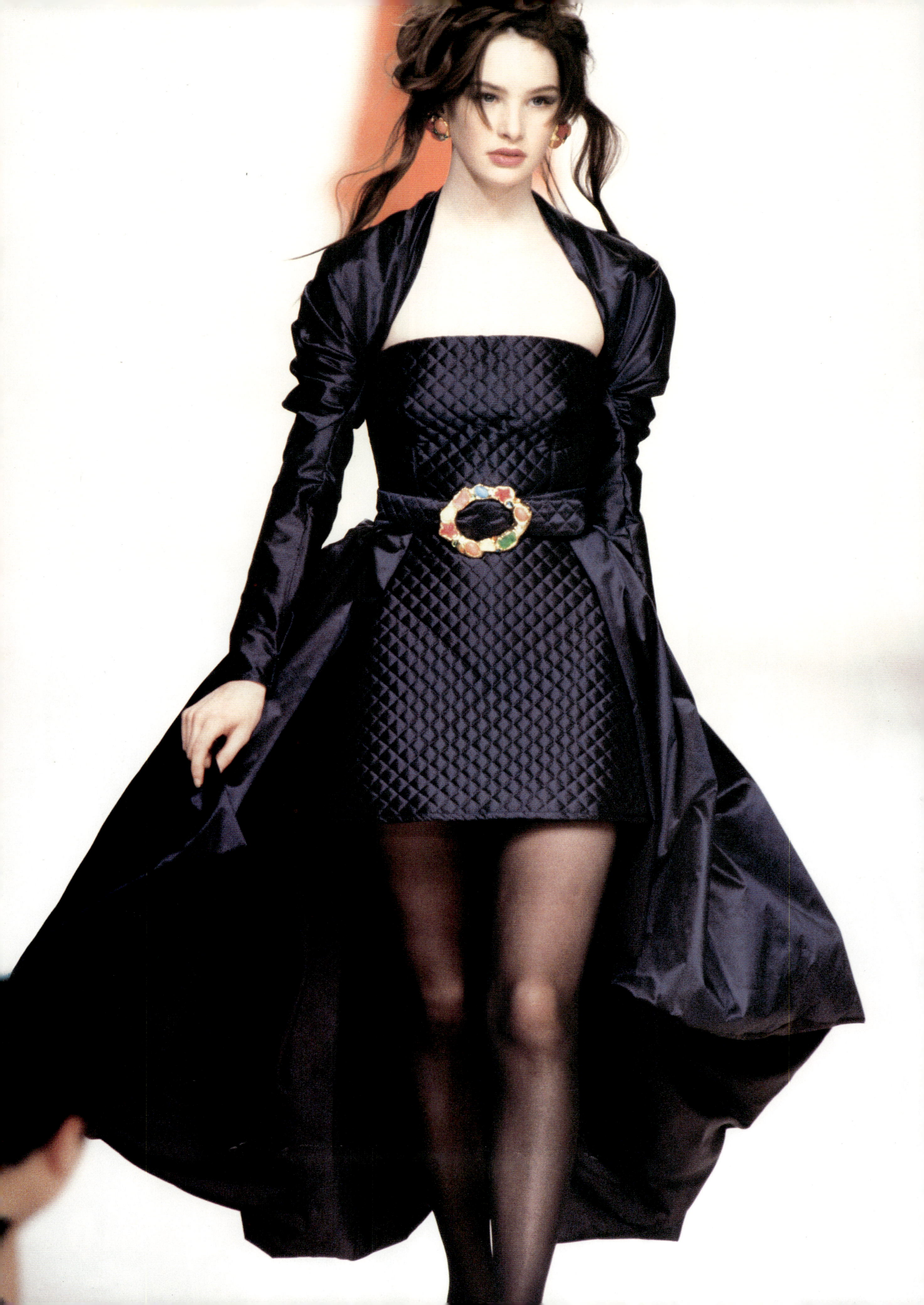

DANIEL HECHTER

ダニエル・エシュテル

オープニングは若々しいカレッジ・スタイルで。ブライトなカラーワークのセーター・ドレスやアイシー・パステルのコーディネイトは軽快でスポーティブなダニエルのスタイルを表現。
Displayed a college style at the opening. Daniel's light and sporty style shown in his sweater dresses with bright color work and a coordination of icy pastel colors.

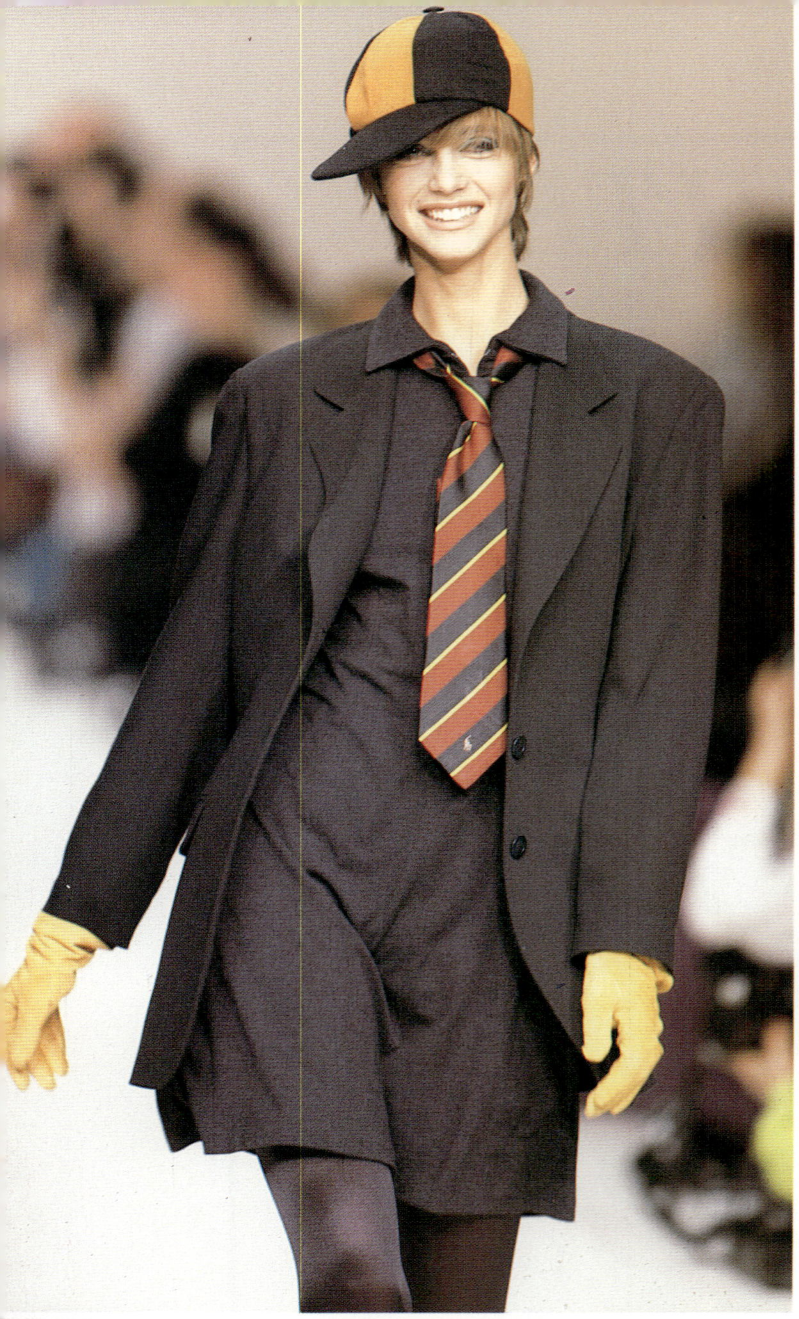
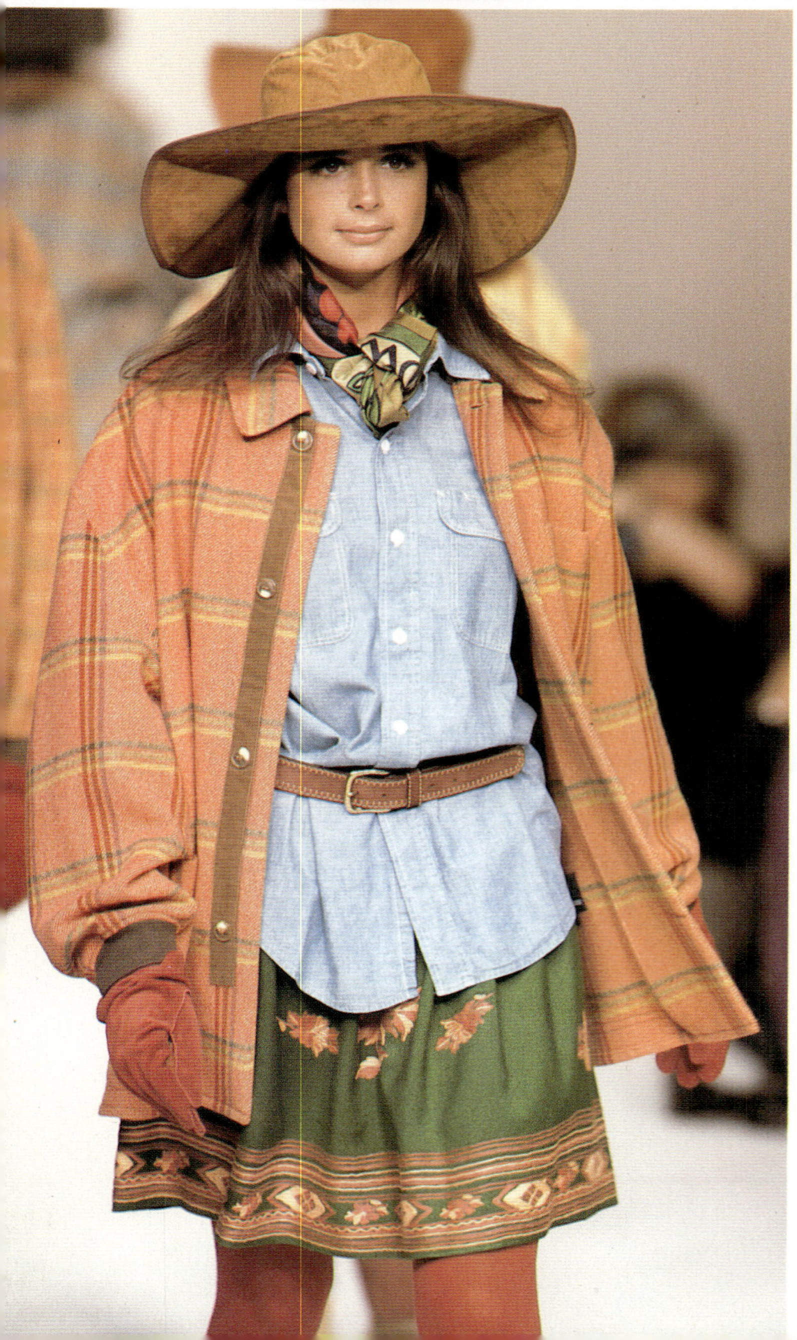
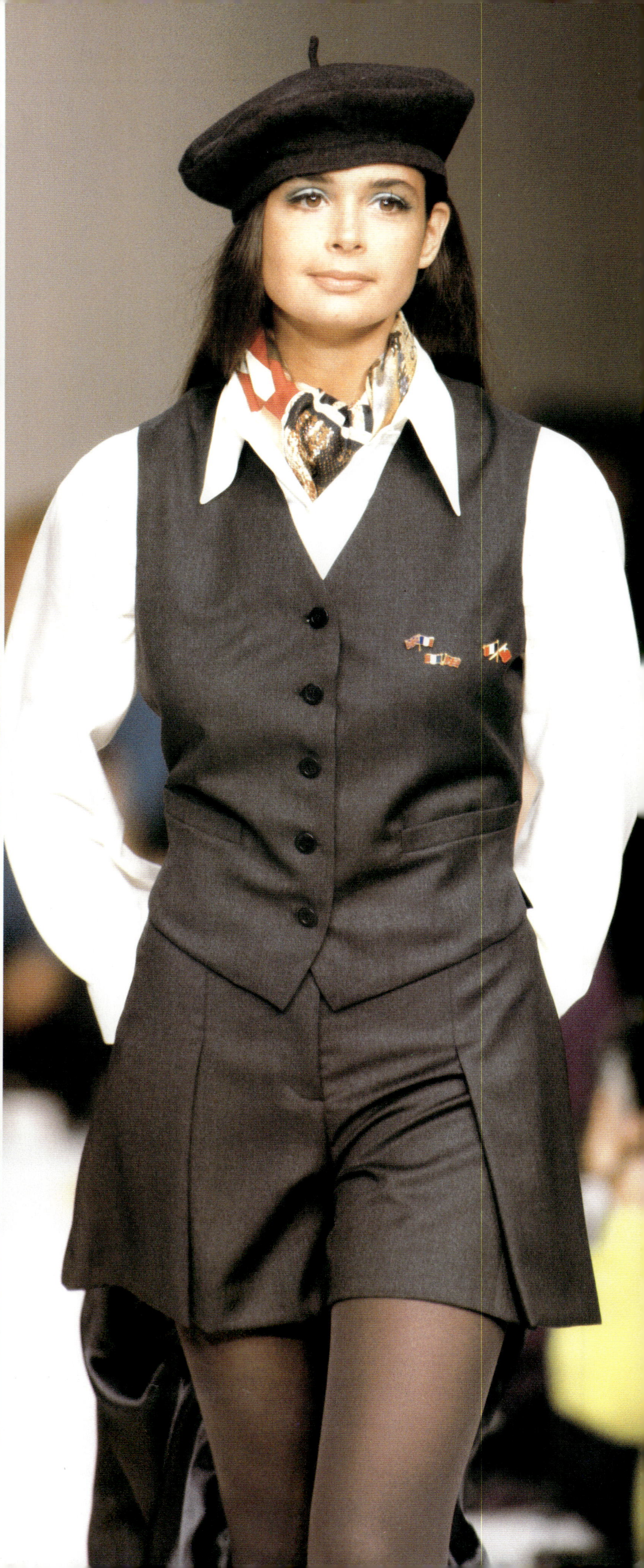

DANIEL HECHTER

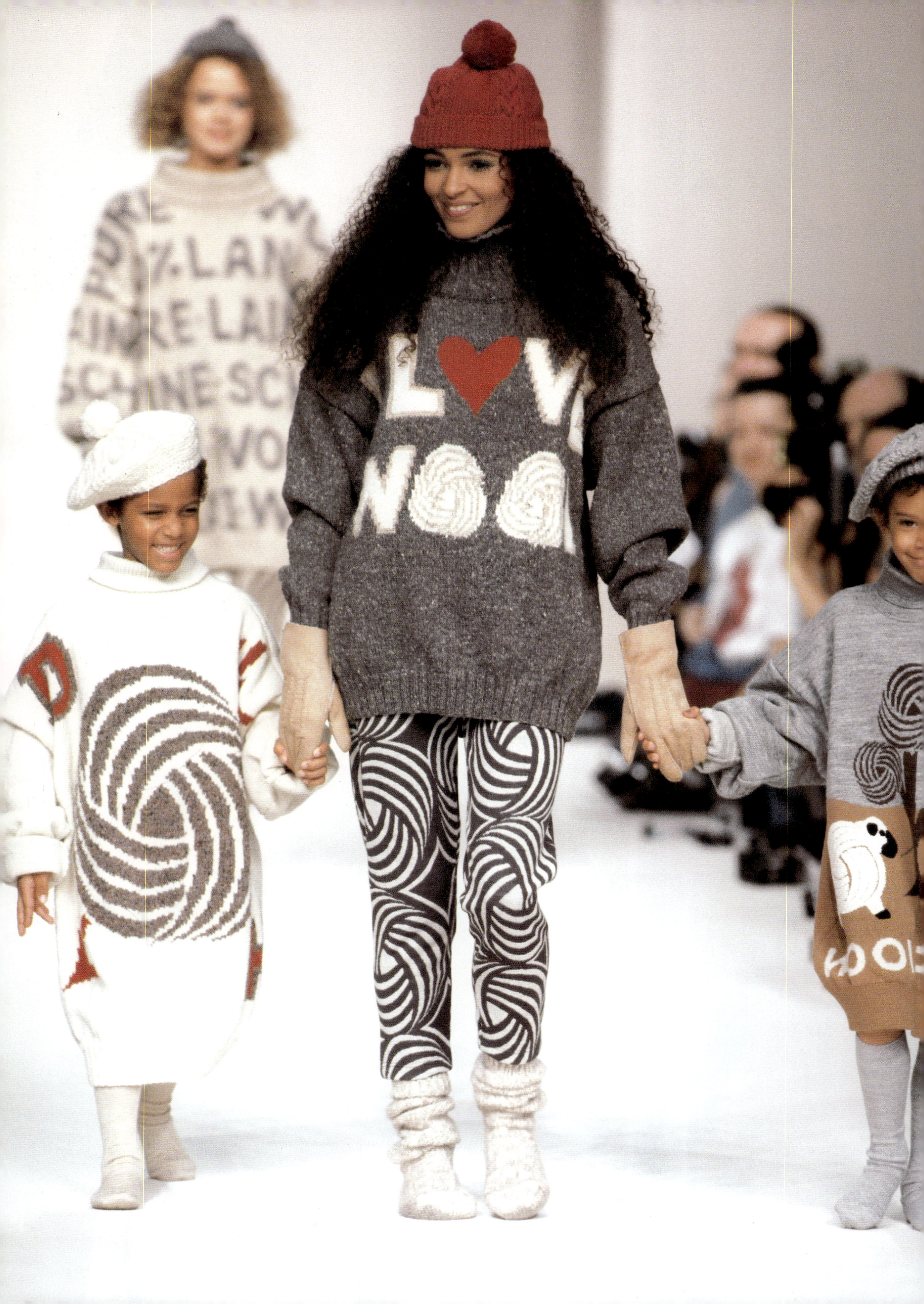

PARIS-24

BARBARA BUI

バルバラ・ビュイ

ミニマルなフォルムをエナメルやラメ、コーティングなどの光る素材で演出。赤と黒のカラー・ブロックやスタッド・ディテール、手編み風のレースもとりいれて新しさを。

Using illuminous materials with coatings such as enamel and lamé she displayed minimal forms.
Demonstrating new ideas using red and black color blocks, stud details and lace looking like a hand knit.

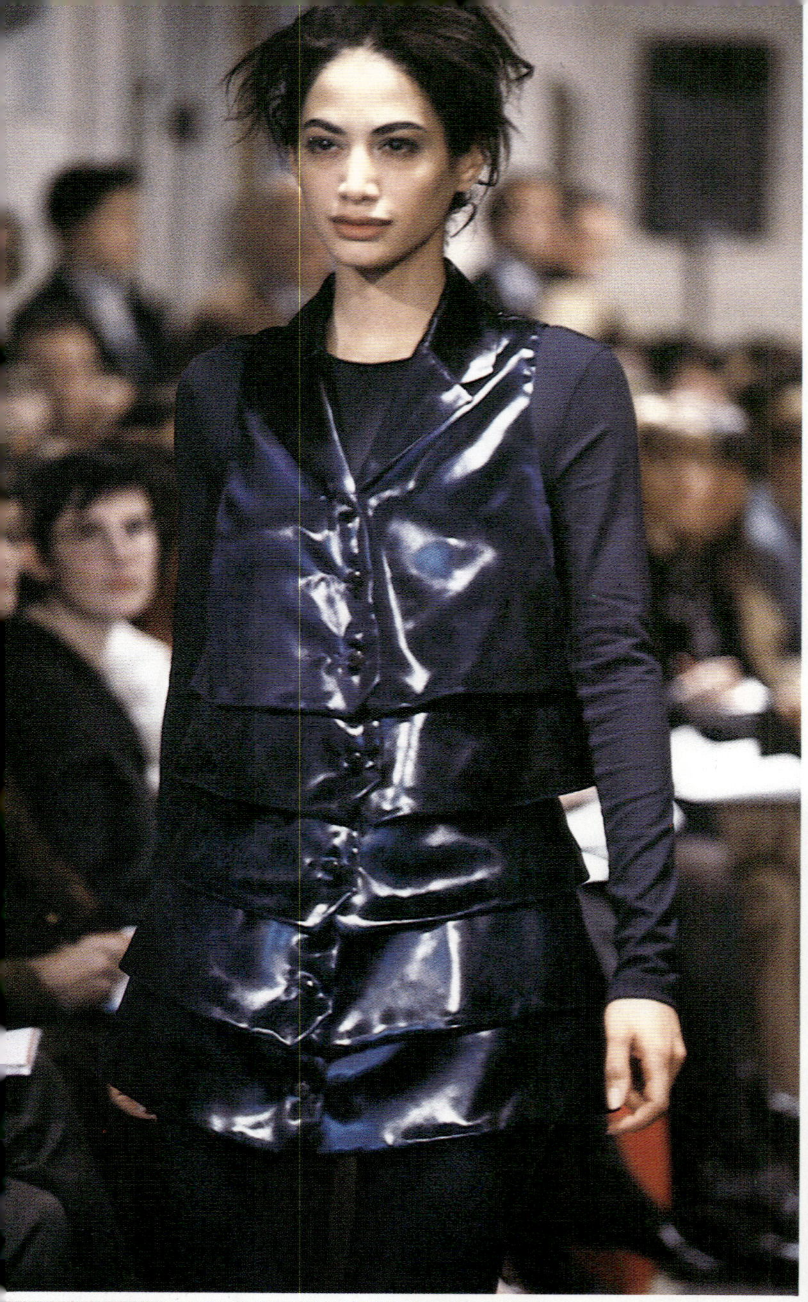

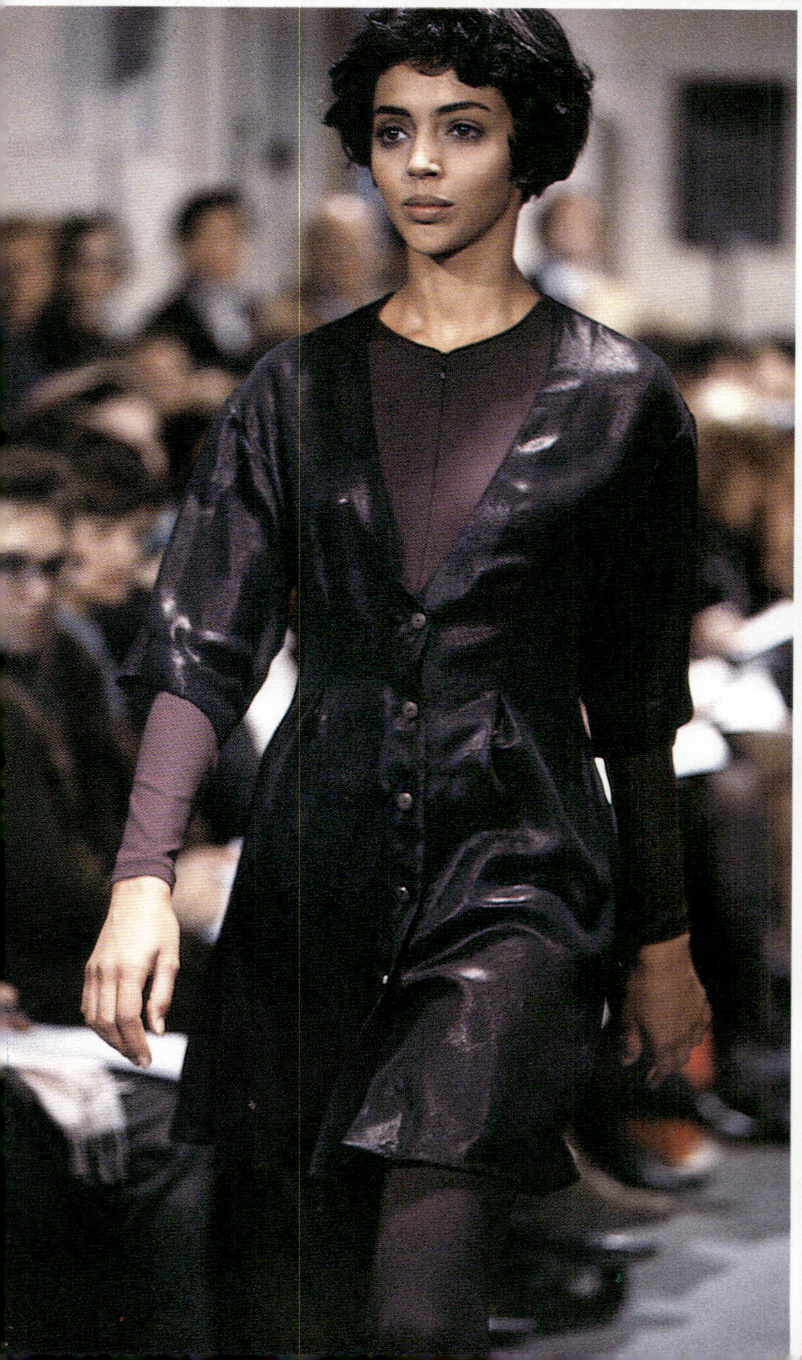

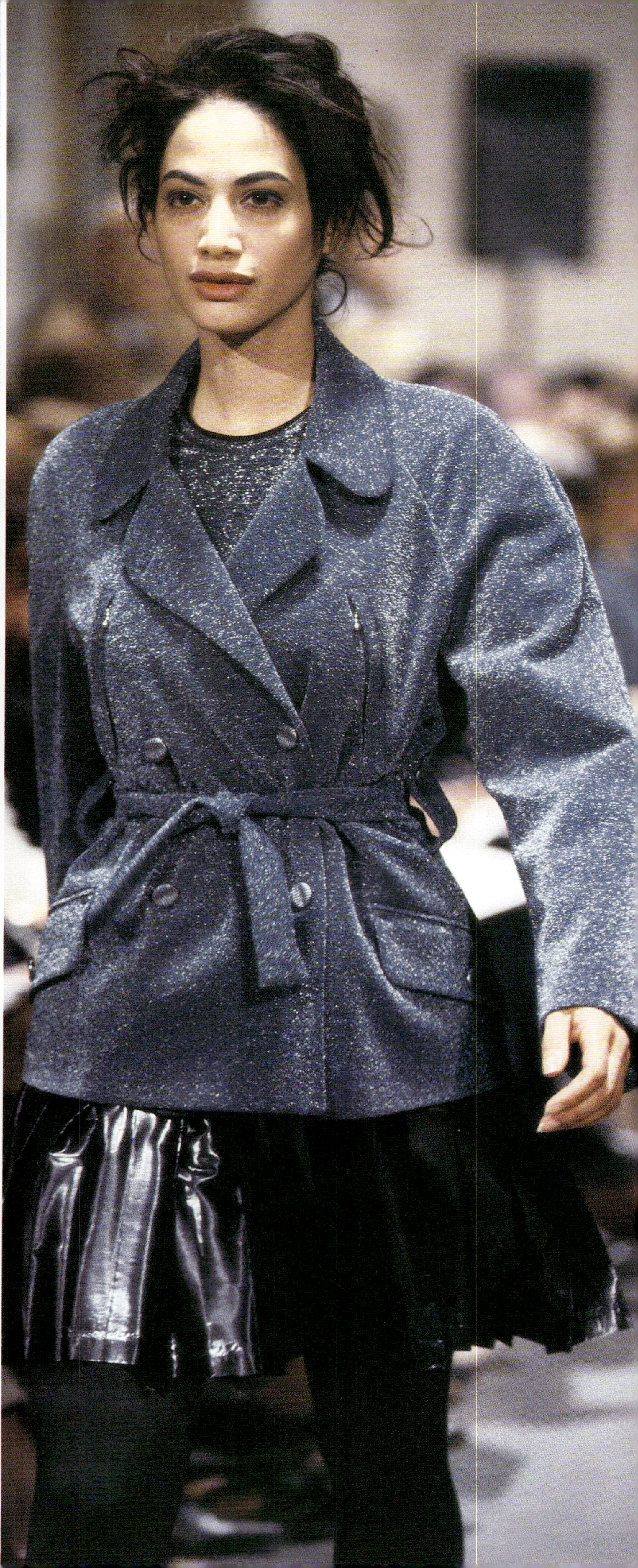

BARBARA BUI

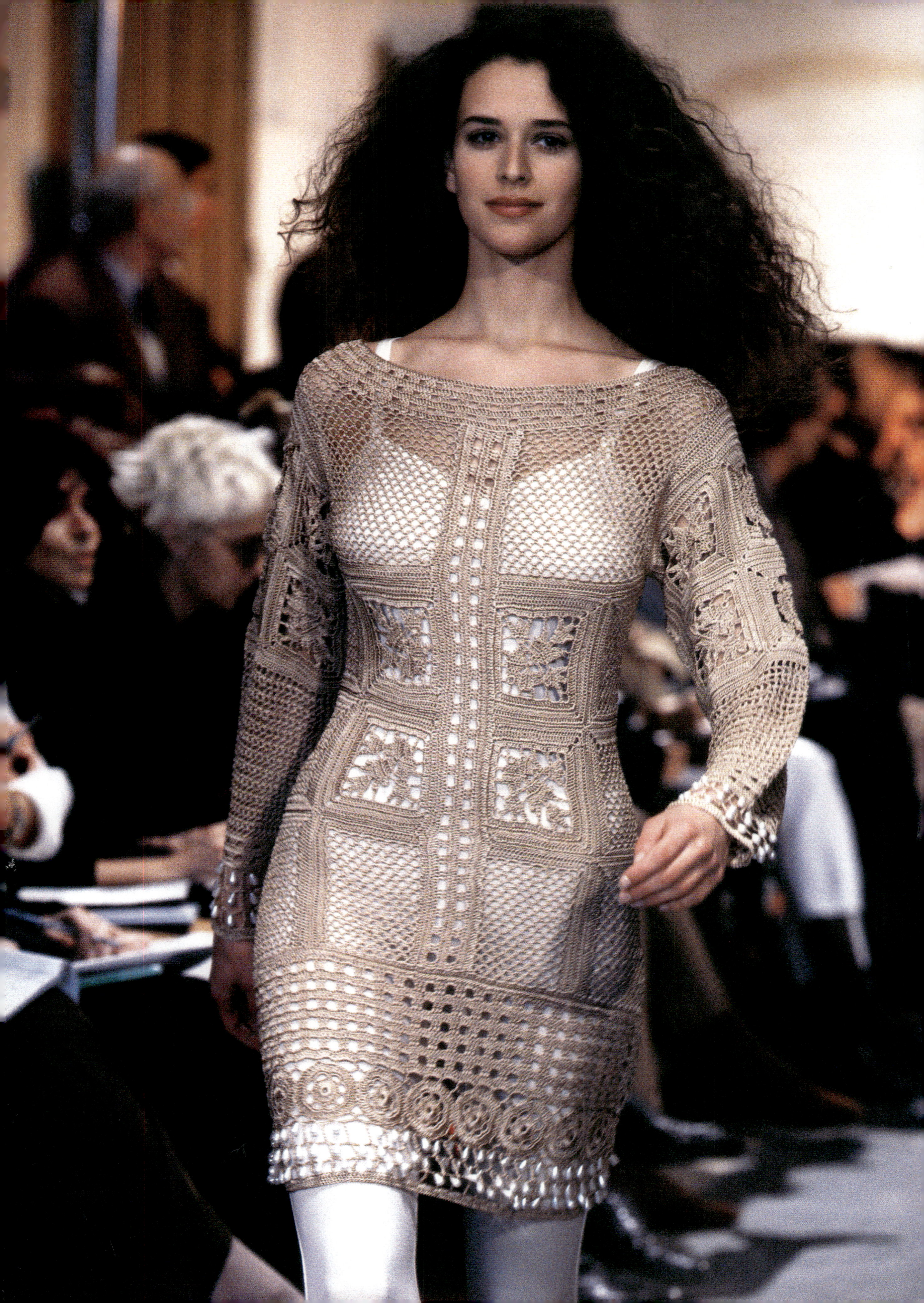

PARIS-25

CHLOÉ

クロエ

ブライト・カラーのボディコンシャス・スーツやセーター・ドレスの若々しさと、シフォンの透けた感覚や羽毛トリムのセクシーな世界が交錯する。

The worlds of brightly colored body-conscious suits, youthful sweater-dresses,
the transparent feel of chiffon and sexy feather trimmings were all mixed together.

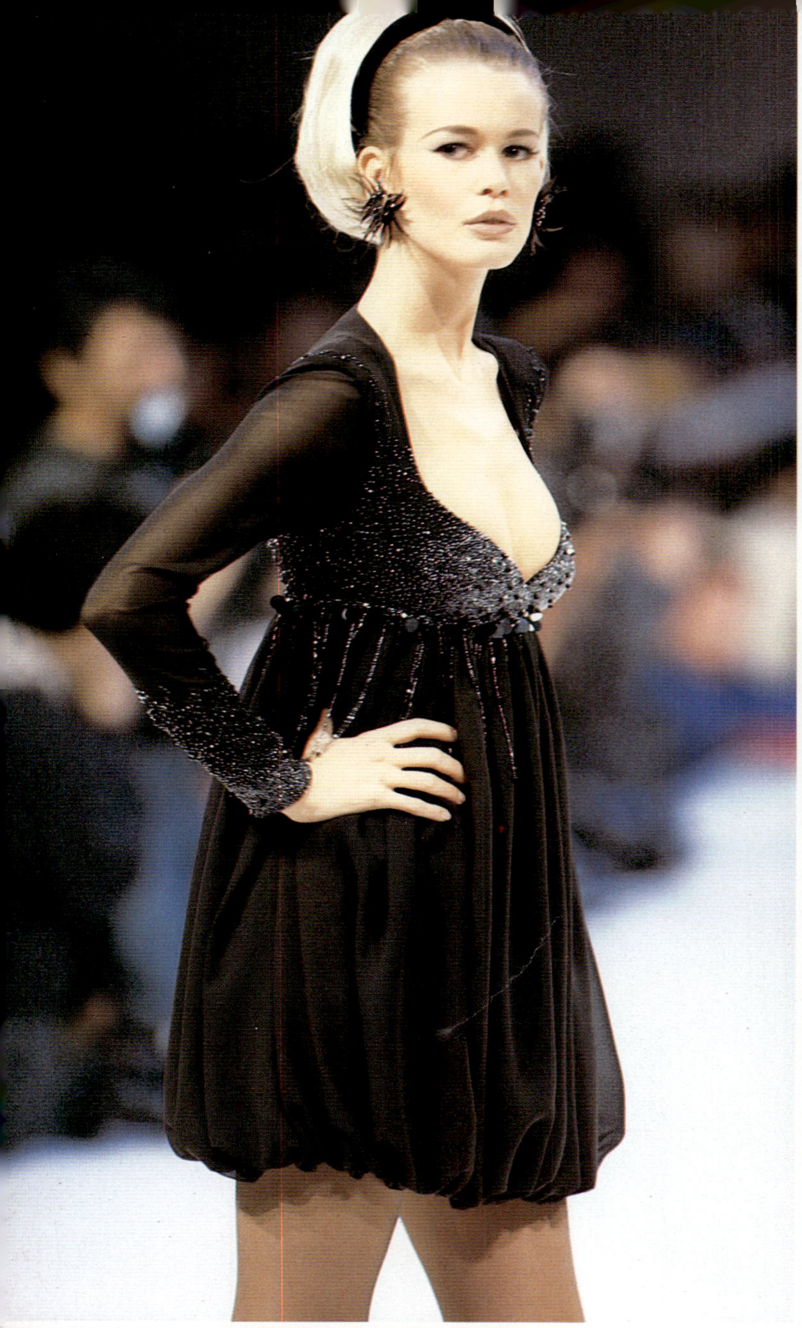

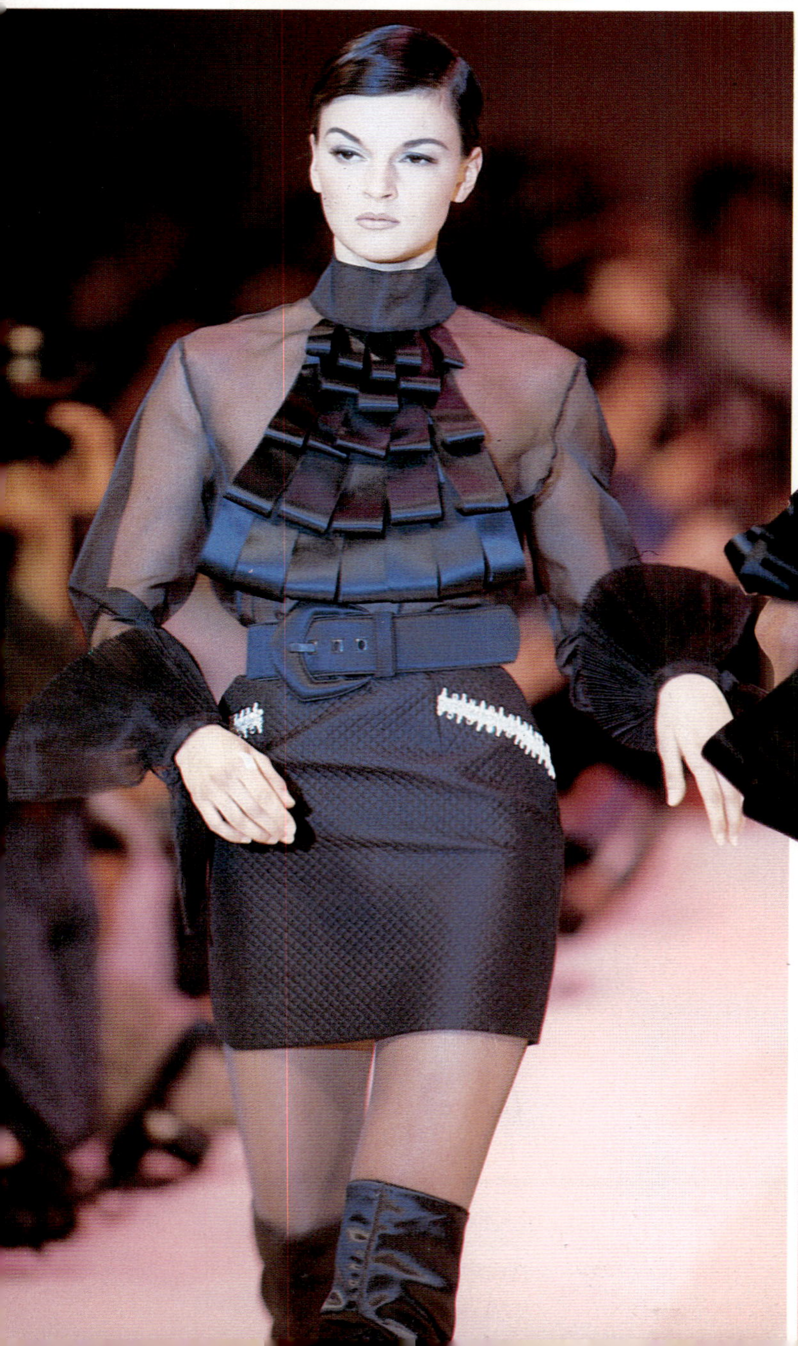

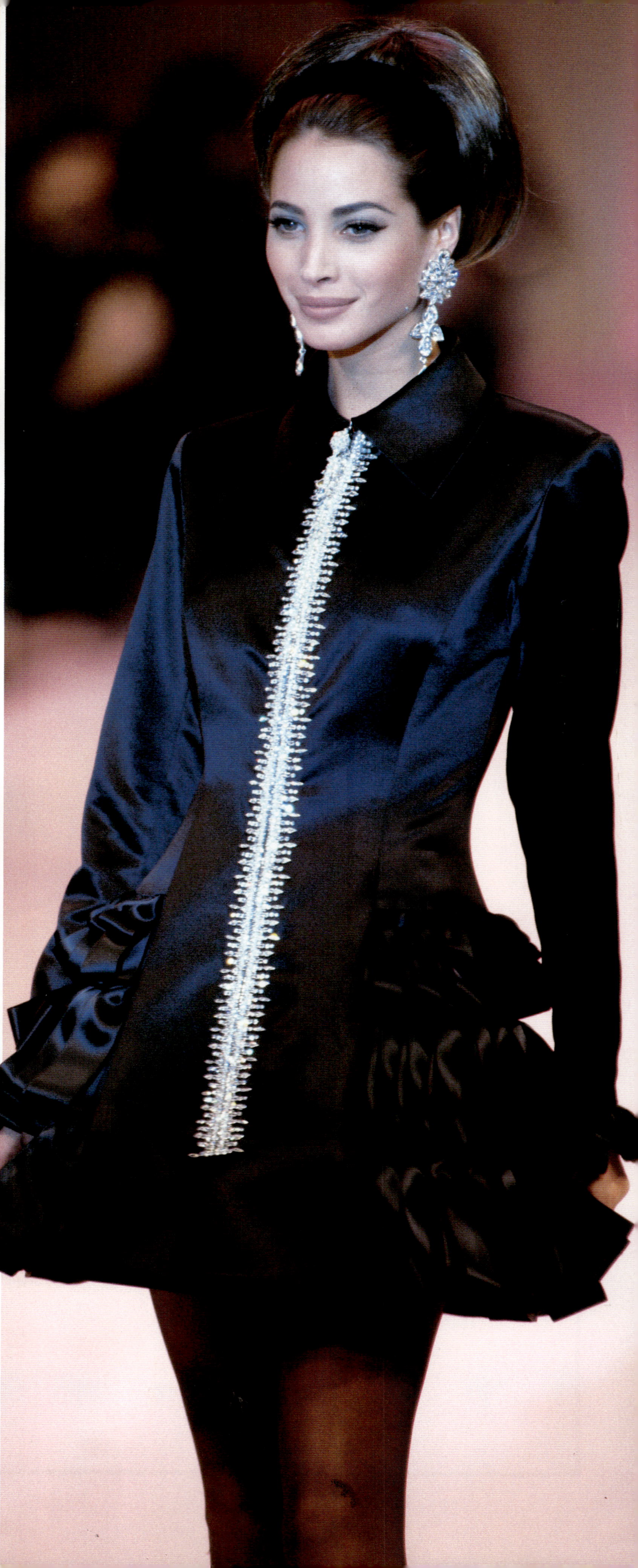

CHLOÉ

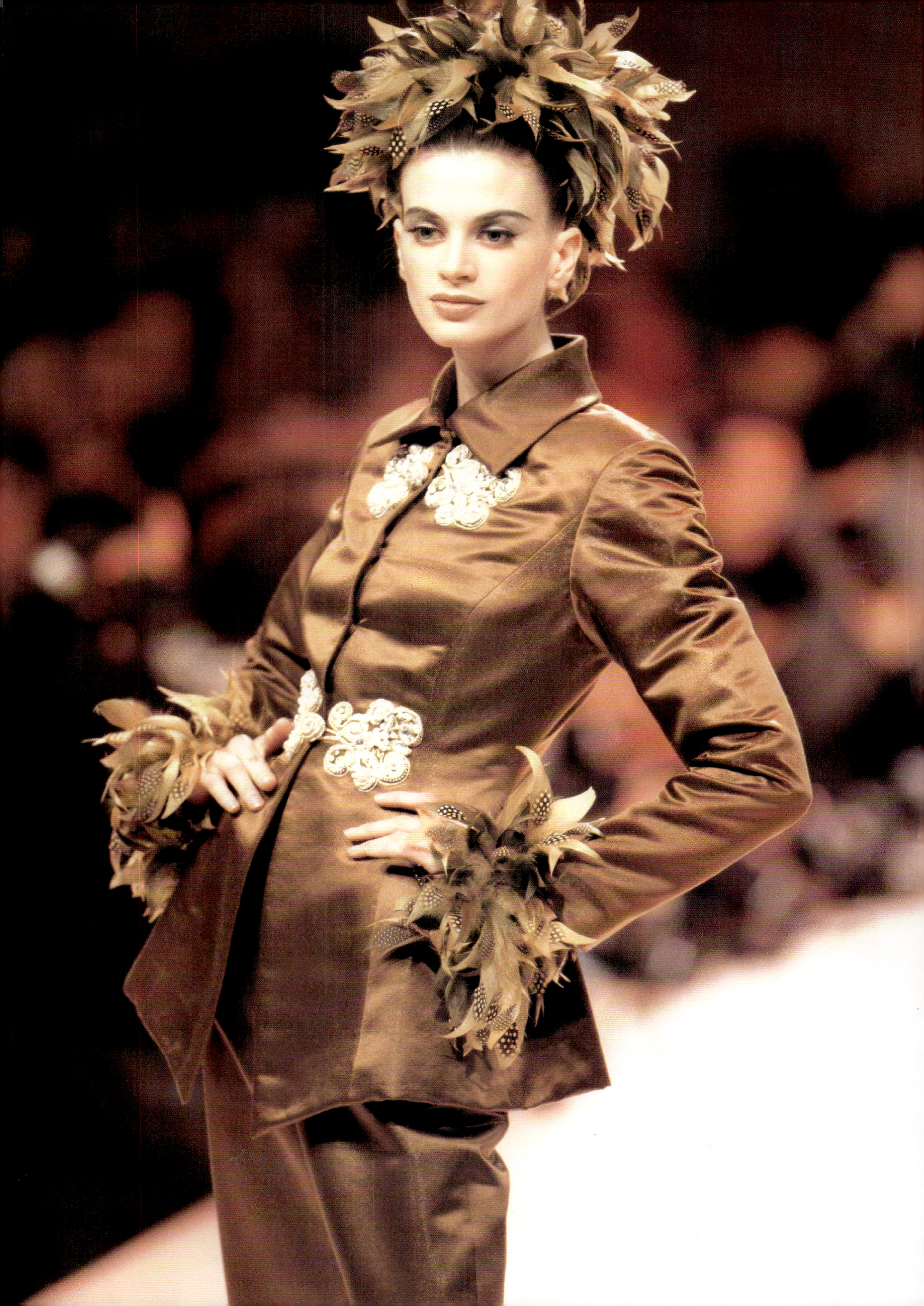

ANGELO TARLAZZI

アンジェロ・タルラッツィ

ジオメトリックなパターンやシェイプの大胆さ、異素材の斬新なコーディネイトが、タルラッツィのセクシーでダイナミックな世界を伝える。

Tarlazzi's sexy and dynamic world was conveyed by geometric patterns along with new and original coordinations of different materials.

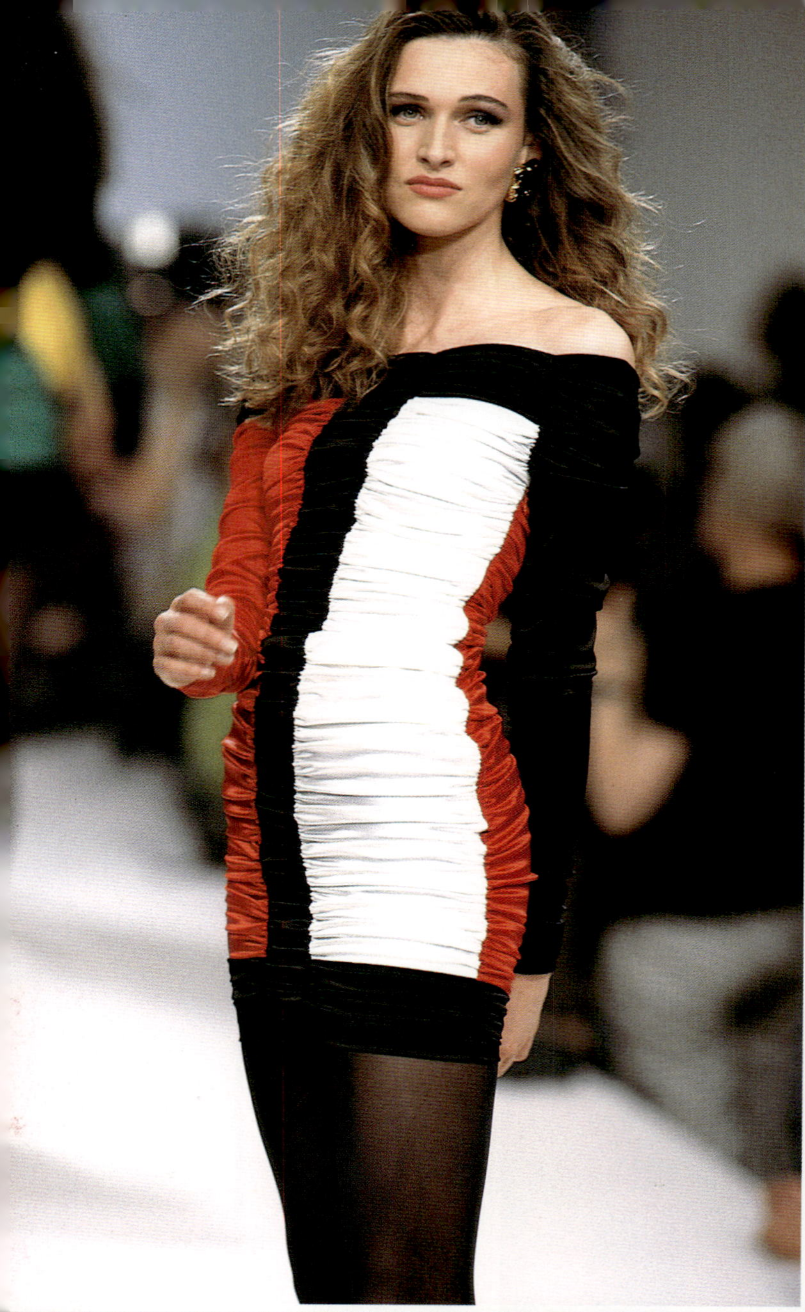
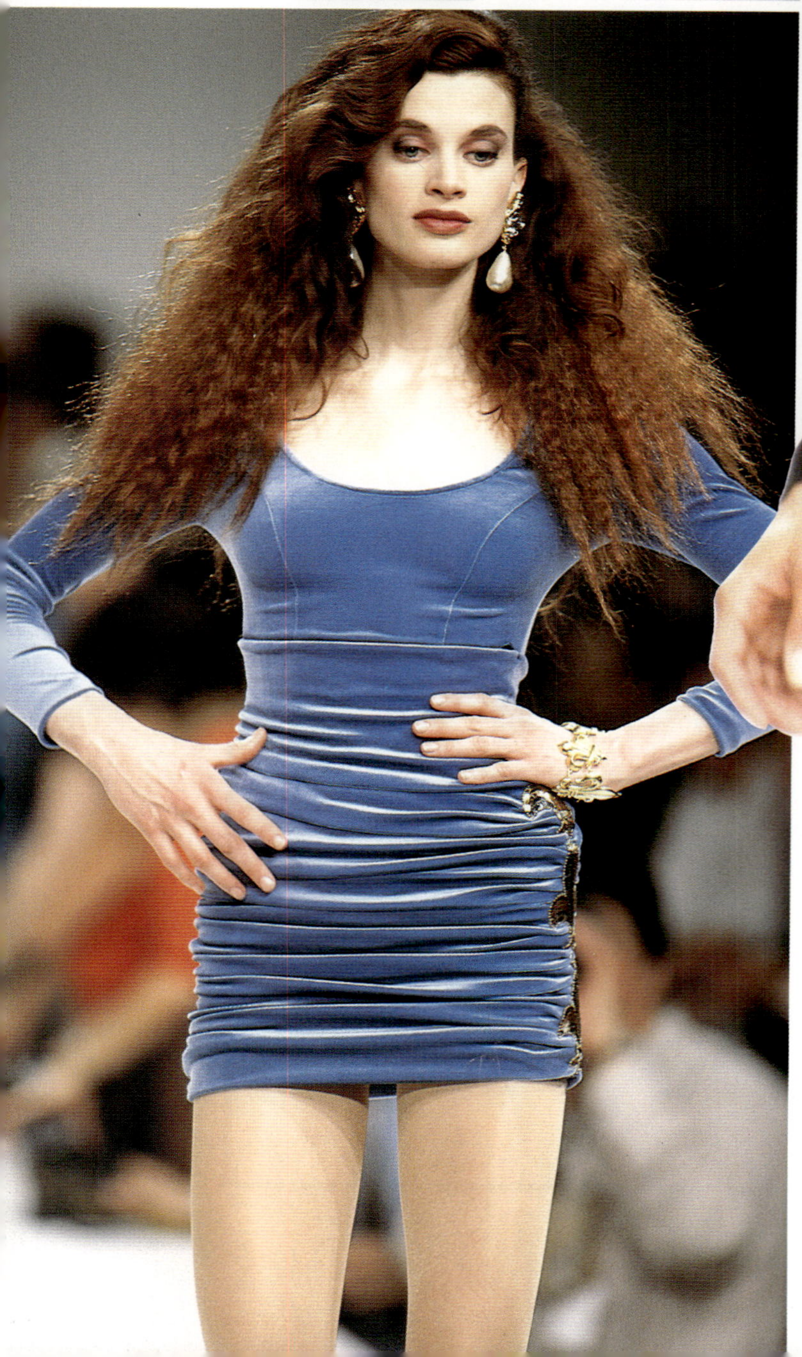
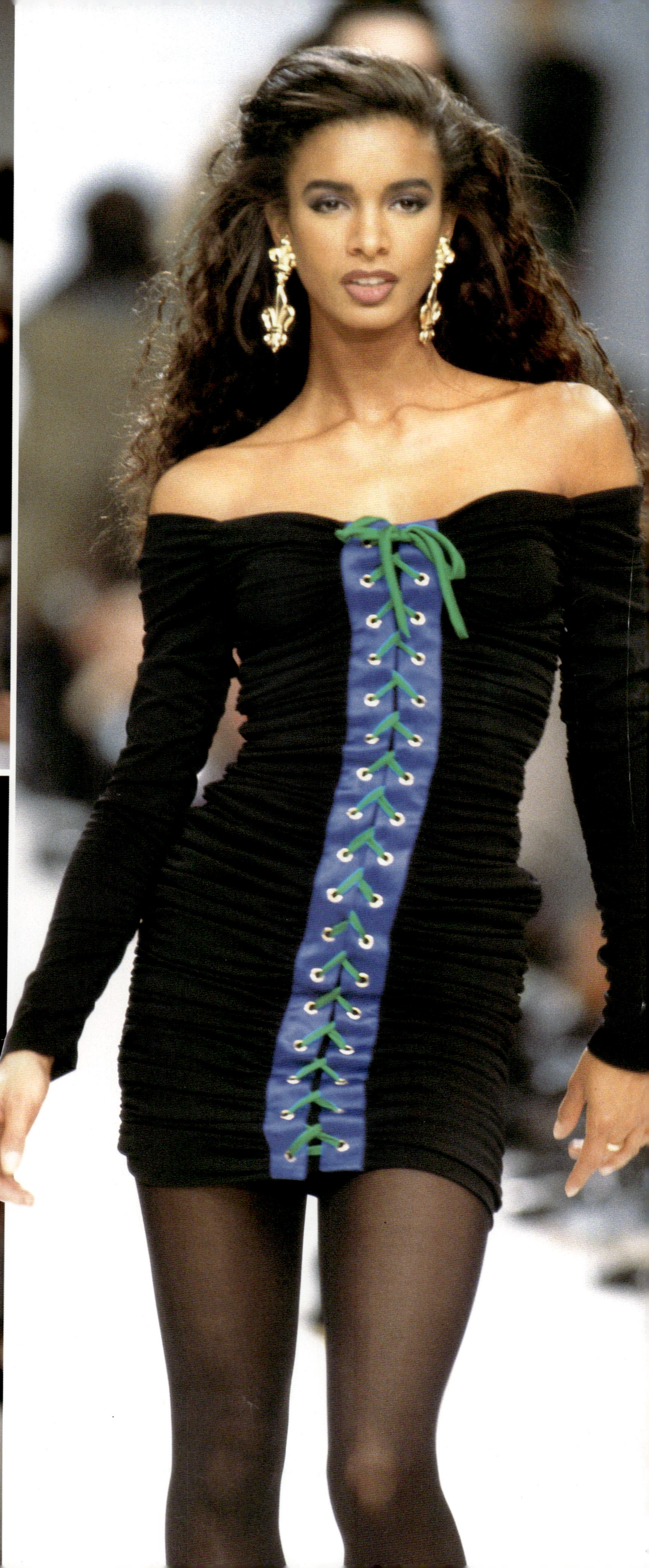

ANGELO TARLAZZI

225

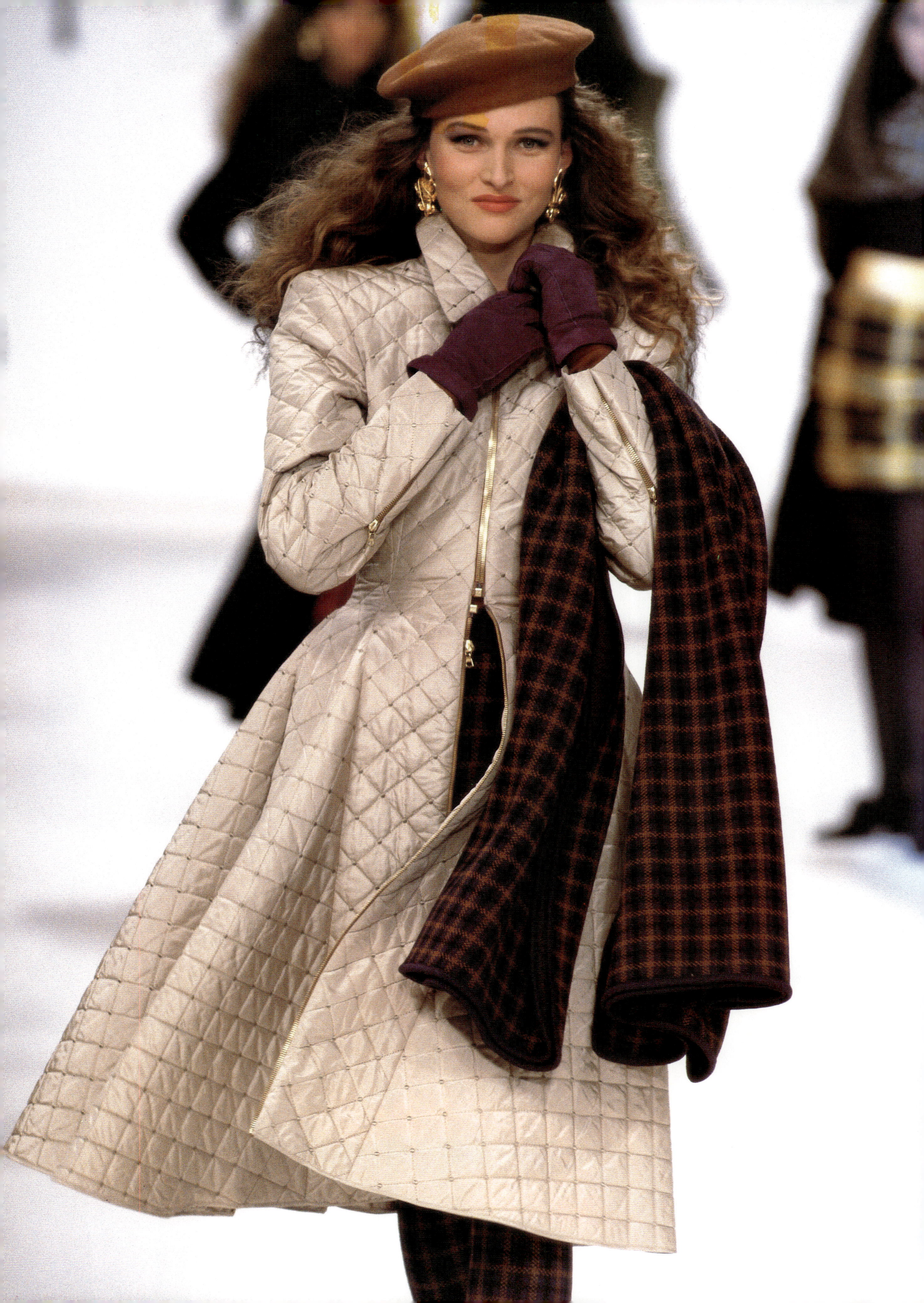

DOROTHÉE BIS

ドロテ・ビス

メンズ・ライクなスタイルにカジュアル要素を加えて表現。チューブラー・シルエットやバルーン・シルエットが今シーズンのラインとして登場。

She displayed manly styles with a casual air.

This season's line saw the release of tubular and balloon silhouettes.

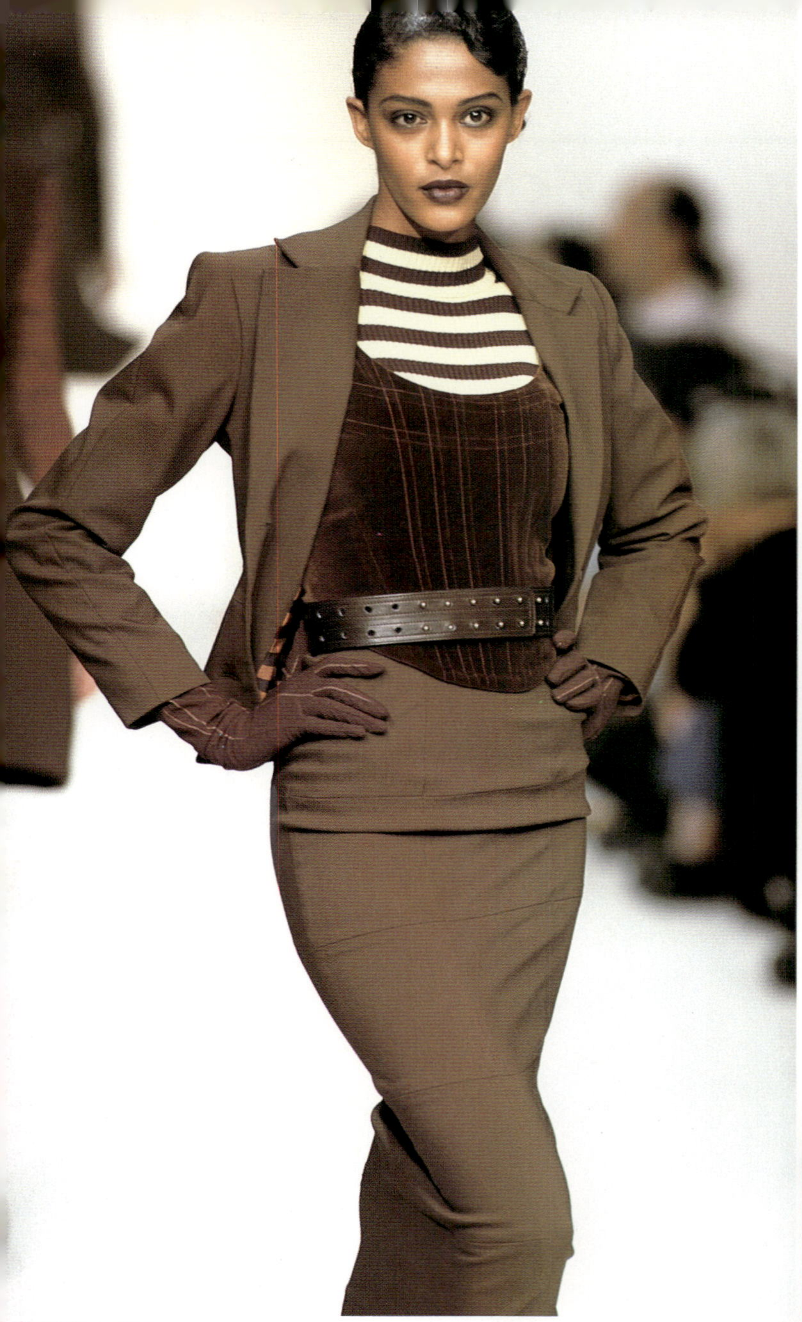
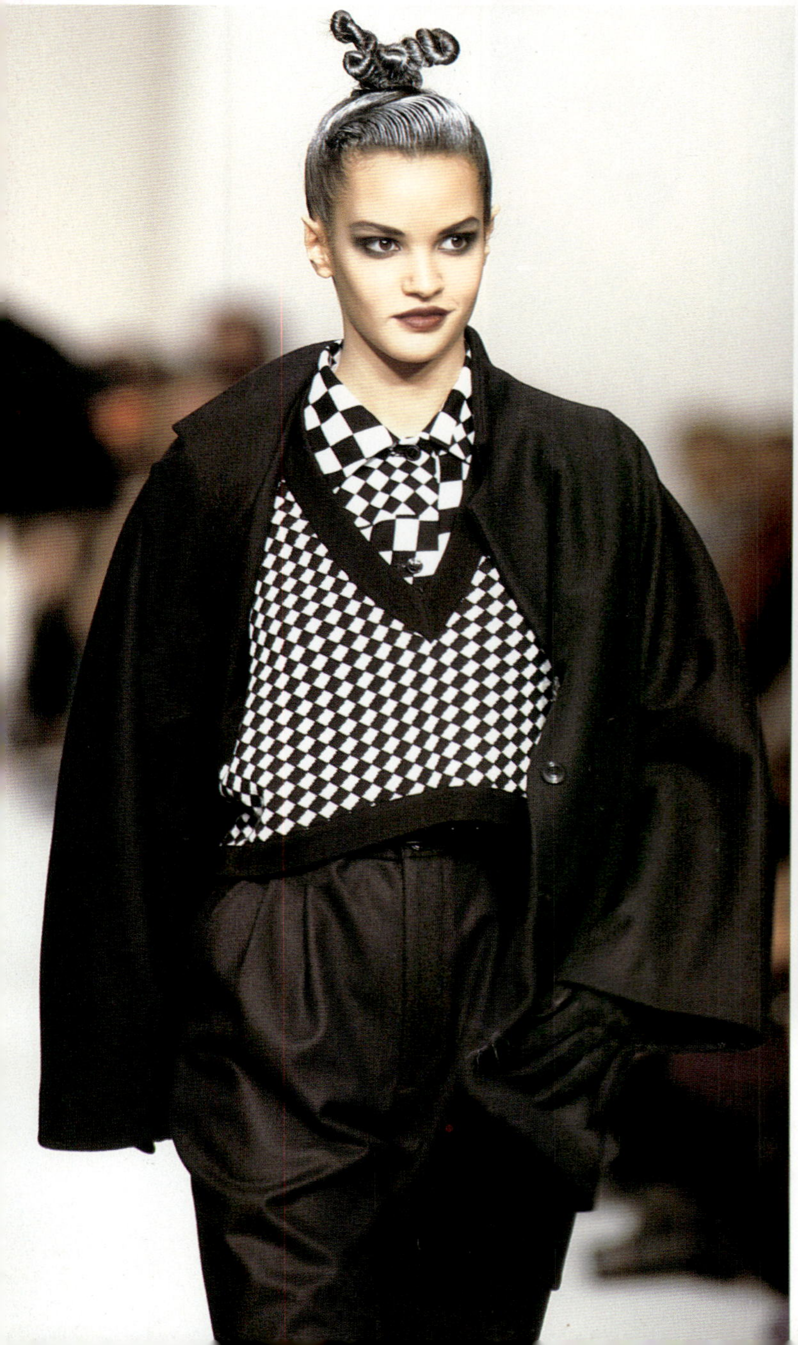
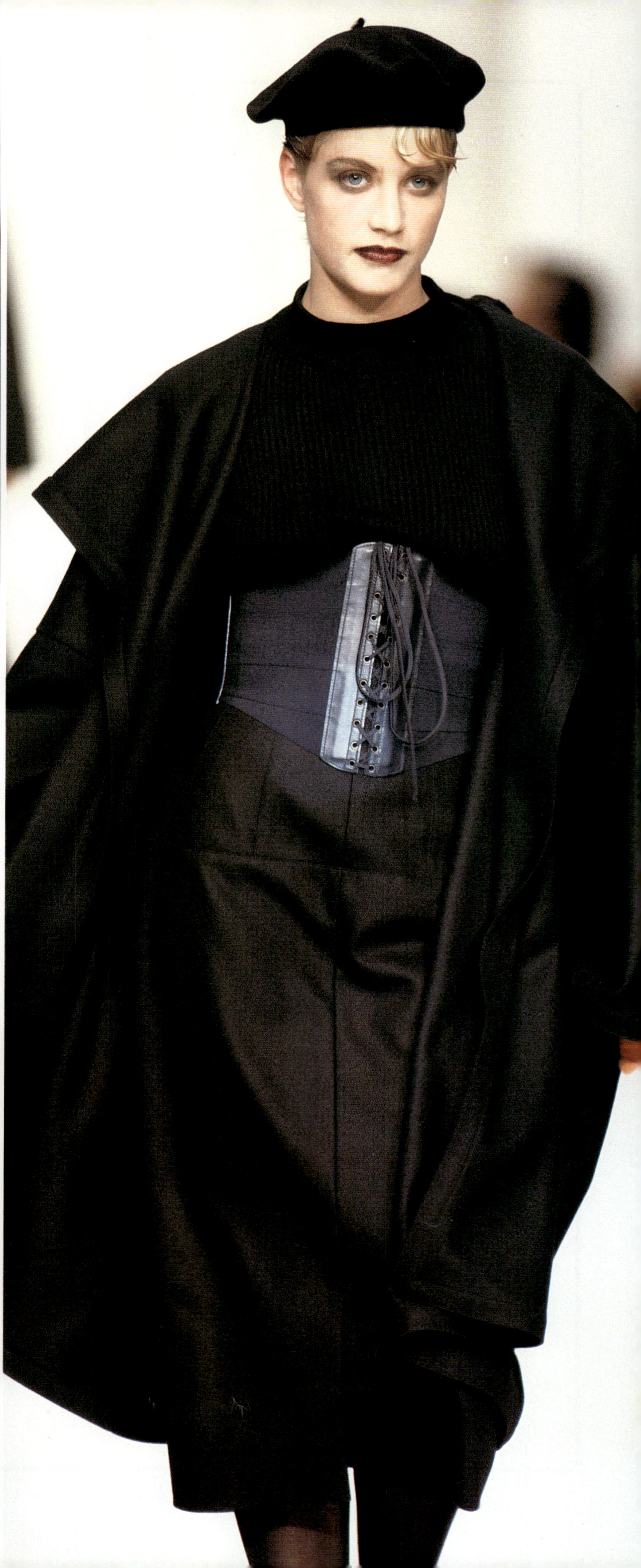

DOROTHÉE BIS

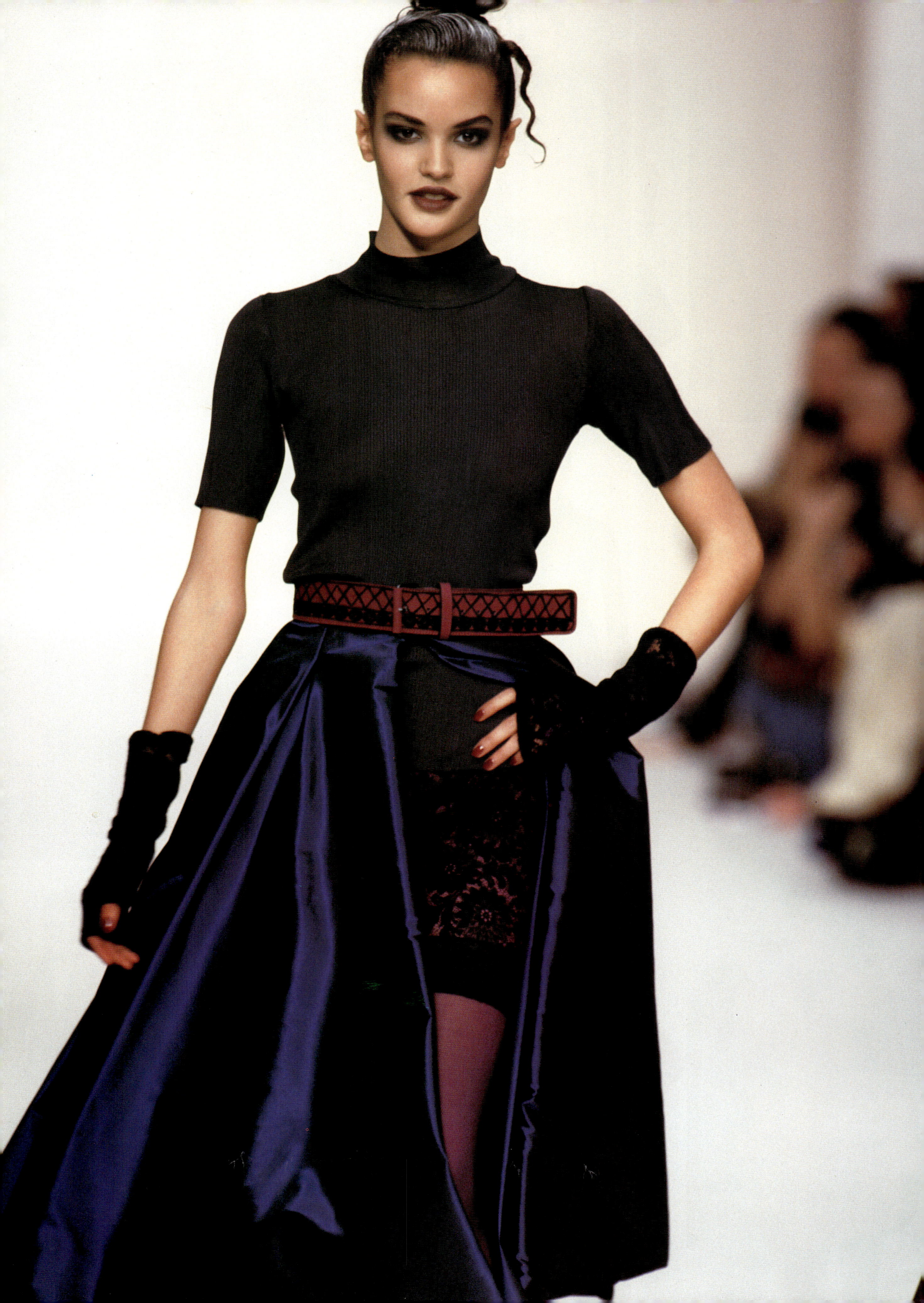

CHANEL

KENZO

'91-'92 AUTUMN & WINTER

PRET-Á-PORTER COLLECTIONS

CHANEL

CHRISTIAN DIOR

CHRISTIAN DIOR

'91-'92
AUTUMN & WINTER
PRÊT-Á-PORTER
COLLECTIONS

YVES SAINT LAURENT

PIERRE BALMAIN	 PACO RABANNE	 KENZO
 JUNKO SHIMADA	 YVES SAINT LAURENT	 HANAE MORI
 HANAE MORI	 DANIEL HECHTER	 YVES SAINT LAURENT

YUKI TORII

PIERRE BALMAIN

'91-'92 AUTUMN & WINTER PRET-Á-PORTER COLLECTIONS

KENZO

JIN ABE

CHRISTIAN DIOR

CHRISTIAN DIOR

SYBILLA

シビラ

パリのショップ・オープンを兼ねて、パーティでショーを見せたシビラ。トラペーズの優しいシルエットやナイーブなハンドメイドは変わらない。

Sybilla held a party for the opening of her Paris shop, and combined it with a show.
The gentle silhouettes of the trapèze, and the innocence of the handmade items haven't changed.

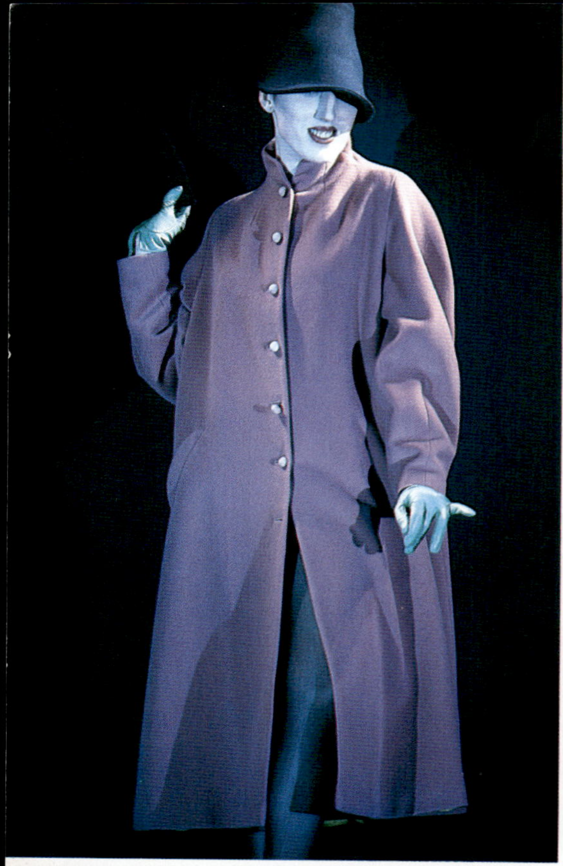
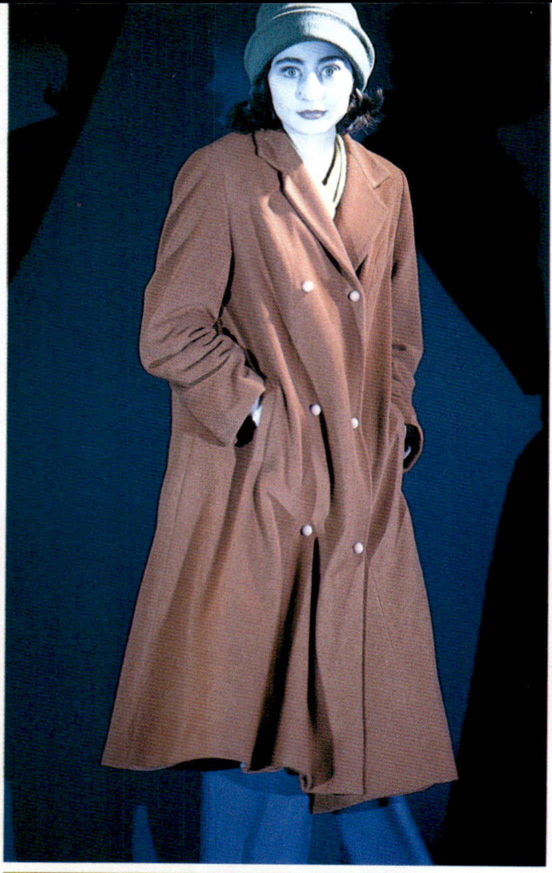
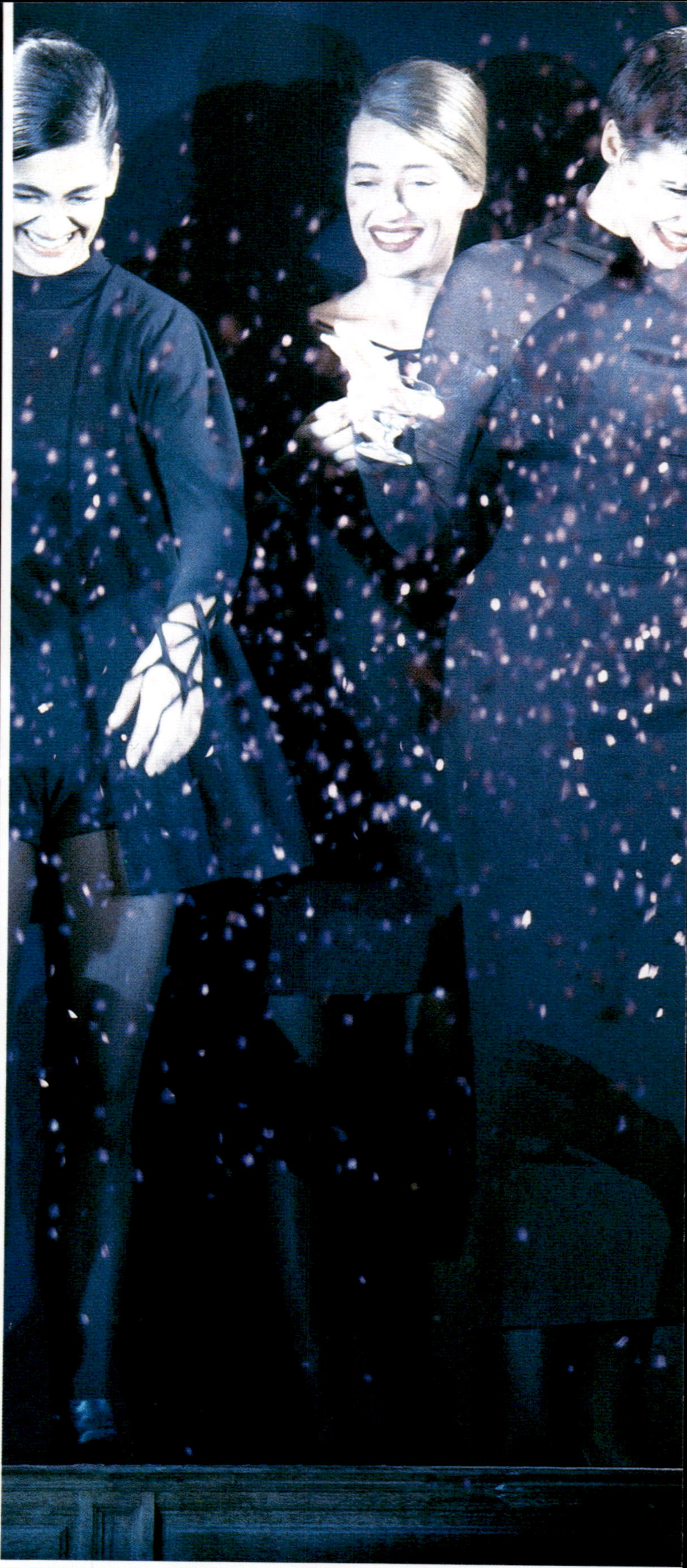
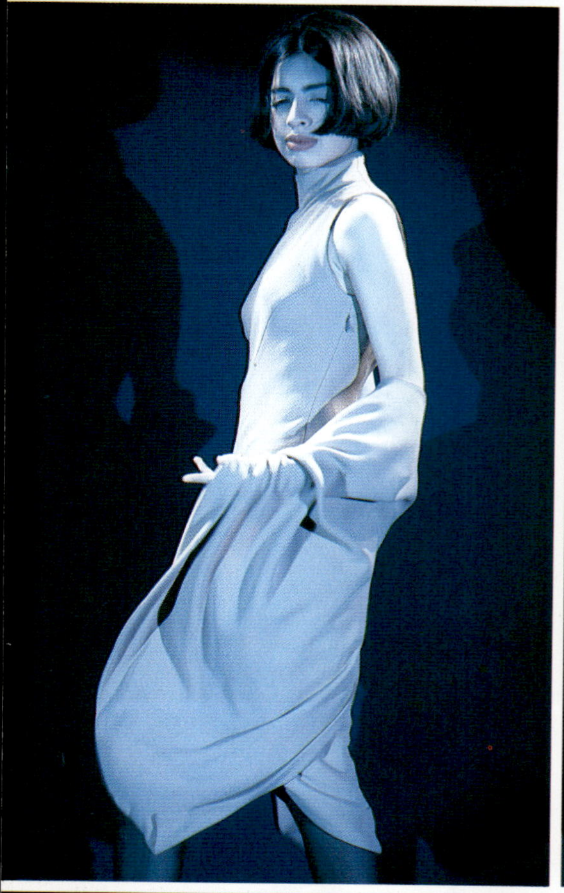
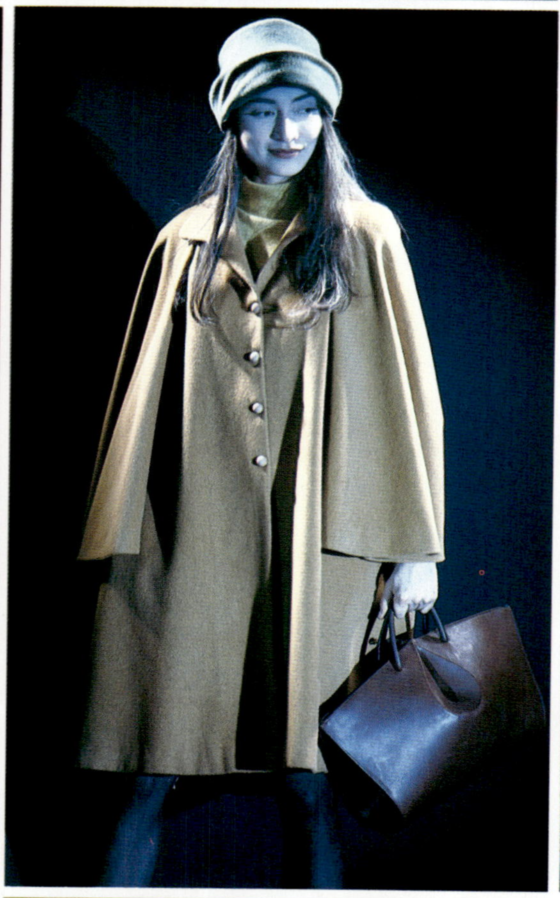
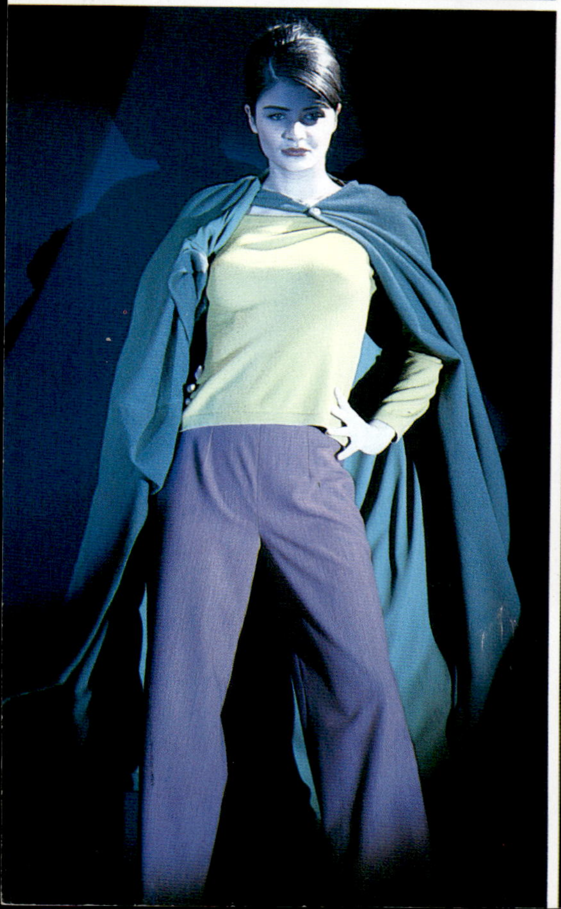
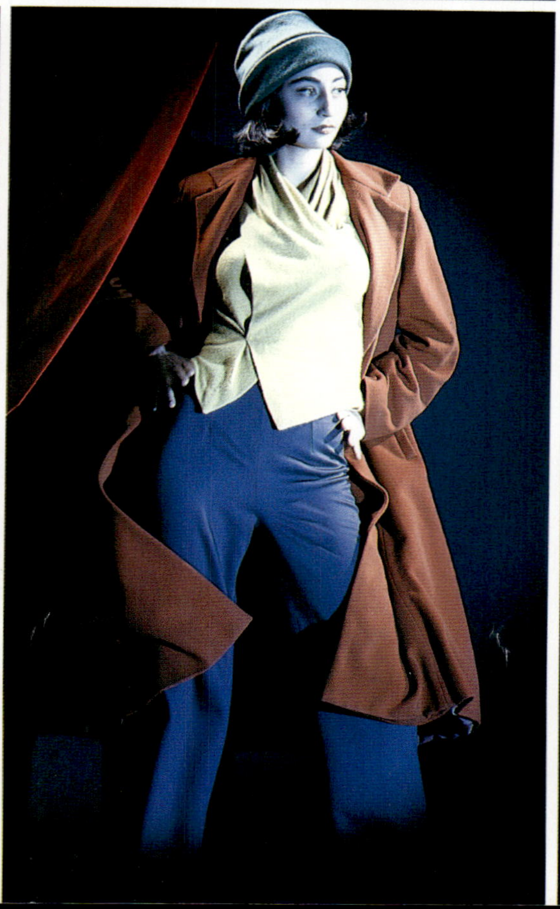
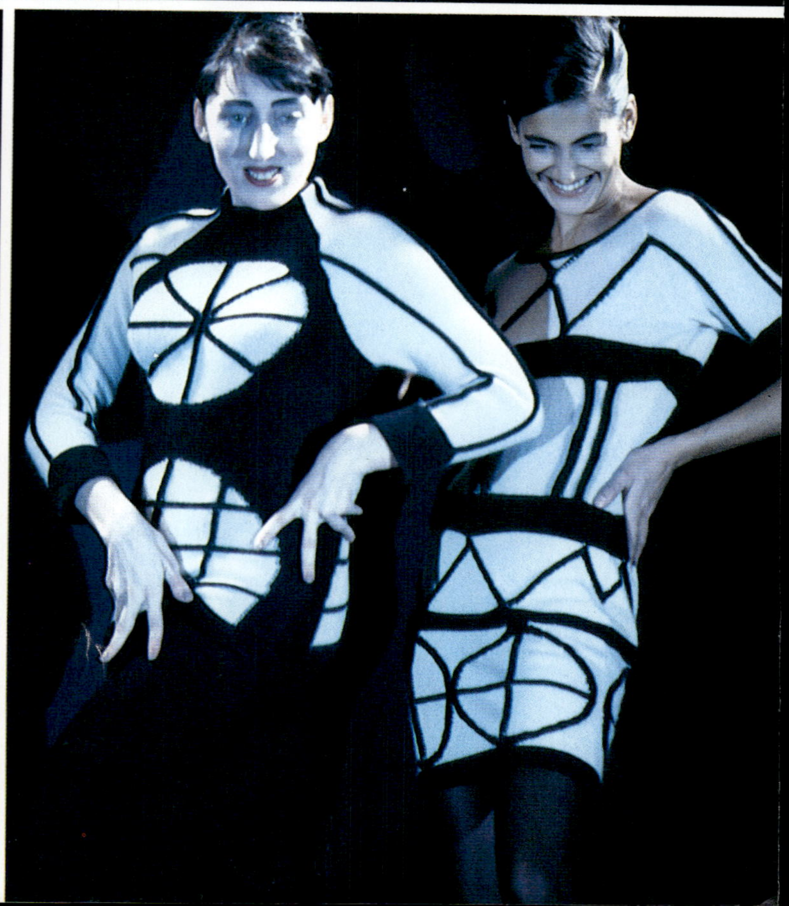

PARIS-29

MARTIN MARGIELA

マルタン・マルジェラ

今回はショーは行わず、ビデオとプレゼンテーションのみのマルジェラ。アバンギャルドなレイヤードとマキシスカートは、ヒッピーたちを彷彿させる。
For this collection, rather than putting on a show. Margiela merely made a video and presentation.
Reminding us of the hippies, avant-garde layered and maxi skirts.

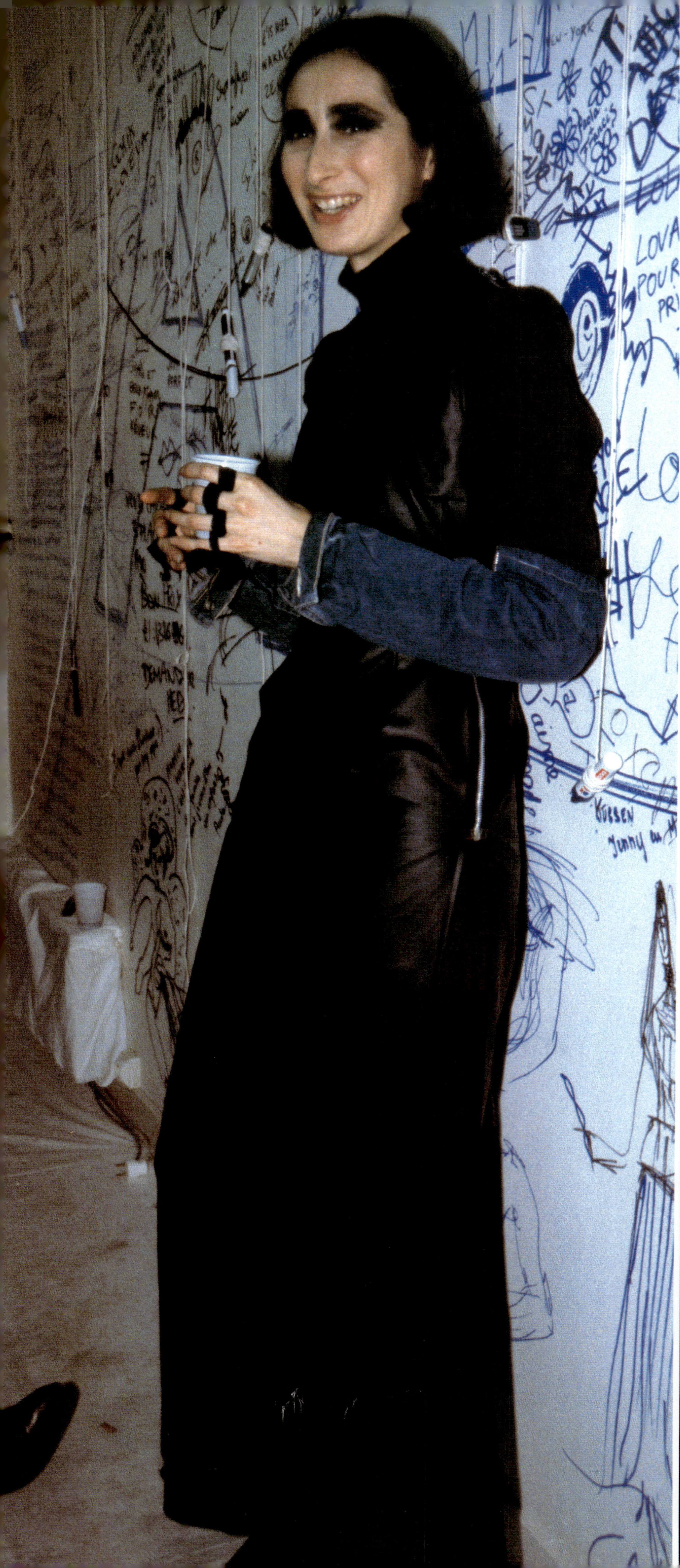

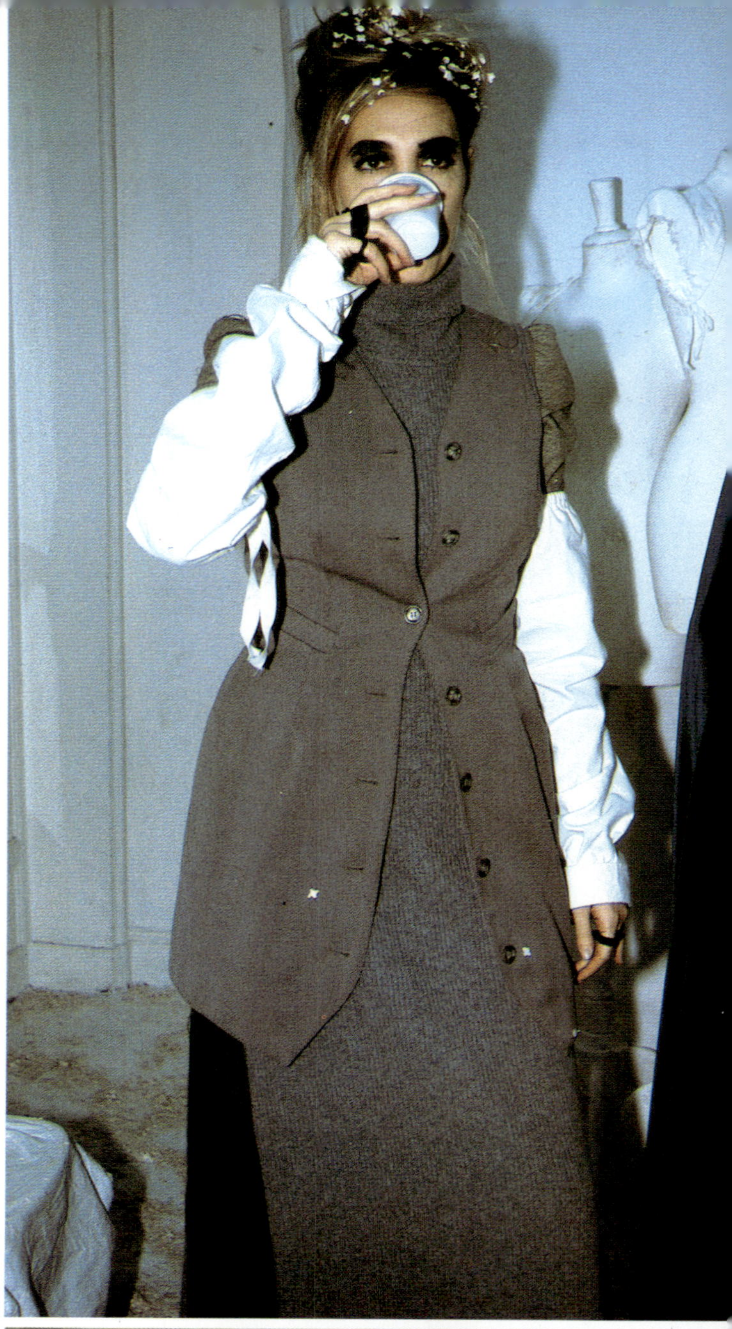

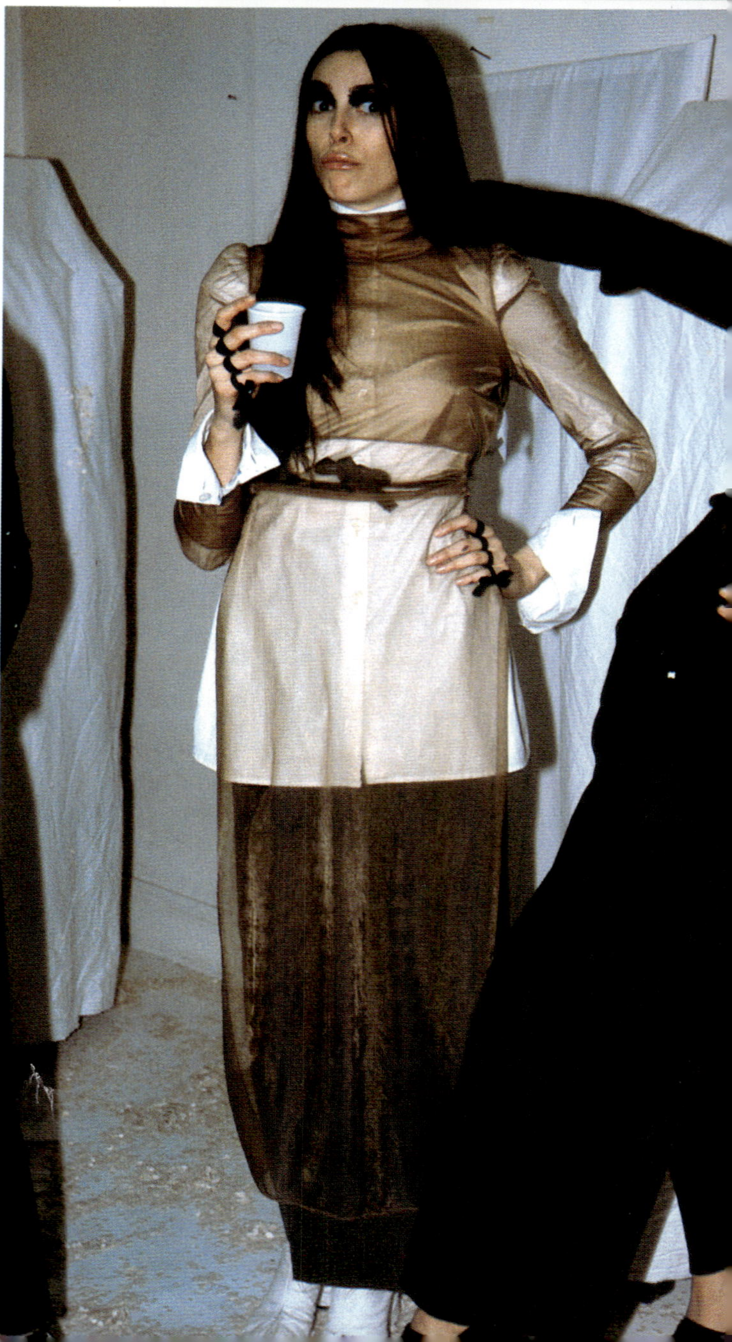

PARIS-30

ZUCCA

ズッカ

ナイーブで爽やかな印象のコレクション。チェック・パターンやプリーツのデザイン性が無彩色の世界に彩りを加える。
The collection gave a refreshing impression of innocence.
The check patterns and the pleat design added color to an otherwise monotone collection.

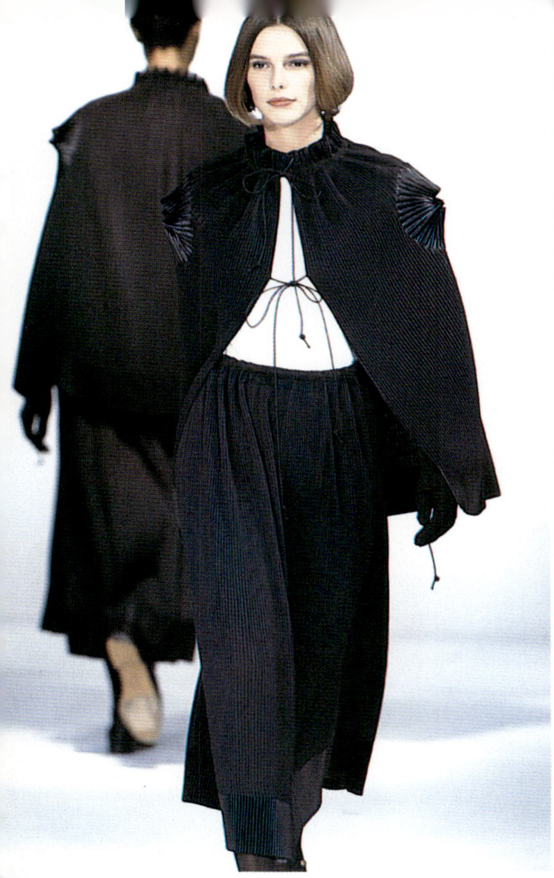
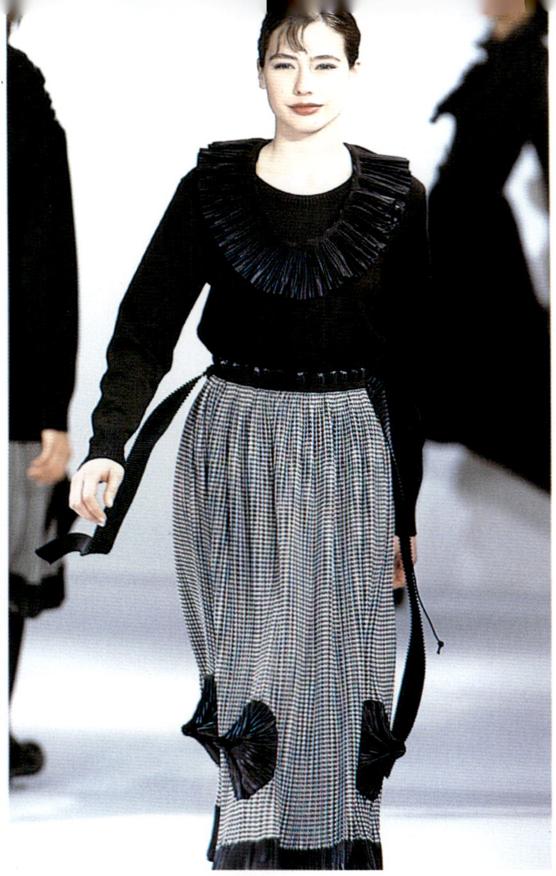
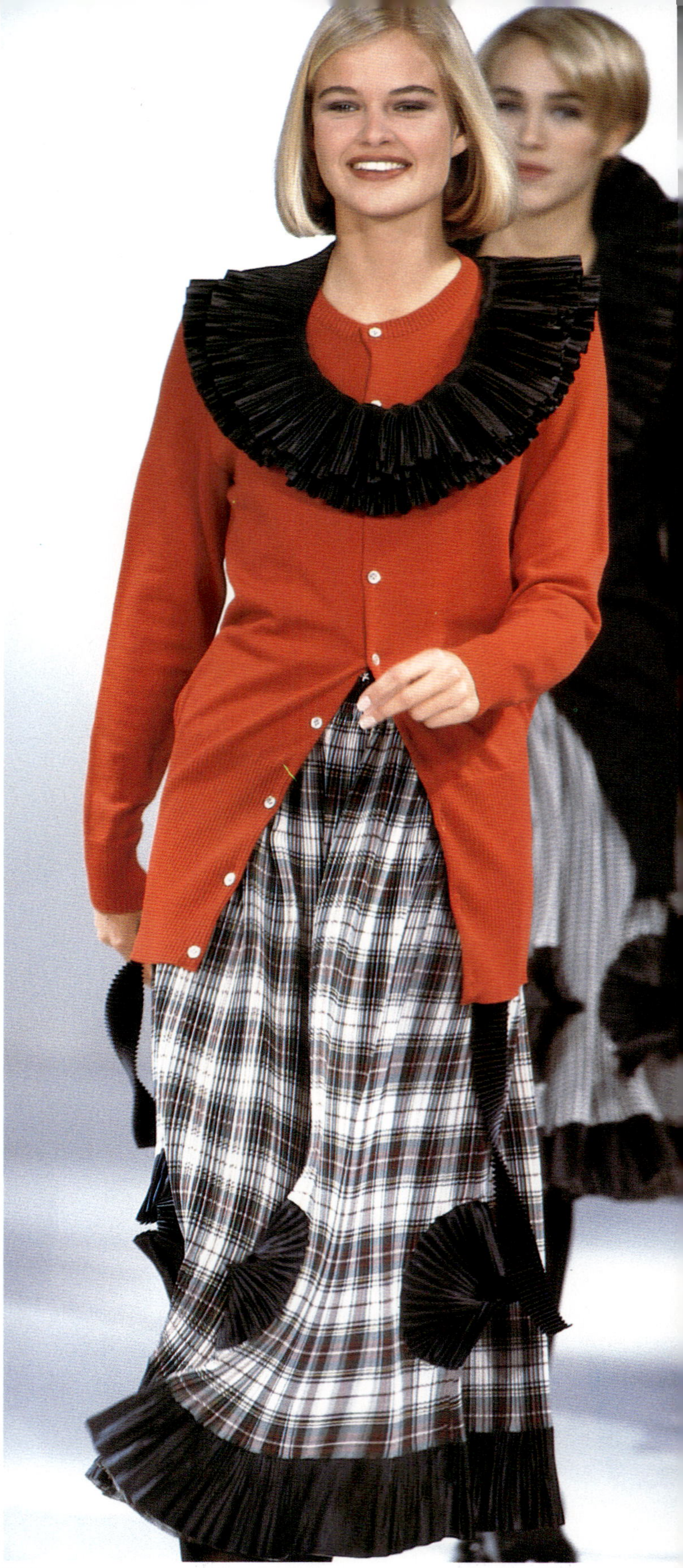
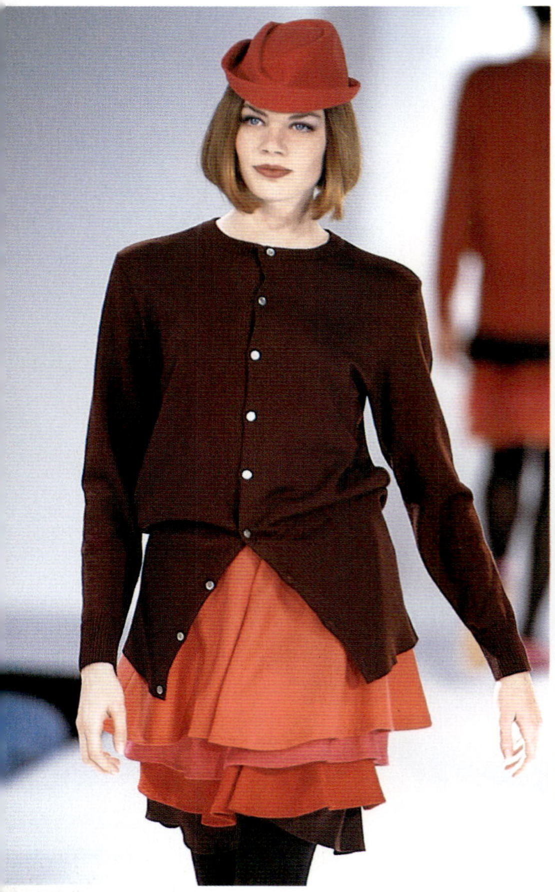
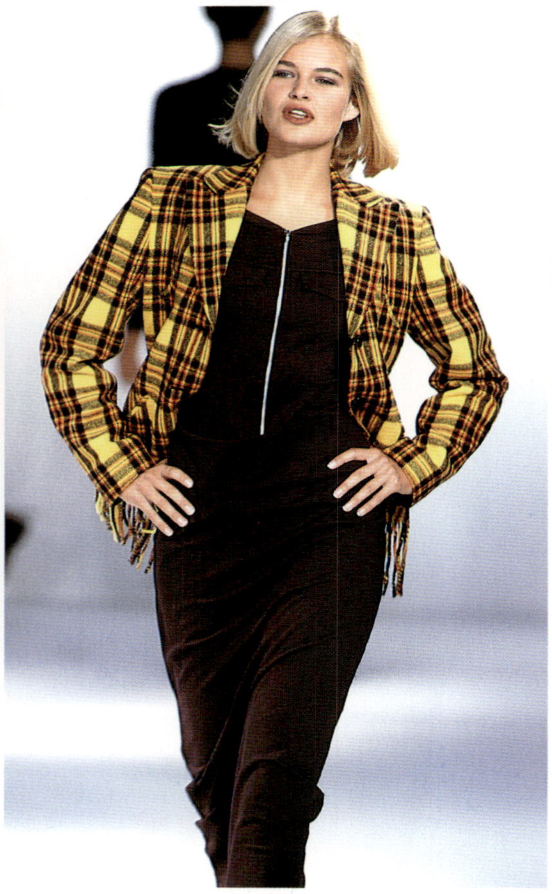
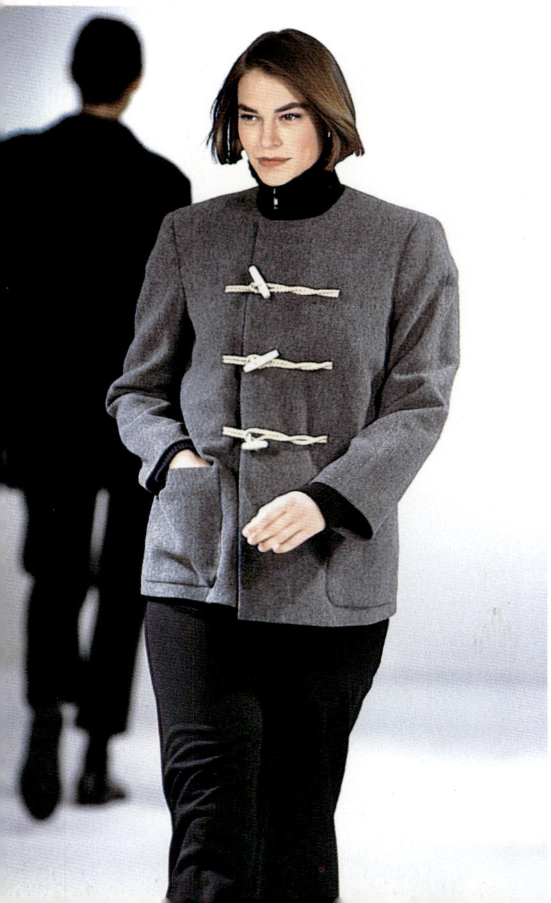
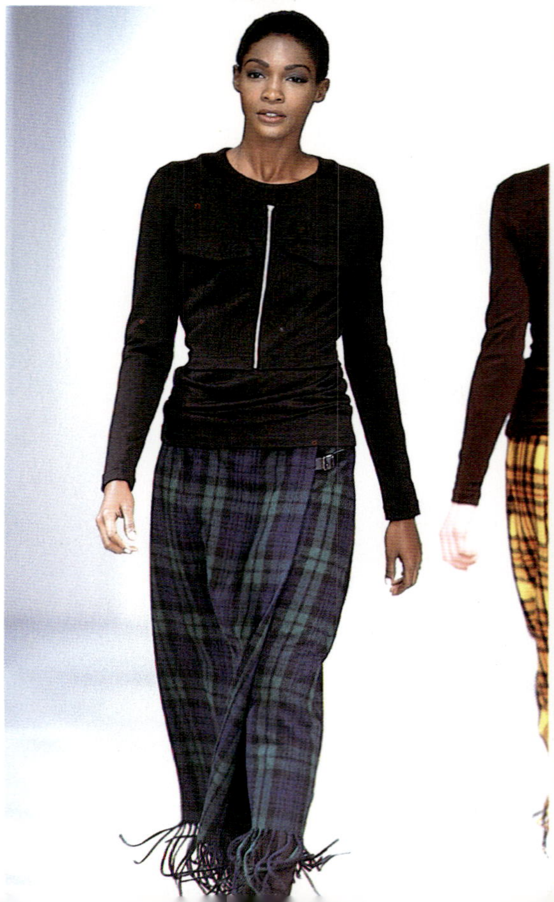
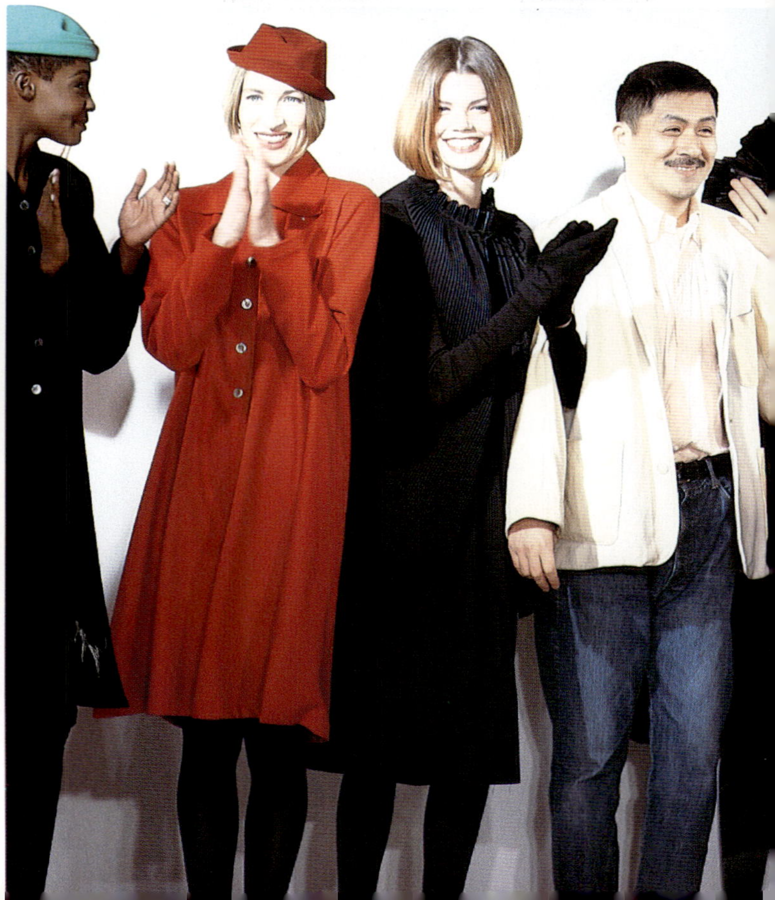

PARIS-31

JEAN-LOUIS SCHERRER

ジャン＝ルイ・シェレル

エキゾティックなプリントやチェックなどのパターンの魅力が生きるコレクション。あくまでも品のあるエレガントな女性を象徴している。
The collection utilized the charm of such patterns as exotic prints and checks.
Every detail symbolizes the refined elegant woman.

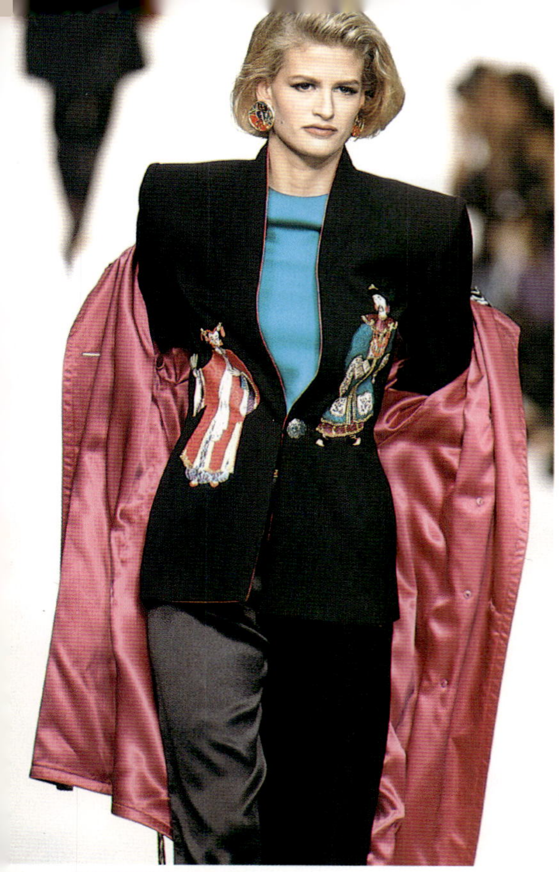
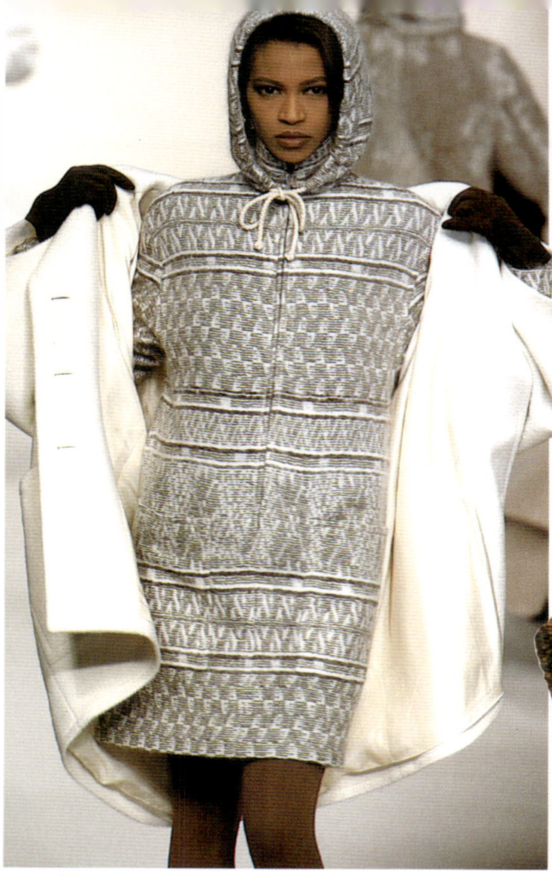
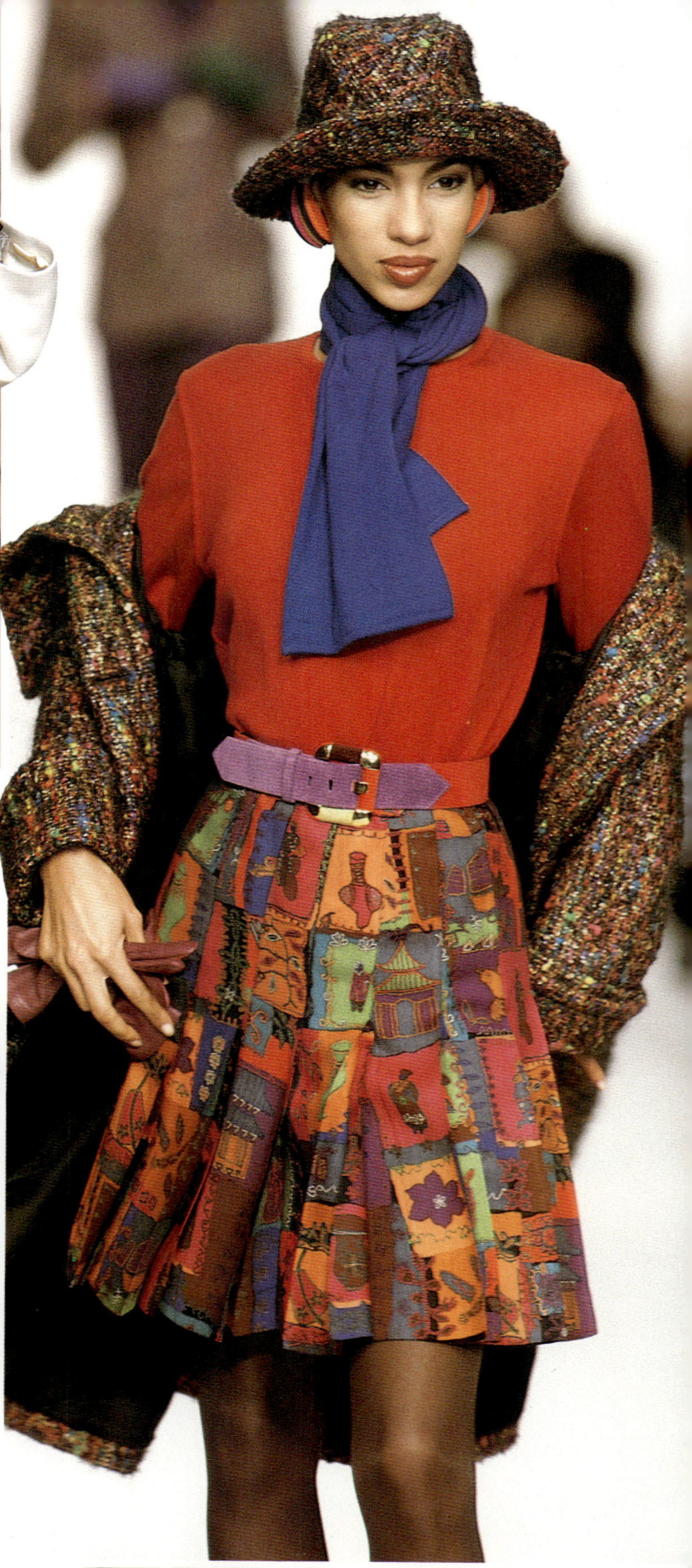
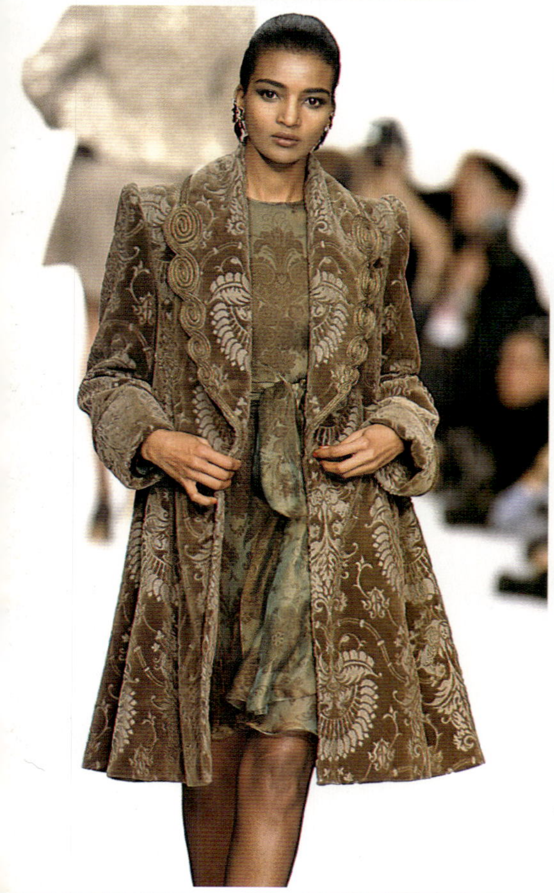
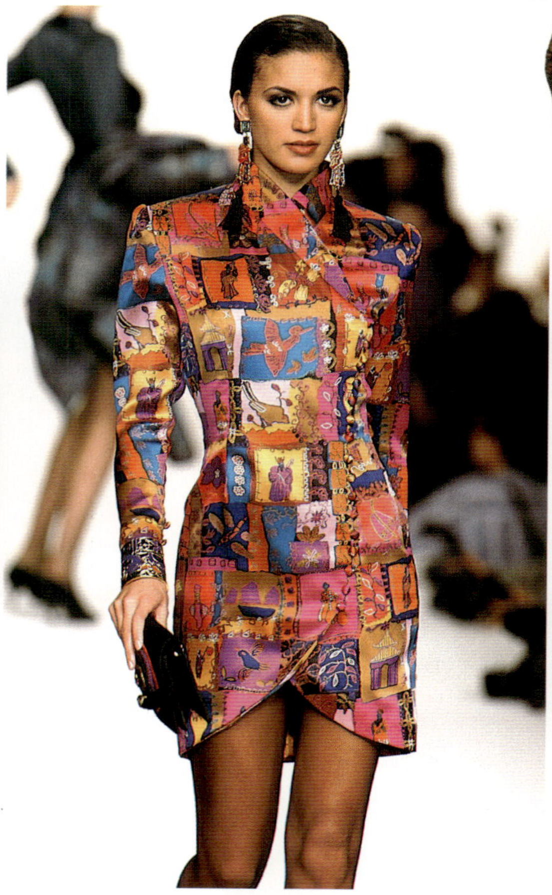
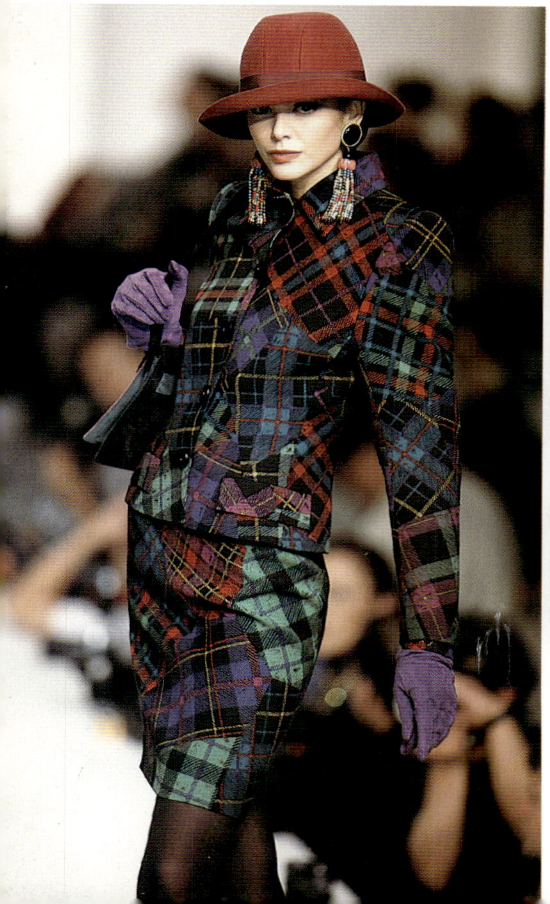
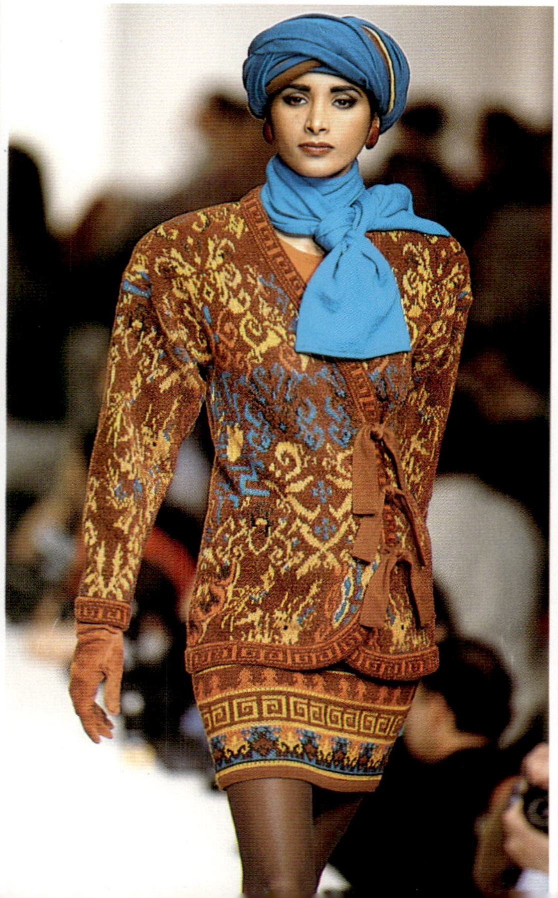
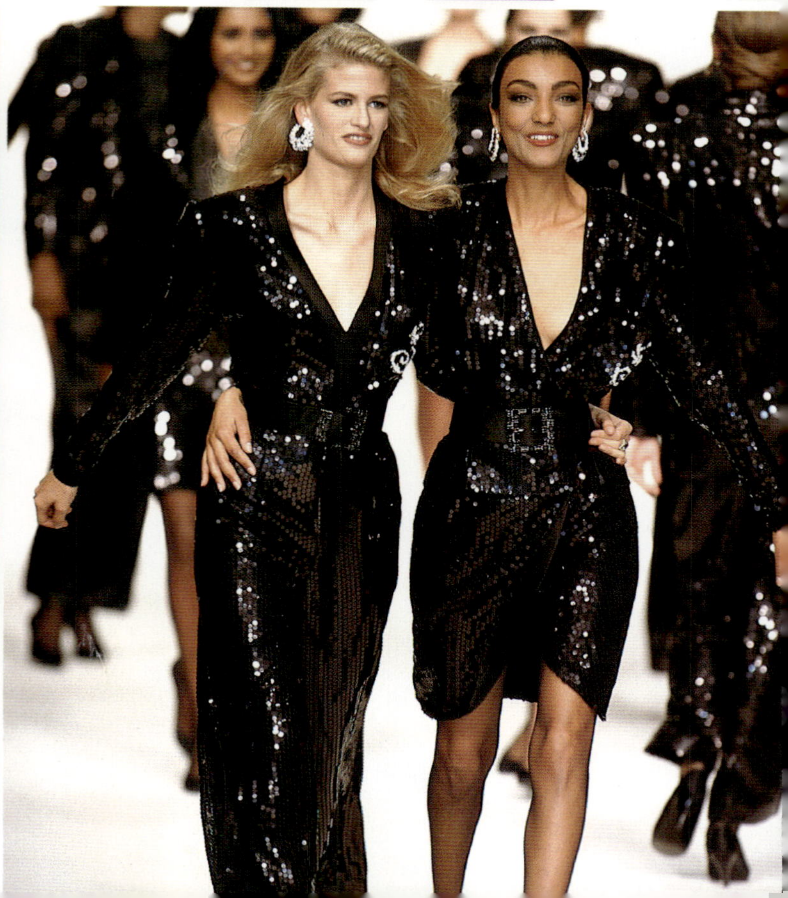

GIVENCHY

ジバンシー

クラシックな優雅さは相変わらず。コート・スーツ等のセットアップ的なアイテムがその味を増す。夜のドレスは豪華できらびやかなベルベットを中心に。

The classic elegance, deepened by set-up items such as coats and suits, hasn't changed.
The evening dresses were mainly made of gorgeous, flashy velvet.

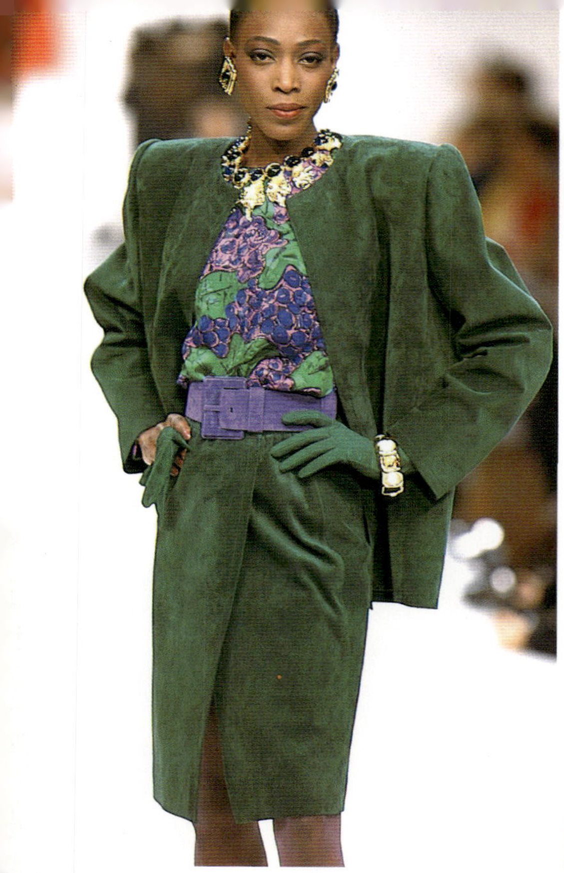
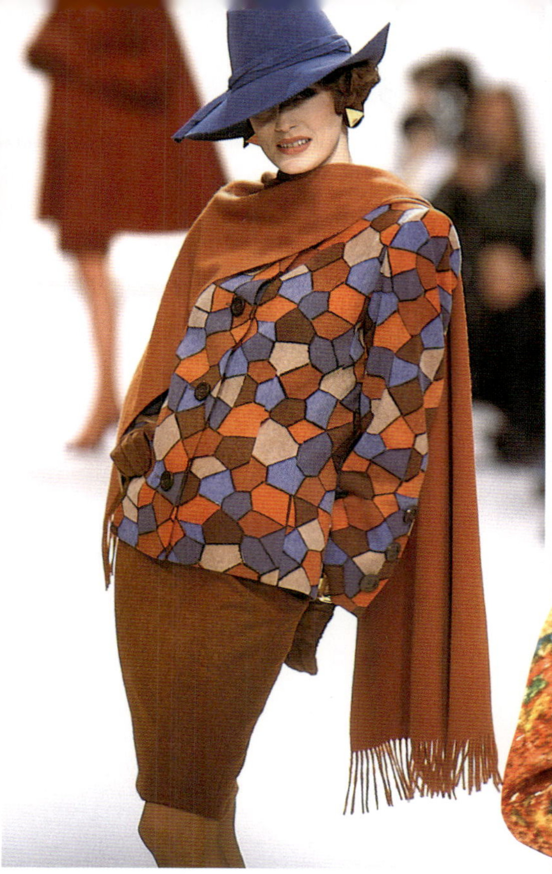
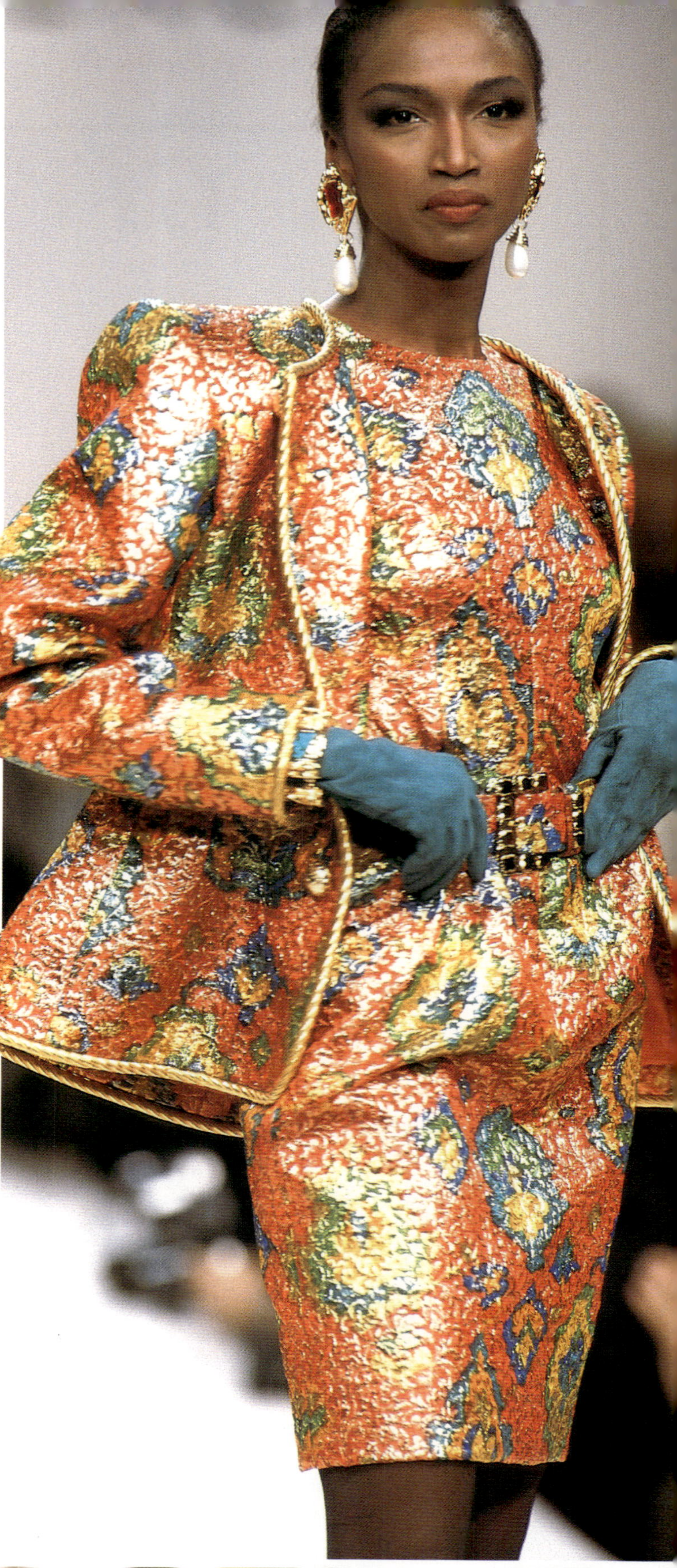
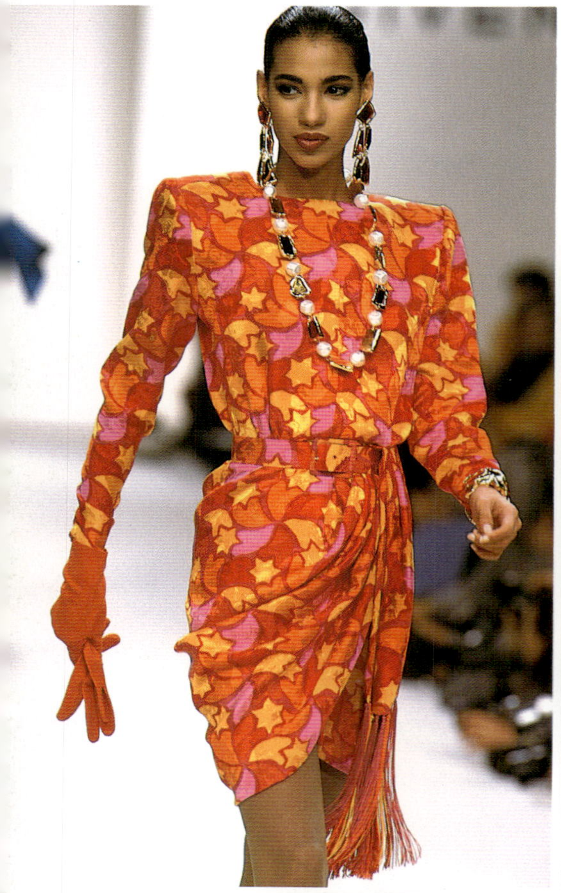
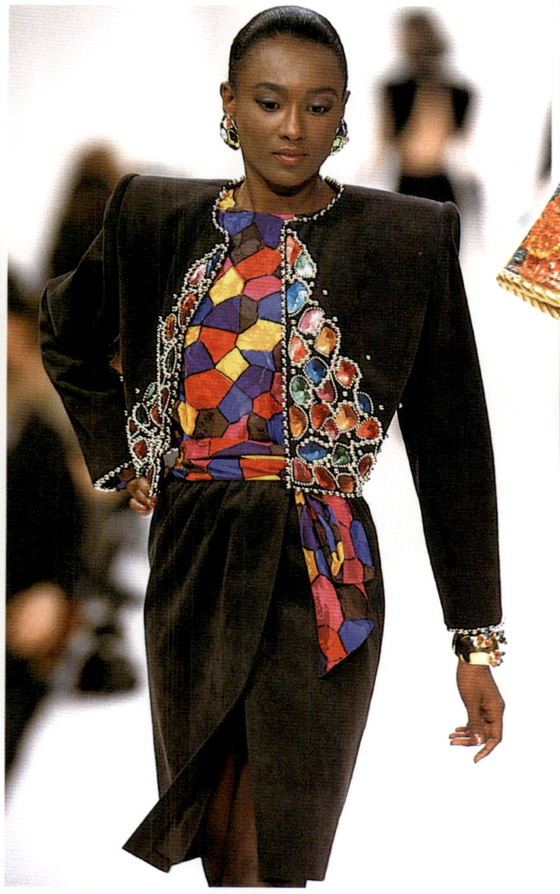
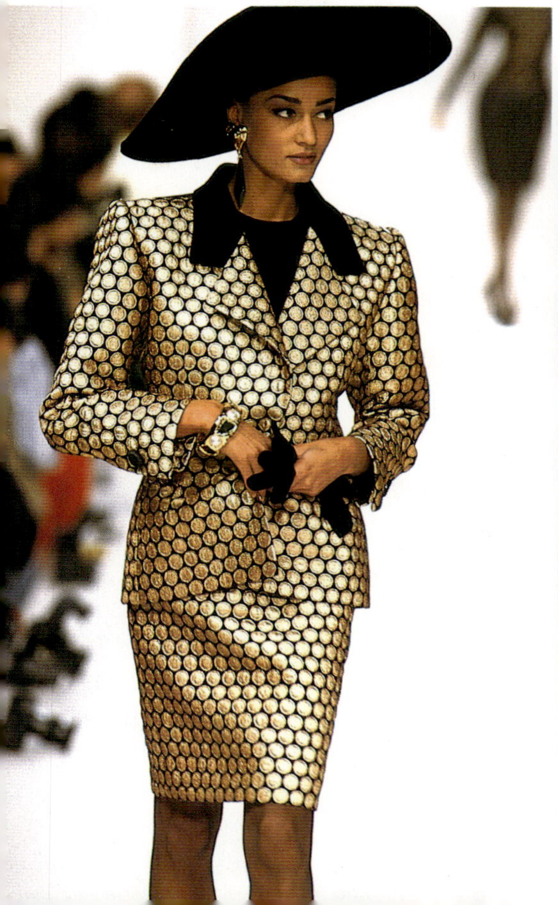
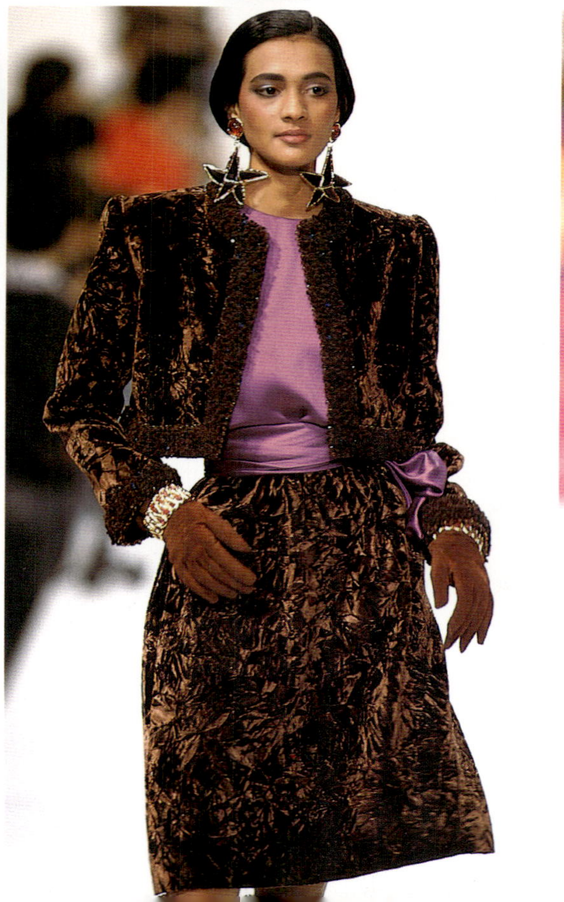
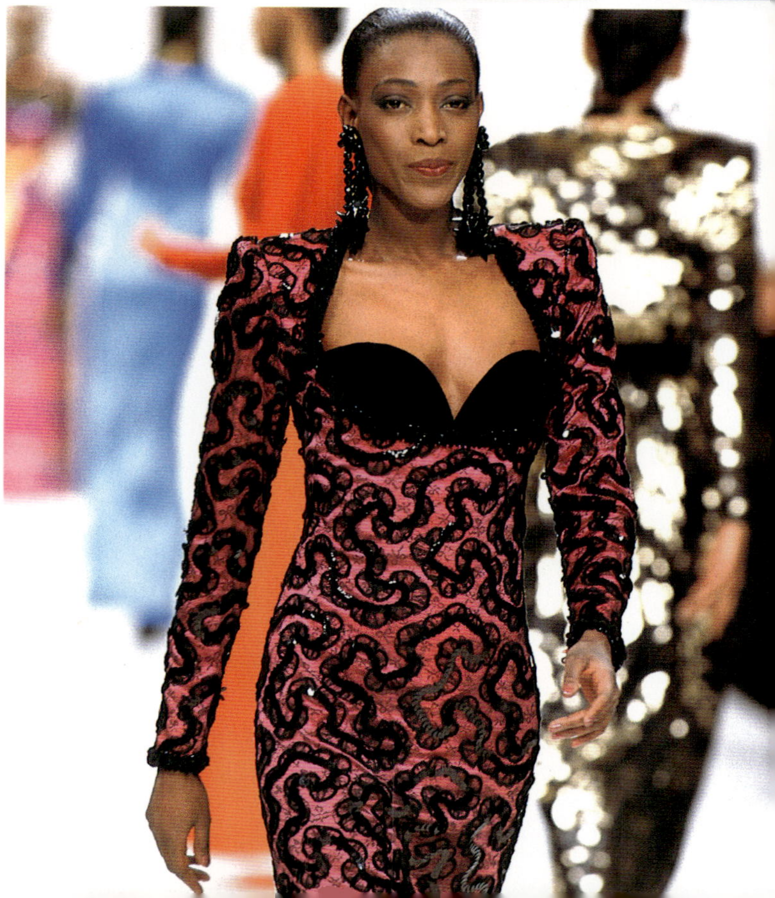

PARIS-33

GUY LAROCHE

ギ・ラロッシュ

丸味をもたせたバルーン・シルエットを多用したコレクション。デイ・ウェアには、ブライト・カラーのスーツやドレスを展開。

A collection which liberally employed the round, balloon silhouette.
Brightly colored dresses and suits were displayed in the day wear.

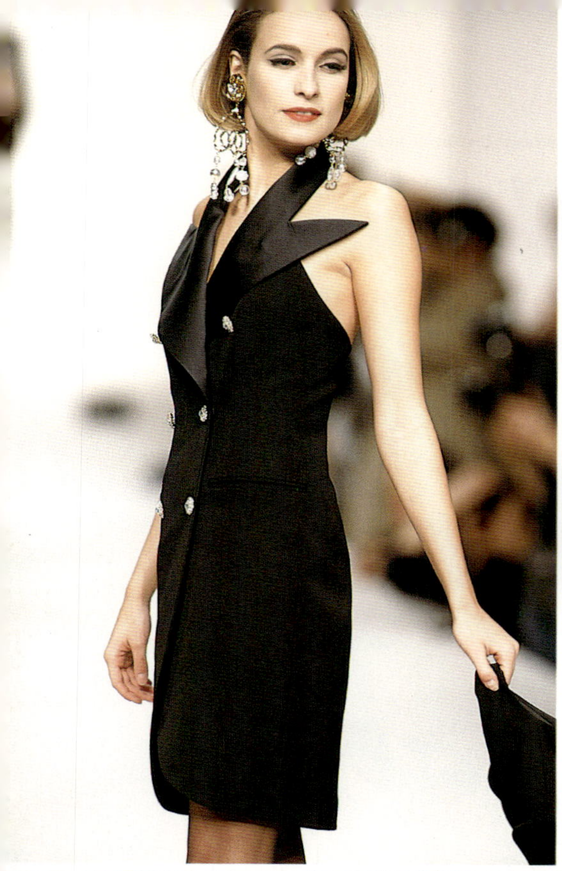
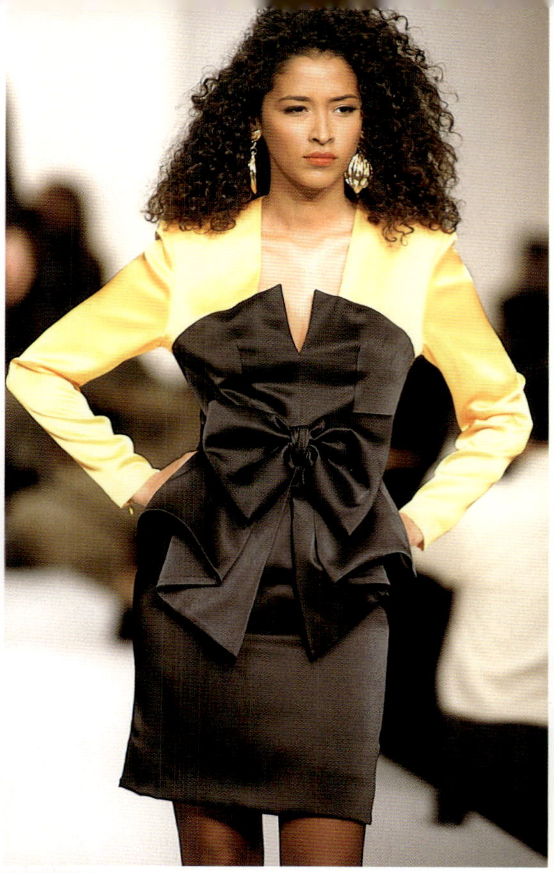
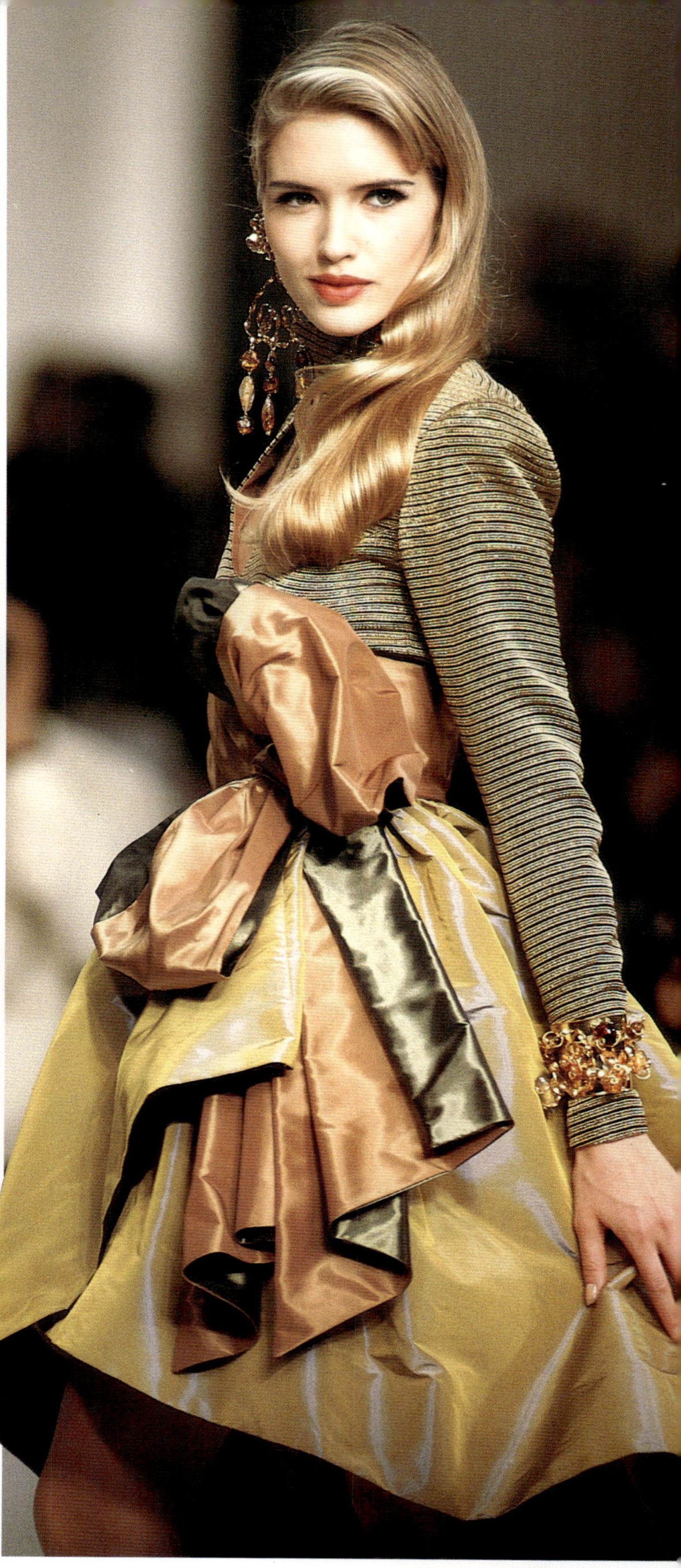
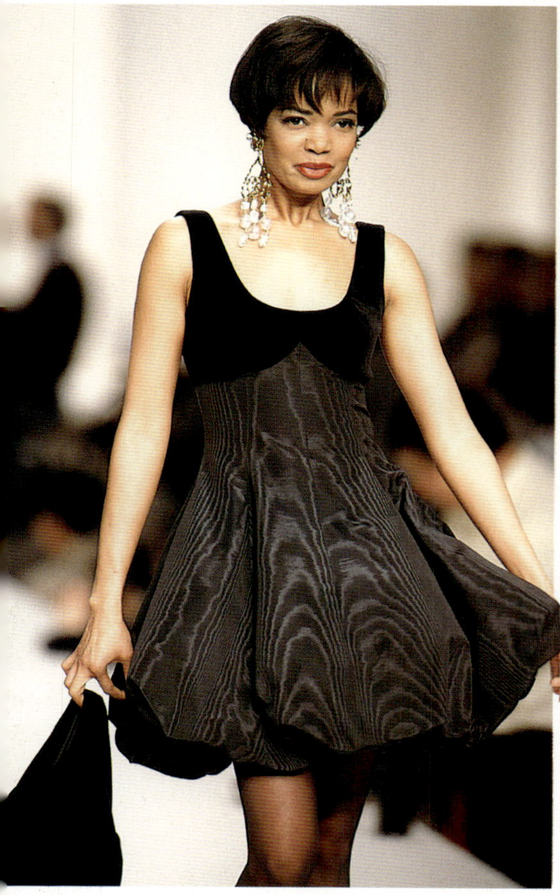
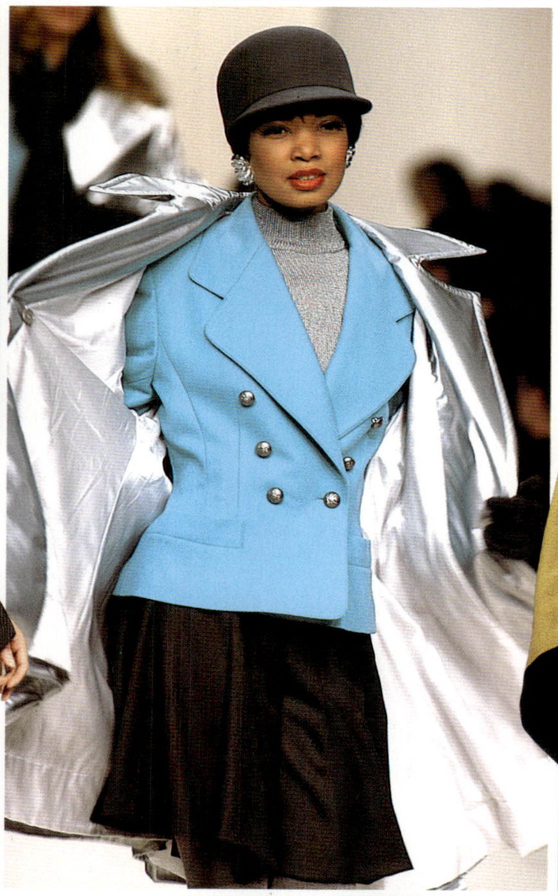
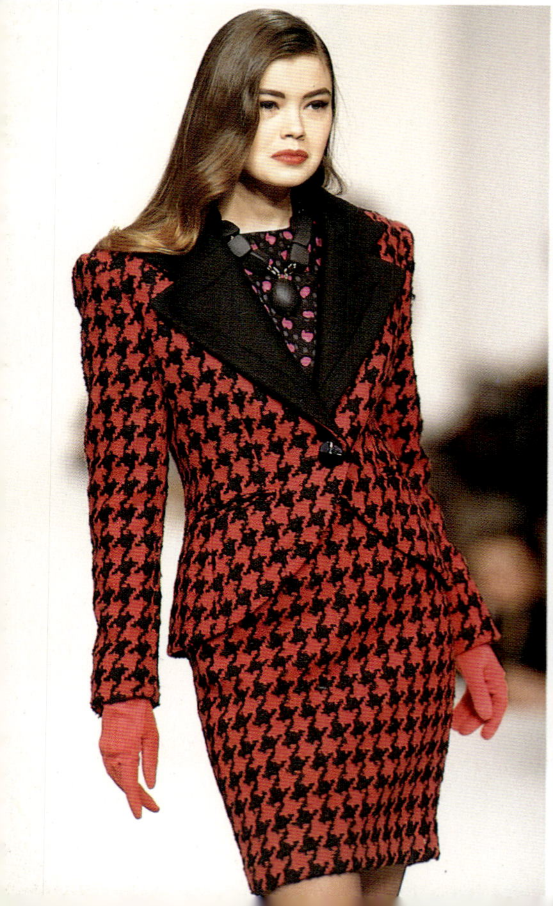
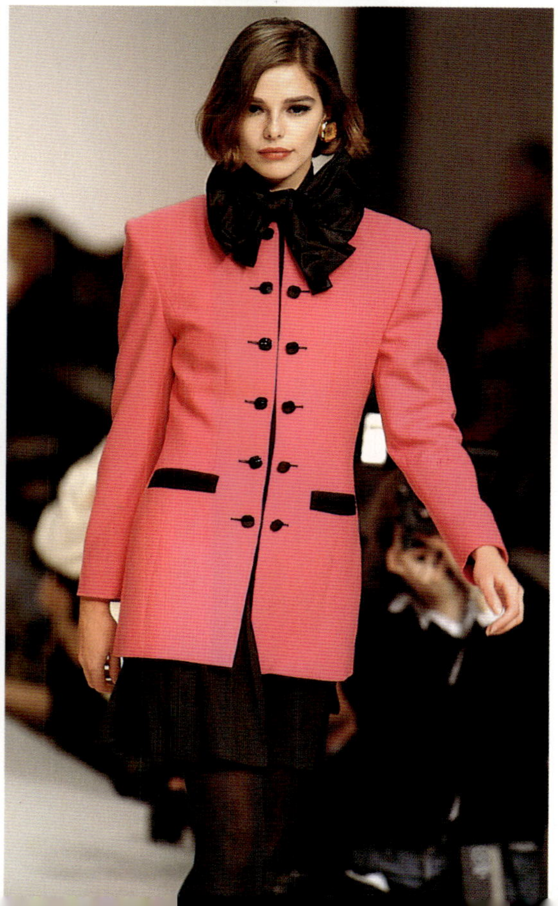
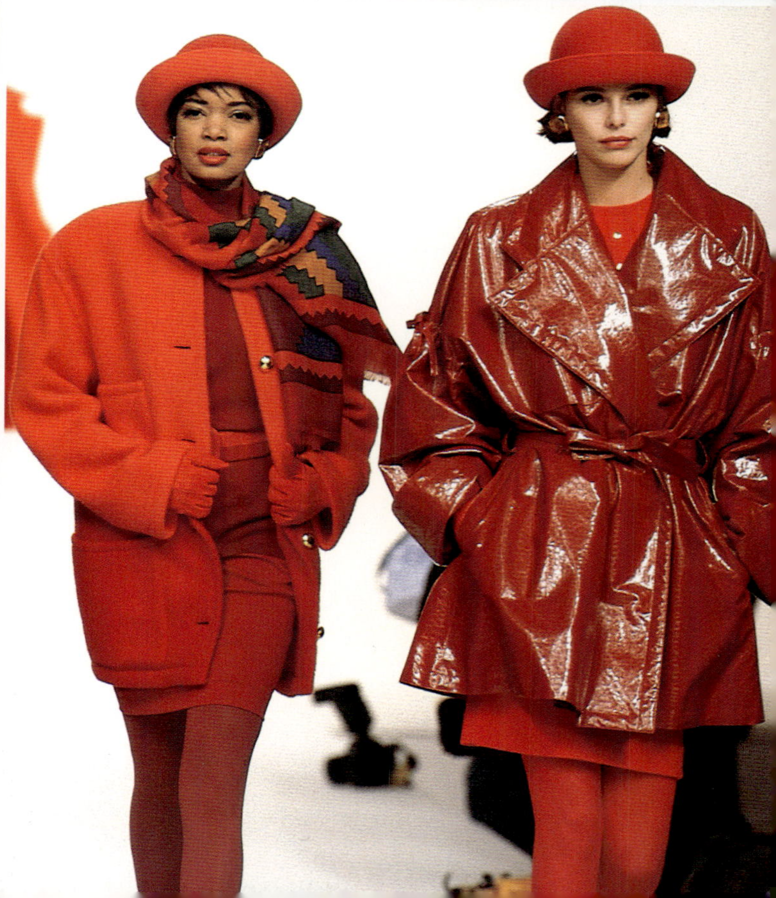

PARIS-34

BALENCIAGA

バレンシアガ

バレンシアガの伝統的優雅さに、今シーズンは若々しい軽快さを加えたコレクション。デイ・ウェアにはスポーティブな要素、夜のためにはゴージャスさを。
This season's collection saw a youthful, light feeling added to Balenciaga's traditional elegance.
On display were sporty day were and gorgeous evening wear.

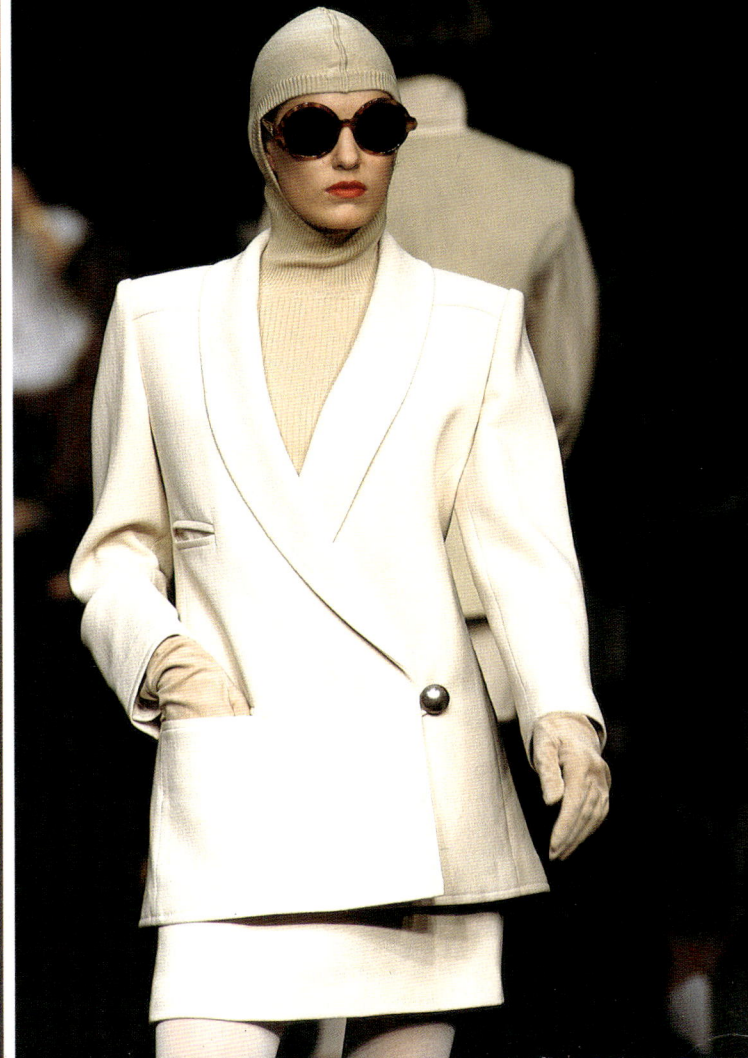

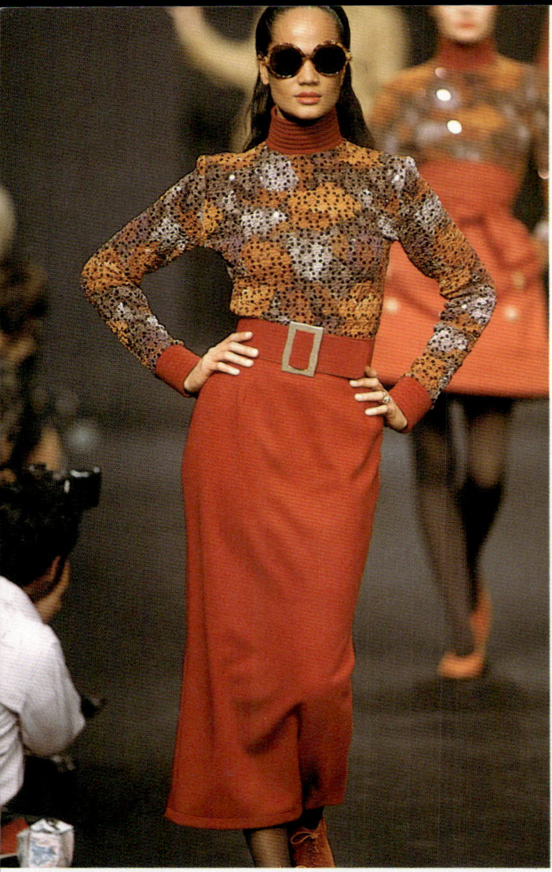
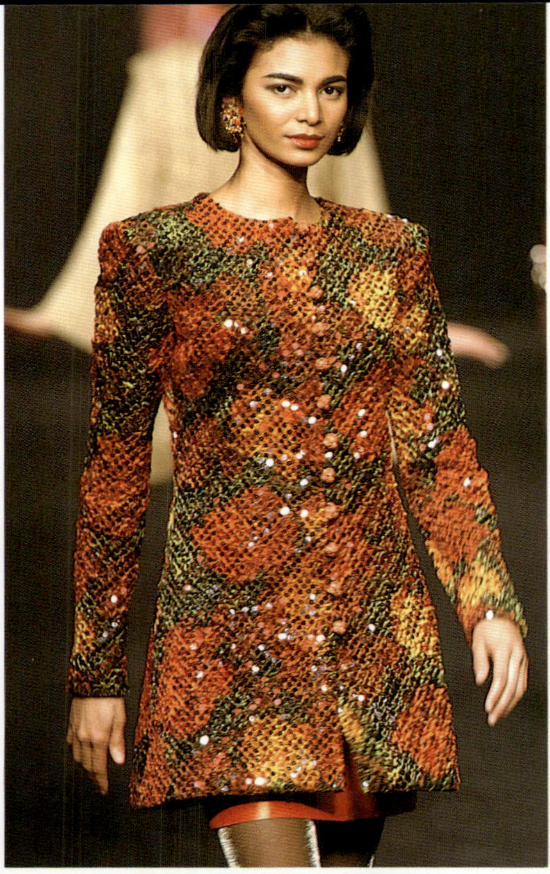
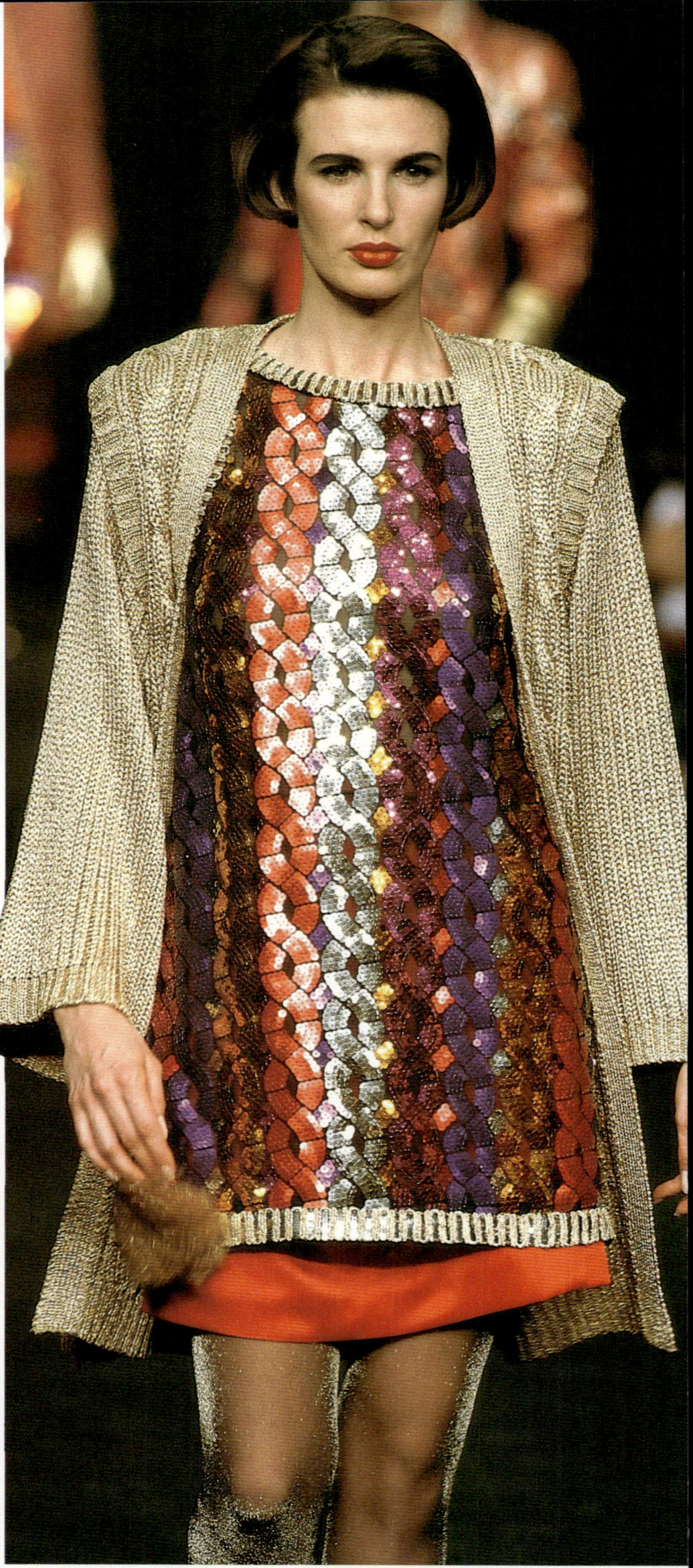
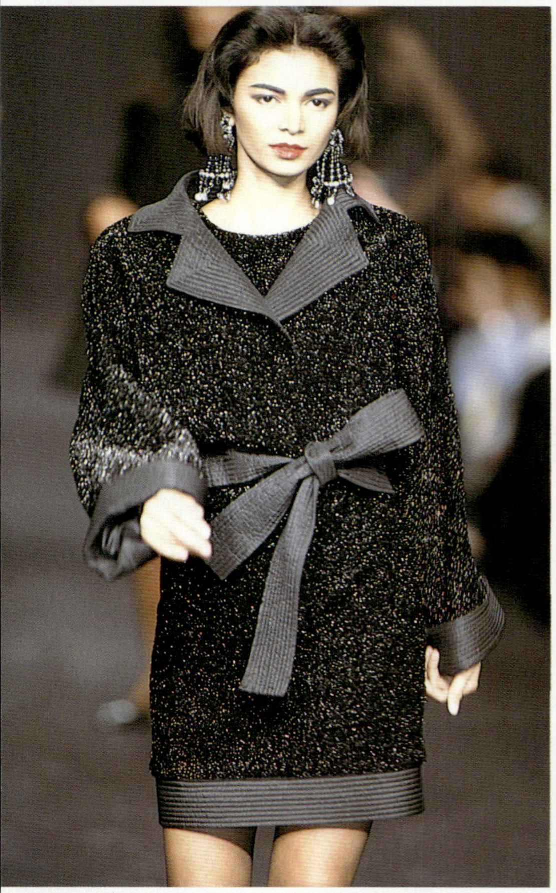
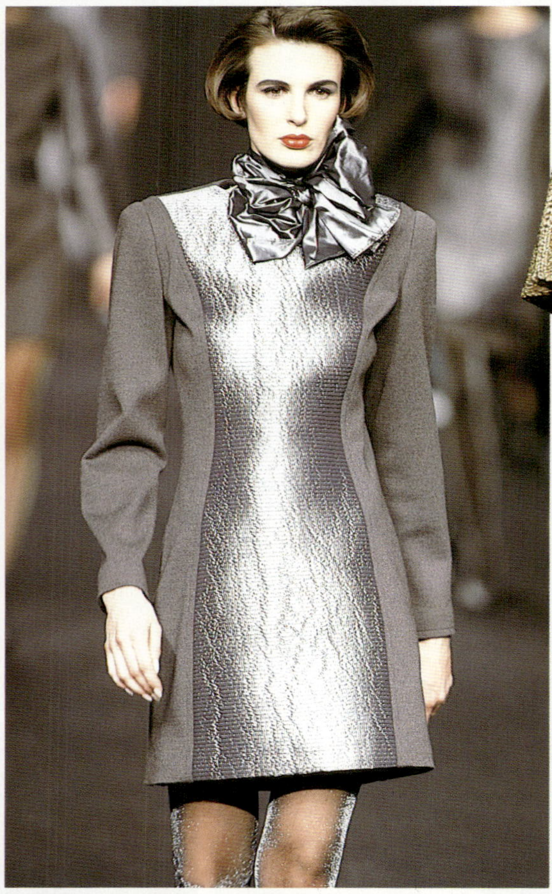
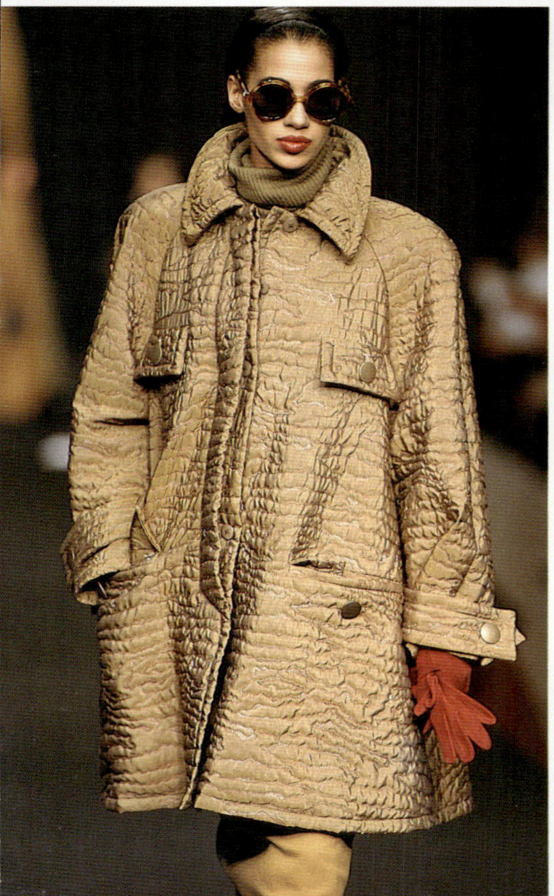
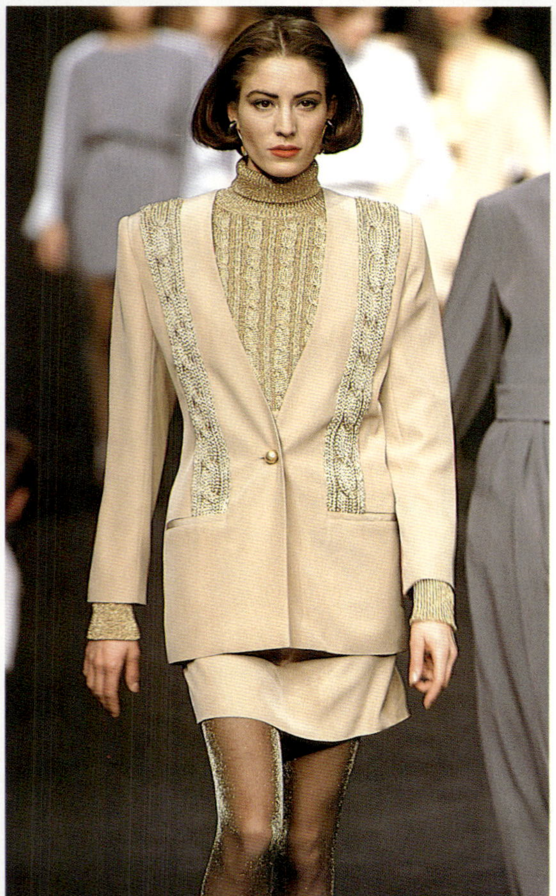
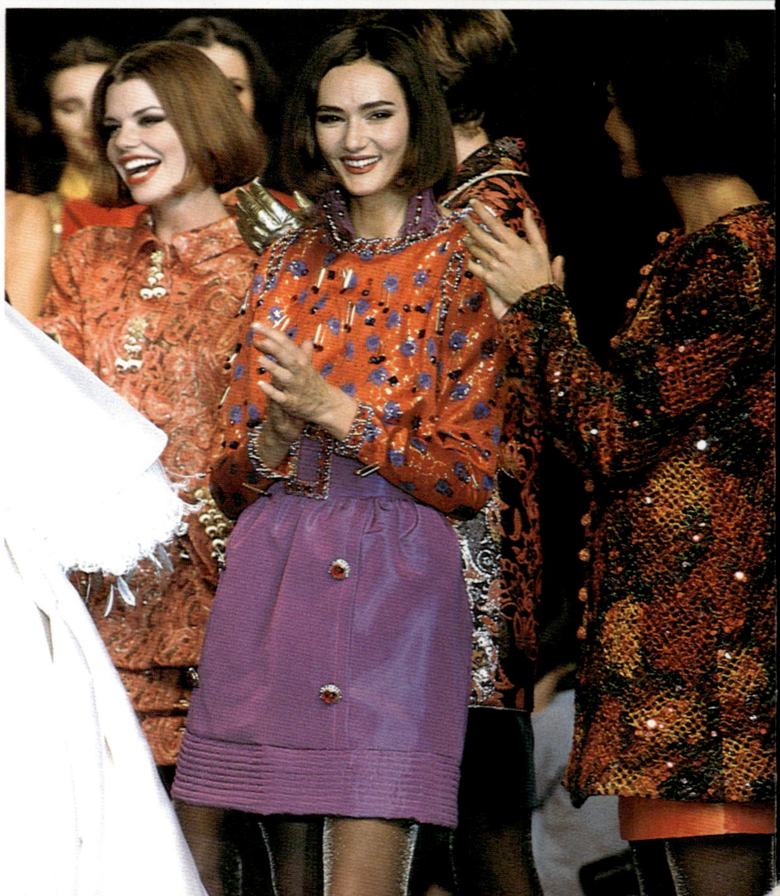

MICHEL KLEIN

ミッシェル・クライン

シンプルでシックな服作りのミッシェル・クライン。今シーズンは、着易い素材、ジャージィやニット、ストレッチ素材でイージー・エレガンスを追求している。

Michel Klein makes simple and chic clothes. The season an easy elegance was sought, using such easy-to-wear materials as jersey and knit stretch material.

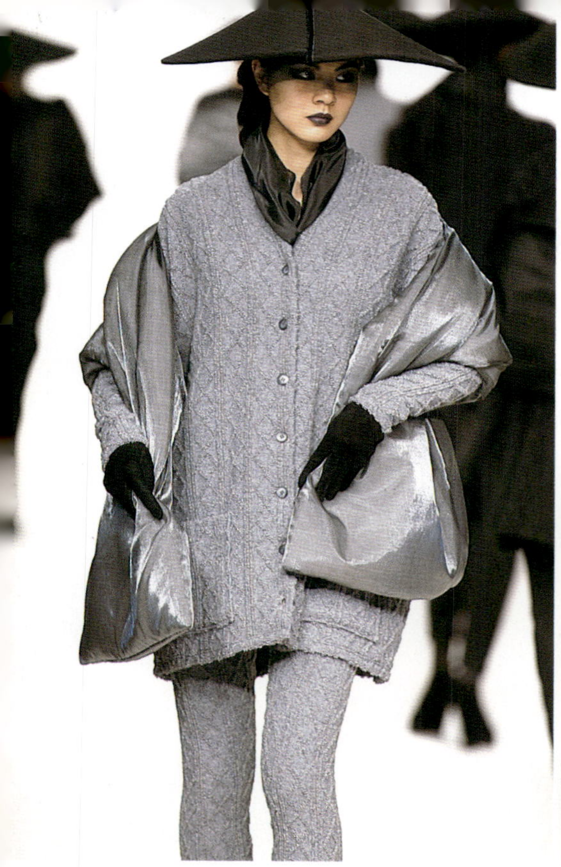
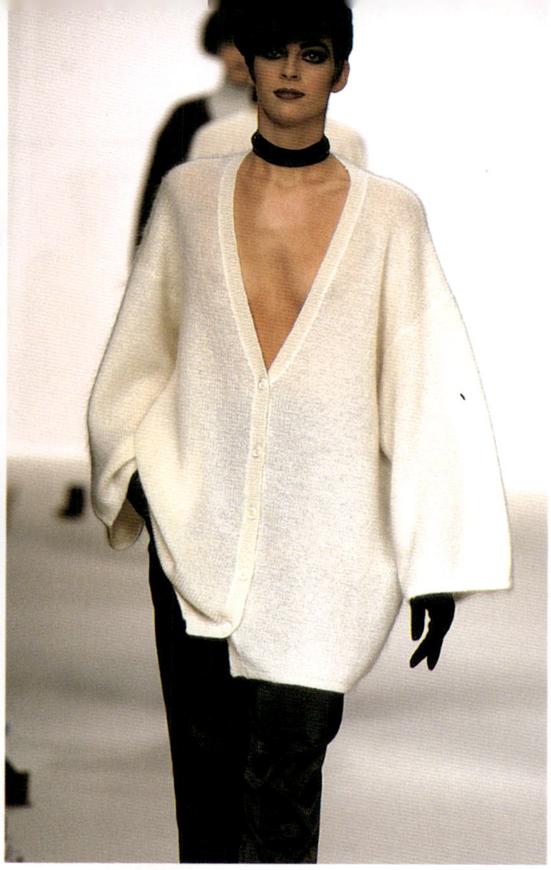
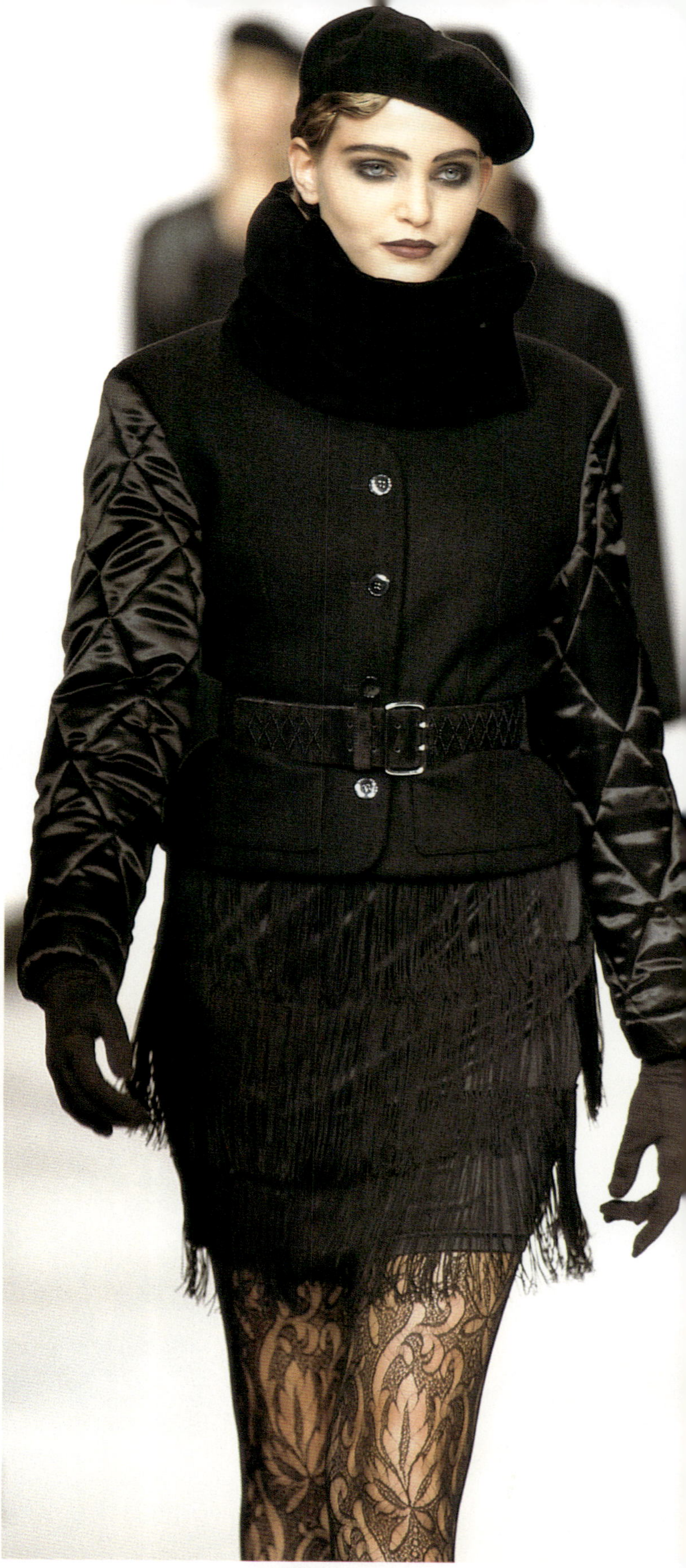
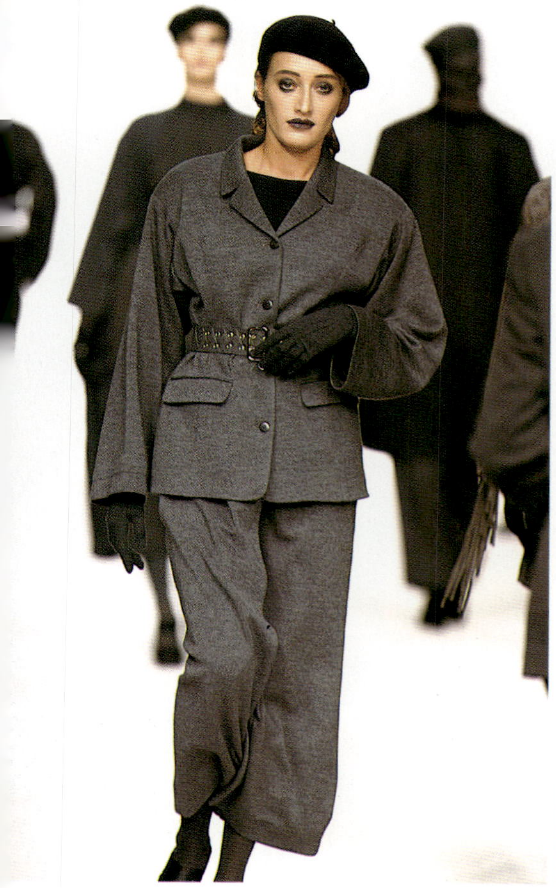
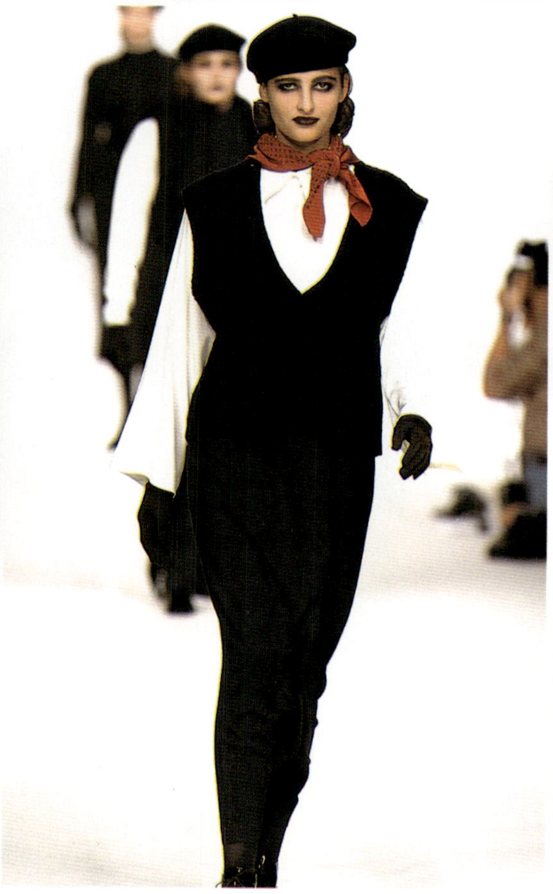
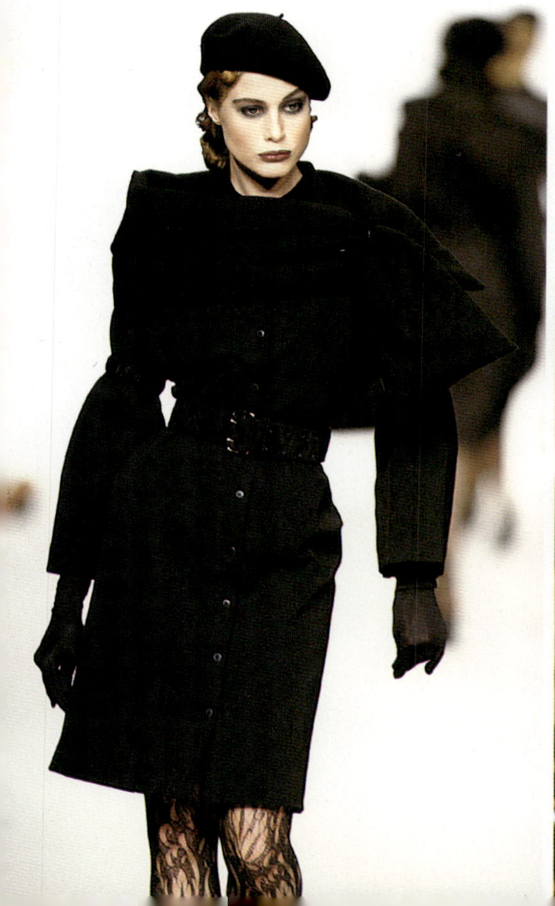
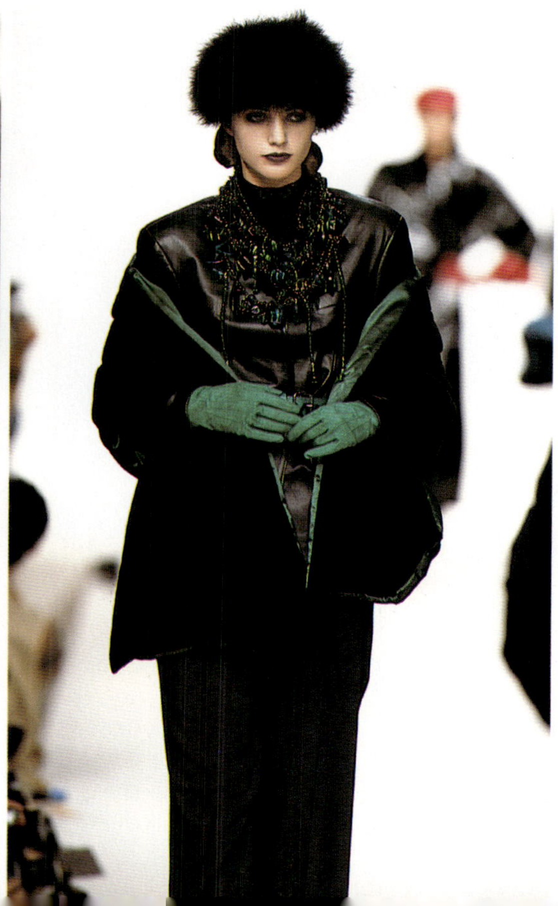
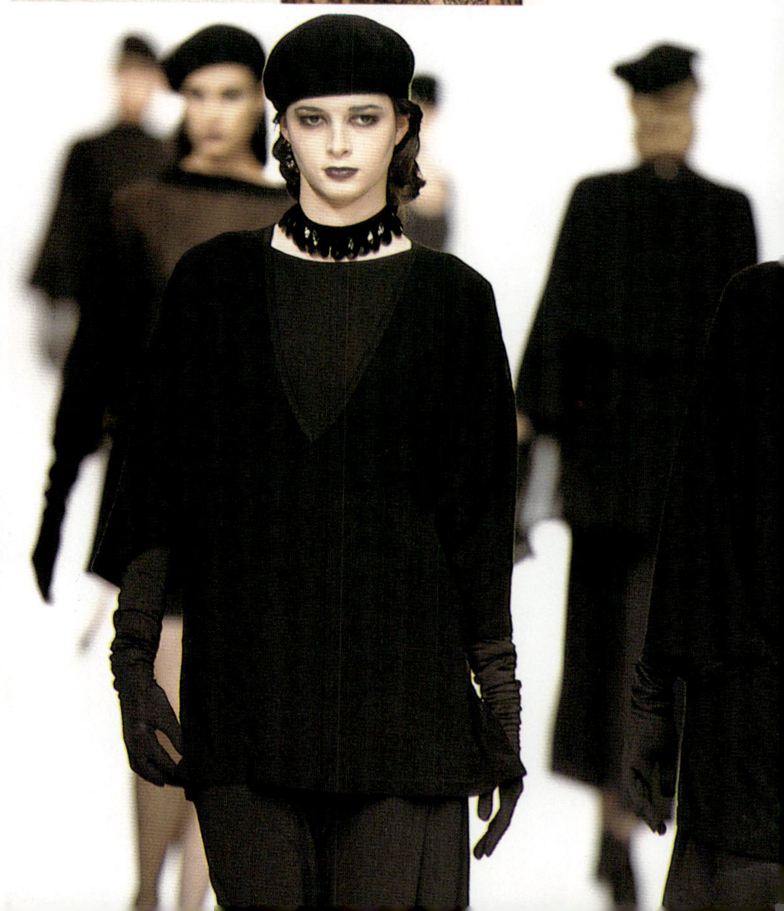

PARIS-36

MATSUDA

マツダ

手編み風のニットの手の凝んだ美しさはマツダの得意とするところ。メンズ・ライクなコーディネーションにアイディアを潜ませている。

Matsusa's favourite is the elaborate beauty of knits, looking like they are handmade.
There is a feeling of new ideas in the manly coordination.

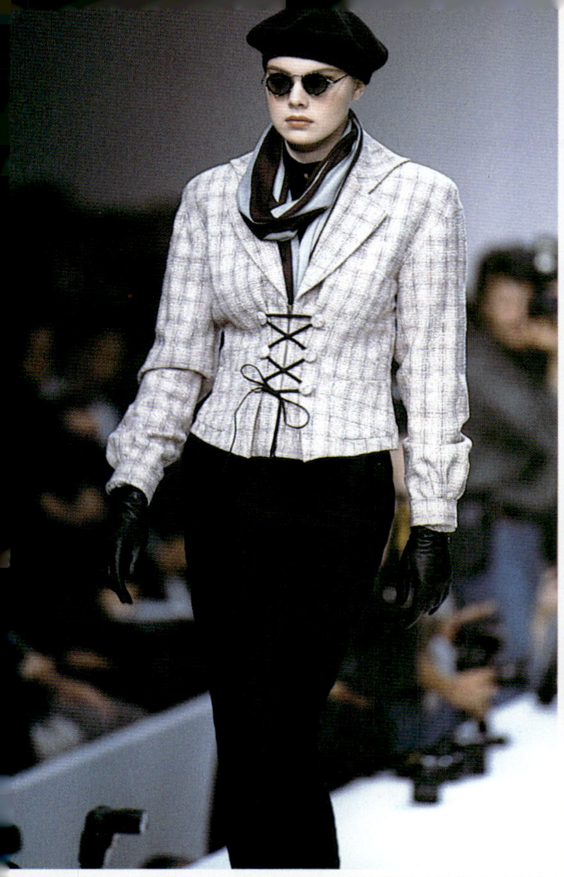
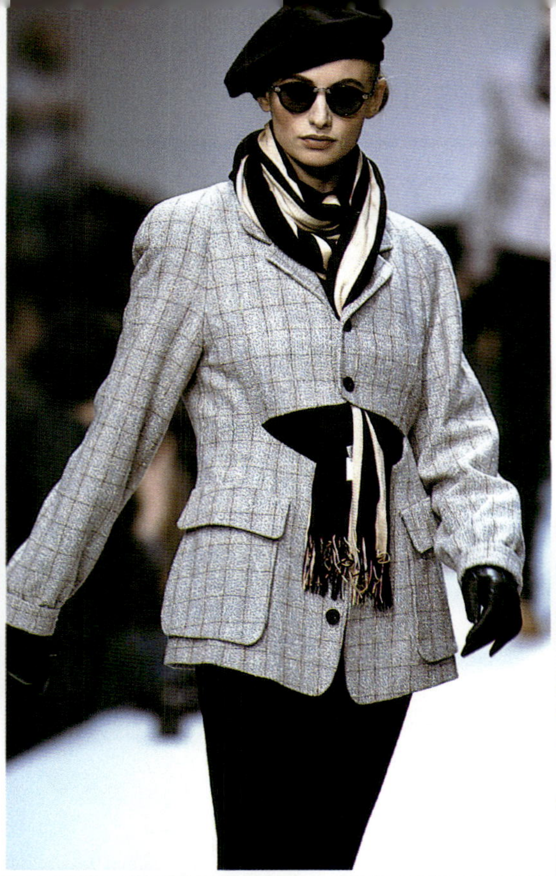
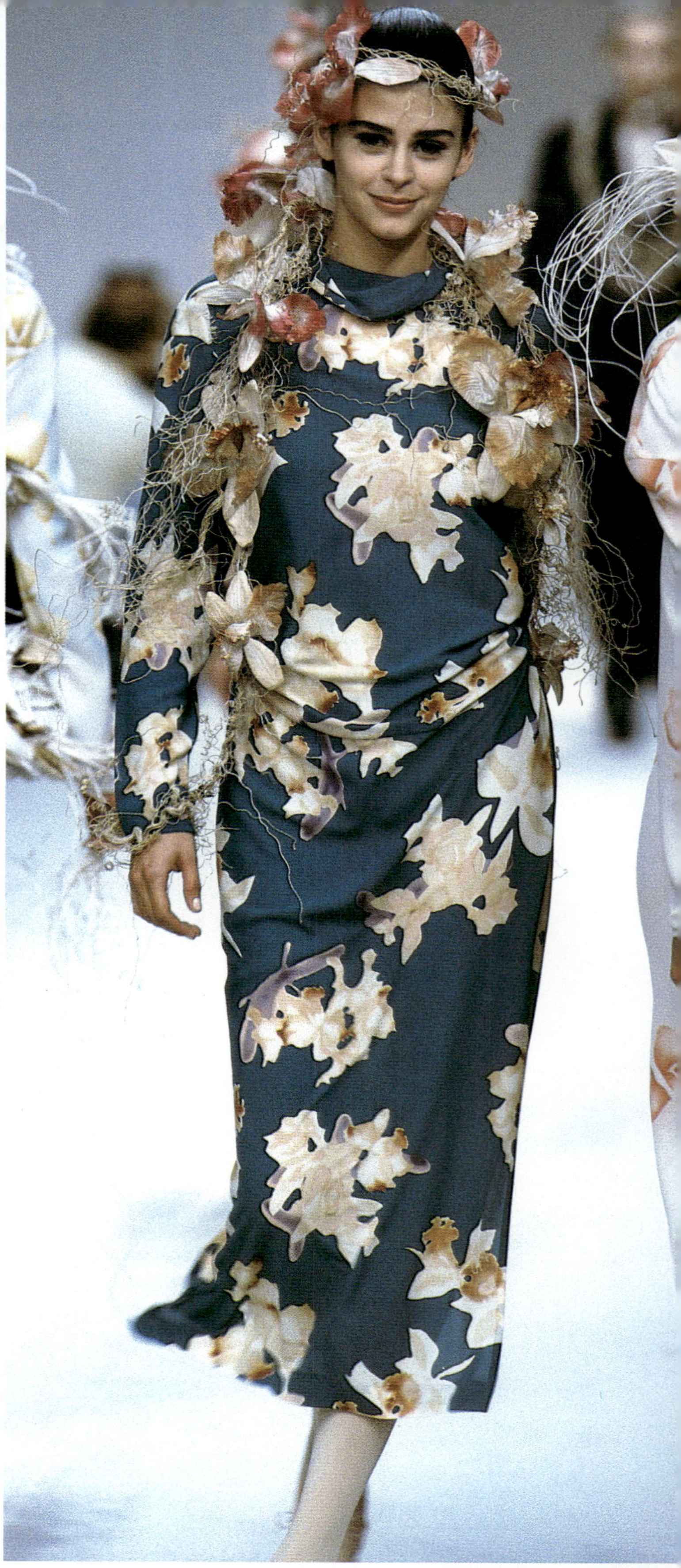
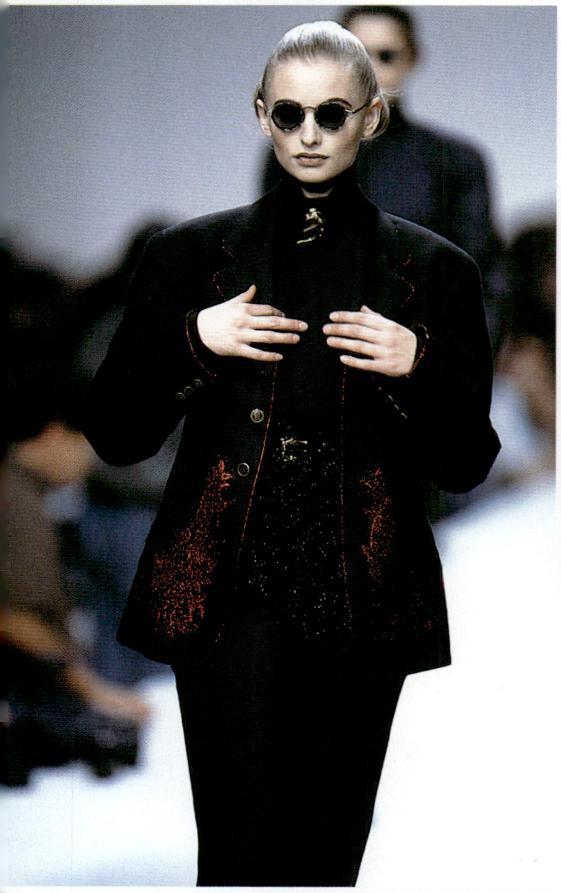
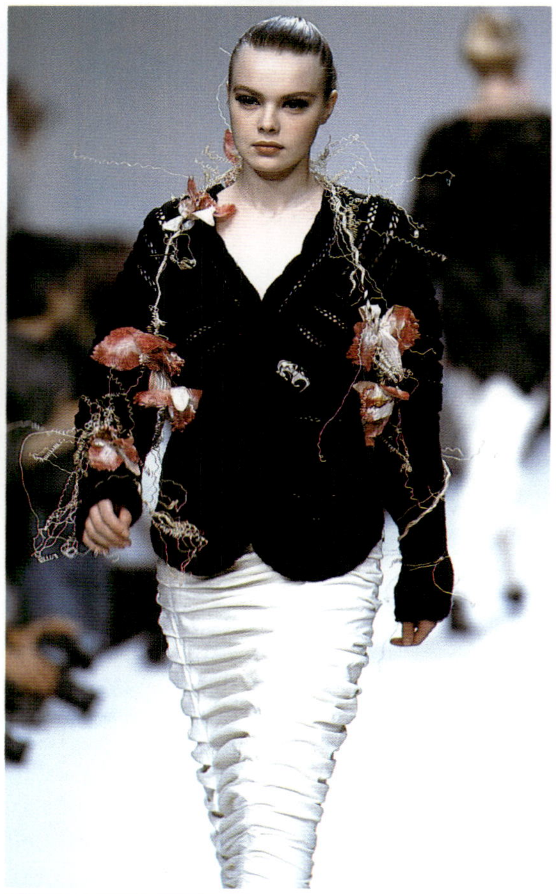
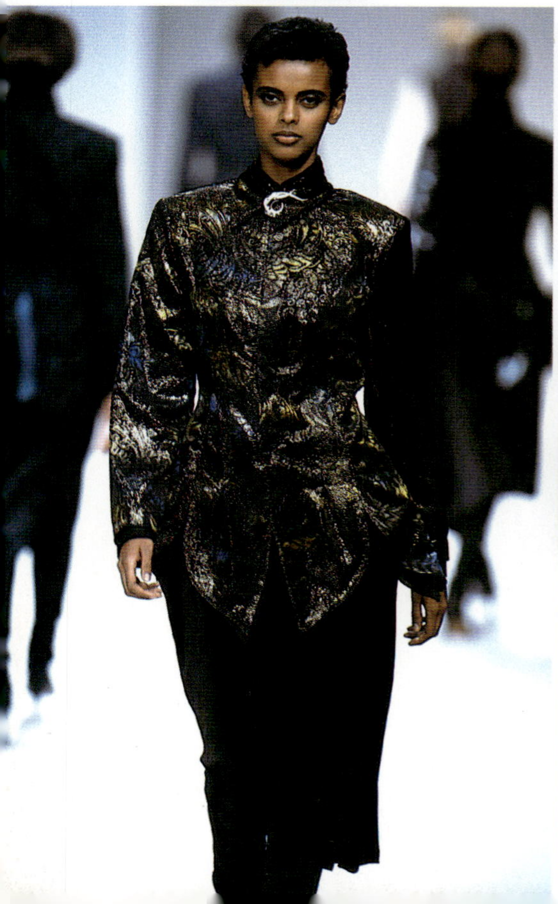
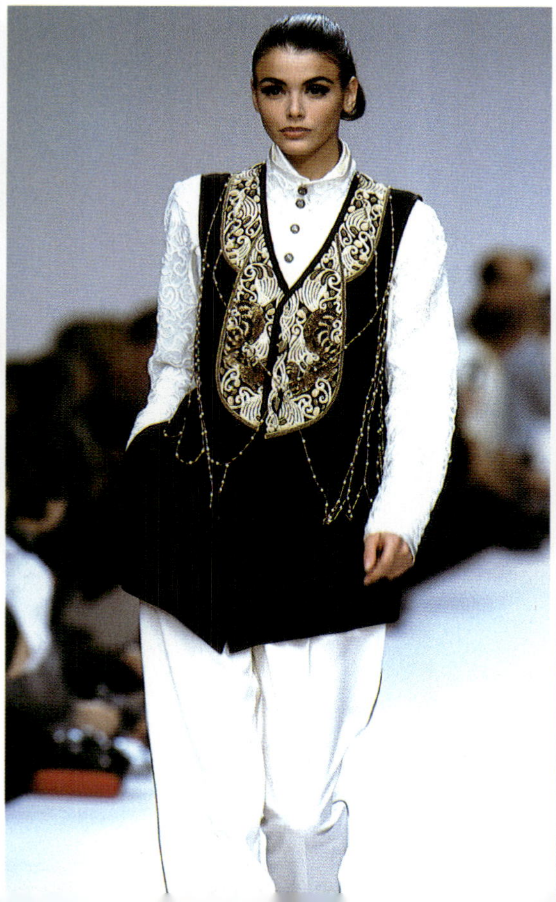
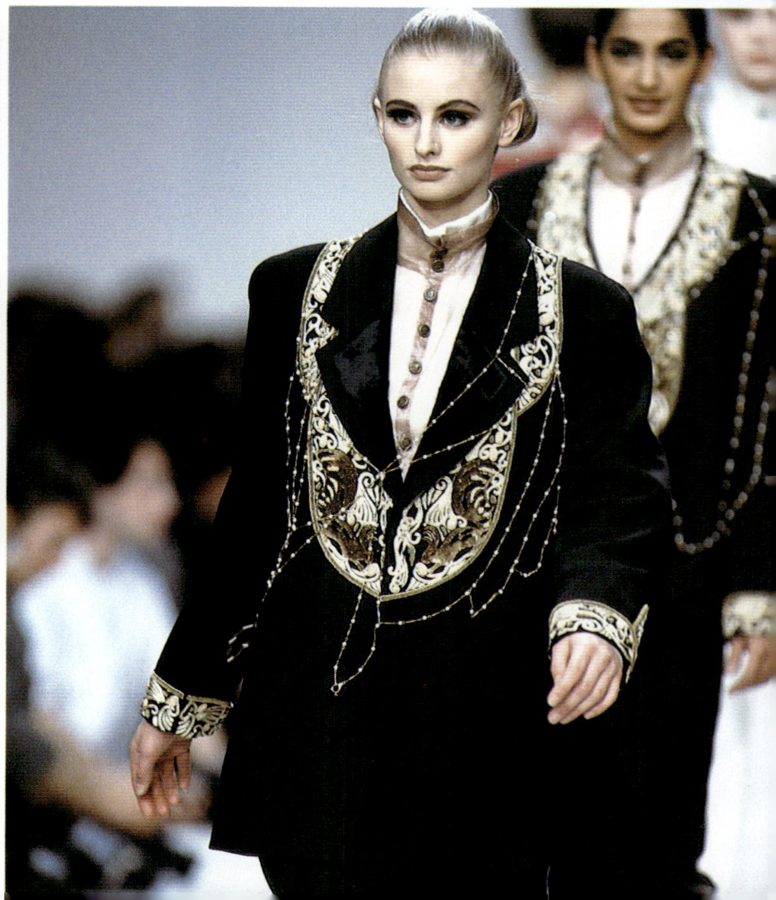

PARIS-37
HIROKO KOSHINO
ヒロコ・コシノ

"ハイ・バランス"をテーマに、造形のバランスや素材のバランス、色彩のバランスを見せるコレクション。オリエンタルの雰囲気もヒロコ・コシノならでは。
Based on a "high balance" theme, the collection displayed a balance of forms, materials and colors.
Also peculiar to Hiroko Koshino, the atmosphere of the Orient.

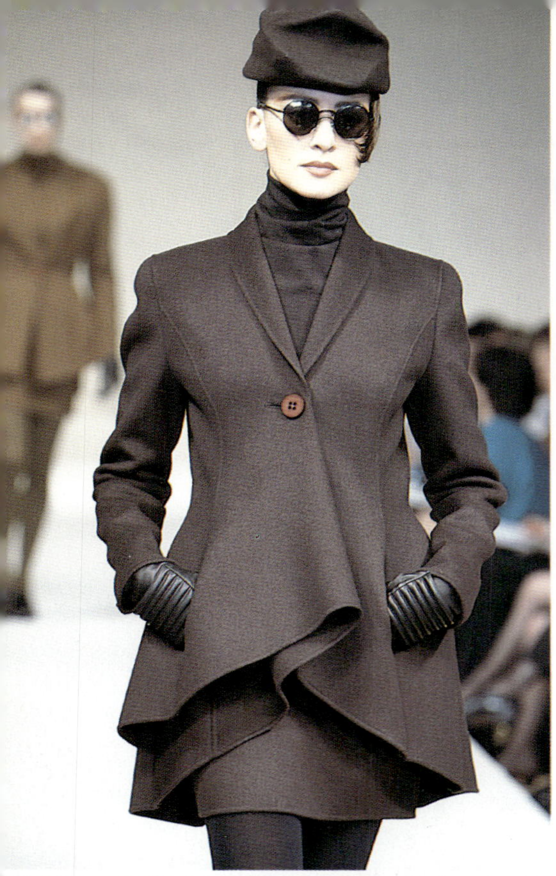
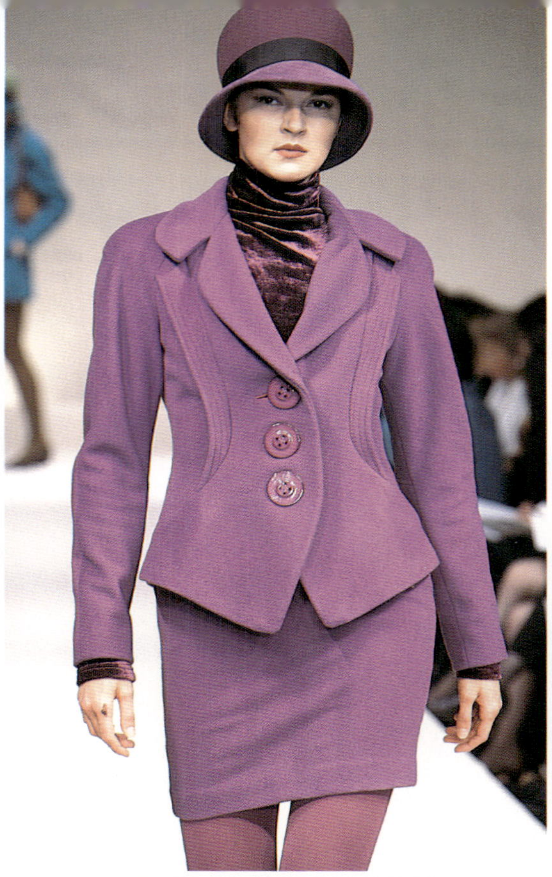
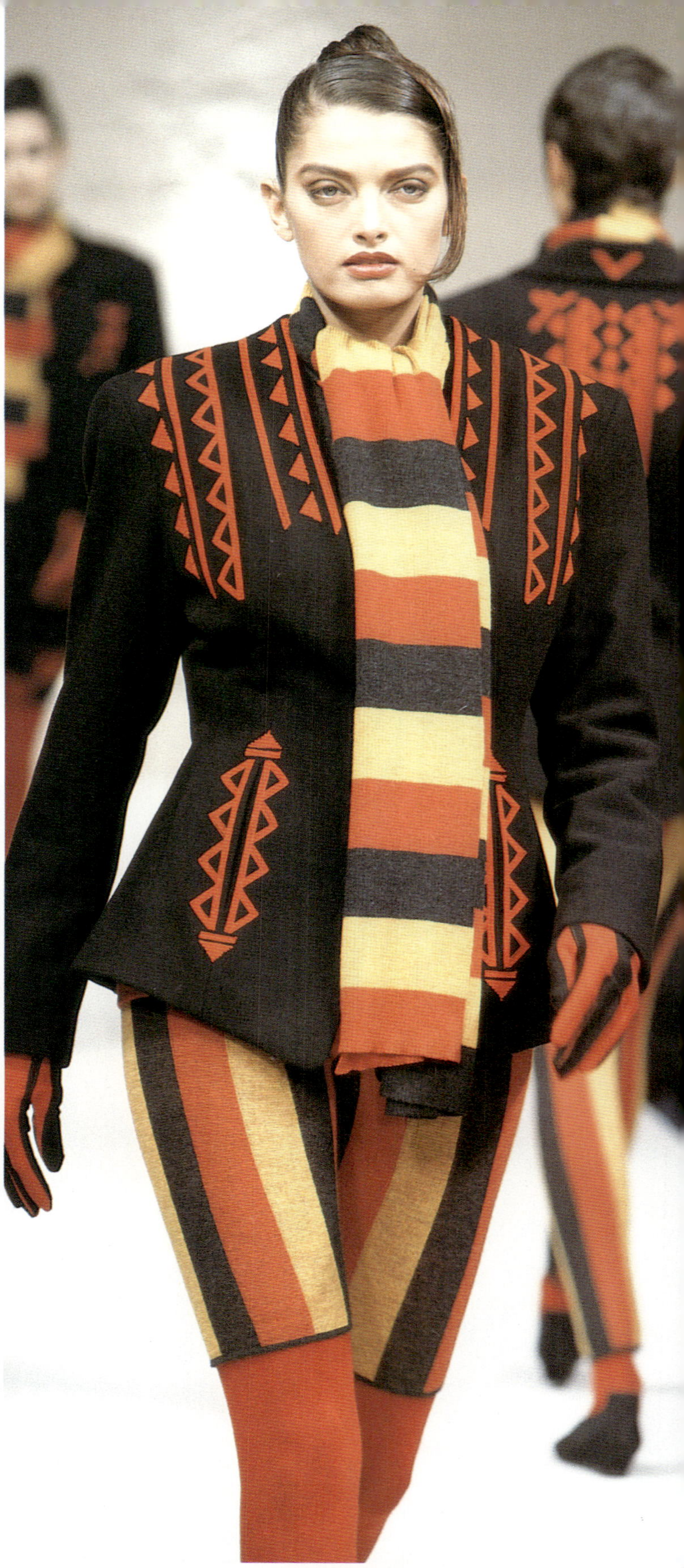
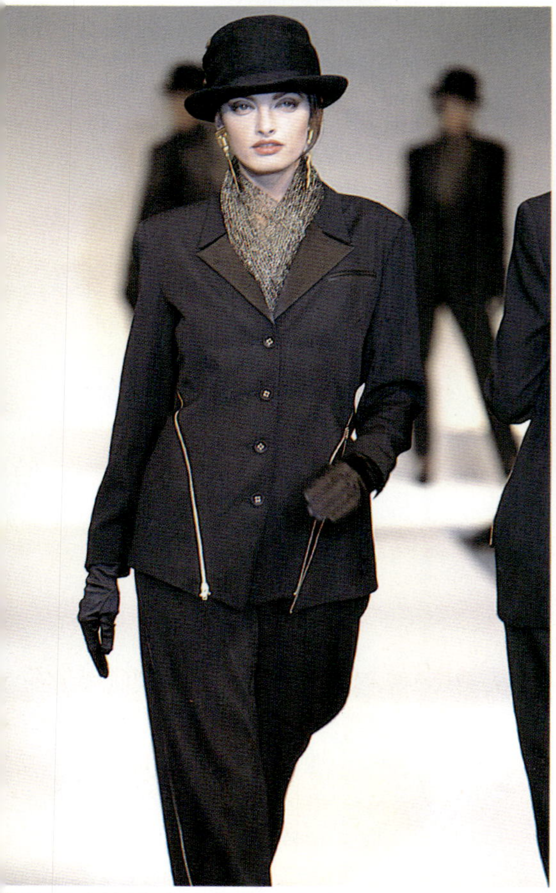
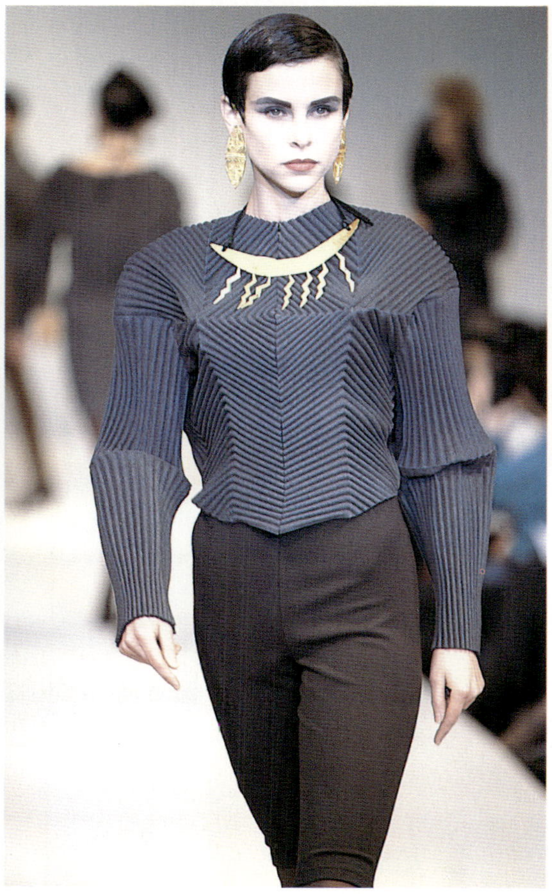
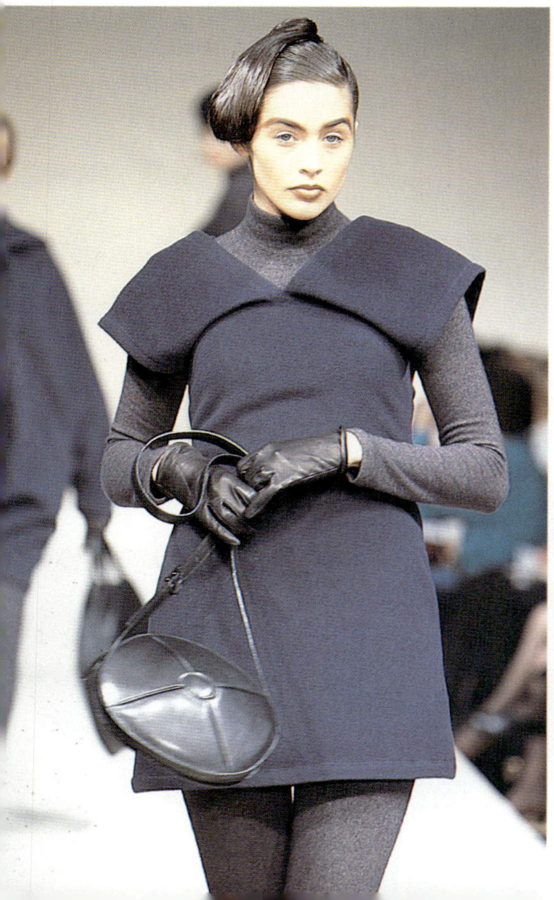
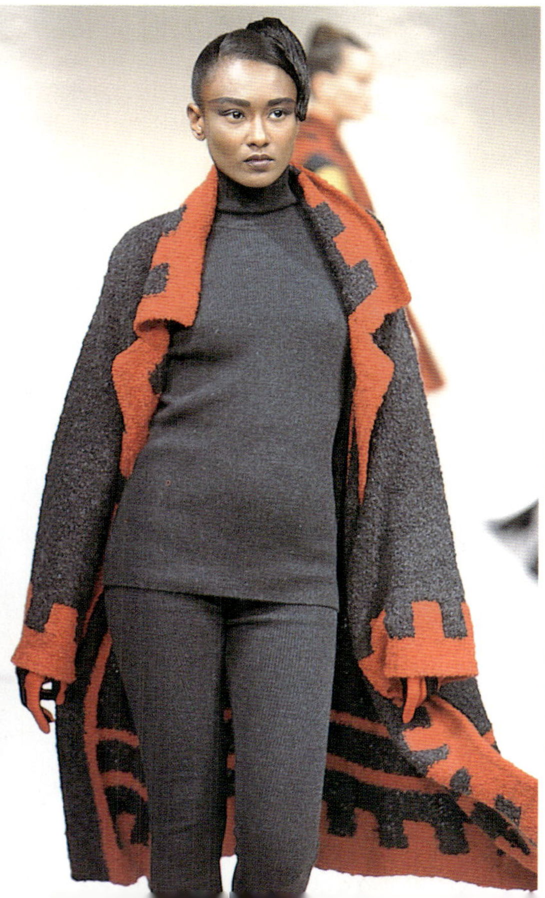
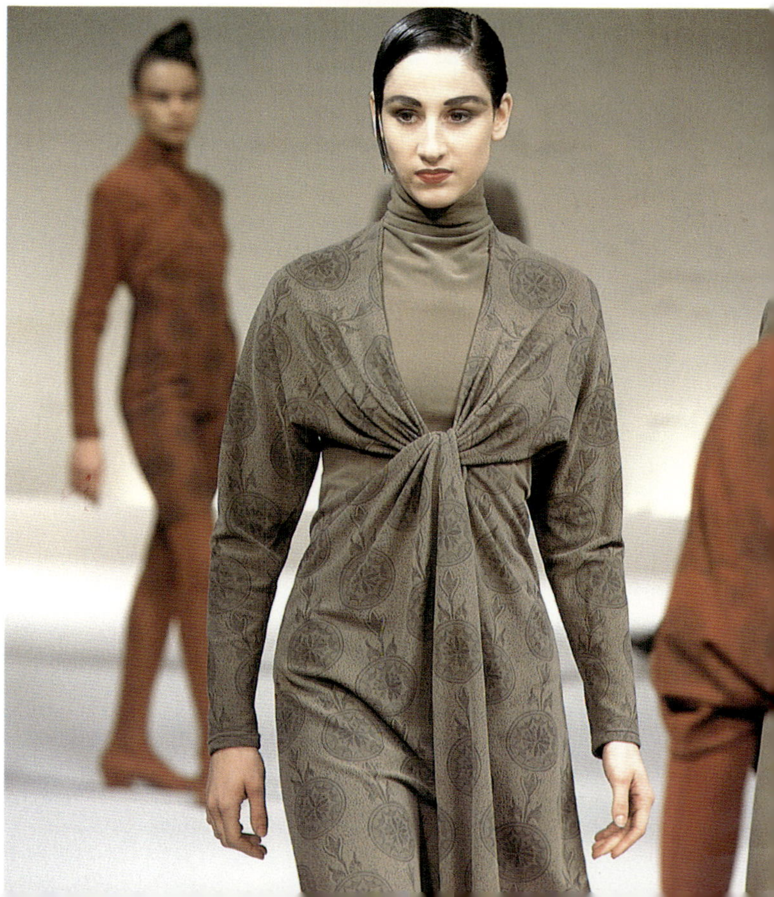

CHANTAL THOMASS

YVES SAINT LAURENT

'91-'92 AUTUMN & WINTER

PRÊT-Á-PORTER COLLECTIONS

EMANUEL UNGARO

YVES SAINT LAURENT

YVES SAINT LAURENT

'91-'92
AUTUMN & WINTER
PRÊT-Á-PORTER
COLLECTIONS

YVES SAINT LAURENT

CHANTAL THOMASS	VALENTINO	CHRISTIAN DIOR
ENRICO COVERI	HANAE MORI	SONIA RYKIEL
EMANUEL UNGARO	EMANUEL UNGARO	CHRISTIAN DIOR

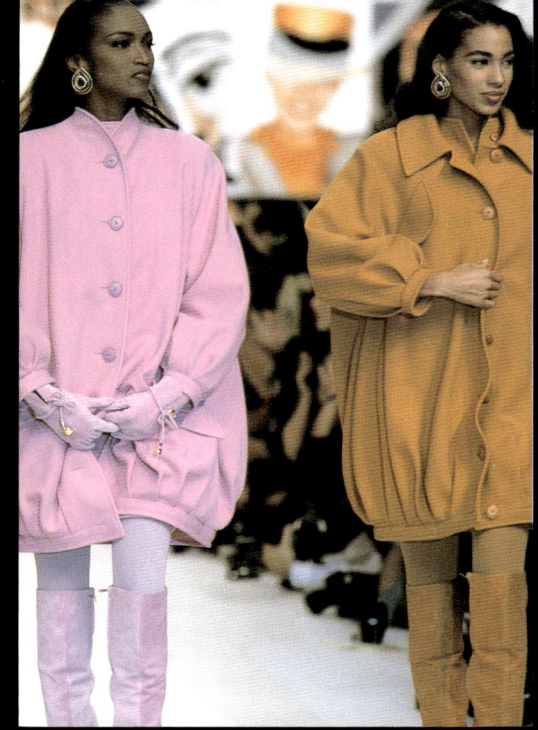

KENZO

MICHEL KLEIN

JIN ABE

ジン・アベ

ジオメトリックなニット・パターンはジン・アベの得意とするところ。今シーズンは伝統的な柄やエスニック柄を大胆な色分割でダイナミックに表現。
Jin Abe's favourite is the geometric knit pattern. This season saw the dynamic display of traditional and ethnic patterns, in a bold color coordination.

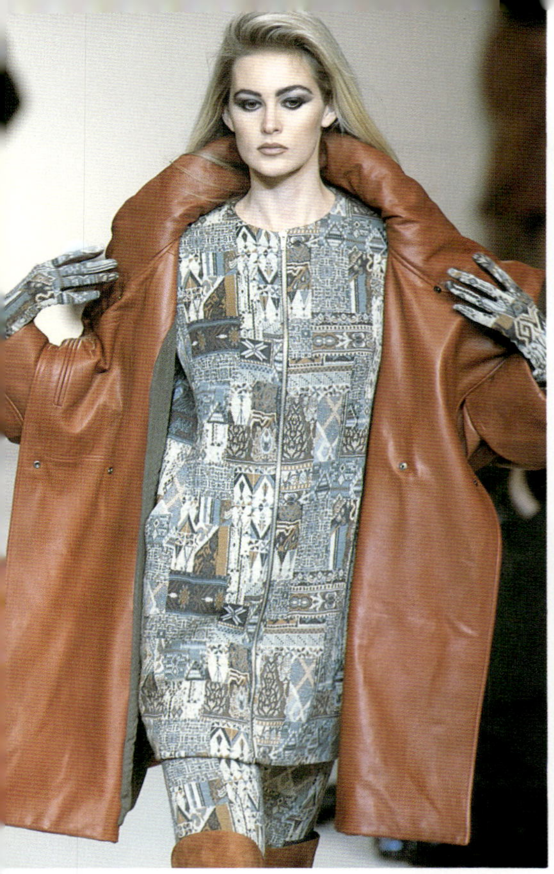
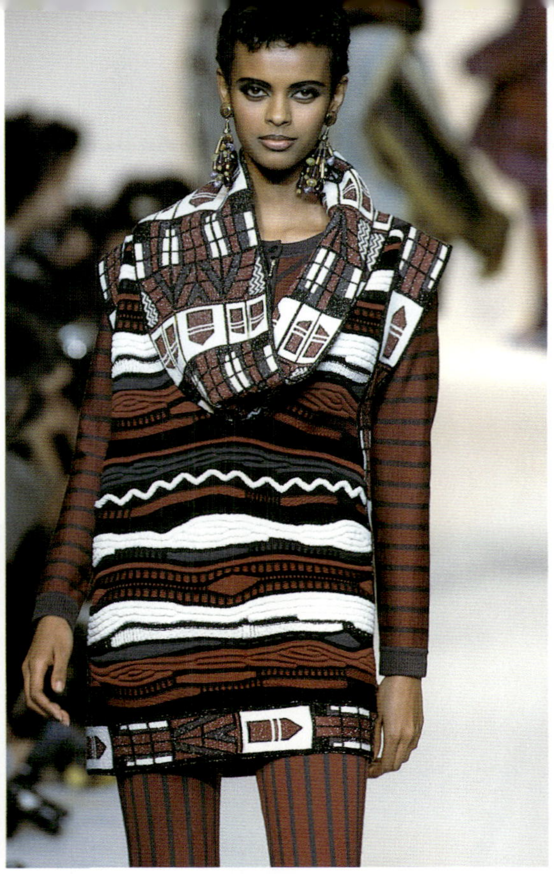
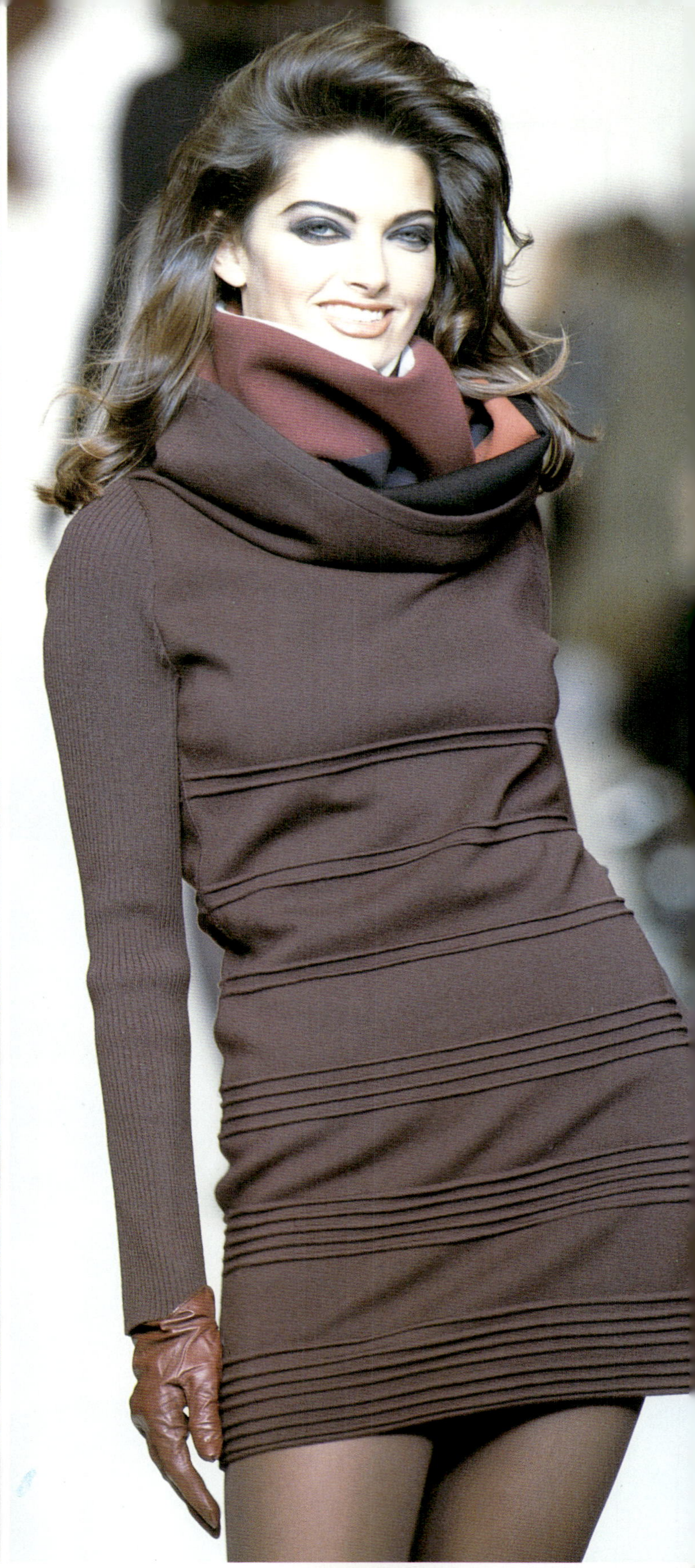
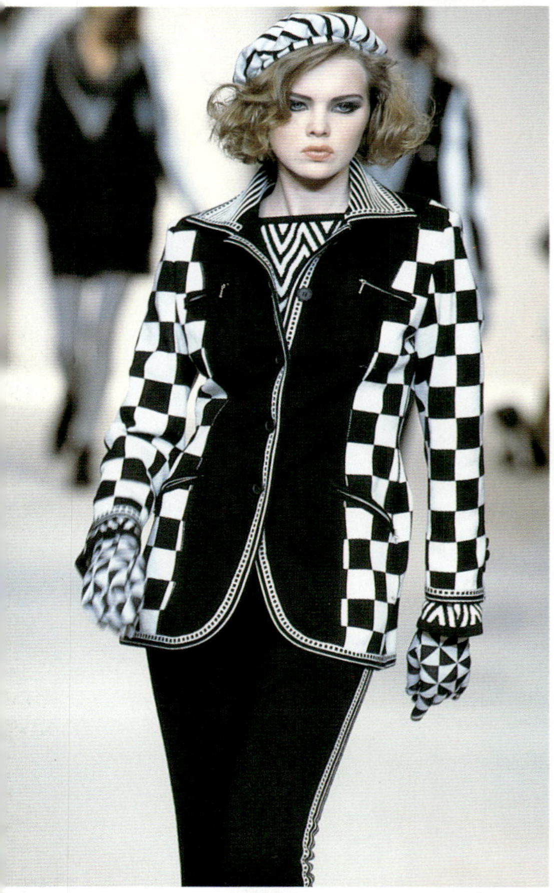
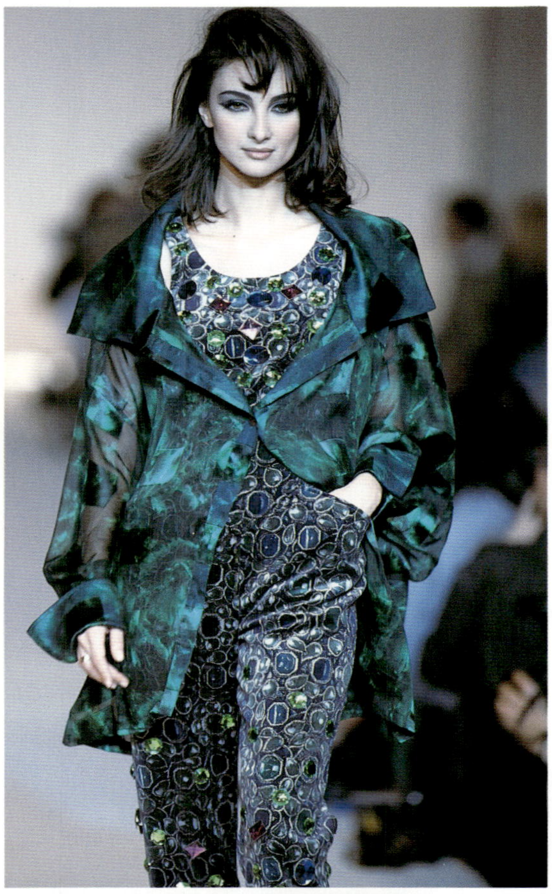
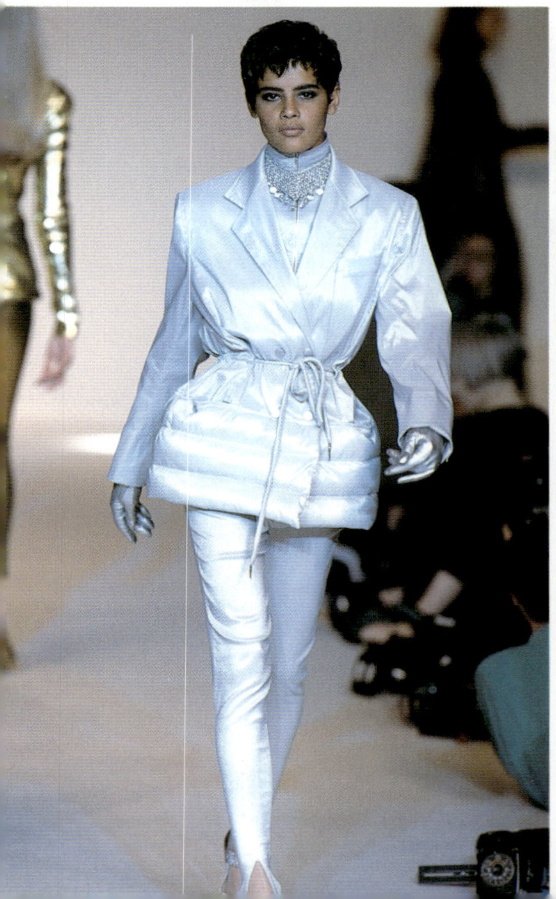
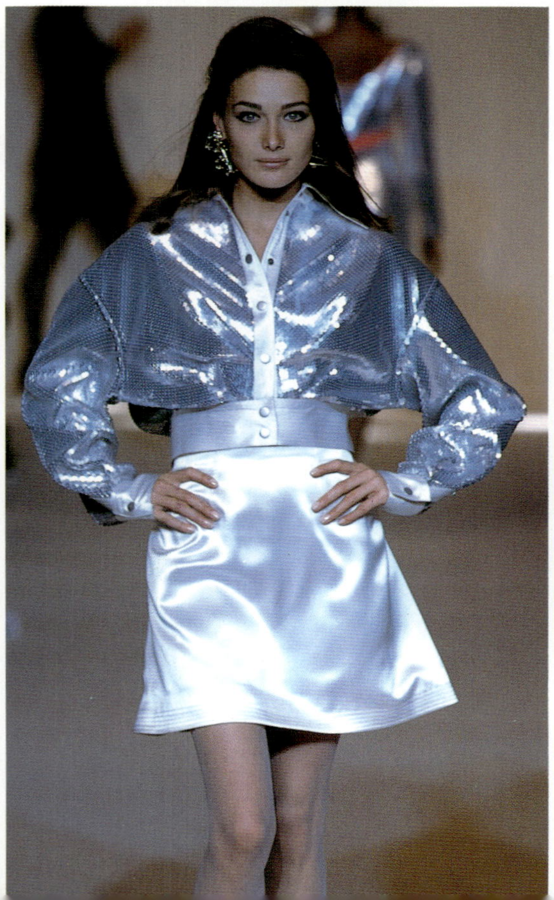
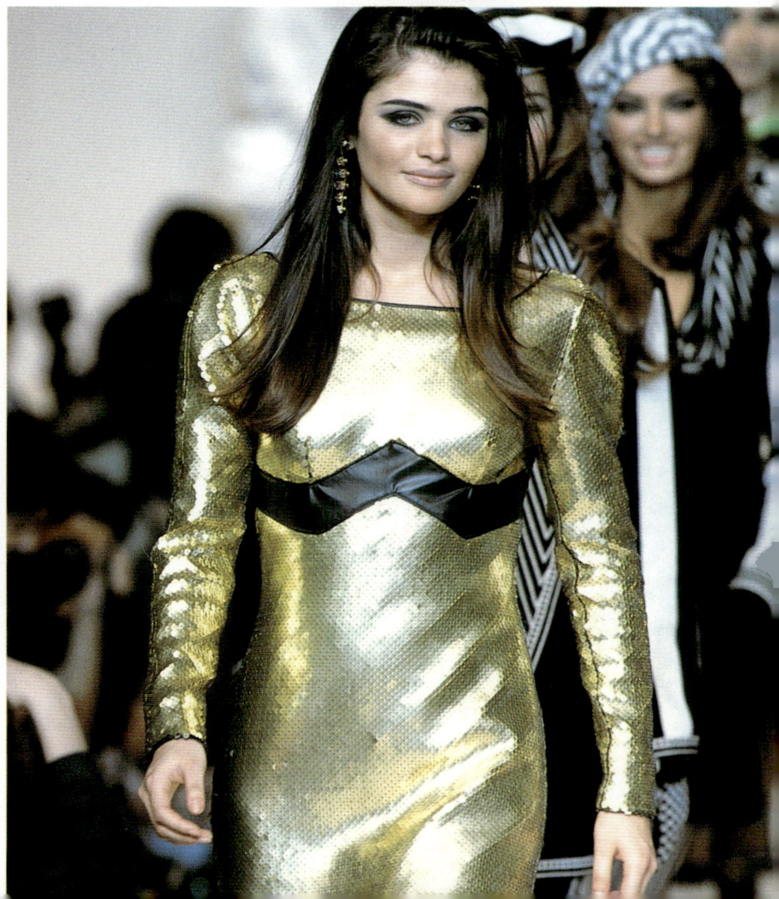

PARIS-39
PACO RABANNE

パコ・ラバンヌ

ジオメトリックなパターンを色彩効果で、よりダイナミックに表現したドレスや、光るメタリックな素材と他素材を組み合わせるアイディア等、斬新さは彼ならでは。

Exclusive to Paco Rabanne, novelties such as geometric patterned dresses,
displayed with the color effect idea of combining luminous metallic materials with other materials.

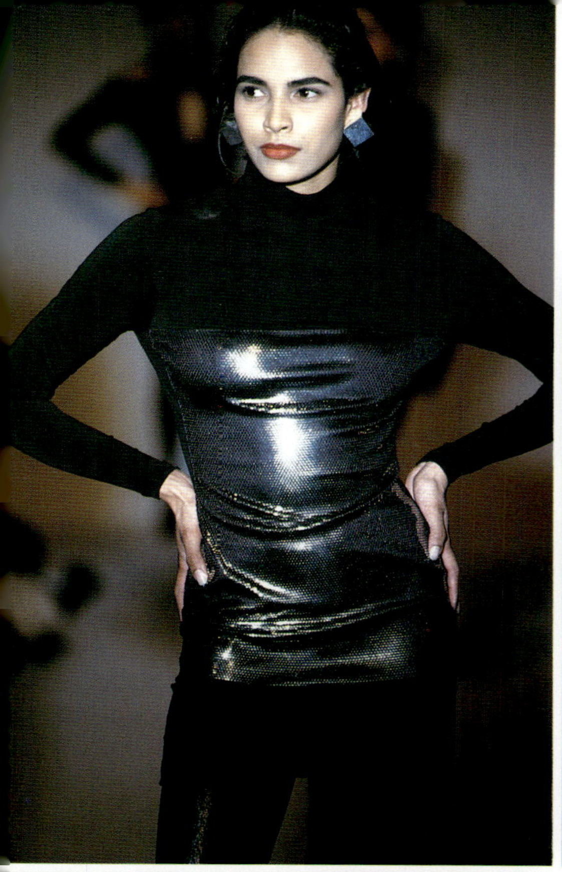
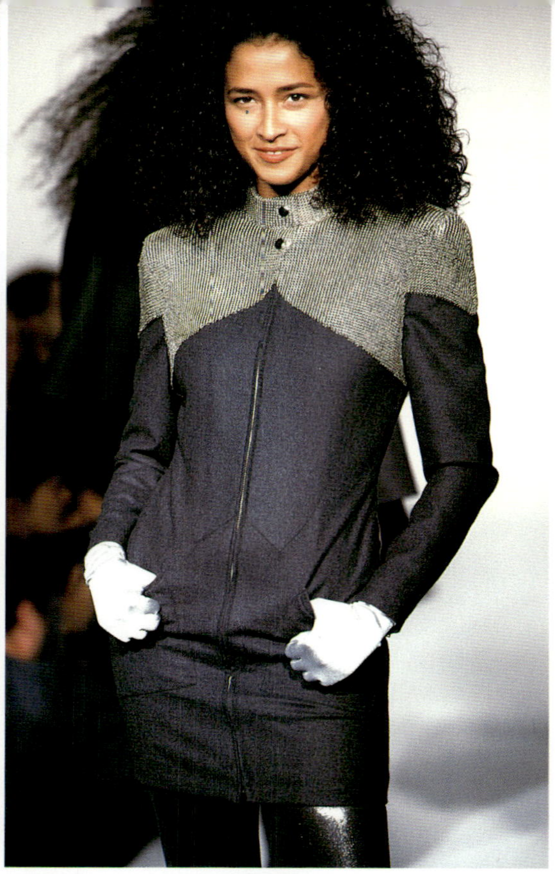
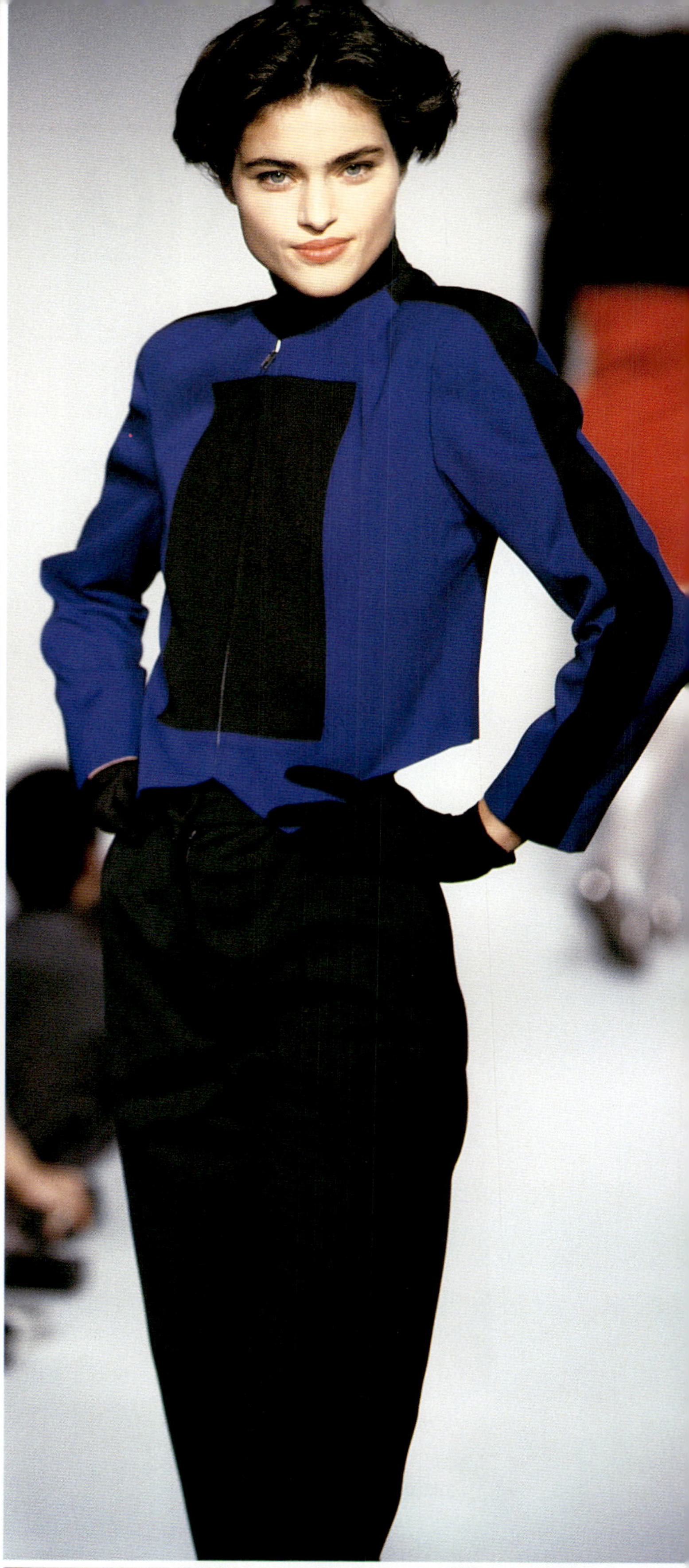
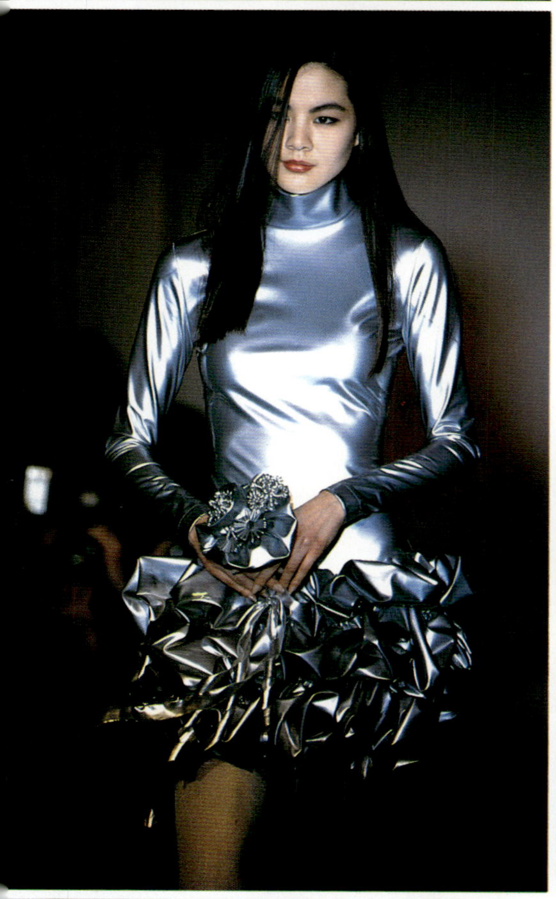
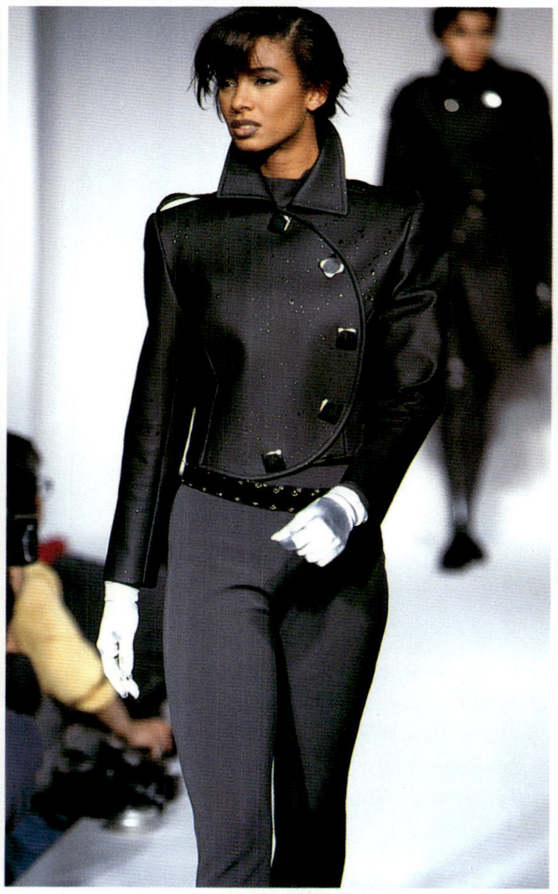
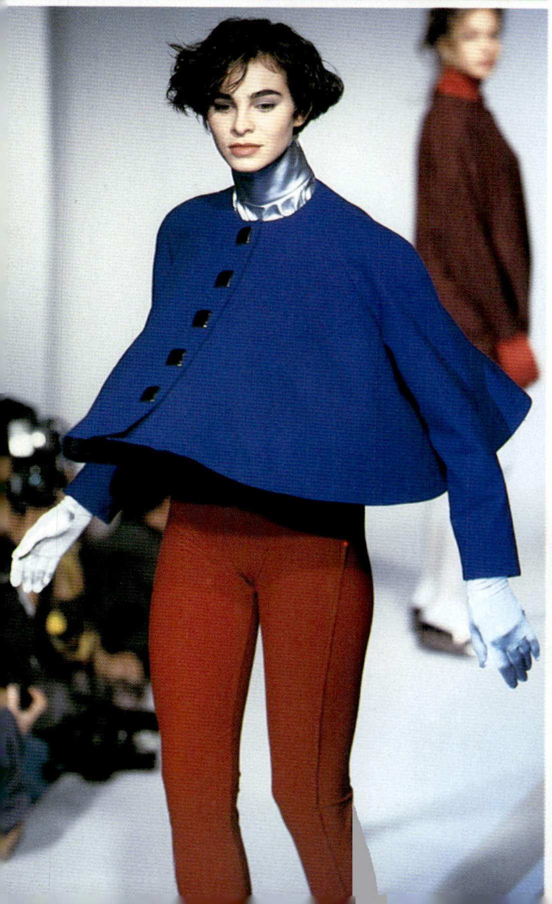
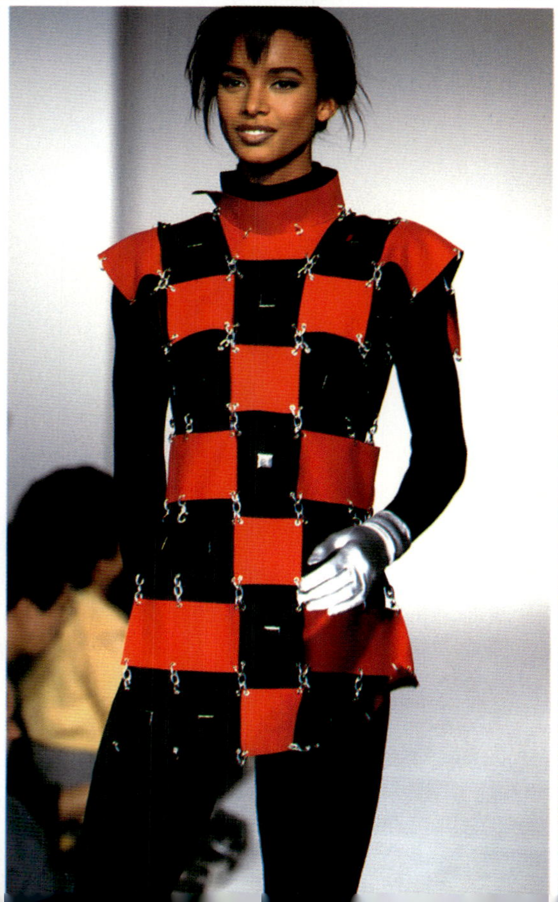
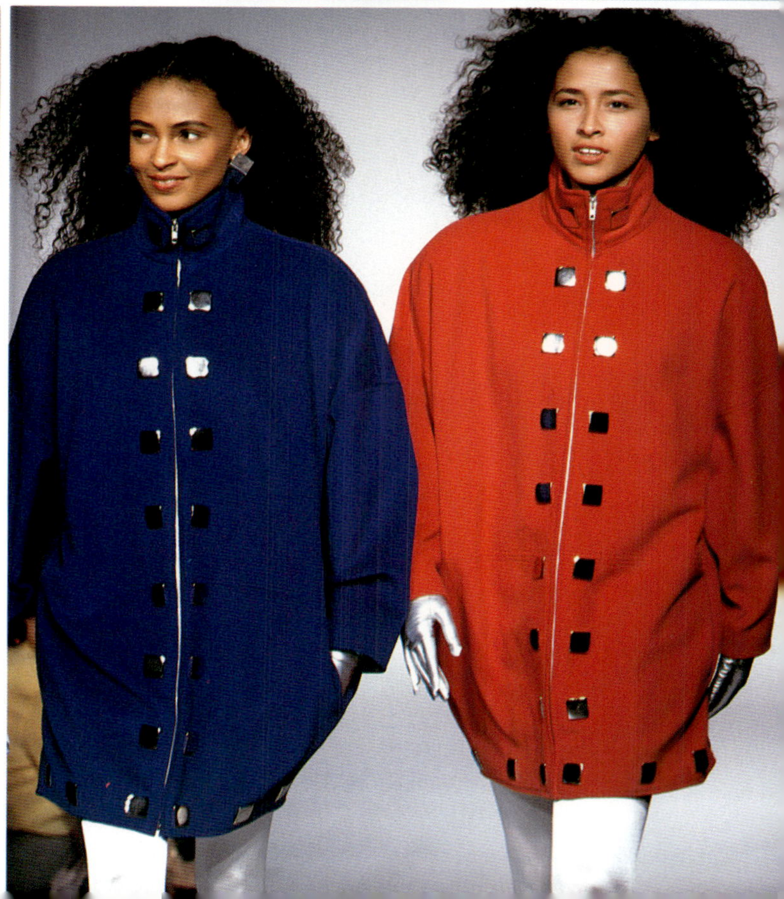

HANAE MORI

ハナエ・モリ

ブライトなカラー使いで、若々しさを演出。ヘアリー・ツイードやハウンド・トゥース柄もハナエ・モリらしい品の良さを保っている。帯風のベルベットは新しいアイディア。
Youthfulness was demonstrated with the use of bright colors. Hanae Mori—like elegance was maintained with hairy tweeds and hound's-tooth patterns. A belt with the appearance of an "obi (a kind of Japanese belt)" is one new idea.

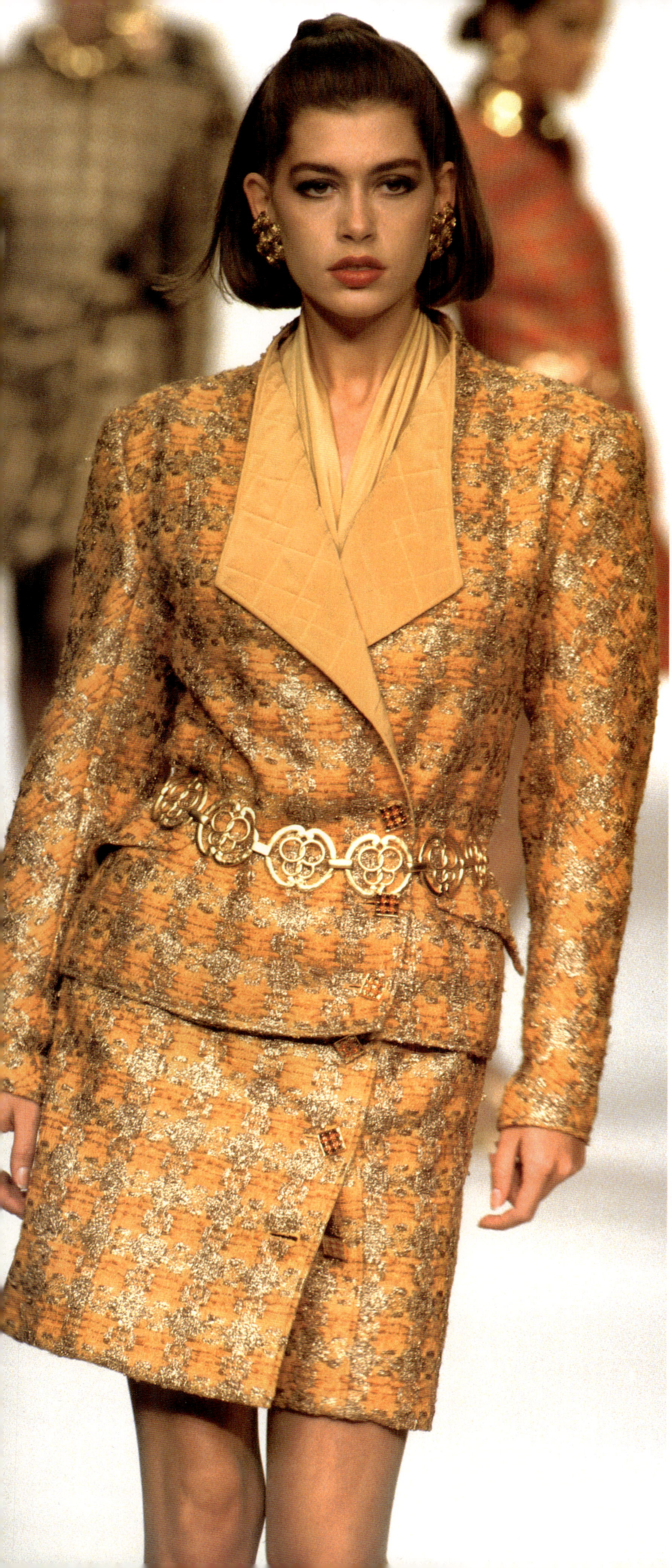
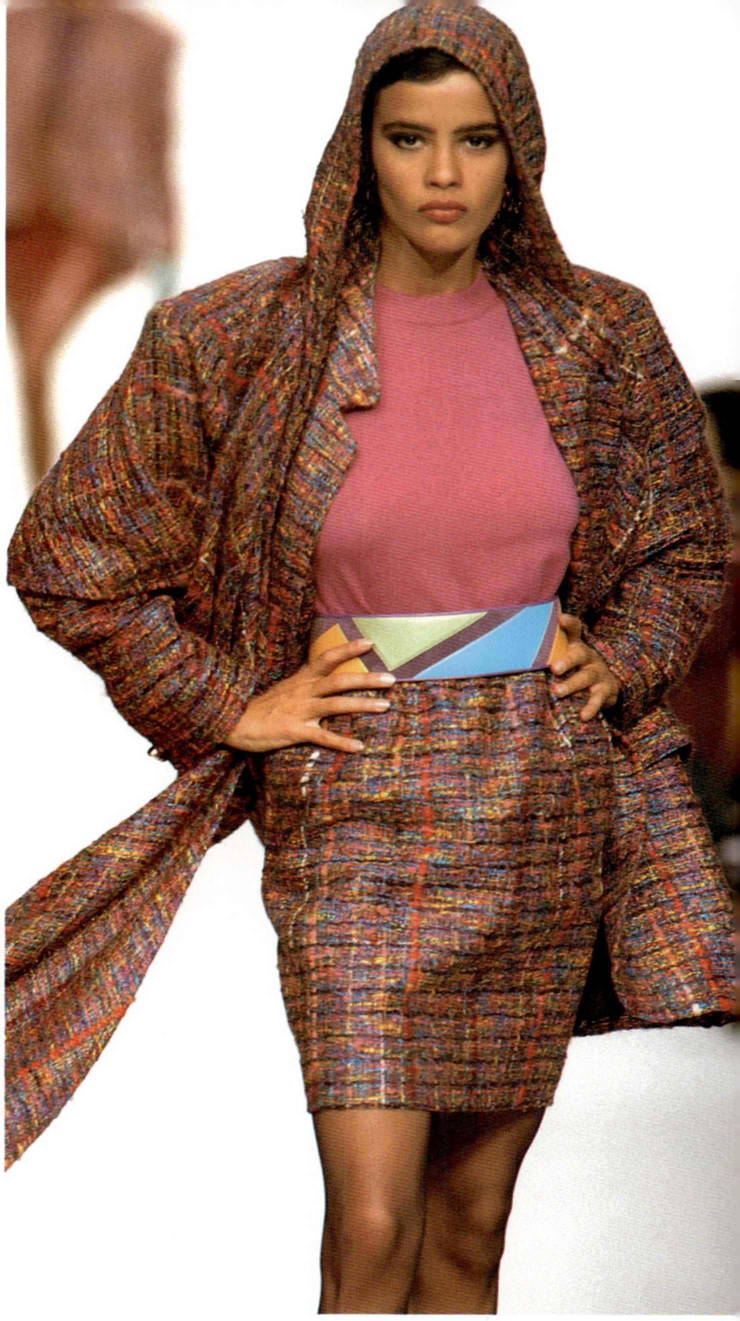
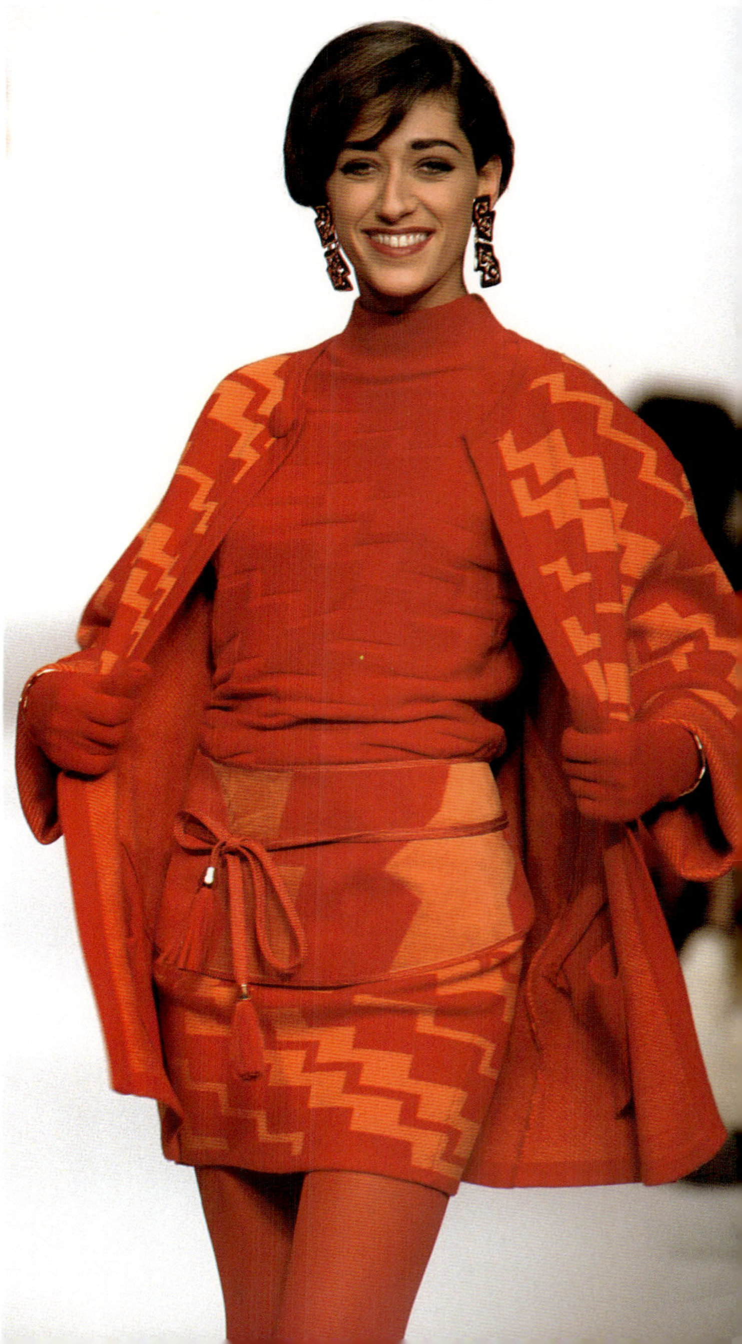

J. C. DE CASTELBAJAC

ジャン=シャルル・ド・カステルバジャック

カラフルな色分割のブロック・チェックのコートやスーツ、ポップな、プリントの世界は、カステルバジャックのスポーティで楽しいオリジナリティを伝える。

Castelbajac's spodrty and fun-loving originality was displayed in coats and suits with colorfully coordinated block checks and pop prints.

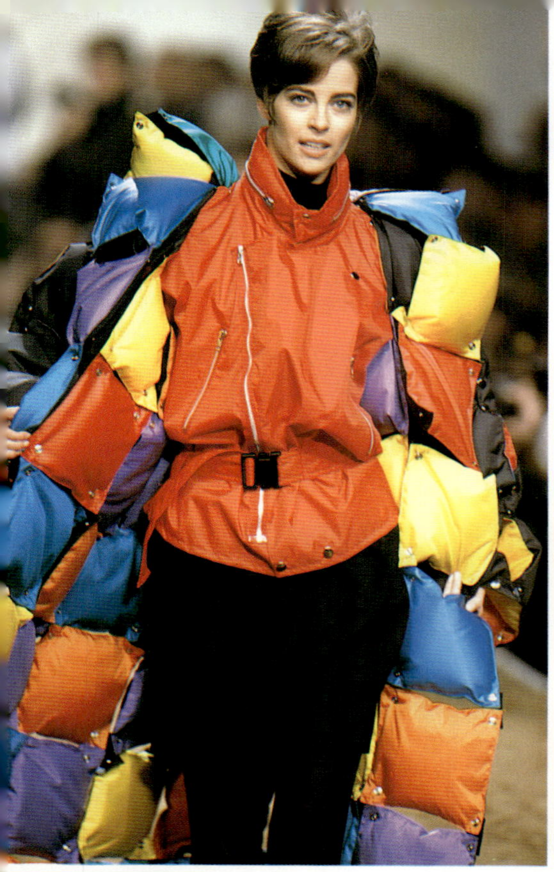

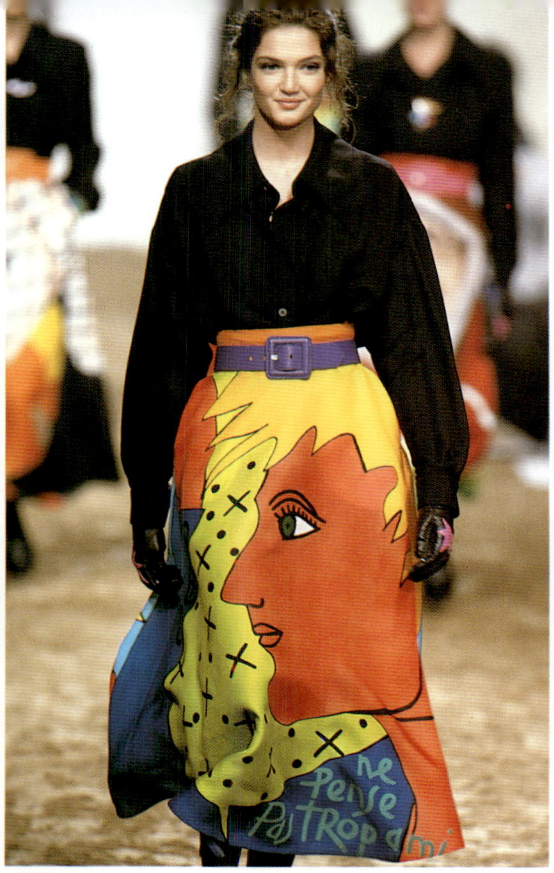
ne
pense

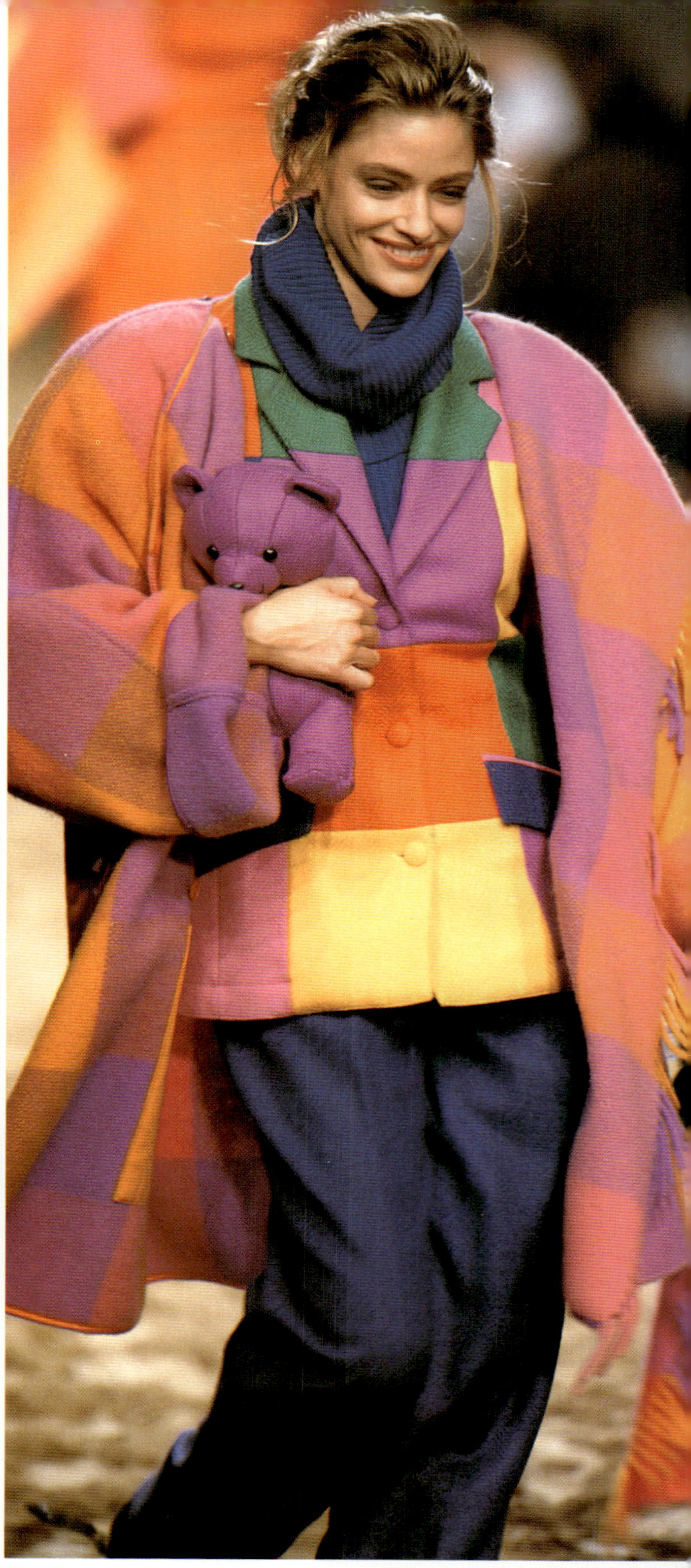

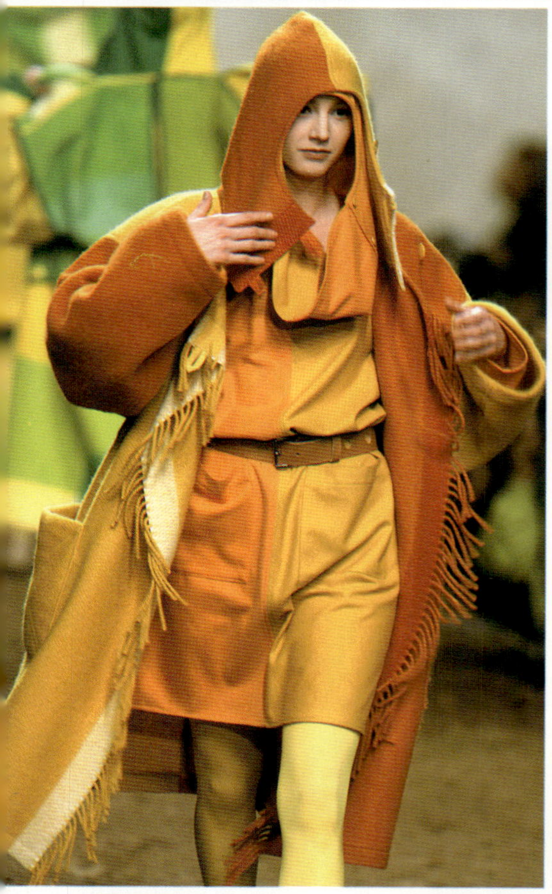

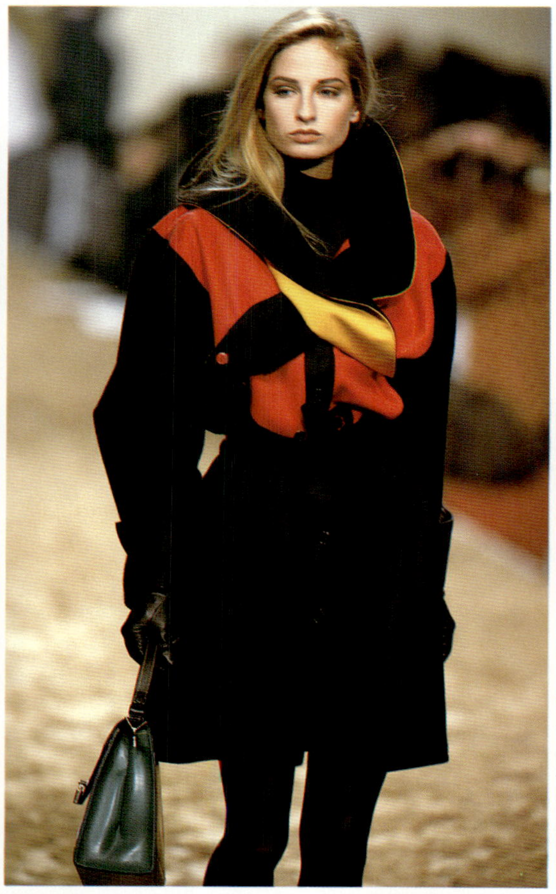

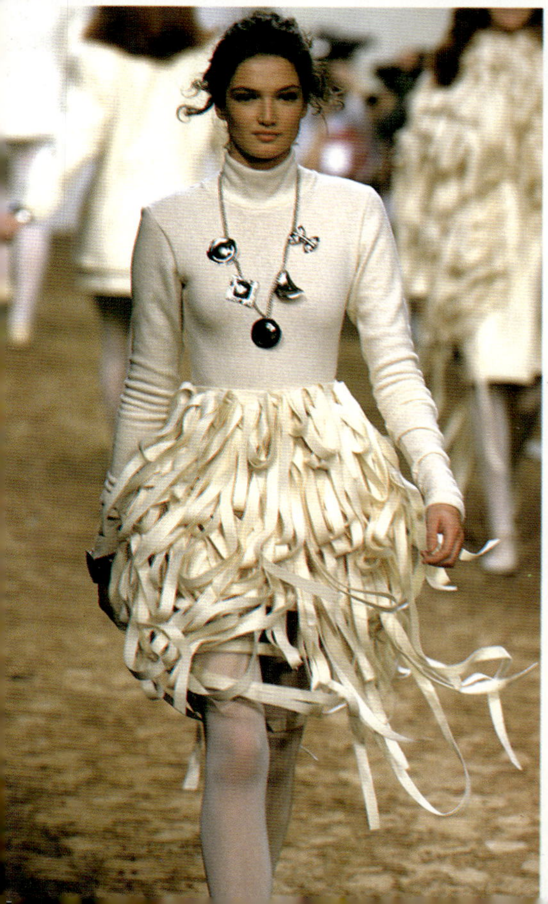

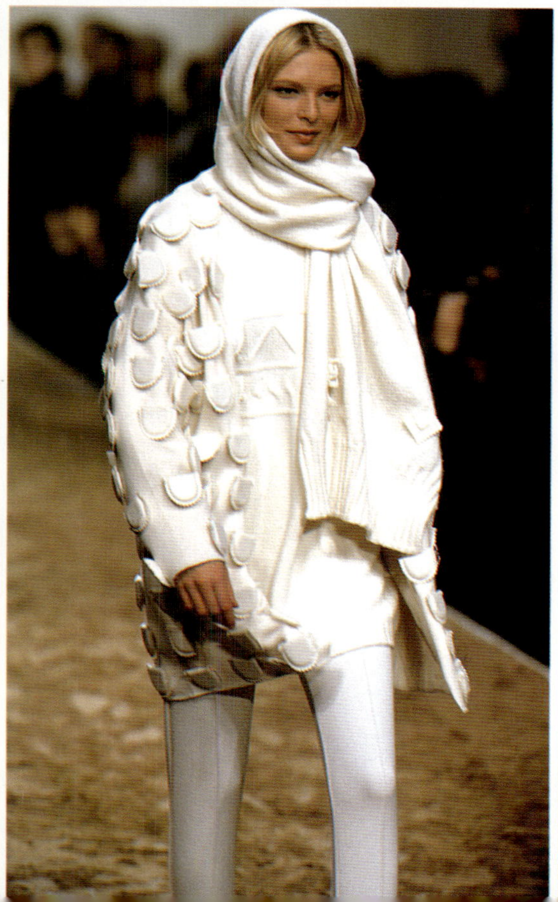

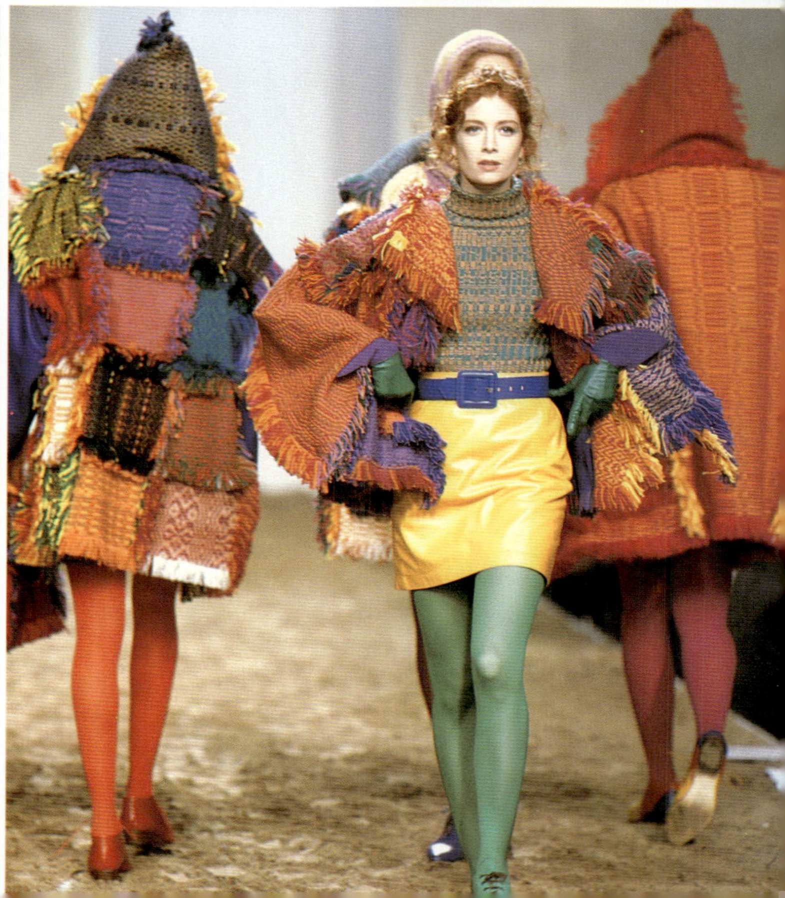

OSCAR DE LA RENTA

オスカー・デ・ラ・レンタ

フリンジやボーダーのスーツやウール・メルトン・ジャケットを生き生きとしたカラー・スペクトルで見せたデ・ラ・レンタのパリコレ・デビュー。
Making his debut in Paris Collection, showing suits with fringes and borders and wool melton Jackets in a vivid color spectrum.

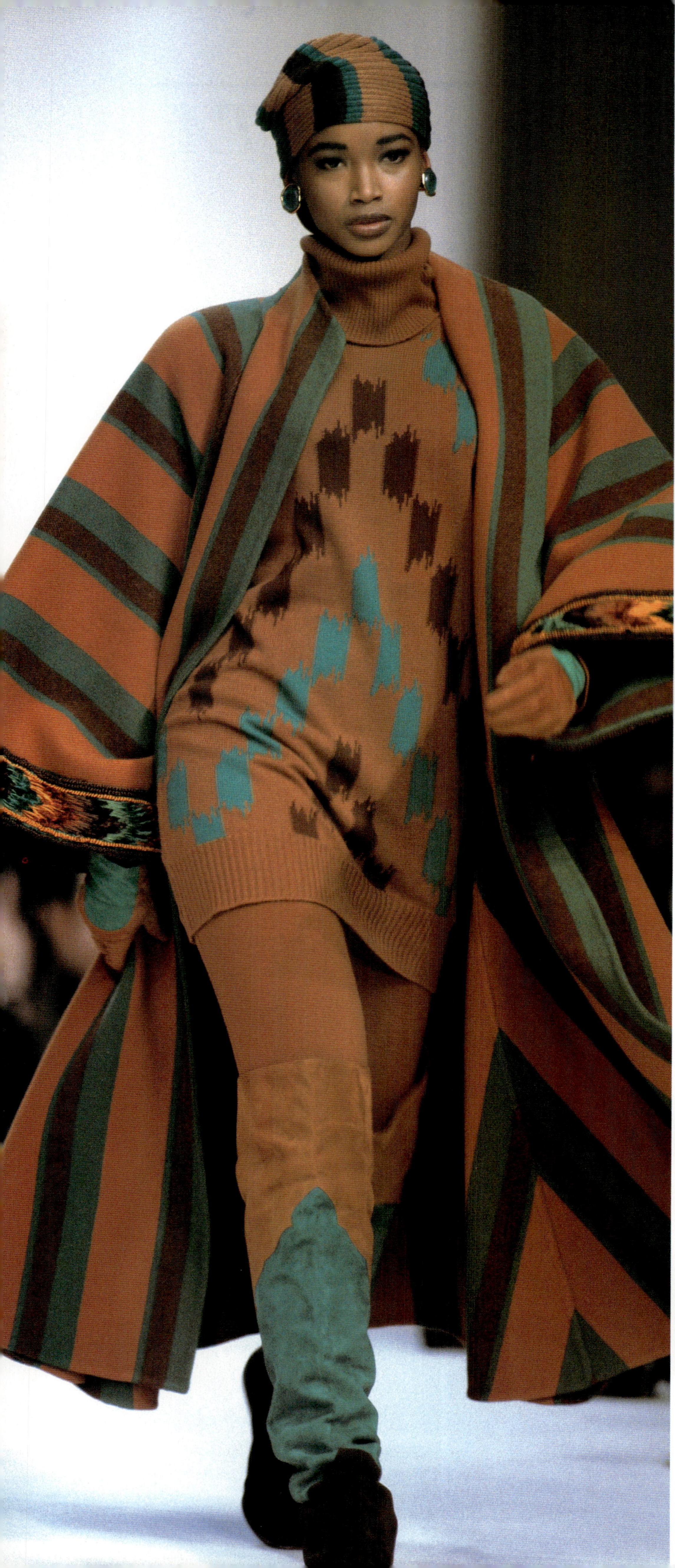
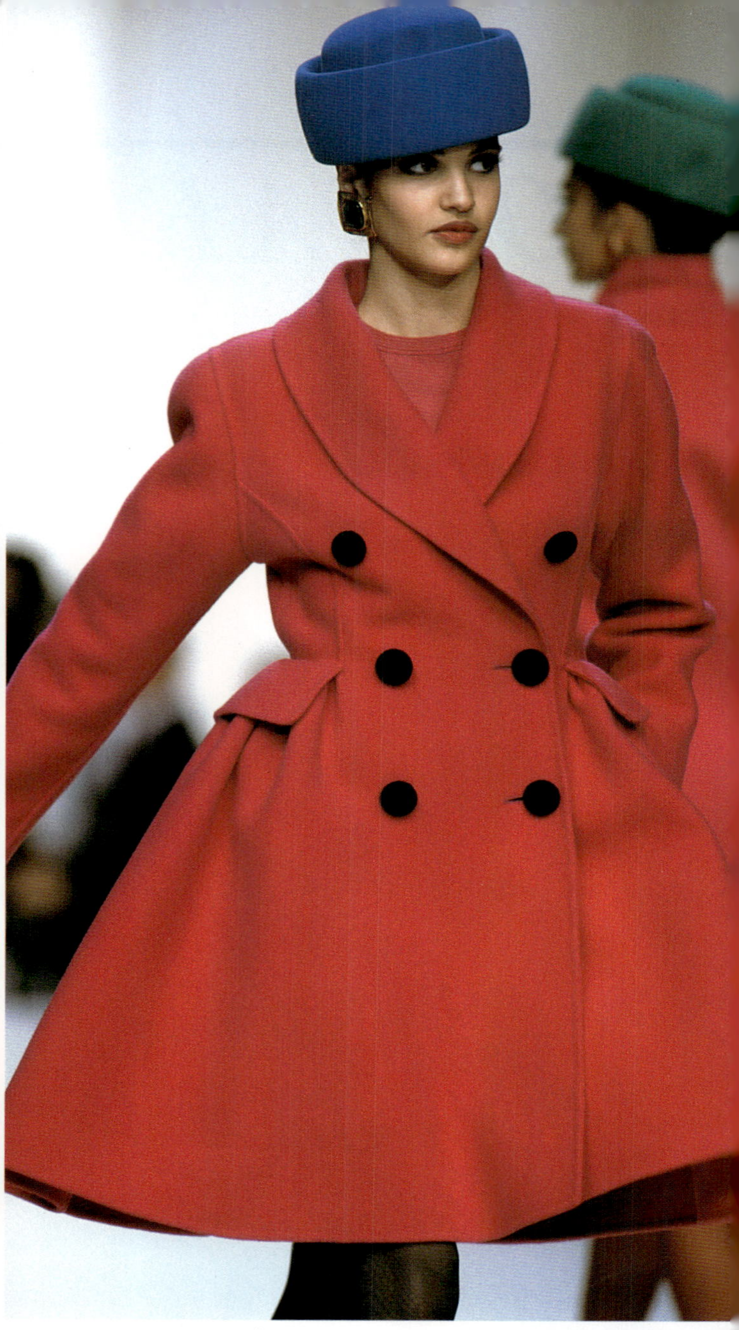
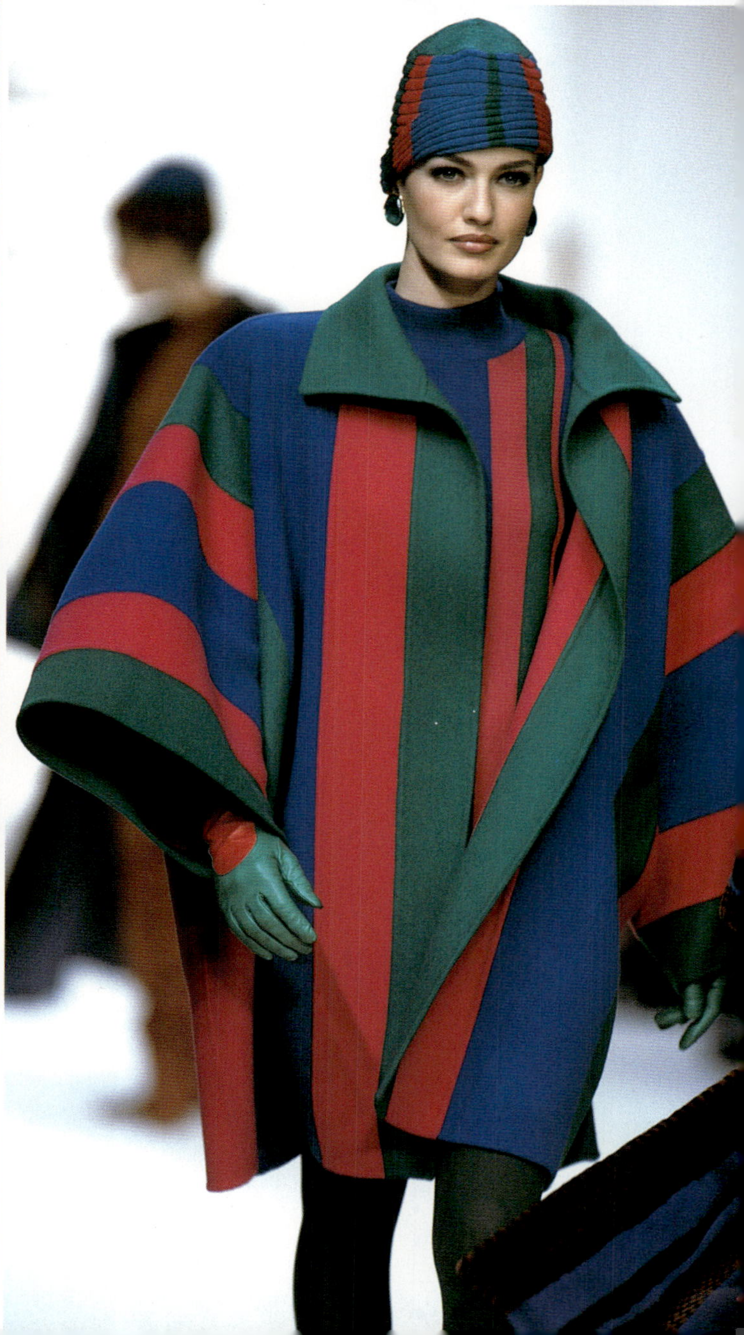

GRÊS

グレ

夜のドレスにはドレープをふんだんに使った黒と赤の世界を、デイ・スーツにはシャープなカットとファブリック・コンビネーションで新鮮さを。

Dresses for the evening were shown in black and red with the liberal use of drapes.
Adding novelty to the daysuits were the sharp cuts and fabric combinations.

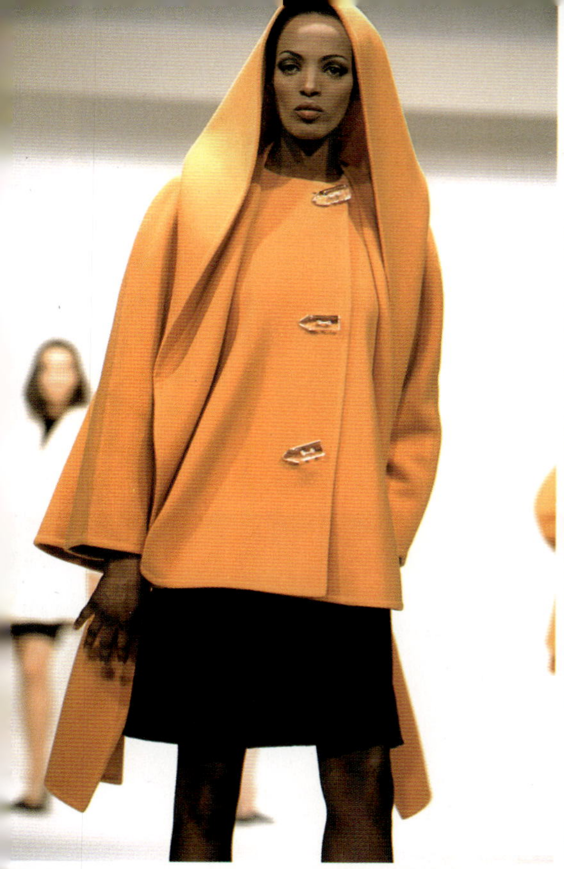
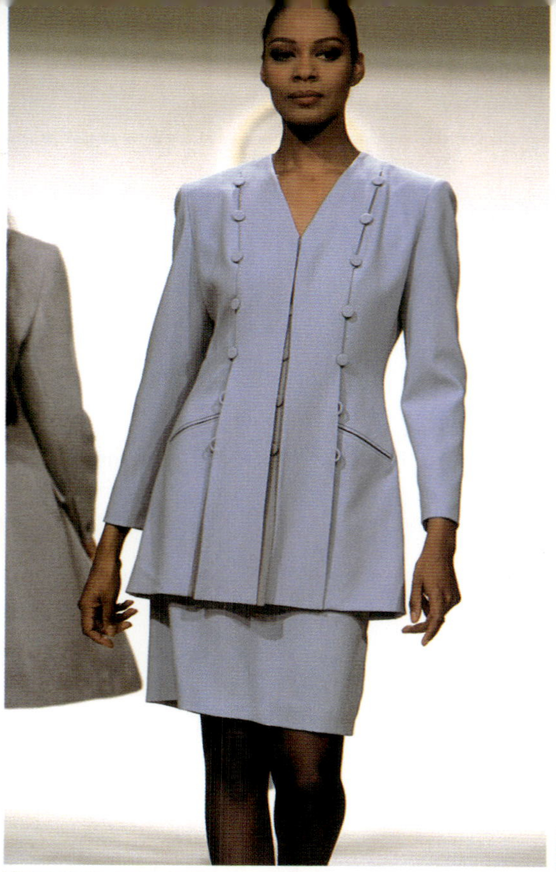
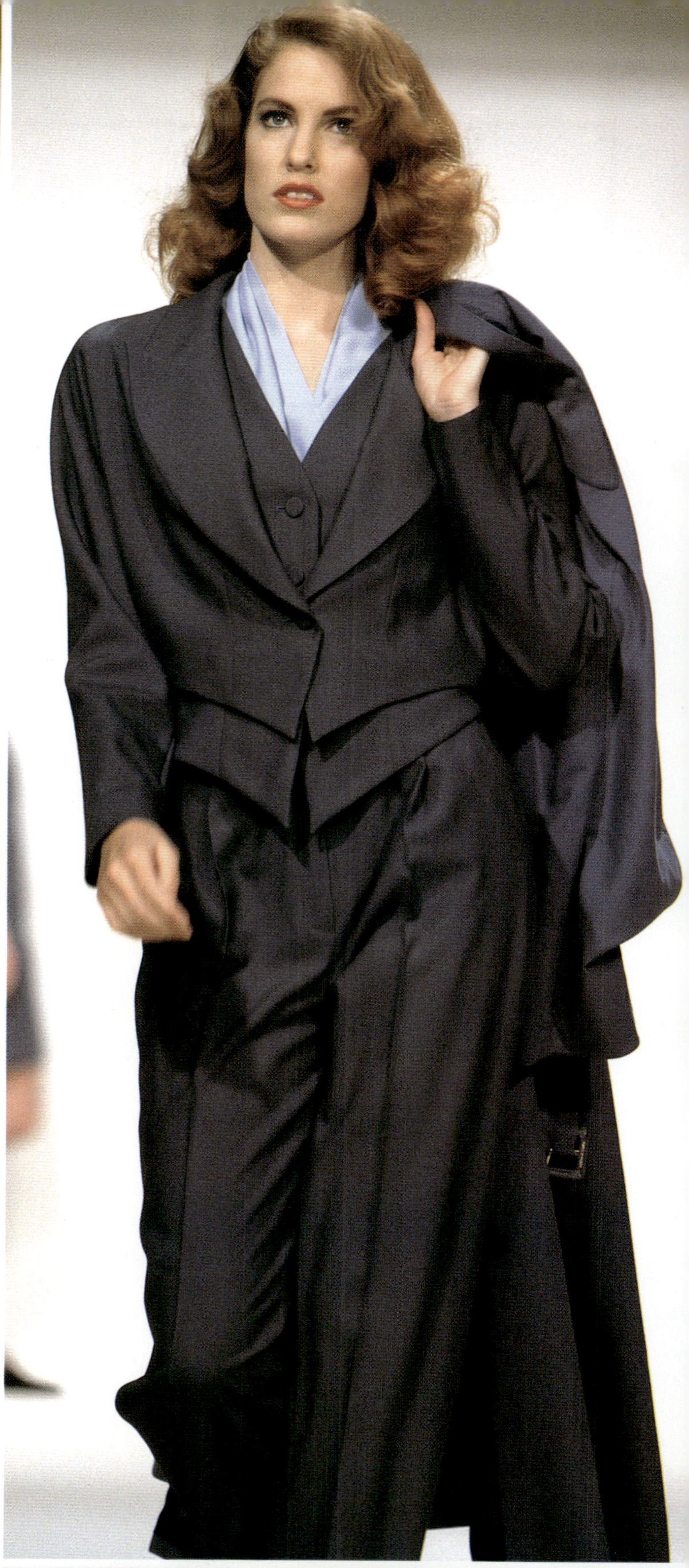
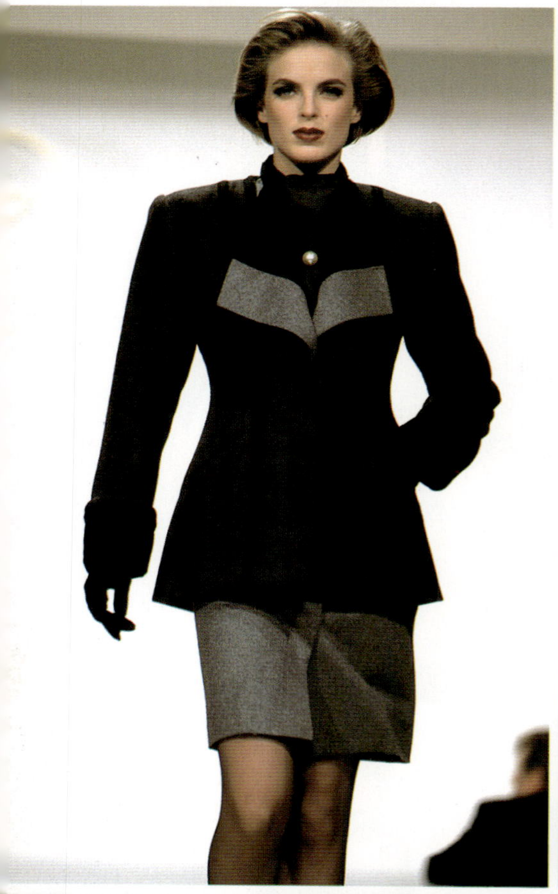
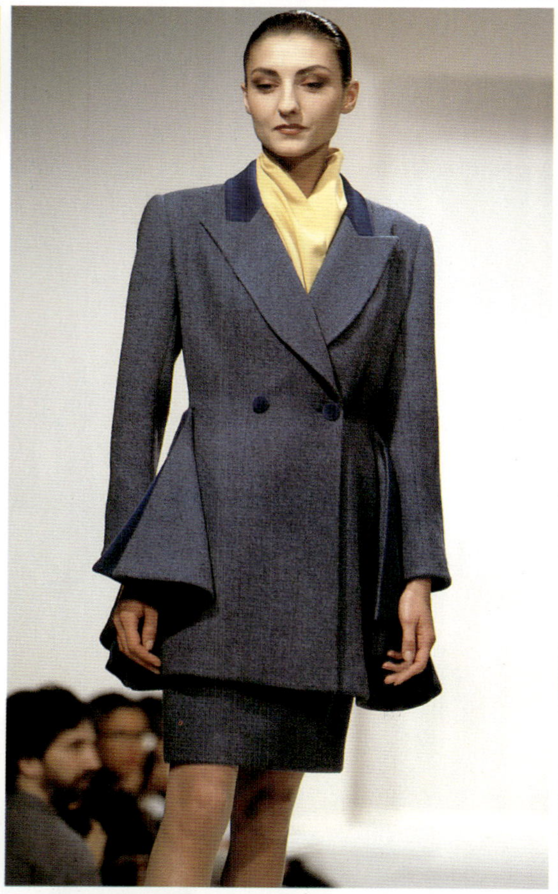
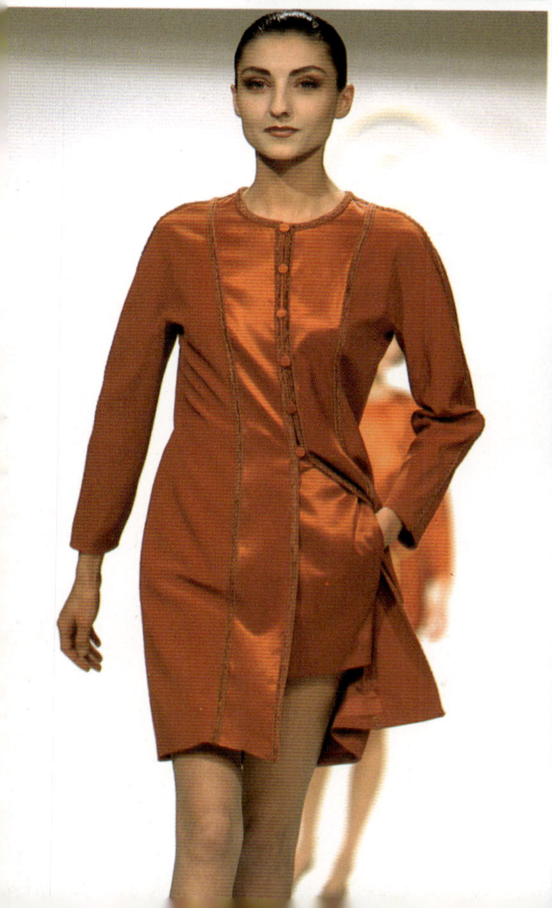
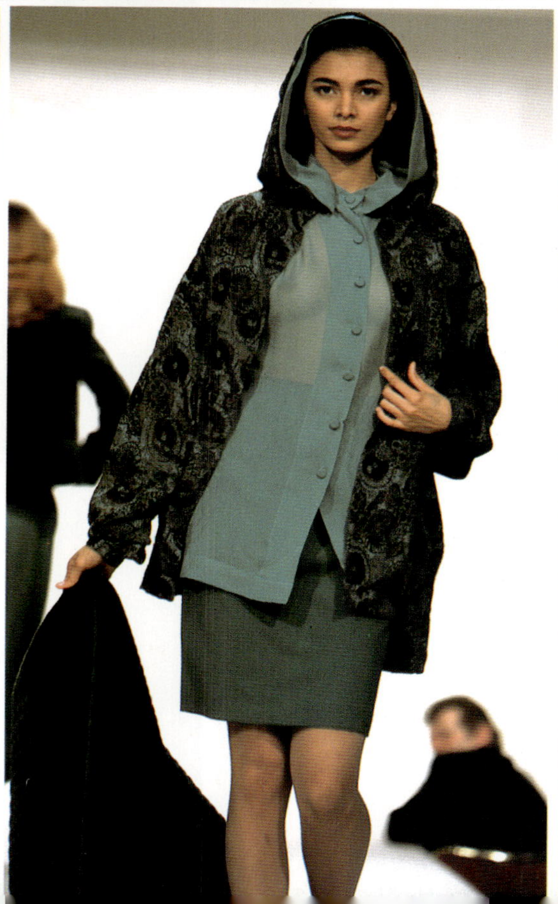
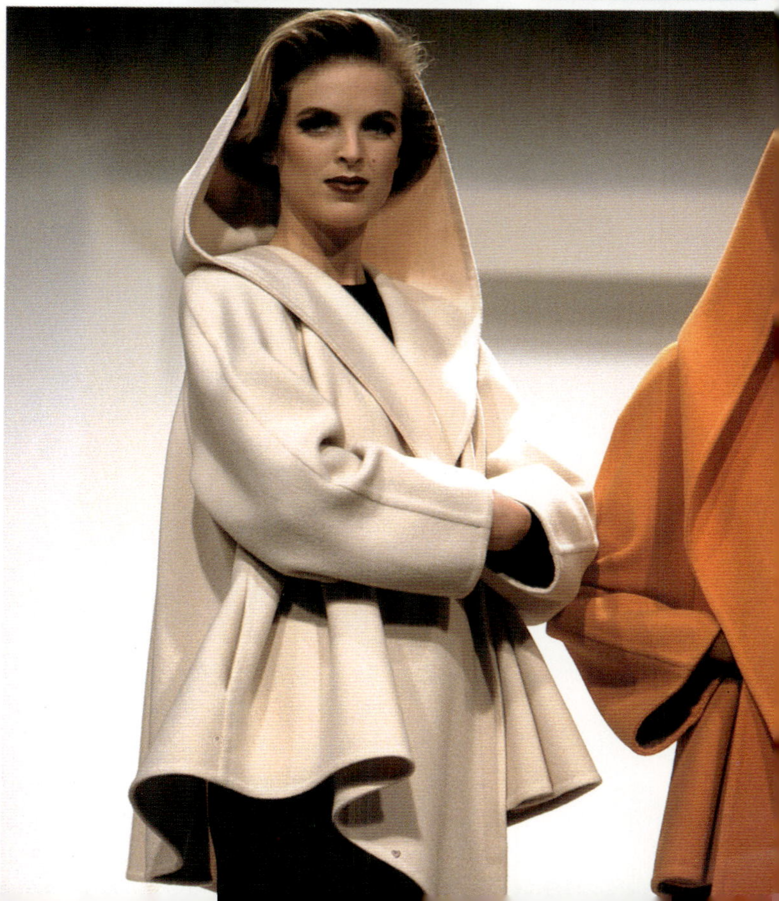

NINA RICCI

ニナ・リッチ

久しぶりのニナ・リッチのプレタポルテ・コレクション。エレガントさを残したまま、より消化された表現になった今シーズン。
The first prêt-à-porter in a while for Nina Ricci. Keeping its elegance, the collection became more sophisticated this season.

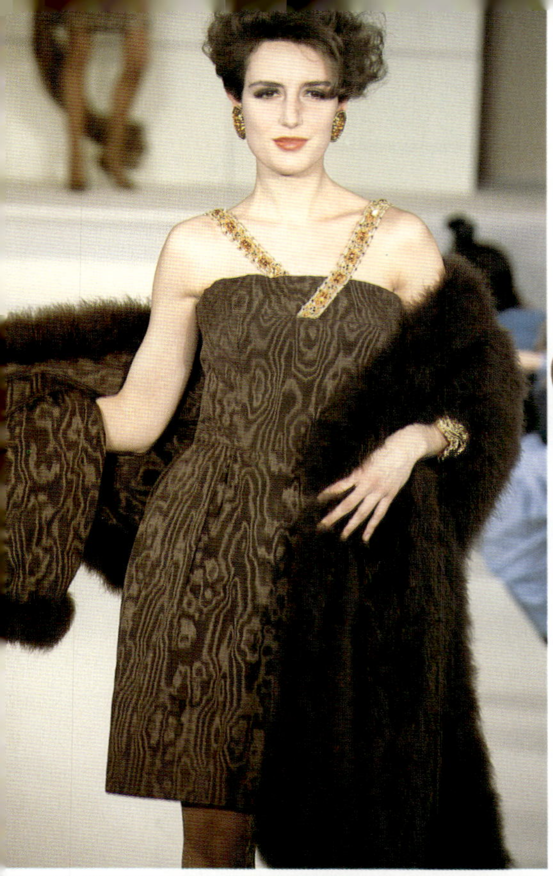
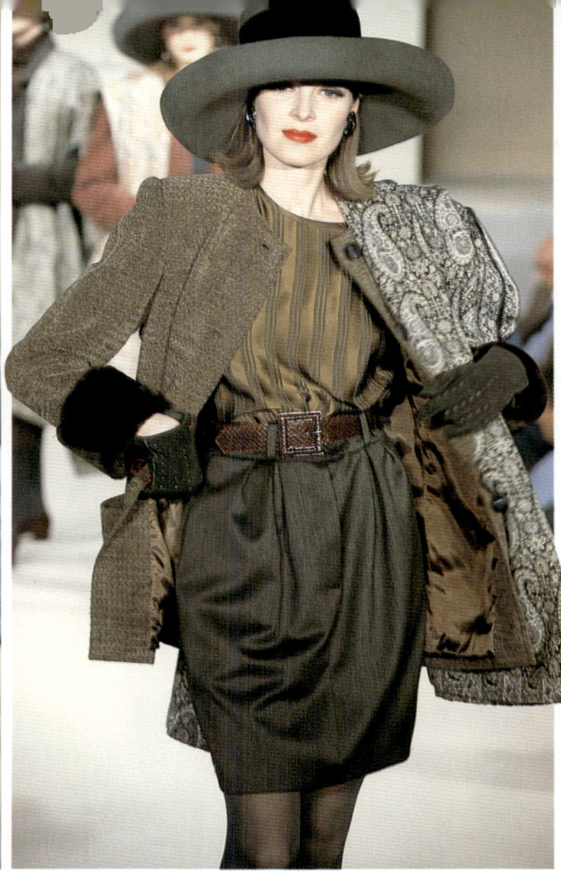
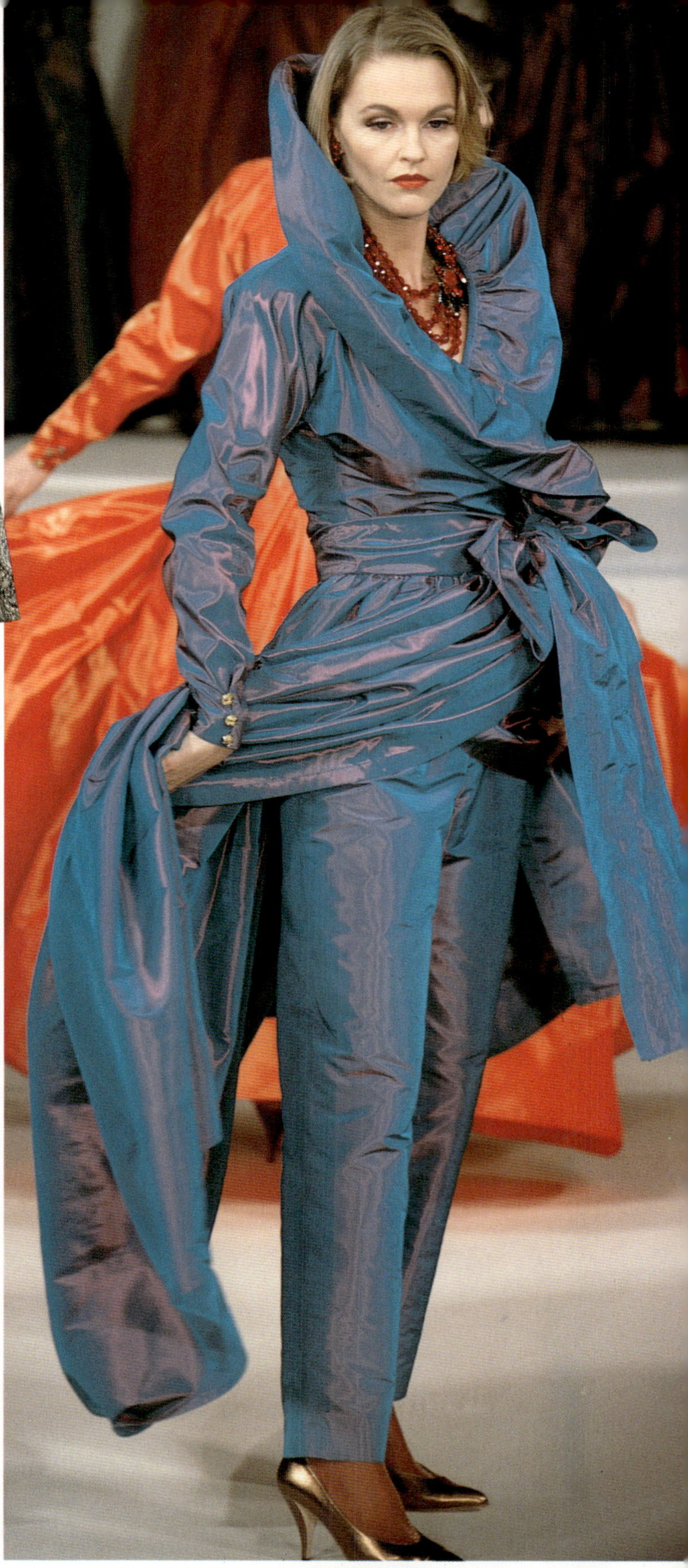
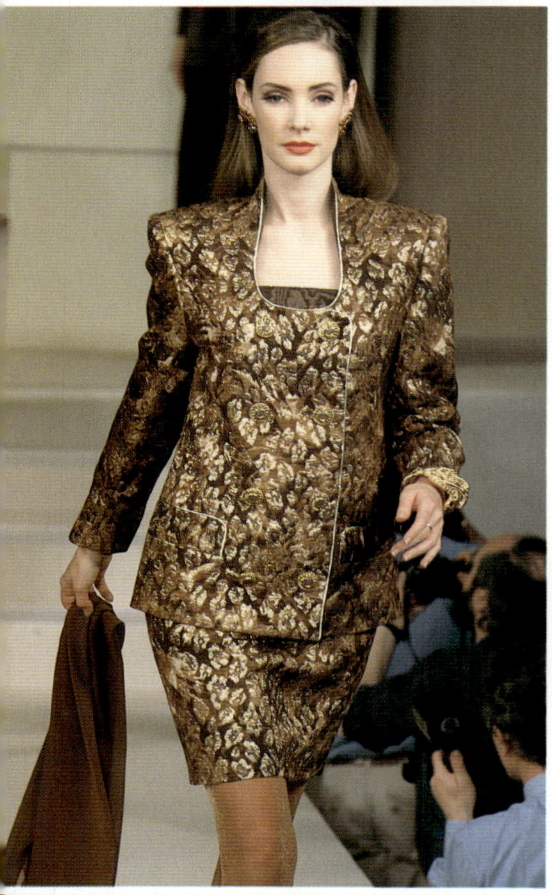
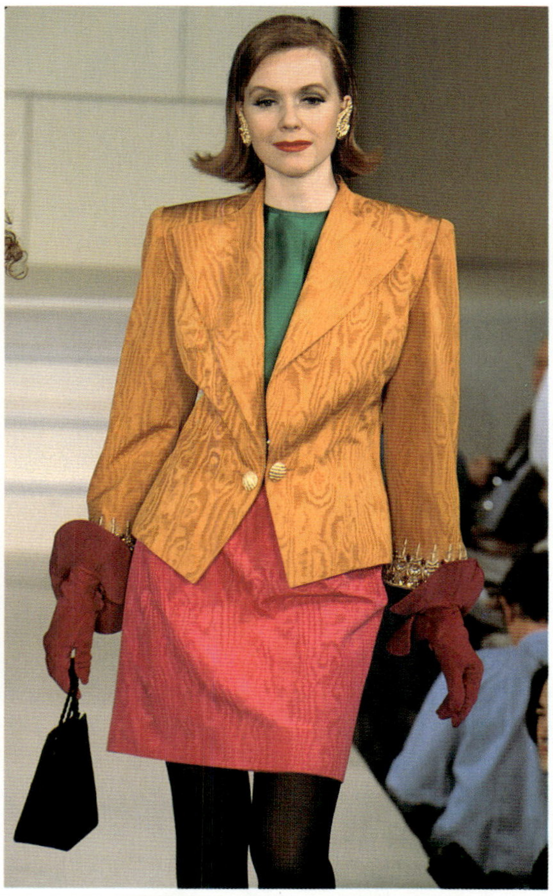
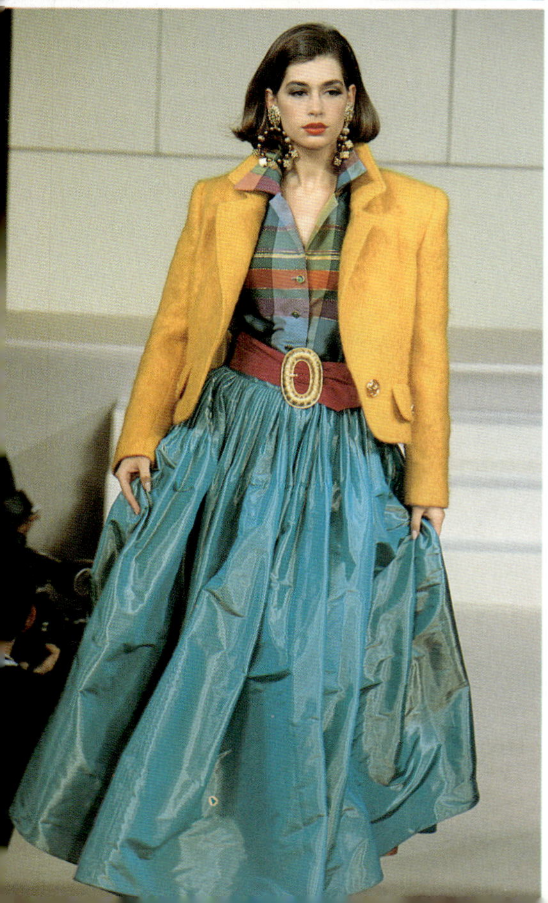
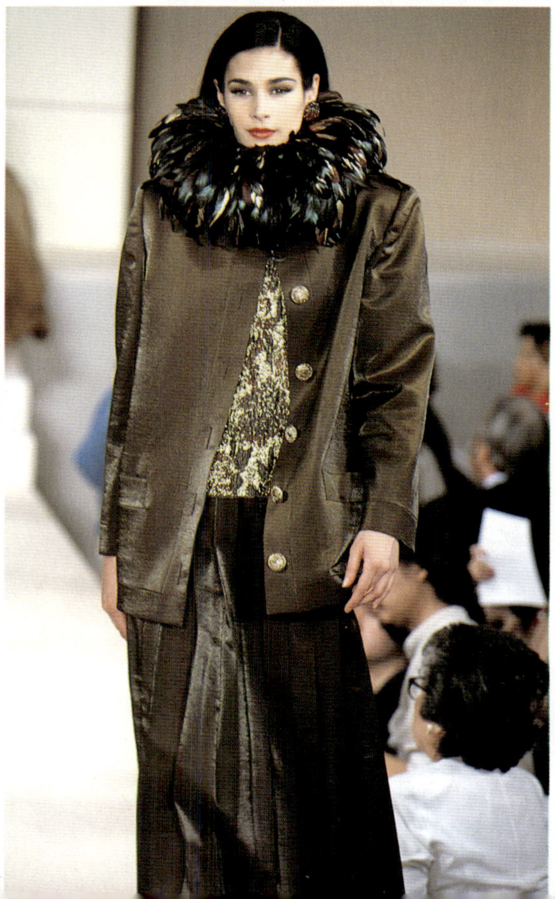
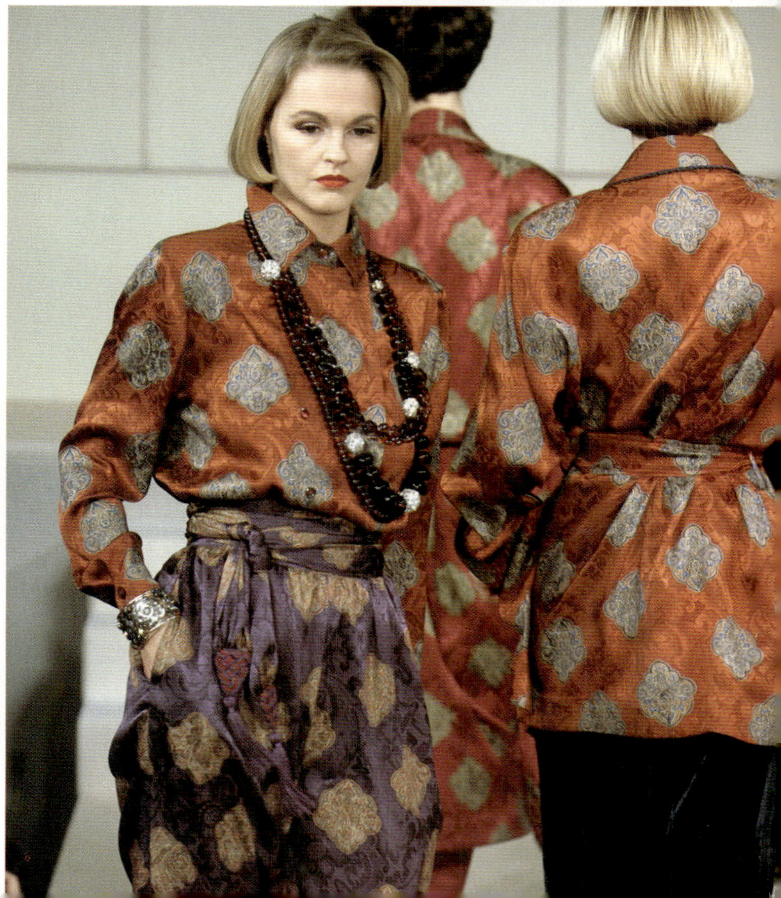

PARIS-45

BERNARD PERRIS

ベルナール・ペリス

視覚効果のある大胆なジオメトリックを生かした面分割がシャープな印象。夜のためにはアシメトリー・ヘムの光沢素材のドレスと、幾何学的処理が特徴。
Giving a sharp impression were the divided patterns, using eye-catching bold geometric forms. For the evening, dresses made of shiny material were shown, using asymmetric hems. The special feature was the use of geometric patterns.

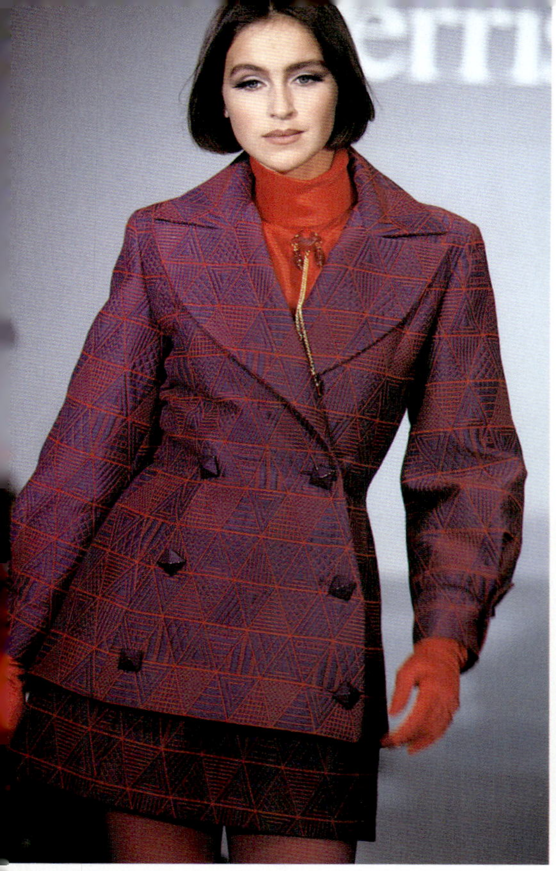
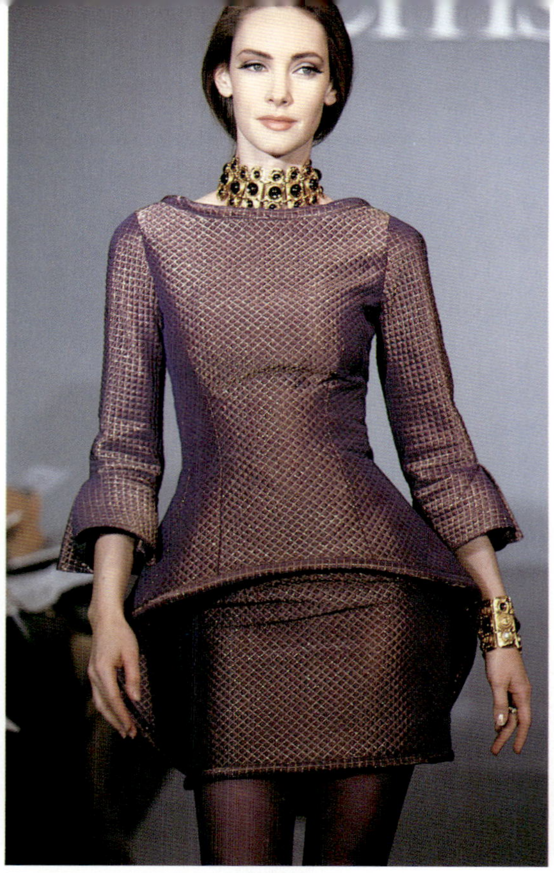
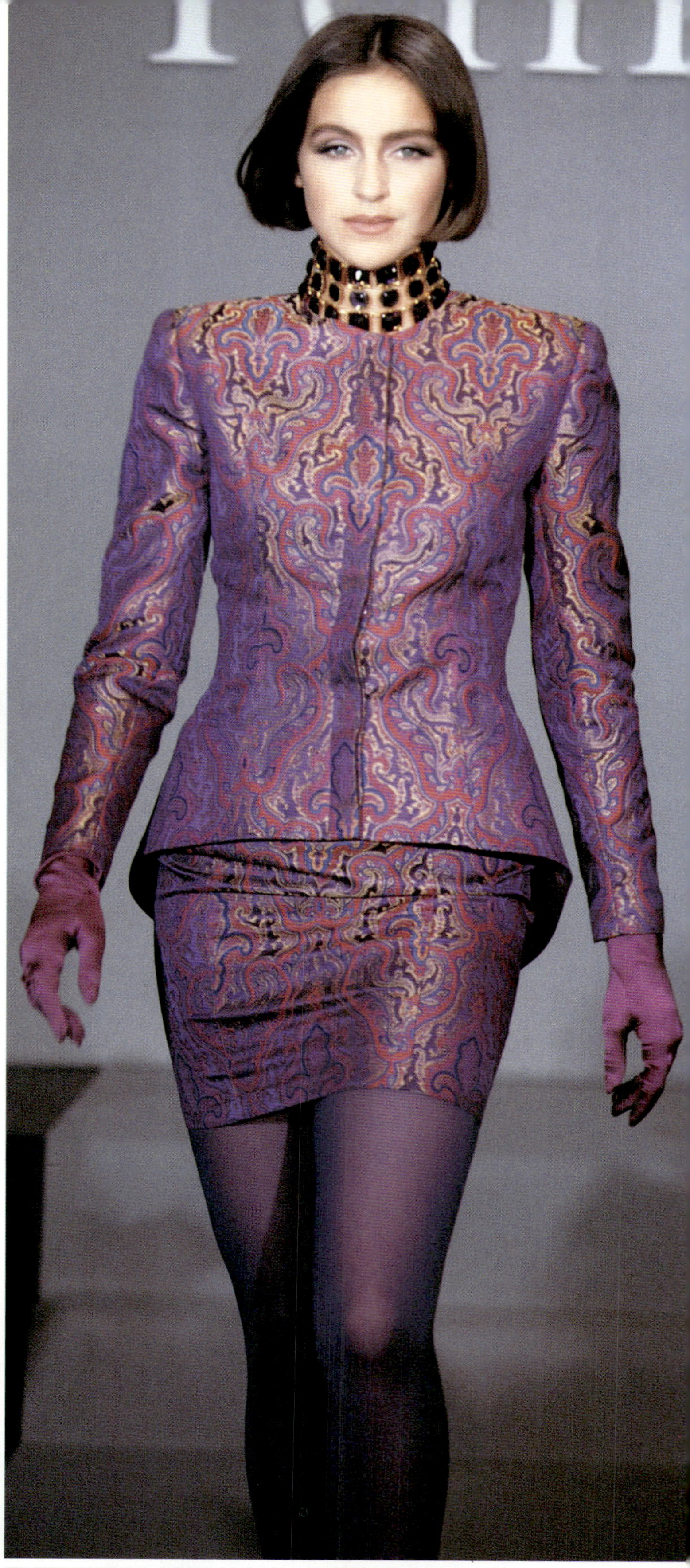
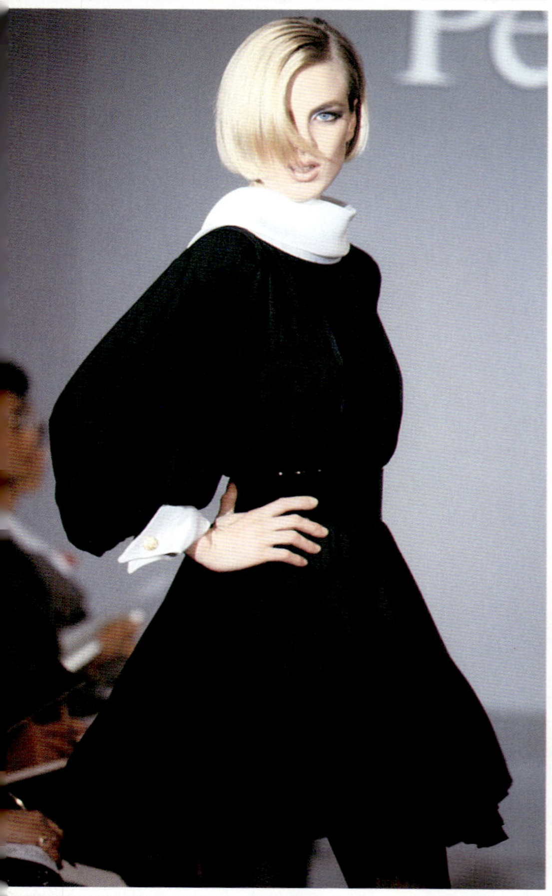
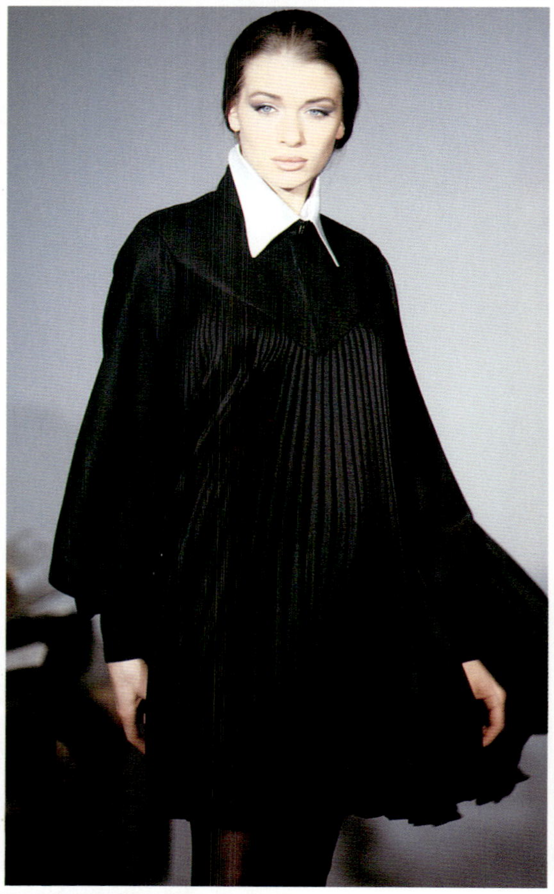
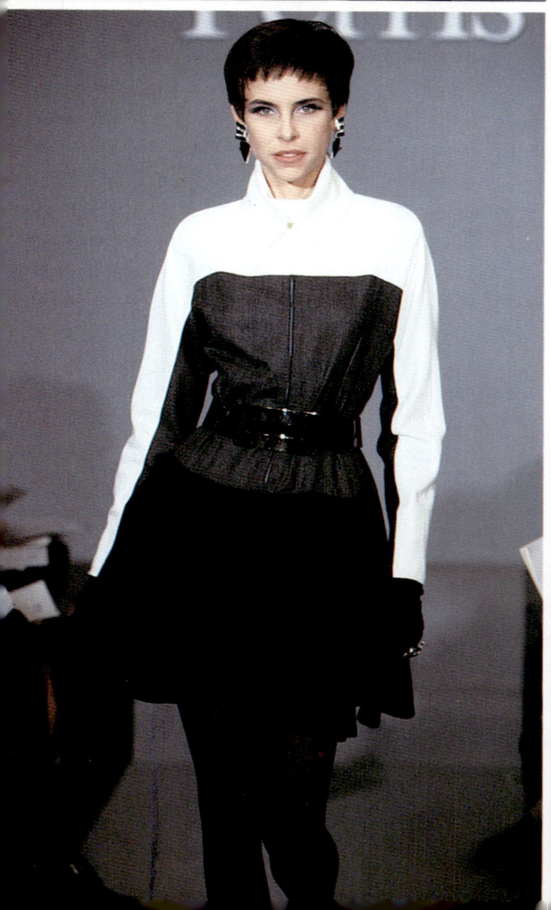
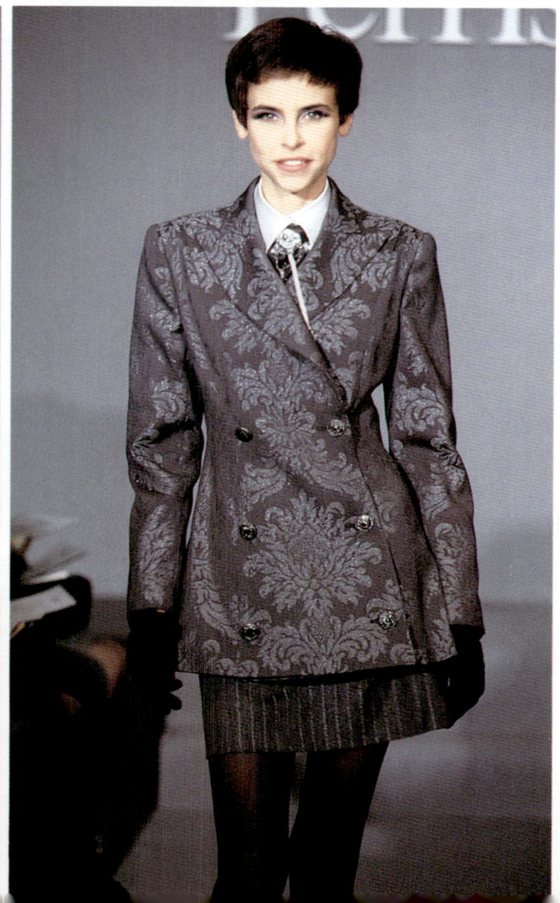
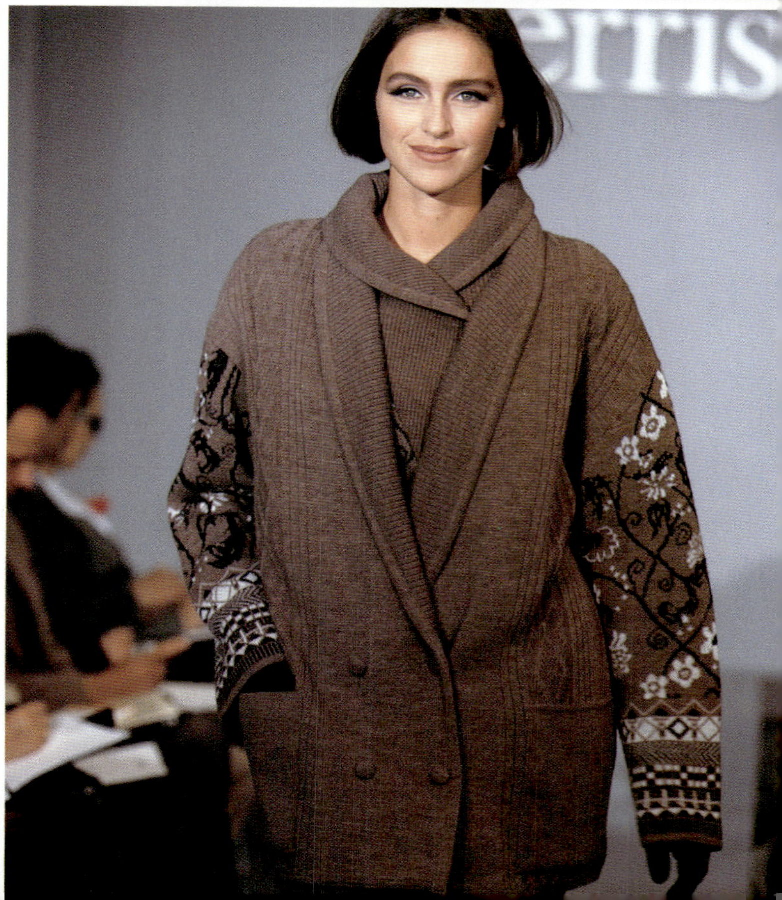

ENRICO COVERI

エンリコ・コーベリ

ファー・トリムのスーツや光沢のあるカクテル・ドレスなど'60年代のハリウッド・シックをベースにクチュールのエスプリを垣間見せる。

Showing the esprit of couture, based on the chic style of Hollywood in the '60's, including suits with fur trimmings and shiny cocktail dresses.

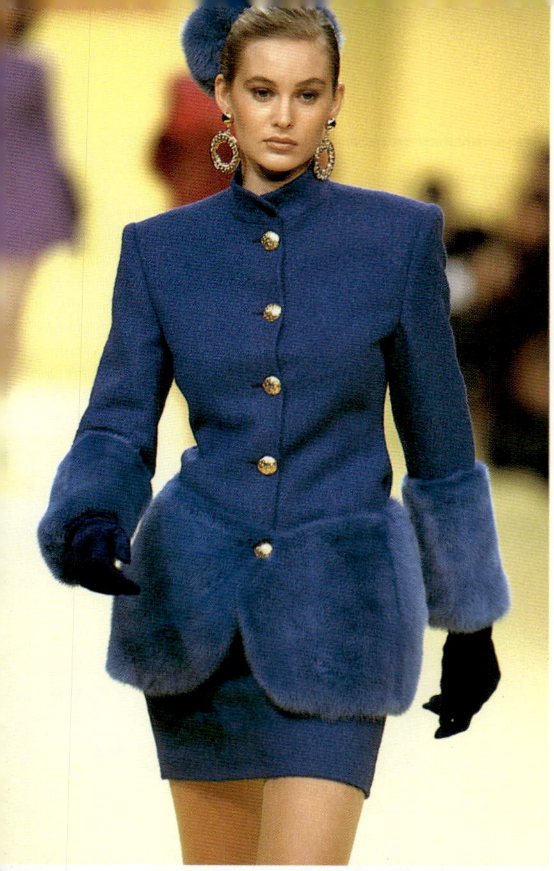
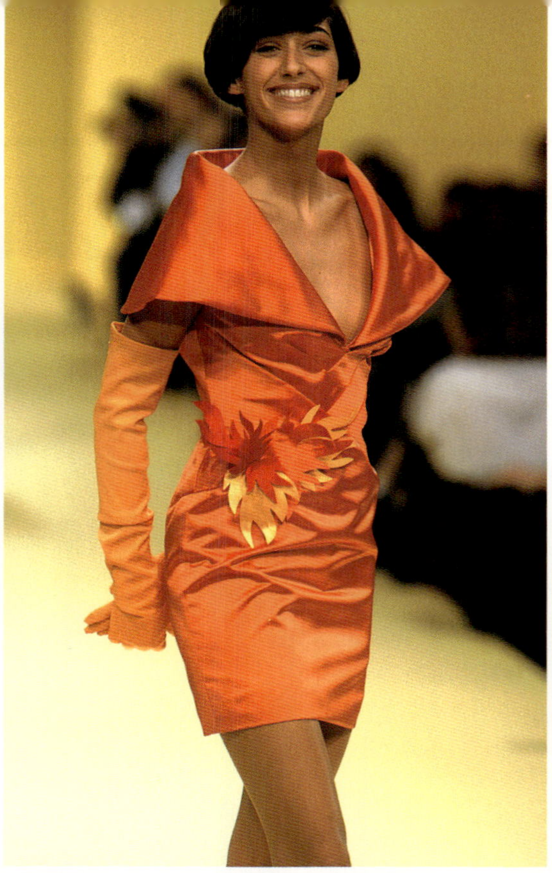
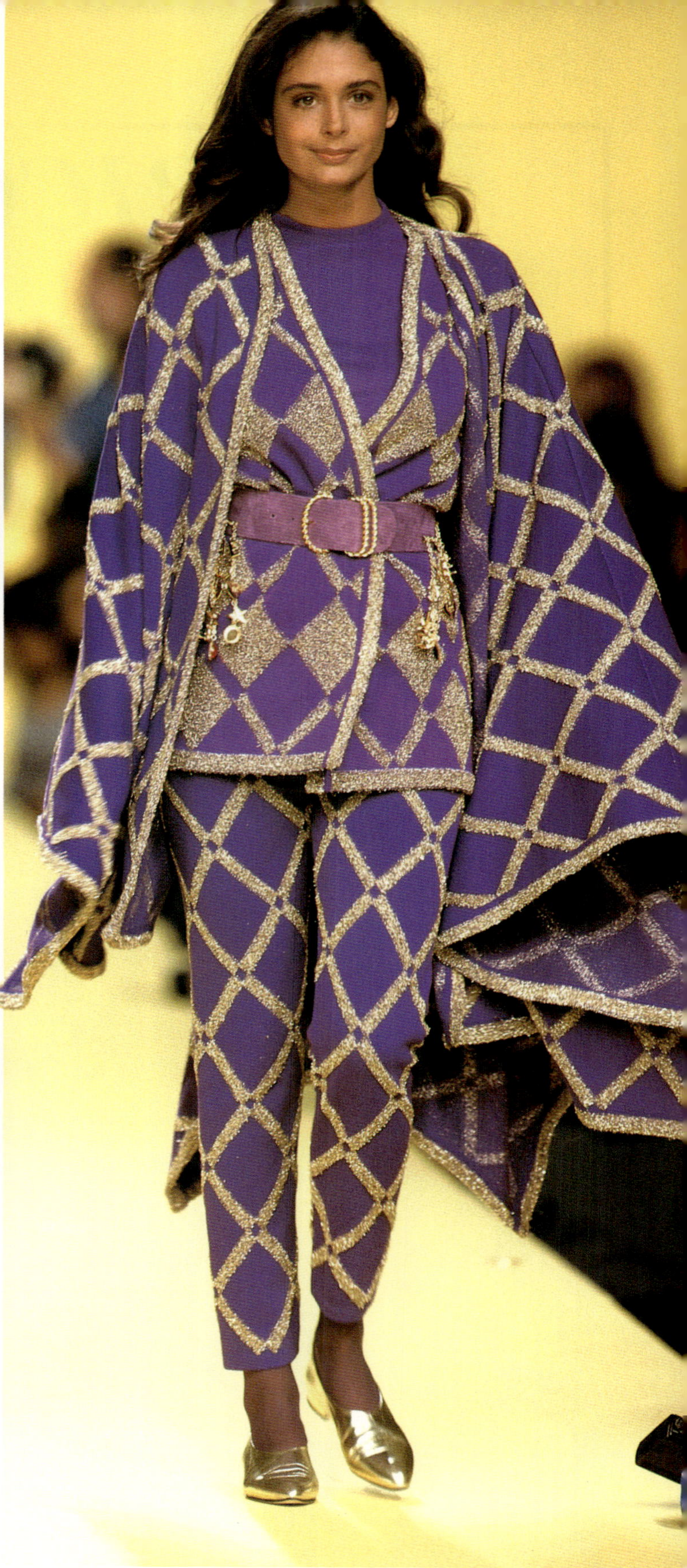
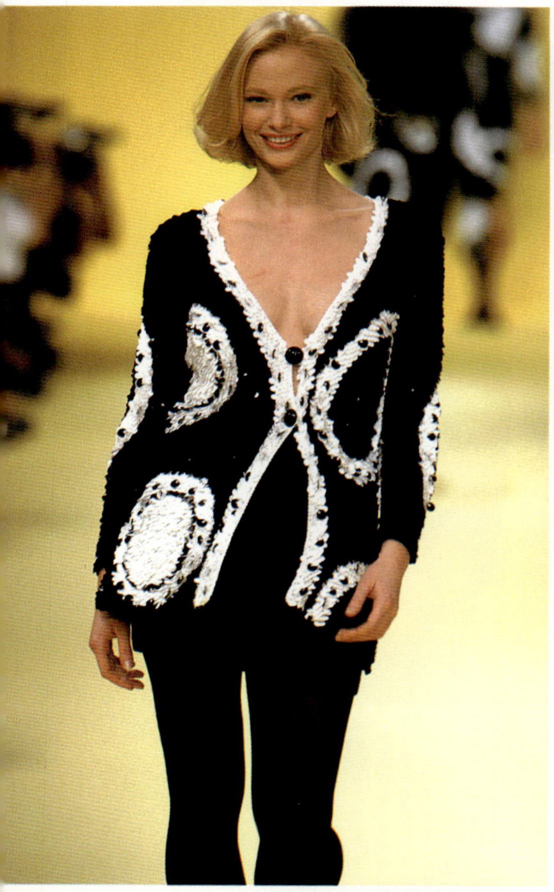
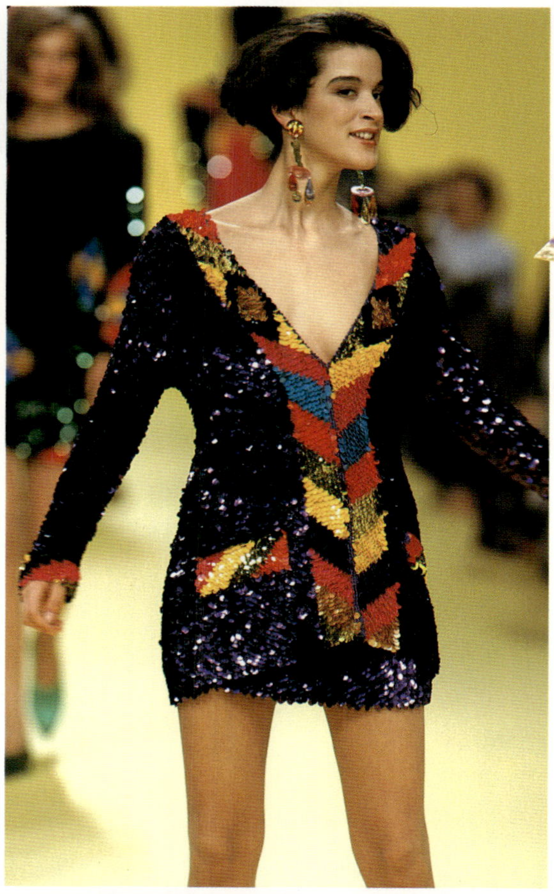
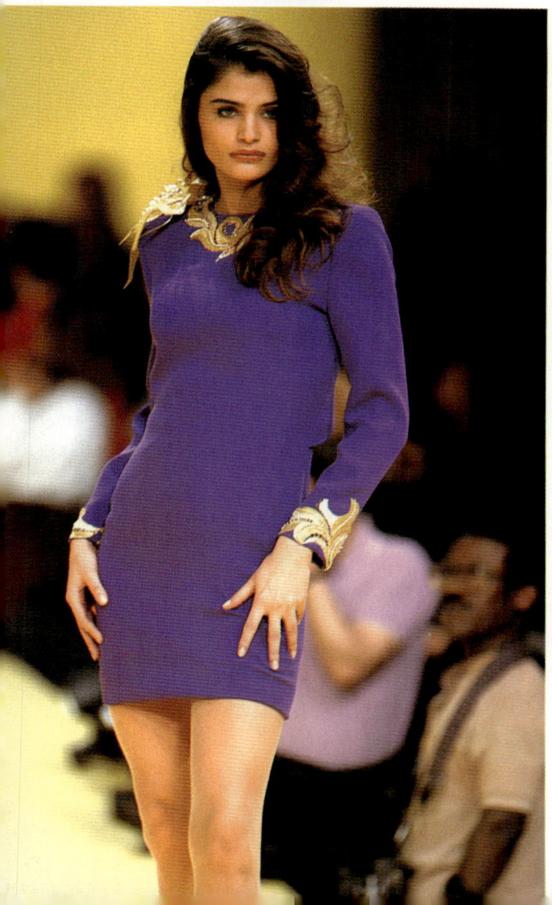
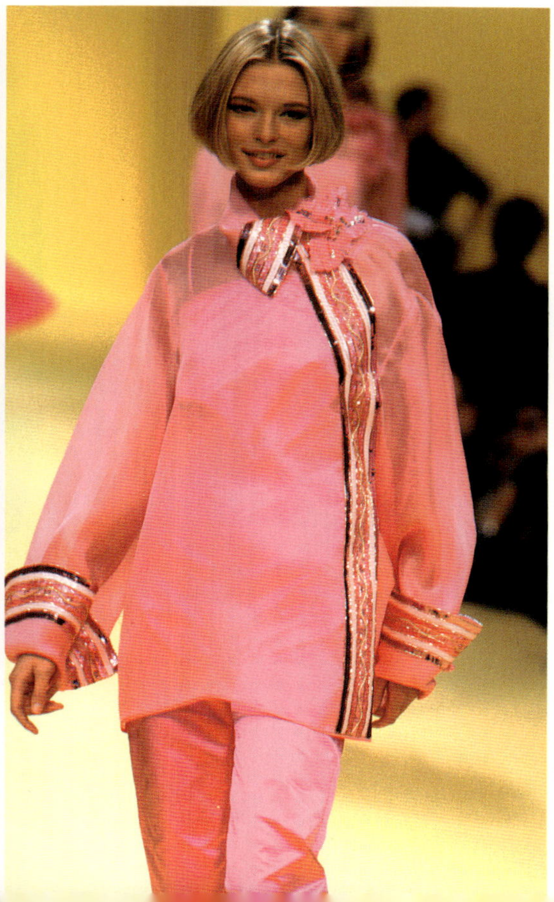
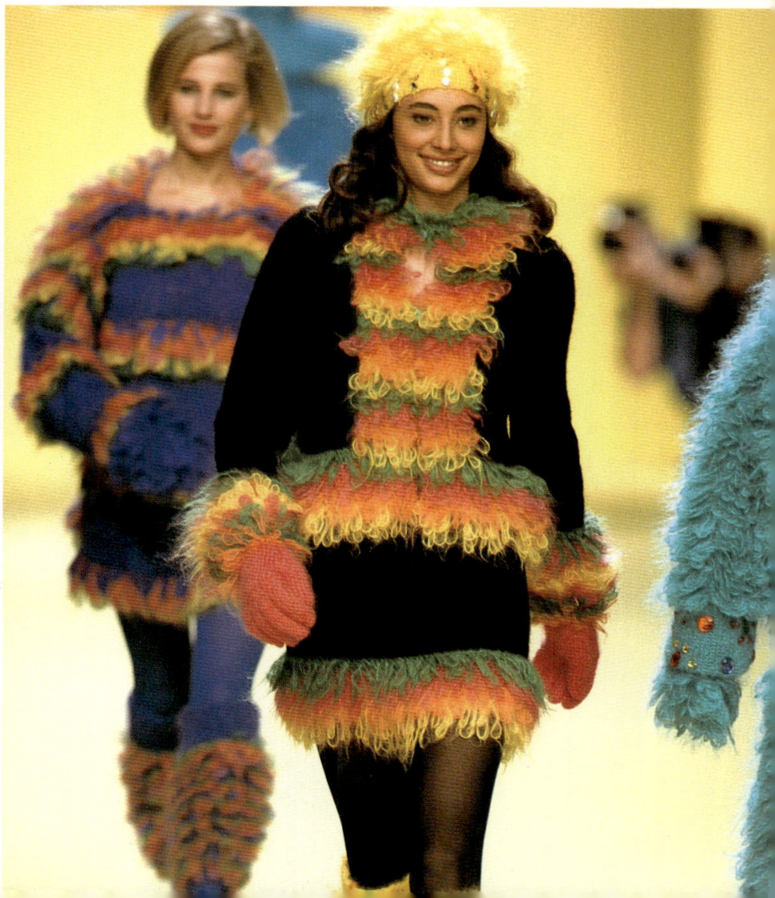

FREDERIC CASTET

フレデリック・カステ

従来のフェイク・ファーとは異なる自然の素材からなるカステ考案のファブリック"Castiss"によるトラペーズ・ラインのコートが印象的。
Impressive were the trapèze-lined coats made of "Castiss", a natural material devised by Castet that is differrent from existing fake fur.

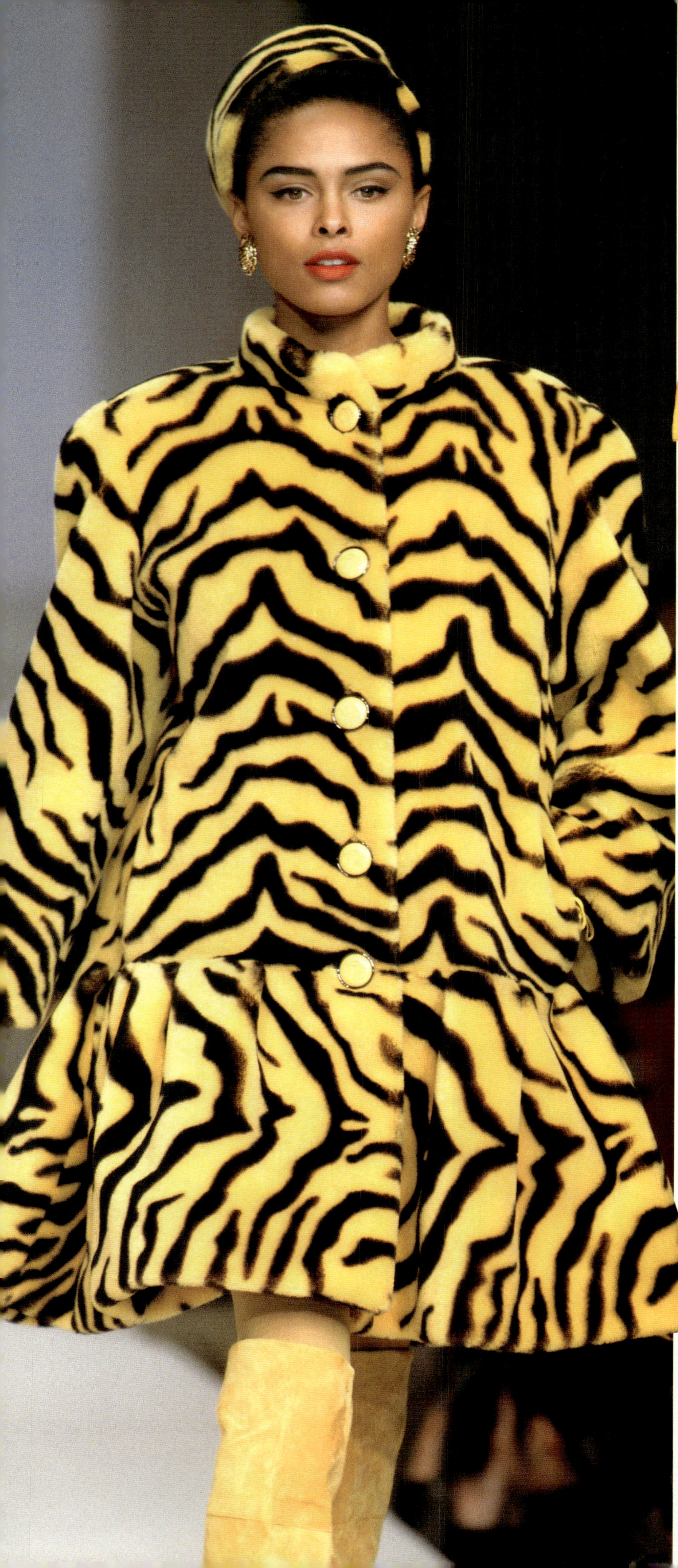
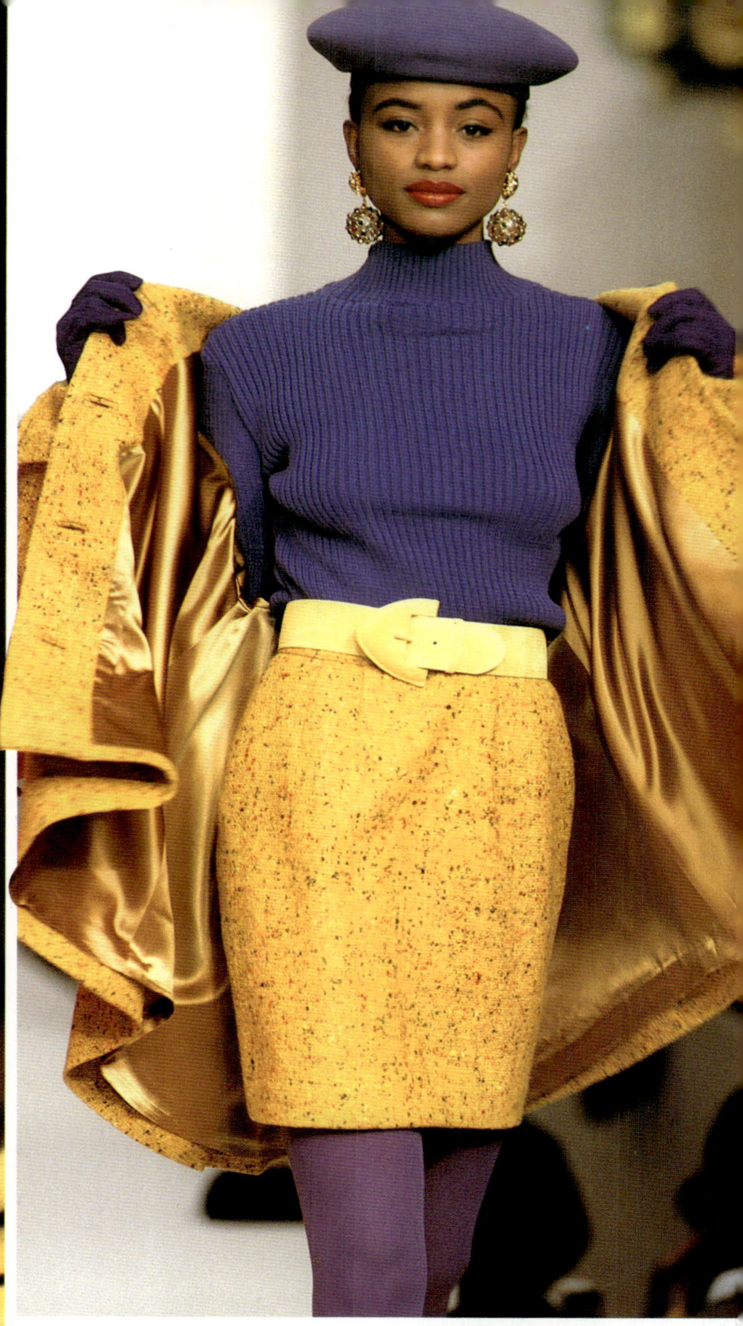
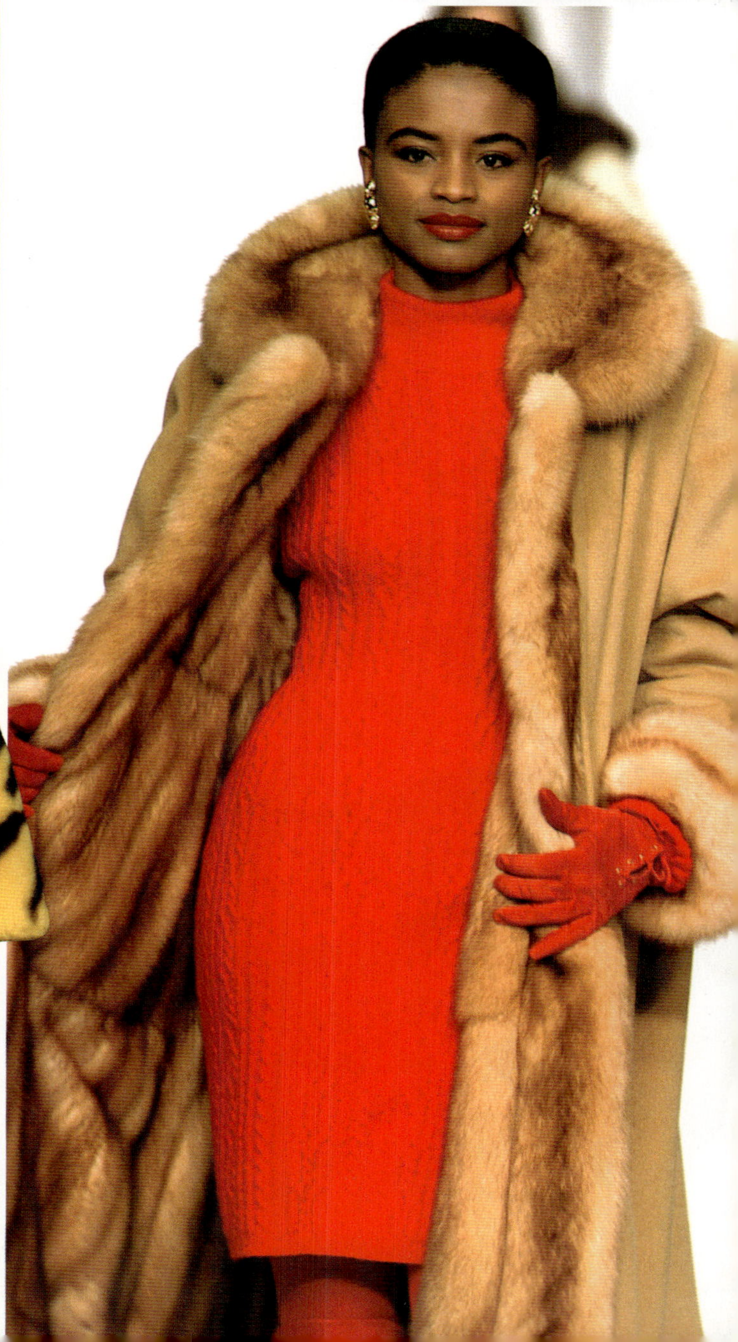

PARIS-48

PIERRE BALMAIN

ピエール・バルマン

アリステア・ブレアがデザイナーに就任して2シーズン目のコレクション。ドレープやチュニック・スカートなどボトムにデザイン性があるのが特徴。
This was the second collection since Allister Blair became the designer.
The special was the design of the bottom part, including drapes and tunic skirts.

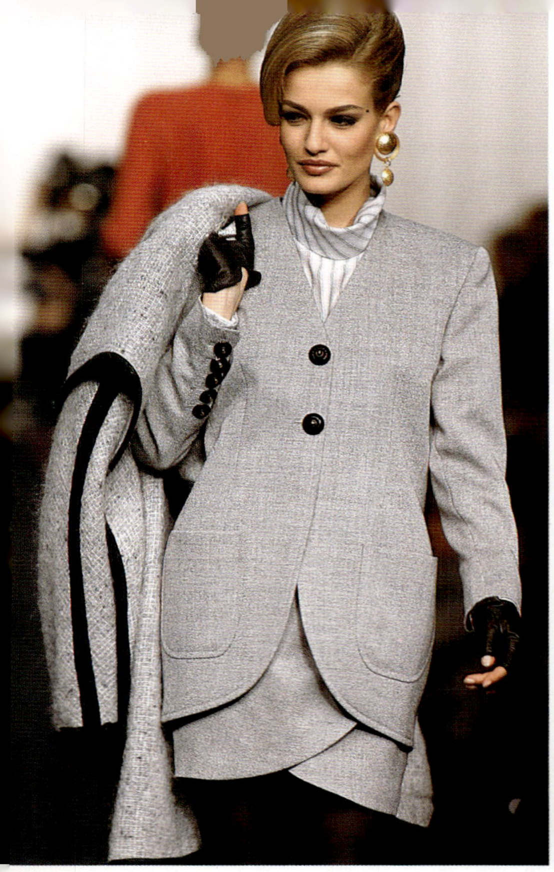
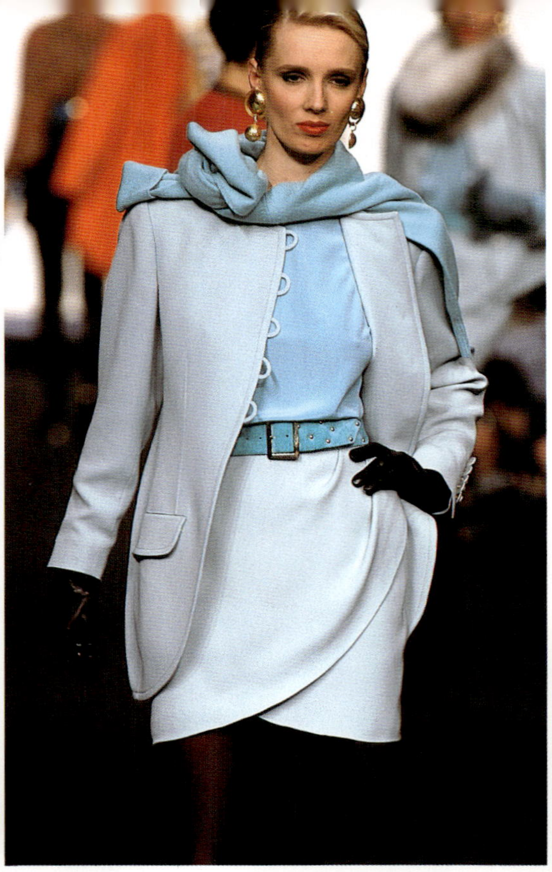
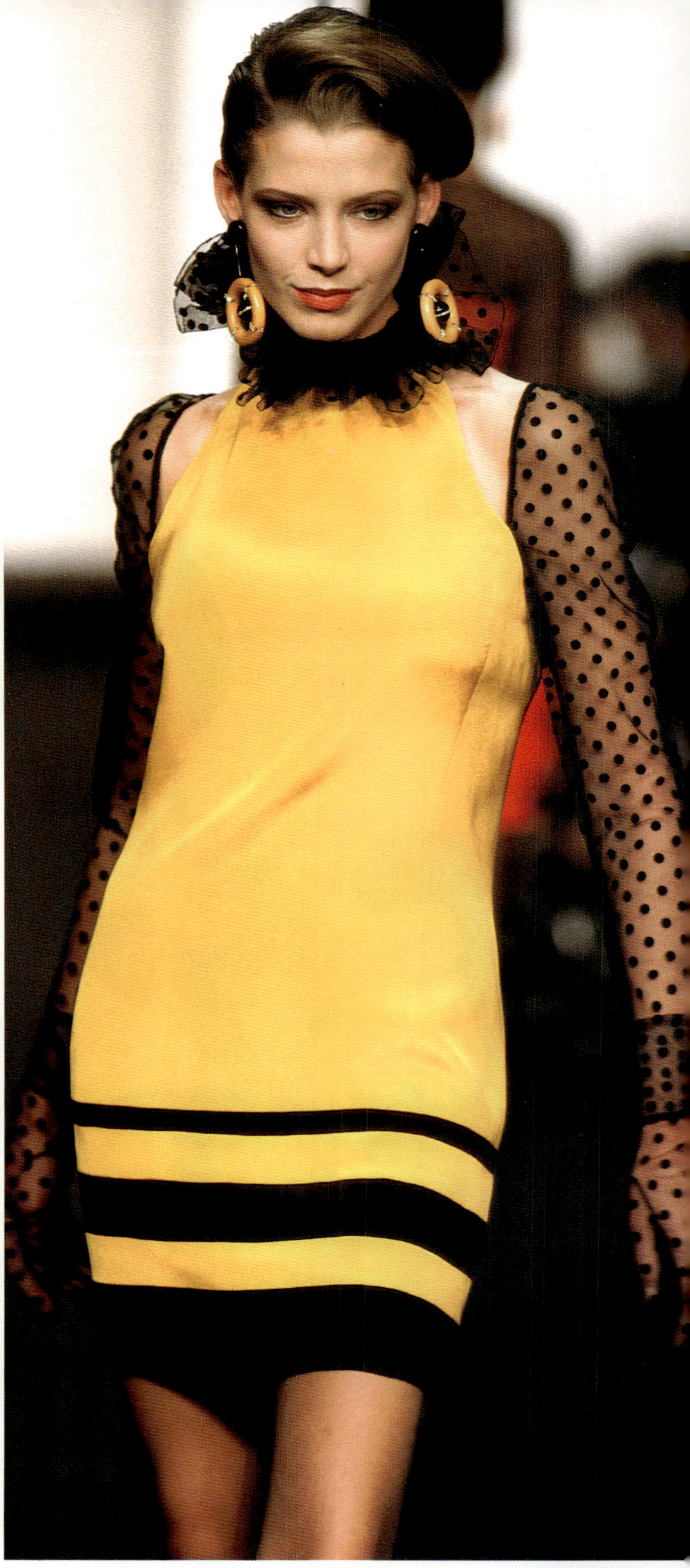
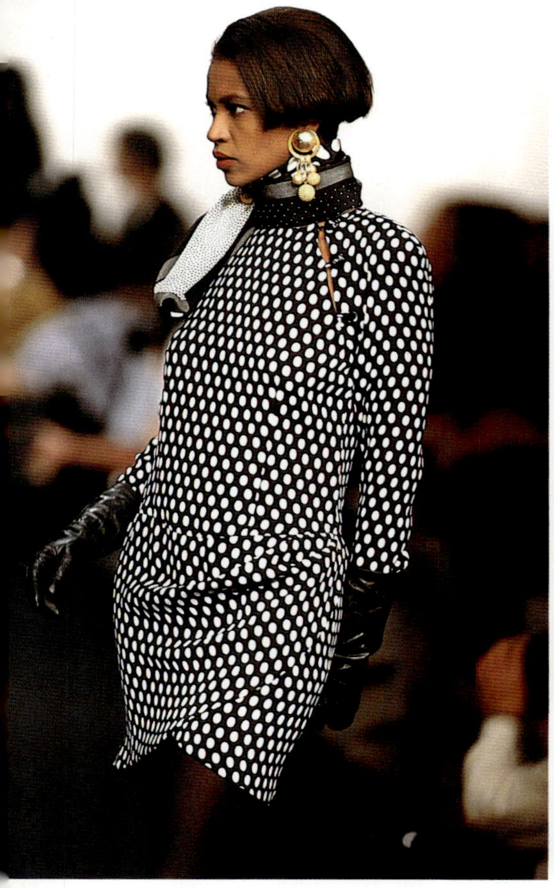
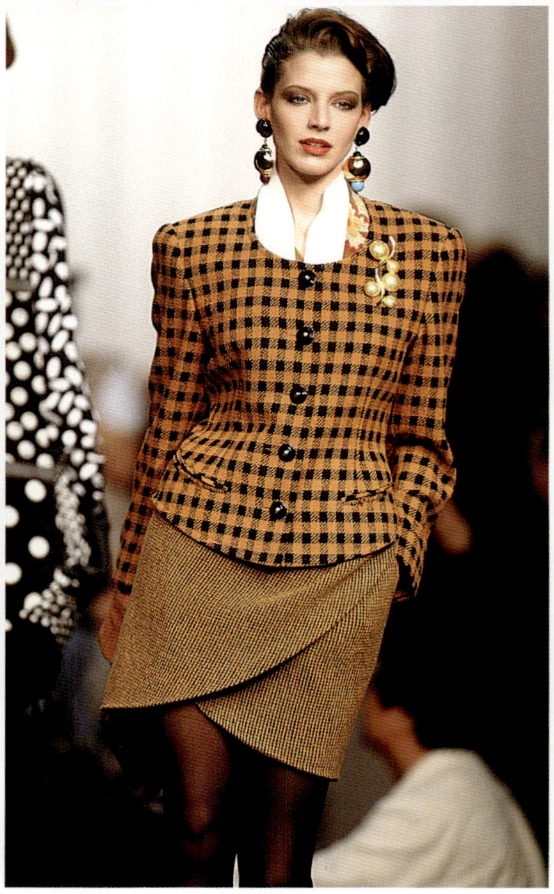
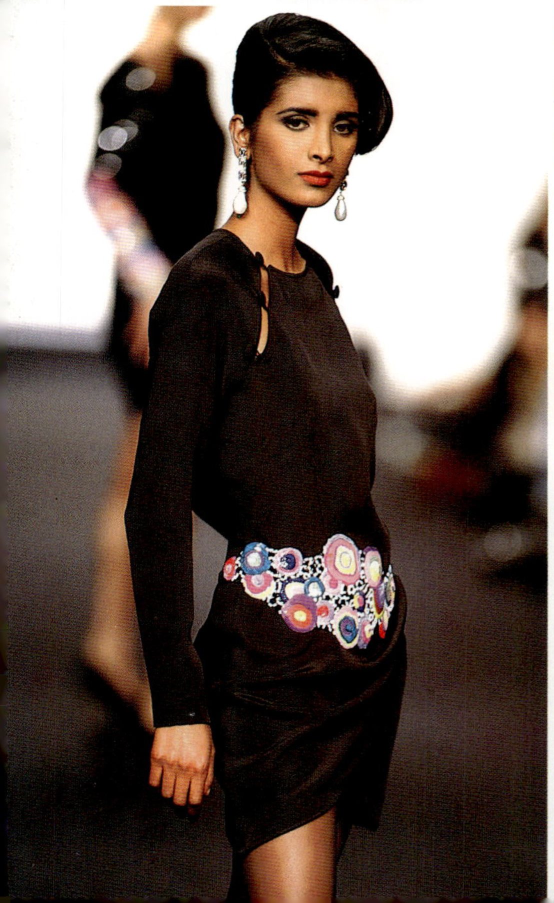
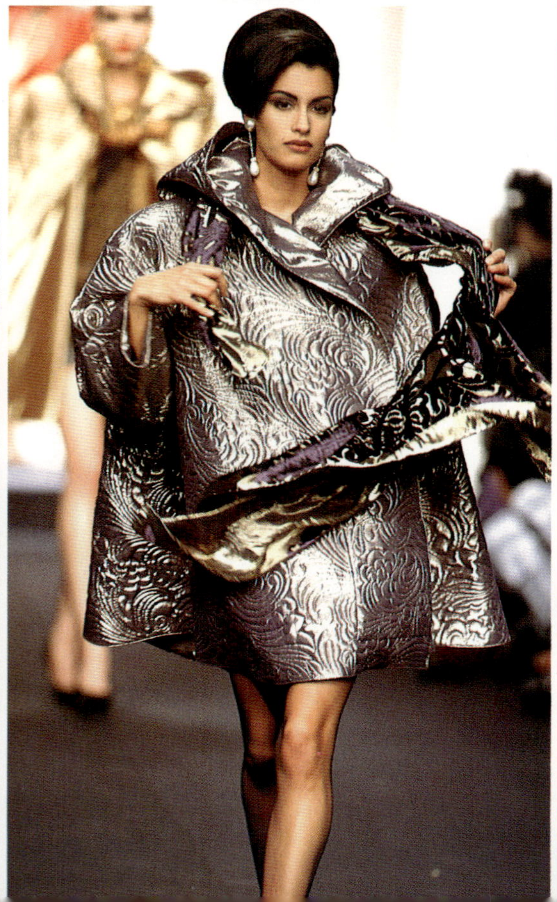
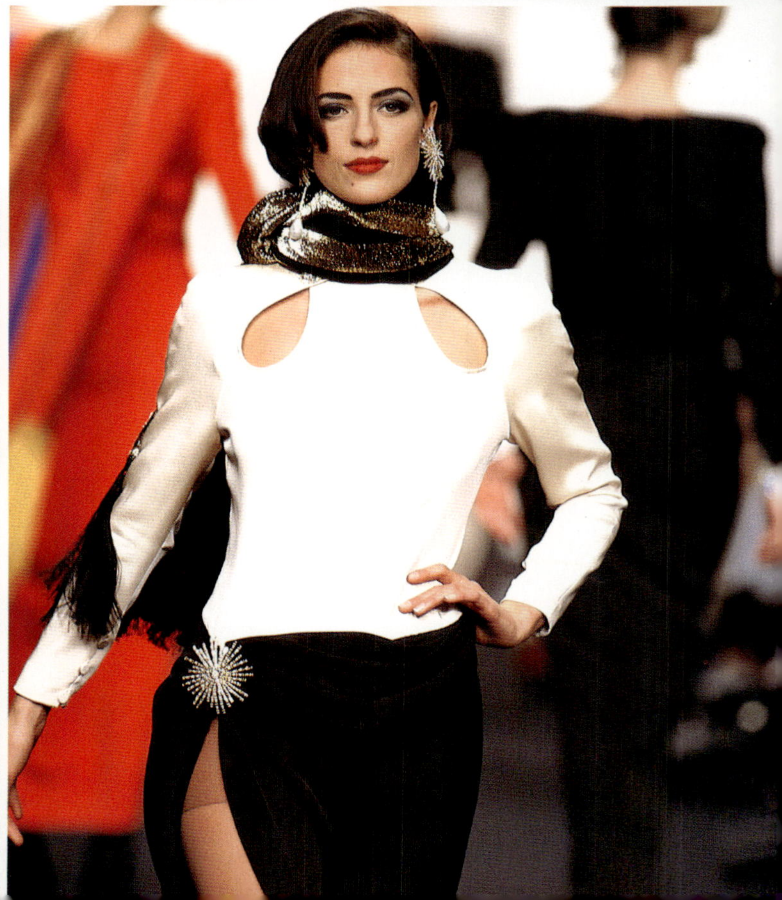

JUNKO KOSHINO

ジュンコ・コシノ

メディテイションの風景の中で、伸縮性のあるプリーツ、リング・フリンジ、スクエア、サークルといった立体の美学が冴える。
The beauty of such forms as stretch pleats, ring fringes, squares and circles, shone out in the meditation scenes.

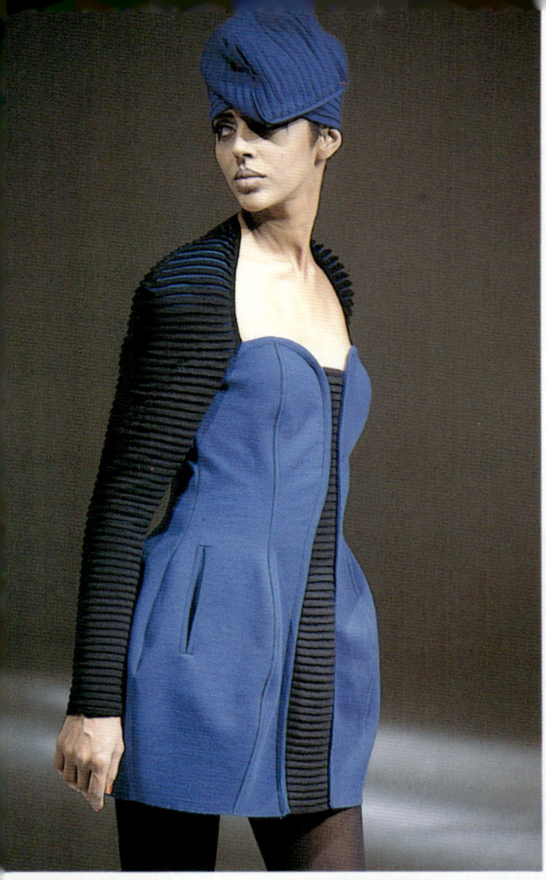
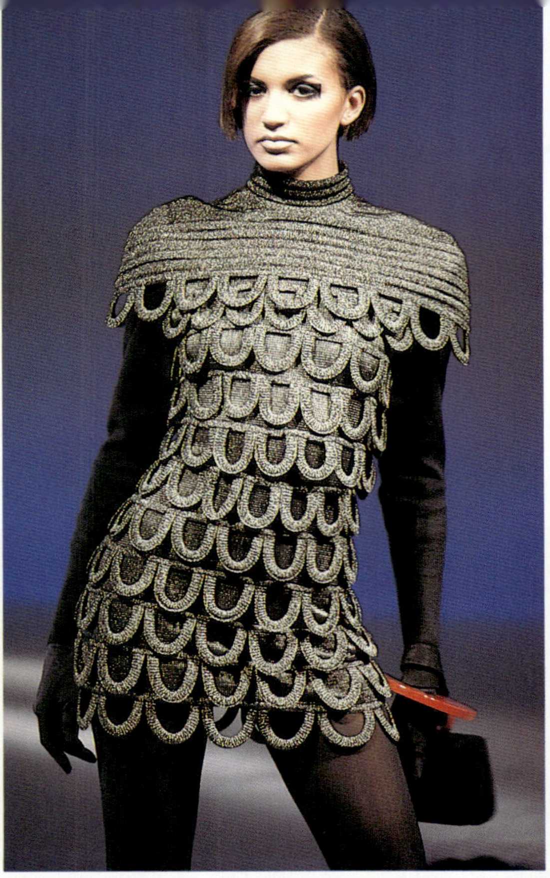
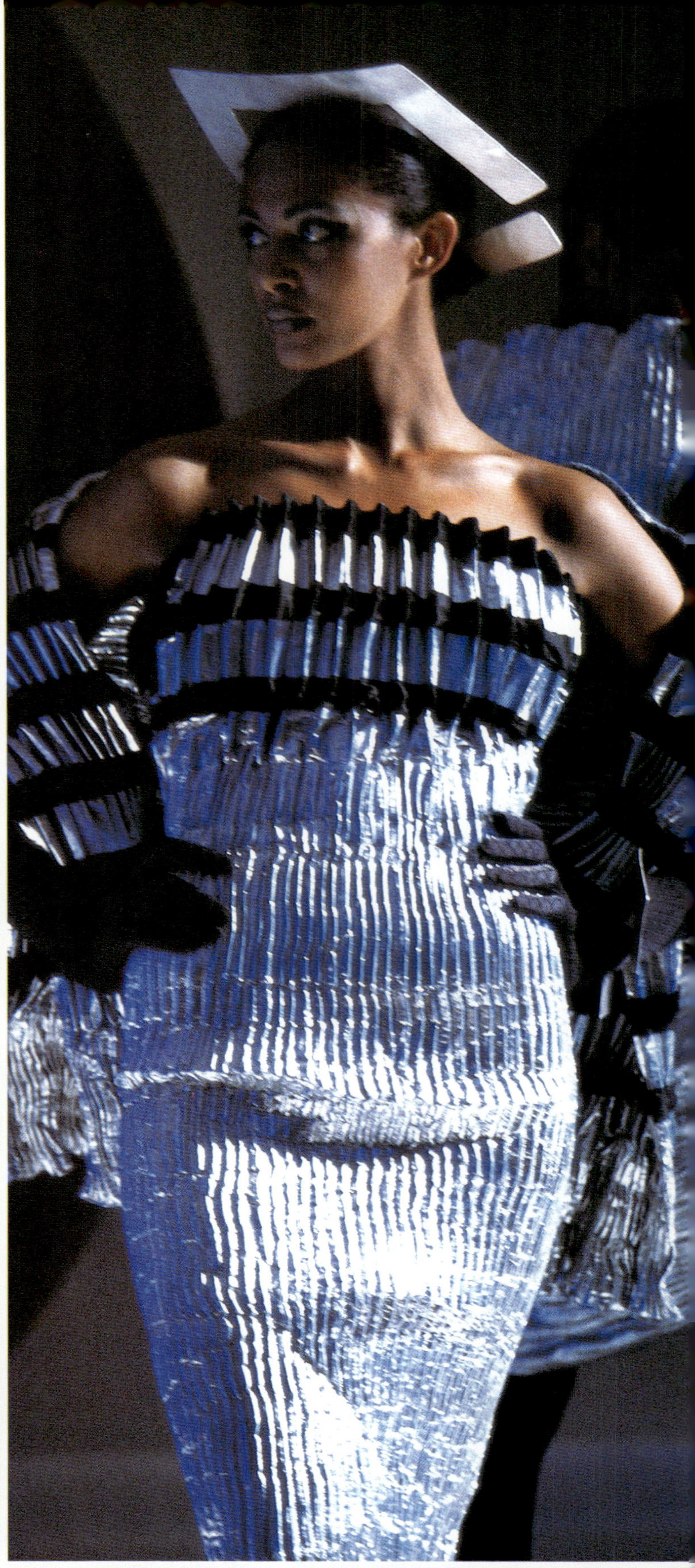
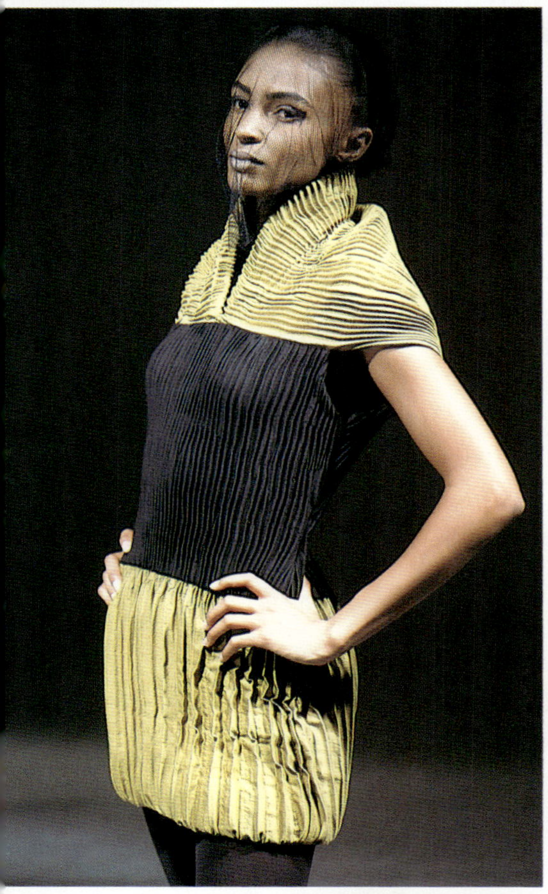
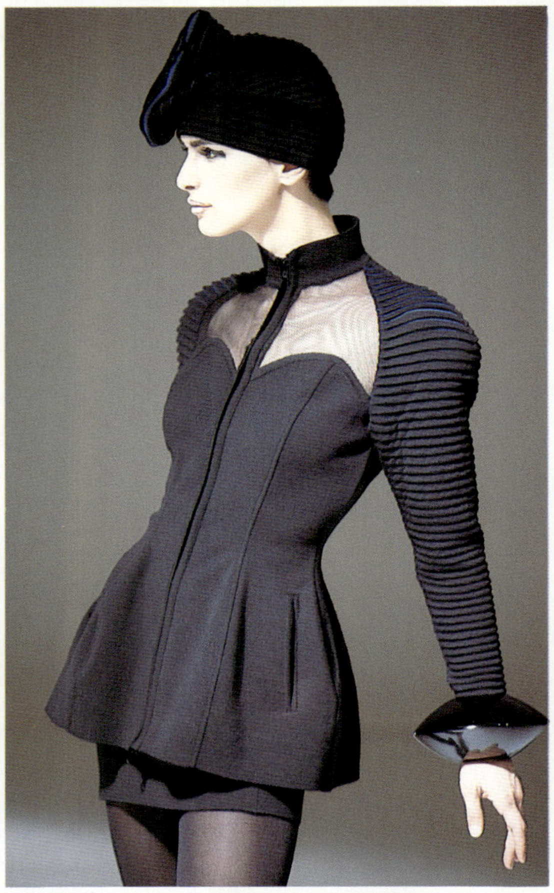
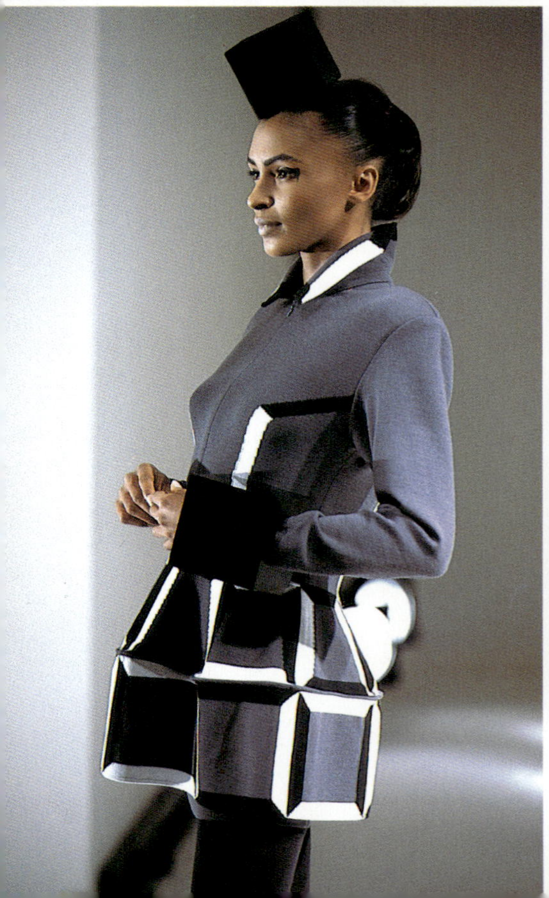
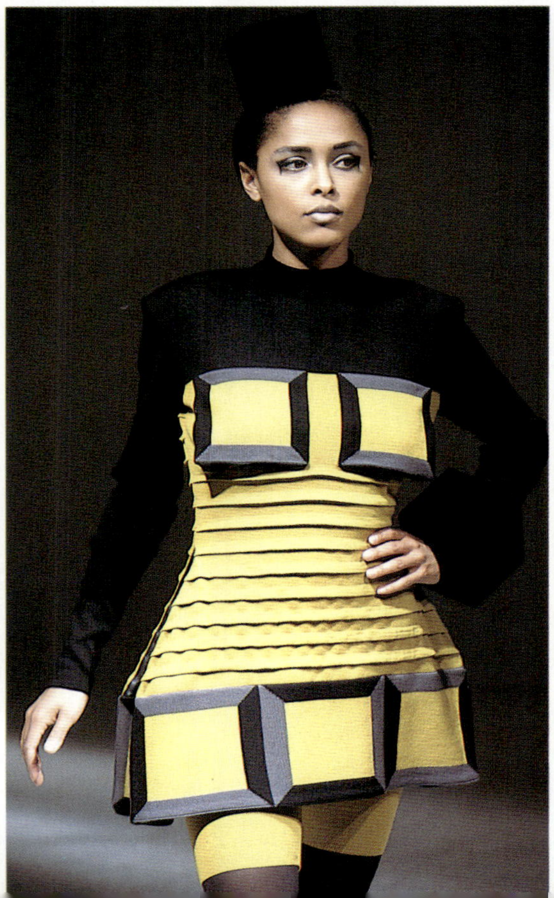
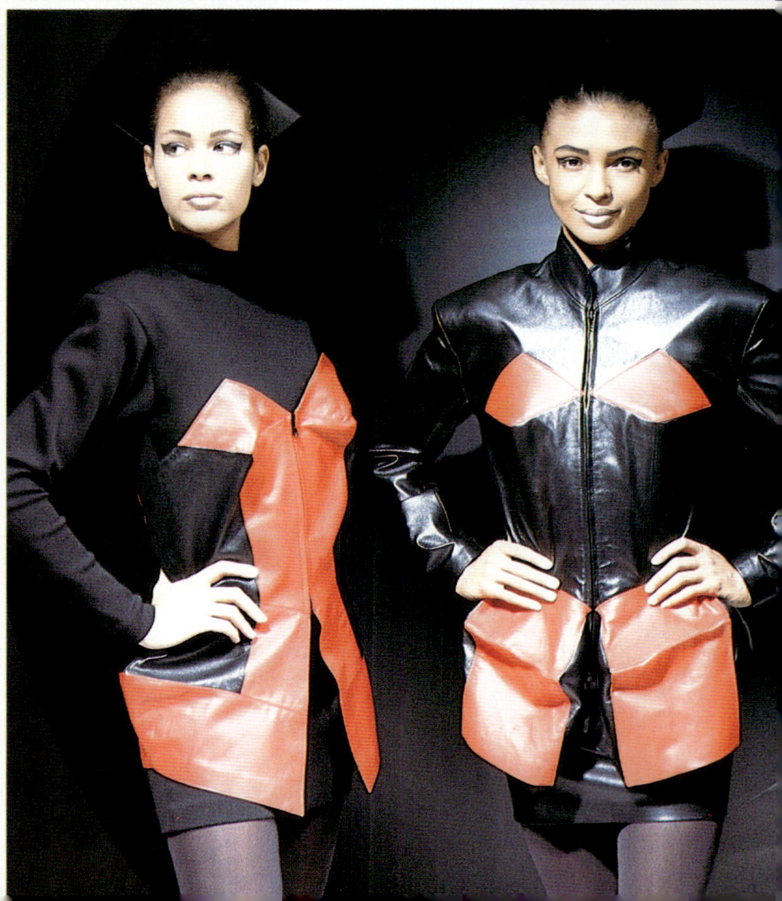

KANSAI YAMAMOTO

カンサイ・ヤマモト

ステンド・グラスのモチーフをはじめ、立体的なフォルムから生じる光、色そのものが有する光など、人が自ら発信する光"AURA"がテーマ。
The theme was "Aura", beginning with motifs of stained glass.
"Aura" refers to the aura arising from three-dimensional shapes, the aura in colors, and the aura coming from people.

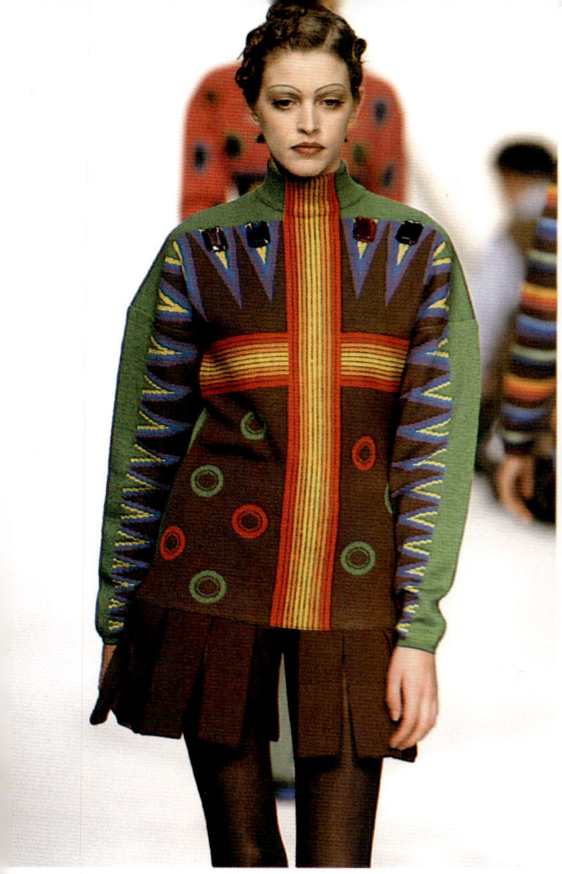
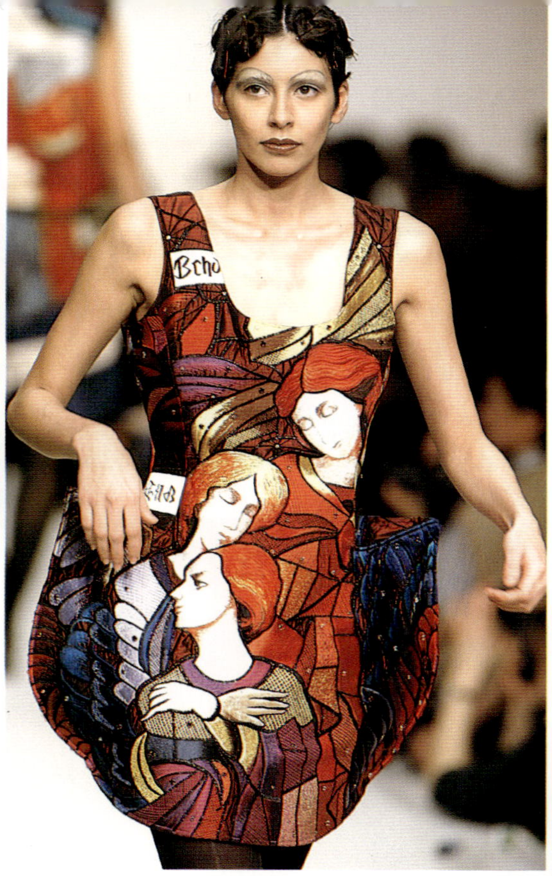
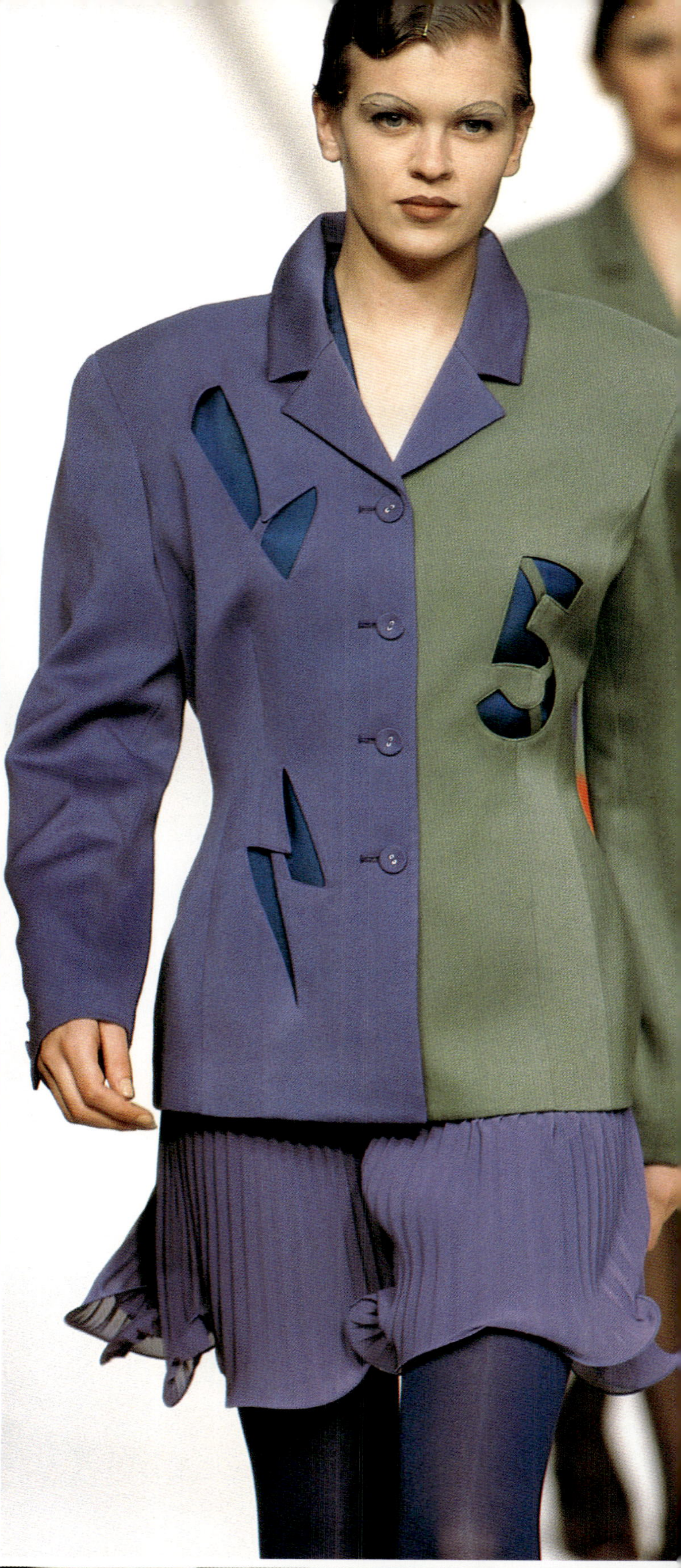
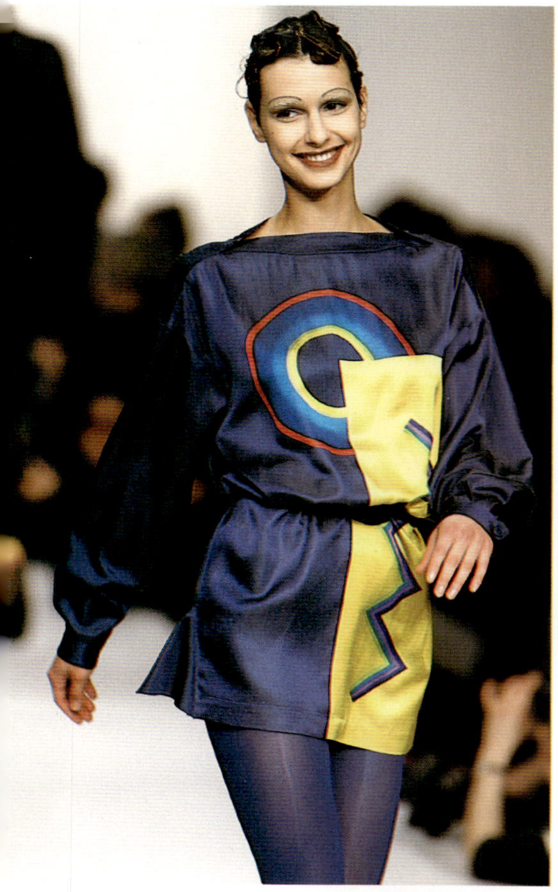
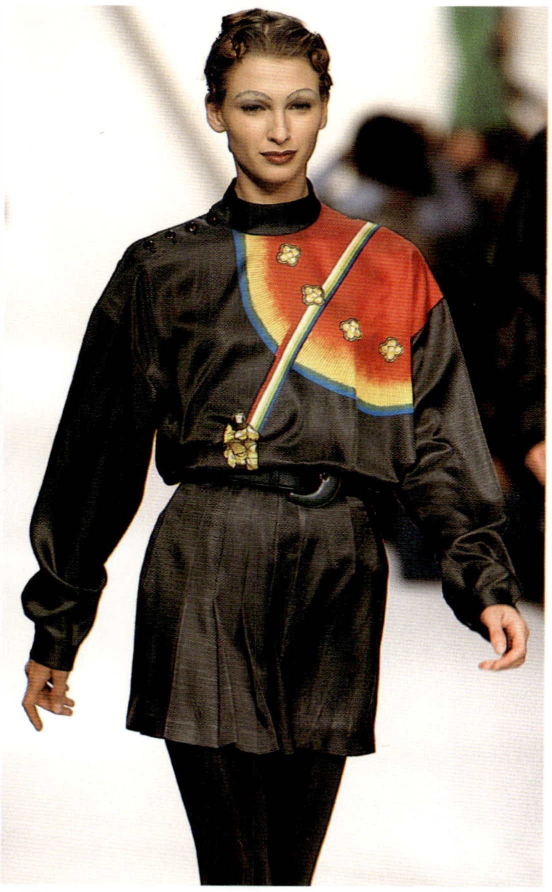
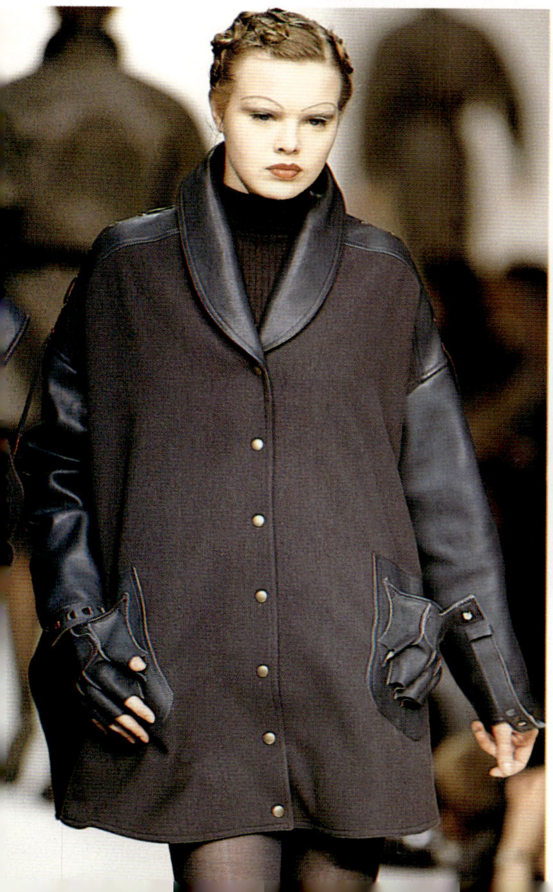
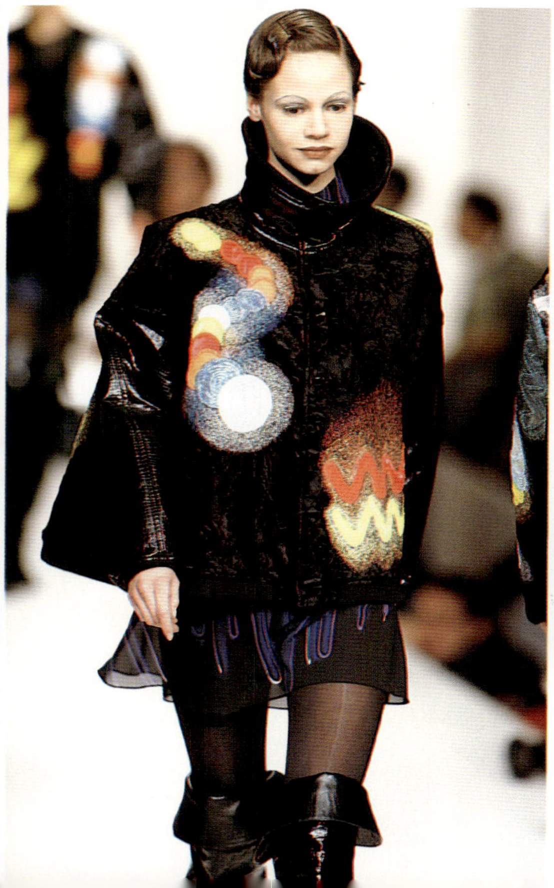
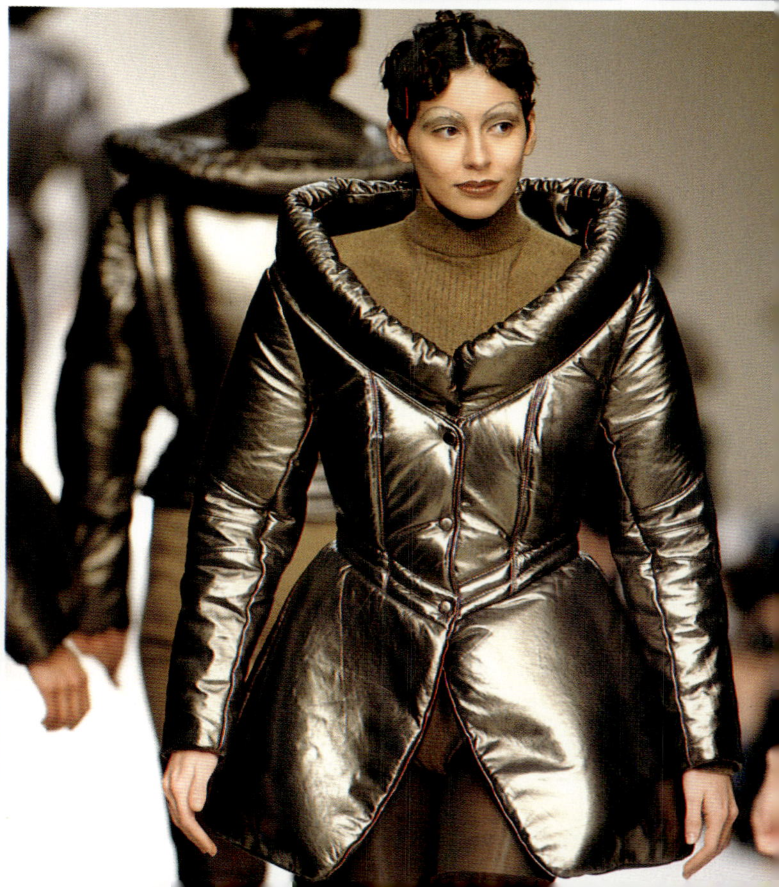

MICHEL KLEIN

HIROKO KOSHINO

'91-'92 AUTUMN & WINTER

PRÊT-Á-PORTER COLLECTIONS

MICHEL KLEIN

KENZO

NINA RICCI

ANGELO TARLAZZI

ANGELO TARLAZZI

LONDON

JACQUELINE HANCHER

The 1991/'92 Autumn & Winter London Collection was held just after the end of the gulf war. The British Fashion Council (BFC) set up a tent to act as the main venue on the Duke of York's King's Road premises. The London Collection has, for the last few years, been accused of being somewhat dull. Some of the people gathered at this collection were even so nasty as to speculate as to how many of the boutiques could survive until autumn. The spectre of conflict in the gulf led to ever bleaker prospects for the London fashion industry.

During the collection, an exhibition was held, entitled the "London designer show." However, the number of buyers was down some 30% from the previous season. Speculation in London before the opening of the collection that buyers and journalists from the U.S. and Japan wouldn't turn up proved correct.

The conventional cat-walk show was employed by 15 of the maisons this season. Not participating for the second time since the 1990/'91 autumn & winter collection, was London fashion industry leader, Jasper Conran, who had taken part in the 1991 spring & summer collection. He merely held a presentation instead. Another top London designer who didn't participate was Vivienne Westwood, who only put on a tea-party style preview in London, and saved a more formal one for Paris. It would appear that Vivienne Westwood has finally finished with London. Losing one star after another, this season's London collection was stripped of its shine.

The trend this season seemed to follow on from last year. From the '60's style of last season, this season displayed styles from the late '60's to the '70's. Most maisons showed maxies, hot-pants and long zip-up vests. Also on display were the see-through shirts and mini jumper skirts often worn in dance scenes from that time. Another remarkable feature was "skin conscious". Following the 1991 spring & summer collection, Ozbek put African folklore on display this season, employing materials such as suade and wool. The most creative designer of this London collection, he demonstrated his talent in his display of a chic ethnic style. Two new designers both put on energetic collections, Helen Storey and Val Piriou, who made the debuts last season. Helen Storey, known for wild elegance, enjoys enormous popularity in the club scene. Val Piriou, emphasizes the soft, feminine feel, based on the same sense of fitness as Helen Storey. Also worthy of mention is Pam Hogg. The mainstay of her collection was body suits, made from a variety of materials, and with emphasis on the breast line.

With the best of London's designers leaving, and with the middle ranks lacking in power, only the new designers shone out. This season's collection showed nothing original, but merely followed world trends. I was left wondering when the next truly original designer, like Vivienne Westwood, will make an appearance. Then, the next wave of London fashion will come.

Original creativity is now expected from new London designers.
今、ロンドンの新人デザイナーに期待されるオリジナル・クリエイティビティ

'91-'92年秋冬ロンドン・コレクションは、湾岸戦争が一応の終結をみせた直後、キングス・ロードのヨーク公邸内に設けられたBFC（ブリティッシュ・ファッション・カウンシル）のテントをメイン会場に開催された。ここ数年、ロンドン・コレクションの低調ぶりが云々され続ける中で迎えた今回のコレクションであるが、今秋までに一体いくつのブティックが生き残るだろうという意地悪な声さえも聞こえてくる不振のロンドン・ファッション業界を、戦争はさらにシビアな状況へと追いこんでいった。

期間中、同会場にて、「ロンドン・デザイナー・ショー」なる展示会が催されたが、バイヤーの出席率は前シーズンに比べ30％のダウンである。コレクションの開幕前から、アメリカ、日本のバイヤーやジャーナリストたちの集まりが悪いのではと、ロンドンではささやかれていたが、そのとおりの結果となった。

今シーズンは、従来のキャットウォークのショー・スタイルをとったのは15メゾン。ロンドン・ファッション界をリードする立場のジャスパー・コンランは'91年春夏ではコレクションに参加したものの、今シーズンは'90-'91年秋冬に引き続きショーをやらずプレゼンテーションのみ。また、ロンドン筆頭デザイナーのヴィヴィアン・ウエストウッドはロンドンでは、ティーパーティ・スタイルのプレビューだけで、本格的なものはパリで開かれた。ついにV. ウエストウッドもロンドンに見切りをつけたかという印象であるが、ロンドンはまた一つ色彩を失い何とも寂しいシーズンとなってしまった。

今回のロンドンの傾向として、昨シーズンの'60'sの後を引き継ぐかのように、'60年代後半から'70年代のアイテムであるマキシ、ホットパンツ・スタイル、ジップアップのロング・ベスト、当時のダンス・シーンなどでよく見うけられたシースルーのシャツにミニのジャンパー・スカートなどが、かなりのメゾンで登場していた。そしてさらに著しいスキン・コンシャスであろう。'91年春夏でアフリカン・フォークロアを取り入れたオズベックは、今シーズンもスウェードやウールといった素材でアフリカン・フォークロアを表現し、シックなエスニックを演出。ロンドン・コレクションにおいてもっともクリエイティブな才能を発揮した。また昨シーズン、デビューしたヘレン・ストーリーとバル・ピローの2人の新人はかなりエネルギッシュである。かたやクラブ・シーンで絶大な人気を誇るワイルド・エレガンスの主。そして後者は同じフィット感をベースにおきながらも女性らしいソフトな感触を強調している。もう1人忘れてならないのがパム・ホッグ。作品のほとんどをボディ・スーツでカバーし、さまざまな素材を使って特に胸のラインを強調。

才能あるデザイナーたちの相次ぐロンドン脱出、中堅デザイナーのパワー不足の中で元気なのは新人デザイナーだけだが、ロンドン・コレクションの今シーズンのトレンドにしてもそれは世界のトレンドと同一化されたものであり、ロンドンのオリジナリティではない。果して、V. ウエストウッドに代表されるような、次のオリジナリティを生みだすデザイナーがいつ登場してくるのか、ロンドン・ファッションのビッグ・ウェイブが起こるのはその時である。

JACQUELINE HANCHER

TOMASZ STARZEWSKI

PAM HOGG

'91-'92 AUTUMN & WINTER COLLECTIONS
LONDON

PAM HOGG

JOE CASELY-HAYFORD

VAL PIRIOU

PAM HOGG

PAM HOGG

LONDON-1

OZBEK

オズベック

'91年春夏にみせたアフリカン・フォークロアをキルティングやベルベットでモダンに表現。エスニックなセクシー・ラインを打ちだした。

Following the '91 spring-summer collection,
he used quilting and velvet to display modern African folklore. An ethnic sexy line was striking.

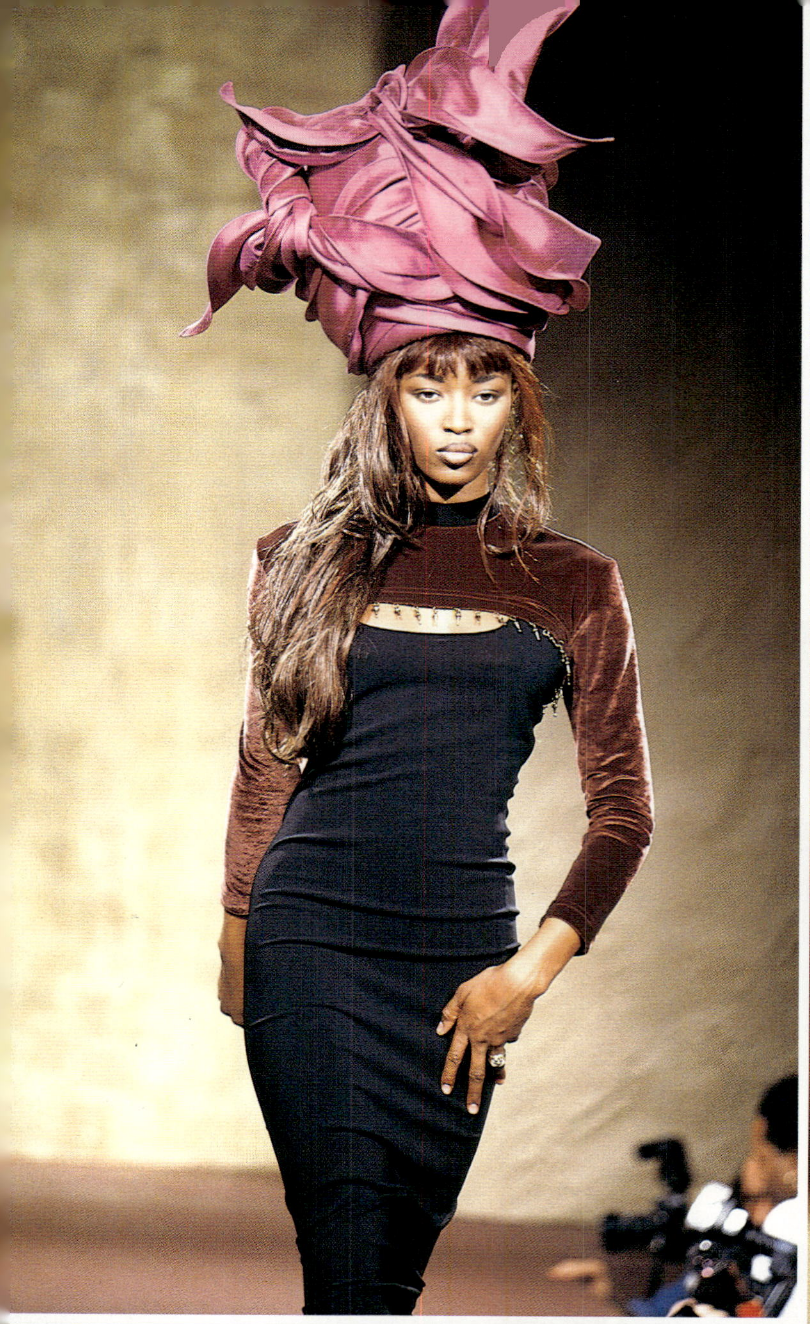
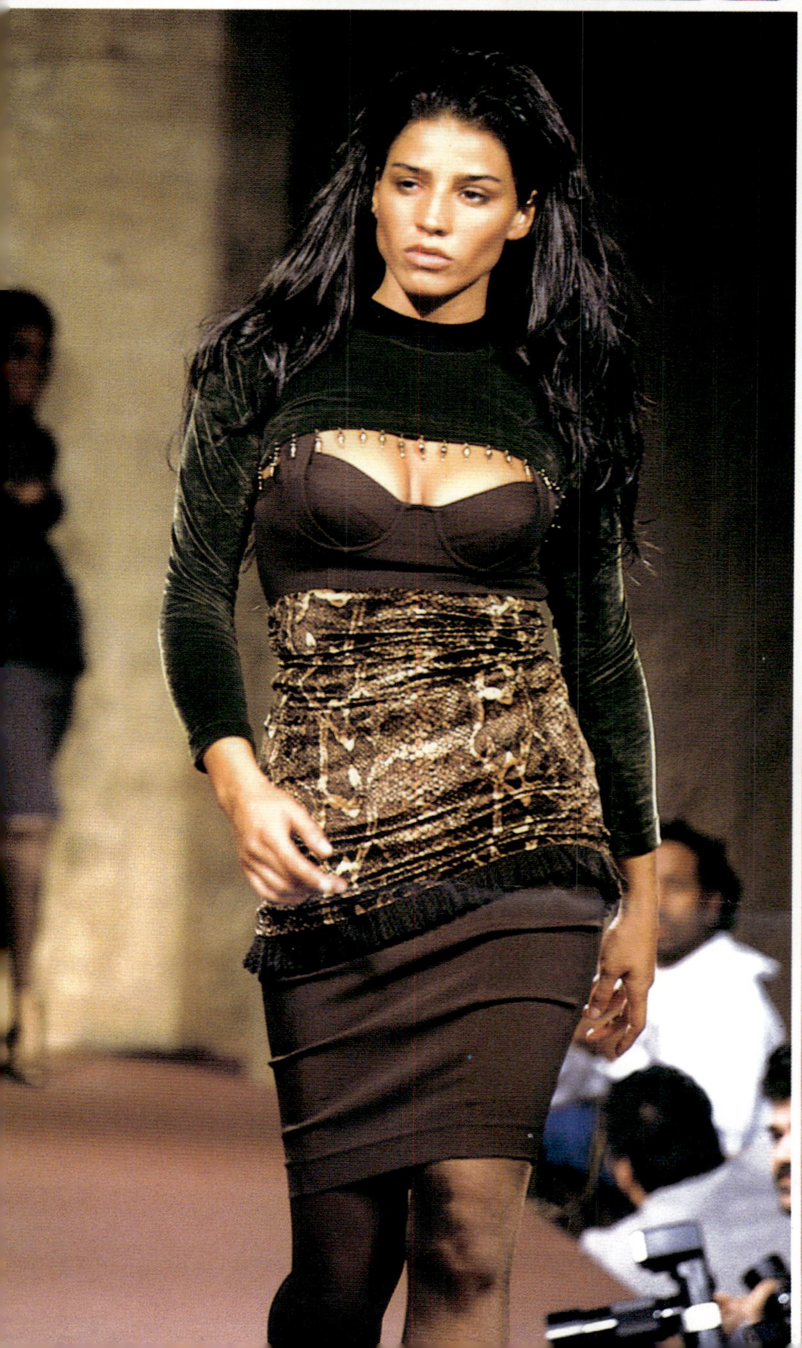
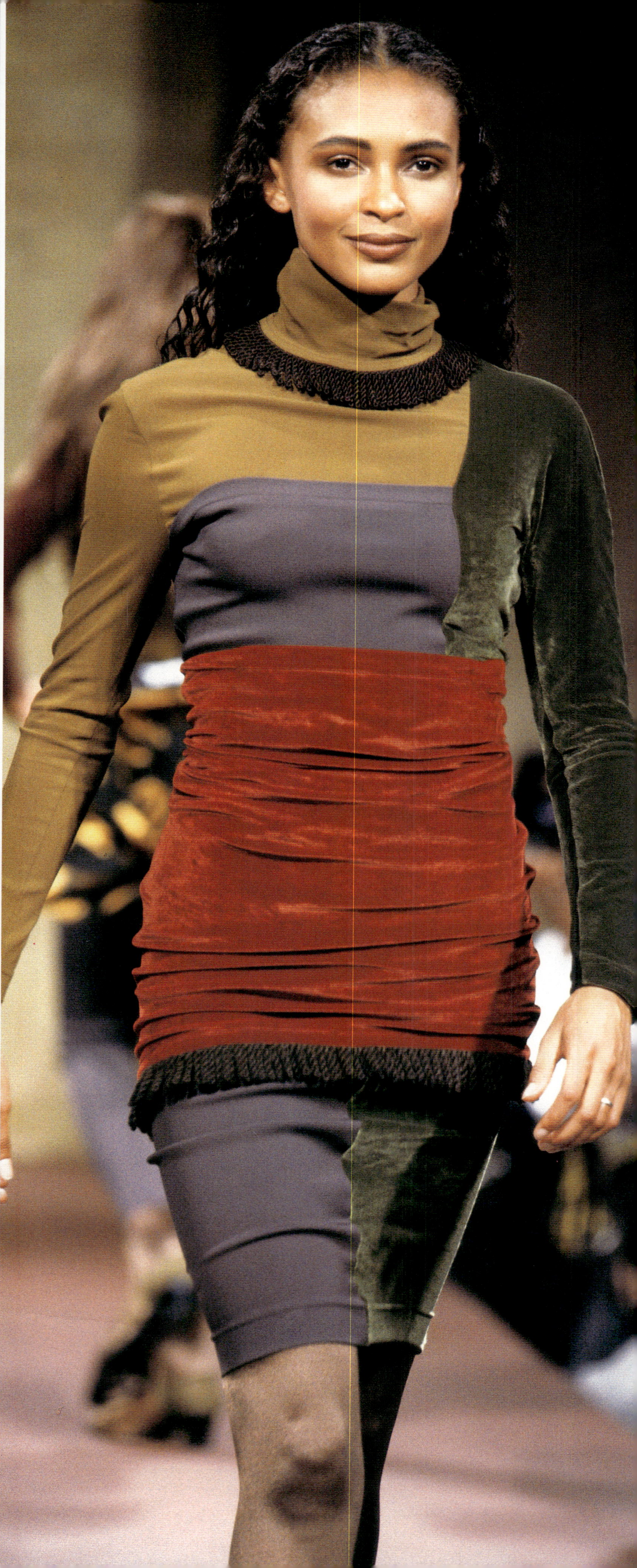

OZBEK

295

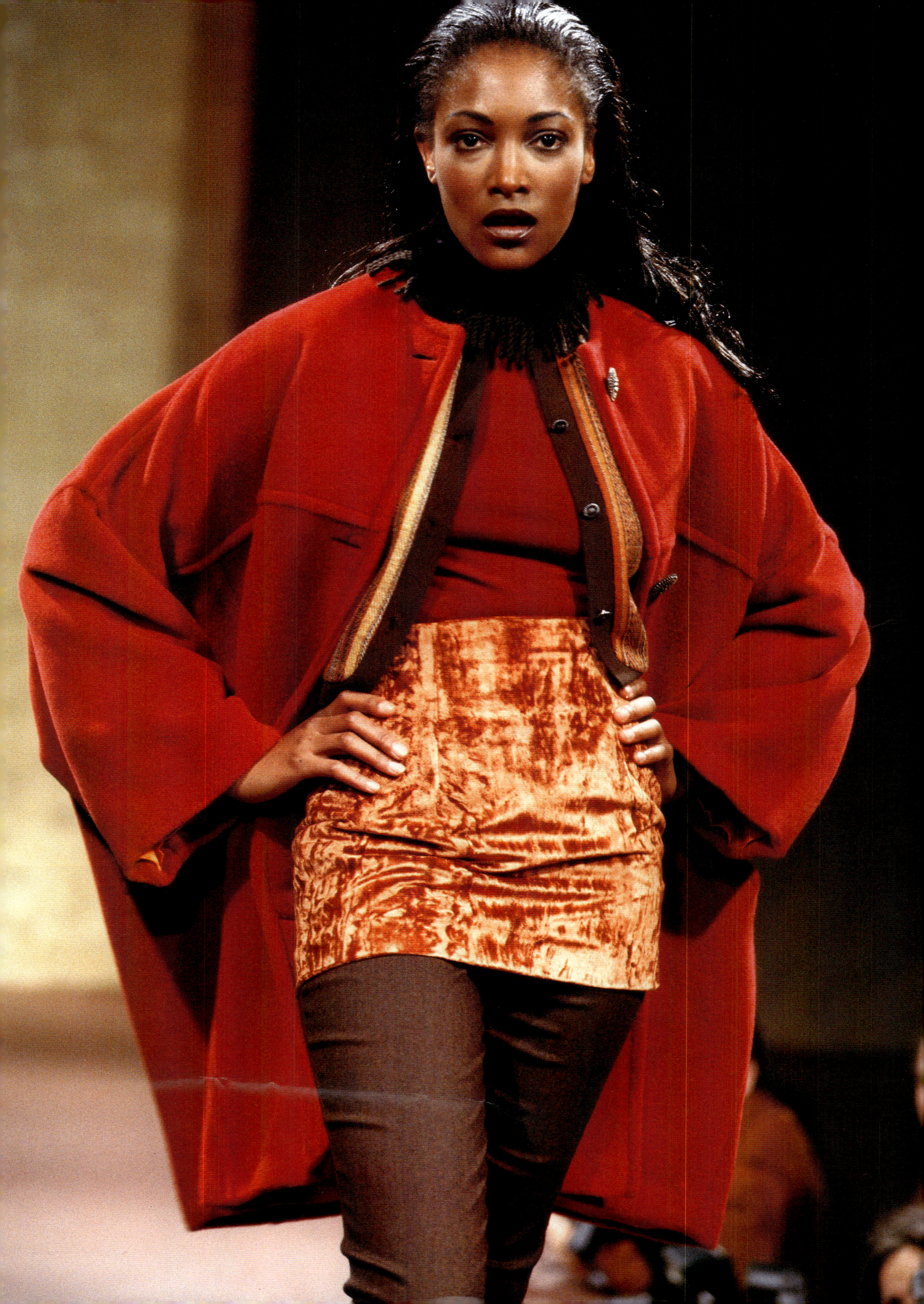

VAL PIRIOU

バル・ピロー

ボディ・フィットをセクシーよりもエレガントでみせたコレクション。カットワークの巧みさにも洗練の兆が見えてきた。

Her collection was elegant rather than sexy in its "body fit" display. The skillful cut work had the make of sophistication.

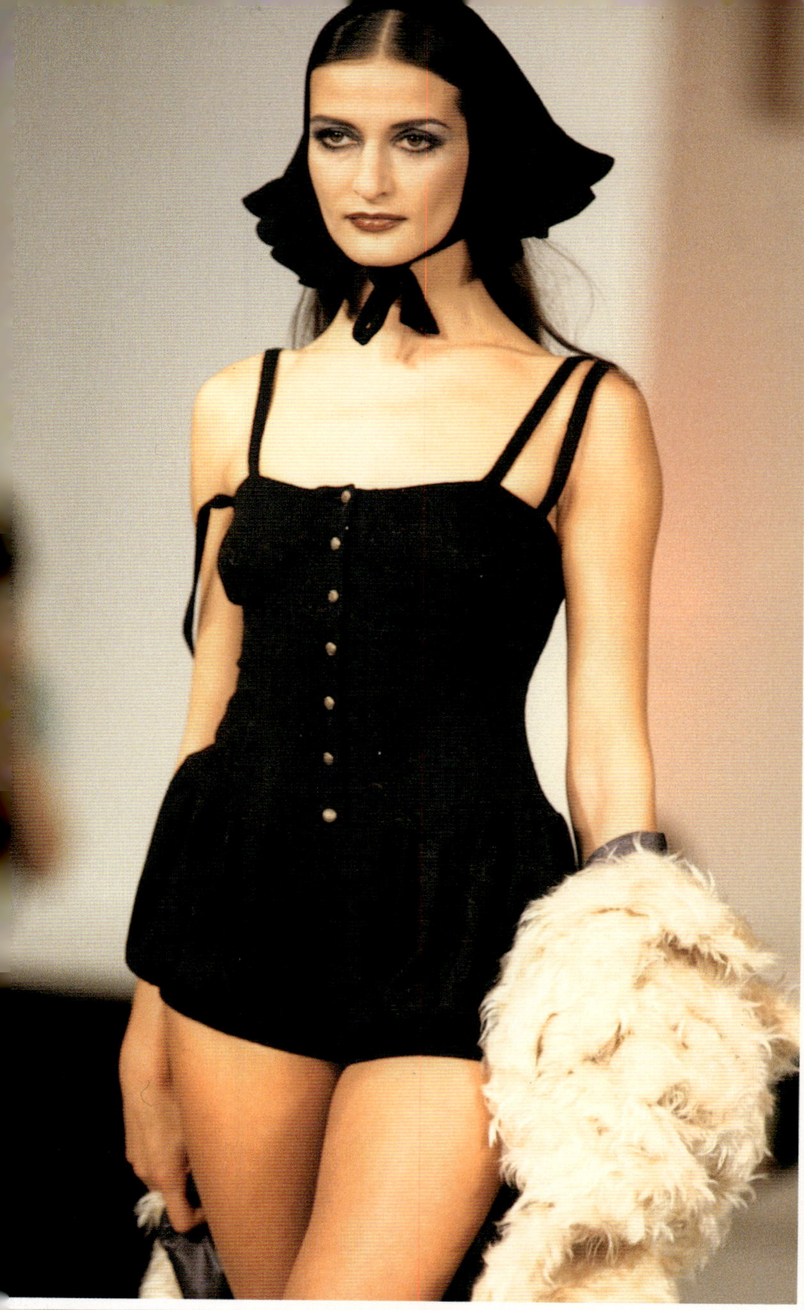

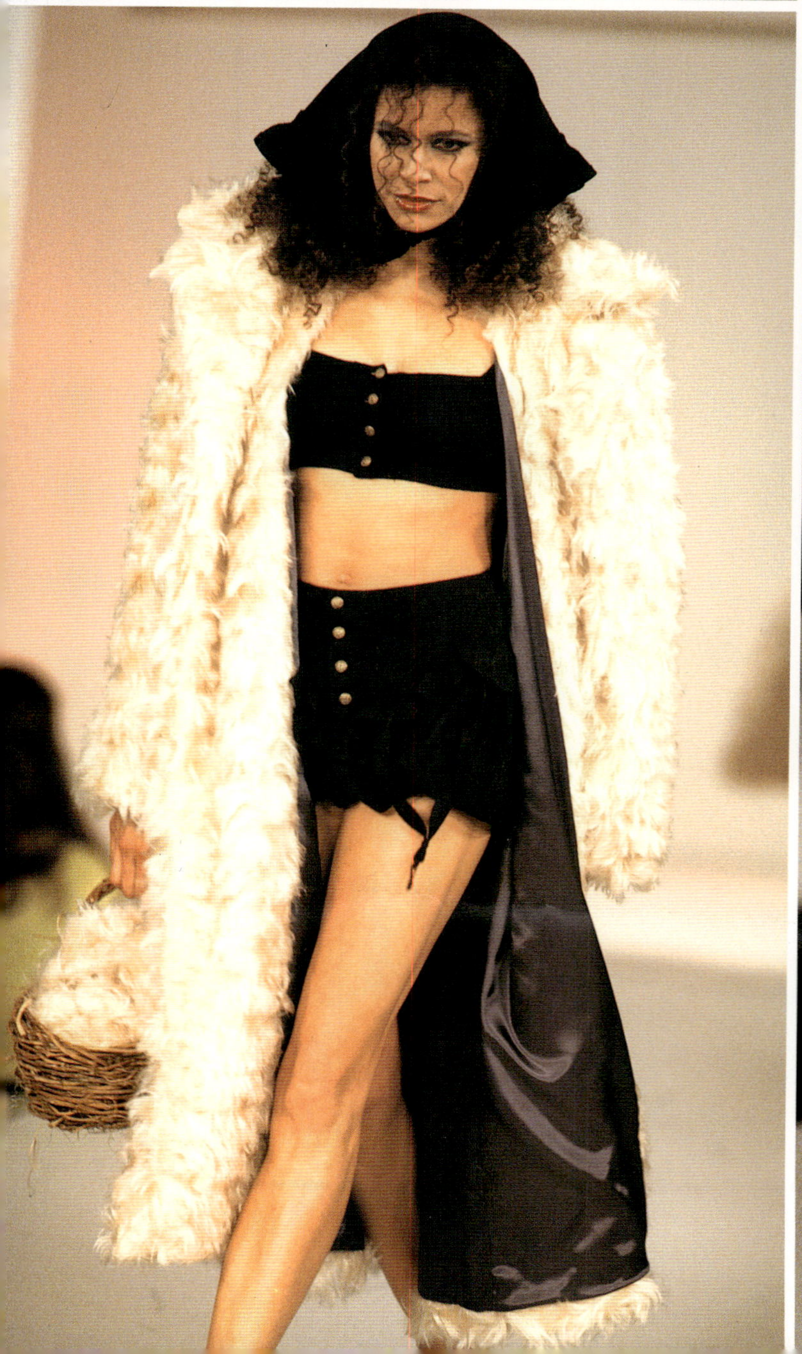

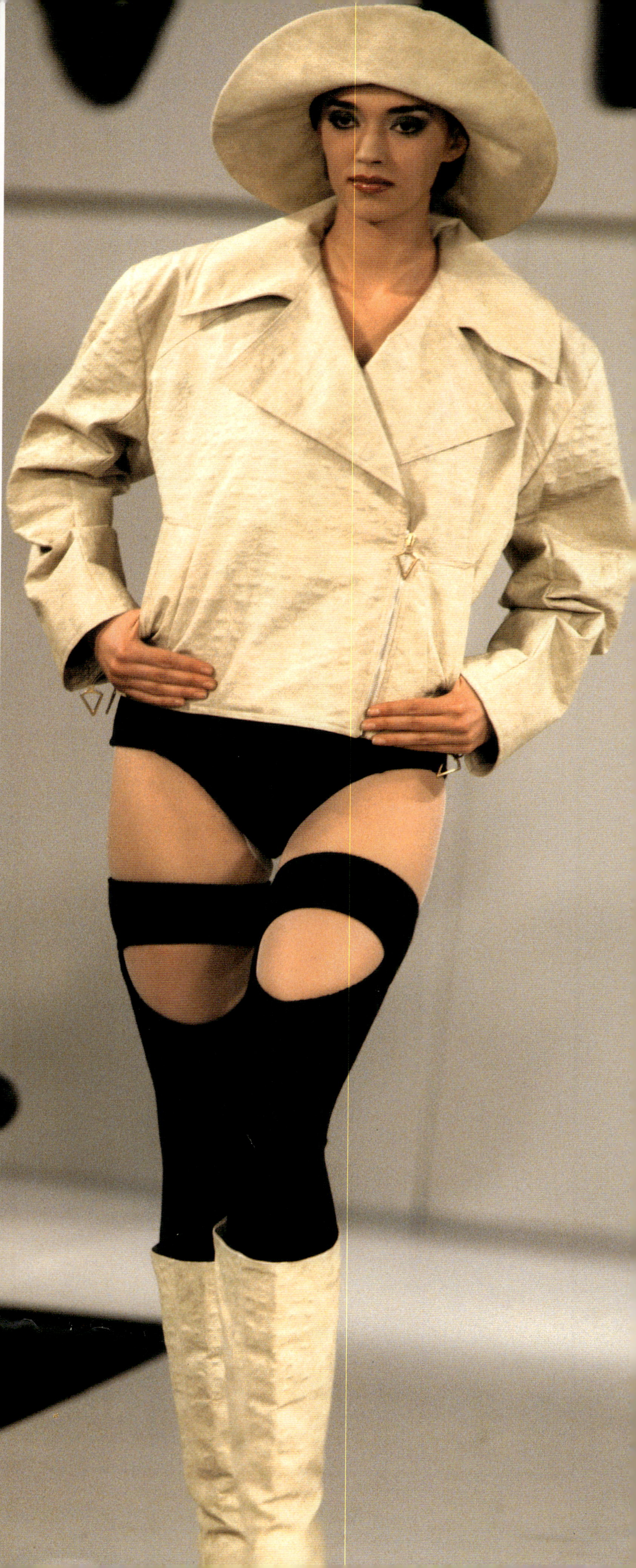

VAL PIRIOU

299

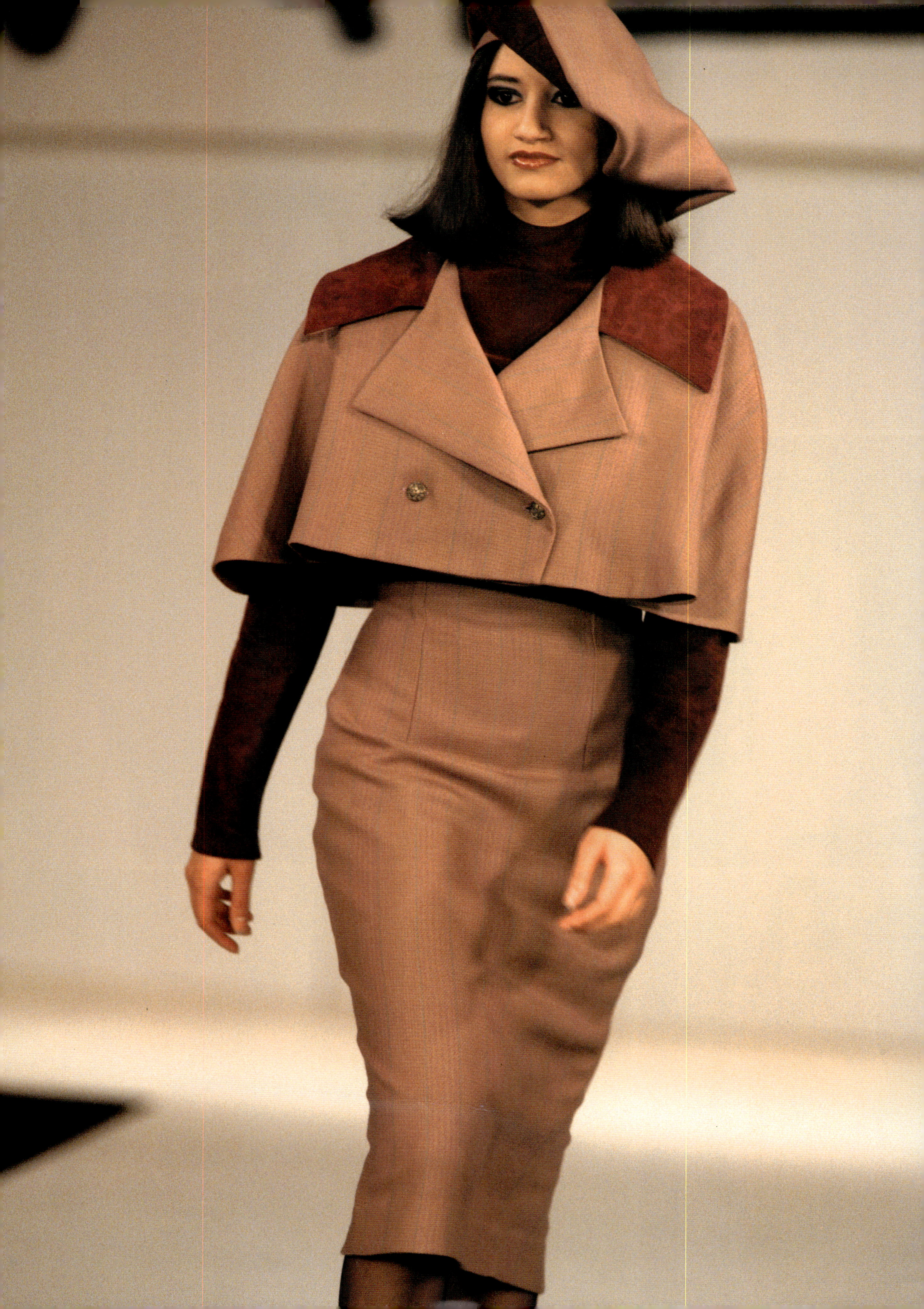

LONDON-3

TOMASZ STARZEWSKI

トーマス・スターゼウスキィ

クチュールのデザイナーだけあってエレガントさはロンドン・コレクション随一。ベルベットやサテンのプリーツ・ドレス、ツイードのスーツが大人の秋に彩りを添える。

A couture designer, he was the best at the London collection in expressing elegance.
His autumn adult wear was colored with pleated dresses of velvet and satin, along with tweed suits.

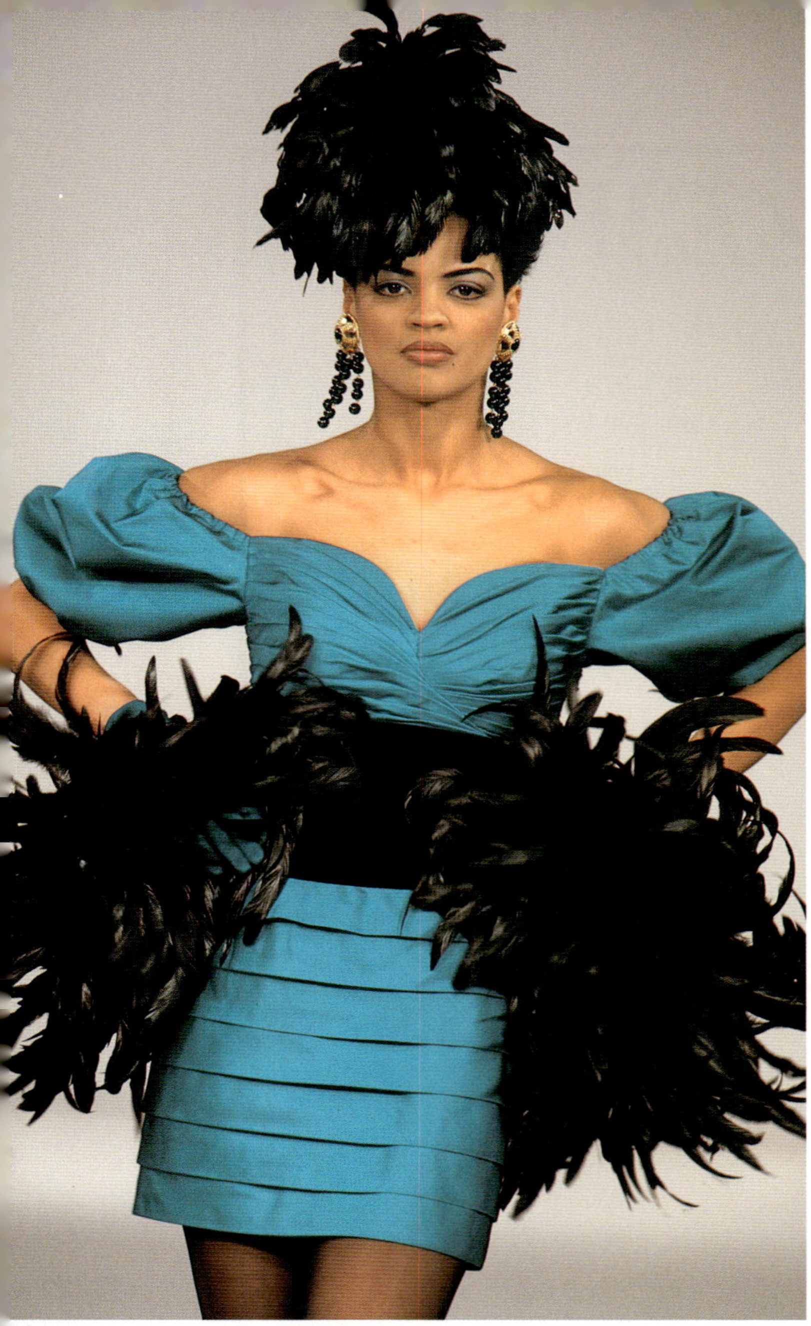
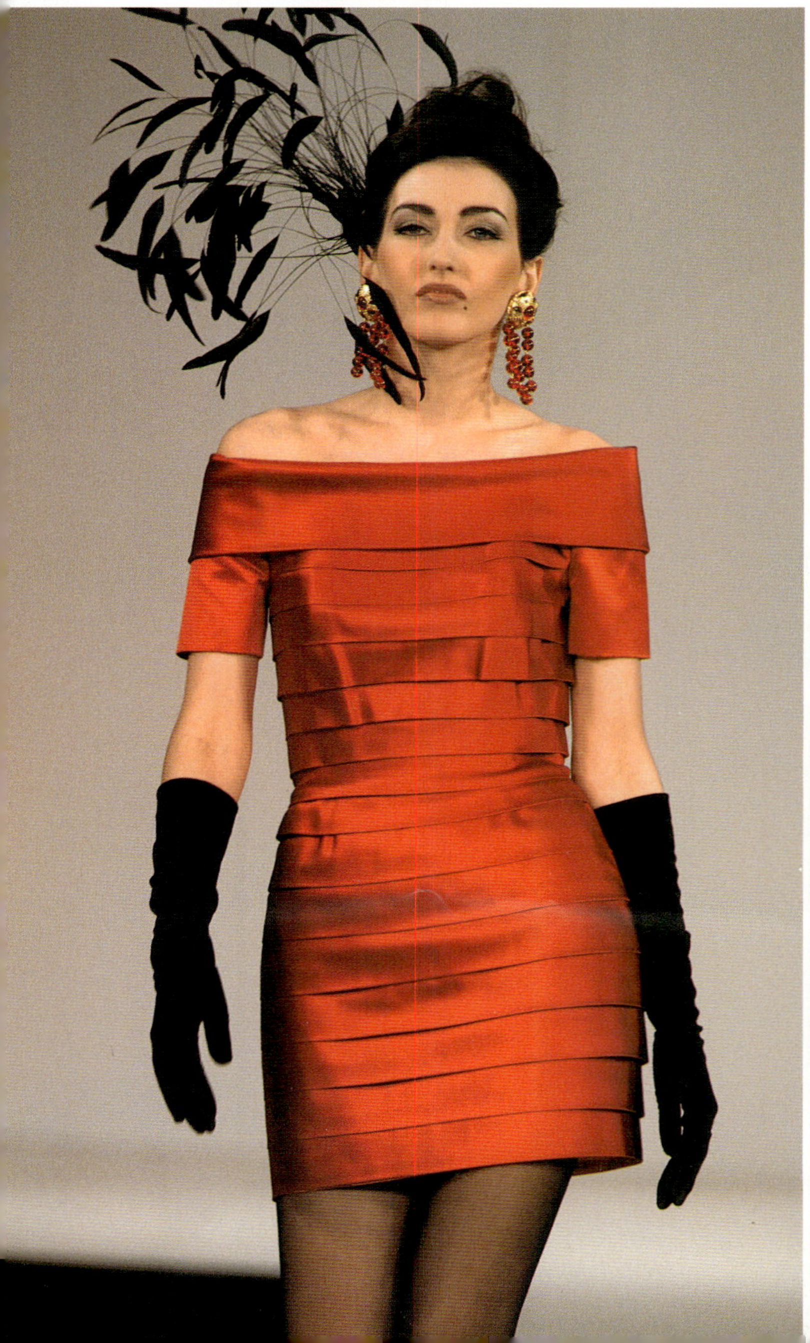
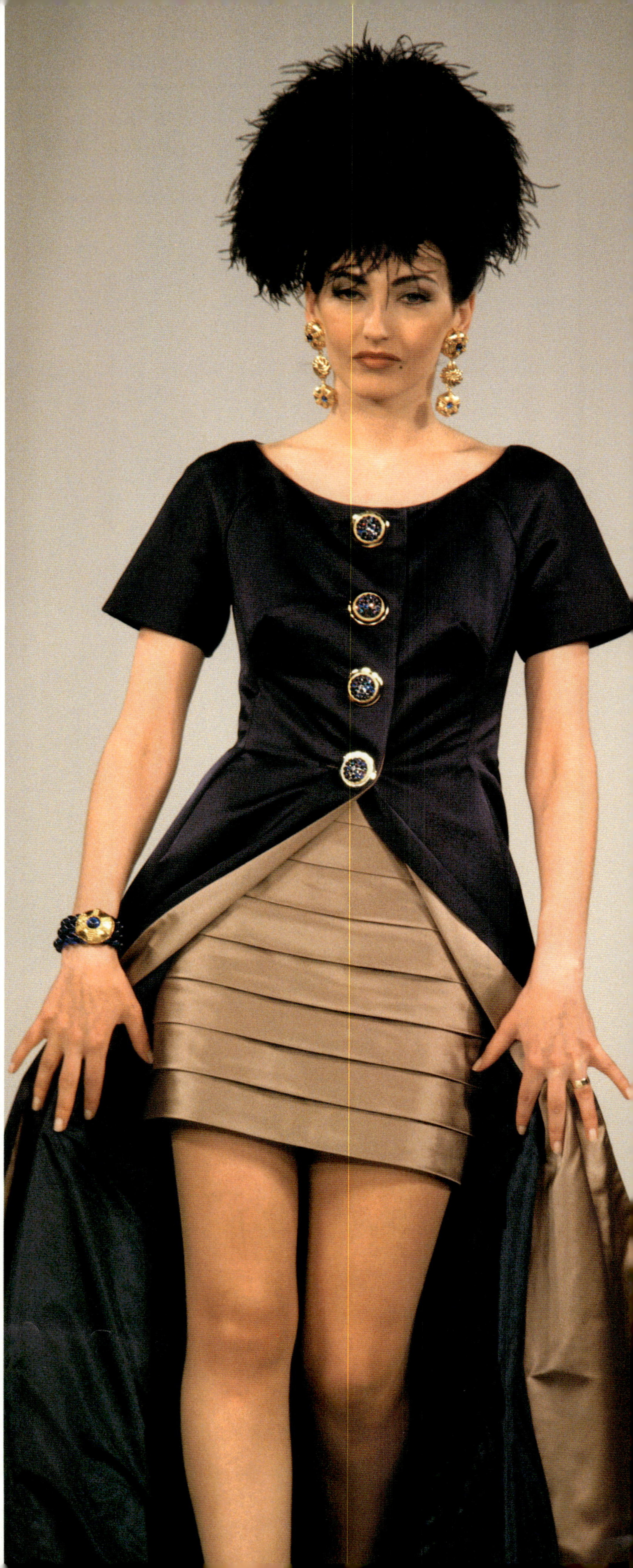

TOMASZ STARZEWSKI

303

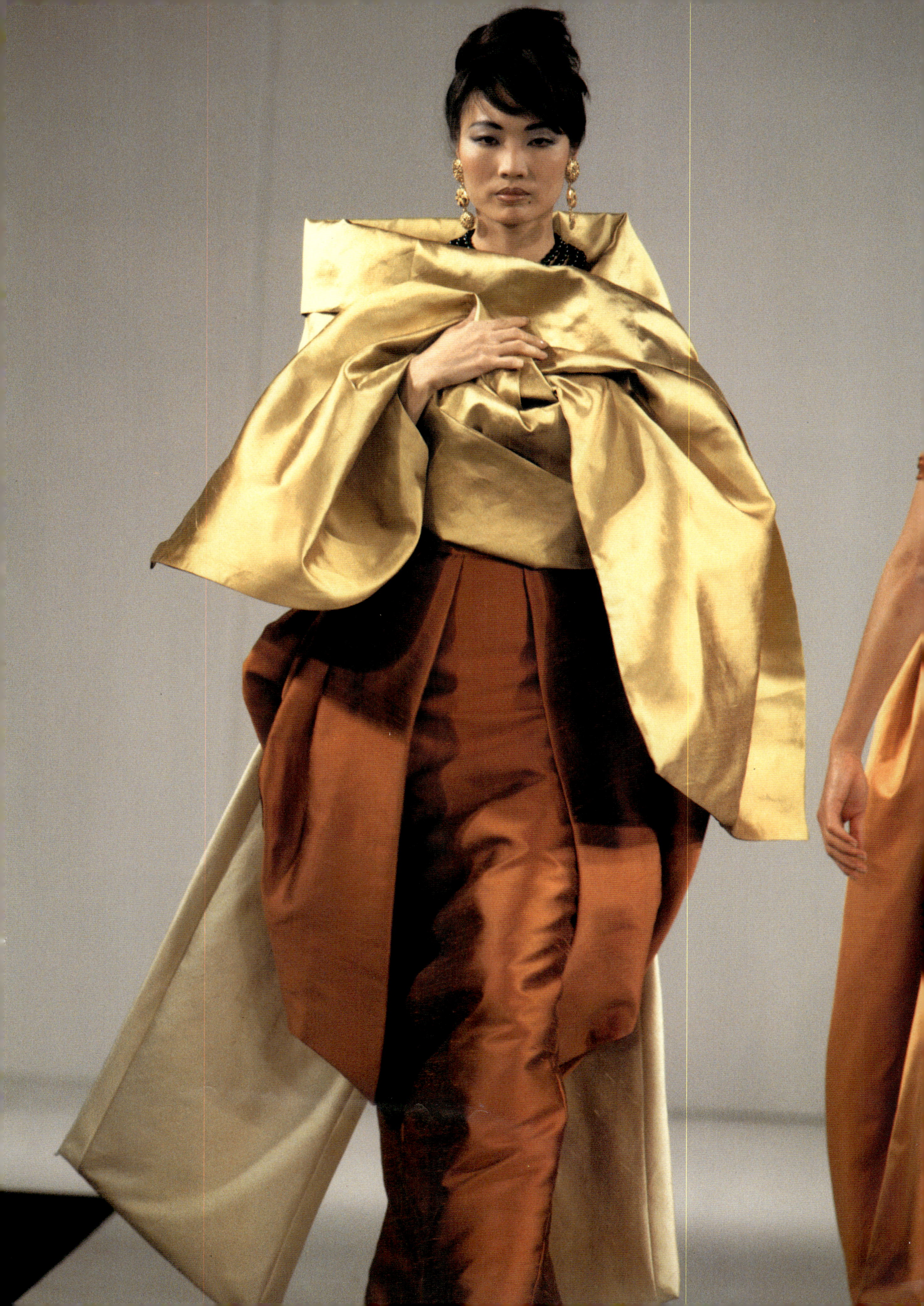

HELEN STOREY

ヘレン・ストーリー

ビニール、レザー、ラメといった冷たい感触の素材を使って、ボディ・スーツからイヴニングまでをカバーしたエレガント・パンク。

Displaying an elegant pank style, her collection ranged from body suits to evening wear, using materials with a cold feel such as vinyl, leather and lamé.

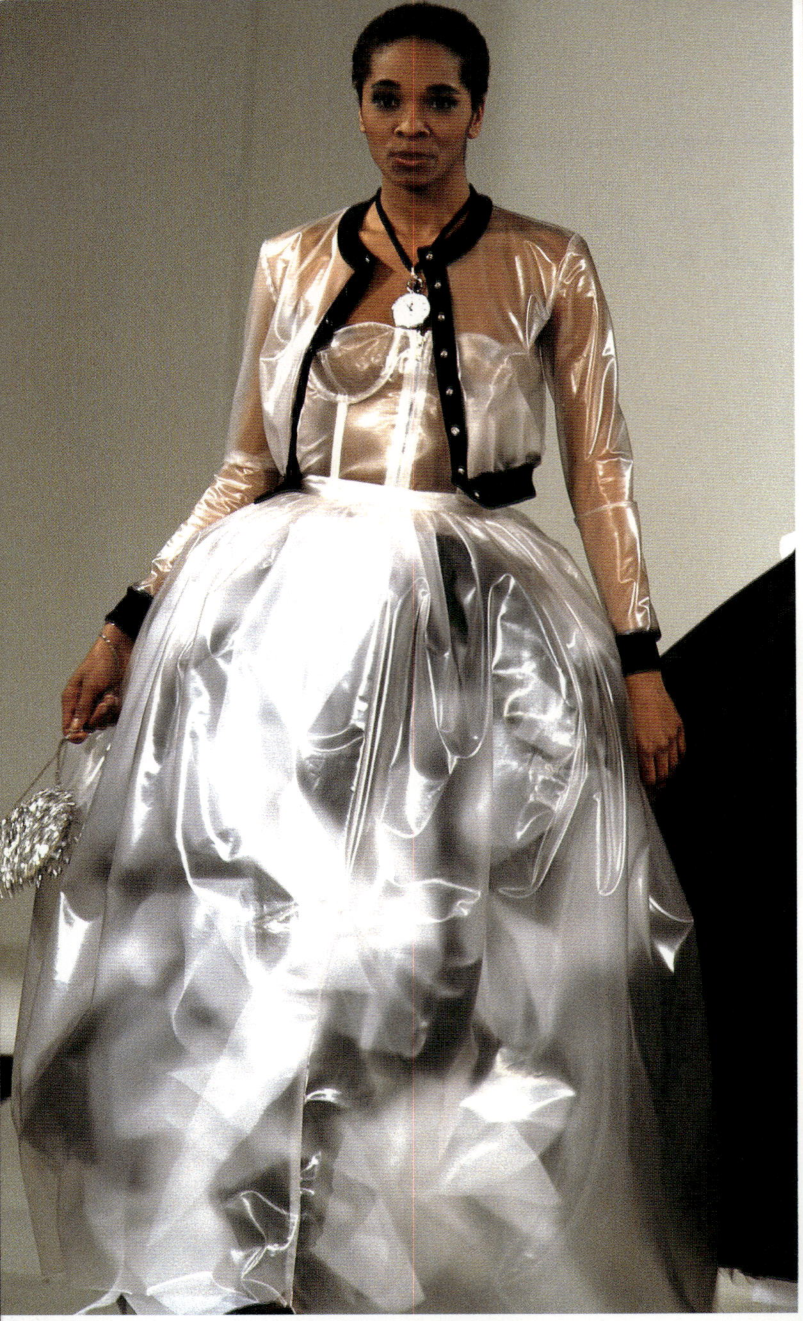
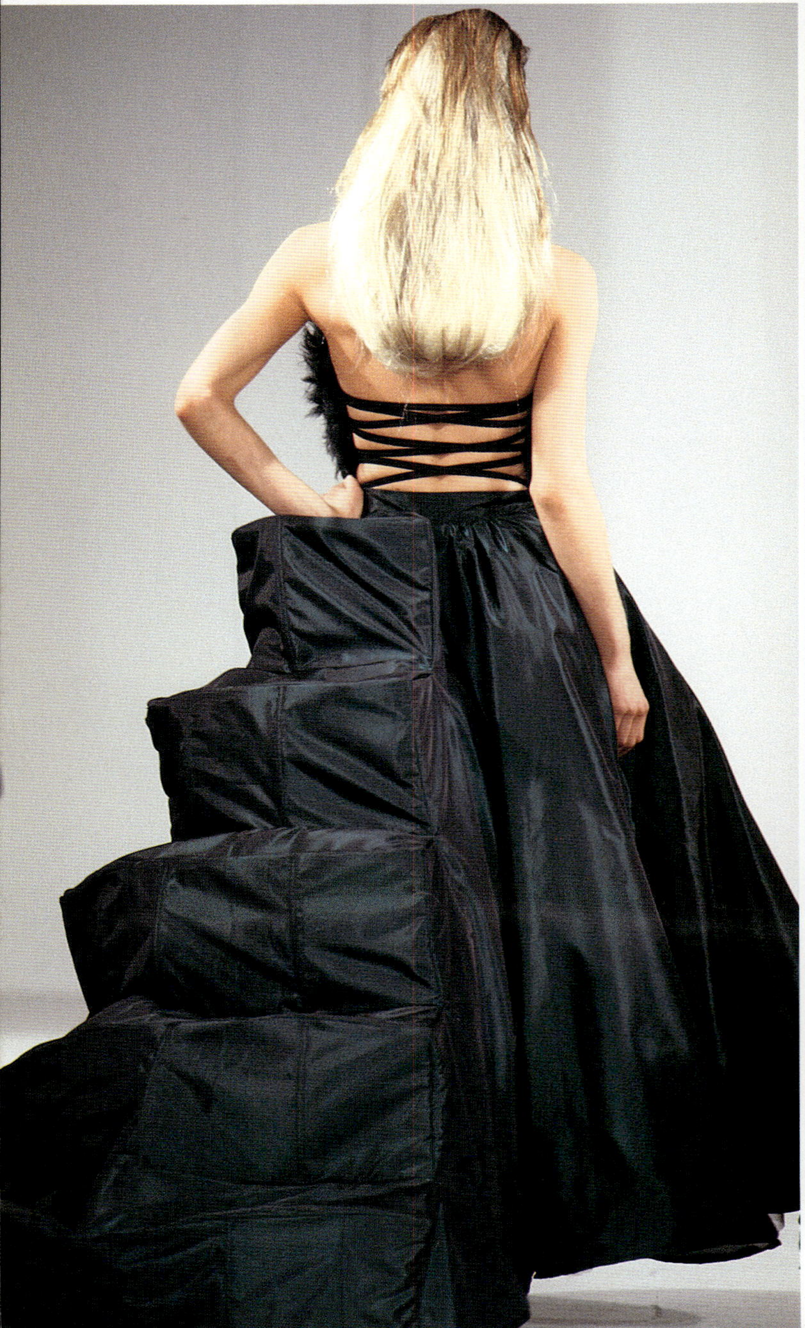
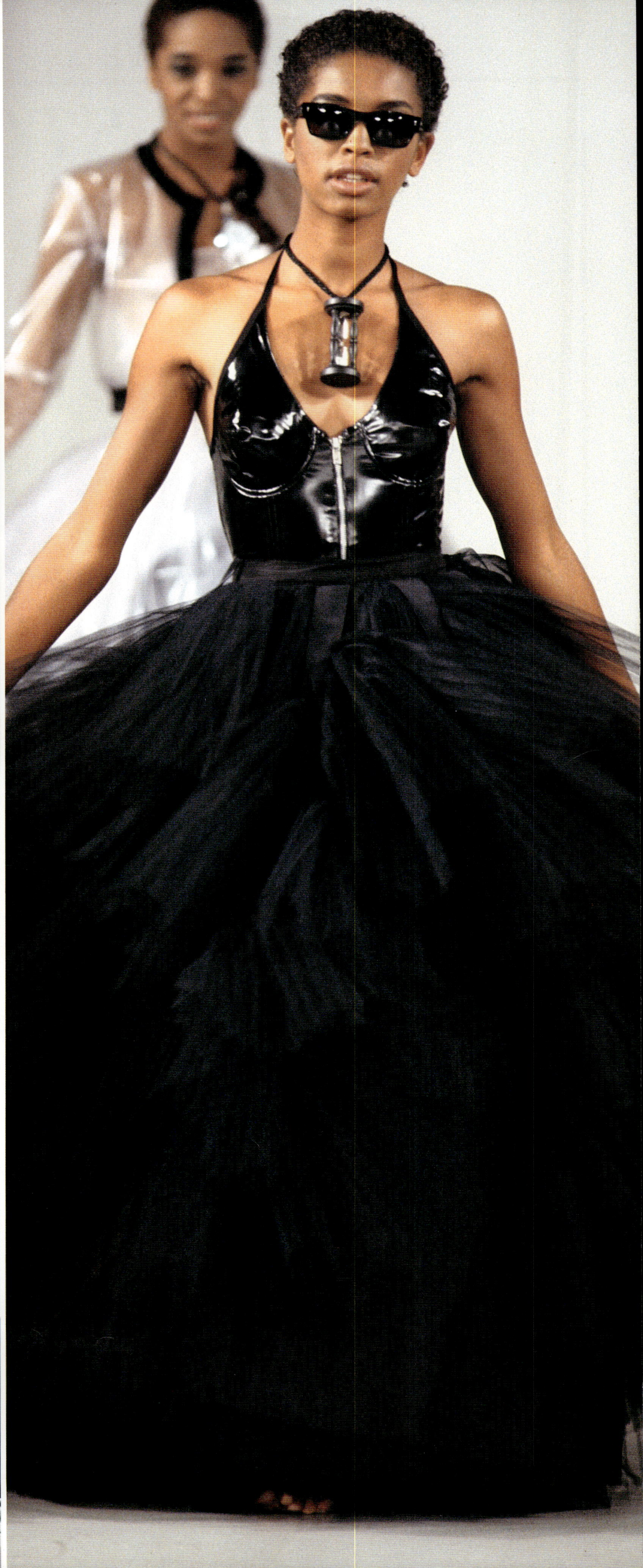

HELEN STOREY

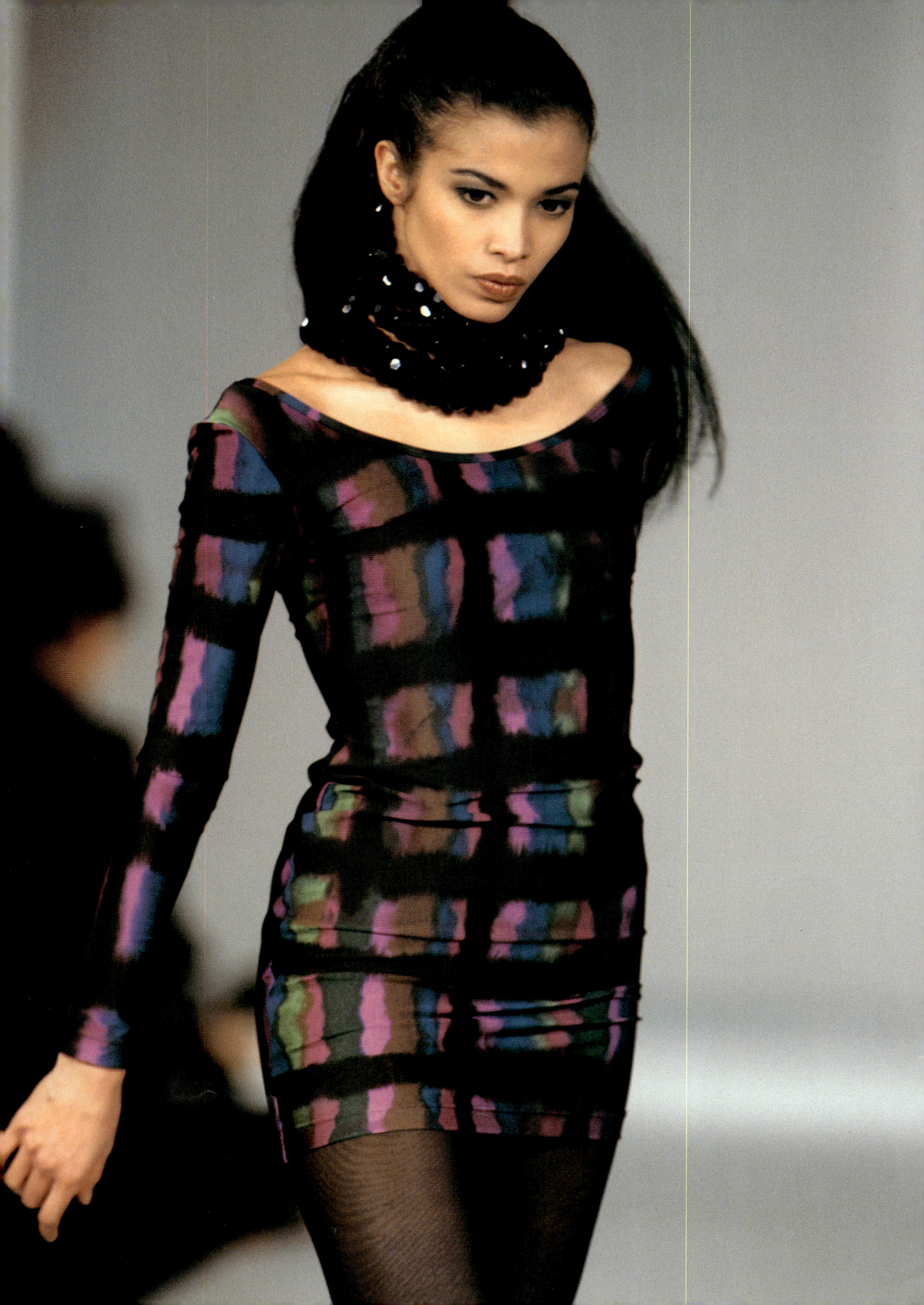

PAM HOGG

パム・ホッグ

パム・ホッグといえばボディ・スーツ。今回も多種多様な素材で特に胸を強調している。シースルーのシャツが'70年代を彷彿させる。

Her work was represented by the body suit, displayed in a variety of materials. Special emphasis was given to the breast line. Her see-through shirts reminded us of the '70's.

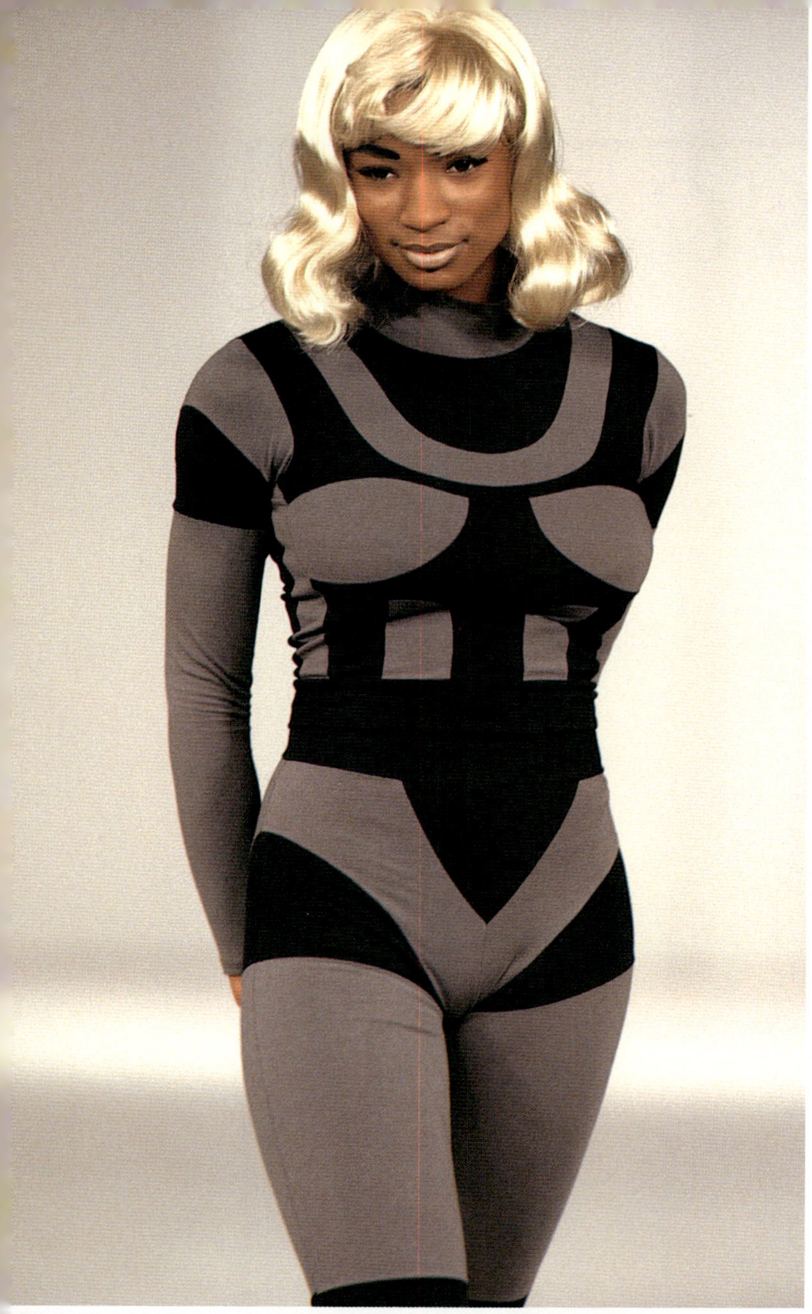
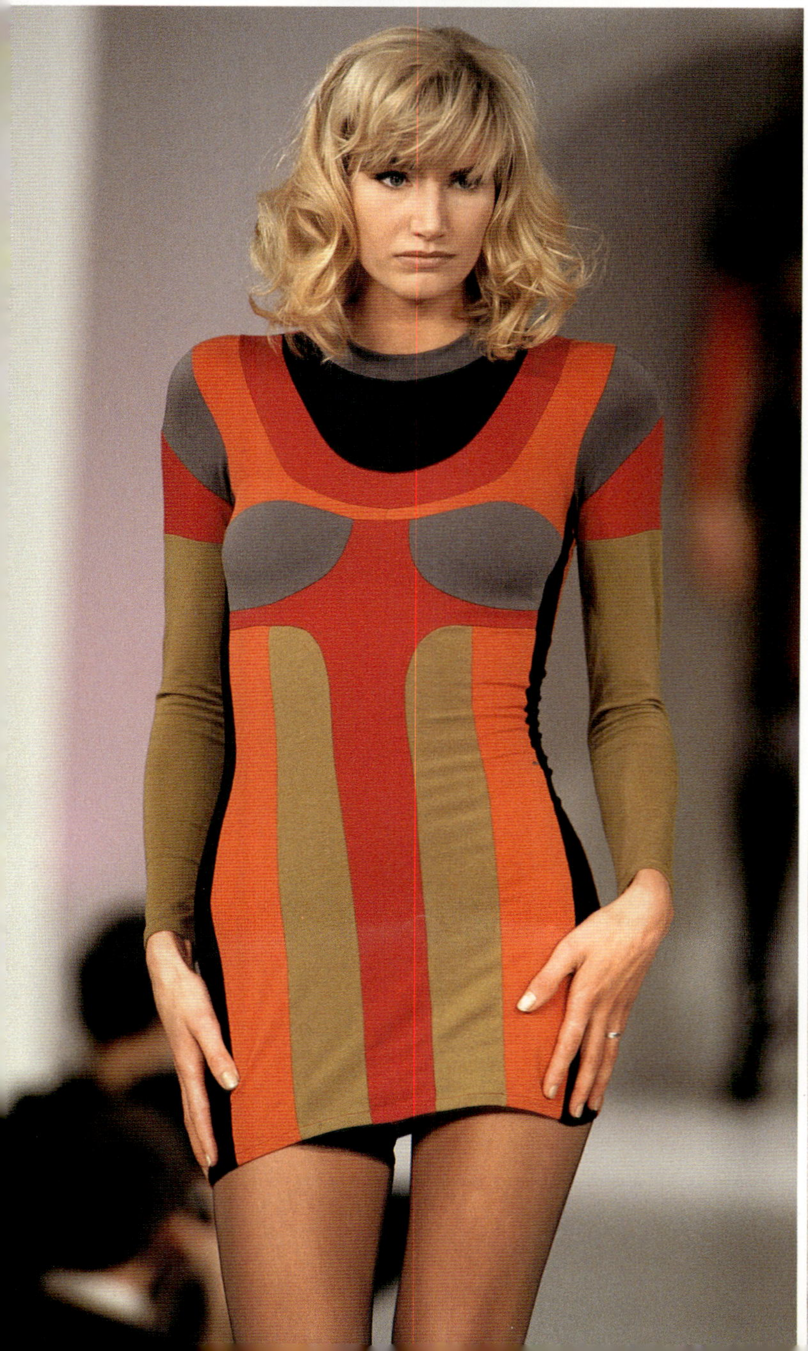
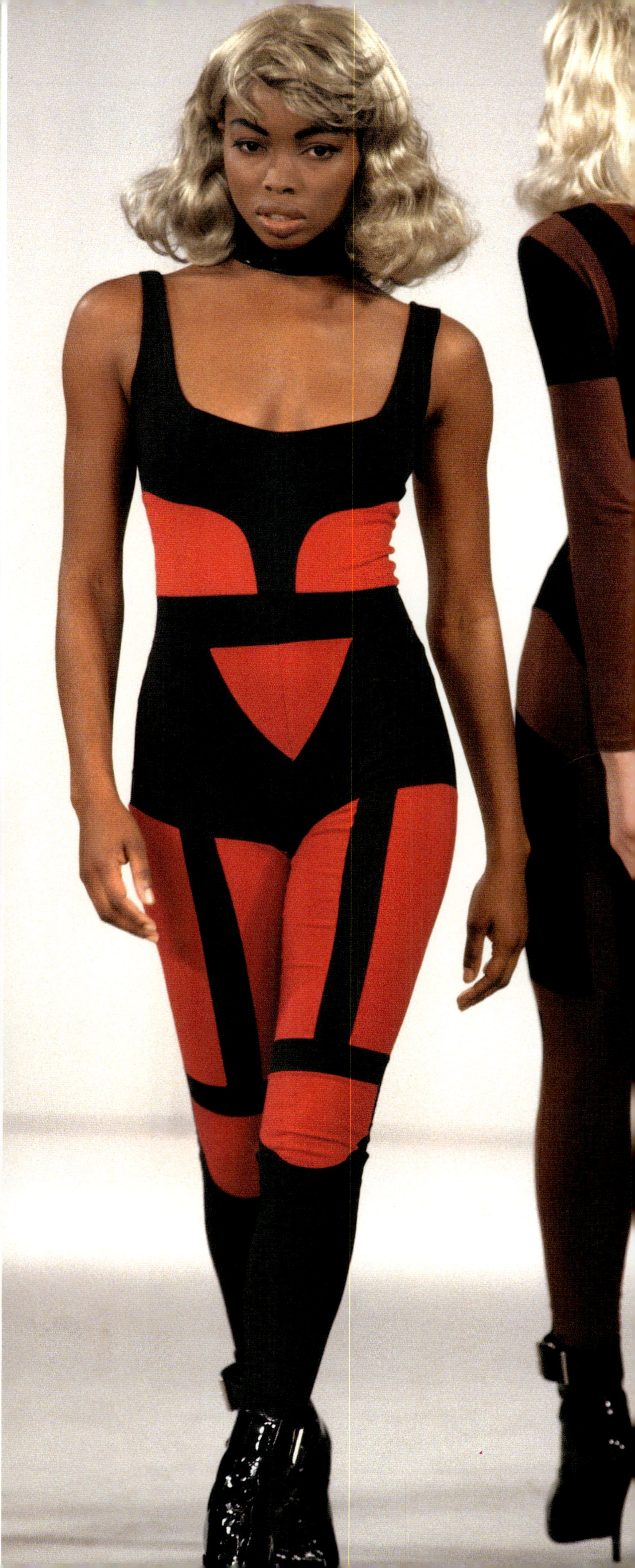

PAM HOGG

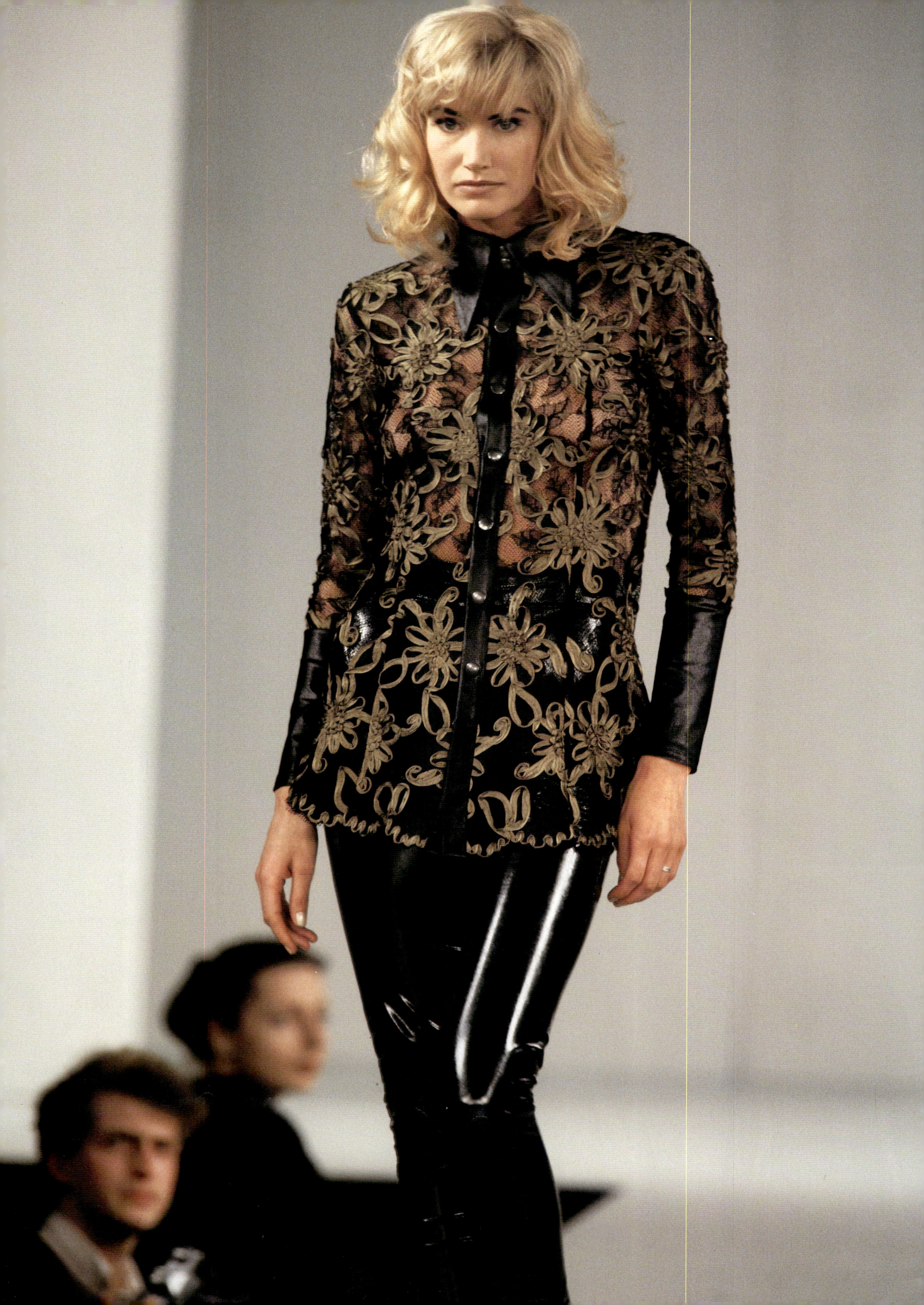

CAROLINE CHARLES

キャロライン・チャールズ

鮮やかな色彩とソフィスティケートされたデザインで、ノーブルな女性たちへのライフ・スタイルを提案している。
Proposing a life style for the noble women, she displayed vivid colors and a sophisticated design.

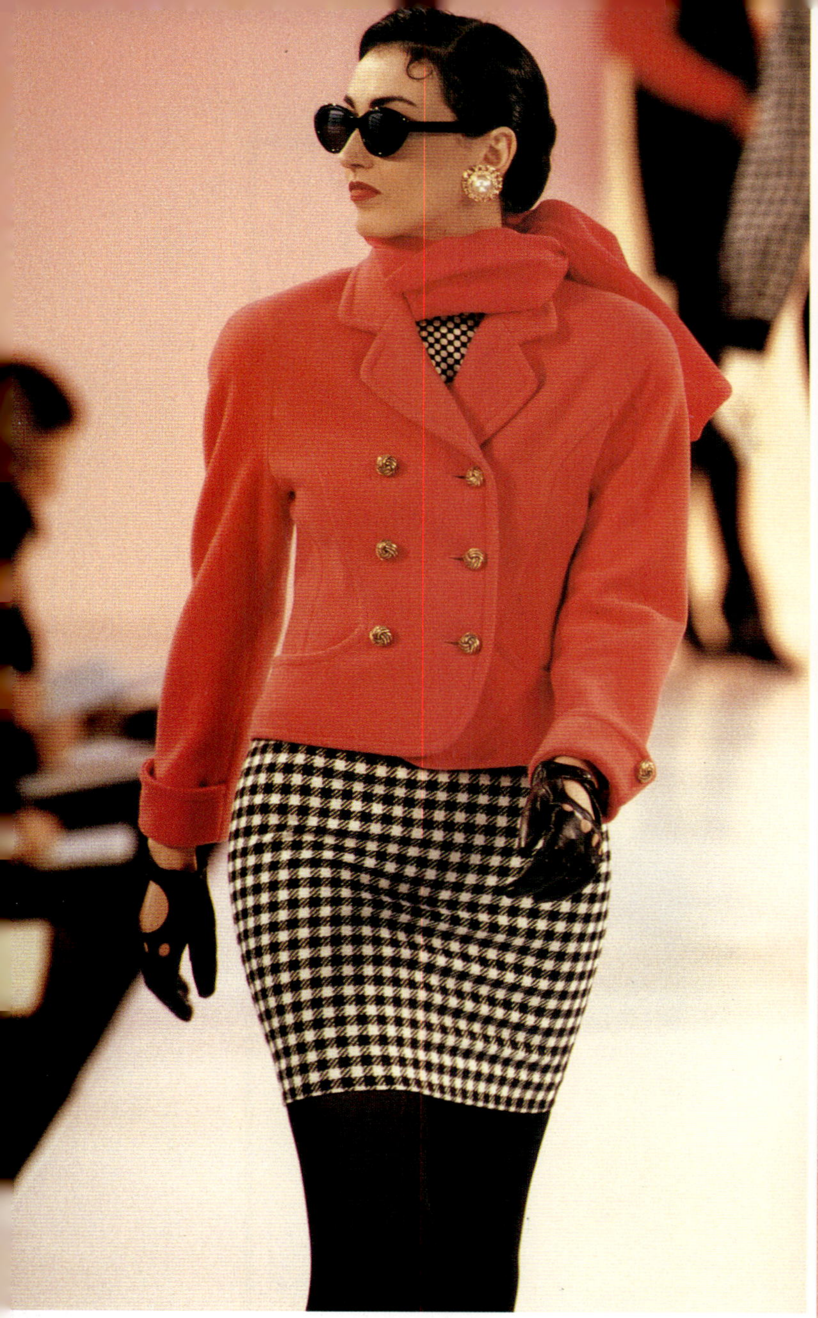
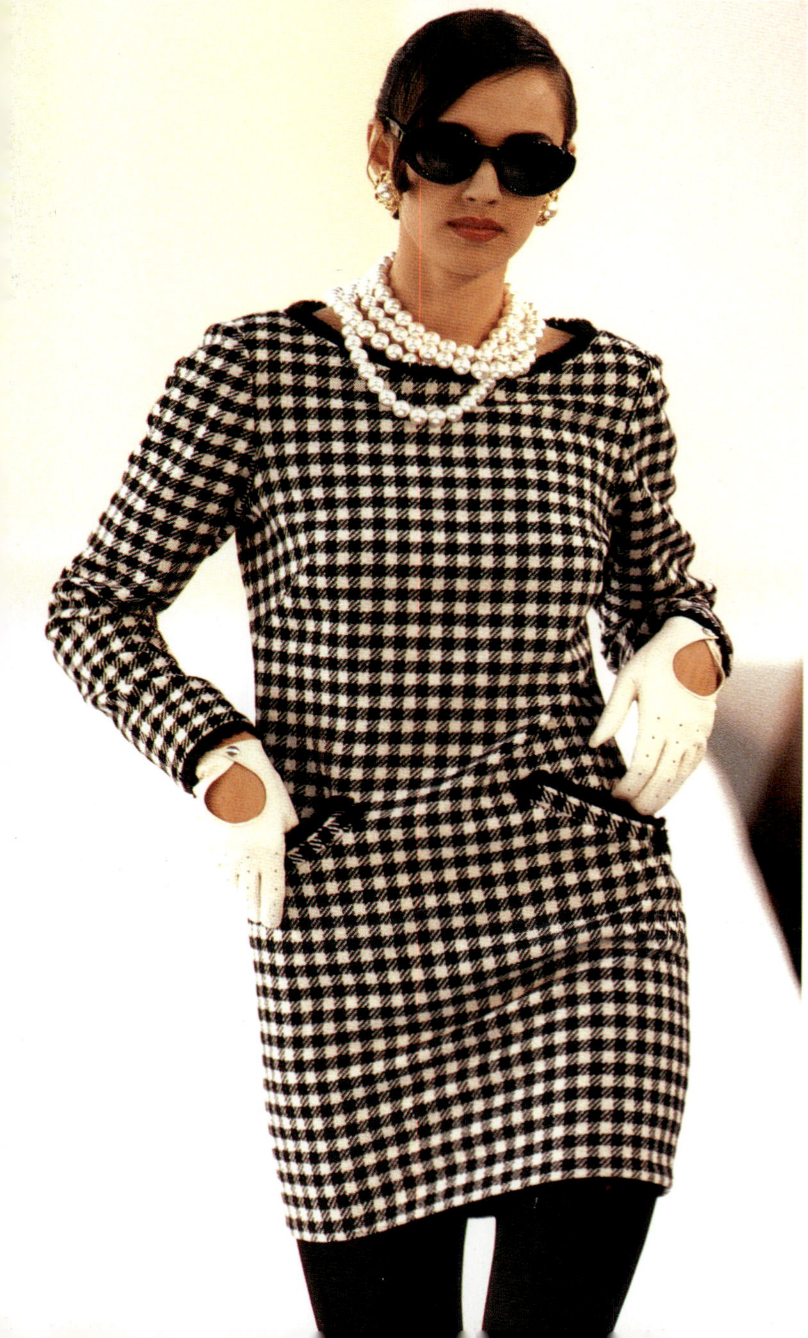
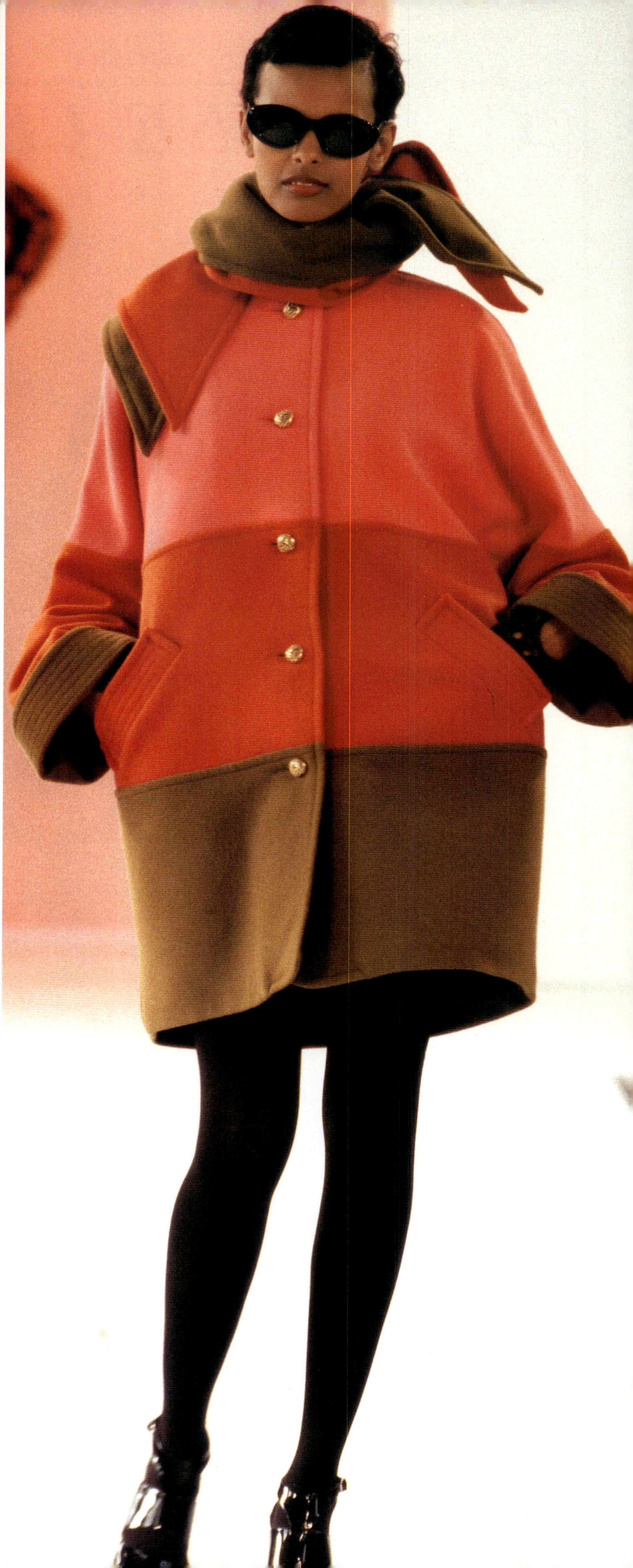

CAROLINE CHARLES

315

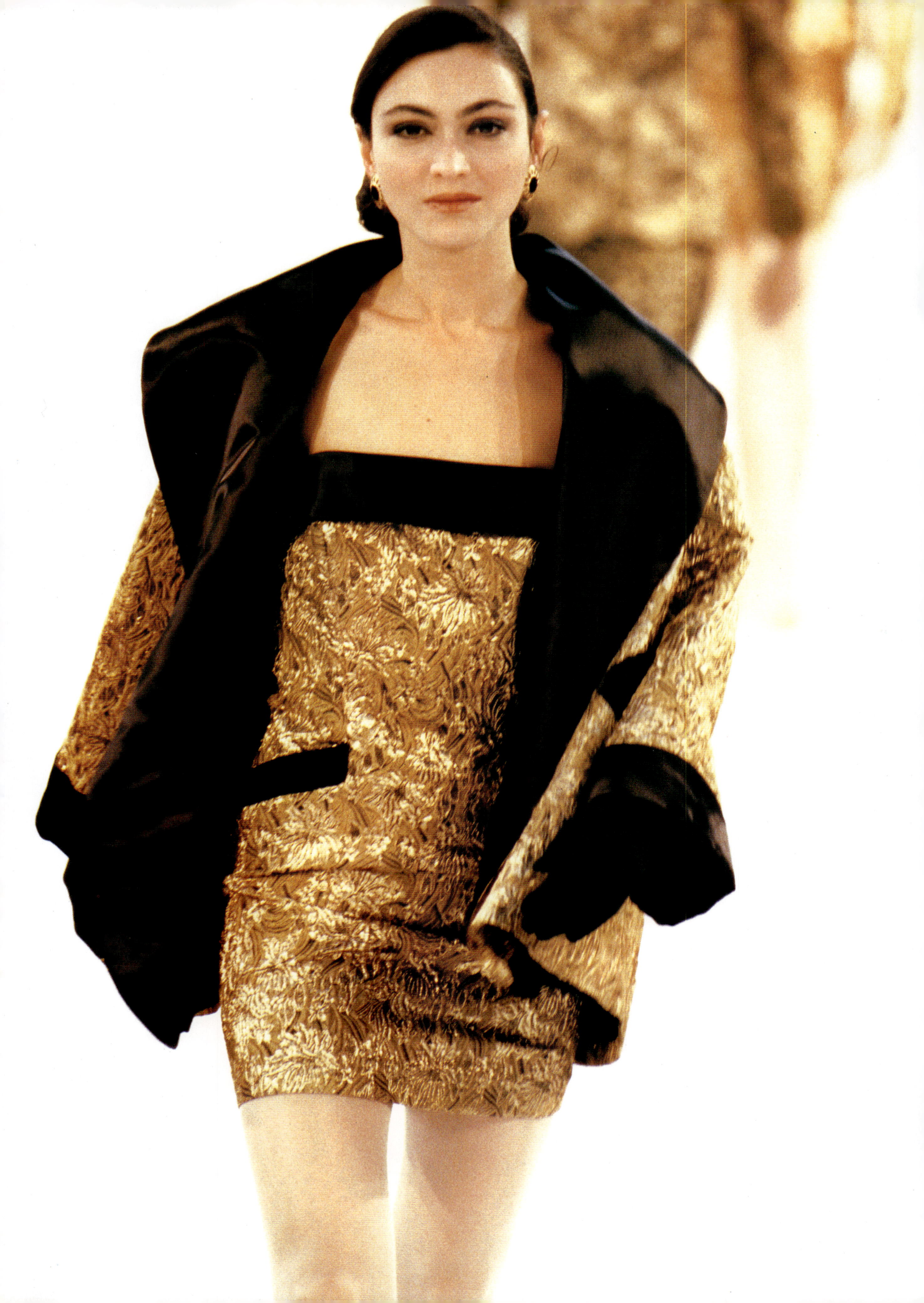

LONDON-7

ARABELLA POLLEN

アラベラ・ポーラン

ボディ・スーツにロングのベスト、ハイ・ウエストのワンピース、シースルーのシャツにジャンパー・スカートと、'60年代後半から'70年代の要素が盛りだくさん。

She produced a collection filled with the essence of the late '60's to the '70's,
Presenting body suits with long vests, high waisted one-pieces and see-through shirts with jumper skirts.

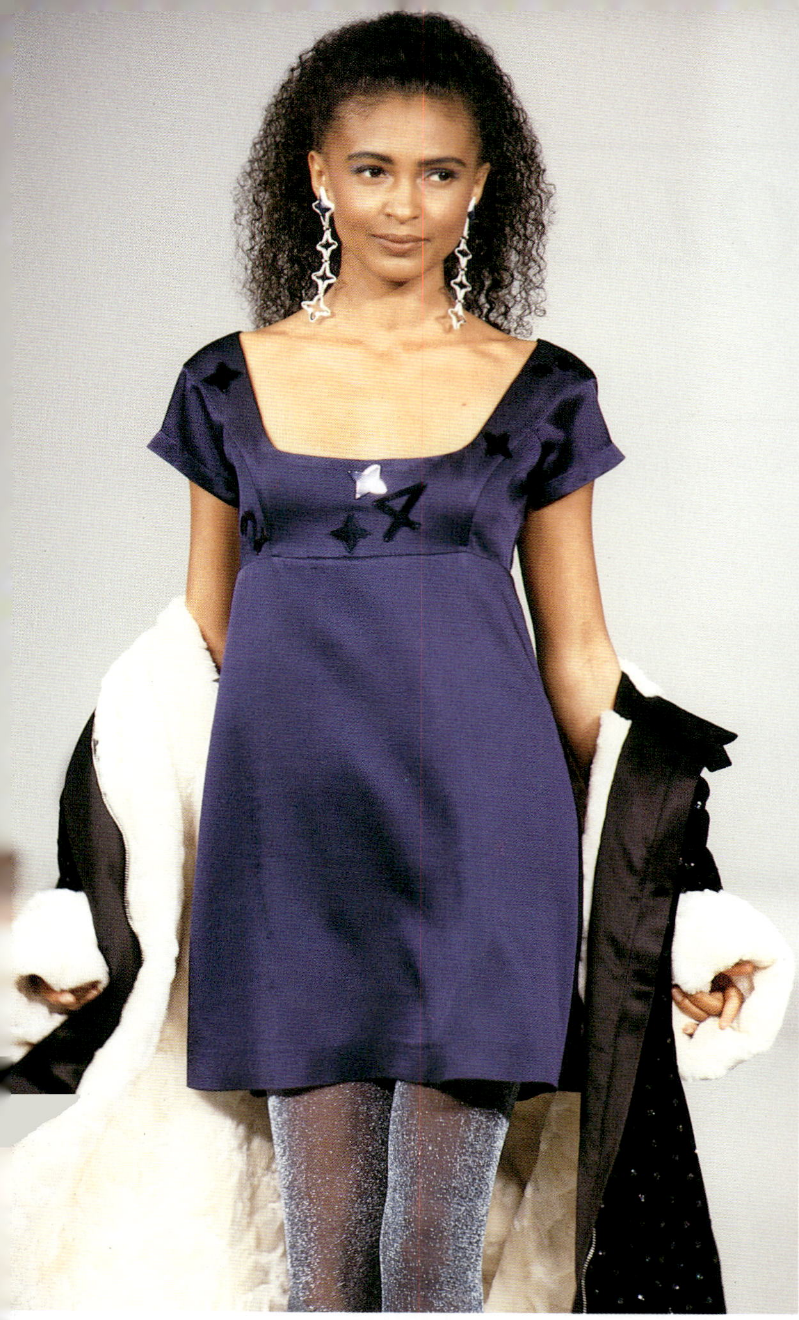
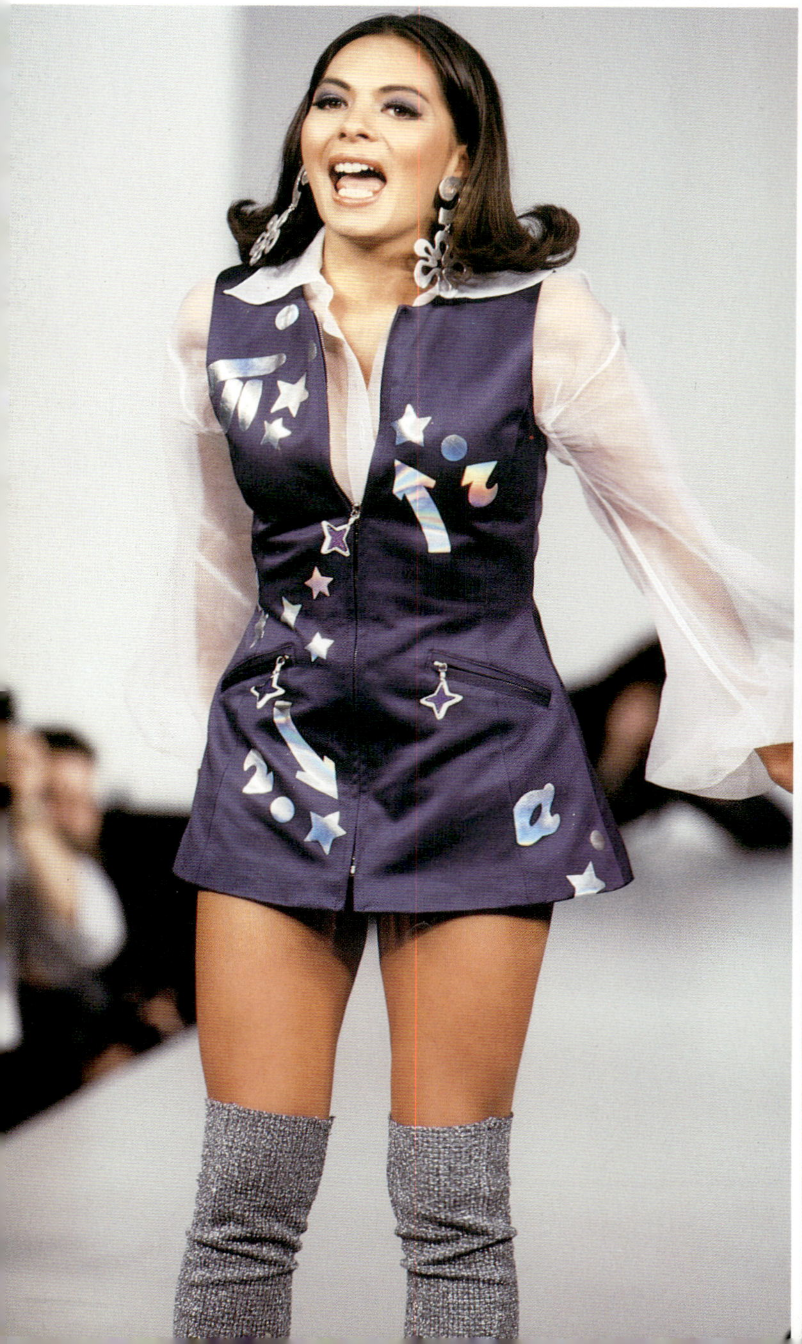
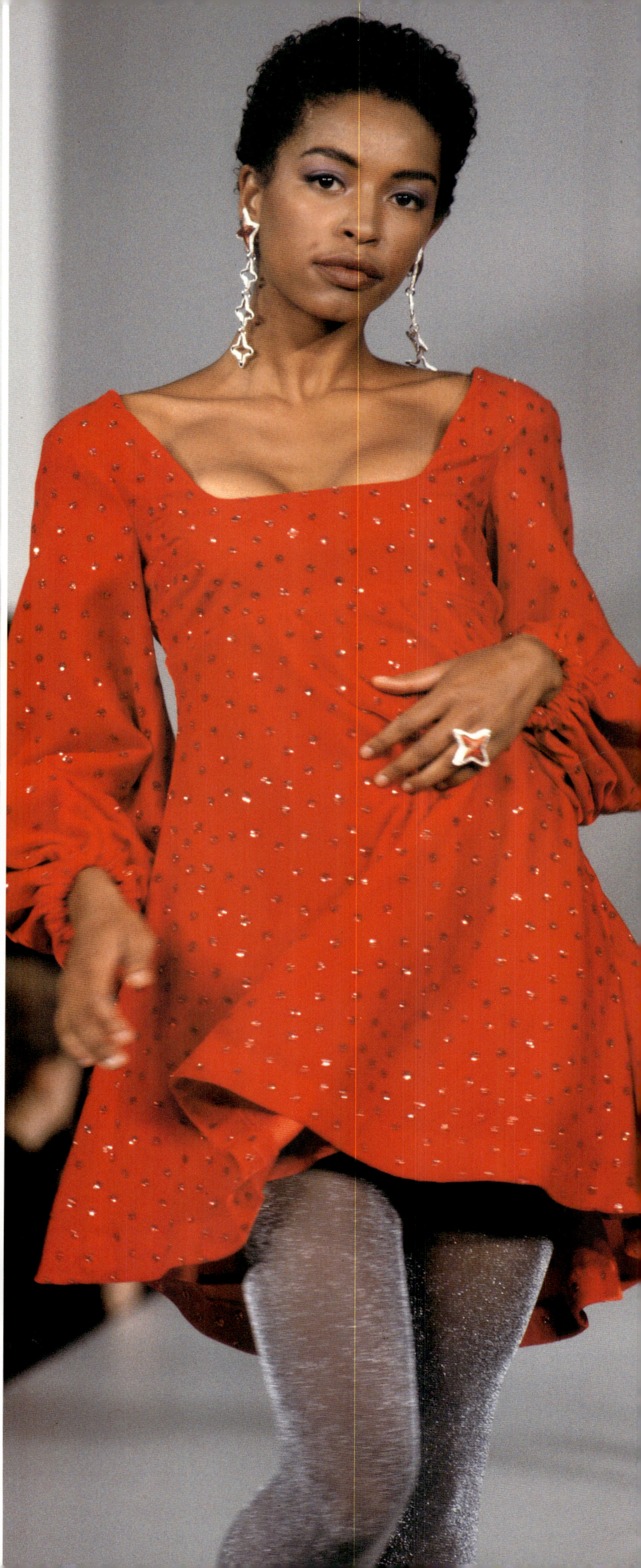

ARABELLA POLLEN

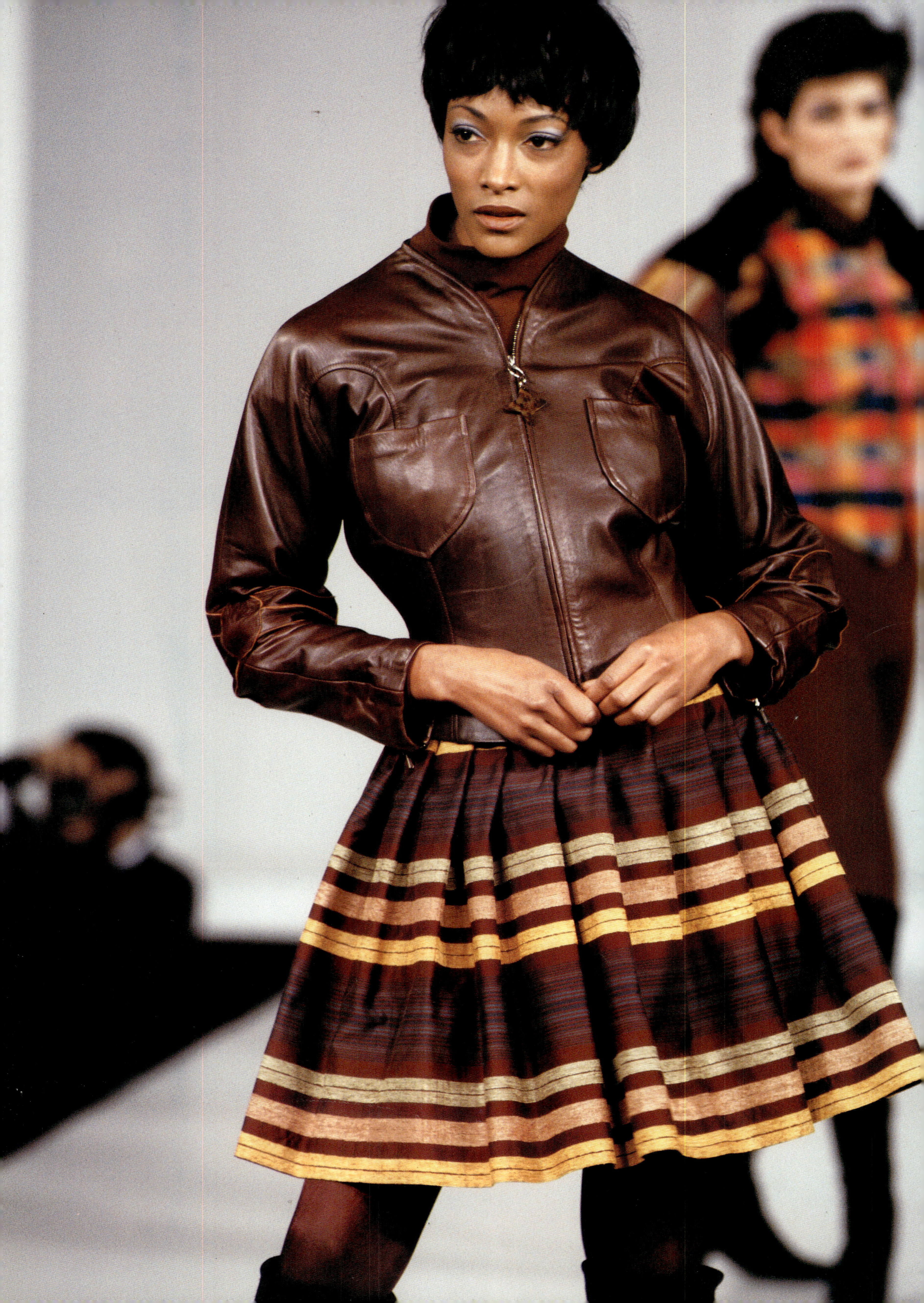

RED OR DEAD

レッド・オア・デッド

犬猫プリントのビニールのレインコートをはじめ遊び心たっぷりのコレクションのテーマは"オリバー・ツイスト、ベガスでエルビスに会う"。
The collection was displayed in a playful way, beginning with such items as vinyl raincoats with cat and dog prints. The theme was "Oliver Twist meets Elvis in Las Vegas."

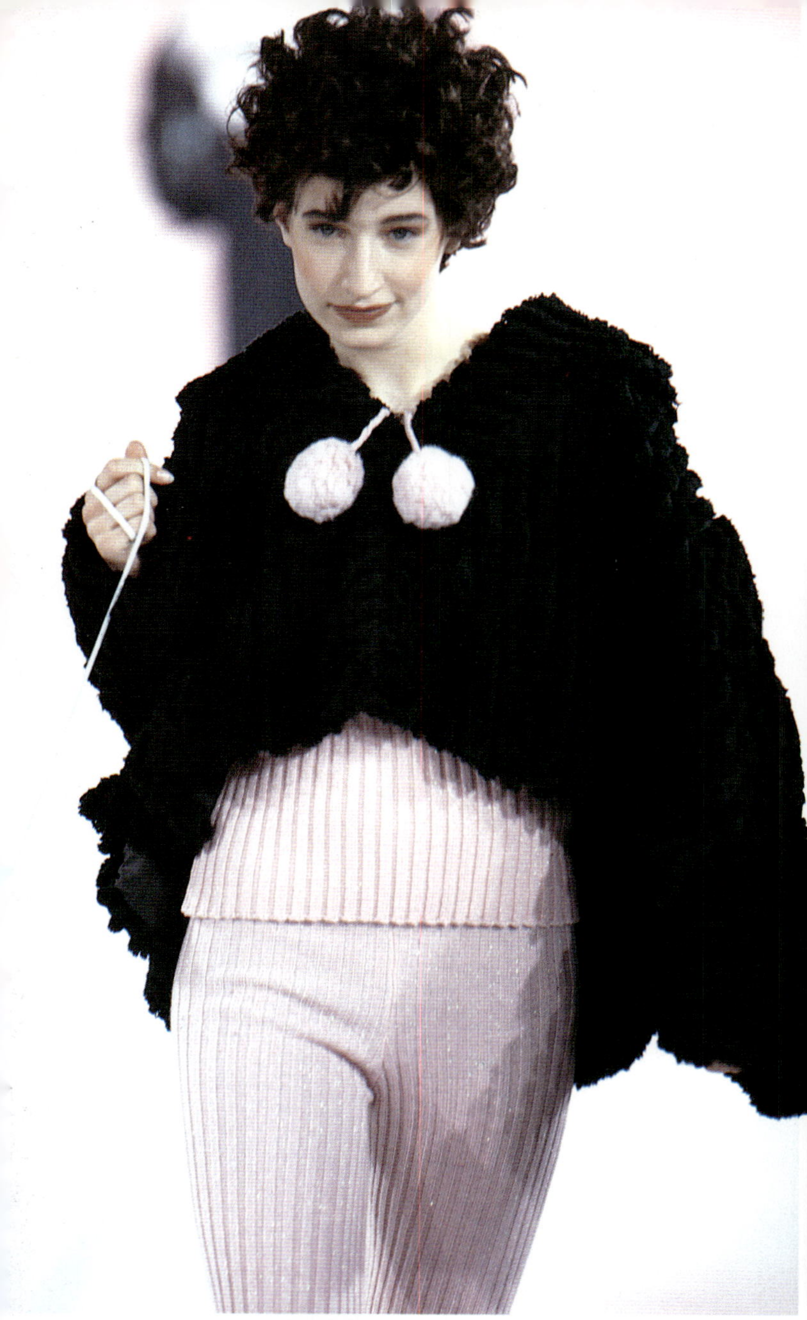
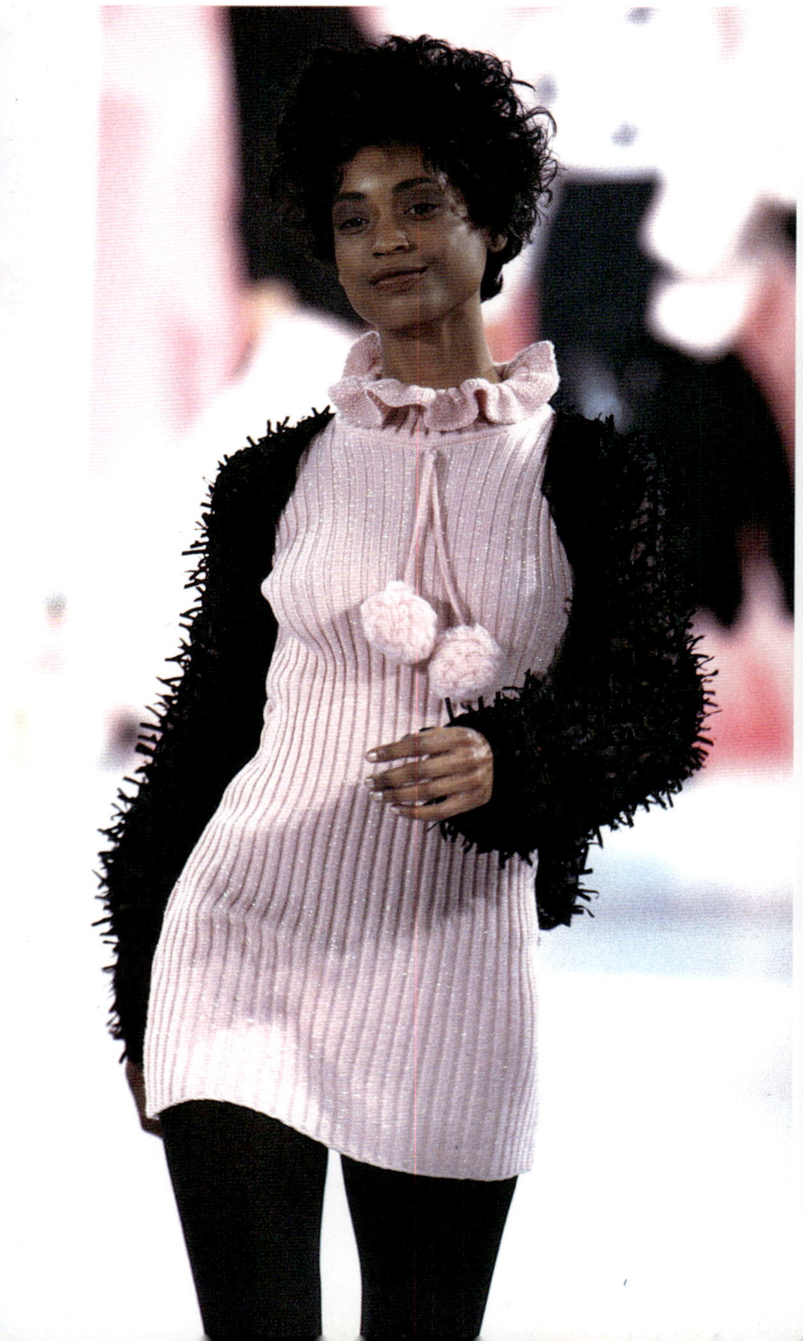
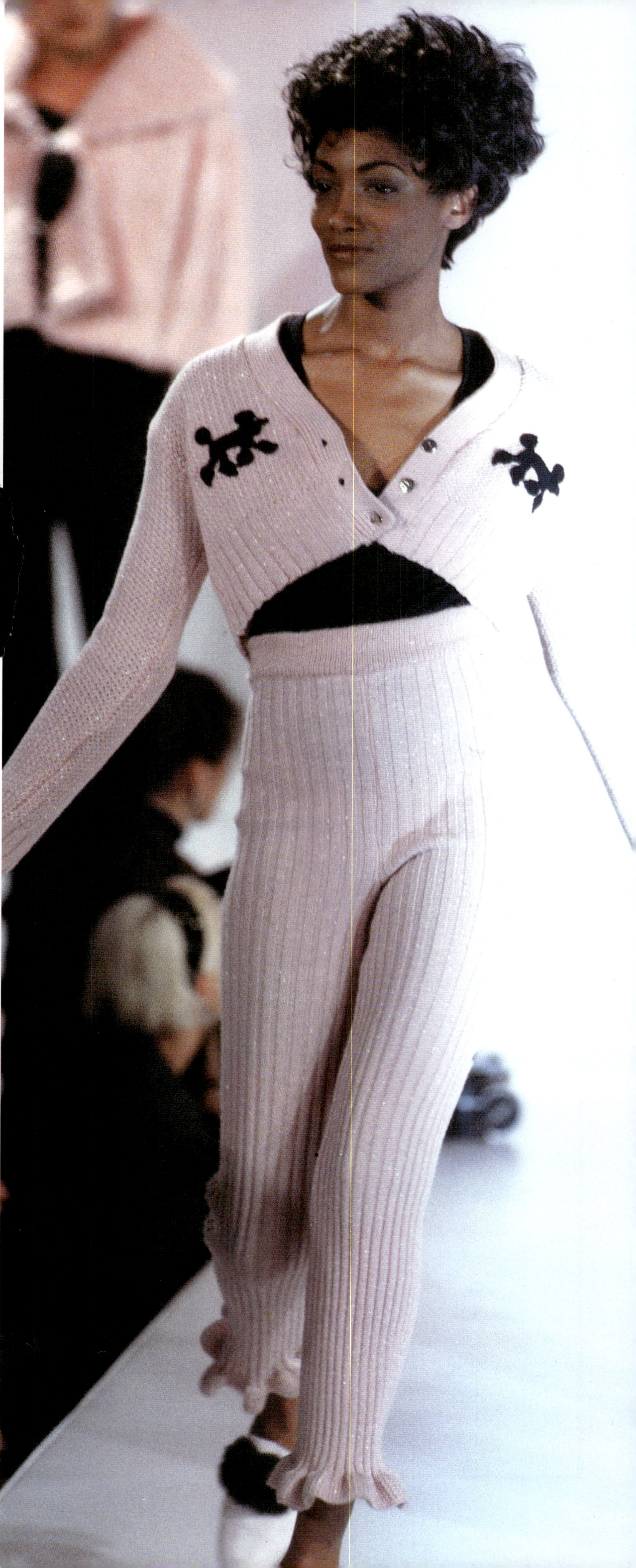

RED OR DEAD

323

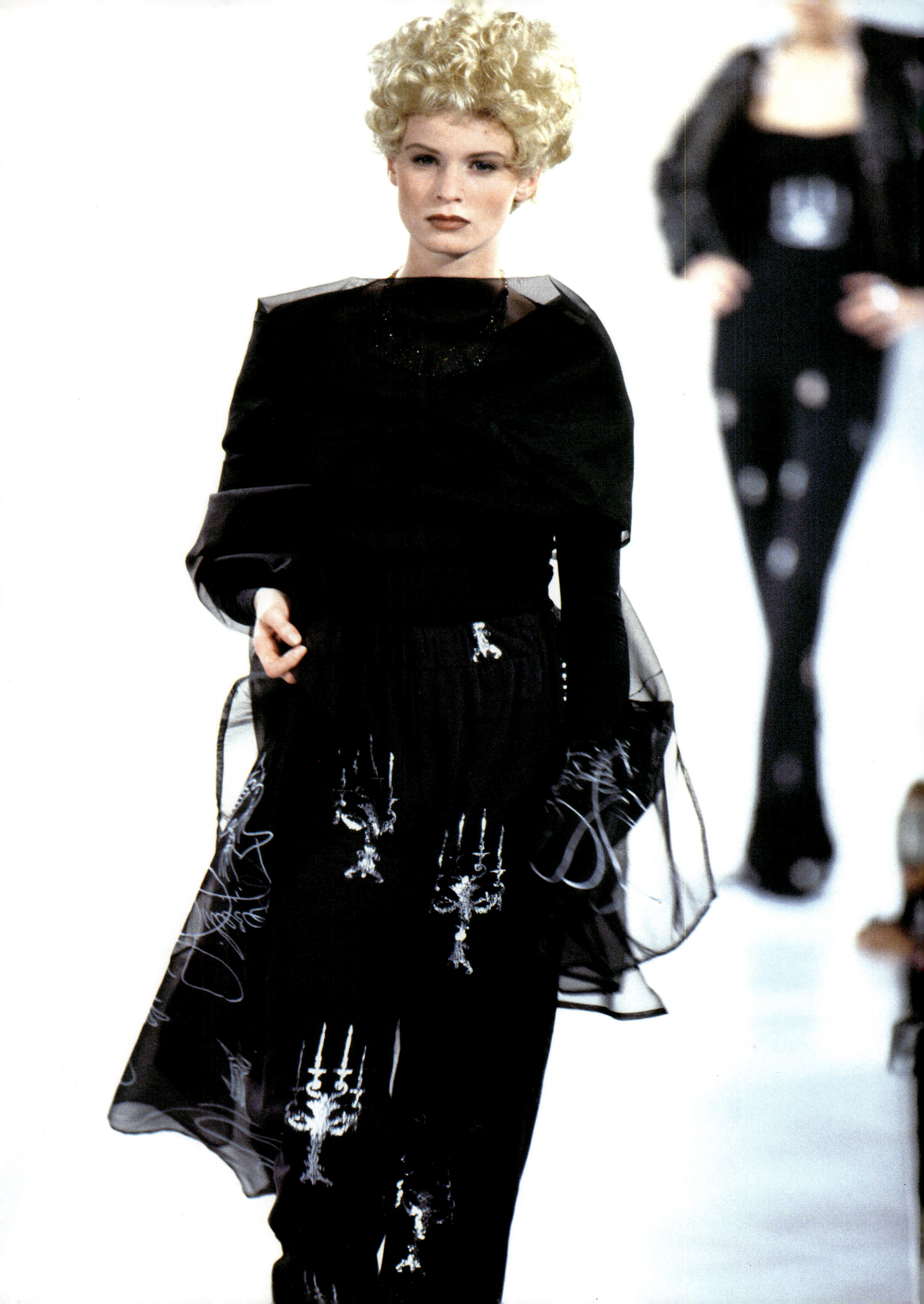

EDINA RONAY

エディーナ・ロネイ

カラフルな色使いがデザインのシンプルさを引き立てる。ステンド・グラスを思わせるドレスが、エキゾチックな趣を添えている。
Her simple designs were highlighted by their full use of colors. Dresses reminding us of stained glass added exotic features.

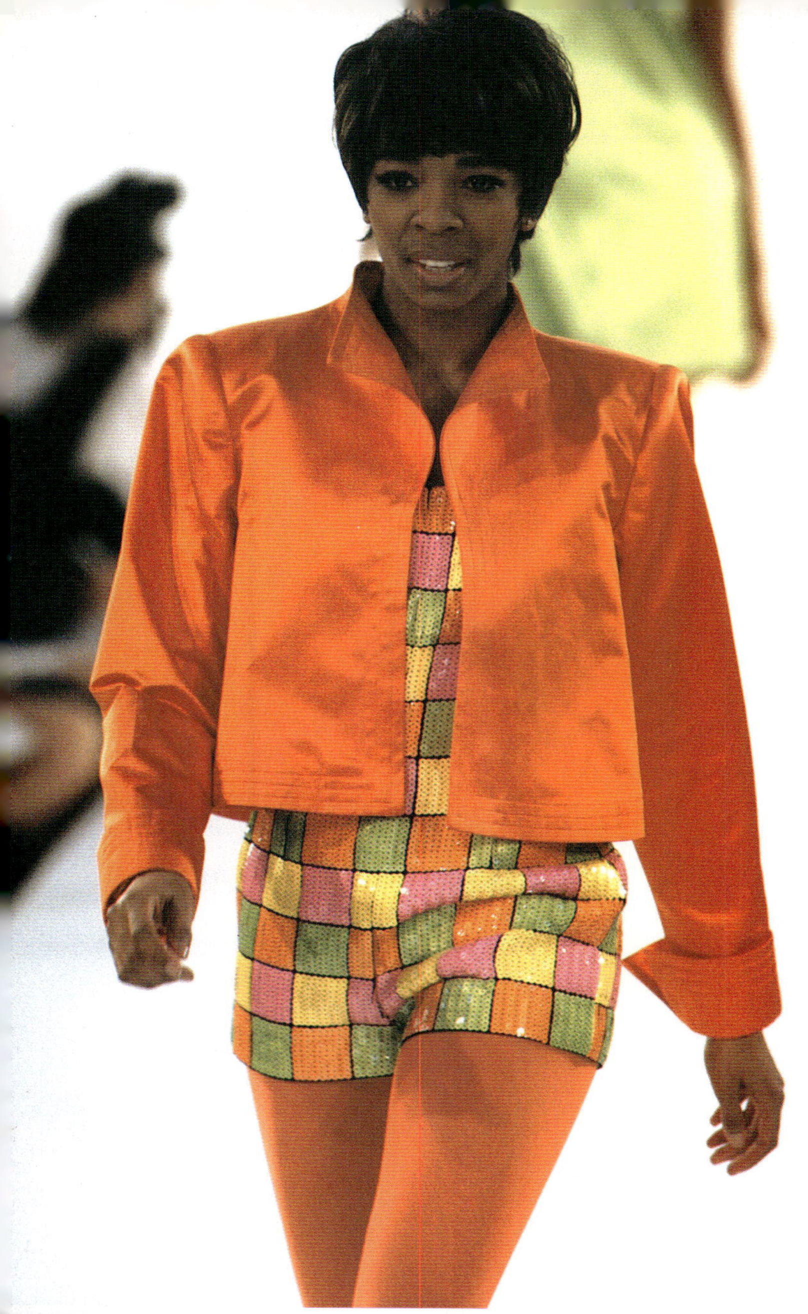

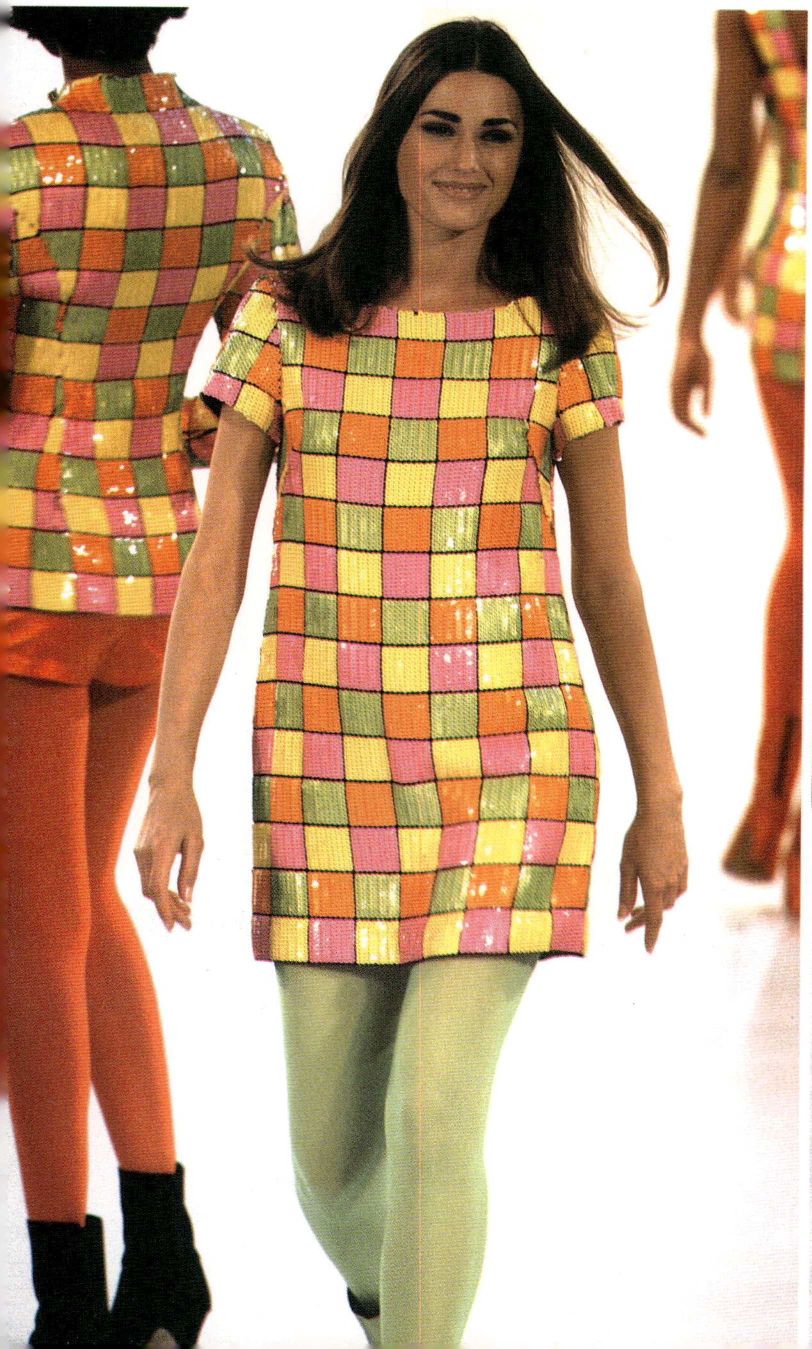

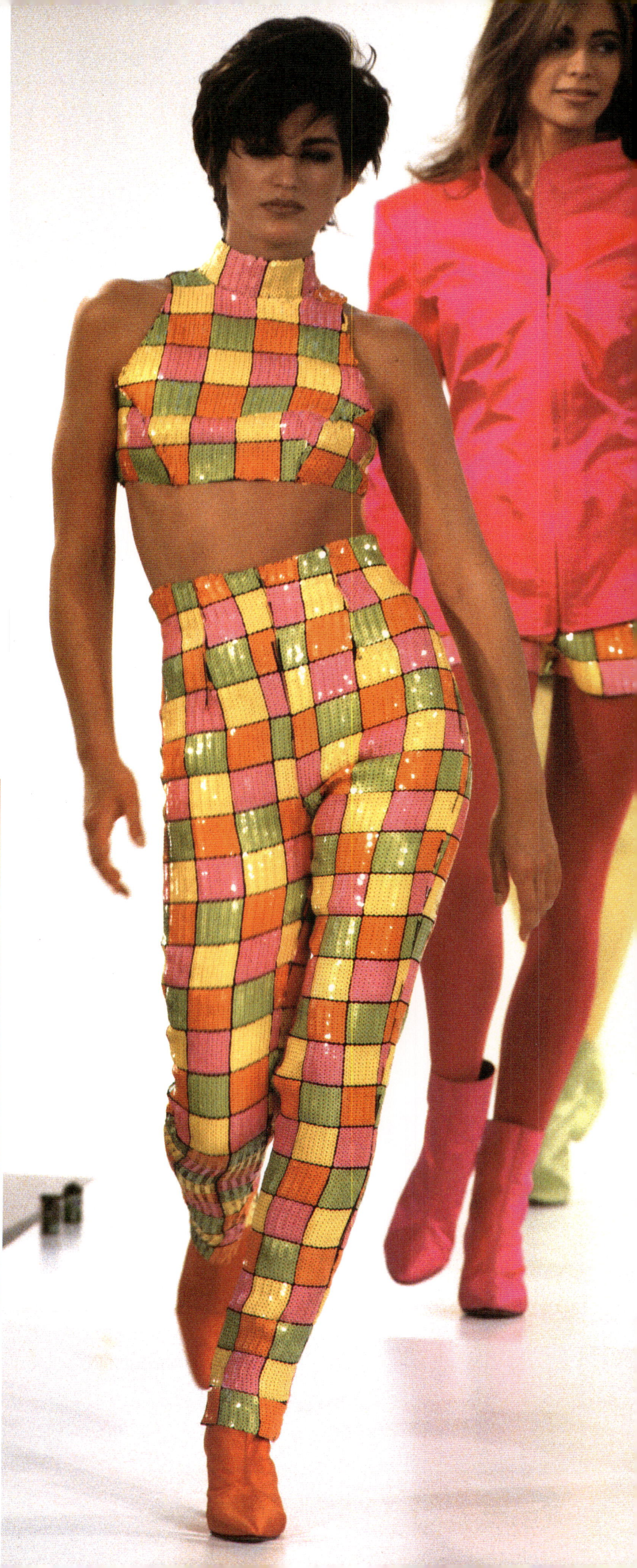

EDINA RONAY

327

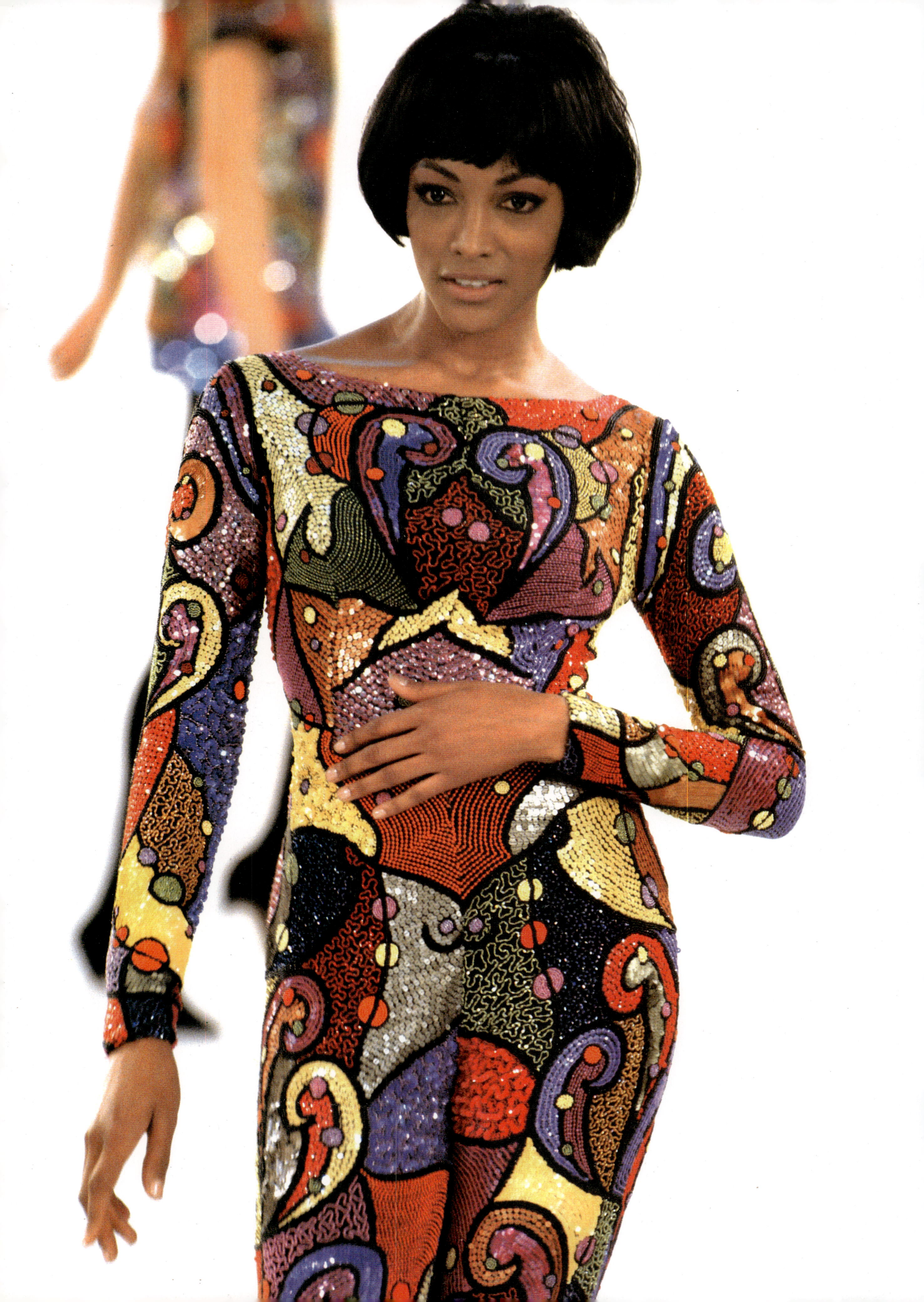

LONDON-10

JACQUELINE HANCHER

ジャクリーヌ・ハンチャー

さすがレザーで知られるデザイナーだけに、ファーをあしらったり、ダイヤモンドをちりばめたりと、レザーをエレガントに見せるコツを心得ている。
A designer associated with leather, she has the knack of presenting leather in an elegant manner, using fur and studded diamonds.

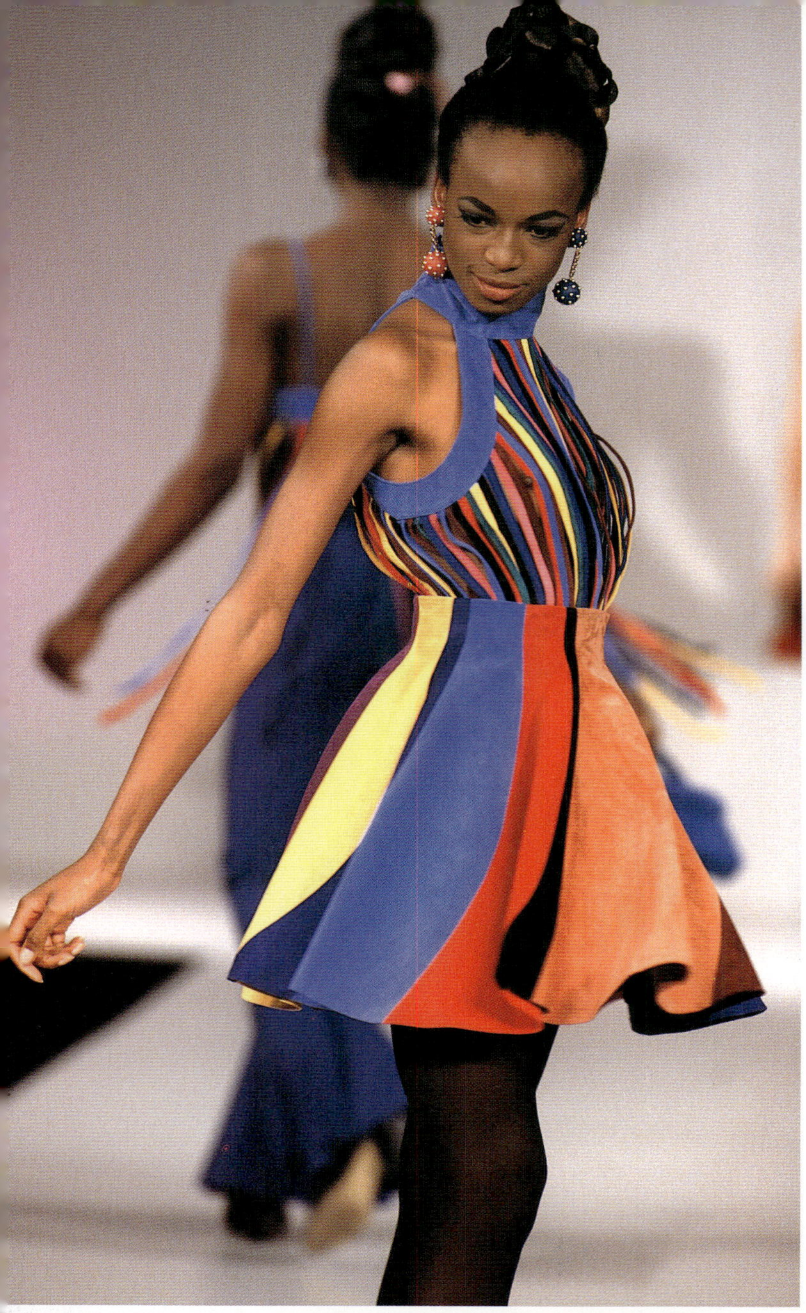
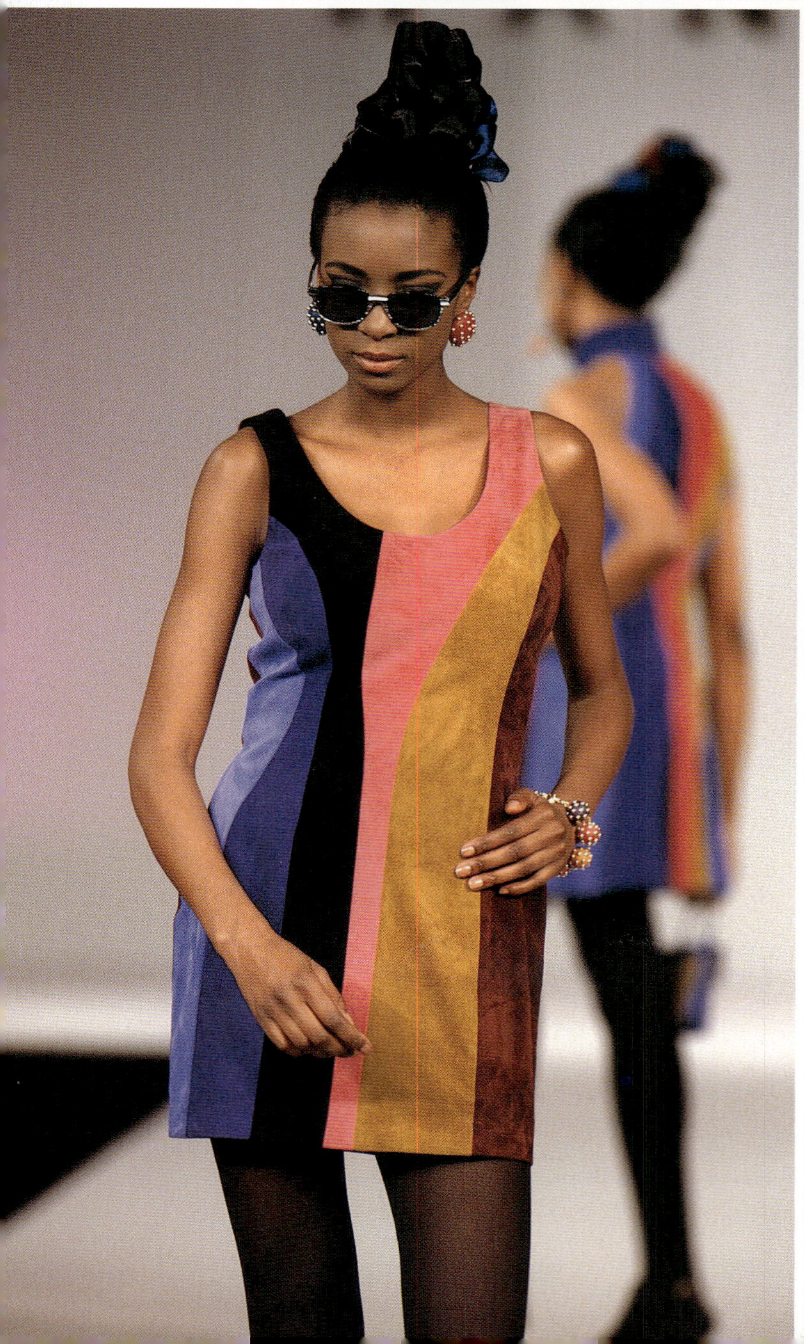
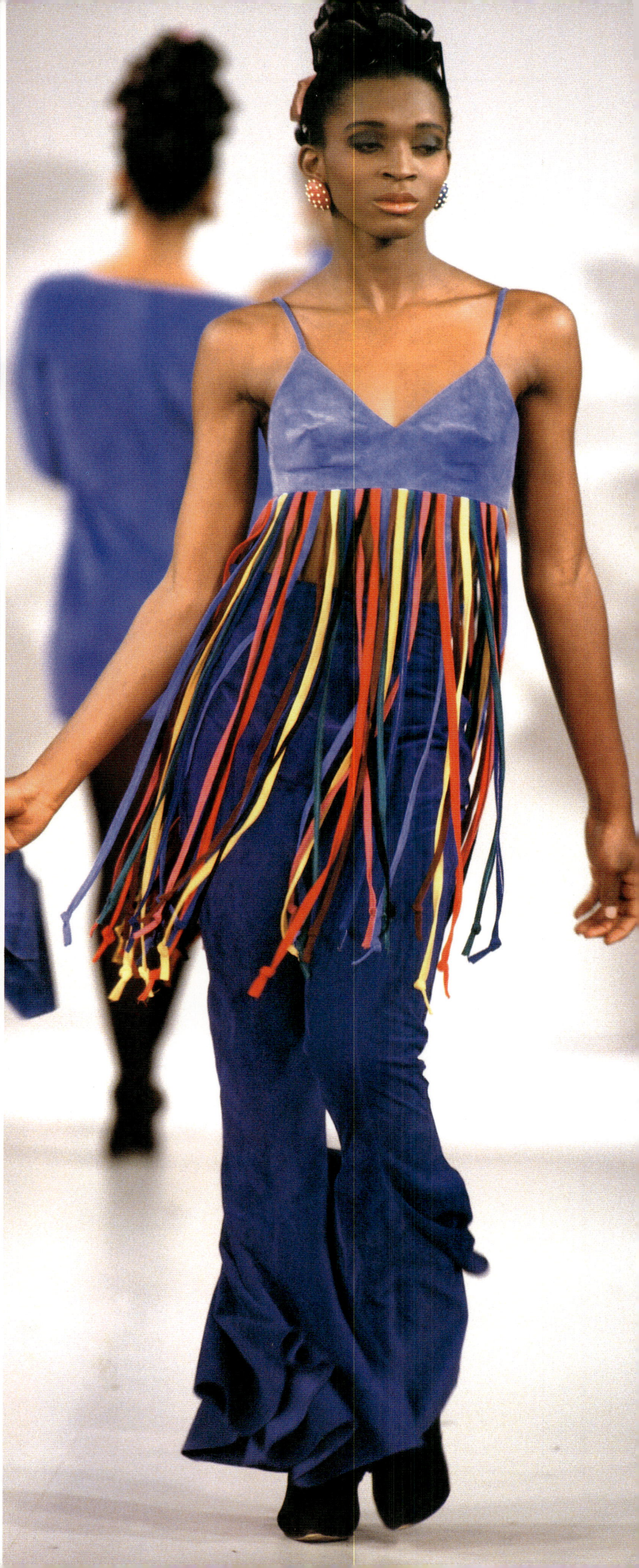

JACQUELINE HANCHER

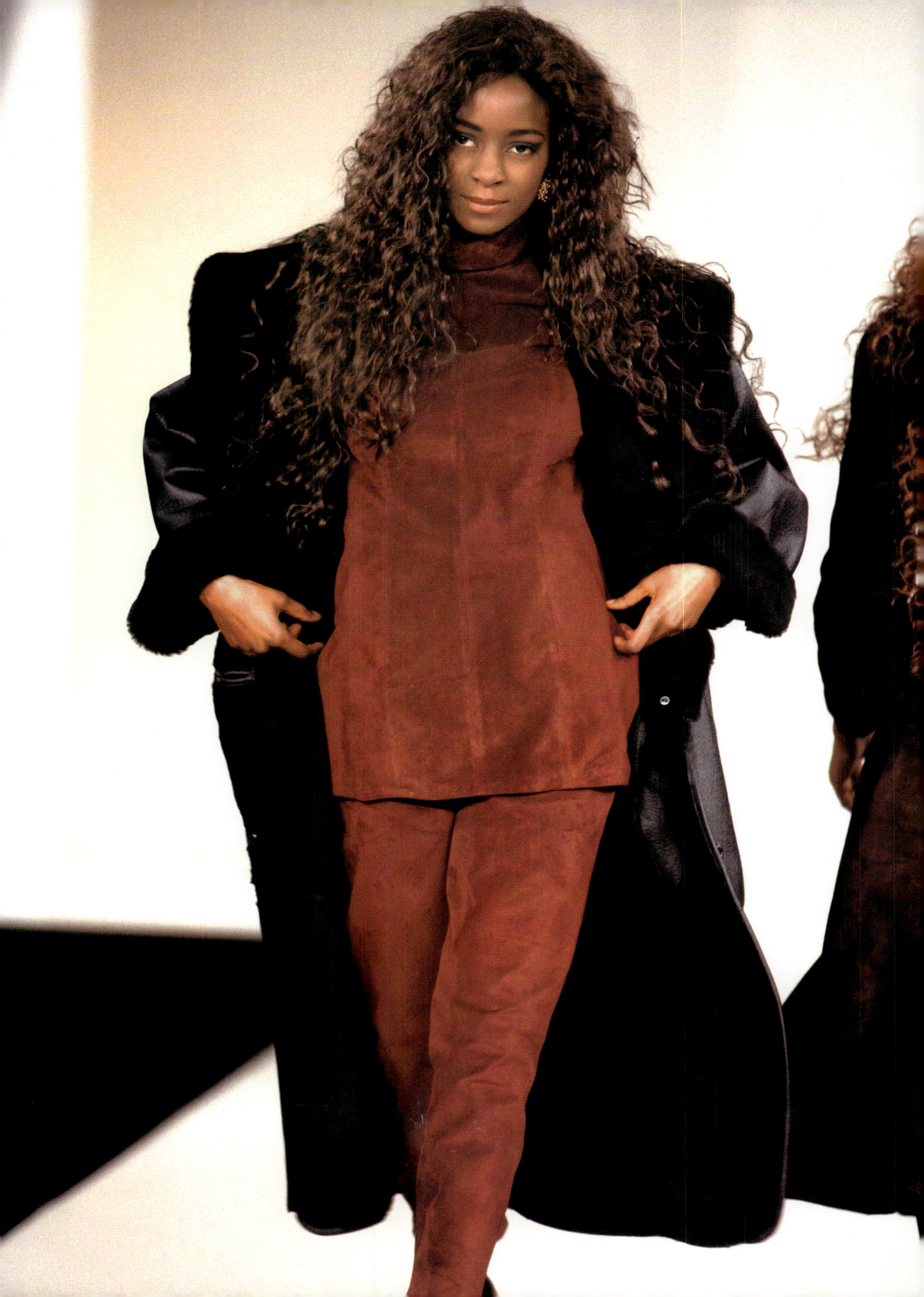

PAUL COSTELLOE

ポール・コステロ

よけいなものを取り除いたシャープなラインのショート・コートやスーツのバリエーションを中心に、都会的な女性のライフ・シーンを演出。

Creating life scenes for the urban women, he dispensed with all the unnecessaries.
Short coats with sharp lines and suits in various styles were the backbone of his collection.

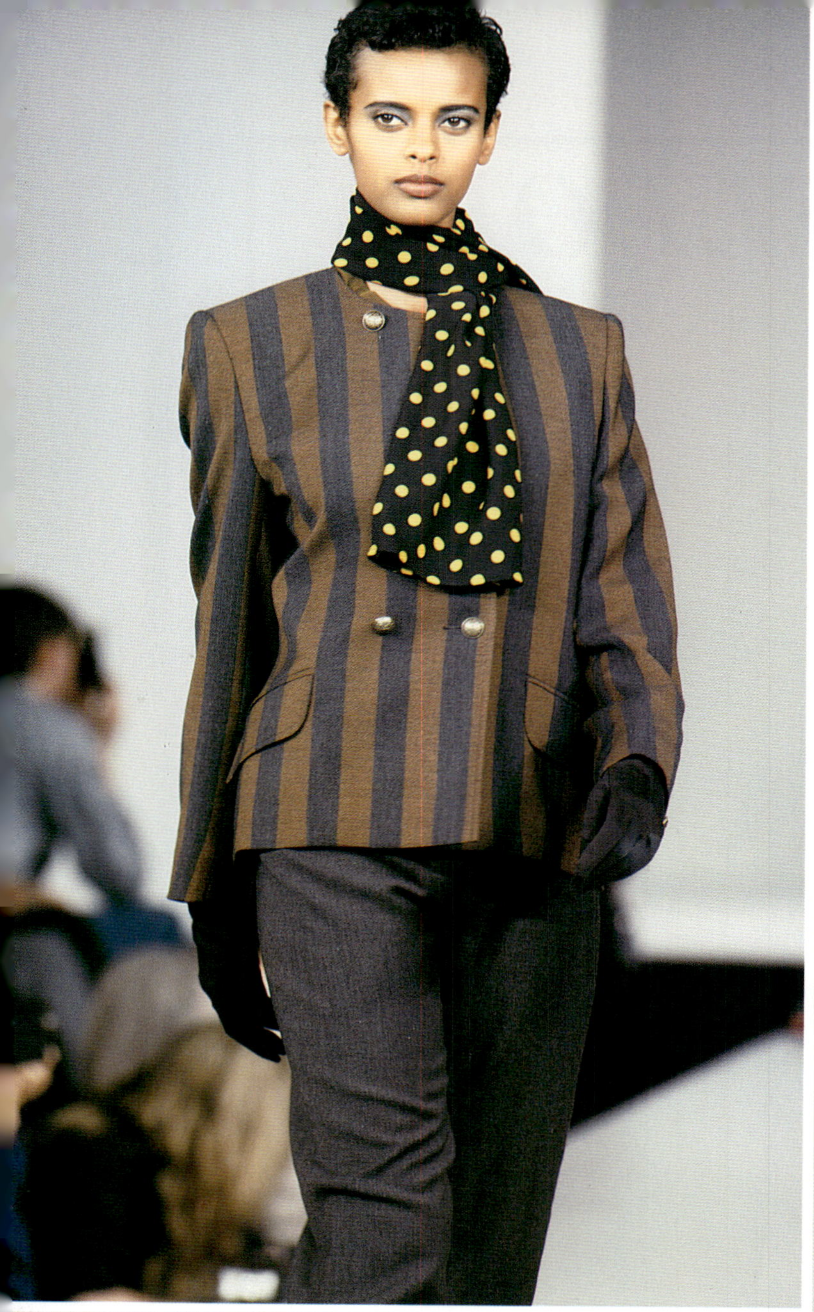
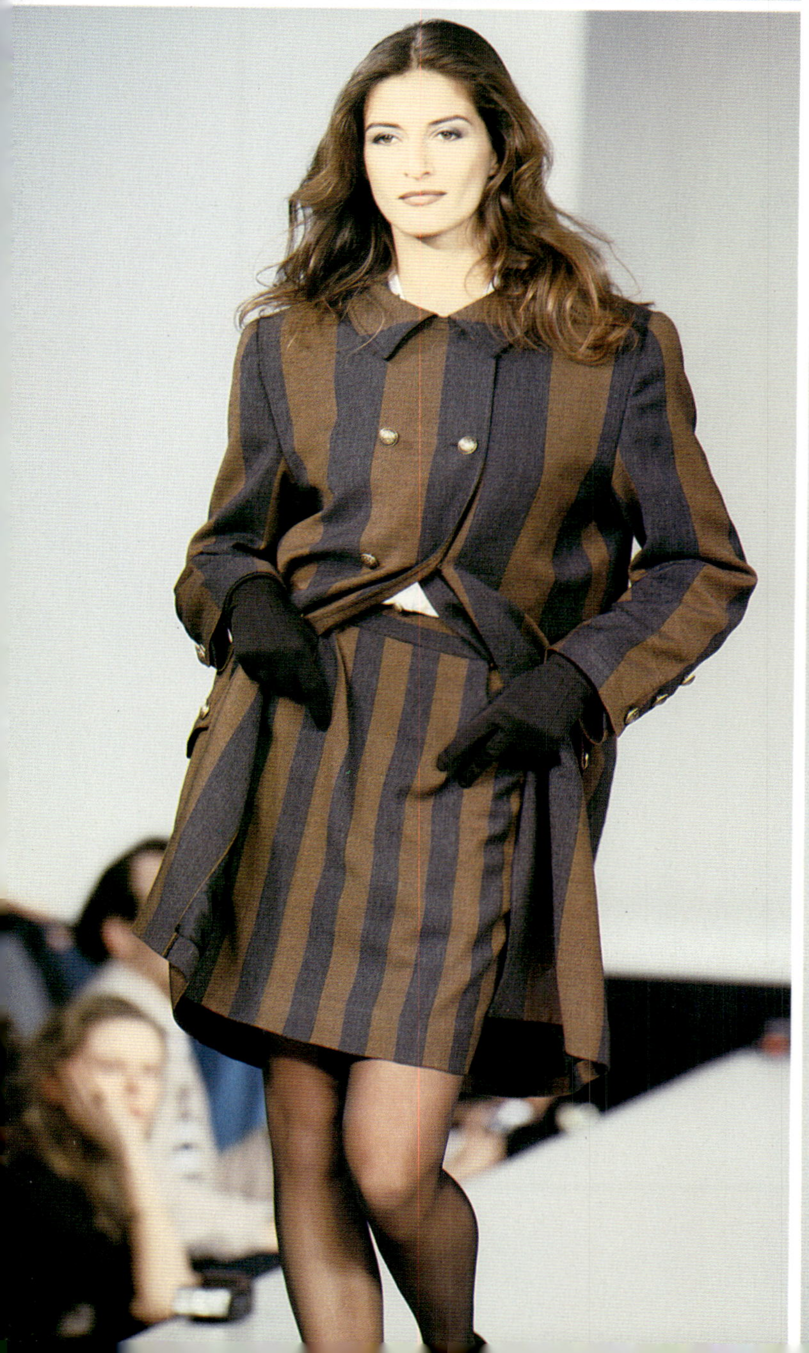
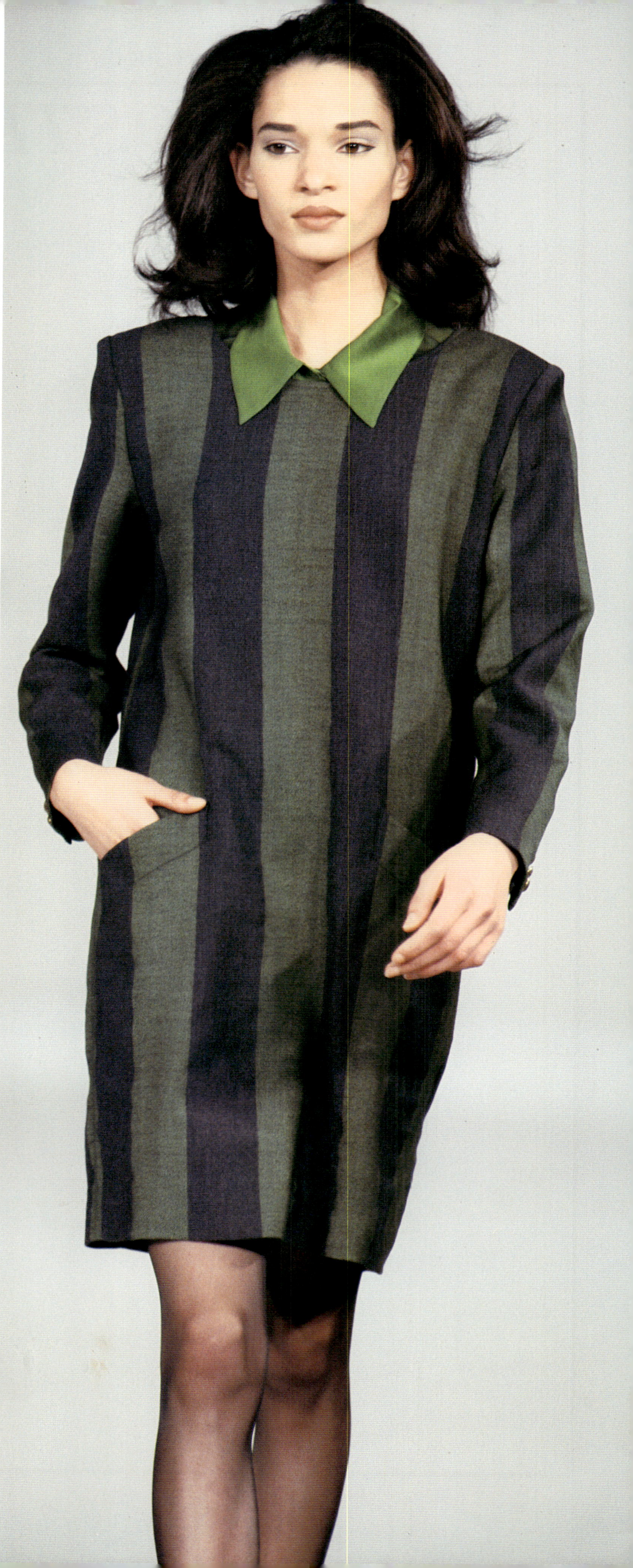

PAUL COSTELLOE

335

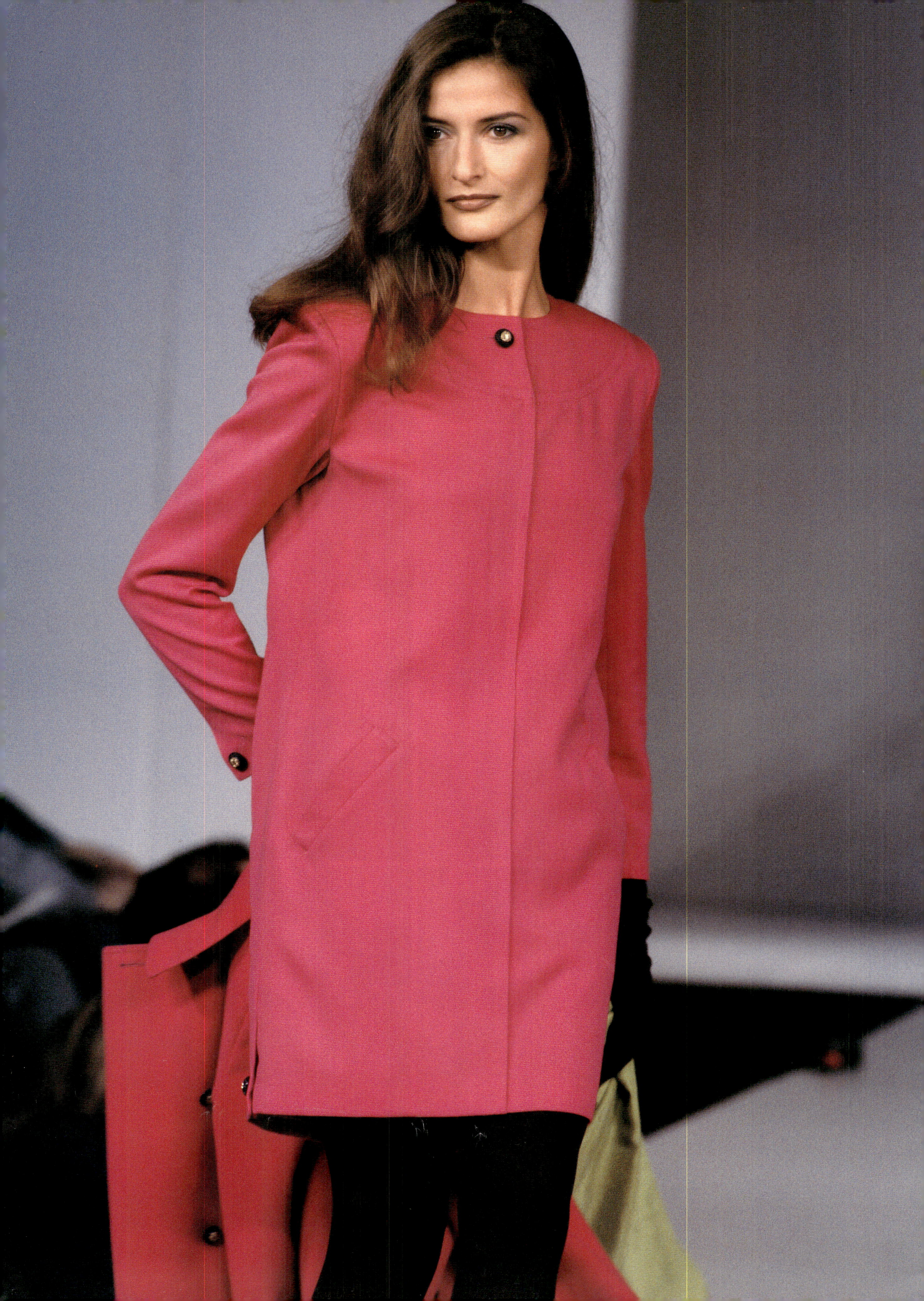

… LONDON-12

BETTY JACKSON

ベティ・ジャクソン

プリントのオーバー・シャツやざっくりとしたニットなど異素材のコンビネーションで、パンツ・スタイルの楽しみ方を提案。
Suggesting ways of enjoying the pants style in combination with such different materials as print overshirts and loose knitwear.

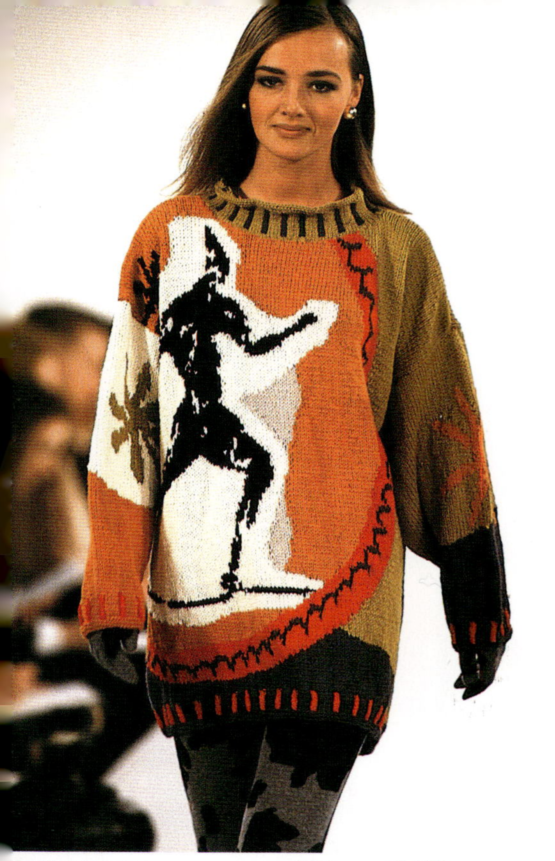
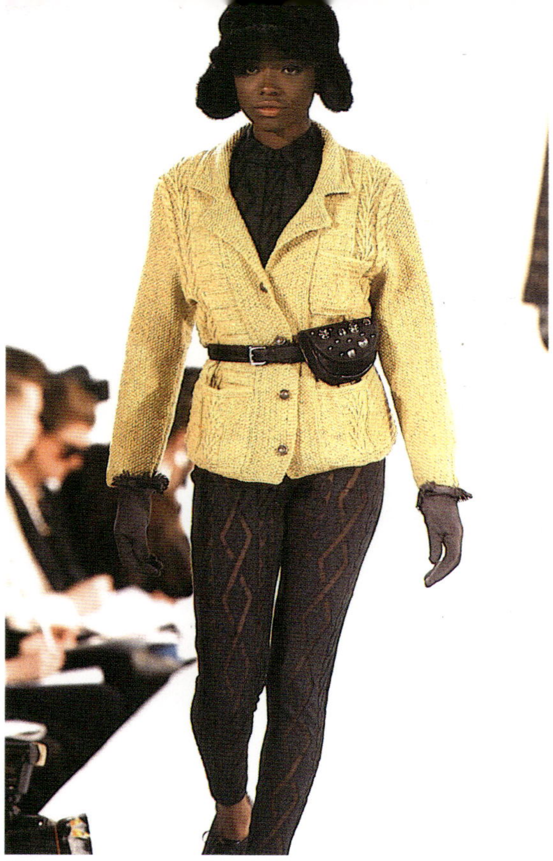
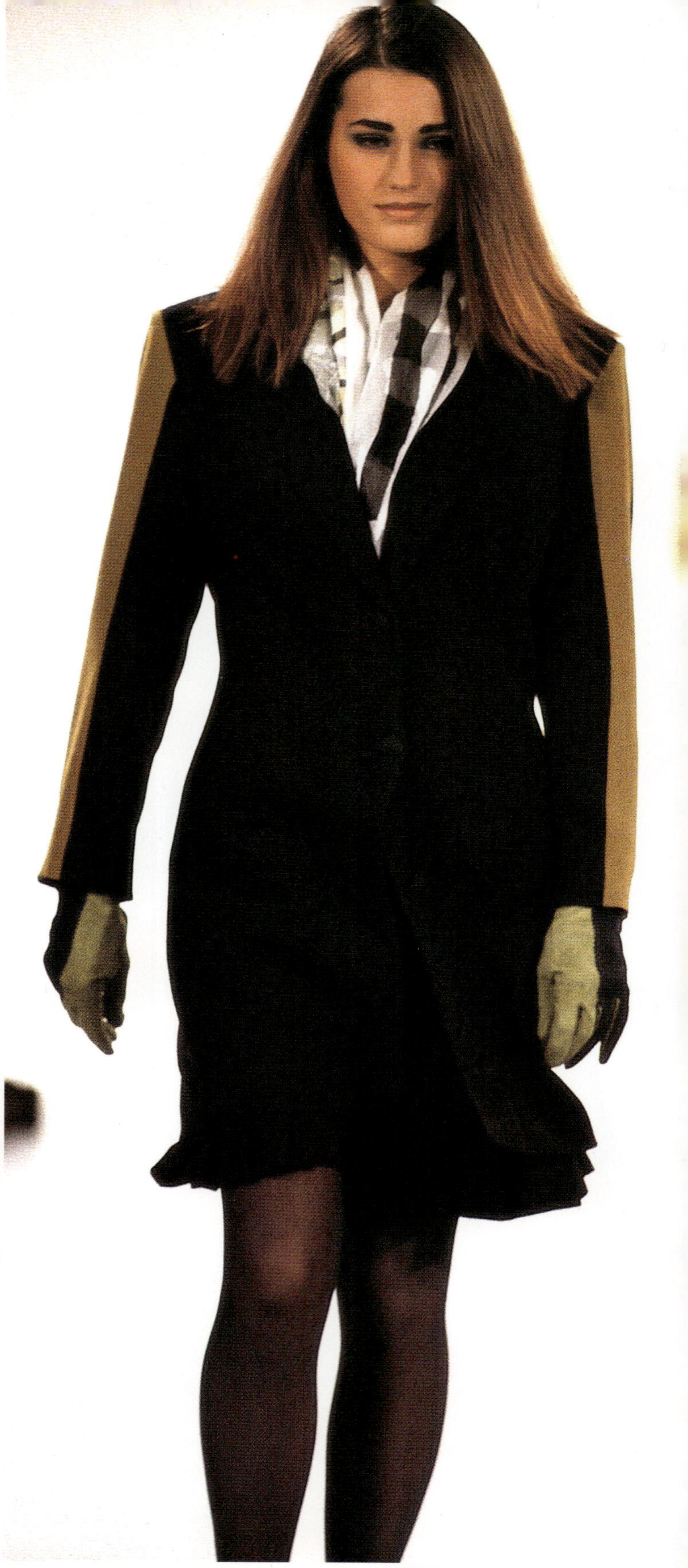
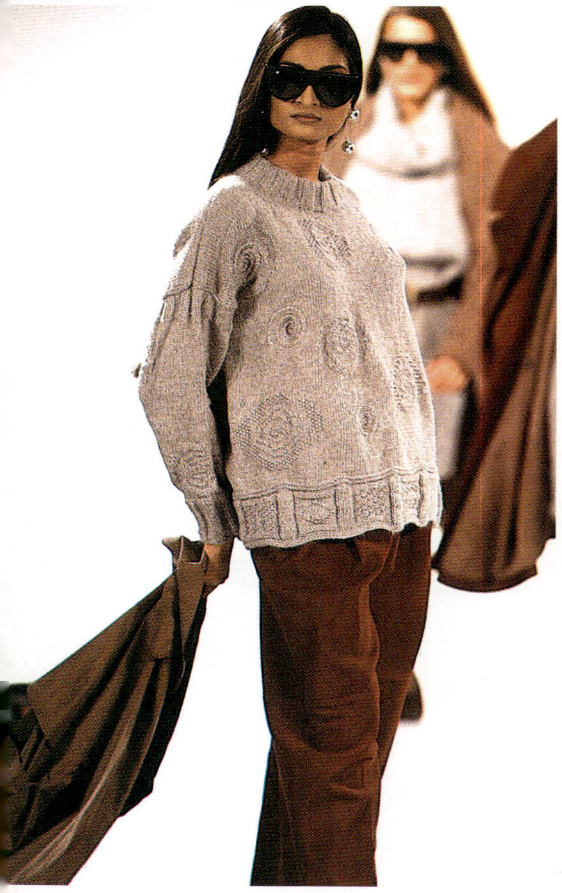
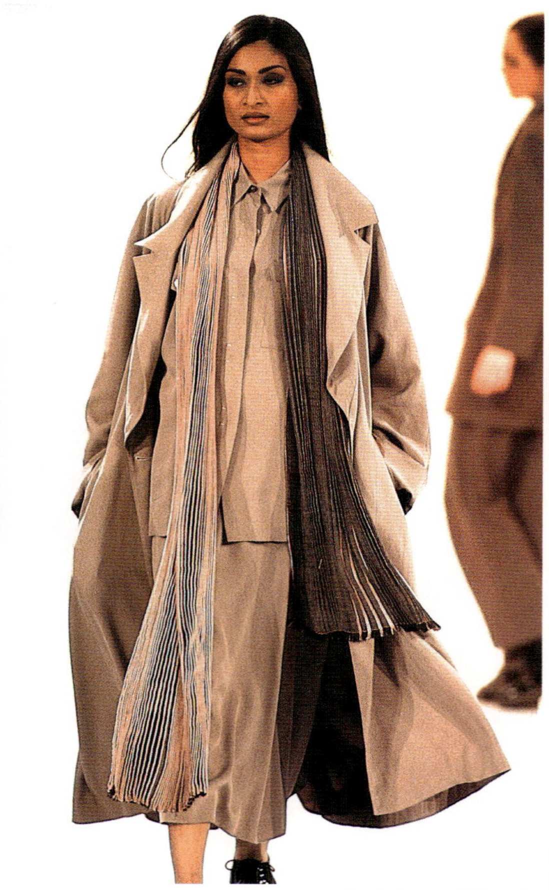
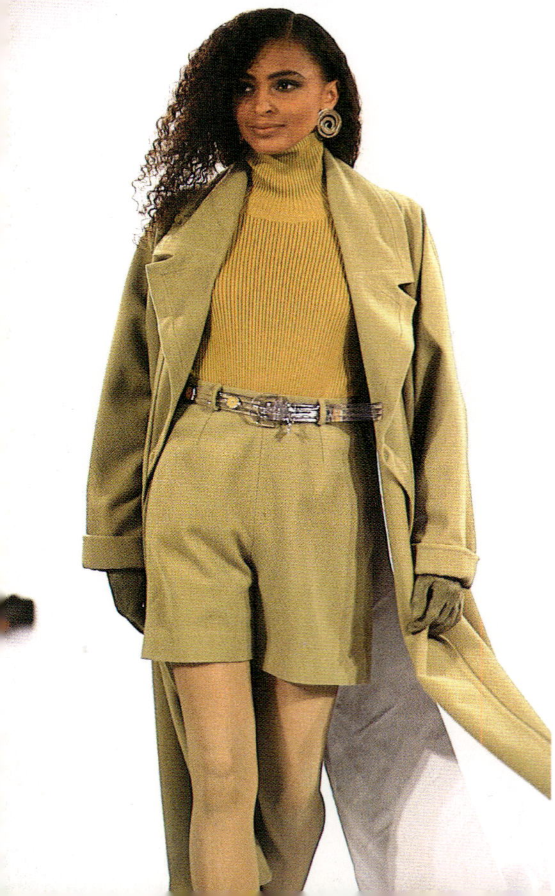
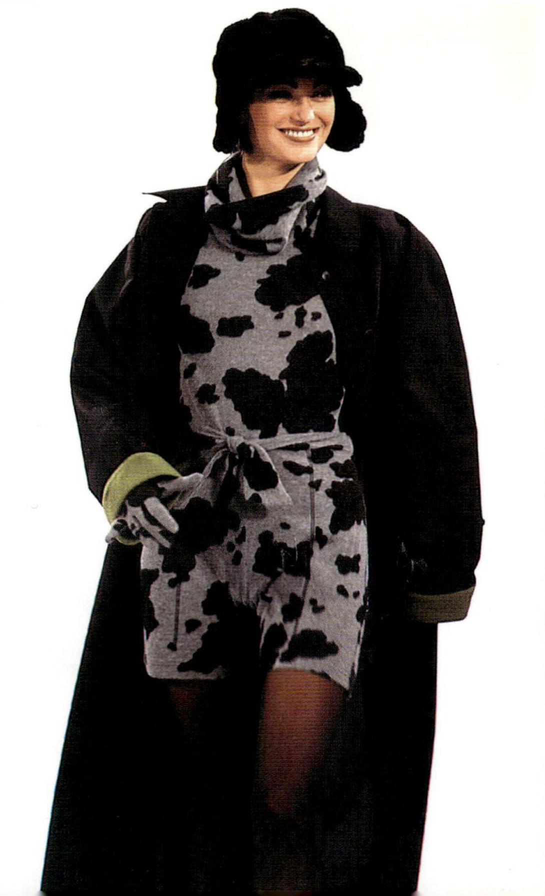
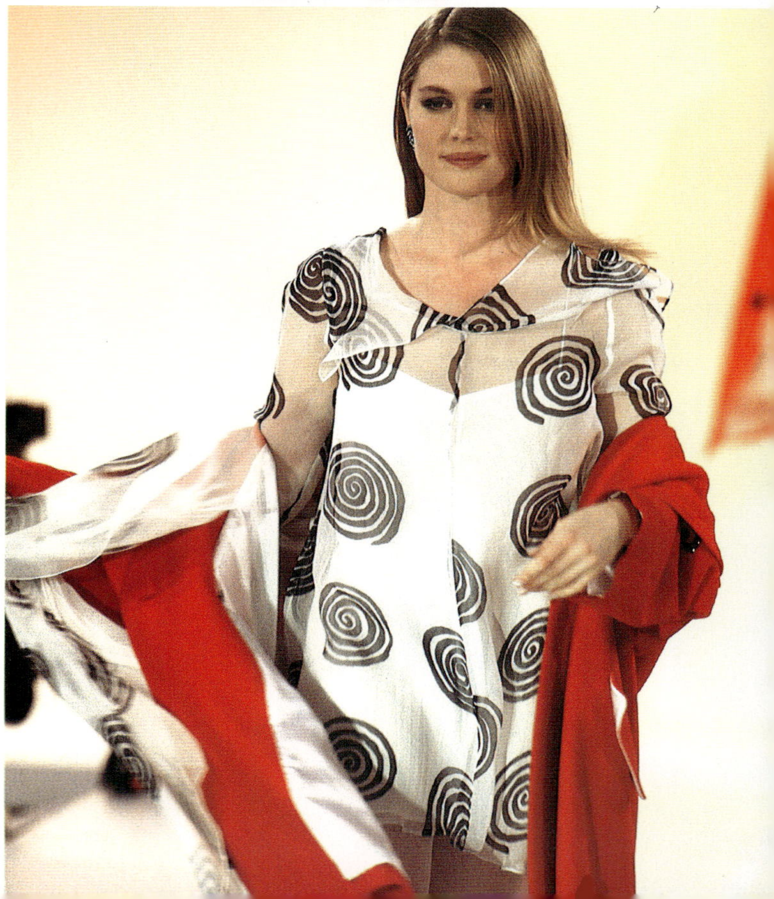

LONDON-13
JOE CASELY-HAYFORD
ジョー・ケイスリー・ヘイフォード

マキシ、シースルー、チョーカーと、今シーズンの傾向である'60年代後半から'70年代の特徴を集約したコレクションとなった。
Displaying a collection epitomizing this season's trend for the late '60's to the '70's, including maxies, see-throughs and chokers.

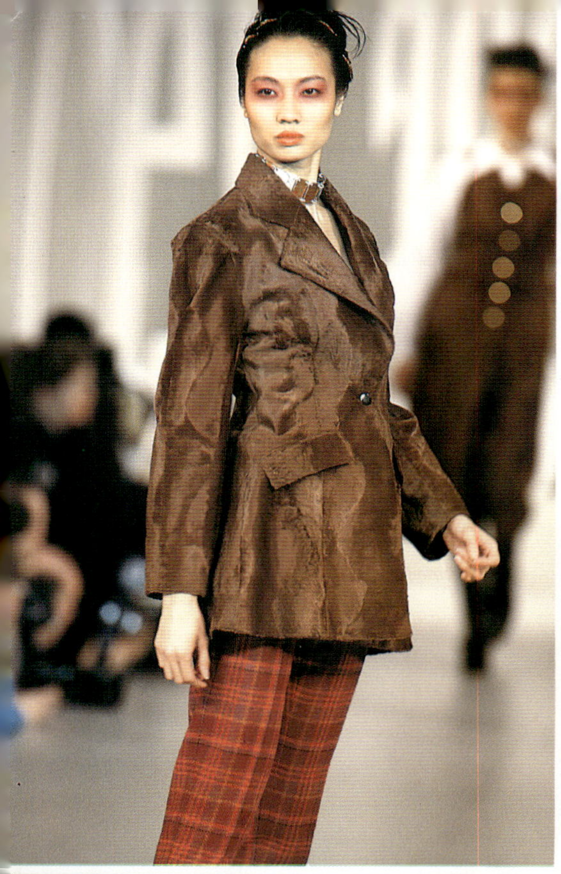
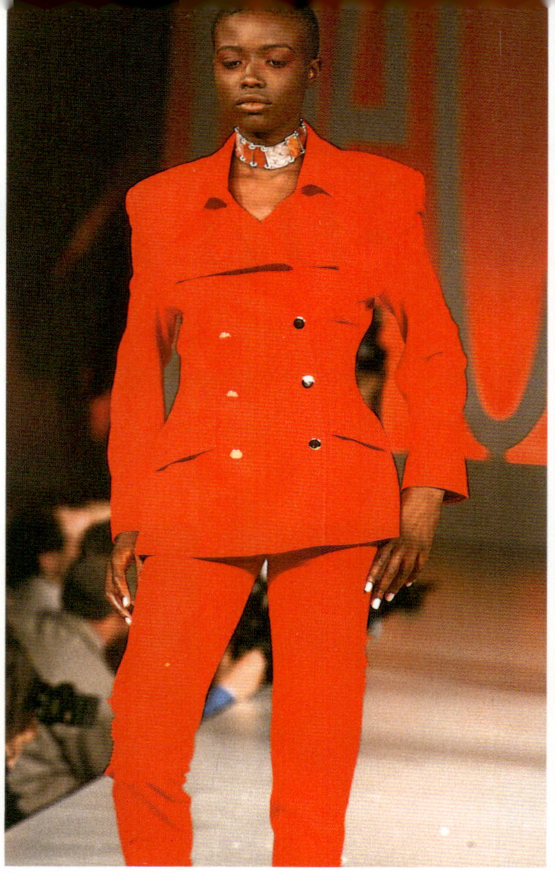
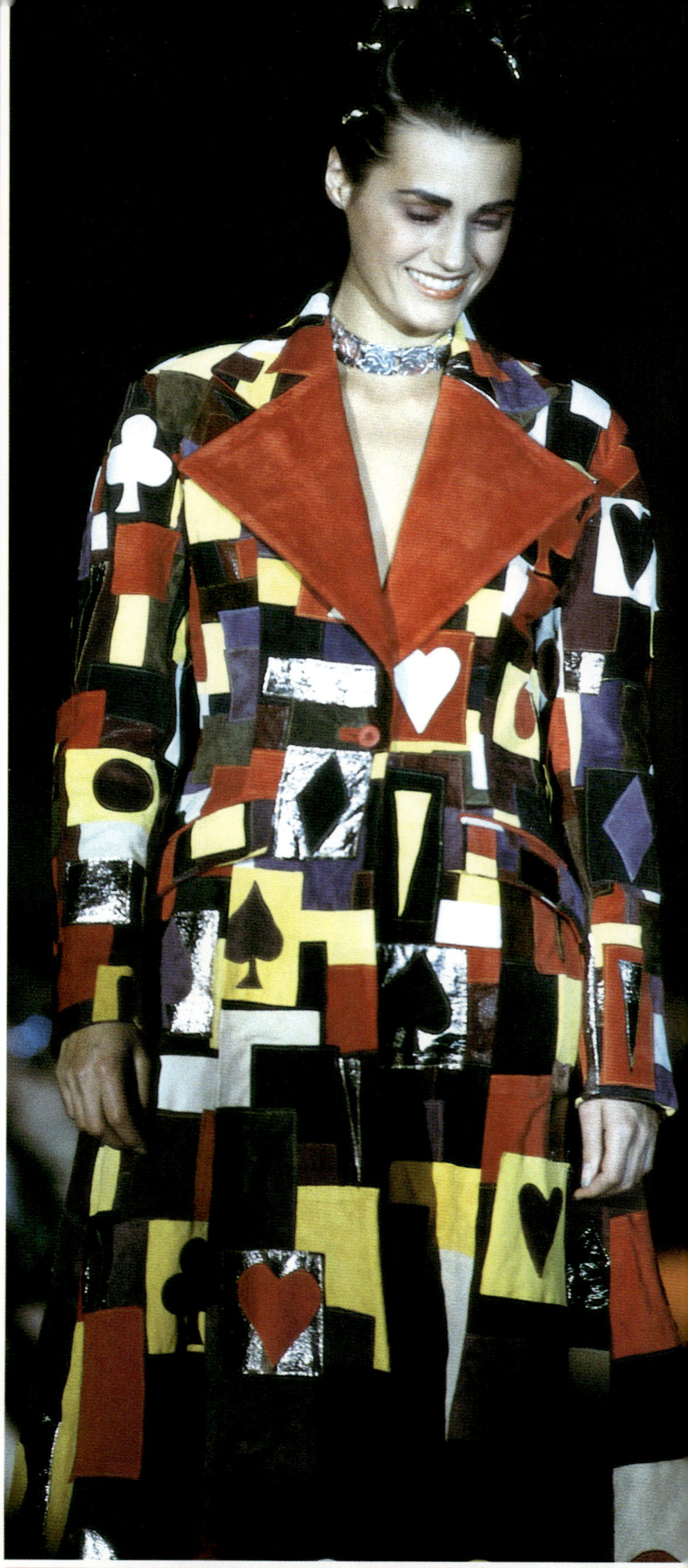
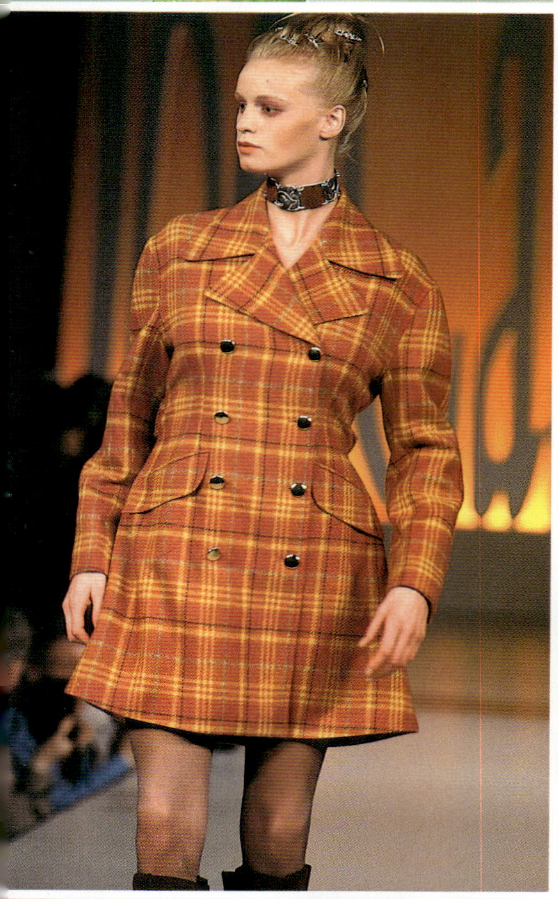
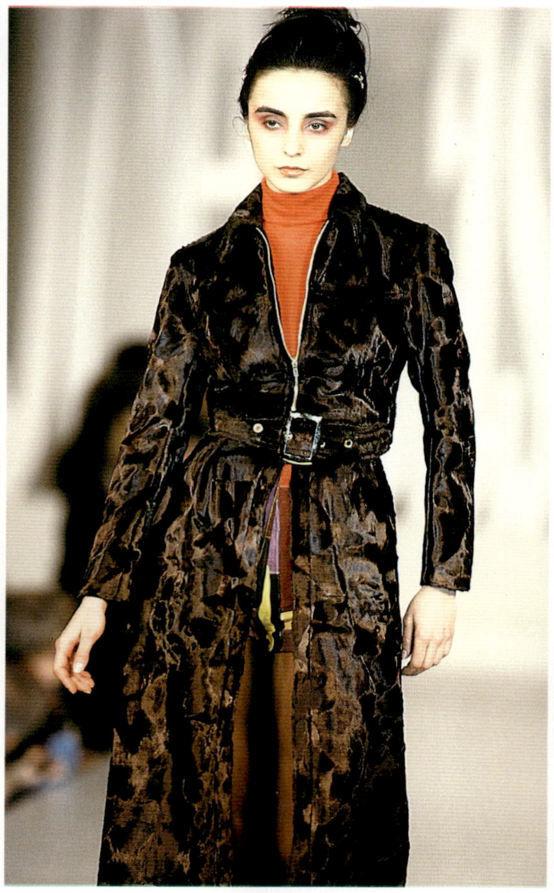
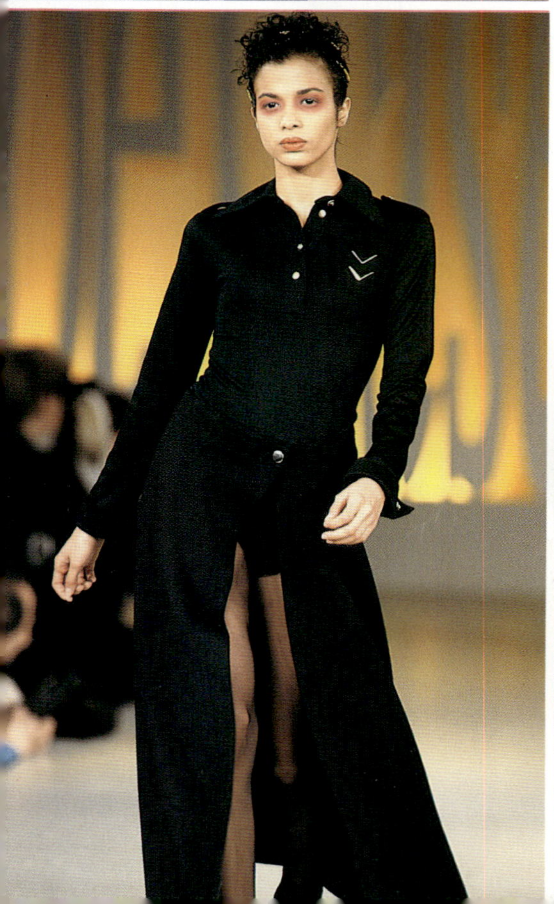
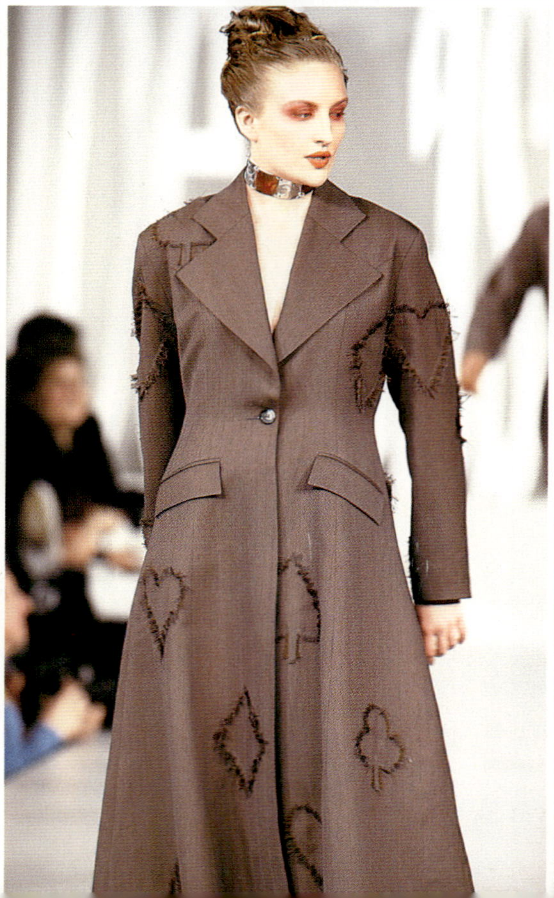
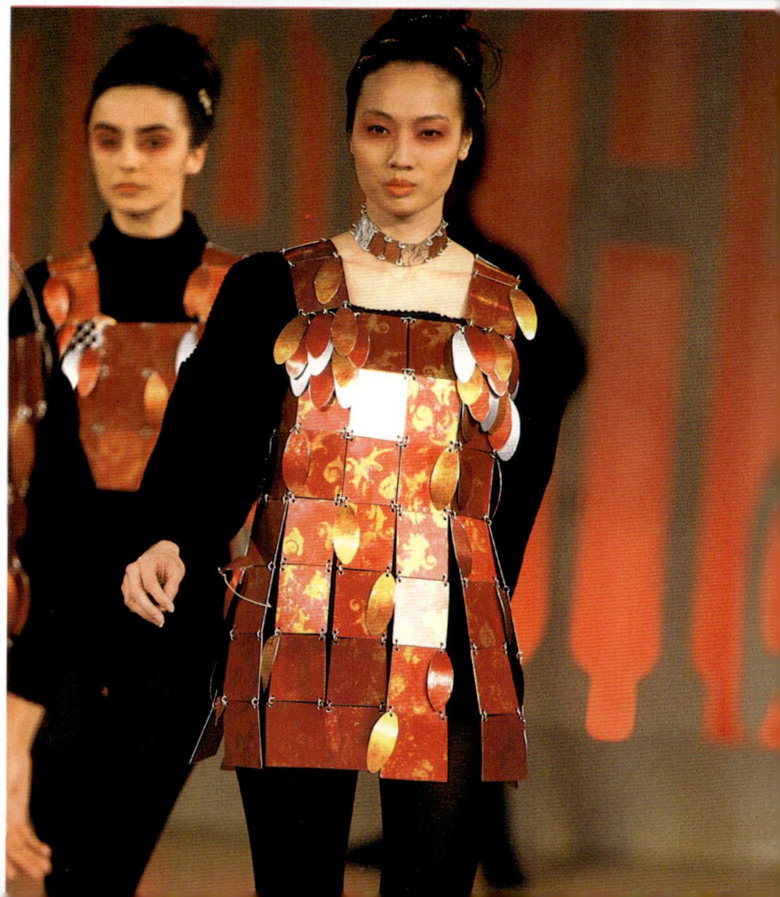

LONDON-14

ZANDRA RHODES

ザンドラ・ローズ

どちらかといえばアバンギャルドで知られるデザイナーが、光る素材とスカーフを巧みに使ってクラシカルなエレガンスの分野に挑戦。
Known for avant-garde fashion, challenging the field in classical elegance, skillfully using illuminous materials and scarves.

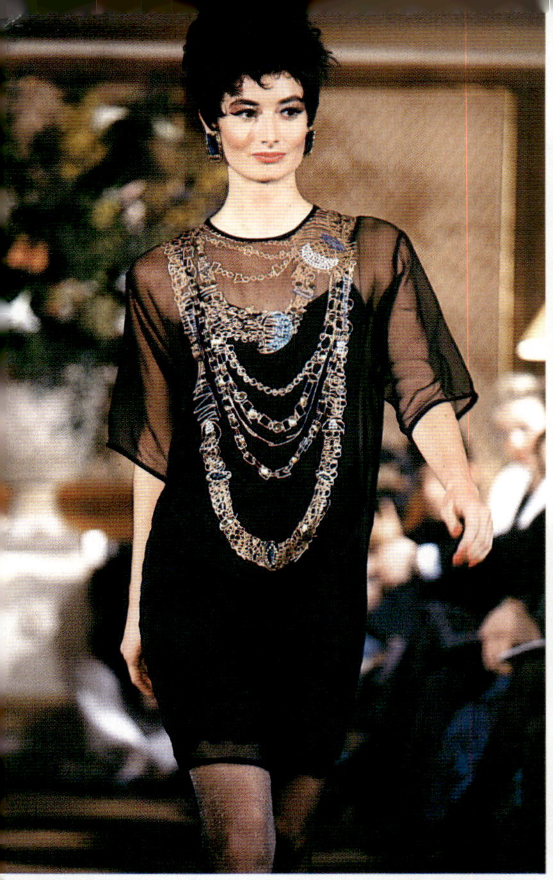
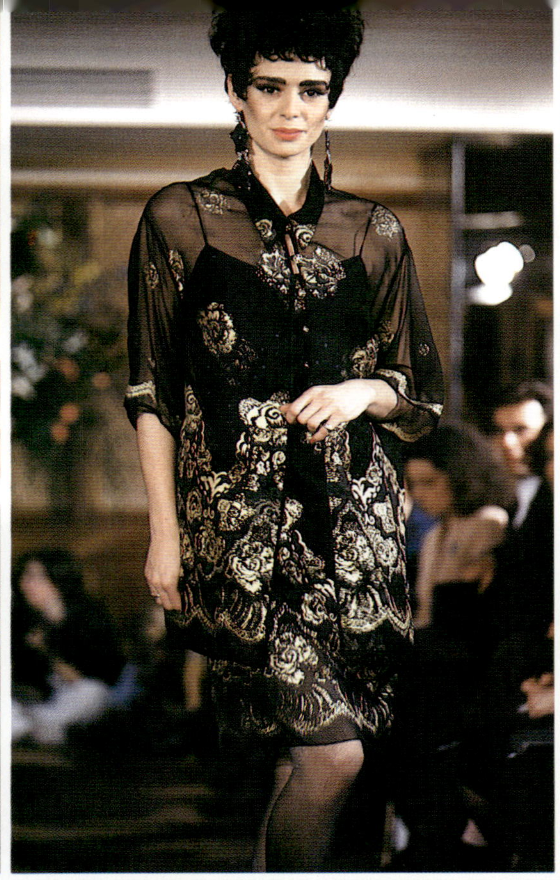
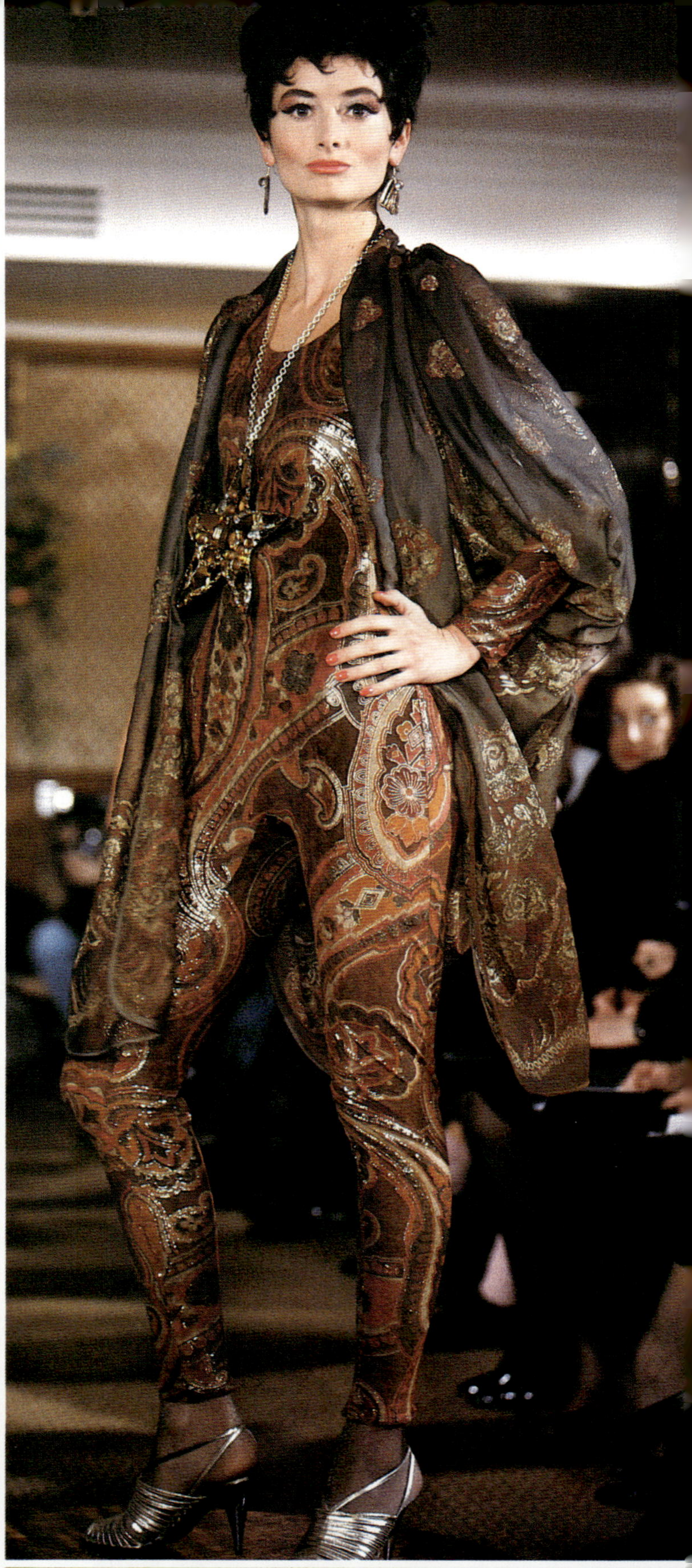
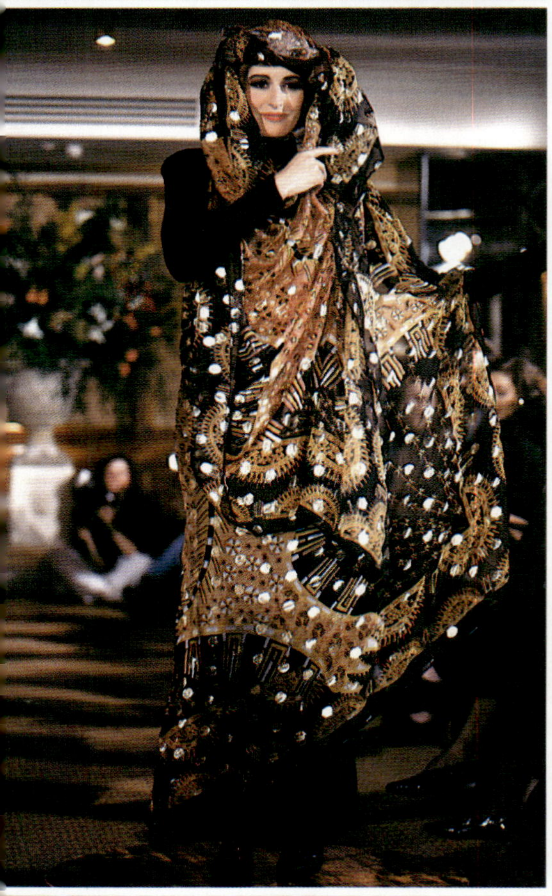
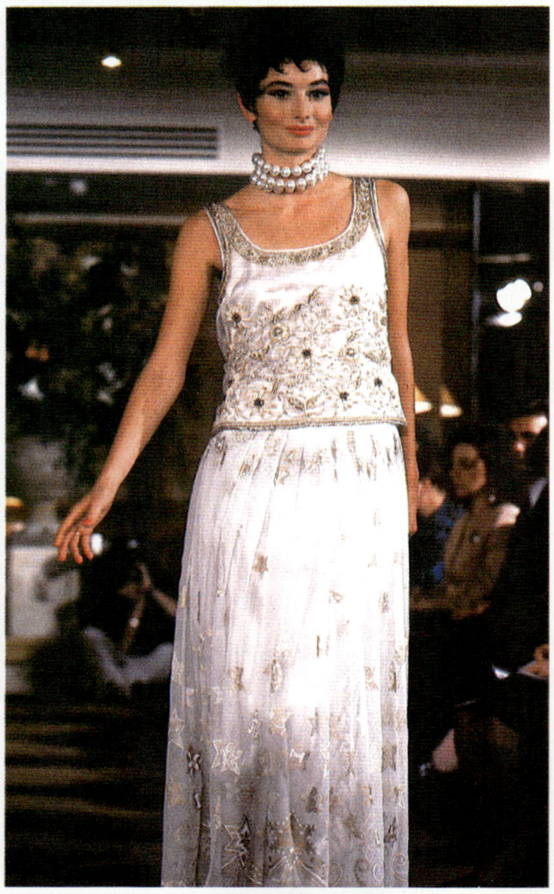
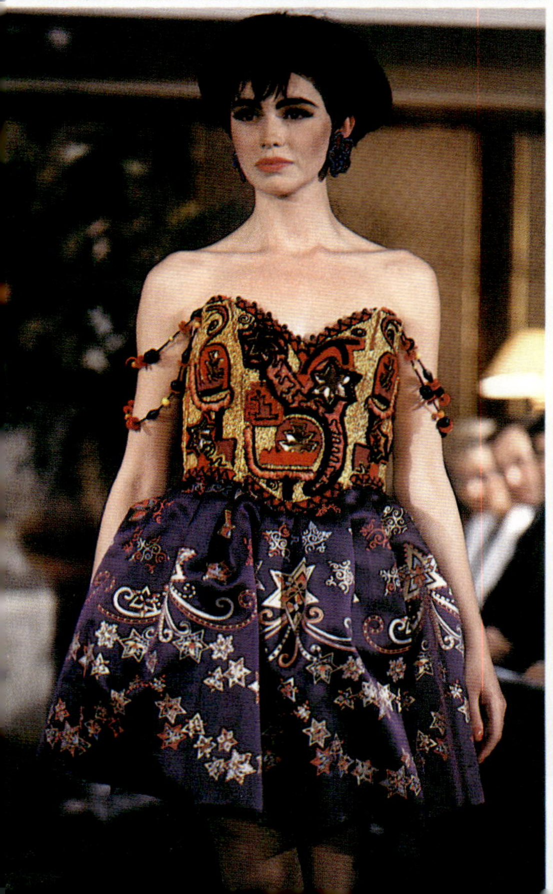
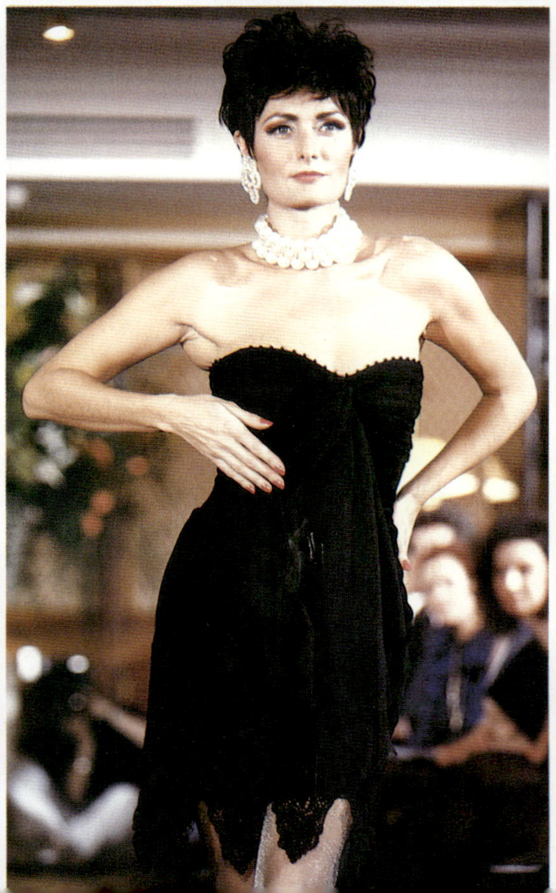
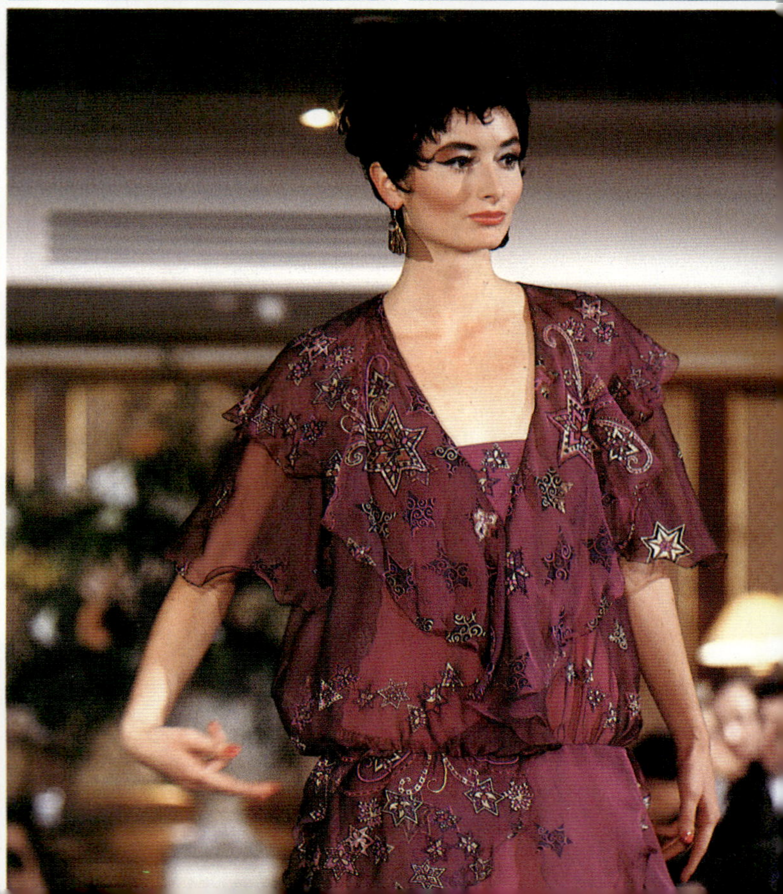

VAL PIRIOU

JACQUELINE HANCHER

'91-'92 AUTUMN & WINTER

PRÊT-Á-PORTER COLLECTIONS

JACQUELINE HANCHER

OZBEK

ARABELLA POLLEN

La Porte de La Vie Créative.

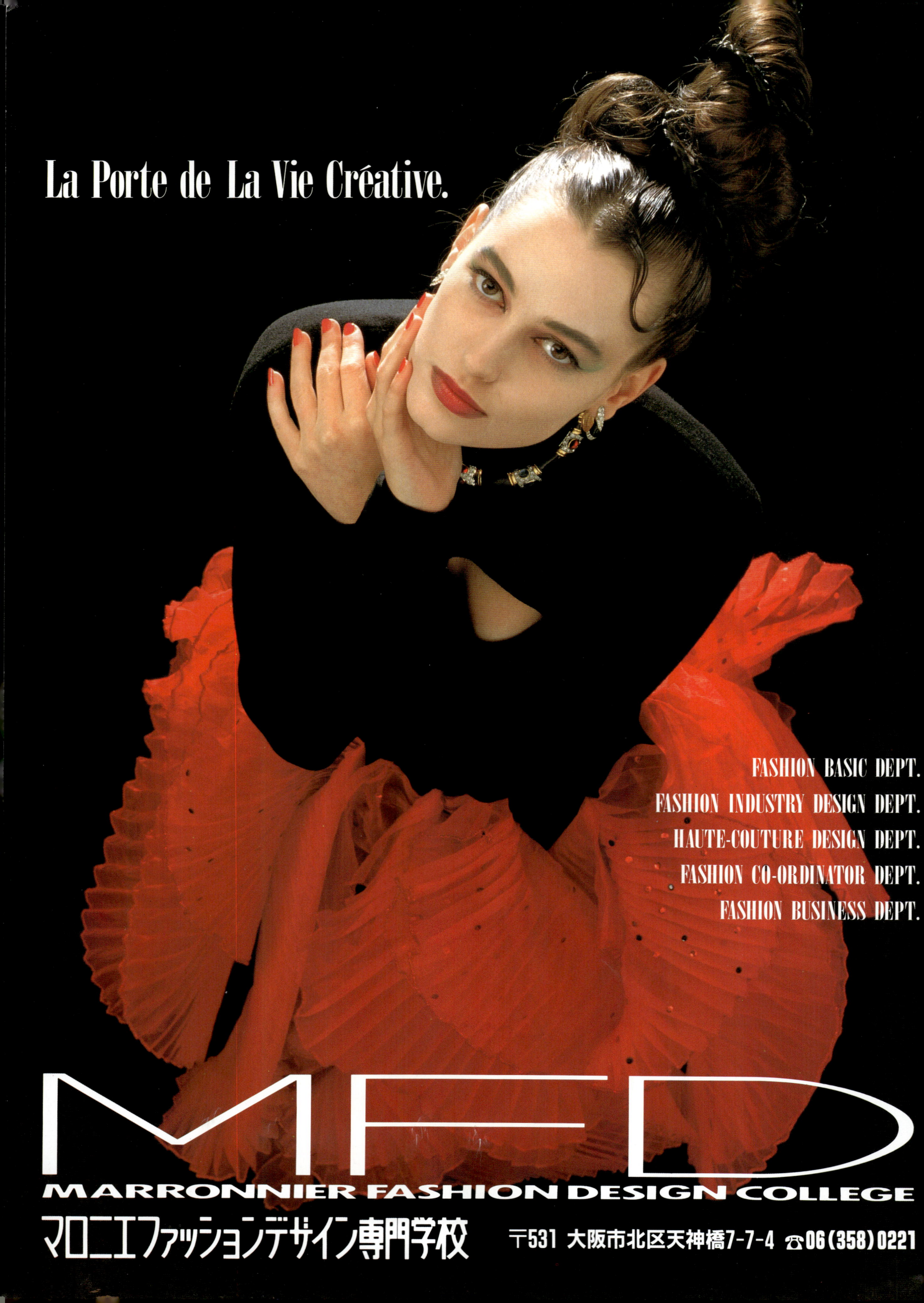

FASHION BASIC DEPT.
FASHION INDUSTRY DESIGN DEPT.
HAUTE-COUTURE DESIGN DEPT.
FASHION CO-ORDINATOR DEPT.
FASHION BUSINESS DEPT.

MFD
MARRONNIER FASHION DESIGN COLLEGE

マロニエファッションデザイン専門学校　〒531 大阪市北区天神橋7-7-4 ☎06(358)0221

ACCESSORIES

'91-'92 AUTUMN & WINTER COLLECTIONS

PARIS/LONDON

JEAN-PAUL GAULTIER

ACCESSORIES

SCARF & MUFFLER

EMANUEL UNGARO

CHANTAL THOMASS

KENZO

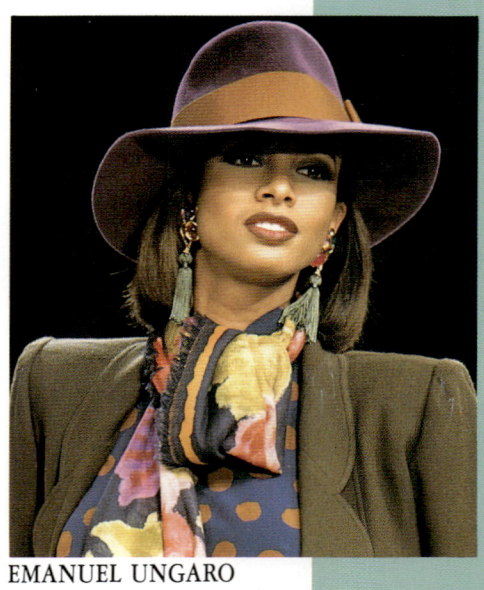

EMANUEL UNGARO

YVES SAINT LAURENT

CHRISTIAN DIOR

NECKTIE & CORSAGE

COMME DES GARÇONS

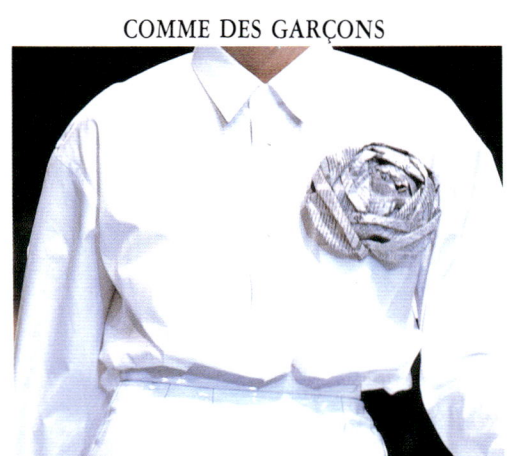

KENZO

'91-'92 AUTUMN & WINTER
COLLECTIONS
PARIS / LONDON

CHRISTIAN DIOR

MATSUDA

NECKLACE & BELT

CHLOÉ

'91-'92 AUTUMN & WINTER
COLLECTIONS
PARIS / LONDON

LOLITA LEMPICKA

MARTINE SITBON

CHANEL

CHANEL

CHANEL

CHANEL

CHANEL

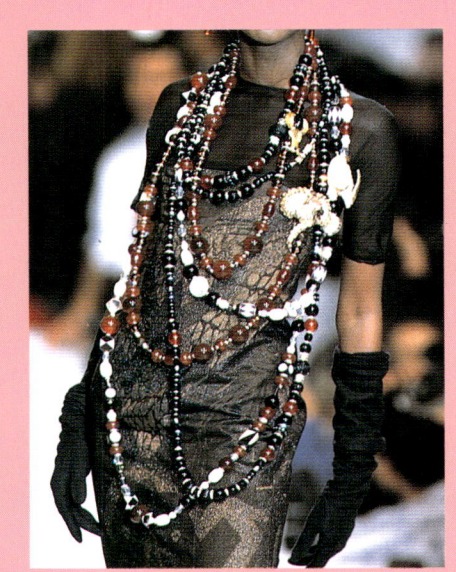

YVES SAINT LAURENT

CHANEL

CHRISTIAN DIOR

ACCESSORIES

Accessories

HAT & BAG

PIERRE BALMAIN

J. C. DE CASTELBAJAC

KARL LAGERFELD

CHANTAL THOMASS

YVES SAINT LAURENT

EMANUEL UNGARO

JEAN-PAUL GAULTIER

CHRISTIAN DIOR

'91-'92 AUTUMN & WINTER
COLLECTIONS
PARIS / LONDON

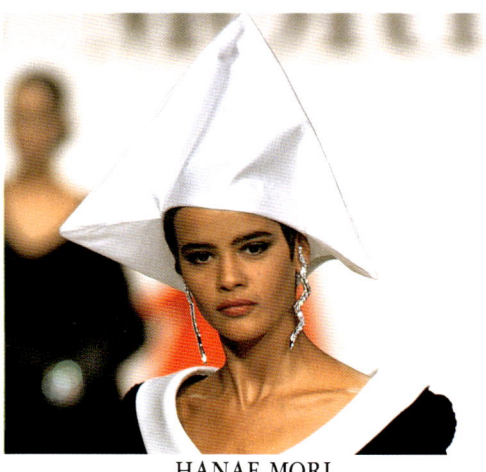

HANAE MORI

CHANTAL THOMASS

KENZO

CHRISTIAN DIOR

J. C. DE CASTELBAJAC

EMANUEL UNGARO

'91-'92 AUTUMN & WINTER

PRÊT-Á-PORTER COLLECTIONS

MATSUDA

J. C. DE CASTELBAJAC

YVES SAINT LAURENT

'91-'92
AUTUMN & WINTER
PRÊT-Á-PORTER
COLLECTIONS

YVES SAINT LAURENT

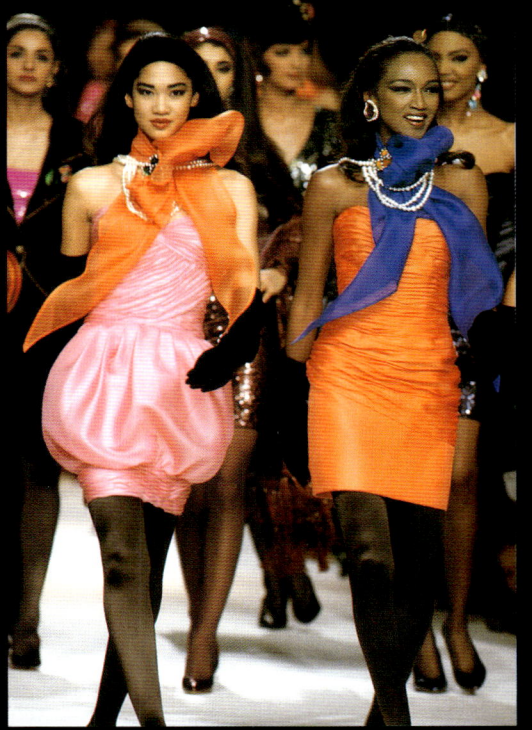

EMANUEL UNGARO	ENRICO COVERI	CLAUDE MONTANA
CHRISTIAN DIOR	JIN ABE	JUNKO KOSHINO
EMANUEL UNGARO	CHRISTIAN DIOR	KANSAI YAMAMOTO

'91-'92 AUTUMN & WINTER PARIS LONDON COLLECTIONS

発行日　1991年5月20日
発行元　㈱ギャップ・ジャパン
発売元　㈱ジャパン・プランニング・アソシエーション
〒107　東京都港区南青山3-10-7　Tel.03-3403-5221代　Fax.03-3478-1414

■

'91-'92 AUTUMN & WINTER MILAN MADRID COLLECTIONS ¥15,450(本体¥15,000)
'91-'92 AUTUMN & WINTER PARIS LONDON COLLECTIONS ¥15,450(本体¥15,000)
'91-'92 AUTUMN & WINTER TOKYO NEW YORK COLLECTIONS ¥15,450(本体¥15,000)

■

編集発行人/梁田義秋
編集スタッフ/尾上陽子　二見屋良樹
デザイナー/三浦絵里
フォトグラファー/ピエロ・クリスタルディ
イングリッシュ・テキスト/㈱バベル・インターナショナル
アソシエイテッド・コーディネイター/文平泰子　山田 茂　木塚 睦　浅川美樹

■

GAP JAPAN Co.,Ltd.
3-10-7 Minami Aoyama Minato-ku Tokyo Japan
Tel.03-3403-5221　Fax.03-3478-1414
Publisher/Yoshiaki Yanada
Editor/Yoko Ogami　Ryoju Futamiya
Designer/Eri Miura
Photographer/Piero Cristaldi
English Text/BABEL INTERNATIONAL INC.
Associated Coordinator/Yasuko Fumihira　Shigeru Yamada　Hiromu Kizuka　Miki Asakawa